W9-DDP-326

KING ARTHUR FLOUR WHOLE GRAIN BAKING

WHOLE GRAIN
BAKING

DELICIOUS RECIPES USING NUTRITIOUS WHOLE GRAINS

The Countryman Press
WOODSTOCK, VERMONT

Copyright © 2006 by The King Arthur Flour Company, Inc.

First Paperback Edition 2014

All rights reserved. No part of this book may be reproduced in any way by any electronic or mechanical means, including information storage and retrieval systems, without permission in writing from the publisher, except by a reviewer, who may quote brief passages.

King Arthur Flour, the King Arthur Flour logo and *The Baker's Catalogue* are registered trademarks of The King Arthur Flour Company, Inc., of Norwich, Vermont.

An invitation to the reader
If you like this book, you'll love King Arthur's bimonthly baking newsletter, *The Baking Sheet*. For information or to subscribe, call *The Baker's Catalogue* at 1-800-827-6836. Also, if you have questions about the recipes in this book, call our baker's hotline at 802-649-3717, 8 a.m.–9 p.m. Monday–Friday, 9 a.m.–5 p.m. Saturday and Sunday (EST).

The Library of Congress has cataloged the hardcover edition as follows:
King Arthur flour whole grain baking : delicious recipes using nutritious whole grains.
    p. cm.
ISBN-13: 978-0-88150-719-5
ISBN-10: 0-88150-719-9
1. Baking. 2. Cookery (Cereals) I. King Arthur Flour (Firm). II. Title.

TX765.K558 2006
641.8'15--dc22

                    2006046313

Paperback ISBN 978-1-58157-262-9

Cover and interior design by Vertigo Design, NYC

Color section layout by Janet Matz

Instructional illustrations by Laura Hartman Maestro

Photos for instructional illustrations by Brenda Hickory

Front cover photo of Lemon Raspberry Cake (recipe on p. 375) and food photography by John Sherman of John Sherman Photography, Inc., Hartford, Vermont

Food styling by Sue Gray

Copyediting by Wendy Ruopp

Index by Elizabeth Parson

Published by The Countryman Press, P.O. Box 748, Woodstock, Vermont 05091

Distributed by W.W. Norton & Company, Inc., 500 Fifth Avenue, New York, 10110

PRINTED IN CHINA

10 9 8 7 6 5 4 3 2 1

Acknowledgments

This book is dedicated to all the employee-owners of King Arthur Flour Company, past and present. It took all of us, including the pioneers from the Sands, Taylor and Wood families back in 1790 right through our most recent employee-owner, to create a book with this much depth of knowledge and this many delicious and creative recipes. We are truly a family of bakers and the teamwork that was displayed while developing this manuscript is heartwarming.

Special thanks go to Susan Miller, who left her role as baking instructor and director of our Baking Education Center for a year to work on this book, and to bakers extraordinaire P.J. Hamel and Susan Reid. This is their third book in five years, all the while juggling their other responsibilities at work and at home. Also helping on practically a daily basis were Brenda Hickory, Janet Matz, Sue Gray, Robby Kuit and our many taste testers throughout the company. Thanks to our president Steve Voigt for seeing how important it was that we put other projects on hold to create this book.

Thanks and heaps of praise, too, to Kermit Hummel, our editor at Countryman, for his guidance and enthusiasm and to another Countryman editor, Jennifer Thompson, who kept us on track.

A handful of employee-owners, from accounting to purchasing, took on pieces of this project from time to time—and always with great passion and dedication to the goal—to create a book that pushes forward the cookbook literature dedicated to baking with whole grains. Creating this book took vision and a lot of hard work—all books do, and this one felt like it held the two in perfect balance.

We also thank our loyal customers who guided us along the way with their valuable opinions. And, we want to thank publicly and lovingly the people who made it all possible, our families. —*Toni Apgar*

CONTENTS

10 ways to get more whole grains into your life

1. Buy some whole wheat flour and put it in your freezer. You can't bake with it if you don't have it.

2. Make your own granola and use it for breakfast or as a trail mix. See recipe on p. 25.

3. Commit to eating and using more oats. Put oats in streusel toppings, cookies, muffins, cakes and so on. Grind them up like a flour and use liberally.

4. Cook a cup of hulled barley (p. 583), refrigerate it and use a tablespoon or two in your bread recipes and in your soups, stews, chili, pot pies and so on.

5. Start today by substituting ⅓ cup of white whole wheat flour for ⅓ cup of all-purpose flour in all your recipes.

6. Chocolate and whole wheat are a great combo—make the Chocolate Crinkle Cookies on p. 328, the Chocolate–Chocolate Chip Waffles on p. 301 or the Double Fudge Brownies on p. 341.

7. Mix up your morning breakfast cereal routine with whole grain muffins, such as our Morning Glory Muffin on p. 35.

8. Give up store-bought white bread. If you can't do that, make sandwiches with one slice of white bread and one slice of whole wheat (if you buy from the store, make sure it is 100 percent whole wheat or 100 percent whole grain). Better yet, make the Golden Malted Wheat Bread on p. 184 and use that for sandwiches and toast.

9. Bake from scratch. You absolutely have no way of knowing how much whole grain nutrition you are getting in store-bought baked goods. You'll love the results of your own baking, and think how much more wholesome you can make even decadent treats.

10. Don't fret about it. Change your diet gradually. If something doesn't taste good, forget about it. Life's too short to eat food that doesn't taste great.

How to create delicious recipes using nutritious whole grains

This book is about flavor. It's not a lecture on why you ought to eat more whole grains because you know that already. We set out to make whole grains taste great, in the firm belief that if they don't taste great, you and your family won't eat whatever amount you determine is good for you. Turns out, that was pretty easy. It didn't take obnoxious chemical additives or weird-sounding ingredients, either.

Whole grains have gotten a bad rap. When they are pure and fresh and used creatively in your favorite recipes—or, in the case of this book, in *our* favorite recipes—they taste great. In our experiments with whole wheat flour, barley flour, oats, spelt, corn and other whole grains, we couldn't believe how versatile and yummy they are, and how they work wonders in so many recipes. We knew all along that whole grains are not just for breads, but can be used in all manner of baked goods. When the first whole grain croissant came out of the test kitchen and our jaws dropped at how light and flaky it was, we knew we were on to something. Ditto with piecrust, cookies, cakes, muffins and so on. Our goal is to make your jaw drop too—to make you say, or at least think, "I had *no* idea you could make something that wonderful with whole grains." The whole grains we use often improve the flavor and texture of tried-and-true recipes (barley flour in pie crusts, p, 452), and in some cases they create their own nuance of flavor that adds depth (Toasted Almond–Mocha Cake, p. 395). We believe the whole grain we use in every recipe in this book *adds* to the result—otherwise we wouldn't have included the recipe.

That brings us to the recipes. We tested thousands of recipes and we were mighty picky about whether a recipe was good enough for this book. We used testing sheets that asked testers what they liked or didn't like about the recipe and whether they would make it at home for their family, because that's really the ultimate test. We were determined to not accept any recipe with a comment something like, "Tastes good *for whole grain*." So in many cases we didn't let our testers know if the recipe included whole grains or not. Each recipe had to stand on its own, as great tasting *and* a

---

GETTING STARTED

You may find this useful when gathering ingredients for the recipes in this book:

Butter is unsalted.

Eggs are large.

Salt is regular table salt.

Sugar is granulated sugar.

Brown sugar can be either light or dark, unless specified.

Vegetable oil can be vegetable, canola, safflower or sunflower oil.

Chocolate chips are semi-sweet chips, unless otherwise specified.

Raisins can be Thompson or golden, your choice.

Baking powder is double-acting baking powder.

Milk is 1% unless otherwise specified.

Yogurt is usually low-fat or full-fat, not nonfat.

Cream cheese is reduced-fat (Neufchâtel) or full-fat.

Molasses is unsulfured golden or dark (not blackstrap).

Yeast is almost always instant yeast, unless noted otherwise. If all you can find is active dry yeast, you'll need to "proof" it first. See more on yeast on p. 174. Do not use rapid rise yeast; it is not the same as instant yeast.

significant source of whole grains. We discovered whole grains are not something to hide; not something to shy away from in your baking; embrace and celebrate them!

OK, fine, but what about the kids? How do you get them to eat nutritious whole grains? If you try our brownies, cookies, cupcakes, breads and muffins, they'll never know (unless you tell them) about the whole grains in the recipe. How about a short stack of Triple Ginger Pancakes (p. 11) that meet their entire recommended daily amount of whole grains? We're not advocating hiding whole grains; however, many of us are parents and we know how hard it can be to get picky eaters to eat what's good for them. We have taken a giant step forward in that realm for you. Trust us—make the brownies on p. 341 and follow that with the cupcakes on p. 371 and see what happens.

Substitutions

One of the first questions usually asked about whole grains is, "Can I substitute whole wheat flour for all-purpose unbleached flour in my favorite recipes?" Our answer is yes, and no. Yes, you can take your favorite recipes and start substituting whole wheat flour for a portion of the white flour. That portion depends on the recipe and on the type of flour you're using. In most cases you can't just take out the white flour and put in whole wheat flour. But with almost 400 recipes in this book that we know all taste great, why turn to substitutions? If you work your way through 10 or so recipes in any of these chapters, you'll be a whole grain expert and will be able to convert just about any of your favorite recipes into whole grain goodness. Have a favorite piecrust recipe? Fool around with ours and maybe you'll want to convert your own, or maybe you'll just use ours from now on.

How to use this book

This book is dedicated to great flavor in combination with whole grains; it isn't a health-food book. We created recipes that all have a significant number of grams of whole grains. How much is enough? The U.S. government's Dietary Guidelines recommend 3 servings, or 48 grams, of whole grains per day. At the bottom of each recipe you'll find a nutritional analysis containing the grams of whole grain per serving as well as other information.

In our testing, we found that lots of whole grain recipes benefit from an overnight rest. We just hate it when we're reading a cookbook, decide on a recipe, gather all the ingredients and then read in the instructions that something needs to rest for 8 hours or overnight. So we've included an overnight icon ⬛ and placed it at the top of all recipes that require, or benefit greatly from, an overnight rest either before or after baking.

We pushed the envelope on ingredients in this book, especially whole grain flours. We gently encouraged wheat and barley and spelt to do things that may never have been done before. Not everything was a success—that's why we do so much testing. On the other hand, we also turned to the advice of our grandmothers, vintage cookbooks and ethnic recipes that have always made good use of whole grains. After all, white flour is a relatively recent development in the history of humankind. At times our test kitchen looked more like a lab than a kitchen, with bowls and bowls of sourdough starter bubbling and gurgling away, and notes being taken every few hours. Each and every recipe had to answer the questions: "Does it taste fantastic?" and "Would the average baker be able to make this at home?" The answer had to be yes to both. We ventured into some unusual territory, sometimes with common ingredients (you'll see orange juice as a preferred liquid in many recipes calling for whole wheat) and sometimes unusual ingredients (malted wheat flakes, boiled cider, vital wheat gluten). In all cases we know that you can get these items and we have some suggestions about where to buy them on page 588.

While developing the premise for this book, we kept asking ourselves: "Is that a whole grain?" We were sure about King Arthur Flour Traditional Whole Wheat and King Arthur Flour White Whole Wheat (for more detail on these two types of flour, see p. 173), and our Whole Wheat Pastry Flour and our cornmeal. But we quickly found that not all of what is marketed or perceived as whole grain is really "whole."

We turned to the experts for help and adopted the definition offered by The Whole Grains Council, an advocacy group that wants us all to consume more whole grains. "Whole grains or foods made from them contain all the essential parts and naturally occurring nutrients of the entire grain seed. If the grain has been processed (e.g., cracked, crushed, rolled, extruded, and/or cooked), the food product should deliver approximately the same rich balance of nutrients that are found in the original grain seed. Examples of generally accepted whole grain foods and flours are: amaranth, barley, brown and colored rice, buckwheat, bulgur, corn and whole yellow cornmeal, emmer, farro, Kamut® grain, millet, oatmeal and whole oats, popcorn, quinoa, sorghum, spelt, teff, triticale, whole rye, whole wheat or cracked wheat, wheat berries, and wild rice."

We've included whole grains in every recipe in this book, but not every recipe is 100 percent whole grain. We strove for the right ratio of whole grain to other ingredients to get the best flavor, rise and workability of the dough. You will see unbleached all-purpose flour or bread flour in some recipes and our rationale for using it is made clear whenever we do. In all cases the recipes using wheat flours were tested using King Arthur Flour or a King Arthur Flour product.

We've included a helpful primer on most of the grains used along with a recipe for each major grain that we think perfectly highlights the unique flavor and baking qualities of that grain. You'll find this beginning on p. 537.

We are fanatics about weighing ingredients. If you don't have a scale, may we suggest that you treat yourself to one now, justifying it by all the nutritious whole grains you're going to be feeding your family. Each recipe ingredient in this book has a volume measurement (such as ½ cup) and a weight measurement (2 ounces). We prefer using the weight measurement and hope that you'll get used to it as well. It is much more precise (and it cuts down on dirty dishes). Here's how we do it: Turn on the scale, put your mixing bowl on it, push "tare" to get the weight back to zero, add your first ingredient to the proper weight, push "tare" to get the weight back to zero, then add the second ingredient to the proper weight, and so on. No more dirty measuring cups.

We are also fanatics about how to measure a cup of flour. We teach hundreds of home bakers around the country every year, and by far the majority of them are stunned when we show them how to measure flour. Do this: Use a fork or spoon to vigorously fluff up the flour in the bag or container that it's in. This, of course, incorporates air into

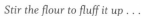

Stir the flour to fluff it up . . .

. . . sprinkle it into the measuring cup . .

. . . and sweep off the excess with the edge of the flour scoop or the flat end of a knife.

the flour, and air is one of nature's very best leaveners, and a powerful one to boot. Then dip a flour scoop or spoon into the container and sprinkle the flour into your dry measuring cup. This will assure that you don't pack in the flour—a certain path to dry, hard, crumbly bread or cookies and so on. Take the edge of the flour scoop or the flat edge of a knife and level the cup. There—you have a cup of flour that weighs approximately 4¼ ounces, depending on the type of flour you are measuring. If you make this a habit and measure all flour this way, we guarantee you will be pleased with the results.

A word about whole grains and storage: You know that whole grains contain the bran and the natural oils from the entire grain. (For more on this, see p. 542.) When the entire grain is milled, exposing the oil to air, it begins a slow oxidation process and can, without proper storage, go rancid, affecting the flavor of your flour and your baked goods. You can handle this two ways: Unmilled grains such as wheat berries stay fresh for a very long time (some have been found intact in Egyptian tombs). Buy some fresh wheat berries from a local health food store or food co-op (or use the Internet to buy by mail) and a small electric or battery-powered mill and grind the wheat berries as you need them. The flavor of freshly milled wheat flour is divine. If that's too much of a bother, then after you purchase your whole wheat flour, whole grain cornmeal and other whole grain flours, store them in the freezer. Pull them out to measure and use and then put the container back in the freezer.

We invite you to get familiar with the recipes in this book—thumb through the index and see what grabs your eye. If you are new to baking with whole grains, start with something familiar; the Devil's Food Cupcakes on p. 371, the Chewy Chocolate Chip Cookies on p. 304 or the Simple Spelt Pancakes on p. 2. Work some of these recipes and some more adventurous ones (Light Sourdough Rye Bread, p. 293 and Classic Whole Wheat Croissants, p. 504) into your baking repertoire and in no time, you'll be turning to them as if they were old friends. In fact, many of them are old friends, looking a bit like some of the recipes our ancestors turned to day after day, no matter what continent your ancestors came from. So once again, come into the kitchen with us and let's bake with whole grains.

BREAKFASTS

Ahhh, breakfast!

For so many of us, it's our favorite meal of the day, and most nutritionists agree it's the most important. We awake each morning with the opportunity to start afresh, all our resolutions intact, and breakfast is the chance to begin with a blast of nutrition to set us on the day's path. There are nights when we go to sleep already anticipating the next morning's meal; we can smell the coffee and taste the waffles as we drift off to sleep. Other days, we just need to grab something fast on the way out the door, deadlines looming. Whether you're breaking fast with a feast or a quick bite, chances are your first meal includes something with grains: a slice of toast, a bowl of cereal, a short stack of pancakes or even a breakfast bar. The trouble is, if you're just pouring another bowl of heart-healthy cereal from a box or toasting a slice of the same whole grain loaf, it can get boring.

We don't believe in boring breakfasts and we found it was easy and fun to shift from grains to whole grains. Many of these breakfast recipes have enough whole grains to keep you fueled through the day and many of them lend themselves to variation. As you make your way through the pancakes and waffles and even the granola, experiment with the grains you like; you'll be amazed at how delicious it can be to incorporate whole grains into the mix.

PANCAKES

Who doesn't love pancakes? There's even a chain of restaurants built around them, and they've long been the stars of breakfast for dinner! Whole grain pancakes are a great discovery; now we can indulge our infatuation with breakfast cakes without the customary guilt. While we were testing the recipes that follow, we noticed that the whole grain pancake batters behaved a little differently on the griddle. Instead of bubbling across the surface, only a couple little bubbles would form around the edges; if we waited for the bubbling, the cakes were overdone, no matter how low we turned the heat. Instead, we learned to look for other signs that the pancakes were done—bubbles at the edges or a change in the surface texture from shiny to matte. We experimented with a wide variety of grains here, and we've included the best of the bunch, so grab your fork and maple syrup and help yourself to a short stack that's long on nutrition!

Simple Spelt Pancakes

YIELD: 16 (4-inch) pancakes
COOKING TIME: 4 to 6 minutes

The sweet flavor of spelt shines through in these simple pancakes. You can dress up these pancakes with fresh fruit, spices or nuts, but we find the flavor of the grain is good enough to stand on its own.

> 2 cups (7 ounces) whole spelt flour
> 2 tablespoons ($7/8$ ounce) sugar
> 1 tablespoon baking powder
> $3/4$ teaspoon salt
> $13/4$ cups (14 ounces) milk
> 2 tablespoons (1 ounce) unsalted butter, melted
> 2 teaspoons vanilla (optional)

TO MAKE THE PANCAKE BATTER: Whisk together the spelt flour, sugar, baking powder and salt in a medium bowl. Combine the milk and melted butter, and the vanilla if you're using it. Form a well in the center of the dry ingredients and pour the wet ingredients into the dry. Stir the batter just until the dry ingredients are thoroughly moistened: it will seem very wet, but will thicken as it sits. Let the batter sit for 15 minutes.

TO MAKE THE PANCAKES: Heat a nonstick griddle if you have one, or a heavy skillet, preferably cast iron. If your surface is not nonstick, brush it lightly with vegetable oil. When the surface of your pan is hot enough that a drop of water sputters across it, give the pan a quick swipe with a paper towel to eliminate excess oil, and spoon the batter onto the hot surface, ¼-cupful at a time. Let the pancakes cook on the first side until bubbles begin to form around the edges of the cakes, 2 to 3 minutes.

You may need to adjust your heat up or down to get the pancakes to cook through without scorching the surface or being too pale. When the cakes are just beginning to set, flip them and let them finish cooking on the second side, until they're golden brown on both sides, about 1 minute more.

NUTRITION INFORMATION PER SERVING (2 PANCAKES, 89G): 27g whole grains, 137 cal, 4g fat, 5g protein, 20g complex carbohydrates, 4g sugar, 4g dietary fiber, 11mg cholesterol, 376mg sodium, 189mg potassium, 57RE vitamin A, 1mg iron, 192mg calcium, 309mg phosphorus.

When the liquid is first added, the batter is very thin and soupy.

After 15 minutes, the spelt has absorbed the liquid, and the batter is much thicker.

The bubbles around the edge and the matte surface of the pancake indicate it's ready to flip.

PATIENCE, PLEASE

While most pancake recipes call for a rest between making and baking the batter, it's especially important to do this with whole grain batters. A 10- to 15-minute rest allows the grains to absorb the liquid, making the batter fluffier and the baked pancakes smoother in your mouth. This time-out also lets the leaveners get a head start, giving you a cakier pancake than you would get without the rest. If you prefer thinner, eggier pancakes, try cooking them immediately after mixing, but be prepared for a grainier texture. We find 15 minutes the perfect amount of time to gather syrup and other toppings, get the coffee going, preheat the oven to a low heat for keeping the baked cakes warm, and alert everyone that breakfast is almost ready!

Homemade Whole Grain Pancake Mix

YIELD: 10 cups dry mix; a batch using 1 cup of the mix will make about 10 (3½-inch) pancakes.
COOKING TIME: 3 to 5 minutes

This is a wonderful alternative to store-bought, bleached-flour, boxed pancake mixes. You may use this mix as the base for all sorts of imaginative pancakes—pineapple-coconut, cranberry-apple, peach-walnut, cinnamon-banana, to name a few—or simply pile them high on your plate, with maple syrup on the side: these are delicious enough to stand alone.

3½ cups (12¼ ounces) old-fashioned rolled oats
4 cups (1 pound) white whole wheat flour
1 cup (4¼ ounces) unbleached all-purpose flour
3 tablespoons (1¼ ounces) sugar
3 tablespoons (1½ ounces) baking powder
1 tablespoon salt
1 tablespoon baking soda
¾ cup (5¼ ounces) vegetable oil

TO MAKE THE MIX: Grind the oats in a food processor until they're chopped fine but not a powder. Put the ground oats, flours and the remaining dry ingredients into the bowl of a mixer with a paddle. Mix on slow speed, and drizzle the vegetable oil into the bowl slowly while the mixer is running. When all the oil has been added, stop the mixer and squeeze a clump of mix in your hand. If it holds together, it's just right. If it won't hold together, stir in 1 tablespoon of oil at a time until the consistency is correct. Store in an airtight container indefinitely in the freezer.

> ### ORANGE JUICE IN MY PANCAKES?
>
> We've found that the acidity and sweetness of orange juice helps mellow the tannic taste some people perceive in whole wheat flour; while the pancakes won't have any orange flavor, they may taste slightly milder to you than without it. Try it!

TO MAKE THE PANCAKES: Whisk together 1 cup of mix, 1 cup buttermilk (or you may use ½ cup plain yogurt plus ½ cup milk), 1 tablespoon orange juice and 1 large egg. Don't worry if the batter seems thin at first: the whole grains will soak up the liquid, and the mixture will thicken as it stands. Let the batter stand for at least 15 minutes before cooking.

Heat a nonstick griddle if you have one, or a heavy skillet, preferably cast iron. If your surface is not nonstick, brush it lightly with vegetable oil. When the surface of your pan is hot enough that a drop of water sputters across it, give the pan a quick swipe with a paper towel to remove excess oil and spoon the batter onto the hot surface, ¼-cupful at a time. After 3 to 4 minutes, when the surface of the cake is no longer shiny and small bubbles are beginning to form around the edges, it's time to flip the cake. Cook on the other side until it's browned, 1 to 2 minutes more and serve immediately, or keep warm in a 200°F oven while you finish cooking the rest of the cakes.

NUTRITION INFORMATION PER SERVING (2 PANCAKES, 86G): 16g whole grains, 139 cal, 6g fat, 6g protein, 16g complex carbohydrates, 1g sugar, 2g dietary fiber, 44mg cholesterol, 254mg sodium, 155mg potassium, 17RE vitamin A, 1mg vitamin C, 1mg iron, 67mg calcium, 133mg phosphorus.

Blueberry-Corn Pancakes

YIELD: 14 (3-inch) pancakes
COOKING TIME: 5 to 6 minutes

Sunny pancakes are a great way to start the day, and these are 100 percent whole grain. The secret to their fluffy texture is letting the batter sit for 15 minutes before you bake them. It also helps reduce the grittiness of the cornmeal. If you want a thinner pancake, use a little more milk and bake them as soon as the batter is mixed.

> ½ cup (2⅜ ounces) whole yellow cornmeal
> ⅔ cup (5⅜ ounces) boiling water
> 3 tablespoons (1½ ounces) butter, melted
> ¼ to ⅓ cup (2 to 2⅜ ounces) milk
> 1 egg, beaten
> ½ cup (1⅝ ounces) whole wheat pastry flour
> 2 tablespoons (⅞ ounce) sugar
> 1 tablespoon baking powder
> ½ teaspoon salt
> 1 cup (5 ounces) blueberries, fresh or frozen

Place the cornmeal in a medium bowl. Pour the boiling water over it, stir the mixture thoroughly and let it sit for 15 minutes. This step allows the cornmeal to absorb the liquid, and it will be quite stiff at the end of the 15 minutes. Stir in the melted butter to loosen the mixture. Measure the milk in a small liquid measuring cup; use the smaller amount of milk if your berries are frozen. Beat the egg into the milk and stir the mixture into the cornmeal. Combine well to be sure there are no lumps. In a separate bowl, combine the pastry flour with the sugar, baking powder and salt. Add the dry ingredients to the cornmeal mixture and combine with a few swift strokes. Let the batter sit for 15 minutes, then stir in the blueberries.

Heat a nonstick griddle if you have one, or a heavy skillet, preferably cast iron. If your surface is not nonstick, brush it lightly with vegetable oil. You'll need very little fat to cook these pancakes, as there's butter in the batter. When the surface of your pan is hot enough that a drop of water sputters across it, give the pan a quick swipe with a paper towel to remove excess oil and spoon the batter onto the hot surface, ¼-cupful at a time. Let the pancakes cook on the first side until bubbles begin to form around the edges, about 3 minutes. These pancakes take a little longer to set than most. You may need to adjust your heat up or down to get the pancakes to cook through without scorching the surface or being too pale. When the cakes are set through the center, flip them and let them finish cooking on the second side, until they're golden brown, 1 to 2 minutes more. Serve immediately.

NUTRITION INFORMATION PER SERVING (2 PANCAKES, 92G): 16g whole grains, 153 cal, 7g fat, 4g protein, 17g complex carbohydrates, 3g sugar, 2g dietary fiber, 45mg cholesterol, 339mg sodium, 104mg potassium, 62RE vitamin A, 2mg vitamin C, 1mg iron, 167mg calcium, 279mg phosphorus.

FRUITFUL ADDITIONS

As soon as you're comfortable with a basic pancake recipe, the adventure begins; your head swivels around the kitchen in search of an addition to make the recipe your own—fruit, nuts, chocolate chips, spices—"Hey, what's in that jar over there? Let's try that!" For successful experiments, it's best to keep a couple things in mind. When you're adding fruit, it makes a big difference to the batter whether it's fresh, dried or frozen. Fresh fruit can usually be added without affecting the batter too much, unless it's especially juicy, like pineapple. Dried fruit will absorb liquid from the batter, so you may want to increase the liquid by a tablespoon or two before you mix together the ingredients. Frozen fruit has the opposite effect, flooding the batter with extra liquid as it thaws, so cut back a tablespoon or two of the liquid before you mix. Also, you'll find that many fruits can clump together in one part of the batter. Try sprinkling them across the uncooked top of the pancake just after it goes on the griddle; this helps keep them from scorching on the hot griddle, too, for that first, longer-cooking side.

SLOW AND STEADY

Pancakes made with whole grains bake a little differently than their white-flour counterparts. The batters tend to be a bit thicker. To be sure they bake through without scorching, you'll want to turn the heat down a bit and give the cakes a slightly longer time on the griddle—as much as 4 minutes on the first side. We also noticed fewer of the characteristic bubbles forming in our pancakes as they baked, so don't wait for bubbles to cover the entire cake before you flip, or you may wind up with pancakes that are too brown. Instead, check the edges to see if the cakes are beginning to set; the surface of the pancakes starts to change from shiny to matte, and that's an indication it's time to flip the cakes.

Orange Cloud Pancakes

YIELD: 12 (4-inch) pancakes
COOKING TIME: 6 to 7 minutes

Orange and whole wheat is a natural combination, and these feathery pancakes make a complete breakfast. They're so light it's hard to believe they're made with whole wheat flour. Eat them as soon as they're made, topped with maple syrup, and begin your day with a full tummy and enough protein to last you till lunch!

¾ cup (6 ounces) cottage cheese
3 eggs, separated
4 tablespoons (½ stick, 2 ounces) unsalted butter, melted
1 tablespoon orange juice
½ cup (2 ounces) white whole wheat flour
1 tablespoon sugar
½ teaspoon salt
Pinch of ground cinnamon
1 tablespoon orange zest

Place the cottage cheese, egg yolks, melted butter and orange juice in a food processor, and process until the cottage cheese is smooth, about 30 seconds. Add the flour, sugar, salt and cinnamon and process again. Scrape the mixture into a medium bowl and stir in the orange zest. Let this mixture sit for 10 minutes. In the bowl of your electric mixer, whip the egg whites until they're stiff but not dry. Use a rubber spatula to stir a spoonful of the whites into the batter to loosen it, and then gently fold in the rest of the whites. This batter does not need to rest; cook the pancakes right away as directed below.

Heat a nonstick griddle if you have one, or a heavy skillet, preferably cast iron. If your surface is not nonstick, brush it lightly with vegetable oil. When the surface of your pan is hot enough that a drop of water sputters across it, give the pan a quick swipe with a paper towel to remove excess oil, and spoon the batter onto the hot surface, ⅓-cupful at a time. Cook the cakes, checking them frequently to be sure they're not browning too quickly. When they're beginning to set, and you see small bubbles starting to form around the edges, flip them and finish cooking until both sides are golden brown. Serve immediately. These pancakes are light and fluffy and do not hold well in the oven. We suggest serving them as they come off the griddle.

NUTRITION INFORMATION PER SERVING (2 PANCAKES, 78G): **9g whole grains,** 175 cal, 12g fat, 8g protein, 9g complex carbohydrates, 2g sugar, 1g dietary fiber, 130mg cholesterol, 341mg sodium, 102mg potassium, 88RE vitamin A, 1mg vitamin C, 1mg iron, 34mg calcium, 120mg phosphorus.

Banana-Oat Pancakes

YIELD: About 10 (4-inch) pancakes
COOKING TIME: 5 to 6 minutes

Fluffy and fragrant, these pancakes are a tempting treat for banana lovers. The oats add a nutty flavor and a light, moist feel, and the spices remind us of that perennial favorite, banana bread. For a special treat, sprinkle toasted walnuts over the batter just before cooking.

3 small (9½ ounces) bananas, mashed
2 tablespoons (1 ounce) unsalted butter, melted
1 tablespoon lemon juice
1 tablespoon sugar
2 eggs
1 cup (3¼ ounces) oat flour
½ teaspoon baking soda
½ teaspoon salt
½ teaspoon ground cinnamon
½ teaspoon ground nutmeg

Stir together the mashed bananas, butter, lemon juice and sugar in a medium bowl. Beat in the eggs. Whisk together the oat flour, baking soda, salt and spices in a small bowl.

Form a well in the center of the dry ingredients and pour in the wet ingredients. Stir the batter just until the dry ingredients are thoroughly moistened. Check to be sure the batter is thin enough for your pancakes: you may need to add a touch of milk or water. Let the batter sit for 10 minutes before using.

Heat a nonstick griddle if you have one, or a heavy skillet, preferably cast iron. If your surface is not nonstick, brush it lightly with vegetable oil. When the surface of your pan is hot enough that a drop of water sputters across it, give the pan a quick swipe with a paper towel to remove excess oil, and spoon the batter onto the hot surface, ¼-cupful at a time. Let the pancakes cook on the first side until bubbles begin to form around the edges of the cakes, 3 to 4 minutes. You may need to adjust the heat up or down to get the pancakes to cook through without scorching the surface or being too pale. When the cakes are just beginning to set, flip them and let them finish cooking on the second side, until they're golden brown on both sides, about 1½ minutes more. Serve the pancakes immediately, or keep them warm in a 200°F oven.

NUTRITION INFORMATION PER SERVING (2 PANCAKES, 104G): 18g whole grains, 203 cal, 8g fat, 6g protein, 26g complex carbohydrates, 2g sugar, 3g dietary fiber, 98mg cholesterol, 386mg sodium, 308mg potassium, 73RE vitamin A, 6mg vitamin C, 1mg iron, 26mg calcium, 139mg phosphorus.

Müesli Pancakes

YIELD: **10 (4-inch) pancakes**
COOKING TIME: **3 to 5 minutes**

These delightfully wholesome pancakes are a snap to make and give you half the recommended amount of whole grains for the day in a single serving (2 pancakes). There's a lovely crunch from the nuts, but the white whole wheat flour keeps these light enough in flavor and texture that they don't come off as "health food" pancakes.

²⁄₃ cup (2¹⁄₄ ounces) müesli
1¹⁄₂ cups (12 ounces) buttermilk
1 egg
2 tablespoons (⁷⁄₈ ounce) packed light or dark brown sugar
2 tablespoons (⁷⁄₈ ounce) vegetable oil
²⁄₃ cup (2⁵⁄₈ ounces) white whole wheat flour
1 teaspoon baking soda
¹⁄₂ teaspoon salt

Soak the müesli in the buttermilk overnight at room temperature. The next morning, in a separate bowl, whisk the egg with the brown sugar and oil until the ingredients are emulsified, then stir in the müesli mixture. Combine the flour, baking soda and salt and swiftly stir them into the wet ingredients just until they're moistened. Allow the batter to rest for 15 minutes before using.

Heat a nonstick griddle if you have one, or a heavy skillet, preferably cast iron. If your surface is not nonstick, brush it lightly with vegetable oil. When the surface of your pan is hot enough that a drop of water sputters across it, give the pan a quick swipe with a paper towel to remove excess oil, and spoon the batter onto the hot surface, ¹⁄₄-cupful at a time. Let the pancakes cook on the first side until the edges begin to look set, about 3 minutes. You may need to adjust your heat up or down to get the pancakes to cook through without scorching the surface or being too pale. When the cakes are just beginning to set, flip them and let them finish cooking on the second side, until they're golden brown on both sides, about 1 minute more.

NUTRITION INFORMATION PER SERVING (2 PANCAKES, 122G): **24g whole grains,** 203 cal, 8g fat, 8g protein, 21g complex carbohydrates, 5g sugar, 3g dietary fiber, 45mg cholesterol, 559mg sodium, 248mg potassium, 20RE vitamin A, 1mg vitamin C, 1mg iron, 101mg calcium, 184mg phosphorus.

Brown Rice Pancakes

YIELD: 12 (3- to 4-inch) pancakes
COOKING TIME: 3 to 4 minutes

These tender pancakes remind us of rice pudding and are a great way to use up last night's left-overs! We've spiced them with our favorite rice-pudding spices, but feel free to play with the seasonings to suit your own taste. You may substitute other cooked grains in pancakes (see sidebar, below).

4 eggs
¼ cup (2 ounces) buttermilk
2 tablespoons (1 ounce) unsalted butter, melted
1 teaspoon vanilla extract
1 teaspoon grated orange or lemon zest
1 cup (6 ounces) cooked brown rice
½ cup (2 ounces) white whole wheat flour
1 tablespoon sugar
½ teaspoon salt
½ teaspoon ground nutmeg
Pinch of ground cinnamon

Beat the eggs* in a medium bowl and whisk in the buttermilk, melted butter, vanilla and orange (or lemon) zest. Stir in the brown rice. Combine the flour, sugar, salt and spices, and stir them into the wet ingredients. Stir the batter until it's just mixed, and let it sit for 10 minutes before making the pancakes.

SEND IN THE SUBSTITUTIONS

It's wonderful to use up leftover grains the next morning, and breakfast offers a variety of choices for dressing up last night's dinner. You can reheat grains with a bit of milk or cream for a quick hot cereal, or stir them into scrambled eggs, or fold them into pancake or waffle batter. The key is to think about how dinner seasonings will work at the breakfast table. If you've had curried quinoa, it probably won't be welcome in pancakes served with maple syrup, but you might be able to slip it into a curried vegetable omelet at brunch. If you're adding salted grains to an existing recipe, you may need to adjust the salt up or down, depending on how much you've used in the original dish. If you've omitted salt in the grain preparation, you'll likely want to increase the salt in your pancake batter. In general, the milder the dish, the more flexible it is in its encore. A little creativity and a lot of flexibility will make those leftovers as magnificent as the main event.

Heat a nonstick griddle if you have one, or a heavy skillet, preferably cast iron. If your surface is not nonstick, brush it lightly with vegetable oil. When the surface of your pan is hot enough that a drop of water sputters across it, spoon the batter onto the hot surface, ¼-cupful at a time. These pancakes set up pretty quickly, but don't really bubble as they cook; as soon as they start to look set, flip the pancakes and bake until both sides are golden brown. Be sure to check the first pancake you make for salt content; depending on how you've prepared the rice, you may need to adjust the salt in the batter. Serve the pancakes immediately, or keep them warm in a 200°F oven until you've finished baking them.

*For an especially delicate texture, separate the eggs, whip the whites and fold them into the batter before the 10-minute rest. Put the yolks in the bowl as directed in the first step and continue the recipe.

NUTRITION INFORMATION PER SERVING (2 PANCAKES, 111G): 38g whole grains, 176 cal, 8g fat, 7g protein, 16g complex carbohydrates, 2g sugar, 2g dietary fiber, 152mg cholesterol, 254mg sodium, 149mg potassium, 81RE vitamin A, 2mg iron, 54mg calcium, 148mg phosphorus.

Triple Ginger Pancakes

YIELD: 12 (3-inch) pancakes
COOKING TIME: 3 to 5 minutes

These pancakes, with the zing of fresh ginger, are so light you won't believe they're 100 percent whole grain! You may make them using all wheat flour if you like, but the barley flour adds a nice touch. If you're a true ginger fan, use the larger amount of fresh ginger and, for even more bite, serve the pancakes with an equal mixture of maple and ginger syrups.

1 cup (4 ounces) white whole wheat flour
½ cup (2 ounces) whole barley flour
1 tablespoon ground ginger
1 teaspoon baking soda
½ teaspoon salt
1 teaspoon grated lemon zest
1 to 2 tablespoons minced crystallized ginger
1 egg, beaten
3 tablespoons (1½ ounces) butter, melted
1 cup (8 ounces) buttermilk
¾ cup (6 ounces) orange juice
1 tablespoon grated fresh ginger

Combine the flours with the ground ginger, baking soda and salt in a medium bowl. Toss in the grated lemon zest and crystallized ginger to taste. In a separate bowl, beat the egg lightly, then stir in the melted butter. Stir in the buttermilk, orange juice and fresh ginger.

Form a well in the center of the dry ingredients and pour in the wet ingredients. Stir the batter just until the dry ingredients are thoroughly moistened. Check to be sure the batter is thin enough for your pancakes: you may need to add more liquid.

Heat a nonstick griddle if you have one, or a heavy skillet, preferably cast iron. If your surface is not nonstick, brush it lightly with vegetable oil. When the surface of your pan is hot enough that a drop of water sputters across it, spoon the batter onto the hot surface, ¼-cupful at a time. Let the pancake cook on the first side until bubbles begin to form around the edges, 2 to 3 minutes. You may need to adjust your heat up or down to get the pancakes to cook through without scorching the surface or being too pale. When the cakes are just beginning to set, flip them and let them finish cooking on the second side, until they're golden brown on both sides, about 1 minute more. Serve immediately, or keep warm in a 200°F oven.

NUTRITION INFORMATION PER SERVING (2 PANCAKES, 76G): **27g whole grains,** 136 cal, 5g fat, 4g protein, 17g complex carbohydrates, 2g sugar, 3g dietary fiber, 32mg cholesterol, 268mg sodium, 149mg potassium, 40RE vitamin A, 7mg vitamin C, 1mg iron, 37mg calcium, 88mg phosphorus.

Quinoa Pancakes

YIELD: 16 (3½-inch) pancakes
COOKING TIME: 4 to 5 minutes

Quinoa packs a lot of protein punch, making it an ideal grain for the morning. These pancakes are spicy with ginger, sweet with applesauce and tart with cranberries. They manage to be both tender and fluffy, with a flavor bright enough to wake you up. For extra zing, try them with maple syrup mixed with ginger syrup.

> 1 cup (3⅞ ounces) quinoa flour
> ¼ cup (¾ ounce) whole wheat pastry flour
> 2 teaspoons baking powder
> 1 teaspoon ground ginger
> ½ teaspoon ground allspice
> ¼ teaspoon salt
> 1 cup (8 ounces) milk
> ½ cup (4 ounces) applesauce

1 egg

½ cup (2 ounces) dried cranberries

¼ cup (1⅝ ounces) minced crystallized ginger

Combine the flours, baking powder, spices and salt in a medium bowl. In a separate bowl, whisk together the milk, applesauce and egg. Form a well in the center of the dry ingredients and pour in the wet ingredients. Stir the batter just until the dry ingredients are thoroughly moistened. Fold in the cranberries and crystallized ginger. Let the batter sit for 10 minutes.

Heat a nonstick griddle if you have one, or a heavy skillet, preferably cast iron. If your surface is not nonstick, brush it lightly with vegetable oil. When the surface of your pan is hot enough that a drop of water sputters across it, spoon the batter onto the hot surface, ¼ cupful at a time. Let the pancake cook on the first side until bubbles begin to form around the edges, 2 to 3 minutes. You may need to adjust your heat up or down to get the pancakes to cook through without scorching the surface or being too pale. When the cakes are just beginning to set, flip them and let them finish cooking on the second side, until they're golden brown on both sides, about 1½ minutes more.

NUTRITION INFORMATION PER SERVING (2 PANCAKES, 88G): **16g whole grains,** 151 cal, 2g fat, 5g protein, 24g complex carbohydrates, 6g sugar, 2g dietary fiber, 28mg cholesterol, 189mg sodium, 264mg potassium, 27RE vitamin A, 2mg vitamin C, 2mg iron, 236mg calcium, 183mg phosphorus.

Buckwheat Pancakes

YIELD: **20 (3½-inch) pancakes**

COOKING TIME: **2 to 3 minutes**

These hearty pancakes go well with orange butter and maple syrup. The buckwheat flour has a unique flavor and texture; its nutty quality is accented by the molasses in this recipe. If you don't have buttermilk on hand, use a combination of milk and orange juice instead.

1 cup (4¼ ounces) whole buckwheat flour

¾ cup (3⅛ ounces) unbleached all-purpose flour

2 teaspoons baking powder

1 teaspoon baking soda

½ teaspoon salt

1 egg

2 tablespoons (1½ ounces) molasses

2 cups (16 ounces) buttermilk

1 tablespoon unsalted butter, melted

Combine the flours, baking powder, baking soda and salt in a medium bowl. In a smaller bowl, beat the egg lightly with the molasses. Whisk in the buttermilk and melted butter. Form a well in the center of the dry ingredients and pour in the wet ingredients. Stir the batter swiftly with a few strokes, just until the dry ingredients are thoroughly moistened.

Heat a nonstick griddle if you have one, or a heavy skillet, preferably cast iron. If your surface is not nonstick, brush it lightly with vegetable oil. When the surface of your pan is hot enough that a drop of water sputters across it, spoon the batter onto the hot surface, ¼-cupful at a time. Let the pancake cook on the first side until bubbles begin to form around the edges, 2 to 3 minutes. You may need to adjust your heat up or down to get the pancakes to cook through without scorching the surface or being too pale. When the cakes are just beginning to set, flip them and let them finish cooking on the second side, until they're golden brown, about 1 minute more. Serve immediately, with orange butter (*below*) and maple syrup.

NUTRITION INFORMATION PER SERVING (2 PANCAKES, 83G): 12g whole grains, 125 cal, 3g fat, 5g protein, 18g complex carbohydrates, 3g sugar, 2g dietary fiber, 26mg cholesterol, 375mg sodium, 220mg potassium, 21RE vitamin A, 1mg iron, 142mg calcium, 197mg phosphorus.

BUCKWHEAT

Buckwheat is not really wheat at all, but more of a bush, along the lines of sorrel. It helps to keep that in mind when baking with it. Rather than trying to bake with it alone, add it to baked goods as a sort of seasoning. It gives a beautiful, speckled color to breads and pancakes, and adds a hearty, grassy flavor. Buckwheat flour comes in two varieties: white and whole. Whole buckwheat flour is the whole grain: it has a much stronger flavor and is far more nutritious. The white is milder in flavor, but like white flour, less nutritious.

Orange Butter

½ cup (1 stick, 4 ounces) unsalted butter
2 tablespoons (⅞ ounce) packed light or dark brown sugar
Zest of 1 orange
2 tablespoons (1 ounce) orange juice

Beat the butter with the brown sugar until it's soft and creamy. Beat in the orange zest and juice until light. Serve with warm pancakes.

Buckwheat Crêpes

YIELD: 10 to 12 (8-inch) crêpes
COOKING TIME: 2 to 3 minutes

What could be more elegant and delicious than crêpes? And they're so easy. The buckwheat flour gives a beautiful, speckled appearance to these crêpes, and its flavor is heightened by the brandy. These are great with savory accompaniments like sour cream and caviar, but our favorite is the sweet variation, served with caramelized apples (see recipes, below and next page) and whipped cream.

½ cup (1¾ ounces) whole spelt flour
¼ cup (1 ounce) whole buckwheat flour
2 teaspoons sugar
⅛ teaspoon salt
¾ cup (6 ounces) milk
2 tablespoons (1 ounce) brandy
2 large eggs
1 tablespoon unsalted butter, melted

TO MAKE THE CRÊPE BATTER: This batter is especially easy in a food processor, but if you don't have one, you can simply whisk everything together in a big bowl. Combine the flours, sugar and salt in your food processor. Give a quick buzz to combine. Pour the milk into a measuring cup and add the brandy, eggs and melted butter. Pour the liquid ingredients into the food processor and process until the batter is well combined. Scrape down the sides once during the processing.

TO COOK THE CRÊPES: Heat an 8-inch crêpe pan over medium heat and brush it lightly with melted butter. Use a ¼-cup measure to ladle the crêpe batter into the pan, tilting so that the batter coats the entire surface. Cook the crêpe until the bottom is firm and speckled with brown spots, less than 1 minute. Loosen the edges and flip the crêpe to cook the second side. When the crêpe is speckled and golden on both sides, slide it out onto a plate. Repeat until the batter is gone, stacking the crêpes on the plate to keep them warm.

NUTRITION INFORMATION PER SERVING (2 CRÊPES, 74G): 13g whole grains, 129 cal, 4g fat, 6g protein, 15g complex carbohydrates, 1g sugar, 2g dietary fiber, 77mg cholesterol, 37mg sodium, 151mg potassium, 58RE vitamin A, 1mg iron, 47mg calcium, 126mg phosphorus.

VARIATION: SWEET BUCKWHEAT CRÊPES *Make the crêpe batter as above, except increase the sugar to 2 tablespoons and add 1 teaspoon vanilla. These are extraordinary wrapped around warm, carmelized apples (see recipe, next page) and topped with whipped cream.*

Caramelized Apple Filling

2 tablespoons (1 ounce) butter
2 apples, peeled and thinly sliced
2 tablespoons (⅞ ounce) packed light or dark brown sugar
1 tablespoon brandy (optional, but delicious!)

Heat the butter in a medium saucepan, and sauté the apples in the warm butter until they're just getting tender. Stir in the brown sugar and brandy (if using), and continue to cook until the apples are tender and the sauce has thickened, 5 to 7 minutes. Serve the filling rolled in sweet buckwheat crêpes, topped with whipped cream.

WAFFLES

Waffles are the sophisticated cousin of pancakes. They take a little more effort to make, but the crispy rewards are worth any extra exertion. They're a simple way to dress up breakfast, brunch or even dinner. We like to make them right at the table, with a variety of toppings and fillings on hand to please everyone. Whole grain waffles are generally best made in a Belgian waffle maker; the deep pockets make for a crisper waffle, and a bonus of extra room for maple syrup or other toppings! If you're making these in a conventional waffle maker, try to spread the batter a little thinner to get that crisp result. Whether you're looking for a hearty breakfast or something to masquerade as an elegant dessert, there's a recipe here that's perfect for you.

Peanut Butter–Chocolate Chip Waffles with Banana Cream

YIELD: 12 (4-inch-square) Belgian waffles
BAKING TIME: 3 to 5 minutes per waffle

These extravagant waffles, piled high with banana cream, are way too good to be whole grain! Serve them for special occasions or to tempt those picky palates in your family. The chocolate chips didn't stick at all in our nonstick waffle iron, but if you're worried about it, use the technique described on page 19.

> 1 cup (3$\frac{1}{2}$ ounces) spelt flour
> 2 tablespoons (1 ounce) baking powder
> $\frac{3}{4}$ teaspoon salt
> $\frac{1}{2}$ cup (4$\frac{3}{4}$ ounces) extra-crunchy peanut butter
> $\frac{1}{4}$ cup (1$\frac{3}{4}$ ounces) sugar
> 4 tablespoons ($\frac{1}{2}$ stick, 2 ounces) unsalted butter, melted
> 2 eggs
> 1 cup (8 ounces) milk
> $\frac{1}{2}$ cup (3 ounces) chocolate chips

TO MAKE THE WAFFLE BATTER: Combine the flour, baking powder and salt in a small bowl. Cream the peanut butter with the sugar until it softens, then pour in the melted butter. Beat in the eggs, one at a time, until the mixture is completely smooth. You'll need to scrape down the sides of the bowl. Add the milk gradually; the mixture will be very wet. Stir in the flour mixture on the slowest speed and mix until just combined. Stir in the chocolate chips. Let the batter sit for at least 10 minutes before you use it; this is especially important with spelt, as the batter starts out very soupy, but thickens as the grain absorbs the liquid.

TO BAKE THE WAFFLES: Preheat your waffle iron; if your waffle iron is not nonstick, spray it with a nonstick cooking spray before preheating. When the iron is hot enough, drop about ⅓ cup of batter onto the center of each square. The batter will not fill to the edges of the iron until the top is closed. Close the iron.

When the steam has stopped pouring out the sides of the waffle iron, gently open the iron to see if the waffle is done. If it's not ready, it will resist your pull; don't force it, or you may split the waffle. Close the iron and let the waffle cook a bit longer. When the waffle is done, the iron will open easily. Use a fork to gently lift the cooked waffle from the iron. Both sides should be golden brown. Serve immediately with banana cream (below).

NUTRITION INFORMATION PER SERVING (1 WAFFLE, 66G): 8g whole grains, 194 cal, 12g fat, 6g protein, 9g complex carbohydrates, 9g sugar, 2g dietary fiber, 46mg cholesterol, 389mg sodium, 167mg potassium, 43RE vitamin A, 1mg iron, 200mg calcium, 333mg phosphorus, 6mg caffeine.

Banana Cream

YIELD: About 2 cups

2 large bananas (about 14 ounces)
¼ cup (1¾ ounces) sugar
½ teaspoon ground cinnamon
½ teaspoon lemon juice
1 cup (8 ounces) heavy cream

Mash the bananas in a small bowl and sprinkle them with the sugar, cinnamon and lemon juice. Whip the cream in a separate bowl until it's stiff. Fold the banana mixture into the whipped cream and serve immediately.

STRIKE WHILE THE IRON IS HOT!

If you try to rush your breakfast by pouring batter onto a waffle iron that isn't sufficiently preheated, you'll wind up scraping stuck waffles off the iron. Instead, give the iron plenty of time to warm up before you start cooking the waffles. If your iron is nonstick, all you have to do is turn it on and wait for the indicator light. If it's not, give it a generous squirt with a nonstick oil spray before you heat it. That way, your waffles will release easily, and you'll save yourself the time spent cleaning cooked-on batter from the grid.

SMOOTH SAILING

Hooray for nonstick waffle irons! If you don't already have one, and you eat a lot of waffles, it's definitely worth the investment. We tested waffles with chocolate chips, pearl sugar, fresh fruit and jam, and not one of them stuck to the iron. Everything, even caramelized sugar, wiped off easily, leaving an iron ready to bake the next batch of waffles. This really opens the doors for varying your waffles to suit your mood. If you don't have a nonstick iron, don't despair; you can turn your waffle add-ins into toppings! Or, if you're bent on crispy waffles with all the ingredients baked in, be sure your batter has enough fat incorporated into it to keep the waffles slick and spray the iron with a nonstick vegetable oil spray before you heat it and between waffles, if they start to stick. You also may try pouring on part of the batter, sprinkling additions on, and then cloaking them with a bit more batter. Or try giving your waffles an extra minute or two to bake; sometimes a sticky waffle just needs a little more baking time to separate easily from the iron.

Hazelnut Waffles with Pear Compote

YIELD: 12 (4-inch-square) Belgian waffles
BAKING TIME: 3 to 5 minutes per waffle

The ground hazelnuts bring a crisp elegance to these light waffles, and the pear compote dresses them up enough to serve for dessert. They're 100 percent whole grain, but using spelt and oats means there's no hint of the bitterness you sometimes find in whole wheat. These waffles reheat well in the toaster, but watch them to be sure the nuts don't overtoast.

1 cup (3$\frac{1}{2}$ ounces) whole spelt flour
$\frac{1}{3}$ cup (1 ounce) oat flour
$\frac{1}{2}$ cup (2$\frac{1}{2}$ ounces) hazelnuts, toasted and finely ground
1$\frac{1}{2}$ teaspoons baking powder
$\frac{1}{2}$ teaspoon salt
$\frac{1}{4}$ teaspoon baking soda
$\frac{1}{4}$ cup (1$\frac{3}{4}$ ounces) sugar
2 eggs
4 tablespoons ($\frac{1}{2}$ stick, 2 ounces) unsalted butter, melted
1$\frac{1}{2}$ cups (12 ounces) buttermilk
1 teaspoon vanilla extract

Combine the flours, ground hazelnuts, baking powder, salt and baking soda in a large bowl. In a separate bowl, whisk the sugar into the eggs, and whisk in the melted butter, buttermilk and vanilla. Stir the wet ingredients into the dry ingredients just until the dry ingredients are thoroughly moistened. Let the batter sit for 15 minutes before making the waffles. Prepare the pear compote (see recipe, next page) while you wait.

Preheat your waffle iron; if your waffle iron is not nonstick, spray it with a nonstick cooking spray before preheating. When the iron is hot, drop the batter by ¼-cupfuls onto each square. Bake the waffles until the steam stops pouring out the sides of the iron, or until the light indicates they're done, 3 to 5 minutes. Serve immediately with warm pear compote spooned over the top.

NUTRITION INFORMATION PER SERVING (1 WAFFLE, 65G): 11g whole grains, 144 cal, 9g fat, 4g protein, 14g complex carbohydrates, 4g sugar, 2g dietary fiber, 47mg cholesterol, 205mg sodium, 138mg potassium, 48RE vitamin A, 1mg iron, 93mg calcium, 158mg phosphorus.

Pear Compote

YIELD: About 2 cups

2 pears (about 1 pound), peeled, cored and sliced
¼ cup (2 ounces) apple juice
2 tablespoons (⅞ ounce) granulated sugar
2 teaspoons unsalted butter
1 teaspoon minced fresh ginger
Pinch of ground cinnamon
1 tablespoon Grand Marnier (optional)

Place the pears in a saucepan with all the ingredients except the Grand Marnier. Bring the mixture to a simmer over medium heat and simmer until the syrup has thickened and the pears are soft, about 10 minutes. Remove from the heat and stir in the Grand Marnier, if using.

NUTRITION INFORMATION PER SERVING (2½ TABLESPOONS, 41G): 35 cal, 1g fat, 5g complex carbohydrates, 2g sugar, 1g dietary fiber, 2mg cholesterol, 1mg sodium, 44mg potassium, 6RE vitamin A, 1mg vitamin C, 3mg calcium, 4mg phosphorus.

DON'T STACK THOSE WAFFLES!

There's an undeniable satisfaction in the sight of a towering stack of just-baked pancakes or waffles, and plunking a stack of pancakes in a slow oven is a great way to keep them warm while you wait to finish the batch. In the case of waffles, however, a stack is a guarantee of a soggy meal. The heat from the neighboring waffles ruins the crispy texture you get from a hot waffle iron. Instead, bring your waffle iron to the table, and bake the waffles to order for your friends and family. Or, if you must make them ahead, spread them out to let them cool, and reheat them individually in the toaster or a warm oven.

Cornmeal-Rye Waffles

YIELD: 16 (4-inch square) waffles
BAKING TIME: 3 to 5 minutes per waffle

These taste like warm corn muffins and are very filling and satisfying. With maple syrup, they are sublime. If you prefer a savory waffle, cut back on the sugar and spice them up with a bit of jalapeño, or fold in some cheese and bacon. These are also great as a base under a hearty stew—the perfect Sunday night supper.

3 cups (24 ounces) buttermilk
2 eggs
6 tablespoons (¾ stick, 3 ounces) butter, melted
2 cups (9¾ ounces) yellow cornmeal
1 cup (3¾ ounces) whole rye (pumpernickel) flour
¼ cup (1¾ ounces) sugar
2 teaspoons baking powder
2 teaspoons salt
1 teaspoon baking soda

Whisk together the buttermilk, eggs and melted butter in a medium bowl. In a separate bowl, blend the dry ingredients, then quickly and gently combine the wet and dry ingredients. Let the batter sit for 10 minutes to allow the cornmeal to soften. The batter will be quite thick by the time you're ready to use it.

Preheat your waffle iron; if it's not nonstick, spray it with a nonstick cooking spray before preheating. When the iron is hot enough, drop the batter onto it by ⅓-cupfuls, and bake until the waffle iron stops steaming, 3 to 5 minutes. These waffles are best with a crispy, browned exterior, so be sure to bake them long enough for the exterior to get quite firm. They will crisp even more as they cool, especially if they're baked in a Belgian waffle iron. Serve warm with maple syrup.

NUTRITION INFORMATION PER SERVING (1 WAFFLE, 86 G): 23g whole grains, 161 cal, 6g fat, 5g protein, 20g complex carbohydrates, 3g sugar, 3g dietary fiber, 40mg cholesterol, 475mg sodium, 177mg potassium, 52RE vitamin A, 1mg iron, 106mg calcium, 195mg phosphorus.

FRENCH TOAST

Day-old (or 2- or 3-day-old) bread makes a great starting point for breakfast. For one thing, simply toasting bread revitalizes it, and if you're using a whole grain bread, that can be the basis for a healthy meal in and of itself. With just a little doctoring, however, Day-old bread can be elevated to extraordinary heights. These recipes, using leftover bread as their base, are perfect for special breakfasts, and they lend themselves especially well to individual creativity. We took the concept of stuffed French toast from *The King Arthur Flour Baker's Companion* (Countryman Press, 2003), and thought to fill it with something a little stronger than cream cheese to complement the nuttier quality of whole grain bread, and presto, French toast with nut butters.

French Toast Fit for a King

YIELD: 6 servings

COOKING TIME: 7 to 9 minutes

We started with the recipe in our original The King Arthur Flour Baker's Companion, *and couldn't help but think of that other King, Elvis, who loved peanut butter and banana sandwiches. This recipe also works well as an impromptu breakfast sandwich, if your bread isn't sliced too thick. This is really a complete meal, with grains, protein and fruit all in one! The variations below are divine—so be sure to try them, too.*

> ½ cup (4¾ ounces) chunky peanut butter
> 2 tablespoons (1½ ounces) honey
> 2 large (about 12 ounces) bananas
> 6 ½-inch-thick slices (about 12 ounces) stale 100% whole wheat bread, cut in half
> 4 large eggs
> 1½ cups (12 ounces) milk, or cream if you're feeling extravagant
> 2 tablespoons (⅞ ounce) sugar
> 1 teaspoon vanilla extract
> ½ teaspoon ground cinnamon
> ¼ teaspoon salt

TO ASSEMBLE THE SANDWICHES: Cream the peanut butter with the honey and spread a thin layer on each slice of bread. Spread the peanut butter on the bread so that when the slices are closed into a sandwich they match perfectly with no overhanging edges.

Slice the banana thinly over the peanut butter and press the pieces of bread together to form half-sandwiches.

Beat the eggs with the milk (or cream), sugar, vanilla, cinnamon and salt and pour the mixture into a shallow dish.

TO BAKE THE FRENCH TOAST: Heat your griddle to 300°F, or medium-low heat. If your surface isn't nonstick, brush the pan with butter or oil. While the pan is heating, drop the first half-sandwich in the egg mixture. Let it sit on one side for about 5 seconds, then use a slotted spatula to flip it; soak the other side for 5 seconds. Lift the sandwich out of the egg and plunk it on the hot griddle. Let the sandwich sauté on the first side until it's golden brown and the filling is beginning to soften, 4 to 5 minutes. Flip the sandwich to finish baking on the second side, about 3 minutes more. Remove the sandwich to a plate for serving and keep warm while you bake the remaining sandwiches. Serve warm with maple syrup.

Be sure to match the slices up so that the sides with spread on them correspond when you close them together.

NUTRITION INFORMATION PER SERVING (1/2 FRENCH TOAST SANDWICH MADE WITH 100% WHOLE WHEAT SANDWICH BREAD ON P. 182, 184G): **21g whole grains,** 323 cal, 16g fat, 15g protein, 20g complex carbohydrates, 13g sugar, 4g dietary fiber, 144mg cholesterol, 348mg sodium, 465mg potassium, 81RE vitamin A, 3mg vitamin C, 2mg iron, 97mg calcium, 258mg phosphorus.

VARIATIONS: GINGERED CASHEW BUTTER *Made with roasted, salted cashews, this is delicious. If you can find cashew butter at the store, use that, sweetened with a bit of honey.*

> 1 cup (4 ounces) roasted, salted cashews
> 2 tablespoons (⁷/₈ ounce) vegetable oil
> 2 tablespoons (1½ ounces) honey
> 3 tablespoons (1¼ ounce) diced crystallized ginger

Turn on your food processor and pour about half the cashews in through the feed tube. Once they begin to turn to butter, turn off the food processor, scrape down the sides, and add the oil and honey. Process for another minute, then add the remaining cashews. Continue to process until you get the texture you want. When you make the sandwiches for French toast, sprinkle ½ tablespoon crystallized ginger over the cashew butter, and bake as in the main recipe.

HAZELNUT BUTTER WITH CHOCOLATE CHIPS

> 1 cup (5 ounces) roasted, blanched hazelnuts
> 2 tablespoons (⁷/₈ ounce) vegetable oil
> 2 tablespoons (1½ ounces) honey
> ⅓ cup (2 ounces) chocolate chips

Prepare the hazelnut butter as described for the cashew butter. When you make the French toast, sprinkle chocolate chips evenly over the hazelnut butter and bake as in the main recipe.

CEREALS

Cold cereal is omnipresent in the United States, most likely because it's so fast and easy to eat; you can pour a bowl of cereal and milk with your eyes closed, making it ideal for the morning. The trouble with boxed cereal is that the box is often as flavorful as the cereal and about as nutritious, too! Our cereal recipes are packed with flavor and nutrition. As you're rediscovering the joy of warm porridge with maple syrup or crunching your way through a nutty granola, you'll appreciate how nourishing cereal is when it's made with whole grains and how easy it is to rise and shine when you have a bowl of homemade cereal waiting on the table.

GRANOLAS GALORE! Who would have predicted back in the '60s, when being a granola-eater was a political slur, how pervasive granola would become? We see it paired with yogurt in the grocery store, taking up half the cereal aisle, fashioned into breakfast and candy bars and baked into just about everything. Granola is remarkably easy to make and easy to adapt to your own taste, since so many of the ingredients are interchangeable, with a few exceptions. We discovered, for instance, that rye and wheat absorb less fat than oats, so if you're substituting one flake for another, keep in mind that you may need to adjust the fat content up or down. We loaded up on flaked grains at the grocery store, rolled up our sleeves and began to play. The recipes that follow are some of our favorite combinations, but feel free to experiment with your own favorite flavors. Every baker should have a granola unique to his or her household! Make it by the tubful—it stores well. A half cup of any of these granolas in the morning—or anytime—is a super way to meet the daily guidelines for whole grains.

Maple Granola

YIELD: **16 cups**
BAKING TEMPERATURE: **250°F**
BAKING TIME: **2 hours**

This granola was the hands-down favorite in our test kitchen, and it's a great recipe to use as a base for variations. We love the mix of dried fruits, the toasty flavor of the nuts and the sweet, smoky maple syrup. If you don't have one of the ingredients, feel free to substitute another or omit it if you like. If you can find other rolled grains, by all means substitute them for part of the oats. Mix this up, plop it in the oven and turn your attention to something else—granolas are pretty low-maintenance baking. Note that just ½ cup of this delicious granola gives you 19 grams of whole grains, and that's over a third of what you need each day.

7 cups (24½ ounces) old-fashioned rolled oats
1 cup (3 ounces) flaked coconut
1 cup (4 ounces) wheat germ
1 cup (5 ounces) almonds, sliced or broken up
1 cup (3¾ ounces) pecans or walnuts, chopped or broken up
1 cup (5 ounces) sunflower seeds, raw or toasted
½ teaspoon salt
1 cup (11 ounces) maple syrup
¾ cup (5¼ ounces) vegetable oil
1 tablespoon vanilla extract
1 cup (5¼ ounces) golden raisins
1 cup (4 ounces) dried cranberries
1 cup (4½ ounces) chopped dried apricots

Preheat the oven to 250°F. Combine the oats, coconut, wheat germ, nuts, seeds and salt in a very large bowl. Mix well. In a separate bowl, whisk together the maple syrup, oil and vanilla. Pour the syrup mixture over the dry mixture, stirring and tossing till everything is very well combined; it's probably easiest to do this with your hands.

Spread the granola over 2 large baking sheets with rims. Your cleanup will be much easier if you line them with parchment paper.

Bake for 2 hours, stirring the mixture after 1 hour or so. Remove the pans from the oven and let cool completely. Transfer the granola to a large bowl and mix in the dried fruit. Store in an airtight container at room temperature.

NUTRITION INFORMATION PER SERVING (1/2 CUP, 68G): **19g whole grains,** 292 cal, 15g fat, 7g protein, 28g complex carbohydrates, 8g sugar, 5g dietary fiber, 47mg sodium, 344mg potassium, 70RE vitamin A, 1mg vitamin C, 2mg iron, 48mg calcium, 214mg phosphorus.

Wheat Granola with Walnuts & Apricots

YIELD: 10 cups
BAKING TEMPERATURE: 300°F
BAKING TIME: 25 to 35 minutes

The wheat germ in this recipe emphasizes the nutty flavor of the wheat flakes and walnuts. The honey is subtle as a sweetener, but you may want to play with some different varieties to see how they interact with the other flavors in the cereal.

4 cups (1 pound) wheat flakes
1 cup (4 ounces) wheat germ
2 cups (9 ounces) walnuts, chopped
½ teaspoon salt
½ cup (6 ounces) honey
⅓ cup (2⅜ ounces) oil
1 tablespoon vanilla extract
2 cups (9 ounces) dried apricots, chopped

Preheat the oven to 300°F.

Combine the wheat flakes, wheat germ, walnuts and salt in a large bowl. Measure the honey and oil and stir in the vanilla. Pour the oil mixture over the wheat flakes and mix until the dry ingredients are thoroughly moistened; it's probably easiest to do this with your hands.

Pour the granola out onto 2 baking sheets with rims. If you line the sheets with parchment paper, your cleanup will be much easier.

Bake until the cereal is evenly toasted, 25 to 35 minutes. Halfway through the baking process, remove the pans from the oven, give the cereal a stir and put the pans back in the oven to finish baking. Remove the granola from the oven and allow it to cool on the baking sheets. When it's cooled, stir in the dried apricots. Store in an airtight container at room temperature.

NUTRITION INFORMATION PER SERVING (1/2 CUP, 60 GRAMS): 17g whole grains, 240 cal, 11g fat, 6g protein, 26g complex carbohydrates, 26g sugar, 5g dietary fiber, 60mg sodium, 382mg potassium, 236RE vitamin A, 2mg iron, 32mg calcium, 174mg phosphorus.

Cinnamon-Nut Granola

YIELD: **10 cups**

BAKING TEMPERATURE: **300°F**

BAKING TIME: **30 to 40 minutes**

This buttery, spicy granola is the perfect balance of salt and sweet, crisp and crunch, fruit and nuts. The flavor of the butter is terrific, especially with cinnamon, but if you're worried about cholesterol, substitute oil in the recipe. As with every granola, varying the fruits and nuts is the fun part, so feel free to substitute your favorites.

4 cups (14 ounces) old-fashioned rolled oats

1 cup (5 ounces) whole almonds, coarsely chopped

1 cup (5 ounces) whole dry-roasted peanuts, salted or unsalted

1 cup (3 ounces) flaked coconut

1½ teaspoons ground cinnamon

½ teaspoon salt (less if you're using salted peanuts)

½ cup (1 stick, 4 ounces) unsalted butter

½ cup (6 ounces) honey

½ cup (2⅝ ounces) golden raisins

½ cup (2¼ ounces) dried apricots, coarsely chopped

½ cup (2½ ounces) dried cherries

½ cup (2 ounces) dried cranberries

Preheat oven to 300°F.

Combine the oats, nuts, coconut, cinnamon and salt in a large bowl. Melt the butter and stir it into the honey. Pour the butter-honey mixture over the oats and mix until they are thoroughly moistened; it's probably easiest to do this with your hands.

Pour the granola out onto 2 baking sheets with rims. If you line the sheets with parchment paper, your cleanup will be much easier.

Bake until the cereal is evenly toasted, 30 to 40 minutes. Halfway through the baking process, remove the pans from the oven, give the cereal a stir and put the pans back in the oven to finish baking. Remove the granola from the oven and allow it to cool on the baking sheets. When it's cooled, stir in the dried fruit. Store in an airtight container at room temperature.

NUTRITION INFORMATION PER SERVING (1/2 CUP, 66G): **17g whole grains,** 280 cal, 14g fat, 7g protein, 27g complex carbohydrates, 8g sugar, 4g dietary fiber, 13mg cholesterol, 72mg sodium, 325mg potassium, 109RE vitamin A, 1mg vitamin C, 2mg iron, 41mg calcium, 164mg phosphorus.

PORRIDGE

Although porridge is not usually baked, it's so fundamental to a book on whole grains we simply couldn't leave it out of our breakfast chapter. You can make porridge from virtually any form of any grain, and over the centuries, man (or more likely woman) has tried every conceivable combination of processing and preparing grain to make it palatable. It's been cracked, rolled, pounded, milled into flour, boiled, sprouted, fermented, baked and, most recently, microwaved, and still for breakfast we come back to the simple satisfaction of warm porridge with cream and fruit to fortify us for the day.

Of course, we're all capable of preparing a packet of instant oatmeal, but if that's all you've had in the hot-cereal department, you're in for a treat. The secret to great whole grain porridge is to use the freshest possible grain and cook it slowly. In general, the larger the form of the grain, the more liquid you'll need to cook it and the longer it will take to prepare—but the better the flavor and texture. See page 583 for a chart of cooking directions for different grains. You may even make porridge from flour—try toasting the flour first, before adding liquid and cooking it. Remember that heat increases the opportunity for rancidity, and any grains on the edge of being rancid will likely be bitter by the time you've cooked them into porridge, so be sure you have a source for fresh whole grains, especially when it comes to corn and wheat.

Irish Oatmeal with Dried Fruit and Maple Cream

YIELD: 1½ cups, 2 servings
COOKING TIME: 10 to 12 minutes

This recipe came to us from Rosemary Hubbard, who dressed it up to serve for dessert by turning the porridge into a brûlée and serving it alongside the elegant maple cream. We've toned it down a little for morning, but the overnight soak makes it relatively quick to cook: just 10 minutes on the stovetop or 3 minutes in the microwave. The maple cream is an exceptional accompaniment to any morning grain; you may want to make up a large batch just to have some on hand.

½ cup (2⅞ ounces) steel-cut oats

1½ cups (12 ounces) water

¼ teaspoon salt

2 tablespoons (1 ounce) dried apricots, chopped

2 tablespoons (⅝ ounce) dried cherries

2 tablespoons (⅝ ounce) raisins, prunes or dates, chopped

PLAN AHEAD

To have hot cereal in a snap for morning, make a large batch of it ahead of time. Cook the grains a few minutes shy of being done, while they still look a bit soupy. Stir in dried fruit to taste, place it in a covered container and store it in the refrigerator for up to 2 weeks. When you're rushed in the morning, scoop the porridge into your bowl, microwave it for 2 to 3 minutes, and breakfast is ready!

TO MAKE THE PORRIDGE: The night before you want to serve the porridge, soak the oats in enough water to cover them plus an inch. The next morning, drain the oats and place them in a saucepan with 1½ cups of water and the salt. Bring the oats to a simmer over medium heat and simmer, stirring, until they're tender, about 10 to 12 minutes total cooking time. Stir in the dried fruits and let the porridge sit for 5 minutes. To serve the porridge, divide the oatmeal between 2 bowls and serve with a sprinkle of brown sugar and the maple cream (see recipe, next page).

NUTRITION INFORMATION PER SERVING (3/4 CUP PORRIDGE, 232G): **39g whole grains,** 190 cal, 3g fat, 6g protein, 37g complex carbohydrates, 5g dietary fiber, 271mg sodium, 269mg potassium, 64RE vitamin A, 2mg iron, 31mg calcium, 184mg phosphorus.

Maple Cream

YIELD: 1 cup, 8 servings
COOKING TIME: 20 minutes

This is sinfully rich, and a little goes a long way. There's enough here to have a dollop with your porridge for two or three mornings in a row. It keeps well in the refrigerator, and a quick zap in the microwave warms it just enough to serve.

1 cup (8 ounces) heavy cream
1 cinnamon stick
1 small strip orange peel
1 star anise (optional)
¼ cup (2¾ ounces) maple syrup

Combine the cream with the cinnamon stick, orange peel and anise, if you're using it, in a small saucepan. Bring the mixture to a simmer over medium heat. Reduce the heat to low and simmer for 10 minutes. Remove the cinnamon stick, orange peel and star anise, if using, and whisk in the maple syrup. Increase the heat and simmer, stirring, until the mixture thickens enough to coat the back of a spoon, about 10 minutes more. Serve with porridge.

QUICK BREADS,
muffins, coffeecakes,
biscuits & scones

Quick breads are an early step into the wider world of baking for many beginning bakers. Quick breads are the family of baked goods that don't require yeast for leavening: they depend mostly on baking powder and baking soda to get their rise, and therefore don't need as much time as yeast breads.

The recipes aren't intimidating: measure, add wet to dry, put in a pan, bake. Ah, but what delights can be made with just a bowl, a spoon, the right recipe and ingredients! From a warm muffin for breakfast to the perfect biscuit with dinner, quick breads bring the baker's caring touch to the table, in an amount of time that still fits in with our busy lives. Because of the comforting familiarity of these recipes, there's no better place to start introducing the goodness of whole grains to your family's diet. Whole wheat performs yeoman service, bringing a nutty, robust flavor to quick breads that only adds to their appeal. Oats take their rightful place, both as a welcome bit of crunch in a streusel, and as a moisture-giving addition in batters. Spelt, with its slightly sweet flavor and affinity for moisture, steals the show in popover batter. And corn and barley bring their own unique flavors and textures to muffins and scones, respectively.

You'll find lots of familiar flavors within, as well as a few fresh and unusual ideas to help round out a meal. All of them capitalize on the intense flavors and unique texture that whole grains provide. Once we found the right balance of liquids to grains, and the techniques to handle the batter and dough, we discovered that most of our mealtime standbys were just as pleasing (often more so) in their whole grain incarnations.

MUFFINS

Muffins are a wonderfully personal treat: everyone gets a (preferably) warm package of fresh-baked goodness. A wide range of flavors can show up in a muffin: There are sweet, cakelike muffins with a drizzle of sugary glaze on top, vegetable and fruit-filled muffins that make a good on-the-go breakfast and savory muffins that can stand in for a sandwich next to a bowl of soup or salad.

Muffins are very quick to make: from motivation to first nibble takes under an hour; even less if you've made the batter ahead of time and have it ready in the refrigerator.

This strategy is particularly effective with whole grain batters, which usually benefit from having extra time for the bran in the flour to fully absorb the batter's liquid. Making the batter ahead softens and tenderizes the bran and improves the flavor of the finished product. It also means you can bake as few or as many muffins as you need from your refrigerated batter, enjoying a fresh, warm snack or breakfast each time you have the urge. When you consider the prepackaged, preservative-laden, artificially flavored breakfast baked goods on store shelves everywhere, it's a relief to know that there's a more healthful alternative available, for much less money. Come with us on a tour of muffin possibilities, and get ready to warm up the oven!

MIX TODAY, BAKE TOMORROW, AND THEN AGAIN THE DAY AFTER THAT

Our sour cream muffin recipe has a proven record of rising reliably, even after 4 days in the refrigerator. If you plan to make it ahead, simply mix up the batter as directed, but leave out the fruit until you're ready to bake. Cover and refrigerate the batter, baking as many muffins as you need over the course of a few days. Mix the fruit or berries of your choice into the batter just before you scoop it into the muffin pan. If the batter is cold from the refrigerator, you may have to increase the baking time by 3 to 5 minutes.

TO PAPER OR NOT TO PAPER

If you have a well-seasoned muffin pan, you may prefer not to line its wells with papers before baking in it. Muffins baked directly on the metal of the pan will form their own bottom crusts, giving them a texture many people prefer. If the recipe you're baking has a lot of berries or fruit mixed in, or has a lot of streusel on top, using a paper liner can be a very good idea. The liners will help keep the fruit from sticking and help to keep the base of a heavy-crowned muffin attached when it comes out of the pan. We recommend spraying the insides of paper muffin liners with nonstick spray before filling them. This step only takes a moment, but it will keep the muffin from tearing itself apart when the paper is removed. Whichever you chose, paper or no paper, be sure to allow the hot muffins a few minutes to cool and set up before removing them from the safety of the pan. (See sidebar, page 39.)

Sour Cream Muffins

YIELD: 1 dozen muffins
BAKING TEMPERATURE: 400°F
BAKING TIME: 22 to 26 minutes

This is the most dependable, most versatile whole grain muffin recipe we know. The batter is a little on the stiff side, the better to hold together when juicy berries and fruits are stirred in, yet the muffins themselves are very tender. As with many whole grain recipes, the batter benefits when made ahead and refrigerated at least an hour, although it's not strictly necessary. Toppings can range from simple, such as coarse sugar or cinnamon-sugar, to stunning, such as streusel.

> 2 cups (8 ounces) white whole wheat flour
> ½ cup (2⅛ ounces) unbleached all-purpose flour
> 1½ teaspoons baking powder
> ½ teaspoon baking soda
> 1 teaspoon salt
> 4 tablespoons (½ stick, 2 ounces) unsalted butter
> 1 cup (7 ounces) sugar
> 2 large eggs
> 1 teaspoon vanilla extract
> 1 cup (8 ounces) sour cream
> 1½ cups (7½ ounces) fresh or frozen berries or diced stone fruits (such as peaches or plums) of your choice
> Coarse sugar for sprinkling

Lightly grease a muffin tin, or line with papers and coat the papers with nonstick spray. Whisk together the flours, baking powder, baking soda and salt in a medium bowl. Cream together the butter and sugar in a large mixing bowl until light and fluffy and almost white in color. Scrape down the bowl to make sure all the butter is incorporated, then turn the mixer back on and add the eggs, one at a time, beating well after each addition. Add the vanilla and sour cream, and mix until incorporated. Add the dry ingredients, mixing on low speed just until the batter is smooth. Scrape the sides and bottom of the bowl once more, to be sure everything is evenly combined. Gently fold in the fruit and refrigerate at least an hour.

Preheat the oven to 400°F. Scoop the batter by the ¼-cupful into the prepared pan and sprinkle with sugar or other topping. Bake the muffins until a cake tester inserted in the center comes out clean, 22 to 26 minutes. Remove from the oven and allow the muffins to cool in the pan for 5 minutes, then turn them out onto a rack to finish cooling.

NUTRITION INFORMATION PER SERVING (1 MUFFIN, MADE WITH BLUEBERRIES, 90G): 20g whole grains, 221 cal, 5g fat, 5g protein, 26g complex carbohydrates, 16g sugar, 3g dietary fiber, 43mg cholesterol, 297mg sodium, 141mg potassium, 49RE vitamin A, 2mg vitamin C, 2mg iron, 73mg calcium, 166mg phosphorus.

Milk and Honey Corn Muffins

YIELD: **1 dozen muffins**

BAKING TEMPERATURE: **400°F**

BAKING TIME: **20 to 23 minutes**

Packed with whole grains, tender and moist, just a bit on the crumbly side, but not overly sweet, this is a wonderful muffin recipe. You may use white whole wheat instead of whole wheat pastry flour; the muffins won't be quite as ethereal, but they'll also be a little less crumbly, too.

¾ cup (1½ sticks, 6 ounces) unsalted butter

¼ cup (1¾ ounces) sugar

1 teaspoon salt

3 tablespoons (2¼ ounces) honey

2 large eggs

2 cups (6¾ ounces) whole wheat pastry or white whole wheat flour

2 cups (9¾ ounces) whole yellow cornmeal

1 tablespoon baking powder

1½ cups (12 ounces) milk

Preheat the oven to 400°F. Lightly grease a muffin tin or line with papers and coat the papers with nonstick spray.

Cream together the butter, sugar and salt in a large mixing bowl until fluffy. Beat in the honey and the eggs, one at a time, stopping to scrape the sides and bottom of the mixing bowl after each addition.

In a separate bowl, whisk together the whole wheat flour, cornmeal and baking powder. Add the dry ingredients to the butter mixture in thirds, alternating with the milk. Mix until the batter is smooth.

Scoop the batter by generous ½-cupfuls into the prepared pan. Bake the muffins until the tops are golden brown and a cake tester inserted in the center comes out clean, 20 to 23 minutes. Remove from the oven and allow the muffins to cool in the pan for 5 minutes, then turn them out onto a rack to finish cooling.

DON'T LET YOUR MUFFINS GET TOUGH

Leaving muffins in their pan to cool causes moisture from inside the muffin to condense when it reaches the cooling metal. This causes the outer edges to steam, and consequently overcook and become tough. To keep your muffins tender, flip them out of the pan after 5 minutes of cooling and let them finish cooling on a rack.

NUTRITION INFORMATION PER SERVING (1 MUFFIN, 104G): **36g whole grains,** 291 cal, 14g fat, 7g protein, 29g complex carbohydrates, 8g sugar, 3g dietary fiber, 85mg cholesterol, 340mg sodium, 191mg potassium, 158RE vitamin A, 2mg iron, 122mg calcium, 184mg phosphorus.

Morning Glory Muffins

YIELD: 1 dozen muffins
BAKING TEMPERATURE: 375°F
BAKING TIME: 25 to 28 minutes

Anyone who reads the recipe-swap column of the local newspaper's food section knows that one of the most requested recipes is for Morning Glory Muffins. These beauties are almost a cross between a granola bar and a whole wheat carrot cake, full of all kinds of good things to get you started for breakfast. This is a muffin that holds well and will also reheat well. You could top it off with cream cheese, but they're quite nice all by themselves or with a cup of coffee or tea. If you have kids who can't be talked into sitting down to breakfast, send them out the door with one of these and you'll know they'll have a decent start to their day.

½ cup (3 ounces) raisins

2 cups (8 ounces) whole wheat flour, traditional or white whole wheat

1 cup (7½ ounces) packed light or dark brown sugar

2 teaspoons baking soda

2 teaspoons ground cinnamon

½ teaspoon ground ginger

½ teaspoon salt

2 cups (7 ounces) peeled and grated carrots

1 large tart apple, peeled, cored and grated

½ cup (1½ ounces) sweetened coconut

½ cup (1½ ounces) sliced almonds or chopped walnuts

⅓ cup (1⅝ ounces) sunflower seeds or wheat germ (optional)

3 large eggs

⅔ cup (4⅝ ounces) vegetable oil

¼ cup (2 ounces) orange juice

2 teaspoons vanilla extract

Preheat the oven to 375°F. Lightly grease a muffin tin or line with papers and coat the papers with nonstick spray.

Put the raisins in a small bowl and cover them with hot water; set aside to soak while you assemble the rest of the recipe. Whisk together the flour, sugar, baking soda, spices and salt in a large mixing bowl. Stir in the carrots, apple, coconut, nuts and sunflower seeds (or wheat germ, if using). In a separate bowl, beat together the eggs, oil, orange juice and vanilla. Add to the flour mixture, and stir until evenly moistened. Drain the raisins and stir them in.

Scoop the batter evenly into the prepared pan (the muffin cups will be almost full to the top; that's OK). Bake the muffins until nicely domed and a cake tester inserted in the center comes out clean, 25 to 28 minutes. Remove from the oven and allow the muffins to cool in the pan for 5 minutes, then turn them out onto a rack to finish cooling.

NUTRITION INFORMATION PER SERVING (1 MUFFIN, 106G): 20g whole grains, 342 cal, 18g fat, 6g protein, 26g complex carbohydrates, 19g sugar, 4g dietary fiber, 53mg cholesterol, 347mg sodium, 322mg potassium, 541RE vitamin A, 3mg vitamin C, 2mg iron, 47mg calcium, 131mg phosphorous.

HOW DO YOU TOP THAT?

Any muffin can dress up simply by adding a little extra something to the top before baking. Why not sprinkle a few sunflower seeds on your Morning Glory Muffins before they go into the oven? If you have a favorite streusel, sprinkling it on any kind of muffin adds texture and visual interest. A pumpkin muffin is jauntier with a few pumpkin seeds sprinkled on top. A quick sprinkle of coarse sugar or cinnamon-sugar is an easy way to add a satisfying crunch to the top of a tender muffin. Demerara sugar, with its large crystals and slight butterscotch taste, is a terrific finishing touch for a banana muffin. So before you open the oven door to bake your muffins, take a quick peek in the pantry, and see if you can't find a little something special for them to wear.

 # Cranberry-Orange Spelt Muffins

YIELD: 1 dozen muffins
BAKING TEMPERATURE: 400°F
BAKING TIME: 24 minutes

Spelt is a distant cousin and ancestor to wheat, containing more gluten than wheat. When spelt is given time to absorb the batter's moisture, it creates a moist, tender crumb in quick breads.

These muffins combine spelt's admirable baking qualities with the sparkle and tang of cranberry and orange flavors, plus a bit of crunchy pecan streusel to add to the fun. They can be baked right after they're mixed up, but they'll be a bit more tender and have a higher rise if you let the batter rest overnight in the refrigerator.

Muffin batter
1 cup (4 ounces) diced dried cranberries
½ cup (4 ounces) orange juice

1¼ cups (4⅜ ounces) whole spelt flour

1 cup (4¼ ounces) unbleached all-purpose flour

1 tablespoon baking powder

½ teaspoon salt

¾ cups (6 ounces) milk

¼ cup (3 ounces) honey

2 large eggs

1 tablespoon sunflower or vegetable oil

1 tablespoon orange zest

½ cup (1⅞ ounces) chopped pecans

Streusel

3 tablespoons (1½ ounces) unsalted butter, softened

½ cup (3¾ ounces) packed light or dark brown sugar

¼ cup (¾ ounce) oat flour

¼ cup (1 ounce) unbleached all-purpose flour

½ cup (1⅞ ounces) chopped pecans

THE NIGHT BEFORE YOU WANT TO BAKE THE MUFFINS: Place the cranberries in a small, heatproof bowl. Heat the orange juice in the microwave, at high power for 30 seconds and pour it over the cranberries. Cover the bowl, and set aside to cool

Whisk together the flours, baking powder and salt in a large mixing bowl. In a separate bowl, mix together the milk, honey, eggs and oil. Add to the dry ingredients, stirring just until you see no more dry clumps of flour. The batter will look a bit soupy; that's OK. Stir in the orange zest, pecans, cranberries and juice. Cover the batter and refrigerate for an overnight rest. If you can't wait for an overnight rest, let the batter sit for at least 2 hours before baking.

Make the streusel while the batter is resting. Combine the butter and sugar until well mixed; work in the flours until you have a crumbly mixture. Stir in the pecans.

When you're ready to bake the muffins, remove the batter from the refrigerator. Preheat the oven to 400°F. Lightly grease a muffin tin or line with papers and coat the papers with nonstick spray,

Scoop the batter by ⅓-cupfuls into the prepared pan; the muffin cups will be almost full. Sprinkle the streusel over the batter. Bake the muffins until golden brown and a cake tester inserted in the center comes out clean, about 24 minutes. Remove from the oven and allow the muffins to cool in the pan for 10 minutes, then turn them out onto a rack to finish cooling.

NUTRITION INFORMATION PER SERVING (1 MUFFIN, 92G): **17g whole grains,** 230 cal, 12g fat, 5g protein, 19g complex carbohydrates, 12g sugar, 4g dietary fiber, 44mg cholesterol, 201mg sodium, 199mg potassium, 55RE vitamin A, 7mg vitamin C, 2mg iron, 121mg calcium, 240mg phosphorus.

Peanut Butter Muffins

YIELD: 1 dozen muffins
BAKING TEMPERATURE: 375°F
BAKING TIME: 23 to 25 minutes

These muffins could well be the answer for parents of problem eaters. Almost anyone who likes peanut butter will be a fan of these very moist, very tender, as-crunchy-as-you want-them-to-be morsels. Try substituting some strawberry jam for the peanut butter glaze, and watch them disappear. They can be made with white whole wheat flour or traditional whole wheat flour instead of whole wheat pastry flour, but the texture will be less ethereal and a little more sturdy.

Muffin batter
2¼ cups (7½ ounces) whole wheat pastry flour
1 teaspoon baking soda
1 teaspoon baking powder
½ teaspoon salt
4 tablespoons (½ stick, 2 ounces) unsalted butter
½ cup (3¾ ounces) firmly packed light or dark brown sugar
¾ cup (7⅛ ounces) peanut butter, crunchy or smooth
1½ teaspoons vanilla extract
2 large eggs
¾ cup (6 ounces) buttermilk
1 cup (6 ounces) chocolate chips, optional

Glaze (optional)
¼ cup (2⅜ ounces) smooth peanut butter
3 tablespoons (¾ ounce) confectioners' sugar
¼ cup (2 ounces) heavy cream
Chopped peanuts for garnish (optional)

Preheat the oven to 375°F. Lightly grease a muffin tin or line with papers and coat the papers with nonstick spray.

Whisk together the flour, baking soda, baking powder and salt in a medium bowl.

Cream together the butter and brown sugar in a large mixing bowl until light. Add the peanut butter, mixing until incorporated. Beat in the vanilla and the eggs, one at a time, scraping the sides and bottom of the bowl to make sure everything is evenly mixed. Add one-third of the dry ingredients, and mix until moistened. Add half of the buttermilk, mix until combined, then add the remaining dry ingredients and the remaining buttermilk. Scrape the bowl again during this process; the peanut butter tends to stick to the bottom. When the batter is evenly mixed, stir in the chocolate chips, if using.

Scoop the batter into the prepared pan. Bake the muffins until golden brown and a cake tester inserted in the center comes out clean, 23 to 25 minutes. Remove from the oven and allow the muffins to cool in the pan for 5 minutes, then turn them out onto a rack to finish cooling.

IF MAKING THE GLAZE: Mix together the peanut butter and confectioners' sugar, then add the heavy cream, a bit at a time, and stir until smooth and spreadable. Use to coat the tops of the cooled muffins. Sprinkle chopped peanuts on top after frosting, if desired.

NUTRITION INFORMATION PER SERVING (1 MUFFIN, WITHOUT GLAZE, 73G): **18g whole grains,** 249 cal, 14g fat, 8g protein, 15g complex carbohydrates, 10g sugar, 3g dietary fiber, 47mg cholesterol, 332mg sodium, 251mg potassium, 55RE vitamin A, 1mg iron, 66mg calcium, 183mg phosphorus.

WHEN TO TAKE A MUFFIN OUT OF ITS PAN

Muffins are delicate creatures when they're hot right out of the oven. If they have a nice, rounded dome on top, lifting them out of their pan too early puts them at risk for decapitation. Leaving the muffins in the pan for too long will cause them to steam themselves (after all, they're more than halfway submerged in the pan). This will make muffins tough and rubbery—not a pleasant prospect.

You can try to lever the warm muffins out with a fork or kitchen knife, but that usually results in a bunch of dented muffins.

It's best to allow muffins to cool in their pans for 5 minutes or so, so they set up enough to be handled. After letting them rest in their pan on a rack for 5 minutes, gently tilt the pan and slide the muffins out, one by one, starting on the high side.

After 5 minutes of cooling time, tilt the muffin pan at a 45° angle. Take the muffins out of the tin, one by one, starting on the uphill side.

Gingered Oatmeal Muffins

YIELD: 1 dozen muffins
BAKING TEMPERATURE: 400°F
BAKING TIME: 20 minutes

These muffins debuted to universal hosannas from our tasters, who proclaimed them to have just the right amount of spice, and who liked the way their light, fluffy texture contrasted with the chewy appeal of the old-fashioned rolled oats. The white whole wheat earns its nickname of "sweet wheat" in this recipe.

Muffin batter
1 cup (4 ounces) white whole wheat flour
½ cup (1⅝ ounces) oat flour
¾ cup (2⅝ ounces) old-fashioned rolled oats
¾ cup (5⅝ ounces) packed light or brown sugar
1 tablespoon baking powder
½ teaspoon salt
1 cup plus 2 tablespoons (9 ounces) milk
¼ cup (1¾ ounces) vegetable oil or melted unsalted butter
2 large eggs
1 teaspoon vanilla extract
½ cup (3¼ ounces) diced crystallized ginger

Topping (optional)
2 tablespoons (⅞ ounce) granulated sugar
½ teaspoon ground cinnamon
¼ teaspoon ground ginger

Preheat the oven to 400°F. Lightly grease a muffin tin or line with papers and coat the papers with nonstick spray.

Stir together the flours, oats, sugar, baking powder, and salt in a large bowl. In a separate bowl, beat together milk, oil (or butter), eggs and vanilla. Gently stir the wet ingredients into the dry ingredients, mixing only enough to blend. Stir in the crystallized ginger. If making the topping, stir the sugar and spices together.

Scoop the batter into the prepared pan. Sprinkle the muffins with the topping, if using. Bake the muffins until golden brown and a cake tester inserted into the center comes out clean, 20 minutes. Remove from the oven and allow the muffins to cool in the pan for 5 minutes, then turn them out onto a rack to finish cooling.

NUTRITION INFORMATION PER SERVING (1 MUFFIN, WITHOUT TOPPING, 72G): 14g whole grains, 183 cal, 6g fat, 4g protein, 12g complex carbohydrates, 19g sugar, 2g dietary fiber, 36mg cholesterol, 213mg sodium, 152mg potassium, 30RE vitamin A, 2mg vitamin C, 1mg iron, 139mg calcium, 139mg phosphorus.

Corn and Oat Muffins

YIELD: 1 dozen muffins
BAKING TEMPERATURE: 375°F
BAKING TIME: 23 to 25 minutes

If you'd rather have a muffin that's not overly sweet, this one's for you. These tender muffins would be right at home in the supper breadbasket. You also could have them for breakfast and feel like you've started your day in a wholesome manner. The dates within provide a nice counterpoint to the tweediness of the oats and corn. If you prefer a sweeter muffin, you can double the brown sugar.

½ cup (1¾ ounces) old-fashioned rolled oats
¾ cup (6 ounces) boiling water
1 cup (5¼ ounces) chopped dates
4 tablespoons (½ stick, 2 ounces) unsalted butter
¼ cup (1⅞ ounces) packed light or dark brown sugar
1 cup (4⅞ ounces) whole yellow cornmeal
1 cup (4¼ ounces) unbleached bread flour
½ cup (1⅝ ounces) oat flour
1 tablespoon baking powder
½ teaspoon baking soda
½ teaspoon salt
¾ cup (6 ounces) buttermilk
2 large eggs

Preheat the oven to 375°F. Lightly grease a muffin tin or line with papers and coat the papers with nonstick spray.

Place the oats in a large mixing bowl and pour the boiling water over them. Add the dates, butter and brown sugar, stirring to combine. Set the bowl aside to cool to room temperature. Whisk together the cornmeal, flours, baking powder, baking soda, and salt in a large bowl. Stir the buttermilk and eggs into the cooled date mixture, then add to the dry ingredients and mix until everything is evenly moistened.

Scoop the batter by heaping ¼-cupfuls into the prepared pan. Bake the muffins until the tops are domed and golden brown, and a cake tester inserted in the center comes out clean, 23 to 25 minutes. Remove from the oven and allow the muffins to cool in the pan for 5 minutes, then turn them out onto a rack to finish cooling.

NUTRITION INFORMATION PER SERVING (1 MUFFIN, 125G): 14g whole grains, 315 cal, 4g fat, 5g protein, 30g complex carbohydrates, 36g sugar, 2g dietary fiber, 44mg cholesterol, 306mg sodium, 278mg potassium, 51RE vitamin A, 2g iron, 127mg calcium, 100mg phosphorus.

THE MUFFIN SCOOP: AN INDISPENSABLE TOOL

Finding the right tool for evenly dividing muffin batter into the muffin pan can be a pain. Serving spoons are clumsy and inexact. Measuring cups are accurate (most pans need a heaping ¼ to ⅓ cup of batter for each muffin), but time-consuming to scrape out and refill. As far as we're concerned, the *only* way to portion muffins is with a scoop, sometimes called a "disher," in restaurant parlance. It's similar to an ice cream scoop, with a blade that helps push the batter out of the scoop's bowl. We prefer a scoop that holds a heaping ¼ cup. Once the batter is mixed, all it takes is 12 dips into the mixing bowl and a squeeze of the lever after each scoop. The batter plops, beautifully rounded, into the muffin pan. The muffins are all the same size, bake evenly and look their best. You can find "dishers" at most kitchen-supply stores and specialty shops, and by mail order.

Chocolate Malted Muffins

YIELD: 1 dozen muffins
BAKING TEMPERATURE: 375°F
BAKING TIME: 25 minutes

If you're a fan of malted milk flavor, this muffin highlights it by combining malted milk powder with barley flour (a natural fit, since malt is made from barley) and whole wheat. The result is a not-too-sweet muffin, nicely balancing the flavors of chocolate and malt. The occasional nugget of melted chocolate from the chips is a nice touch.

Muffin batter
1 cup (4 ounces) whole barley flour
½ cup (2 ounces) whole wheat flour, traditional or white whole wheat
½ cup (2⅛ ounces) unbleached bread flour
¾ cup (2¼ ounces) unsweetened cocoa powder
¼ cup (1¼ ounces) malted milk powder
1 cup (7½ ounces) packed light or dark brown sugar
1 teaspoon baking powder
½ teaspoon baking soda
½ teaspoon salt
4 tablespoons (½ stick, 2 ounces) unsalted butter, melted
1¼ cups (10 ounces) buttermilk
2 large eggs
1 teaspoon vanilla extract
1 cup (6 ounces) chocolate chips (optional)

Glaze

6 tablespoons (2¾ ounces) packed light or dark brown sugar

2 tablespoons (⅝ ounce) malted milk powder

2 tablespoons (⅜ ounce) unsweetened cocoa powder

1 tablespoon corn syrup

¼ cup (2 ounces) plain yogurt

½ teaspoon vanilla extract

Preheat the oven to 375°F. Lightly grease a muffin tin or line with papers and coat the papers with nonstick spray.

TO MAKE THE BATTER: Whisk together the flours, cocoa, malted milk powder, brown sugar, baking powder, baking soda and salt in a large mixing bowl. In another bowl, whisk together the butter, buttermilk, eggs and vanilla. Stir the wet ingredients into the dry, mixing until the batter is evenly moistened. Stir in the chocolate chips, if using.

Scoop the batter by the ½-cupfuls into the prepared pan. Bake the muffins until you can smell the chocolate and a cake tester inserted in the center comes out clean, 25 minutes. Remove from the oven and allow the muffins to cool in the pan for 5 minutes, then turn them out onto a rack to finish cooling.

TO MAKE THE GLAZE: Place all the ingredients in a small saucepan. Bring to a simmer, stirring occasionally, then remove from the heat and drizzle over the tops of the cooled muffins.

NUTRITION INFORMATION PER SERVING (1 MUFFIN, WITH GLAZE, 106G): 15g whole grains, 287 cal, 7g fat, 7g protein, 25g complex carbohydrates, 25g sugar, 4g dietary fiber, 49mg cholesterol, 269mg sodium, 354mg potassium, 63RE vitamin A, 1mg vitamin C, 2mg iron, 130mg calcium, 199mg phosphorus, 16mg caffeine.

Sailor Jacks

YIELD: 1 dozen muffins

BAKING TEMPERATURE: 375°F

BAKING TIME: 20 to 23 minutes

These muffins seem to be native to the Pacific Northwest, where they can be found in Oregon's bakeries. There you'll find these moist raisin-and-spice muffins turned upside down, and wearing a lemon glaze that's the perfect touch for the muffin below. We've left ours right side up, but feel free to turn them on their heads before glazing for the full experience.

Raisin-and-spice mixture

½ cup (3½ ounces) granulated sugar

½ cup (3¾ ounces) packed light or dark brown sugar

4 teaspoons ground cinnamon

1 teaspoon salt

1 teaspoon ground ginger

¾ teaspoon ground nutmeg

½ teaspoon ground cloves

1 cup (8 ounces) water

½ cup (3 ounces) raisins

2 tablespoons (1½ ounces) molasses

Muffin batter

1 cup (4 ounces) whole wheat flour

½ cup (1⅝ ounces) oat flour

½ cup (1¾ ounces) old-fashioned rolled oats

1 teaspoon baking soda

¾ teaspoon baking powder

⅓ cup (2⅜ ounces) vegetable oil

1 large egg

Glaze

½ cup (2 ounces) confectioners' sugar

2 teaspoons fresh lemon juice

1 teaspoon milk

Preheat the oven to 375°F. Lightly grease a muffin tin or line with papers and coat the papers with nonstick spray.

TO MAKE THE RAISIN-AND-SPICE MIXTURE: Place the ingredients in a medium saucepan and cook, stirring occasionally, over medium heat, until the mixture comes to a boil. Simmer for 5 minutes, then remove from the heat and let cool, overnight if desired.

TO MAKE THE BATTER: Whisk together the flours, oats, baking soda and baking powder in a medium mixing bowl. Add the cooled raisin-and-spice mixture, oil and egg. Stir to combine (there's no need to beat the batter; it'll become tough if you do).

TO BAKE THE MUFFINS: Scoop the batter into the prepared muffin pan, filling each cup about three-quarters full. Bake the muffins until a cake tester inserted into the center comes out clean, about 20 to 23 minutes. Remove from the oven and allow the muffins to cool in the pan for about 15 minutes, then turn them out onto a rack to finish cooling.

FOR THE GLAZE: Mix all the ingredients until smooth; drizzle over the cooled muffins.

NUTRITION INFORMATION PER SERVING (1 GLAZED MUFFIN, 85G): **18g whole grains,** 245 cal, 7g fat, 3g protein, 19g complex carbohydrates, 3g dietary fiber, 18mg cholesterol, 329mg sodium, 183mg potassium, 9RE vitamin A, 1mg vitamin C, 2mg iron, 64mg calcium, 131mg phosphorus.

Moist Bran Muffins

YIELD: **1 dozen muffins**
BAKING TEMPERATURE: **375°F**
BAKING TIME: **23 to 26 minutes**

While bran is only part of any whole grain, its health benefits have been well documented. In the case of wheat bran, there are many fans of the flavor it imparts, as well. These muffins are moist and chewy without being heavy, with a hint of caramel sweetness from the brown sugar. They're a great choice for breakfast or a wholesome snack. The batter can be mixed up and held in the refrigerator for up to a week, then scooped and baked as needed, so you can have fresh, warm muffins whenever you like.

¾ cup (6 ounces) boiling water
1¼ cups (2⅜ ounces) bran cereal (not flakes), divided
¾ cup (4½ ounces) raisins
¾ cup (5⅝ ounces) packed light or dark brown sugar
¼ cup (1¾ ounces) vegetable oil
2½ cups (10 ounces) whole wheat flour, traditional or white whole wheat
1 teaspoon baking soda
½ teaspoon baking powder
1 teaspoon salt
1 large egg
¾ cup (6 ounces) buttermilk
½ cup (4 ounces) orange juice

Pour boiling water over ¾ cup of the bran cereal in a small mixing bowl. Add the raisins, brown sugar and oil. While the bran mixture cools, blend together the flour, baking soda, baking powder and salt in a large mixing bowl.

Beat the egg with the buttermilk and orange juice in a large measuring cup. Add this mixture to the dry ingredients. Stir in the remaining ½ cup bran cereal, then the bran-raisin mixture. Cover the bowl and refrigerate overnight.

The next day, preheat the oven to 375°F. Lightly grease a muffin tin or line with papers and coat the papers with nonstick spray. Fill each cup two-thirds full. Bake the muffins until a cake tester inserted in the center comes out clean, 23 to 26 minutes. Remove from the oven and allow the muffins to cool in the pan for 5 minutes, then turn them out onto a rack to finish cooling, or serve warm, as desired.

NUTRITION INFORMATION PER SERVING (1 MUFFIN, 106G): **25g whole grains,** 241 cal, 6g fat, 6g protein, 32g complex carbohydrates, 14g sugar, 6g dietary fiber, 18mg cholesterol, 386mg sodium, 346mg potassium, 43RE vitamin A, 9mg vitamin C, 3mg iron, 82mg calcium, 203mg phosphorus.

Whole Corn and Green Chili Muffins

YIELD: **1 dozen muffins**
BAKING TEMPERATURE: **400°F**
BAKING TIME: **20 minutes**

These muffins demonstrate how easily whole grains can support savory recipes as well as sweet ones. Corn, cheese and chilies with a little bit of spice in the background create a memorable southwestern flair. The cheese and chilies on top make a lovely pastiche while they're baking. Bring these to the table with some tortilla soup and a salad, and supper's ready.

1 cup (4$\frac{7}{8}$ ounces) whole yellow cornmeal
$\frac{1}{2}$ cup (2 ounces) whole wheat flour, traditional or white whole wheat
$\frac{3}{4}$ cup (3$\frac{1}{8}$ ounces) unbleached all-purpose flour
2 tablespoons ($\frac{7}{8}$ ounce) sugar
1 tablespoon baking powder
1 teaspoon salt
$\frac{1}{2}$ teaspoon chili powder or $\frac{1}{4}$ teaspoon cayenne pepper
1 large egg
1 cup (8 ounces) milk
$\frac{1}{2}$ cup (3$\frac{1}{2}$ ounces) corn oil
1 cup (5$\frac{3}{4}$ ounces) frozen corn kernels, thawed
1 can (4$\frac{1}{2}$ ounces) diced green chilies, well drained, divided
$\frac{3}{4}$ cup (3 ounces) grated sharp Cheddar cheese, divided

Preheat the oven to 400°F. Lightly grease a muffin tin or line with papers and coat the papers with nonstick spray.

Whisk together the cornmeal, flours, sugar, baking powder, salt and chili powder (or cayenne) in a medium bowl. In a separate bowl, lightly beat the egg with the milk and oil. Stir in the corn kernels and all but 2 tablespoons of the chilies. Add the wet ingredients to the dry ingredients, stirring just until evenly moistened. Stir in $\frac{1}{2}$ cup of the grated cheese.

Scoop the batter by heaping $\frac{1}{4}$-cupfuls into the prepared muffin pan, and sprinkle each muffin with 1 teaspoon of the remaining cheese and $\frac{1}{2}$ teaspoon of the reserved chilies. Bake the muffins until a toothpick inserted in the center comes out clean, 20 minutes. Remove from the oven and allow the muffins to cool in the pan for 5 minutes, then turn them out onto a rack to finish cooling.

NUTRITION INFORMATION PER SERVING (1 MUFFIN, 85G): **18g whole grains,** 223 cal, 13g fat, 6g protein, 21g complex carbohydrates, 2g sugar, 2g dietary fiber, 26mg cholesterol, 337mg sodium, 123mg potassium, 55RE vitamin A, 1mg vitamin C, 1mg iron, 165mg calcium, 233mg phosphorus.

Ham-and-Cheese Rye Muffins

YIELD: 1 dozen muffins
BAKING TEMPERATURE: 375°F
BAKING TIME: 25 to 27 minutes

Here's an easy way to round out a quick breakfast or lunch while adding to your daily intake of whole grains, in a most delicious fashion. The rye flour, pointed up just slightly by the onion powder, brings to mind the flavors of the classic ham and Swiss cheese sandwich. The grated Swiss on top of the muffins gets wonderfully toasty while they bake. These muffins created a stampede when they made their debut, disappearing in record time.

2 cups (7½ ounces) whole rye (pumpernickel) flour
¾ cup (3⅛ ounces) unbleached bread flour
2½ teaspoons baking powder
½ teaspoon baking soda
1 teaspoon salt
½ teaspoon onion powder
1½ cups (6 ounces) grated Swiss cheese, divided
1 large egg
1½ cups (12 ounces) buttermilk
½ cup (1 stick, 4 ounces) unsalted butter, melted
4 ounces diced ham or ½ pound bacon, cooked crisp and crumbled

Preheat the oven to 375°F. Lightly grease a muffin tin or line with papers and coat the papers well with nonstick spray; the cheese tends to make them stick a bit.

Whisk together the flours, baking powder, baking soda, salt and onion powder in a large mixing bowl. Add 1¼ cups of the Swiss cheese, tossing it in the flour mixture to coat it.

In a separate bowl, whisk together the egg, buttermilk and melted butter. Add, all at once, to the flour mixture, and stir until evenly moistened. Stir in the ham (or bacon).

Scoop the batter into the prepared pan, and sprinkle the remaining ¼ cup of cheese over the tops. Bake the muffins until the cheese on top is toasted golden brown and a cake tester inserted into the center comes out clean, 25 to 27 minutes. Remove from the oven and allow the muffins to cool in the pan for 5 minutes, then turn them out onto a rack to finish cooling, or serve warm.

NUTRITION INFORMATION PER SERVING (1 MUFFIN, 100G): 21g whole grains, 254 cal, 14g fat, 11g protein, 23g complex carbohydrates, 5g dietary fiber, 59mg cholesterol, 448mg sodium, 278mg potassium, 122RE vitamin A, 2mg iron, 260mg calcium, 385mg phosphorus.

QUICK BREAD LOAVES: VERSATILE AND DELICIOUS

Few baked goods can hold a candle to a good quick bread. It serves admirably from the brunch table to holiday gifts to housewarming gestures to the bake sale table. Quick breads taste great, they keep well, and they're a welcome addition at practically any meal of the day (or in between). Quick breads can be sweet and cakelike, or more reserved, wanting only a bit of butter or a slice of cheese.

Practically all quick breads benefit from an overnight rest before slicing. The moisture in the dough redistributes itself as the bread sits, improving its texture and slicing qualities. This characteristic couldn't be better suited for whole grains, which become even more appetizing when given some extra time to absorb the loaf's moisture. The bran softens, the flavors meld, and any spices or vanilla have more time to evenly suffuse the bread.

New England Nut Bread

YIELD: **One 9 x 5-inch loaf, 16 servings**
BAKING TEMPERATURE: **300°F**
BAKING TIME: **1 hour 10 minutes to 1¼ hours**

This loaf isn't overly sweet; it pairs as well with a slice of cheese as it does with butter and jam. The flavor is a bit reminiscent of brown bread, with a lighter touch. Baking the whole wheat batter at a lower temperature for a longer time helps to moisten the bran, making the loaf tender. The nuts take on a lovely toasted flavor, too. Tent the loaf with foil for the last 15 minutes of baking, if it's darkening too quickly on top.

2 cups (8 ounces) whole wheat flour, traditional or white whole wheat
1 cup (4¼ ounces) unbleached bread flour
2 teaspoons baking powder
½ teaspoon baking soda
1¼ teaspoons salt
½ cup (1 stick, 4 ounces) unsalted butter
½ cup (3¾ ounces) packed light brown sugar
2 large eggs
⅓ cup (4 ounces) molasses
1¼ cups (10 ounces) milk
2 tablespoons (1 ounce) orange juice
1¼ cups (5 ounces) chopped nuts

Preheat the oven to 300°F. Grease a 9 x 5-inch loaf pan.

Whisk together the flours, baking powder, baking soda and salt in a medium bowl.

Cream together the butter and brown sugar in a large mixing bowl until light. Add the eggs, one at a time, stopping to scrape the bottom and sides of the bowl and mixing until smooth. Beat in the molasses. Mix in half the flour mixture, then half the milk. Scrape the bowl again, then add the remaining flour mixture, the remaining milk, and the orange juice. When the batter is evenly moistened, stir in the nuts.

Transfer the batter to the prepared pan. Bake for 1 hour 10 minutes to 1 hour 15 minutes. Check the bread after 1 hour; cover the top with foil for the remaining baking time if it's darkening too quickly.

Remove the pan from the oven and place on a rack to cool for 20 minutes. After 20 minutes, run a table knife around the edges of the pan and turn the loaf out. Place the bread on a rack to cool completely before slicing or wrapping in plastic wrap to rest overnight before serving.

NUTRITION INFORMATION PER SERVING (1 SLICE, 73G): 15g whole grains, 202 cal, 7g fat, 5g protein, 18g complex carbohydrates, 12g sugar, 2g dietary fiber, 44mg cholesterol, 282mg sodium, 169mg potassium, 80RE vitamin A, 1mg vitamin C, 2mg iron, 90mg calcium, 153mg phosphorus.

Lemon–Poppy Seed Bread

YIELD: One 9 x 5-inch loaf, 16 servings
BAKING TEMPERATURE: 350°F
BAKING TIME: 1 hour to 1 hour 5 minutes

This perennial favorite sparkles with lemon flavor throughout, and by using white whole wheat flour, the only difference you'll see from an all-white flour recipe is a slightly creamier-looking background color. The batter can be scooped and baked for muffins, as well as making a stately loaf for slicing. The extra fillip of the lemon glaze makes it a great treat for company.

Bread
1½ **cups (6 ounces) white whole wheat flour**
½ **cup (1⅝ ounces) oat flour**
¾ **cup (3⅛ ounces) unbleached all-purpose flour**
2 **teaspoons baking powder**
½ **teaspoon baking soda**
½ **teaspoon salt**

½ cup (1 stick, 4 ounces) unsalted butter

1 cup (7 ounces) sugar

2 large eggs

2 tablespoons grated lemon zest

½ cup (4 ounces) fresh lemon juice

¾ cup (6 ounces) lemon yogurt, non-fat to full fat

¼ cup (1⅜ ounces) poppy seeds

Lemon glaze (optional)

½ cup (2 ounces) confectioners' sugar

2 teaspoons fresh lemon juice

1 teaspoon milk

Preheat the oven to 350°F. Grease a 9 x 5-inch loaf pan.

TO MAKE THE BREAD: Whisk together the flours with the baking powder, baking soda and salt in a medium bowl.

Cream together the butter and sugar in a large mixing bowl until fluffy. Add the eggs, one at a time, scraping the sides and bottom of the bowl between additions. Add the lemon zest, then one-third of the dry ingredients. Add the lemon juice, then another third of the dry ingredients. Mix in the yogurt and poppy seeds, then the remaining dry ingredients.

Pour the batter into the prepared pan. Bake until a toothpick inserted in the center comes out clean, 1 hour to 1 hour 5 minutes. Remove from the oven, place on a rack, and cool in the pan for 15 to 20 minutes. After that time, run a table knife around the edge of the pan, and tip the bread out. Return the bread to the rack to cool completely before glazing.

TO MAKE THE GLAZE: Whisk together all the ingredients until smooth. Brush or drizzle over the top of the cooled bread just before serving.

NUTRITION INFORMATION PER SERVING (1 SLICE, WITHOUT GLAZE, 67G): 14g whole grains, 204 cal, 8g fat, 4g protein, 17g complex carbohydrates, 13g sugar, 3g dietary fiber, 45mg cholesterol, 169mg sodium, 117mg potassium, 70RE vitamin A, 4mg vitamin C, 1mg iron, 103mg calcium, 163mg phosphorus.

VARIATION: *To make muffins, make the batter as directed, and scoop into a muffin pan lined with papers. Bake in a preheated 375°F oven until a toothpick inserted in the center comes out clean, 22 to 24 minutes. Remove from the oven and cool on a rack for 5 minutes before removing the muffins from the pan. Place the muffins on the rack to finish cooling completely, before brushing or drizzling with the glaze, if desired.*

Pumpkin Bread

YIELD: One 9 x 5-inch loaf, 16 servings
BAKING TEMPERATURE: 350°F
BAKING TIME: 1 hour

Pumpkin as an ingredient is a natural for a whole grain loaf. The moisture of the pumpkin is absorbed by the whole grain's bran, making a moist and tender bread. The more pronounced flavor of the wheat berry combines in harmony with the spices.

2 cups (8 ounces) whole wheat flour, traditional or white whole wheat
1 teaspoon baking soda
½ teaspoon baking powder
½ teaspoon salt
½ teaspoon ground cinnamon
½ teaspoon ground cloves
¼ teaspoon ground nutmeg
½ cup (1 stick, 4 ounces) unsalted butter
1 cup (7½ ounces) packed light or dark brown sugar
¼ cup (1¾ ounces) granulated sugar
3 large eggs
1 teaspoon vanilla extract
1 cup (9½ ounces) canned pumpkin
¾ cup (3 ounces) chopped nuts
¾ cup (4½ ounces) raisins, dried cranberries, or chocolate chips

Preheat the oven to 350°F. Grease a 9 x 5-inch loaf pan.

Whisk together the flour, baking soda, baking powder, salt and spices in a medium bowl.

Cream together the butter and sugars in a large mixing bowl until light and fluffy. Beat in the eggs, one at a time, stopping to scrape the sides and bottom of the mixing bowl. Beat in the vanilla and pumpkin. Add the dry ingredients, mixing until evenly moistened. Stir in the nuts and raisins, cranberries or chips.

Pour the batter into the prepared pan. Bake until a cake tester inserted in the center comes out clean, 1 hour. Remove the bread from the oven and place it on a rack to cool for 15 minutes. After 15 minutes, run a table knife around the edges of the pan to make sure the bread isn't sticking, turn it out of the pan, and place it on the rack to finish cooling completely before slicing.

NUTRITION INFORMATION PER SERVING (1 SLICE, MADE WITH WALNUTS, 63G): 15g whole grains, 242 cal, 11g fat, 4g protein, 18g complex carbohydrates, 18g sugar, 3g dietary fiber, 56mg cholesterol, 209mg sodium, 209mg potassium, 75RE vitamin A, 1mg vitamin C, 1mg iron, 44mg calcium, 113mg phosphorus.

VARIATION: *To make pumpkin muffins, make the batter as directed and scoop into a muffin pan lined with papers. Sprinkle the tops with pumpkin seeds, if desired. Bake in a preheated 375°F oven until a toothpick inserted in the center comes out clean, 22 to 24 minutes. Remove from the oven and cool on a rack for 5 minutes before removing the muffins from the pan.*

 # Broonie

YIELD: One 8¹/₂ x 4¹/₂-inch loaf, 16 servings
BAKING TEMPERATURE: 350°F
BAKING TIME: 50 to 55 minutes

This recipe is a descendant of a traditional oatmeal gingerbread from the Orkney Islands, in the North Sea above Scotland. The word comes from the Norse Bruni, *meaning a thick bannock. Bannocks are the ancestors of today's scones, made with barley and oats. We've lightened up the original a bit and enhanced it with a touch of crystallized ginger, to make a loaf that's equally at home with some peach ice cream for dessert or a little butter or cream cheese for breakfast.*

1¹/₂ cups (5¹/₄ ounces) old-fashioned rolled oats
1 cup (4 ounces) whole barley flour
1 cup (4¹/₄ ounces) unbleached all-purpose flour
¹/₂ cup (3³/₄ ounces) packed light or dark brown sugar
1¹/₂ teaspoons baking powder
1¹/₂ teaspoons ground ginger
¹/₂ teaspoon salt
¹/₂ cup (1 stick, 4 ounces) unsalted butter
3 large eggs, beaten
1 cup (8 ounces) buttermilk
¹/₄ cup (3 ounces) molasses
¹/₂ cup (3¹/₄ ounces) diced crystallized ginger

Preheat the oven to 350°F. Grease an 8¹/₂ by 4¹/₂-inch loaf pan.

Whisk together the oats, flours, brown sugar, baking powder, ginger and salt in a large bowl. With a fork, two knives, or a pastry cutter, cut in the butter until the mixture resembles coarse cornmeal.

In a separate bowl, combine the eggs, buttermilk and molasses. Stir this mixture into the dry ingredients, stirring until the batter is evenly moistened. Stir in the crystallized ginger.

Spoon the batter into the prepared pan. Bake until a cake tester inserted in the center comes out clean, 50 to 55 minutes. Remove from the oven and cool on a rack. After the Broonie is cooled, remove from the pan and wrap well; it's best to hold it overnight before slicing, if possible.

NUTRITION INFORMATION PER SERVING (1 SLICE, 66G): **15g whole grains,** 163 cal, 1g fat, 5g protein, 17g complex carbohydrates, 15g sugar, 2g dietary fiber, 41mg cholesterol, 143mg sodium, 137mg potassium, 21RE vitamin A, 1mg vitamin C, 1mg iron, 75mg calcium, 126mg phosphorus.

Whole Wheat Zucchini Bread

YIELD: **One 9 x 5-inch loaf, 16 servings**
BAKING TEMPERATURE: **350°F**
BAKING TIME: **1 hour to 1¼ hours**

This classic is made all the better because the moisture from the grated zucchini softens the bran in the whole wheat, resulting in an eminently appetizing quick bread. We've used a bit of lemon zest and a smidgen of nutmeg to show off the zucchini, and when made with white whole wheat flour, the bread is a beautiful light golden color.

> 2 cups (8 ounces) whole wheat flour, traditional or white whole wheat
> 1 cup (4¼ ounces) unbleached bread flour
> ¾ cup (5¼ ounces) sugar
> 1 tablespoon baking powder
> 1 teaspoon salt
> ¼ teaspoon ground nutmeg
> 2 large eggs
> ¾ cup (6 ounces) milk
> ¼ cup (1¾ ounces) vegetable oil
> 1½ cups (12⅜ ounces) shredded zucchini
> ½ cup (3 ounces) raisins
> ½ cup (2 ounces) chopped walnuts
> 1 tablespoon grated lemon zest

Preheat the oven to 350°F. Lightly grease a 9 x 5-inch loaf pan.

Whisk together the flours, sugar, baking powder, salt and nutmeg in a large bowl. Whisk the eggs, milk and oil in a small bowl or large mixing cup. Stir into the dry ingredients until everything is evenly moistened; stir in the zucchini, raisins, walnuts and lemon zest.

Pour the batter into the prepared pan. Bake for 1 hour. Check the top; if it's wet looking and wobbles when you touch it, tent the bread loosely with foil and bake until a cake tester inserted in the center comes out clean, 10 to 15 minutes more.

Remove the bread from the oven and cool in the pan for 15 minutes before taking it out of the pan and putting it on a rack to finish cooling completely.

NUTRITION INFORMATION PER SERVING (1 SLICE, 95G): 15g whole grains, 199 cal, 7g fat, 5g protein, 23g complex carbohydrates, 9g sugar, 3g dietary fiber, 14mg cholesterol, 213mg sodium, 174mg potassium, 16RE vitamin A, 3mg vitamin C, 1mg iron, 95mg calcium, 184mg phosphorus.

Maple-Walnut Bread

YIELD: One 9 x 5-inch loaf, 16 servings
BAKING TEMPERATURE: 350°F
BAKING TIME: 1 hour

The sweet, slightly caramel-like flavor of maple in this bread matches up nicely with the flavor of whole wheat and crunch of walnuts. It's simply delicious as is, or with a bit of cream cheese on top. This bread can also be enhanced by adding your favorite dried fruit to the batter before baking.

> **2 cups (8 ounces) whole wheat flour, traditional or white whole wheat**
> **1 cup (4¼ ounces) unbleached all-purpose flour**
> **½ cup (3½ ounces) sugar**
> **1½ teaspoons baking powder**
> **1 teaspoon salt**
> **1 cup (8 ounces) buttermilk**
> **6 tablespoons (¾ stick, 3 ounces) unsalted butter, melted**
> **2 large eggs**
> **½ cup (5½ ounces) maple syrup**
> **½ teaspoon maple flavor (optional, but makes a big difference)**
> **1½ cups (6 ounces) chopped walnuts**

Preheat the oven to 350°F. Grease and flour a 9 x 5-inch loaf pan.

Whisk together the flours, sugar, baking powder and salt in a large mixing bowl. In a separate bowl, mix together the buttermilk, melted butter, eggs, maple syrup and flavoring (if using). Add the wet ingredients to the dry, stirring just until the mixture is evenly combined. Stir in the walnuts.

Spoon the batter into the prepared pan. Bake until the top of the loaf is golden brown and a toothpick or cake tester inserted in the center comes out clean, 1 hour.

Remove the bread from the oven and place it on a rack, in the pan, for 15 minutes. After 15 minutes, run a table knife around the edges of the loaf to make sure it's not sticking, then turn it out of the pan and return it to the rack to cool completely before slicing.

NUTRITION INFORMATION PER SERVING (1 SLICE, 77G): 15g whole grains, 250 cal, 12g fat, 6g protein, 19g complex carbohydrates, 12g sugar, 3g dietary fiber, 39mg cholesterol, 206mg sodium, 176mg potassium, 57RE vitamin A, 2mg iron, 70mg calcium, 128mg phosphorus.

VARIATIONS: MAPLE-CRANBERRY PECAN BREAD: *Substitute ³⁄₄ cup each dried cranberries and diced pecans for the walnuts.*

MAPLE-DATE BREAD: *Add ³⁄₄ cup chopped dates to the batter.*

Cream Cheese and Molasses Bread

YIELD: One 9 x 5-inch loaf, 16 servings
BAKING TEMPERATURE: 350°F
BAKING TIME: 55 minutes to 1 hour

Dark mahogany in color, perfect for an afternoon snack or quick breakfast, this bread has some of the allure of gingerbread, with a bit more toothy substance from the oats, barley, and whole wheat that make up part of its character. Moist and just a little spicy from the ginger; it keeps beautifully for over a week, wrapped in plastic and resting on the counter.

1 cup (3¹⁄₂ ounces) old-fashioned rolled oats
1 cup (8 ounces) boiling water
1 cup (4 ounces) whole wheat flour, traditional or white whole wheat
1 cup (4 ounces) whole barley flour
³⁄₄ cup (3¹⁄₈ ounces) unbleached bread flour
1 teaspoon baking powder
¹⁄₂ teaspoon baking soda
¹⁄₂ teaspoon salt
¹⁄₂ teaspoon ground nutmeg
¹⁄₂ cup (1 stick, 4 ounces) unsalted butter, at room temperature
4 ounces cream cheese, softened
¹⁄₂ cup (3¹⁄₂ ounces) sugar
¹⁄₃ cup (4 ounces) molasses
3 large eggs

½ cup (3¼ ounces) finely diced crystallized ginger
1 cup (3¾ ounces) chopped pecans (optional)

Preheat the oven to 350°F. Lightly grease a 9 x 5-inch loaf pan.

Place the oats in a large mixing bowl and pour the boiling water over them. Set the bowl aside to cool to room temperature. Combine the flours, baking powder, baking soda, salt and nutmeg in a small bowl.

Add the butter, cream cheese and sugar to the oats and cream the mixture until evenly combined. Add the molasses, then add the eggs one at a time, mixing thoroughly after adding each one and stopping once to scrape the bowl. Add the dry ingredients, mixing well, then stir in the crystallized ginger and nuts (if using).

Spoon the batter into the prepared pan. Bake for 55 minutes to 1 hour, checking after 45 minutes to see if the top is browning too quickly. If it is, tent loosely with foil for the last 15 minutes of baking.

Remove the bread from the oven and place it on a rack, in the pan, for 15 minutes. After 15 minutes, run a table knife around the edges of the loaf to make sure it's not sticking, then turn it out of the pan and return it to the rack to cool completely before slicing.

NUTRITION INFORMATION PER SERVING (1 SLICE, WITHOUT NUTS, 63G): 20g whole grains, 197 cal, 10g fat, 4g protein, 15g complex carbohydrates, 9g sugar, 1g dietary fiber, 63mg cholesterol, 111mg sodium, 173mg potassium, 103RE vitamin A, 1mg vitamin C, 2mg iron, 85mg calcium, 72mg phosphorus.

Peach-Oatmeal Bread

YIELD: One 9 x 5-inch loaf, 16 servings

BAKING TEMPERATURE: 350°F

BAKING TIME: 1 hour to 1 hour 10 minutes

The summery flavor of peaches in this bread is surrounded in comforting fashion by whole wheat, with the sturdy accent of old-fashioned rolled oats. The bread is moist and flavorful, as well as being low-fat, so you can relax, as you would in your hammock, with a smile on your face. It's best to use slightly under-ripe peaches if you're using fresh ones in this recipe.

2 cups (12 ounces) peeled, sliced peaches; thawed if using frozen slices, well drained if using canned

2 cups (8 ounces) whole wheat flour, traditional or white whole wheat

¾ cup (3⅛ ounces) unbleached bread flour

½ cup (3½ ounces) granulated sugar

½ cup (3¾ ounces) packed light or dark brown sugar

1 tablespoon baking powder

½ teaspoon baking soda

½ teaspoon salt

1 teaspoon ground cinnamon

¼ teaspoon ground nutmeg

1 cup (3½ ounces) old-fashioned rolled oats

2 large eggs

1 cup (8 ounces) milk

¼ cup (1¾ ounces) vegetable oil

¼ teaspoon almond extract

Preheat the oven to 350°F. Grease a 9 x 5-inch loaf pan. Cut the peaches into small (¼-inch) pieces; place in a strainer to drain. Stir together the flours, sugars, baking powder, baking soda, salt, and spices in a large mixing bowl. Add the oats and peaches; stir to coat the peaches. Beat together the eggs, milk, oil and almond extract in a small bowl or large mixing cup. Add to the flour mixture, stirring just until evenly moistened.

Pour the batter into the prepared pan. Bake for 1 hour. Test the loaf for doneness; if a toothpick inserted in the center doesn't come out clean, cover the top of the bread with foil and bake for 10 minutes. Remove from the oven and cool in the pan for 15 minutes. After 15 minutes, run a table knife around the edges of the loaf to make sure it's not sticking, then turn it out of the pan and return it to the rack to cool completely before slicing.

NUTRITION INFORMATION PER SERVING (1 SLICE, 87G): **20g whole grains,** 198 cal, 5g fat, 5g protein, 22g complex carbohydrates, 13g sugar, 3g dietary fiber, 27mg cholesterol, 127mg sodium, 183mg potassium, 33RE vitamin A, 2mg vitamin C, 2mg iron, 103mg calcium, 198mg phosphorus.

Rieska

YIELD: **2 dozen (2-inch) squares**
BAKING TEMPERATURE: **500°F**
BAKING TIME: **17 to 20 minutes**

Rieska is a very moist, tasty, stir-together quick bread that has the texture of a cakey drop biscuit. One more benefit? Whole grains, low calories and great taste! It's originally from Finland, so if you have any Scandinavian ancestors to honor during holiday season, it's a fine addition to the breadbasket. After cutting, you'll have lots of 2-inch squares, each about an inch tall. We can picture these next to a bowl of soup, under a poached egg or sporting some melted cheese.

The oven temperature here isn't a misprint. Since this is a very moist batter, the bread needs a high baking temperature to cook through properly and to take on a bit of color by the time it's finished baking.

1 cup (3½ ounces) old-fashioned rolled oats
2 cups (7½ ounces) whole rye (pumpernickel) flour
1 cup (4 ounces) whole wheat flour, traditional or white whole wheat
1 cup (4¼ ounces) unbleached all-purpose flour
¼ cup (1¾ ounces) sugar
4 teaspoons baking powder
1 teaspoon baking soda
2 teaspoons salt
½ cup (1 stick, 4 ounces) unsalted butter
3 cups (24 ounces) buttermilk

Preheat the oven to 500°F. Lightly grease a 13 x 18 x 1-inch half-sheet pan.

Whisk together the oats and flours with the sugar, baking powder, baking soda and salt in a large mixing bowl. Cut the butter into the dry ingredients until thoroughly distributed. Stir in the buttermilk; the mixture will be kind of goopy; that's OK.

Transfer the dough to the sheet pan, and spread it out until it's ¾ inch thick and covers the bottom of the pan completely.

Bake until the top is light golden brown and springs back to the touch, 17 to 20 minutes. Remove from the oven and cool on a rack before slicing.

NUTRITION INFORMATION PER SERVING (1 SQUARE, 30G): 19g whole grains, 137 cal, 5g fat, 4g protein, 29g complex carbohydrates, 2g sugar, 4g dietary fiber, 12mg cholesterol, 235mg sodium, 164mg potassium, 40RE vitamin A, 1mg iron, 103mg calcium, 209mg phosphorus.

Buttermilk-Rye Bread

YIELD: One 9 x 5-inch loaf, 16 servings
BAKING TEMPERATURE: 350°F
BAKING TIME: 55 minutes to 1 hour

Dark and soft, nicely balanced between sweet and savory, this is the perfect loaf to pair with some soft cheese, a pâté, or a simple coating of butter. The orange zest and caraway provide an intriguing counterpoint to the hearty flavor of the rye flour. Best of all, this bread goes together quick as a wink, and needs nothing more than two bowls, a spoon and a pan.

2 cups (7½ ounces) whole rye (pumpernickel) flour

1 cup (4¼ ounces) unbleached bread flour

2 teaspoons baking powder

1 teaspoon baking soda

1 teaspoon salt

1¾ cups (14 ounces) buttermilk

¼ cup (3 ounces) molasses

1 large egg

1 tablespoon grated orange zest

1 tablespoon caraway seeds

4 tablespoons (½ stick, 2 ounces) unsalted butter, melted

Preheat the oven to 350°F. Grease a 9 x 5-inch loaf pan.

Whisk together the flours, baking powder, baking soda and salt in a large mixing bowl. In another bowl, whisk together the buttermilk, molasses, egg and orange zest. Pour the wet ingredients into the dry, and stir quickly and lightly until the batter is evenly moistened. Stir in the caraway seeds and melted butter.

Pour the batter into the prepared pan. Bake until a cake tester inserted in the center comes out clean, 55 minutes to 1 hour.

Remove the bread from the oven and place it on a rack to cool for 15 minutes. After 15 minutes, run a table knife around the edges of the pan to make sure the bread isn't sticking, turn it out of the pan, and place it on the rack to finish cooling completely before slicing.

NUTRITION INFORMATION PER SERVING (1 SLICE, 66G): 16g whole grains, 144 cal, 4g fat, 5g protein, 19g complex carbohydrates, 4g sugar, 4g dietary fiber, 22mg cholesterol, 297mg sodium, 201mg potassium, 37RE vitamin A, 1mg vitamin C, 2mg iron, 95mg calcium, 201mg phosphorus.

Hibernian Brown Bread

YIELD: **One 8-inch round loaf, 16 servings**
BAKING TEMPERATURE: **400°F, then 375°F**
BAKING TIME: **40 to 50 minutes**

This bread would be familiar to most rural families in Ireland, where it first became popular. Leavened with baking powder and soda, it was quicker to put on the table after a day in the fields than a yeast-leavened bread. Meant to be eaten the day it's made, the Irish developed the trick of placing a clean tea towel over the warm loaf to keep it soft until everyone came to the table.

The traditional cross that's cut in the top of this bread serves two purposes. The first is to remind the diners whom to thank for the bounty before them. The second is to ensure that the center of the bread cooks through.

3 cups (12 ounces) whole wheat flour, traditional or white whole wheat

1 cup (4¼ ounces) unbleached all-purpose flour

½ cup (1¾ ounces) old-fashioned rolled oats

2 teaspoons baking powder

1 teaspoon baking soda

1 teaspoon salt

1½ cups (12 ounces) buttermilk

1 large egg

½ cup (1 stick, 4 ounces) unsalted butter, melted

Preheat the oven to 400°F. Grease an 8-inch round pan.

Whisk together the flours, oats, baking powder, baking soda and salt in a large mixing bowl. Beat together the buttermilk, egg and melted butter in a large measuring cup. Make a well in the dry ingredients and add the liquid. Stir just until all the ingredients are evenly moistened. Turn the dough out onto a floured surface and knead three or four times. Form the dough into a ball, place it in the prepared pan, and cut a cross an inch deep into the top.

Bake at 400°F for 10 minutes. After 10 minutes, reduce the oven temperature to 375°F and bake until the bread sounds hollow when you tap the base and the top begins to brown, 30 to 40 minutes more. Remove from the oven and transfer the bread to a rack to cool. Drape the warm bread with a clean kitchen towel to keep it soft until you're ready to eat.

NUTRITION INFORMATION PER SERVING (1 SLICE, 60G): **25g whole grains,** 154 cal, 7g fat, 5g protein, 19g complex carbohydrates, 3g dietary fiber, 31mg cholesterol, 287mg sodium, 140mg potassium, 65RE vitamin A, 1mg iron, 81mg calcium, 175mg phosphorus.

Irish American Soda Bread

YIELD: **One 8-inch round loaf, 16 servings**

BAKING TEMPERATURE: **325°F**

BAKING TIME: **1 hour 15 minutes**

Soda bread in Ireland was originally promoted there as a quick, stir together way to get a loaf of bread on the table. As it traveled with the Irish immigrants to these shores, it began to include more and more of the culinary riches that were easier to find here: butter, eggs, and sugar. This soda bread recipe harks back to its roots, in a way, since it's made with whole wheat flour. The creamy beige color of the bread is beautiful, especially with its sparkling sugar top.

The soda bread tastes like a sweet, rich scone, a tiny bit crumbly but moist enough to hold together nicely when it's sliced. We bake it in a tall, round pan, to give it its classic shape. Though you can use raisins or currants, we prefer the tinier currants, as they spread themselves more evenly throughout the loaf.

> **6 tablespoons (¾ stick, 3 ounces) unsalted butter**
> **¾ cup (5¼ ounces) sugar**
> **2 large eggs**
> **1 tablespoon baking powder**
> **¼ teaspoon baking soda**
> **¾ teaspoon salt**
> **2 cups (8 ounces) whole wheat flour, traditional or white whole wheat**
> **1½ cups (12 ounces) buttermilk**
> **1 cup (4¼ ounces) unbleached all-purpose flour**
> **1 cup (5 ounces) currants or golden raisins, firmly packed**
> **2 teaspoons caraway seeds**
> **1 tablespoon milk, for glaze**
> **1 tablespoon coarse sugar, for topping**

Preheat the oven to 325°F. Lightly grease an 8-inch round pan, a soufflé dish, 1½-quart round casserole dish or panettone pan. Whichever pan you choose, make sure its sides are at least 3 inches high.

Beat together the butter and sugar in a large bowl until smooth. Add the eggs and beat on high speed until the mixture is thick and light colored, about 2 minutes. Stir in the baking powder, baking soda and salt, then 1 cup of the whole wheat flour. Gently beat in half of the buttermilk then another cup of the flour. Add the remaining buttermilk and the all-purpose flour, mixing until smooth. Stir in the currants (or raisins) and caraway seeds.

Turn the dough into the prepared pan. Drizzle the milk over it and sprinkle with the coarse sugar.

Bake the bread until a cake tester inserted into the center comes out clean, 1 hour 15 minutes. If you're using a ceramic pan, check the bread at 1 hour, since it may be done sooner. Tent a sheet of foil over the top for the final 15 minutes if it appears to be browning too quickly. Remove the bread from the oven, wait about 5 minutes, then run a dull knife around the edges to loosen them, before carefully turning it out onto a rack to cool, right side up. Allow the bread to cool for at least 1 hour before slicing.

NUTRITION INFORMATION PER SERVING (1 SLICE, 78G): 15g whole grains, 200 cal, 6g fat, 5g protein, 24g complex carbohydrates, 10g sugar, 3g dietary fiber, 40mg cholesterol, 222mg sodium, 199mg potassium, 7 RE vitamin A, 1mg vitamin C, 2 mg iron, 110mg calcium, 191mg phosphorus.

VARIATION: *If you prefer making a loaf shape, preheat the oven to 375°F and grease a 9 x 5-inch loaf pan. Prepare the batter as directed, transfer it to the pan, glaze with milk and top with sugar. Bake the bread until a cake tester inserted in the center comes out clean, 45 minutes to 1 hour.*

Boston Brown Bread

YIELD: One 8½ x 4½-inch loaf, 16 servings
BAKING TEMPERATURE: 325°F, or the high setting on a slow cooker
BAKING TIME: 1 hour 30 minutes to 2 hours

This is a classic recipe whose ingredients needed no rearranging. Brown bread has always been a whole grain, lowfat classic, sweetened with molasses, studded with currants or raisins, made tender and soft by long, slow cooking in a moist environment. While you may love this New England-born staple, the thought of rigging up a steamer on the stove and having to babysit it for up to 2 hours has probably kept you from making it yourself.

We've found two no-fuss alternatives to the stovetop-steaming scenario, both of which give you the familiar texture you expect from brown bread. One method is to bake the bread in a loaf pan in a covered water bath; the other is to use a pudding mold and place it in a slow cooker. Both methods provide moist, slow heat without needing to be checked, adjusted or fussed over. Now you can make hot, fresh brown bread whenever you like.

¾ cup (2¾ ounces) whole rye (pumpernickel) flour
¾ cup (3⅝ ounces) whole yellow cornmeal
¾ cup (3 ounces) whole wheat flour, traditional or white whole wheat
¾ teaspoon baking soda
¾ teaspoon salt
¾ cup (3¾ ounces) currants or raisins
1½ cups (12 ounces) buttermilk
½ cup (6 ounces) molasses

If baking in the oven, grease an 8½ x 4½-inch loaf pan and preheat the oven to 325°F. If using a slow cooker, butter a 2-quart pudding mold and see the slow cooker instructions below.

TO MAKE THE BATTER: Whisk together the pumpernickel, cornmeal, whole wheat flour, baking soda, salt and currants in a medium mixing bowl. In a separate bowl, beat the buttermilk and molasses together till smooth. Add the wet ingredients to the dry ingredients and mix till just combined; there's no need to beat the batter.

TO BAKE THE BREAD IN THE OVEN: Spoon the batter into the loaf pan and place the pan into a 9-inch-square pan. Pour hot water into the outer pan to a depth of 1½ inches.

Butter the center of a piece of 12 x 16-inch foil and make a tent over the loaf pan, so the bread has room to expand without hitting the foil. Secure the foil tightly to the edges. Tear off a 12-inch square of foil, cut it in half diagonally, and use the two resulting triangles to close up the ends of the tent.

Place the nested pans in the oven, and bake for 1 hour 30 minutes. Carefully remove the tent from the loaf pan, and the pans from the oven. The center of the bread may have a slight depression—that's OK; a tester inserted into it should come out clean. Serve warm or cool on a rack to be eaten later.

TO COOK IN A SLOW COOKER: Check to see that your pudding mold will fit into your slow cooker with the cooker's lid in place. Put 2 inches of water in the cooker, turn it on high, and replace the lid to heat the water.

Spoon the batter into the prepared pudding mold. Butter the lid and clip it tightly on top. Place the mold into the prepared slow cooker (no rack is necessary), and cover with the cooker's lid. The water should come halfway up the mold; if not, add more hot water as needed. Cook until a cake tester inserted in the center comes out clean, 1 hour 30 minutes to 2 hours.

NUTRITION INFORMATION PER SERVING (1 SLICE, 35G): 18g whole grains, 112 cal, 2g protein, 18g complex carbohydrates, 8g sugar, 3g dietary fiber, 176mg sodium, 192mg potassium, 1mg iron, 22mg calcium, 84mg phosphorus.

Use a piece of foil to create a tent shape over the loaf pan in its water bath.

Use two more pieces of foil to seal up the ends.

COFFEECAKES

Coffeecakes are immensely sociable treats. Nothing says, "Have a seat, stay awhile, let's chat" like a cup of coffee and a slice of moist, crumb-topped, cinnamon-scented cake. A coffee cake is simpler to make than an iced, dressed-to-the-nines layer cake, and doesn't really require an occasion.

Often graced with a smattering of fruit or a sprinkling of nuts, coffeecakes turn out to be eminently well suited to baking with whole grains. Depending on the size and shape of the cake, white whole wheat flour, oat flour, or whole wheat pastry flour proved to be the most suitable for making coffeecakes that struck our tasters as true and familiar. Even the most sumptuous part of a coffeecake, the topping, happily included whole grains and whole grain flours, with the added benefit of needing a little less fat to keep them together.

There are many different types of toppings in this section, from the luxurious pile of cinnamon-scented crumbs atop the Crumb Coffeecake to the oat and nut-flecked topping on the Banana Crunch Cake to the tried-and-true streusel that graces the Blueberry Buckle Coffeecake. Perhaps one of these will become your new favorite; if so, we hope you'll exercise the home baker's prerogative, and mix and match toppings and cakes as much as you like.

COFFEECAKES IN MINIATURE, OR MAKE MINE A MUFFIN, PLEASE

Any coffeecake recipe that calls for a total of 2½ cups of flour is the right size to make about a dozen muffins. The batter should be mixed according to its recipe, then scooped by the heaping ¼-cupful into a greased or paper-lined muffin tin. If the recipe includes streusel, simply sprinkle enough onto each muffin to cover the batter. As a general rule, a streusel-topped muffin should bake at 375°F until a cake tester inserted in the center comes out clean, 25 to 28 minutes. Remove from the oven, and cool on a rack for 5 minutes before gently taking the muffins out of the pan to finish cooling on a rack.

Crumb Coffeecake

YIELD: Two 8-inch round cakes, one 9 x 13-inch cake, or one 10-inch tube cake; 24 servings

BAKING TEMPERATURE: 350°F

BAKING TIME: 23 to 27 minutes for 8-inch rounds, 30 to 35 minutes for a 9 x 13 cake, 40 to 45 minutes for a 10-inch tube cake

We've found, much to our delight, that the lower protein level of whole wheat pastry flour makes it ideal for including in streusel or in crumbs, as you'll taste in this cake. When you choose white whole wheat for the cake batter, it takes on a lovely golden color while it bakes up beautifully moist and sweet. The proportion of batter to crumbs is just far enough to the decadent side of things to be gloriously indulgent. To highlight those crumbs, dust the top with a little confectioners' sugar after baking.

Crumbs

1¾ cups (6 ounces) whole wheat pastry flour

1 cup (4¼ ounces) unbleached all-purpose flour

1¼ cups (8¾ ounces) sugar

1½ teaspoons ground cinnamon

½ teaspoon salt

¾ cup (1½ sticks, 6 ounces) unsalted butter, melted

1 teaspoon vanilla extract

½ teaspoon almond extract

Cake batter

½ cup (1 stick, 4 ounces) unsalted butter

1 cup (7 ounces) sugar

2 large eggs

1 cup (8 ounces) sour cream

1 teaspoon vanilla extract

2 cups (8 ounces) whole wheat flour, traditional or white whole wheat

¾ cup (3⅛ ounces) unbleached bread flour

1 teaspoon baking soda

1 teaspoon baking powder

½ teaspoon salt

Confectioners' or glazing sugar for dusting, optional

Preheat the oven to 350°F. Grease and flour the pan (or pans).

TO MAKE THE CRUMBS: Whisk together the flours, sugar, cinnamon and salt in a medium mixing bowl. Melt the butter in the microwave or a small saucepan, and add the extracts to it. Pour the butter into the flour mixture, and mix until all of the butter is absorbed and you have a uniformly moistened crumb mixture. Set aside while you make the cake batter.

TO MAKE THE CAKE BATTER: Cream together the butter and sugar in a large mixing bowl until light and fluffy. Add the eggs, one at a time, and beat well between additions. Scrape down the mixing bowl, then beat in the sour cream and vanilla. Whisk together the flours, baking soda, baking powder and salt in a medium bowl. Add to the butter/sour cream mixture, mixing until evenly combined. Pour the batter into the prepared pan(s). Crumble the crumb mixture over the top, until the batter is completely covered.

TO BAKE THE CAKE: Bake according to pan size, or until a tester inserted in the center comes out clean. Remove from the oven and cool on a rack; dust the top with confectioners' sugar (or glazing sugar) before serving, if desired.

NUTRITION INFORMATION PER SERVING (1 SERVING, $\frac{1}{24}$ OF RECIPE, 51G): 17g whole grains, 267 cal, 12g fat, 4g protein, 19g complex carbohydrates, 18g sugar, 47mg cholesterol, 168mg sodium, 98mg potassium, 113RE vitamin A, 1mg iron, 36mg calcium, 102mg phosphorous.

Banana Crunch Cake

YIELD: One 8-inch-square cake, 16 servings
BAKING TEMPERATURE: 350°F
BAKING TIME: 40 to 45 minutes

This cake gets extra whole grain punch from its combination of wheat and oat flours. The bananas keep it moist and tender, while the crunch topping is a satisfying counterpoint to the cake underneath. This is a great lunchbox cake: it will wrap and travel well. For a larger crowd, double the recipe and bake it in a 9 x 13-inch pan.

Cake batter
1 cup (3¼ ounces) oat flour
1 cup (4 ounces) whole wheat flour, traditional or white whole wheat
1 teaspoon baking soda
½ teaspoon salt
½ cup (1 stick, 4 ounces) unsalted butter
⅔ cup (5 ounces) packed light or dark brown sugar
2 large eggs
1 cup (8 ounces) mashed banana (2 large or 3 medium bananas)
½ cup (4 ounces) plain yogurt, non-fat to full-fat
1 teaspoon vanilla extract
½ cup (1⅞ ounces) chopped pecans or walnuts
1 cup (6 ounces) chocolate or toffee chips (optional)

Crunch topping
¾ cup (2⅝ ounces) old-fashioned rolled oats
⅓ cup (2½ ounces) packed light or dark brown sugar
½ teaspoon ground cinnamon
¼ teaspoon salt
2 tablespoons (1 ounce) unsalted butter, melted
¼ cup (1 ounce) chopped pecans or walnuts

Grease and flour an 8-inch-square pan. Preheat the oven to 350°F.

TO MAKE THE CAKE BATTER: Whisk together the flours, baking soda and salt in a medium bowl.

Cream together the butter and sugar in a large mixing bowl until light and fluffy. Beat in the eggs, one at a time, stopping to scrape the sides and bottom of the bowl between additions. Mix in half the dry ingredients until moistened, then mix in the bananas, yogurt and vanilla. Scrape down the sides and bottom of the bowl, then add the remaining dry ingredients and the nuts and chips, if using, mixing until evenly moistened. Transfer the batter to the prepared pan.

TO MAKE THE TOPPING: Combine the oats, brown sugar, cinnamon and salt in a small mixing bowl until well blended. Stir in the melted butter until the moisture forms large crumbs; stir in the chopped nuts. Sprinkle the topping over the batter in the pan.

Bake until the edges pull away from the pan and a cake tester inserted in the center comes out clean, 40 to 45 minutes. Remove the cake from the oven and place on a rack to cool for 20 minutes before serving warm, with ice cream, or cool completely for later use.

NUTRITION INFORMATION PER SERVING (1 SQUARE, WITHOUT CHIPS, 77G): 22g whole grains, 251 cal, 12g fat, 5g protein, 18g complex carbohydrates, 14g sugar, 3g dietary fiber, 46mg cholesterol, 166mg sodium, 225mg potassium, 83RE vitamin A, 1mg vitamin C, 1mg iron, 44mg calcium, 128mg phosphorus.

Blueberry Buckle Coffeecake

YIELD: **One 9-inch-square coffeecake, 16 servings**
BAKING TEMPERATURE: **375°F**
BAKING TIME: **45 to 50 minutes**

This recipe is one of our favorite summer morning treats, when blueberries are ripe and abundant. We've made a few adjustments to the traditional buckle recipe, to give whole grains in the form of oats and whole wheat pastry flour a chance to strut their stuff in the streusel. White whole wheat performs its magic in the cake, bringing whole grain goodness to this moist cake treat, studded with blueberries. This recipe can be made with any berry you like, or cherries, or diced stone fruits, such as peaches, plums or nectarines. Blueberry Buckle Coffeecake is rarely still around for more than an hour out of the oven, but should you have admirable restraint, it will still be just as delicious later for dessert, under a scoop of ice cream.

Streusel
¾ cup (5¼ ounces) sugar
½ cup (1¾ ounces) whole wheat pastry flour
¼ cup (1 ounce) unbleached all-purpose flour
¼ cup (⅞ ounces) old-fashioned rolled oats
1 teaspoon ground cinnamon
¼ teaspoon ground nutmeg
¼ teaspoon salt
6 tablespoons (¾ stick, 3 ounces) unsalted butter, softened

Buckle
2 cups (8 ounces) white whole wheat flour
½ cup (2⅛ ounces) unbleached all-purpose flour
2 teaspoons baking powder
½ teaspoon salt
4 tablespoons (½ stick, 2 ounces) unsalted butter
1 cup (7 ounces) sugar
2 large eggs
½ cup (4 ounces) milk
1 teaspoon vanilla extract
2 cups (10 ounces) blueberries (fresh or, if using frozen, don't thaw them)

Preheat the oven to 375°F. Grease and flour a 9-inch-square pan.

TO MAKE THE STREUSEL: Whisk together the sugar, flours, oats, cinnamon, nutmeg and salt in a medium bowl. Add the butter and mix to make medium-size crumbs.

TO MAKE THE BUCKLE: Whisk together the flours, baking powder and salt in a medium bowl.

Cream together the butter and sugar in a large mixing bowl until light and fluffy, then add the eggs, one at a time, stopping to scrape the sides and bottom of the bowl between additions. Stir in half the dry ingredients, then the milk and vanilla, scraping down the sides. Stir in the remaining dry ingredients, then gently fold in the blueberries. Spread the batter in the prepared pan, and sprinkle the streusel evenly over the top.

Bake the buckle until a cake tester inserted in the center comes out clean, 45 to 50 minutes. Remove it from the oven and let it cool, in the pan, on a rack.

NUTRITION INFORMATION PER SERVING (ONE 2¼-INCH SQUARE, 88G): 19g whole grains, 252 cal, 8g fat, 4g protein, 21g complex carbohydrates, 21g sugar, 3g dietary fiber, 46mg cholesterol, 160mg sodium, 121mg potassium, 85RE vitamin A, 2mg vitamin C, 1mg iron, 67mg calcium, 151mg phosphorus.

Peach Coffeecake

YIELD: Two 9-inch round coffeecakes or one 9 x 13-inch cake, 24 servings
BAKING TEMPERATURE: 350°F
BAKING TIME: 25 to 30 minutes for rounds, 30 to 35 minutes for 9 x 13-inch cake

This is a very quick cake to put together. The scent of baking cinnamon from the crunchy top provides its own allure, and the peaches baked into the whole wheat batter give it a wonderfully comforting moistness. When baked with rhubarb (see variation, below), the stalks tend to melt into the batter, where the rhubarb lends its distinctly citrusy tang and moisture, without drawing too much attention to itself. In either form, this coffeecake is sure to become a favorite.

Cake
2 cups (8 ounces) white whole wheat flour
½ cup (2⅛ ounces) unbleached all-purpose flour
1 teaspoon baking soda
1 teaspoon salt
½ cup (1 stick, 4 ounces) unsalted butter
1 cup (7 ounces) sugar
1 large egg
1 cup (8 ounces) buttermilk
1½ teaspoons vanilla extract
2 cups (12 ounces) peeled, diced fresh peaches, or if frozen, thawed

Topping
2 tablespoons (1 ounce) unsalted butter, softened
½ cup (3½ ounces) sugar

1 tablespoon unbleached all-purpose flour
1 tablespoon ground cinnamon

Preheat the oven to 350°F. Grease and flour two 9-inch round pans or one 9 x 13-inch pan.

TO MAKE THE CAKE: Whisk together the flours, baking soda and salt in a medium mixing bowl. Cream together the butter and sugar in a large bowl. Beat in the egg, stopping afterward to scrape the sides and bottom of the bowl. Add the dry ingredients, one third at a time, alternately with the buttermilk. Add the vanilla. Stir in the peaches until evenly distributed. Pour the batter into the prepared pan(s).

TO MAKE THE TOPPING: Combine the softened butter, sugar, flour, and cinnamon in a small mixing bowl until evenly mixed. Sprinkle this mixture over the batter.

Bake according to pan size, until the top is golden brown and a cake tester inserted in the center comes out clean. Remove from the oven and cool on a rack for at least 20 minutes before serving.

NUTRITION INFORMATION PER SERVING (ONE 2¼-SQUARE OR ¹⁄₁₂-INCH OF ONE ROUND LAYER, 48G): 10g whole grains, 141 cal, 5g fat, 2g protein, 11g complex carbohydrates, 12g sugar, 2g dietary fiber, 22mg cholesterol, 145mg sodium, 76mg potassium, 56RE vitamin A, 1mg vitamin C, 1mg iron, 7mg calcium, 44mg phosphorus.

VARIATION: RHUBARB COFFEECAKE *Substitute finely chopped rhubarb for the peaches, and increase the sugar in the cake batter to 1½ cups. Prepare and bake as directed above.*

Apple-Walnut Coffeecake

YIELD: One 10-inch tube cake, 16 to 20 servings
BAKING TEMPERATURE: 350°F
BAKING TIME: 45 to 50 minutes

Crunchy-sweet and apple-scented, with a hint of tang from the sour cream, this is a very moist coffeecake, its golden brown top dressed up in an apple-flavored glaze. Each slice is glowing with the color of the whole wheat within, and ever-so-slightly hinting of cinnamon.

Cake
2 cups (8 ounces) whole wheat flour, traditional or white whole wheat
½ cup (2⅛ ounces) unbleached bread flour
2 teaspoons baking powder
1 teaspoon baking soda
1 teaspoon salt
1½ cups peeled, diced tart apples (2 medium)

1 tablespoon fresh lemon juice

1½ teaspoons ground cinnamon

1 cup (2 sticks, 8 ounces) unsalted butter

1 cup (7 ounces) granulated sugar

3 large eggs

1½ teaspoons vanilla extract

¼ cup (2 ounces) boiled cider (see Where to Buy, p. 588) or apple juice concentrate

1 cup (8 ounces) sour cream

1½ cups (6 ounces) chopped walnuts

Glaze

½ cup (2 ounces) confectioners' sugar

2 tablespoons (1 ounce) heavy cream

1 tablespoon boiled cider or apple juice concentrate

Preheat the oven to 350°F. Lightly grease a 10-inch tube pan.

TO MAKE THE CAKE: Whisk together the flours, baking powder, baking soda and salt in a medium bowl.

Toss the diced the apples with the lemon juice and cinnamon.

Cream together the butter and sugar in a large mixing bowl until light and fluffy. Add the eggs, one at a time, beating well after each addition and stopping to scrape the sides and bottom of the bowl. Beat in the vanilla and boiled cider (or apple juice concentrate). Mix in half the dry ingredients, stirring until incorporated. Mix in the sour cream and the remaining dry ingredients. Scrape the bottom and sides of the bowl once more to make sure everything is evenly combined, then stir in the apples and walnuts. Spoon the batter into the prepared pan.

Bake until a cake tester inserted in the center comes out clean and the cake just begins to pull away from the outside edge of the pan, 45 to 50 minutes. Remove from the oven and place on a rack for 15 to 20 minutes, before turning the cake out of the pan onto a serving plate. Cool the cake completely before glazing.

TO MAKE THE GLAZE: Whisk together the ingredients until smooth. Spread the glaze over the top of the cooled cake.

NUTRITION INFORMATION PER SERVING (¹/₂₀ CAKE, WITH GLAZE, 79G): 12g whole grains, 296 cal, 19g fat, 5g protein, 17g complex carbohydrates, 13g sugar, 2g dietary fiber, 64mg cholesterol, 155mg sodium, 155mg potassium, 131RE vitamin A, 1mg vitamin C, 1mg iron, 52mg calcium, 123mg phosphorus.

GRINDING NUTS FOR BAKING

Almost any shelled nut can be made into a nut flour; all it takes is a food processor and a careful touch with the pulse button. Nuts have a high percentage of beneficial oils in their kernels, and the heat and friction of the food processor can release enough oil to take nuts to nut butters quickly, if you don't pulse them in short bursts. If you're grinding nuts to use in a baking recipe, we advise placing a cup of the flour from the recipe's dry ingredients into the food processor with the nuts. The flour will absorb the oils as the nuts are processed, allowing you to grind them to a fine texture without turning them into a paste.

Hazelnut-Espresso Coffeecake

YIELD: One 10-inch tube cake, 16 servings
BAKING TEMPERATURE: 300°F, then 350°F
BAKING TIME: 20 to 25 minutes for the hazelnuts; 1 hour to 1 hour 5 minutes for the coffeecake

For coffeehouse fans everywhere, here's a cake that suits both morning wake-up calls and the need for an afternoon pick-me-up. The rich nutty taste of ground hazelnuts serve, as the background note for the robust flavors of whole wheat and espresso. A sprinkling of chocolate chips only adds to the appeal.

Cake
1¾ cups (8¾ ounces) whole, blanched hazelnuts (filberts) or toasted almond flour (5⅞ ounces)
1 cup (4¼ ounces) unbleached all-purpose flour
2¼ cups (7½ ounces) whole wheat pastry flour
1 cup (7 ounces) granulated sugar
2 teaspoons baking powder
½ teaspoon salt
1 teaspoon ground cinnamon
1 cup (2 sticks, 8 ounces) unsalted butter, melted
4 large eggs
¾ cup (6 ounces) milk
1 to 2 tablespoons espresso powder
2 tablespoons (1 ounce) Frangelico liqueur or hazelnut syrup
1 cup (6 ounces) semisweet chocolate chips, or coarsely chopped chocolate

Glaze (optional)
1 cup (4 ounces) confectioners' sugar
1 teaspoon espresso powder
3 tablespoons (1½ ounces) warm milk or heavy cream

Preheat the oven to 300°F. Grease a 10-inch decorative tube pan.

TO TOAST AND GRIND THE HAZELNUTS: Spread the nuts in a single layer on a baking sheet with sides. Place in the oven to toast until golden brown and fragrant, 20 to 25 minutes. Remove the nuts from the oven and place on a rack to cool. Increase the oven temperature to 350°F.

Once the nuts have cooled to lukewarm, place them in the bowl of your food processor with the all-purpose flour. Grind the nuts, pulsing in short bursts, until they are finely chopped. Place the nut-and-flour mixture in a large mixing bowl.

If using toasted almond flour, place it and the all-purpose flour in a large mixing bowl.

TO MAKE THE CAKE: Add the whole wheat pastry flour, sugar, baking powder, salt and cinnamon to the mixing bowl. Mix until well blended. Make a well in the center and add the butter, eggs, milk, espresso powder to taste and Frangelico (or hazelnut syrup). Beat on low speed until combined. Scrape the sides and bottom of the bowl (the dry ingredients will tend to stay on the bottom). Increase the mixer's speed to medium-high and beat for approximately 1 minute, until everything's well blended. Stir in the chocolate chips.

Pour the batter into the prepared pan. Bake until a cake tester inserted in the center comes out clean, 1 hour to 1 hour 5 minutes. Allow the cake to cool in the pan for at least 15 minutes before turning it out onto a rack to cool. Top with the glaze, if you wish.

TO MAKE THE GLAZE: Place the confectioners' sugar in a small bowl. Dissolve the espresso powder in the warm milk (or cream), and add the mixture to the sugar. Brush the glaze over the cake; repeat after the first coat has had a chance to set up.

NUTRITION INFORMATION PER SERVING ($1/16$ CAKE, WITHOUT GLAZE, 97G): 14g whole grains, 414 cal, 24 fat, 6g protein, 18g complex carbohydrates, 28g sugar, 3g dietary fiber, 40mg cholesterol, 145mg sodium, 181mg potassium, 122RE vitamin A, 2mg iron, 80mg calcium, 136mg phosphorus, 15mg caffeine.

BISCUITS, POPOVERS, DUMPLINGS

Biscuits are near and dear to the hearts of legions of bakers. They're a part of the culture and heritage of many families, a dining touchstone that speaks of home and the familiar.

And no wonder. What can be more compelling than a high-rising, multilayered, crisp-on-top, cloudlike-in-the center biscuit? They're very simple to make, yet they add an enormous appeal to any meal.

Whole grain biscuits can proudly take their place on any table. The trick, we've found, is a dough that's a little on the moist side, a bit of bread flour to help with lift, and a light touch with the dough. We'll show you how to shape and cut your biscuits with a gentle hand, to capture the essence of the traditional biscuit, with the added flavor and nutritional benefits of whole grains. Perhaps it will be the beginning of a new tradition in your family.

We've included two other savory side dishes in this section: popovers and dumplings. Dumplings begin with very biscuitlike dough; they're just cooked in a moist heat environment instead of the oven. Popovers require a hot oven, as do biscuits, but use a very wet batter to create steam inside; this makes them "pop." The hot, fast-cooking oven creates the crispy outsides that are the source of our popover cravings. The popovers and dumplings you'll find here defy the conventional perception of whole grain foods. They're as light and airy as a whisper, and incredibly flavorful besides.

Honey–Whole Wheat Biscuits

YIELD: 1 dozen (2-inch) biscuits
BAKING TEMPERATURE: 400°F
BAKING TIME: 20 to 22 minutes

Slightly crunchy on top, full of wheat flavor without being heavy, with a little bit of honey to accent the flavor, these biscuits may well take the place of your regular recipe.
For a lighter color and more subtle wheat taste, choose white whole wheat instead of traditional whole wheat flour.

2$\frac{1}{2}$ cups (10 ounces) whole wheat flour, traditional or white whole wheat
$\frac{1}{2}$ cup (2$\frac{1}{8}$ ounces) unbleached bread flour
2$\frac{1}{2}$ teaspoons baking powder
$\frac{1}{2}$ teaspoon baking soda
$\frac{3}{4}$ teaspoon salt
$\frac{1}{2}$ cup (1 stick, 4 ounces) cold unsalted butter
1 large egg
$\frac{3}{4}$ cup (6 ounces) buttermilk, plus more for brushing
3 tablespoons (2$\frac{1}{4}$ ounces) honey

Preheat the oven to 400°F. Lightly grease a baking sheet or line it with parchment paper.

Whisk together the flours, baking powder, baking soda and salt in a large mixing bowl. With a fork, two knives, a pastry cutter or a food processor, cut in the butter until the mixture resembles coarse crumbs. Whisk together the egg, buttermilk and honey in a small bowl or large measuring cup. Add, all at once, to the flour mixture, and blend lightly and quickly with a fork until the mixture is evenly moistened.

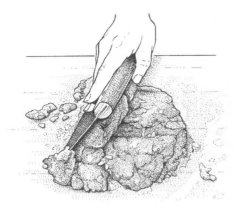

Fold the dough over on itself by picking it up with a bench knife or dough scraper. This will bring the dough together, without making it tough.

By stacking the scraps on top of each other and folding the dough again, you'll be able to cut more biscuits without overworking the dough.

Turn the dough out onto a floured work surface, and using a bench knife or dough scraper, fold the dough over on itself three or four times until it comes together. (See illustrations, above.)

Pat the dough out (or roll very lightly with a rolling pin) until it's ¾ inch thick. Cut the dough into squares or rounds with a 2-inch biscuit cutter, and transfer the biscuits to the prepared baking sheet. Stack the scraps on top of each other, fold them as you did for the original dough, and pat out and cut again.

Brush the tops of the biscuits with buttermilk, if desired.

Bake until the tops are golden brown, 20 to 22 minutes. Remove from the oven and serve warm, or cool on a rack.

NUTRITION INFORMATION PER SERVING (1 BISCUIT, 62G): 23g whole grains, 190 cal, 9g fat, 5g protein, 22g complex carbohydrates, 4g sugar, 3g dietary fiber, 37mg cholesterol, 263mg sodium, 130mg potassium, 78RE vitamin A, 1mg iron, 95mg calcium, 194mg phosphorus.

CUTTING BISCUITS

If you collect old recipes, or cherish the memory of baking with your grandmother, you may remember the days of cutting out biscuits with the top of a drinking glass. Alas, while it makes for a homey memory, this old-fashioned method doesn't make for the best-looking biscuit. The edge of a glass is rounded (otherwise you'd scrape your mouth), and when used to cut biscuits will compress the dough's layers before it finally cuts through them. This pinch around the edges will keep the dough from rising as it should in the oven, making a shorter, dense biscuit. For that reason we recommend using only sharp metal, plastic or nylon cutters for biscuits. Their sharper edges slice cleanly through the dough, revealing lots of beautiful, flaky layers as the biscuits bake.

Barleycorn Biscuits

YIELD: 10 (2-inch) biscuits
BAKING TEMPERATURE: 400°F
BAKING TIME: 20 to 23 minutes

These biscuits feature an interesting combination of textures. The barley flour makes them tender and the whole yellow cornmeal gives them a satisfying bit of crunch. The whole, in the words of one of our tasters, is "beyond tasty."

¾ cup (3 ounces) barley flour
½ cup (2⅛ ounces) unbleached all-purpose flour
¾ cup (3⅝ ounces) whole yellow cornmeal
1 tablespoon sugar
2 teaspoons baking powder
½ teaspoon baking soda
1 teaspoon salt
½ cup (4 ounces, 1 stick) cold unsalted butter
1 large egg
¾ cup (6 ounces) buttermilk
Melted butter or milk for brushing the tops (optional)

Preheat the oven to 400°F. Lightly grease a baking sheet, or line it with parchment paper.

Whisk together the flours, cornmeal, sugar, baking powder, baking soda and salt in a large mixing bowl. With a fork, two knives, a pastry cutter, or a food processor, cut in the butter until the mixture resembles coarse crumbs. Whisk together the egg and buttermilk in a small bowl or large measuring cup. Add, all at once, to the flour mixture, and blend lightly and quickly with a fork until the mixture is evenly moistened.

Turn the dough out onto a floured work surface, and using a bench knife or dough scraper, fold the dough over on itself three or four times until it comes together (see illustration, p. 75).

Pat the dough out (or roll very lightly with a rolling pin) until it's ¾ inch thick. Cut the dough into squares or rounds with a 2-inch biscuit cutter and transfer the biscuits to the prepared baking sheet. Stack the scraps on top of each other, fold them as you did for the original dough, and pat out and cut again. Brush the tops with melted butter or milk for a more pronounced golden color, if desired. Bake until the tops are golden brown, 20 to 23 minutes. Remove from the oven and serve warm.

NUTRITION INFORMATION PER SERVING (1 BISCUIT, 62G): 18g whole grains, 189 cal, 11g fat, 4g protein, 19g complex carbohydrates, 1g sugar, 2g dietary fiber, 48mg cholesterol, 379mg sodium, 84mg potassium, 106RE vitamin A, 1mg iron, 96mg calcium, 154mg phosphorus.

Parmesan–Pine Nut Biscuits

YIELD: 1 dozen to 14 (2-inch) biscuits

BAKING TEMPERATURE: 400°F

BAKING TIME: 20 to 22 minutes

Redolent of toasted cheese and glowing with golden color from the white whole wheat, these biscuits are crisp on top, moist and tender inside, and are just as flavorful at room temperature as they are warm, which makes them a great addition to a picnic. They would pair beautifully with a soup or stew, or even your favorite pasta dish.

2 cups (8 ounces) white whole wheat flour

½ cup (2⅛ ounces) unbleached bread flour

2½ teaspoons baking powder

½ teaspoon baking soda

¾ teaspoon salt

½ cup (1 stick, 4 ounces) cold unsalted butter

1 cup (3½ ounces) freshly grated Parmesan cheese, plus more for the tops

1 cup (5 ounces) pine nuts

1 tablespoon finely chopped fresh rosemary (optional)

1 large egg

1 cup (8 ounces) buttermilk, plus more for the tops

> **HOW DO YOU LIKE YOUR SIDES?**
>
> If you like biscuits for their crisp tops and sides, place them on the baking sheet with 2 inches of space between them. That way air will circulate around them more efficiently, giving a crispy top and a slightly taller rise. If you like the tender, melting, cloud-like part of biscuits, bake them with their sides almost touching. They'll expand into each other as they rise, and as a result their sides will be more moist than crisp.

Preheat the oven to 400°F. Lightly grease a baking sheet or line it with parchment paper.

Whisk together the flours, baking powder, baking soda and salt in a large mixing bowl. With a fork, two knives, a pastry cutter or a food processor, cut in the butter until the mixture resembles coarse crumbs. Stir in the Parmesan cheese, pine nuts, and rosemary (if using).

Whisk together the egg and buttermilk in a small bowl or large measuring cup. Add, all at once, to the flour mixture, and blend lightly and quickly with a fork until the mixture is evenly moistened.

Turn the dough out onto a floured work surface, and using a bench knife or dough scraper, fold the dough over on itself three or four times until it comes together (see illustration, p. 75).

Pat the dough out (or roll very lightly with a rolling pin) until it's ¾-inch thick. Cut the dough into squares or rounds with a 2-inch biscuit cutter and transfer the biscuits to the prepared baking sheet. Stack the scraps on top of each other, fold them as you did for the original dough, and pat out and cut again. Brush the tops with more buttermilk, and sprinkle with more cheese if desired.

Bake until the tops are golden brown, 20 to 22 minutes. Remove from the oven and serve warm, or cool on a rack.

NUTRITION INFORMATION PER SERVING (1 BISCUIT, 70G): 17g whole grains, 233 cal, 15g fat, 9g protein, 19g complex carbohydrates, 3g dietary fiber, 39mg cholesterol, 346mg sodium, 181mg potassium, 83RE vitamin A, 2mg iron, 166mg calcium, 269mg phosphorus.

Spelt–Cream Cheese Biscuits

YIELD: 10 to 1 dozen (2-inch) biscuits
BAKING TEMPERATURE: 400°F
BAKING TIME: 20 to 22 minutes

Spelt is often stone-ground, with larger flakes of bran in the flour than whole wheat flour. This characteristic makes this a more freckled-looking biscuit. The cream cheese gives a tangy background note to these tender biscuits and the slightly sweet spelt lends a bit of contrasting crunch.

2 cups (7 ounces) whole spelt or whole wheat pastry flour
½ cup (2 ounces) white whole wheat flour
1 tablespoon sugar
1 tablespoon baking powder
1 teaspoon salt
4 tablespoons (½ stick, 2 ounces) cold unsalted butter
4 ounces cream cheese
1 large egg
½ cup (4 ounces) milk
Melted butter or additional milk for brushing the tops (optional)

Whisk together the flours, sugar, baking powder and salt in a large mixing bowl. With a fork, two knives, a pastry cutter, or a food processor, cut in the butter until the mixture resembles coarse crumbs. Repeat the cutting-in process with the cream cheese.

Whisk together the egg and milk in a small bowl or large measuring cup. Add, all at once, to the flour mixture, and blend lightly and quickly with a fork until the mixture is evenly moistened.

Turn the dough out onto a floured work surface, and using a bench knife or dough scraper, fold the dough over on itself three or four times until it comes together (see illustration, p. 75).

Pat the dough out (or roll very lightly with a rolling pin) until it's ¾-inch thick. Cut the dough into squares or rounds with a 2-inch biscuit cutter, and transfer the biscuits to the prepared baking sheet. Stack the scraps on top of each other, fold them as you did for the original dough, and pat out and cut again.

Brush the tops of the biscuits with melted butter or milk for a more pronounced golden color, if desired. Bake until the tops are golden brown, 20 to 22 minutes. Remove from the oven and serve warm.

NUTRITION INFORMATION PER SERVING (1 BISCUIT, 65G): 31g whole grains, 182 cal, 9g fat, 6g protein, 33g complex carbohydrates, 1g sugar, 4g dietary fiber, 43mg cholesterol, 335mg sodium, 167mg potassium, 101RE vitamin A, 2mg iron, 119mg calcium, 261mg phosphorus.

Cornmeal-Maple Biscuits

YIELD: 1½ dozen (2-inch) biscuits
BAKING TEMPERATURE: 400°F
BAKING TIME: 15 minutes

Susan Miller, head of the King Arthur Flour Baking Education Center and author of several of the chapters in this book, recited this recipe to us from memory. We took that as a good sign, because it means it's something she bakes again and again, with consistently wonderful results. Sure enough, these biscuits came together in less than 10 minutes and were acclaimed by all who tasted them. They're a classic example of a food that is delicious, simply and absolutely, making the most of each whole grain's simple goodness.

> 1 cup (4⅞ ounces) whole yellow cornmeal
> 1 cup (4 ounces) white whole wheat flour
> 1 tablespoon baking powder
> ½ teaspoon salt
> 5 tablespoons (2½ ounces) unsalted butter
> ½ cup (4 ounces) milk
> ¼ cup (2¾ ounces) maple syrup

Preheat the oven to 400°F. Lightly grease a baking sheet or line it with parchment paper.

Whisk together the cornmeal, whole wheat flour, baking powder and salt in a large bowl. Cut the butter into the dry ingredients with a fork, your fingers, or a pastry cutter, until the mixture resembles coarse crumbs.

In a separate bowl, stir the milk and syrup together, and add to the dry ingredients, stirring just until the dough is evenly moistened. Scoop the dough by heaping tablespoons onto the prepared baking sheet. Press down lightly with your fingers if you like, to flatten the biscuits, or leave them just as they are. Bake the biscuits until the edges are light golden brown, 15 minutes. Remove from the oven and serve warm.

NUTRITION INFORMATION PER SERVING (1 BISCUIT, 25G): 14g whole grains, 64 cal, 2g protein, 11g complex carbohydrates, 3g sugar, 1g dietary fiber, 144mg sodium, 39mg potassium, 7RE vitamin A, 1mg iron, 56mg calcium, 35mg phosphorus.

Onion-Rye Biscuits

YIELD: 12 to 14 (2-inch) biscuits
BAKING TEMPERATURE: 400°F
BAKING TIME: 20 to 22 minutes

These biscuits are a wonderful vehicle for a bit of smoked salmon. Place them next to some corned beef, or a hearty stew, and you and yours will sigh with pleasure at the first bite. Rye bakes particularly well in the presence of acidic ingredients. These biscuits get their distinctly deli-style flavor from their "secret" ingredient: pickle juice.

2 cups (7½ ounces) whole rye (pumpernickel) flour
1 cup (4¼ ounces) unbleached bread flour
1 tablespoon dried onion flakes
2 teaspoons onion powder
2½ teaspoons baking powder
½ teaspoon baking soda
¾ teaspoon salt
½ cup (1 stick, 4 ounces) cold unsalted butter
1 large egg
¾ cup (6 ounces) buttermilk, plus more for brushing
2 tablespoons (1 ounce) dill pickle juice
1 tablespoon dried dill or chives (optional)

Preheat the oven to 400°F. Lightly grease a baking sheet, or line it with parchment paper.

Whisk together the flours, onion flakes, onion powder, baking powder, baking soda and salt in a large mixing bowl. With a fork, two knives, a pastry cutter or a food processor, cut in the butter until the mixture resembles coarse crumbs. Whisk together the egg, buttermilk and pickle juice in a small bowl or measuring cup. Add, all at once, to the flour mixture, and blend lightly and quickly with a fork until the mixture is evenly moistened. Add dill (or chives), if using.

Turn the dough out onto a floured work surface, and using a bench knife or dough scraper, fold the dough over on itself three or four times until it comes together (see illustration, p. 75).

Pat the dough out (or roll very lightly with a rolling pin) until it's ¾ inch thick. Cut the dough into squares or rounds with a 2-inch biscuit cutter, and transfer the biscuits to the prepared baking sheet. Stack the scraps on top of each other, fold them as you did for the original dough, and pat out and cut again.

Brush the tops of the biscuits with more buttermilk, if desired.

Bake until the tops are golden brown, 20 to 22 minutes. Remove from the oven and serve warm, or cool on a rack.

NUTRITION INFORMATION PER SERVING (1 BISCUIT, ¹/₁₄ RECIPE, 86G): **18g whole grains,** 202 cal, 12g fat, 5g protein, 22g complex carbohydrates, 5g dietary fiber, 44mg cholesterol, 284mg sodium, 186mg potassium, 105RE vitamin A, 1mg vitamin C, 2mg iron, 94mg calcium, 230mg phosphorus.

Dumplings

YIELD: 1 dozen (2-inch) dumplings

COOKING TIME: 20 minutes, depending on the size of the dumplings

Dumplings are a first cousin to biscuits, with similar ingredients and mixing methods. At their best, both are light and airy; they just have different ways of getting there. Dumplings are steamed on top of simmering liquid, which allows them to expand to almost double their size. While they're simmering, they give some of their starch to the liquid, thickening it in a most agreeable fashion.

Whole grains don't form gluten bonds that can stand up to steaming all by themselves, so we've given them an assist here with some unbleached bread flour. The method described below will make the most tender, lightest side dish you could ever imagine with a whole grain batter.

1 cup (4 ounces) white whole wheat flour

⅓ cup (1⅜ ounces) unbleached bread flour

1½ teaspoons baking powder

1 teaspoon salt

2 tablespoons (1 ounce) cold unsalted butter

1 large egg

¼ cup (2 ounces) milk

Bring your almost-ready soup or stew to a simmer. Whisk together the flours, baking powder and salt in a medium bowl. Cut in the cold butter until the mixture is the texture of coarse crumbs. Beat together the egg and milk in a small bowl or measuring cup and add to the dry mixture all at once, stirring quickly and as little as possible, just until everything is evenly moistened.

Drop the dough by rounded spoonfuls into the simmering soup or stew. Cook, uncovered, for 10 minutes, then cover and simmer until the dumplings are cooked through, 10 minutes more. Depending on how your soup or stew is seasoned, 1 tablespoon chopped parsley or chives, some black pepper or a pinch of thyme is a flavorful addition to your dumplings.

NUTRITION INFORMATION PER SERVING (1 DUMPLING, ¹/₁₂ RECIPE, 27G): 10g whole grains, 74 cal, 3g fat, 3g protein, 10g complex carbohydrates, 1g dietary fiber, 23mg cholesterol, 232mg sodium, 58mg potassium, 30RE vitamin A, 1mg iron, 55mg calcium, 108mg phosphorus.

Herbed Spelt Popovers

YIELD: 1 dozen popovers
BAKING TEMPERATURE: 450°F, then 350°F
BAKING TIME: 30 minutes

Given the characteristics of spelt's protein, it's a natural for this much-beloved side dish. Spelt made the highest-rising whole grain popover batter we tried, by far; whole wheat pastry flour was a close second. The more assertive flavor of either whole grain pairs well with herbs.

We like the following recipe because it's easily made, doesn't require a popover pan and makes an even dozen popovers. You can make up the batter the day before, if you like, since whole grains benefit greatly from an overnight soak. You can add cheese or spices to the batter to vary the flavor. Be aware, though, that anything heavier than herbs will weigh down the popovers, and they may not rise as high.

3 large eggs
1½ cups (12 ounces) milk
1 cup plus 2 tablespoons (4 ounces) whole spelt flour or 1¼ cups whole wheat
    pastry flour
½ cup (2⅛ ounces) unbleached all-purpose flour
¾ teaspoon salt
2 tablespoons (1 ounce) unsalted butter, melted
2 teaspoons fresh rosemary, finely chopped or 1 teaspoon dried
1 teaspoon dried parsley
½ teaspoon ground sage
½ teaspoon dried thyme

Preheat the oven to 450°F.

TO MAKE THE POPOVERS: Place all the ingredients in a blender in the order indicated. Blend for 30 seconds, stopping halfway through to scrape down the sides. Allow the batter to rest for 15 minutes, while you preheat your oven to 450°F.

If you don't have a blender, whisk together the eggs, milk, flours, salt and butter in a medium bowl. Pour the mixture through a strainer, and press out any lumps. Whisk in the herbs, and set the batter aside to rest.

Grease a muffin pan or popover pan thoroughly, greasing the area around the tops of the cups as well as the cups themselves. Use solid shortening or nonstick vegetable oil spray. Fill the cups about two-thirds full with the batter.

TO BAKE THE POPOVERS: Bake for 20 minutes. Reduce the oven temperature to 350°F and bake for 10 minutes more. Resist the urge to open the oven door at any time during this process.

Remove the baked popovers from the oven, allow them to cool in the pan for 5 minutes, then gently turn them out of the pan to cool on a rack. Serve warm.

NUTRITION INFORMATION PER SERVING (1 POPOVER, 51G): 13g whole grains, 85 cal, 2g fat, 3g protein, 14g complex carbohydrates, 2g dietary fiber, 6mg cholesterol, 149mg sodium, 113mg potassium, 37RE vitamin A, 1mg iron, 41mg calcium, 80mg phosphorus.

VARIATIONS: PLAIN POPOVERS: *Omit the herbs from the recipe; bake as directed. Serve with maple or honey butter.*

PARMESAN-HERB POPOVERS: *Omit the sage and thyme, and add 1 teaspoon each dried oregano and basil to the batter. Stir ½ cup freshly grated Parmesan cheese into the batter.*

ONION POPOVERS: *Omit the herbs, and add 1 tablespoon dried chives and 2 teaspoons onion powder to the batter.*

SCONES

They began as the quickest way to put whole grain nutrition on the table in the form of the Celtic bannock (the ancestor of our native hoecake or johnnycakes). From their beginnings as unsweetened oat or barley cakes, baked on a girdle (griddle), scones gradually evolved over time in Great Britain to include a bit of butter and sugar, eventually taking their place as a teatime staple. Now scones have come full circle, back to their whole grain past, only this time with a little more updating from the abundance of the modern American pantry. They now have more butter and sugar, and often some vanilla or other flavoring. We've also discovered that scones comfortably accommodate almost every kind of treat we can think of to add: where a sprinkling of currants was at one time the height of luxury, today we think nothing of reaching for the chocolate chips, apricots, citrus, or exotic tropical delights like coconut or macadamia nuts.

Oat and Currant Scones

YIELD: 1 dozen scones
BAKING TEMPERATURE: 375°F
BAKING TIME: 22 to 25 minutes

Our friends in Great Britain would find these tasty morsels a familiar sight at teatime, but on this side of the pond we like scones just as much for breakfast too. In this recipe, the scone returns to its heritage in some ways, with the use of oat flour, old-fashioned rolled oats and whole wheat. We've updated the traditional recipe a bit, by adding an egg and some vanilla, which make the scones a little more flavorful, tender and moist.

Feel free to experiment with this recipe, adding nuts, flavored chips or other flavors that you like. We've given you some ideas at the end of the recipe to get you started.

¾ cup (3 ounces) whole wheat flour, traditional or white whole wheat
¾ cup (3⅛ ounces) unbleached all-purpose flour
½ cup (1⅝ ounces) oat flour
¼ cup (1¾ ounces) sugar
½ teaspoon baking soda
¼ teaspoon baking powder
¼ teaspoon salt
½ cup (1 stick, 4 ounces) cold unsalted butter
⅓ cup (1¾ ounces) currants or raisins
⅓ cup (1⅛ ounces) old-fashioned rolled oats
1 large egg
½ cup (4 ounces) buttermilk
1 teaspoon vanilla extract
Milk or cream for brushing the tops
Coarse sugar for sprinkling

Preheat the oven to 375°F. Lightly grease a baking sheet or line it with parchment paper.

Whisk together the flours, sugar, baking soda, baking powder and salt in a large bowl. Using a fork or pastry blender, cut the butter into the dry ingredients until it resembles bread crumbs.

Add the currants (or raisins) and oats, and stir with a fork just to mix them in: you don't want to crush them more than necessary.

Whisk together the egg, buttermilk and vanilla in a separate bowl or large measuring cup. Add, all at once, to the dry ingredients, and stir lightly and quickly with a fork until the dough is evenly moistened.

Turn the dough out onto a floured work surface, and knead two or three times. Divide the dough in half, and pat each half into a circle about ½ inch thick and 6 inches in diameter. Use a baker's bench knife to divide each circle into 6 wedges.

Transfer the scones to a baking sheet, leaving an inch of space between them. Brush the tops with milk (or cream) and sprinkle the tops with coarse sugar. Bake until the scones are puffed and golden brown, 22 to 25 minutes. Serve warm.

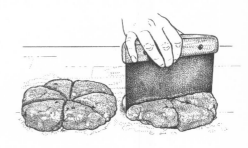

After shaping the dough into 2 disks, use a baker's bench knife to divide each circle into 6 wedges.

NUTRITION INFORMATION PER SERVING (1 SCONE, 55G): 15g whole grains, 187 cal, 9g fat, 4g protein, 19g complex carbohydrates, 4g sugar, 2g dietary fiber, 40mg cholesterol, 122mg sodium, 122mg potassium, 85RE vitamin A, 1mg iron, 33mg calcium, 99mg phosphorus.

VARIATIONS: MAPLE-WALNUT SCONES: *Substitute maple sugar for the granulated sugar in the recipe, and replace the currants with chopped walnuts. Add ¼ teaspoon maple flavoring with the vanilla, and sprinkle the tops with maple sugar.*

CINNAMON-PECAN SCONES: *Substitute chopped toasted pecans for the currants in the recipe, and add ⅓ cup cinnamon-flavored chips to the dry ingredients. Sprinkle the tops of the scones with cinnamon-sugar before baking.*

CHERRY-ALMOND SCONES: *Substitute ⅓ cup dried cherries for the currants in the recipe, and add ¼ teaspoon almond extract with the vanilla. Add ⅓ cup slivered almonds to the dough before cutting.*

PINEAPPLE-ORANGE SCONES: *Substitute ⅓ cup diced dried pineapple for the currants in the recipe. Replace ¼ cup of the buttermilk with ¼ cup orange juice; add 1 tablespoon grated orange zest with the vanilla.*

WARM SCONES, WHENEVER YOU LIKE

Scones are a sweetened, richer relative of the basic biscuit. In both cases, if you don't want to bake a whole batch at once, you can make up the recipe, cut the dough into the desired shape, and freeze what you don't want for your current meal. Place the scones or biscuits on a baking sheet that's lined with parchment or wax paper, and freeze them until they're firm. Once frozen, take the scones or biscuits off the baking sheet, and place them into a zip-top plastic bag. Press out any extra air, seal the bag, and return to the freezer for up to a month. When you want one or two (or three or four) scones or biscuits, take them out of the bag and place them on a baking sheet while the oven is preheating. Bake as directed in the recipe; it's OK if they go into the oven partially frozen. You may need to add 3 to 5 minutes more baking time, but in the end you'll be rewarded with fresh, warm treats with a minimum of fuss.

Cherry-Chocolate Scones

YIELD: 16 scones
BAKING TEMPERATURE: 375°F
BAKING TIME: 22 to 25 minutes

Cherries and chocolate are longtime friends, and they do their part to liven up this scone. Whole wheat pastry flour creates a tender, flavorful scone; the barley flour version is no less tender, but has an ever-so-slight malty taste that matches well with the chocolate. The dried cherries are chewy and tangy, and the chocolate creates wonderful pools of goodness, especially when these scones are enjoyed warm.

2½ cups (8⅜ ounces) whole wheat pastry or 2 cups whole barley flour
1 cup (4¼ ounces) unbleached all-purpose flour
¼ cup (1¾ ounces) granulated sugar
¼ cup (1⅞ ounces) packed light or dark brown sugar
1 teaspoon baking soda
1 teaspoon baking powder
½ teaspoon salt
½ cup (1 stick, 4 ounces) cold unsalted butter
¾ cup (3¾ ounces) dried cherries
¾ cup (4½ ounces) chocolate chunks or chips
1 large egg
1 cup (8 ounces) buttermilk
2 teaspoons vanilla extract
Milk, for brushing the tops
Coarse sugar for sprinkling

Preheat the oven to 375°F. Lightly grease a baking sheet, or line it with parchment paper.

Whisk together the flours, sugars, baking soda, baking powder and salt in a large bowl.

Using a fork or pastry blender, cut the butter into the dry ingredients until the mixture resembles bread crumbs. Add the cherries and chocolate, and stir with a fork just to mix them in.

Whisk together the egg, buttermilk and vanilla in a separate bowl or large measuring cup. Add, all at once, to the dry ingredients, and stir lightly and quickly with a fork until the dough is evenly moistened.

Turn the dough out onto a floured work surface, and knead two or three times.

From here, you can either divide the dough in half and make 2 circles, as described for Oat and Currant Scones, p. 86, dividing each circle into 8 wedges each, or pat the dough into a rectangle 8 inches wide by 10 inches long; it will be about ¾ inch thick. Cut the dough in half lengthwise and in quarters across its width with a lightly greased baker's bench knife, as shown. Cut each resulting rectangle in half diagonally, to make a wedge shape.

Transfer the scones to a baking sheet. Brush the tops with milk and sprinkle the tops with coarse sugar. Bake until the scones are puffed and golden brown, 22 to 25 minutes. Serve warm.

Lightly grease the bottom inch of the bench knife's blade. Cut the scone dough in half lengthwise, then in quarters across its width. Cut each small rectangle diagonally in half, to create 16 wedges.

NUTRITION INFORMATION PER SERVING (1 SCONE, 74G): 15g whole grains, 239 cal, 9g fat, 4g protein, 26g complex carbohydrates, 11g sugar, 3g dietary fiber, 30mg cholesterol, 159mg sodium, 214mg potassium, 64RE vitamin A, 1mg vitamin C, 2mg iron, 58mg calcium, 127mg phosphorus, 6mg caffeine.

Lemon-Barley Scones

YIELD: 16 scones
BAKING TEMPERATURE: 375°F
BAKING TIME: 22 to 25 minutes

Lemon lovers will be thrilled with the light, sunny flavor of these scones; all of our tasters loved them. Barley flour creates a tender scone with just a bit of crunch on top, and the lemon glaze adds its cheerful touch to the whole.

Scones
2 cups (8 ounces) whole barley flour
1 cup (4¼ ounces) unbleached all-purpose flour
¼ cup (1¾ ounces) granulated sugar
¼ cup (1⅞ ounces) packed light or dark brown sugar
1 teaspoon baking soda
1 teaspoon baking powder
½ teaspoon salt
½ cup (1 stick, 4 ounces) cold unsalted butter
1 large egg
¾ cup (6 ounces) buttermilk

¼ cup (2 ounces) fresh lemon juice
1 tablespoon grated lemon zest

Glaze
½ cup (2 ounces) confectioners' sugar
2 tablespoons (1 ounce) fresh lemon juice
1 teaspoon lemon zest

Preheat the oven to 375°F. Lightly grease a baking sheet, or line it with parchment paper.

TO MAKE THE SCONES: Whisk together the flours, sugars, baking soda, baking powder and salt in a large bowl.

Using a fork or pastry blender, cut the butter into the dry ingredients until the mixture resembles bread crumbs.

Whisk together the egg, buttermilk, lemon juice and lemon zest in a separate bowl or large measuring cup. Add, all at once, to the dry ingredients, and stir lightly and quickly with a fork until the dough is evenly moistened.

Turn the dough out onto a floured work surface, and knead two or three times.

From here, you can either divide the dough in half and make 2 circles, as described for Oat and Currant Scones, p. 86, dividing each circle into 8 wedges, or pat the dough into a rectangle 8 inches wide by 10 inches long; it will be about ¾ inch thick. Cut the dough as shown in the illustration on page 88.

Transfer the scones to a baking sheet. Bake until the scones are puffed and golden brown, 22 to 25 minutes. Remove from the oven, and place on a rack to cool for 15 minutes.

TO MAKE THE GLAZE: While the scones are cooling, whisk together the sugar, lemon juice and lemon zest until smooth. Brush the glaze over the tops of the warm scones.

Serve warm or cool completely to be served later.

NUTRITION INFORMATION PER SERVING (1 SCONE, WITH GLAZE, 55G): 14g whole grains, 171 cal, 7g fat, 3g protein, 16g complex carbohydrates, 10g sugar, 3g dietary fiber, 30mg cholesterol, 183mg sodium, 66mg potassium, 63RE vitamin A, 3mg vitamin C, 1mg iron, 40mg calcium, 61mg phosphorus.

Cinnamon-Filled Scones

YIELD: 1 dozen scones
BAKING TEMPERATURE: 375°F
BAKING TIME: 40 minutes

These filled scones feature an extra layer of moist, sumptuous flavor surrounded by tender whole grain dough; they need no further adornment than a hot beverage and the appreciative smiles they deserve. Since they're taller than a regular scone, we divide them into smaller slices.

Filling
²/₃ cup (4¾ ounces) granulated sugar
1 tablespoon ground cinnamon
1 tablespoon unbleached all-purpose flour
3 tablespoons (1½ ounces) soft unsalted butter

Dough
1 cup (3¼ ounces) oat flour
1 cup (4 ounces) whole wheat flour, traditional or white whole wheat
1 cup (4¼ ounces) unbleached all-purpose flour
⅓ cup (2⅜ ounces) granulated sugar
1 tablespoon baking powder
½ teaspoon salt
½ cup (1 stick, 4 ounces) cold unsalted butter
1 large egg
1 cup (8 ounces) half-and-half or evaporated milk
1 teaspoon vanilla extract
1 cup (6 ounces) cinnamon chips (optional)

Topping
Milk for brushing
Demerara sugar, sparkling sugar or cinnamon-sugar

Glaze (optional)
¾ cup (3 ounces) confectioners' sugar
3 to 4 tablespoons (1½ to 2 ounces) milk
1 teaspoon grated orange zest

Preheat the oven to 375°F. Lightly grease a 9-inch round baking pan or line it with parchment paper.

TO MAKE THE FILLING: Stir together the sugar, cinnamon and flour in a small bowl. Work in the butter until you have a spreadable paste; set aside.

TO MAKE THE DOUGH: Whisk together the flours, sugar, baking powder and salt. With a fork, two knives or a pastry cutter, cut the butter into this mixture, leaving some pea-size chunks. Whisk together the egg, half-and-half (or evaporated milk) and vanilla in a small bowl or cup. Add this mixture to the dry ingredients, along with the cinnamon chips (if using), and stir with a fork just until the dough comes together.

Turn the sticky mass out onto a floured work surface and divide it in half. Knead each half gently, then pat into two 9-inch circles. Place one of the circles into the prepared pan. Spread the reserved cinnamon filling over it, then place the second circle on top, pressing down lightly to take out any air gaps.

With a bench knife or a dough scraper, cut the scones straight down into 12 wedges. Brush the tops with milk and sprinkle with the sugar of your choice.

Bake until golden brown and firm to the touch in the center, 40 minutes. Remove the scones from the oven, and place on a rack to cool for 10 minutes. Run a dull knife around the outside edge of the pan, place a plate or rack on top, and flip the scones over. Remove the baking pan and put another plate in its place; flip the scones back so they're right side up.

TO MAKE THE GLAZE: Whisk all of the ingredients together until smooth, adding more milk if necessary. Drizzle the glaze over the scones. Serve warm, or at room temperature.

NUTRITION INFORMATION PER SERVING (1 SCONE, 88G): 18g whole grains, 278 cal, 12g fat, 5g protein, 21g complex carbohydrates, 18g sugar, 3g dietary fiber, 48mg cholesterol, 195mg sodium, 118mg potassium, 110RE vitamin A, 2mg iron, 125mg calcium, 225mg phosphorus.

Place a rack or plate on top of the baking pan and holding the pan and the plate, flip everything over to release the scones.

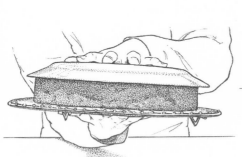

Remove the baking pan, and put a serving plate in its place.

Flip the scones back right side up; remove the top plate, and serve.

Apricot-Filled Cranberry Scones

YIELD: 1 dozen scones
BAKING TEMPERATURE: 375°F
BAKING TIME: 40 minutes

The rich flavor of apricots is a natural filling for scones; here we set them off with the jewel-like accent of dried cranberries. Spelt and its offspring, whole wheat flour, add flavor and an extra dose of nutrients and fiber to the mix.

Filling
1½ cups (6¾ ounces) dried apricots
½ cup (3½ ounces) sugar
½ cup (4 ounces) water
1 tablespoon fresh lemon juice

Dough
1¼ cups (5 ounces) whole wheat flour, traditional or white whole wheat
1 cup (3½ ounces) whole spelt flour
1 cup (4¼ ounces) unbleached all-purpose flour
⅓ cup (2⅜ ounces) granulated sugar
1 tablespoon baking powder
½ teaspoon salt
½ cup (1 stick, 4 ounces) unsalted butter
1 large egg
1 cup (8 ounces) half-and-half or evaporated milk
1 teaspoon vanilla extract
1 cup (4 ounces) dried cranberries
1 tablespoon grated orange zest

Glaze (optional)
1½ cups (6 ounces) confectioners' sugar
3 tablespoons (1½ ounces) milk
½ teaspoon vanilla extract

Preheat the oven to 375°F. Lightly grease a 9-inch round baking pan or line it with parchment paper.

TO MAKE THE FILLING: Place the apricots, sugar, water and lemon juice in a small saucepan. Bring to a simmer, stirring occasionally, and cook until the mixture thickens, 5 to 10 minutes. Remove from the heat and set aside to cool.

TO MAKE THE DOUGH: Whisk together the flours, sugar, baking powder and salt. With a fork, two knives or a pastry cutter, cut the butter into this mixture, leaving some pea-size chunks. Whisk together the egg, half-and-half (or evaporated milk) and vanilla in a small bowl or cup. Add this mixture to the dry ingredients, along with the cranberries and orange zest, and stir with a fork just until the dough comes together.

Turn the sticky mass out onto a floured work surface and divide it in half. Knead each half gently, then pat into two rough 9-inch circles. Place one of the circles into the prepared pan. Spread the apricot filling over it, then place the second circle on top, pressing down lightly to take out any air gaps.

With a baker's bench knife or a dough scraper, cut the scones straight down into 12 wedges.

Bake until golden brown and firm to the touch in the center, 40 minutes. Remove the scones from the oven, and place on a rack to cool for 15 minutes. After 15 minutes, run a dull knife around the outside edge of the pan, and flip the scones over onto a plate. Remove the baking pan and put another plate in its place; flip the scones back so they're right side up (see illustrations, page 91).

TO MAKE THE GLAZE: Whisk all the ingredients together until smooth, adding more milk if necessary. Drizzle the glaze over the scones, if desired. Serve warm or at room temperature.

NUTRITION INFORMATION PER SERVING (1 SCONE, 113G): 24g whole grains, 339 cal, 11g fat, 7g protein, 45g complex carbohydrates, 14g sugar, 6g dietary fiber, 46mg cholesterol, 198mg sodium, 462mg potassium, 217RE vitamin A, 2mg vitamin C, 3mg iron, 135mg calcium, 266mg phosphorus.

Eggnog-Oat Scones with a Whiskey Glaze

YIELD: **16 (2-inch) drop scones**

BAKING TEMPERATURE: **375°F**

BAKING TIME: **25 to 27 minutes**

This recipe received universally high marks from our tasters, many of whom claimed not to like eggnog. The scones are very moist and tender, even the day after baking, and don't need more than a bowl, a fork and a spoon to put together. Since they're a drop scone and don't need to be cut and transferred to a baking sheet, the whole wheat flour provides enough structure to hold them together.

Scones

1¼ cups (5 ounces) white whole wheat flour

1¼ cups (4 ounces) oat flour

½ cup (1¾ ounces) old-fashioned rolled oats

¼ cup (1⅞ ounces) packed light or dark brown sugar

2 tablespoons (⅞ ounce) granulated sugar

1 tablespoon baking powder

½ teaspoon salt

1 teaspoon ground nutmeg

½ cup (1 stick, 4 ounces) cold unsalted butter

1 large egg

¾ cup (6 ounces) eggnog

⅛ teaspoon eggnog flavor

Glaze

¾ cup (3 ounces) confectioners' sugar

1½ tablespoons bourbon or apple juice

1 tablespoon heavy cream or milk

TO MAKE THE SCONES: Preheat the oven to 375°F. Lightly grease a baking sheet, or line it with parchment paper.

Combine the flours, oats, sugars, baking powder, salt and nutmeg in a large bowl. With a pastry cutter, a fork or your fingers, cut the butter into the dry ingredients until the butter pieces are the size of a pea. Whisk together the egg, eggnog and flavoring in a large measuring cup. Make a well in the center of the dry ingredients and add the liquid to the bowl. Lightly mix with a fork until the dough is evenly moistened; it will come together but still be a little wet. Don't stir vigorously, or the scones will be tough. Let the dough sit for 5 minutes to allow the oats to absorb the liquid.

Scoop the dough by the generous tablespoon, placing the scones 2 inches apart on the prepared baking sheet. Wet your fingers and smooth out the tops a bit. Bake until the tops and edges are light golden brown, 25 to 27 minutes.

Remove the scones from the oven and cool on the pan on a rack for 15 minutes before transferring to a rack to cool completely.

TO MAKE THE GLAZE: Whisk together the sugar, bourbon (or apple juice), and cream (or milk) in a small, heatproof bowl until the glaze has no lumps. Heat the glaze for 30 seconds in the microwave, then whisk again. Brush the glaze over the tops of the scones while it's still lukewarm.

NUTRITION INFORMATION PER SERVING (1 SCONE, WITH GLAZE, 62G): 11g whole grains, 215 cal, 9g fat, 5g protein, 19g complex carbohydrates, 11g sugar, 3g dietary fiber, 37mg cholesterol, 172mg sodium, 133mg potassium, 76RE vitamin A, 1mg iron, 85mg calcium, 150mg phosphorus.

HANDLING YOUR LIQUOR WHEN IT COMES TO A FROSTING

The flavor of many liquors or liqueurs is distinctive and brings a lot to a grace note like a frosting; but most people understandably don't want the flavor of raw alcohol to be part of the equation.

When you want the flavor of whiskey or a liqueur in your glaze, but don't want the harsh alcohol taste, microwave the glaze for 30 seconds to heat it. Most of the alcohol will evaporate; briefly heating the frosting will get rid of the raw taste.

Coconut Scones

YIELD: **16 scones**

BAKING TEMPERATURE: **375°F**

BAKING TIME: **22 to 25 minutes**

This recipe is designed to be customized to your taste. You can make these scones a little sweeter and chewier, by using shredded, sweetened coconut in the dough. If you want a scone that's a little less sweet so the chocolate is more noticeable, use unsweetened coconut inside. The whole wheat flour and coconut milk make a dough that handles and cuts with ease. The curly coconut topping on these scones toasts up beautifully while they're baking.

2 cups (8 ounces) white whole wheat flour

1 cup (4¼ ounces) unbleached all-purpose flour

¼ cup (1¾ ounces) granulated sugar

¼ cup (1⅞ ounces) packed light or dark brown sugar

2 teaspoons baking powder

½ teaspoon salt

½ cup (1 stick, 4 ounces) cold unsalted butter

1 cup (4 ounces) unsweetened coconut or sweetened shredded coconut, depending on your taste

1 large egg

1¼ cups (10 ounces) unsweetened coconut milk, well stirred

1 teaspoon vanilla extract

½ teaspoon coconut extract or ⅛ to ¼ teaspoon strong coconut flavor

¾ cup (4½ ounces) chocolate chunks or chips (optional)

Milk, for brushing

¼ cup (¾ ounce) sweetened, shredded coconut for sprinkling

Preheat the oven to 375°F. Lightly grease a baking sheet, or line it with parchment paper.

Whisk together the flours, sugars, baking powder and salt in a large bowl. Using a fork or pastry blender, cut the butter into the dry ingredients until it resembles bread crumbs. Stir in the coconut.

In a separate bowl, whisk together the egg, coconut milk and extracts.

Add the wet ingredients to the dry ingredients and stir gently with a fork just until the dough is evenly moistened. Stir in the chocolate chunks (or chips), if using.

Turn the dough out onto a floured work surface, and knead two or three times. Divide the dough in half, and pat each half into a circle about ½ inch thick and 6 inches in diameter. Use a knife to divide each circle into 8 wedges, or pat the dough into an 8 x 10-inch rectangle, and cut into triangles as shown on page 88.

Transfer the scones to a baking sheet. Brush the tops with milk and sprinkle with the sweetened coconut, pressing it in gently. Bake until the scones are puffed and golden brown, 20 to 25 minutes. Serve warm. Drizzle with Chocolate Glaze (p. 413) if desired.

NUTRITION INFORMATION PER SERVING (1 SCONE, MADE WITH UNSWEETENED COCONUT IN THE DOUGH, 73G): **14g whole grains,** 288 cal, 20g fat, 4g protein, 19g complex carbohydrates, 7g sugar, 4g dietary fiber, 30mg cholesterol, 150mg sodium, 211mg potassium, 63RE vitamin A, 2mg iron, 36mg calcium, 140mg phosphorus.

BAKING WITH COCONUT MILK

Unsweetened coconut milk is wonderful to bake with. It usually settles during shipping, so one half of the can has a clump of dense coconut cream, and the other has a more watery liquid.

This can be a convenient thing for a baker, since the dense coconut cream is a terrific ingredient in coconut-flavored frostings (see Coconut Frosting, p. 374).

In our coconut scones, it's important to stir the solid and liquid parts of the coconut milk together well, to assure a consistency that's similar to buttermilk.

Macadamia-Oat Scones with Orange Glaze

YIELD: **16 (2-inch) drop scones.**

BAKING TEMPERATURE: **375°F**

BAKING TIME: **25 to 27 minutes**

Macadamia nuts have the amazing ability to be crunchy and buttery at the same time. Oats have a similar appealing chewiness, and when paired together with whole wheat, the trio make a toothsome combination. We've used a little vanilla butternut flavor (see Where to Buy, p. 588) to highlight the wonderful taste of the macadamia nuts and dressed up these tender scones with a simple orange glaze.

Scones

1¼ cups (5 ounces) white whole wheat flour

1¼ cups (4 ounces) oat flour

½ cup (1¾ ounces) old-fashioned rolled oats

¼ cup (1⅞ ounces) packed light or dark brown sugar

2 tablespoons (⅞ ounce) granulated sugar

1 tablespoon baking powder

½ teaspoon salt

½ cup (1 stick, 4 ounces) cold unsalted butter

1 cup (5¼ ounces) macadamia nuts, chopped

1 large egg

¾ cup (6 ounces) milk

⅛ teaspoon vanilla butternut flavor, or ½ teaspoon almond extract

Glaze

1 cup (4 ounces) confectioners' sugar

1 tablespoon grated orange zest

2 tablespoons (1 ounce) orange juice

Preheat the oven to 375°F. Lightly grease a baking sheet, or line it with parchment paper.

TO MAKE THE SCONES: Combine the flours, oats, sugars, baking powder and salt in a large mixing bowl. With a pastry cutter, a fork or your fingers, cut the butter into the dry ingredients until the butter pieces are the size of a pea. Stir in the macadamia nuts. Whisk together the egg, milk and flavoring in a large measuring cup. Make a well in the center of the dry ingredients, and add the liquid all at once to the bowl. Lightly mix with a fork until the dough is evenly moistened; it will come together but still be a little wet. Don't stir vigorously, or the scones will be tough. Let the dough sit for 5 minutes to allow the oats to absorb the liquid.

Scoop the dough by the generous tablespoon, placing the scones 2 inches apart on the prepared baking sheet. Wet your fingers and smooth out the tops a bit.

Bake until the tops and edges are light golden brown, 25 to 27 minutes.

Remove the scones from the oven and cool on the pan on a rack for 15 minutes before transferring to a rack to cool completely.

TO MAKE THE GLAZE: Whisk together the sugar, orange zest and orange juice in a small bowl until the glaze has no lumps. Brush over the tops of the cooled scones.

NUTRITION INFORMATION PER SERVING (1 SCONE, WITH GLAZE, 50G): 11g whole grains, 156 cal, 7g fat, 3g protein, 10g complex carbohydrates, 12g sugar, 2g dietary fiber, 30mg cholesterol, 147mg sodium, 89mg potassium, 70RE vitamin A, 2mg vitamin C, 1mg iron, 89mg calcium, 152mg phosphorus.

CRISPS, COBBLERS
& puddings

Warm, bubbling fruit with a crunchy cloak of baked grains, fragrant with spices, and topped with cream. Soft, creamy custards with a hint of whole grain and dried fruit for texture. This is true comfort food: desserts passed down from generation to generation—humble recipes made with whatever's on hand, baked at whatever temperature's available at the back of the oven.

You can hear these being named by modest housewives from the past, as they pulled the warm dishes from the oven. "This one kind of slumped." "I just cobbled this together." "It's supposed to be crumbly."

Apples and berries, when plentiful in backyards, make frequent appearances here, along with old-fashioned flavors like cinnamon, nutmeg, maple syrup and molasses. These simple combinations of fruit and whole grain flours, with a hint of spice or sugar to bring out the flavor, are immensely satisfying, perhaps because they take us back to a simpler time.

Since many of these desserts have roots in the days before white flour was commonly available, it seems natural to return to whole grains, especially corn, barley and whole wheat. We expected the nutty flavors of whole grains to complement the natural sweetness of fruits and nuts, but were surprised to encounter the hurdle of texture. The challenge here was making desserts that feel good to palates accustomed to white flour. Our modern tongues anticipate the smooth, melting texture of a light biscuit, not the grain and bran of whole grains. We found spelt was a ready substitute for many of the recipes where we wanted a light, buttery texture. The crispier textures were easier to come by with oats, corn and whole wheat ready to fill the bill. If you're a beginning baker, these simple recipes are a great place to launch your career; if you're more experienced, let them be the springboard for your creative spirit.

CRISPS AND CRUMBLES

These are among the most simple, most satisfying desserts to make. They go together quickly and fill the house with delectable aromas while they bake. We slide them in the oven as dinner is served, and they're ready to eat just in time for dessert. Every other time we make a crisp or crumble, we double the recipe for the topping and put half away in the refrigerator for next time; that makes it even easier to toss together dessert.

There's a fine line between a crisp and a crumble—each time we think we've got the definition down, we come across another recipe that breaks the mold. For simplicity's sake, if it has oats, we'll call it a crumble. If not, it's a crisp, but we've seen plenty of crisp recipes calling for oats. Whatever the nomenclature, be sure to add these to your baking repertoire—they're an easy way to make a meal heartwarming and are sure to appeal to every palate.

Apple-Raspberry Oat Crumble

YIELD: **16 servings**

BAKING TEMPERATURE: **350°F**

BAKING TIME: **35 to 40 minutes**

What could be cozier than warm apple crumble, with vanilla ice cream melting over the top? To us, this is the quintessential autumn dessert, similar to but not as fussy as a pie, and now that our local orchard grows both apples and fall-bearing raspberries, we can't wait for cool weather! Old-fashioned rolled oats are a traditional topping for these simple desserts; they help to thicken the filling at the same time they crisp the crumble.

Topping

1 cup (3¼ ounces) oat flour

1 cup (7½ ounces) packed light or dark brown sugar

½ cup (1 stick, 4 ounces) cold unsalted butter

1 cup (3½ ounces) old-fashioned rolled oats

½ cup (1½ to 2 ounces) sliced or slivered almonds

1 teaspoon ground cinnamon

¼ teaspoon salt

Filling

7 cups (1⅞ pounds) peeled, cored and sliced crisp, tart apples (7 to 8 medium apples before peeling, about 3 pounds)

1 cup (4¼ ounces) raspberries, fresh or frozen

½ cup (3¾ ounces) packed light or dark brown sugar

¼ cup (¾ ounce) oat flour

½ teaspoon ground cinnamon

Preheat the oven to 350°F and butter a 9 x 13-inch baking dish.

TO MAKE THE TOPPING: Combine the oat flour and brown sugar in a medium bowl. Cut the butter into cubes, and use your fingers, a pastry blender or fork, or a food processor to cut the butter into the flour and sugar. When the flour and sugar start to feel saturated, stop cutting before it becomes a paste. Some of the butter may remain in small chunks—that's OK. Add the oats, almonds, cinnamon and salt, and toss to combine. Set the topping aside while you make the filling.

TO MAKE THE FILLING: Put the apple slices and raspberries in a large bowl. Combine brown sugar, oat flour and cinnamon in a small bowl, then pour the mixture over the fruit and toss to coat. Turn the filling into the prepared pan, and cover it evenly with the topping.

Place the crumble in the oven and bake until the topping is crisp and brown and the filling is bubbling and thick, 35 to 40 minutes. Remove the crumble from the oven, and cool for at least 10 minutes before serving. Careful, the fruit filling is hot! Of course, ice cream helps hurry along the cooling process.

NUTRITION INFORMATION PER SERVING (1 SERVING, 122G): 13g whole grains, 238 cal, 8g fat, 3g protein, 21g complex carbohydrates, 20g sugar, 4g dietary fiber, 15mg cholesterol, 43mg sodium, 230mg potassium, 52RE vitamin A, 5mg vitamin C, 1mg iron, 40mg calcium, 90mg phosphorus.

WHAT APPLES ARE BEST FOR BAKING?

This is a question we hear over and over, and as soon as we think we have an answer in hand, it seems the variety we've selected has disappeared from the market. We're lucky to have a farmstand next door that carries a wide variety of apples most of the year, including some wonderful heirloom varieties, and over each apple bin there's a guide to how it tastes and how it bakes.

We've found that apples you enjoy eating also work well in baking. Be aware that the eating varieties we like for their crisp qualities often melt away in the oven. What we perceive as "crisp" often means a lot of moisture, which makes the apples more apt to turn mushy as they bake. We've had the best luck mixing different varieties in baking. We'll use a couple Macouns to add a tart flavor, or Golden Delicious for the sweet, mellow taste and firm texture. If you're not sure how a specific variety will work in the oven, try adding one or two of that variety to apples you're already sure will work. You'll be able to spot the newcomers and see how they survived the time in the oven and whether or not you like what they bring to the mix. Crisps and cobblers are a great place to experiment; they're a homey dessert with minimal time investment, and you can easily see what does and doesn't work.

Gingery Pear Crisp

YIELD: 8 to 10 servings
BAKING TEMPERATURE: 375°F
BAKING TIME: 35 to 40 minutes

The secret to the snap of this crisp is the fresh ginger in the topping. We combined spelt with whole wheat to keep the crisp from tasting too much of bran, but you can certainly make the topping all spelt or all whole wheat. If you don't have gingerbread on hand for the crumbs, crumbled gingersnaps will add the flavor and texture you need. Be sure to use pears that are ripe and flavorful.

Filling
6 to 7 cups (2 to 2½ pounds) peeled, cored and sliced pears, very ripe
    (about 6 large pears, 3 pounds, before peeling)
2 tablespoons (¾ ounce) crystallized ginger
2 tablespoons (½ ounce) cornstarch
2 tablespoons (⅞ ounce) sugar
2 tablespoons (1 ounce) lemon juice

Topping
⅓ cup (1⅛ ounces) spelt flour
¼ cup (1 ounce) white whole wheat flour
½ cup (3¾ ounces) packed light or dark brown sugar
1 teaspoon baking powder
¼ teaspoon salt
Pinch of ground cinnamon
½ cup (1 stick, 4 ounces) unsalted butter, chilled
¼ cup (¾ ounce) gingerbread crumbs (try the whole wheat Gingerbread on p. 425)
    or crumbled gingersnaps
2 tablespoons (1 ounce) grated fresh ginger

Preheat the oven to 375°F and butter an 8-inch-square baking dish.

TO MAKE THE FILLING: Put the pear slices and crystallized ginger in a large bowl. Combine the cornstarch and sugar in a small bowl, sprinkle over the pears and toss to coat. Turn the pears into the buttered dish and sprinkle with the lemon juice; set aside while you make the topping.

TO MAKE THE TOPPING: Combine the spelt and whole wheat flours with the brown sugar, baking powder, salt and cinnamon. Cut the butter into small pieces, and use a pastry blender, fork or your fingers to cut the butter into the flour mixture until it's crumbly. You want to stop before the mixture becomes a paste, so there may still be some pea-size pieces of butter left—that's OK. Add the gingerbread crumbs (or crumbled gingersnaps) and fresh ginger and stir lightly. Spoon the topping over the pears to cover the fruit completely.

Bake the crisp until the topping is brown and the pear filling is thickened and bubbly, 35 to 40 minutes. Remove from the oven and cool for 10 minutes before serving.

NUTRITION INFORMATION PER SERVING (⅛ CRISP, 173G): **9g whole grains,** 293 cal, 13g fat, 2g protein, 46g complex carbohydrates, 27g sugar, 4g dietary fiber, 33mg cholesterol, 128mg sodium, 260mg potassium, 106RE vitamin A, 7mg vitamin C, 1mg iron, 75mg calcium, 105mg phosphorus.

STAYING FRESH

Are you tired of buying a piece of fresh ginger for a recipe, using just a piece of it and then finding it shriveled and dry a week later? Whenever we buy ginger, we peel the whole piece. We use whatever amount we need, and the rest we break into manageable (2- to 3-inch) pieces. Submerge the pieces in a jar of sherry or sherry vinegar, and store in the refrigerator. The next time you need a piece of fresh ginger, fish one out, and you'll find it's as good as new. The bonus is the ginger-infused vinegar when the ginger is gone; it makes a great addition to all kinds of recipes, from salads to stir-fries.

Apple Brown Betty

YIELD: **10 servings**

BAKING TEMPERATURE: **350°F**

BAKING TIME: **50 minutes**

This simple dessert has been around since Colonial times. The crumbs sprinkled in with the apples thicken the juices and make a nice pudding texture as the betty bakes. You may use any sort of crumbs in the recipe—some of our favorites are cinnamon bread, gingerbread, doughnuts, graham crackers or spice cake. As long as you use whole grain crumbs, you're adding flavor and nutrition to the final dish. As with any apple dessert, this is great served warm with ice cream.

Filling
7 cups (1¾ pounds) peeled, cored and sliced crisp, tart apples
   (7 to 8 medium apples, about 3 pounds before peeling)
¼ cup (1⅞ ounces) packed light or dark brown sugar
2 teaspoons ground cinnamon
1 teaspoon ground nutmeg
⅓ cup (2⅝ ounces) apple cider
1 tablespoon lemon juice

Topping
1½ cups (4½ ounces) crumbs (moist whole grain bread, cake, doughnuts or crackers)
½ cup (1¾ ounces) old-fashioned rolled oats
½ cup (3¾ ounces) packed light or dark brown sugar
6 tablespoons (¾ stick, 3 ounces) unsalted butter, melted
2 tablespoons (½ ounce) walnuts, finely chopped

Preheat the oven to 350°F. Butter a 1½-quart baking dish.

TO MAKE THE FILLING: Combine the apple slices in a medium bowl with the rest of the filling ingredients.

TO MAKE THE TOPPING: Combine the crumbs, oats, brown sugar and melted butter in a small bowl. Sprinkle a thin layer of the crumb mixture over the bottom of the prepared baking dish. Spoon half the apple mixture over the crumbs and top with half the remaining crumb mixture. Add the chopped walnuts to the last of the crumbs. Spoon the last of the fruit into the dish, and sprinkle the last of the crumbs over the top.

Cover the betty with foil and place it in the oven. Bake for about 30 minutes, then remove the foil. Continue baking until the crumb topping is browned and the apples are soft and bubbly, 20 minutes more. Remove the pan from the oven and cool for a few minutes before serving warm.

NUTRITION INFORMATION PER SERVING (1 SERVING, 153G): 15g whole grains, 286 cal, 12g fat, 3g protein, 25g complex carbohydrates, 20g sugar, 4g dietary fiber, 26g cholesterol, 75mg sodium, 262mg potassium, 5mg vitamin C, 1mg iron, 47mg calcium, 84mg phosphorus.

COBBLERS, GRUNTS AND SLUMPS

Here's another dessert category that defies exact definition. It seems to be applied to any combination of fruit and dough. For the purposes of this section, we've chosen to define a cobbler as cooked fruit with biscuit dough on top of it. All the recipes here are baked, though the grunts and slumps could be made on top of the stove in a large, heavy pot, with steamed dough instead of baked—then you'd likely hear the grunts referred to in the recipe title. That method worked well when you had a wood-fired stove that was going all day, with cooler corners where fruit could stew slowly without needing a lot of attention. For most modern bakers, though, it's more practical to put the cobbler in the oven while you attend to other parts of the meal, and pull out a thick, bubbly fruit concoction, topped with golden-brown biscuits to dazzle your diners. Don't be afraid to substitute whole grains in your own recipes. You'll love the way the complex flavors and textures of whole grains work with the deeply flavorful fruits featured here.

Peach-Blueberry Cobbler

YIELD: 12 servings
BAKING TEMPERATURE: 350°F
BAKING TIME: 40 to 45 minutes

Peaches and blueberries are a natural combination, with overlapping seasons, so they've been paired together in every possible way. Here we put them with a light whole wheat biscuit topping, faintly seasoned with nutmeg. This dessert is great in the summer, when peaches and blueberries are in season, but you could easily make it with frozen fruit if you're craving the taste of summer in the middle of the winter.

Biscuit topping
2 cups (8 ounces) white whole wheat flour
2½ teaspoons baking powder
½ teaspoon salt
½ teaspoon ground nutmeg
½ cup (1 stick, 4 ounces) unsalted butter, chilled
2 tablespoons (⅞ ounce) packed light or dark brown sugar
1 large egg, lightly beaten
⅔ cup (5⅜ ounces) milk

Filling
3 cups (1¼ pounds) fresh or frozen sliced peaches
2 cups (10 ounces) fresh or frozen blueberries
½ cup (3¾ ounces) packed light or dark brown sugar
2 tablespoons (½ ounce) cornstarch
½ teaspoon ground nutmeg
Pinch of salt
1 tablespoon lemon juice
Sparkling sugar for top (optional)

Preheat the oven to 350°F. Lightly butter a 9-inch-square baking pan.

TO MAKE THE BISCUIT TOPPING: Combine the flour, baking powder, salt and nutmeg in a mixing bowl or your food processor.

Cut the cold butter into pats, and then cut them into the flour using your fingers, a pastry blender or the metal blade of your food processor, until the largest pieces of butter are the size of peas. Mix in the brown sugar quickly.

Beat the egg with the milk and add to the flour mixture all at once. Mix gently, just until combined; the dough will be a bit wet and sticky. Let it rest while you make the filling.

TO MAKE THE FRUIT FILLING: Combine the peaches and blueberries in a large bowl. In a small bowl, mix the brown sugar with the cornstarch, nutmeg and salt. Add the sugar mixture to the fruit and stir gently to combine. Turn the fruit into the buttered baking pan and sprinkle with the lemon juice. Set aside while you finish the biscuits.

Generously dust your work surface with flour and turn the dough out onto it. Flour your hands and pat the dough into a circle about ¾ to 1 inch thick. During this process, re-flour your hands liberally whenever the dough starts to stick to them.

It's not important that the surface be perfectly smooth for a cobbler—it's named for the process of patching the dough together.

Using a well-floured biscuit cutter, cut the biscuits and "cobble" them together over the peaches and blueberries.

Try to cover the entire surface of the fruit. Sprinkle the top with sparkling sugar, if you like.

Place the pan in the oven. Bake the cobbler until the topping is browned and the fruit is bubbling and thickened, 40 to 45 minutes. Remove from the oven and cool for 10 minutes before serving. Serve warm with whipped cream or ice cream.

NUTRITION INFORMATION PER SERVING (½ COBBLER, 110G): 19g whole grains, 222 cal, 9g fat, 4g protein, 24g complex carbohydrates, 11g sugar, 4g dietary fiber, 39mg cholesterol, 183mg sodium, 239mg potassium, 85RE vitamin A, 1mg iron, 111mg calcium, 197mg phosphorus.

FROM THE FREEZER TO THE OVEN

Freezers have to be one of the best culinary inventions of the last 100 years. It's now simple to store the summer's harvest without spending hours over a steamy stove. We love being able to pull berries from the freezer in the middle of January to brighten our winter tables. If you're freezing fruit from your own harvest, choose fully ripe but still firm fruit. Be sure the fruit is completely dry when you put it in the freezer. Place the fruit on a rimmed baking sheet and pop that whole thing in the freezer; freeze the fruit and then place it in a freezer bag. Even if you don't have the chance to freeze your own fruit, you can now purchase high-quality IQF (individually quick-frozen) fruit of almost every variety.

As you bake with frozen fruit, you'll notice it behaves a little differently than its fresh counterpart. The water in the fruit expands as it freezes and causes the cell walls to burst. As it thaws, that liquid is released and can make for a soupy mess. To compensate for this, be sure to use some sort of thickener in whatever you're making. Apple crisp from fresh apples needs no thickener at all, but if you're using frozen apples, you'll want to add cornstarch, tapioca or another thickener to absorb the extra liquid.

Pear-Hazelnut Cobbler

YIELD: 12 servings
BAKING TEMPERATURE: 400°F
BAKING TIME: 35 to 40 minutes

This is an elegant version of the humble cobbler, and it is imperative to use perfectly ripe pears, since there are no spices to supply the flavor in the filling. The bright flavor of Cointreau brightens the mellow pears, and the toasted nuts help to crisp the topping. Using spelt in the biscuit makes it sweet, light and tender. Add a bit more liquid than you think you'll need, and let the dough sit a few minutes before rolling it; spelt wants a little extra time to absorb moisture.

Biscuit topping
2 cups (7 ounces) spelt flour
2 teaspoons baking powder
$1/4$ teaspoon salt
6 tablespoons ($3/4$ stick, 3 ounces) unsalted butter, chilled
$3/4$ cup ($3^3/4$ ounces) hazelnuts, toasted (see p 598) and ground
$1/4$ cup ($1^7/8$ ounces) packed light or dark brown sugar
$1/2$ cup (4 ounces) milk

Filling
5 ripe pears (about $2^1/2$ pounds), peeled, cored and thickly sliced
2 tablespoons (1 ounce) Cointreau
3 tablespoons ($5/8$ ounce) old-fashioned rolled oats
$1/3$ cup ($2^1/2$ ounces) packed light or dark brown sugar
Pinch of salt
1 tablespoon butter

TO MAKE THE BISCUIT TOPPING: Combine the spelt flour, baking powder and salt in a bowl. Cut the butter into small cubes and work it into the flour mixture, using your fingers, a pastry blender, fork or the metal blade of a food processor. Stop when the largest pieces of butter are about the size of small peas. Stir in the ground hazelnuts and brown sugar and mix well. Make a small well in the center of the dry ingredients, pour the milk into it and quickly stir with a fork—it may look a little sloppy, but resist the temptation to keep mixing. Let the mixture rest for about 10 minutes, while you preheat the oven and prepare the filling.

Preheat the oven to 350°F. Butter a deep, ovenproof dish or a 9-inch-square baking dish.

TO MAKE THE FILLING: Toss the pear slices in a large bowl with the Cointreau. Pulse the oats in your food processor for 30 seconds to grind. Combine the ground oats in a small bowl with the brown sugar and salt. Sprinkle the sugar mixture over the pears, and toss to combine. Turn the pears into the prepared dish. Be sure the pears don't fill the dish; leave about ½ inch at the top for the biscuit topping.

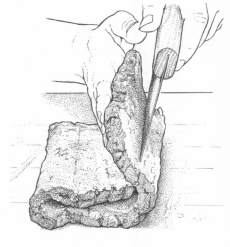

TO ASSEMBLE AND BAKE THE COBBLER: Make sure the biscuit dough has had its 10-minute nap so that the flour absorbs the milk. Flour a work surface, turn the biscuit dough out onto it and roll the dough with a rolling pin. It will be soft and sticky, but keep your pin and the surface well floured and you'll be fine. Use a baker's bench knife to give the dough a couple of folds, as illustrated at right.

Fold the dough into a rough letter shape, pat it and repeat.

Flour your hands generously and pat the dough until it's about ½ inch thick. Cut the biscuits with a sharp well-floured cookie or biscuit cutter and plop the cut pieces directly onto the fruit filling. Patch the pieces together ("cobbling" them) to cover the entire dish.

Place the cobbler into the oven and bake until the biscuits are browned, the pears are tender and the juice has thickened to a syrup consistency, 35 to 40 minutes. Remove the cobbler from the oven and let it cool for 10 minutes before serving. This is wonderful with vanilla ice cream.

NUTRITION INFORMATION PER SERVING (¹⁄₁₂ COBBLER, 126G): 17g whole grains, 229 cal, 12g fat, 4g protein, 25g complex carbohydrates, 4g sugar, 6g dietary fiber, 16mg cholesterol, 112mg sodium, 254mg potassium, 55RE vitamin A, 3mg vitamin C, 1mg iron, 94mg calcium, 185mg phosphorus.

DRESSING UP FOR DINNER

Cobblers, grunts and slumps are named for their humble nature, but there are times when you want to make a "pretty" presentation for your delectable dish. Any biscuit can be rolled and cut into shapes with a cookie cutter. If your recipe is for a drop biscuit, cut back on the liquid by a table-spoon or two to make the dough thick enough to roll. Roll the dough with a light hand, cut it into the desired shapes with a sharp cutter and place the shapes over the fruit in a pleasing pattern. Sprinkle the dough with sparkling sugar for even more pizzazz. Or for a very special presentation, bake the desserts in individual ramekins and top each one with its own individual biscuit or topping. These smaller desserts will bake more quickly, needing only about 25 to 30 minutes, which will still be time enough for the biscuits to rise and brown and for the fruit to soften and thicken.

Pear-Cherry Slump

YIELD: **12 servings**

BAKING TEMPERATURE: **350°F**

BAKING TIME: **40 to 45 minutes**

Slumps and grunts are a little like submerged cobblers. They can be made on the stovetop if you happen to have one of those big cast-iron pots. You'd bring the fruit to a simmer, then drop the dough into the hot fruit, cover the pot and steam until the dough is done. This version is baked, but has a syrup to pour over the dough to help create a steamed effect.

Dumplings

1 cup (4 ounces) whole barley flour

1/4 cup (1 ounce) unbleached all-purpose flour

1 teaspoon baking powder

1/2 teaspoon cinnamon

1/4 teaspoon salt

3 tablespoons (1 1/2 ounces) unsalted butter

2 tablespoons (7/8 ounce) packed light or dark brown sugar

Grated zest of 1 orange

1 large egg

1/2 cup (4 ounces) milk

Filling

4 to 5 cups (1 1/2 to 1 3/4 pounds) peeled, cored and sliced pears (about 4 large pears, 2 pounds before peeling)

1/2 cup (2 1/2 ounces) dried cherries

1/4 cup (1 3/4 ounces) sugar

1/4 cup (2 ounces) orange juice

Pinch of ground cloves

Syrup

1/2 cup (4 ounces) water

1/2 cup (3 3/4 ounces) packed light or dark brown sugar

2 tablespoons (1 ounce) unsalted butter

1/4 teaspoon ground nutmeg

TO MAKE THE DUMPLINGS: Combine the flours, baking powder, cinnamon and salt in a medium bowl or your food processor. Cut the butter into small cubes, and use your fingers, a pastry blender or the metal blade of the food processor to cut it into the flour, until the mixture is the texture of coarse meal. Stir in the brown sugar and orange zest. Beat the egg lightly with a fork in a small bowl and beat in the milk. Add the liquid ingredients all at once to the flour mixture, and mix quickly just until you have a wet, shaggy mass. Let the mixture rest while you prepare the fruit filling and the syrup.

Preheat the oven to 350°F. Butter a 9-inch-square pan.

TO MAKE THE FILLING: Combine the pear slices and dried cherries. Place the fruit in the prepared pan, and sprinkle with the sugar, orange juice and cloves.

TO MAKE THE SYRUP: Combine the water, brown sugar and butter in a small saucepan. Heat the mixture until the brown sugar is completely melted; stir in the nutmeg.

TO ASSEMBLE AND BAKE THE SLUMP: Plop spoonfuls of the dumpling dough over the fruit, leaving space between the dumplings. You don't want a complete cloak here; instead, you want to leave room for the fruit to bubble up around the dough. Pour the syrup over the whole thing to help moisten the dough.

Bake the slump in the oven until the dumplings are golden brown and the fruit is bubbly and starting to thicken, about 40 minutes. Remove the slump from the oven and cool for 10 minutes before serving.

NUTRITION INFORMATION PER SERVING (1 SERVING, 129G): 9g whole grains, 224 cal, 6g fat, 3g protein, 28g complex carbohydrates, 15g sugar, 3g dietary fiber, 31mg cholesterol, 92mg sodium, 240mg potassium, 53RE vitamin A, 5mg vitamin C, 1mg iron, 67mg calcium, 109mg phosphorus.

Blackberry Grunt

YIELD: 12 servings
BAKING TEMPERATURE: 350°F
BAKING TIME: 30 to 35 minutes

There's something so homey about blackberries—they grow wild on the roadside here in Vermont, and nearly everyone has access to a patch of blackberry bushes, if they're willing to risk the thorns. In season, we pick as many as we can and toss them in the freezer to pull out in the heart of winter for a bright, summery surprise under the crisp cloak of a dropped cornmeal biscuit. You may substitute blueberries if your blackberry patch is bare, or try combining berries—blackberries and raspberries, raspberries and blueberries. As long as you have a dark berry as part of the mix, the cornmeal topping is a nice contrast for color and taste. This is heavenly with vanilla ice cream.

Filling

6 cups (about 2 pounds) blackberries or combination of dark berries, fresh or frozen

³/₄ cup (5¹/₄ ounces) sugar

2 tablespoons (¹/₂ ounce) cornstarch

Topping

1¹/₂ cups (7¹/₄ ounces) whole cornmeal

¹/₂ cup (2¹/₈ ounces) unbleached all-purpose flour

1 tablespoon baking powder

¹/₂ teaspoon salt

6 tablespoons (³/₄ stick, 3 ounces) unsalted butter, chilled

¹/₂ cup (4 ounces) milk

¹/₄ cup (2³/₄ ounces) maple syrup

Preheat the oven to 350°F. Butter a 9-inch-square baking dish.

TO MAKE THE FILLING: Place the berries in the dish. Combine the sugar and cornstarch in a small bowl, mix well, and sprinkle over the fruit. Toss to combine thoroughly. Set aside.

TO MAKE THE TOPPING: Combine the cornmeal, flour, baking powder and salt in a medium bowl or your food processor. Cut the butter into small cubes. Using a pastry blender, your fingers or the metal blade of the food processor, cut the chilled butter into the flour until the pieces of butter are the size of small peas. Combine the milk and maple syrup and stir swiftly into the cornmeal mixture, mixing just until it is moistened.

Drop the topping by small spoonfuls onto the fruit, but be sure to leave spaces between the spoonfuls to let the fruit bubble up around the dough.

Place the pan in the oven and bake the grunt until the topping is lightly browned and the fruit is bubbling and thick, 30 to 35 minutes. Remove from the oven and let cool for 10 minutes before serving.

NUTRITION INFORMATION PER SERVING (1 SERVING, 148G): 17g whole grains, 247 cal, 7g fat, 4g protein, 29g complex carbohydrates, 22g sugar, 5g dietary fiber, 16mg cholesterol, 204mg sodium, 223mg potassium, 71RE vitamin A, 16mg vitamin C, 2mg iron, 139mg calcium, 199mg phosphorus.

Apple Crandowdy

YIELD: 10 servings
BAKING TEMPERATURE: 300°F
BAKING TIME: 50 to 55 minutes

This dessert won't win a prize for the most beautiful dish to grace a table, but its sweet/tart flavor and ease of preparation more than make up for its plain appearance. Pandowdies were traditionally made in a cast-iron pan, and one old recipe we found called for 3 hours of baking time. We've updated it here to be made in a baking dish as well as in a more manageable amount of time. The barley crust reflects the dowdy's humble origins; barley and rye were more common than white flour in the days when this dish was invented. We've paired the apples here with dried cranberries to help absorb some of the moisture—it's a very sloppy experience, but delicious, especially with cider and maple syrup as the liquid!

Crust
¾ cup (3 ounces) whole barley flour
¼ cup (1 ounce) unbleached all-purpose flour
1 teaspoon baking powder
¼ teaspoon salt
6 tablespoons (¾ stick, 3 ounces) unsalted butter, chilled
2 to 4 tablespoons (1 to 2 ounces) milk

Filling
7 cups (1¾ pounds) peeled, cored and chopped apples (7 to 8 medium apples, 3 pounds before peeling)
1 cup (4 ounces) dried cranberries
½ cup (3¾ ounces) packed light or dark brown sugar
¼ teaspoon ground nutmeg
¼ teaspoon ground cinnamon
Pinch of salt
¼ cup (2¾ ounces) maple syrup
¼ cup (2 ounces) apple cider or apple juice
2 tablespoons (1 ounce) unsalted butter, cut into small pieces

TO MAKE THE CRUST: Combine the flours, baking powder and salt in a small bowl or your food processor. Cut the butter into small cubes, and use a pastry blender or the metal blade of the food processor to cut the butter into the flour mixture until the largest pieces of butter are the size of small peas. You want to avoid making a paste here, so stop before the butter is fully incorporated into the flour, especially if you're doing this by hand. Add just enough milk to make the dough cohere when you pinch it. Bring the dough together, and use the heel of your hand to press it into a flat circle. Wrap the disk well with plastic wrap, and put it in the refrigerator to chill for 30 minutes while you prepare the filling.

Preheat the oven to 350°. Butter a 9-inch-square pan.

TO MAKE THE FILLING: Toss the apple slices with the cranberries in a large bowl. Combine the brown sugar, nutmeg, cinnamon and salt, and add to the fruit. Pour the maple syrup and cider (or juice) over the fruit and toss again. Turn the fruit into the prepared pan, and dot it all over with the butter.

TO ASSEMBLE AND BAKE THE PANDOWDY: Remove the crust from the refrigerator and, because it's made with all butter, let it rest for 5 minutes before you roll it out on a well-floured surface until it's approximately the size and shape of the pan. The dough may be a bit brittle, but you should be able to squeeze it back together easily—it's not important for the crust to look perfect in this dessert. Use a large spatula or small pizza peel to lift the crust from your work surface and lay it over the apples. Press the edges of the crust onto the edges of the pan, and slash the crust in a few spots.

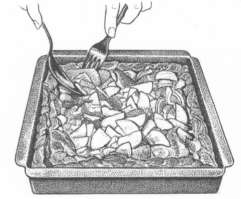

Place the pandowdy in the oven, and bake until the crust is browned and the fruit is bubbling and softened, 50 to 55 minutes: it will still be *very* wet—that's OK. Remove the pan from the oven and let it cool for 10 minutes before you "dowdy" it.

Take a fork and spoon and cut through the crust, lifting the apples and submerging the crust.

Try to leave some fairly large (2-inch-square) chunks of crust for texture. Let the dowdy cool a bit before serving; as it cools, the crust will absorb some of the liquid, and it will become puddinglike. Serve warm with vanilla ice cream.

Use a fork and spoon to "dowdy" the crust.

NUTRITION INFORMATION PER SERVING (1 SERVING, 124G): **9g whole grains,** 257 cal, 10g fat, 2g protein, 28g complex carbohydrates, 16g sugar, 3g dietary fiber, 25mg cholesterol, 100mg sodium, 240mg potassium, 82RE vitamin A, 3mg vitamin C, 1mg iron, 65mg calcium, 80mg phosphorus.

PUDDINGS

How can such simple desserts be so deeply appealing? For most of us, puddings translate directly to comfort, whether they're made from a box or from scratch—they somehow taste as though they *must* be good for you. Well, the surprise is that it's remarkably simple to make pudding that's bursting with the nutrition and flavor of whole grains. These recipes convert some of our traditional favorites into delicious recipes that bring you as much nutrition as they do comfort and pleasure. They range from simple grain puddings to bread puddings to steamed puddings that are more like cake than pudding, each one more compelling than the last, so get out your spoon and get ready to dive into the splendid textures and flavors that follow.

Brown Rice Pudding

YIELD: 8 servings
BAKING TEMPERATURE: 325°F
BAKING TIME: 30 to 35 minutes

Here's a whole grain version of the traditional favorite that's easy to make if you have leftover rice on hand. Brown rice has a bit more bite to it than its white counterpart, and our tasters liked the combination of creamy and chewy, pronouncing it "toothsome." The dried fruit can be varied according to what you have on hand. This makes a delectable dessert and is also great the next morning for breakfast.

> 2 cups (16 ounces) whole milk
> 1 tablespoon unsalted butter
> 2 large eggs
> ¼ cup (1¾ ounces) packed light or dark brown sugar
> 2 tablespoons (1⅜ ounces) maple syrup
> 1 teaspoon vanilla
> ¼ teaspoon salt
> ½ teaspoon cinnamon
> ¼ teaspoon ground nutmeg
> 1½ cups (9 ounces) cooked brown rice
> 1 cup (about 4 ounces) dried fruit (apricots and cherries are nice, or golden raisins and cranberries)

Preheat the oven to 325°F. Butter a 1½-quart baking dish.

Scald the milk (see sidebar, below) and stir in the butter, melting it. Whisk the eggs with the brown sugar, maple syrup, vanilla and salt in a medium bowl. Whisk the hot milk very slowly into the egg mixture, adding the milk just a little at a time and whisking well after each addition to keep the eggs from cooking. Whisk in the spices, then stir in the brown rice and dried fruit. Turn the custard into the prepared dish.

Bake until the pudding is set around the edges, 30 to 35 minutes. Remove the pudding from the oven and let cool for 20 minutes before serving. Serve warm or chilled.

NUTRITION INFORMATION PER SERVING (1 SERVING, 123G): 12g whole grains, 176 cal, 5g fat, 5g protein, 19g complex carbohydrates, 9g sugar, 2g dietary fiber, 63mg cholesterol, 113mg sodium, 352mg potassium, 272RE vitamin A, 1mg iron, 104mg calcium, 121mg phosphorus.

SCALDING MILK

One of our favorite stories is when a gentleman called our customer service phone line because he had been on a quest to make homemade bread as good as his late wife's loaves. We talked him through the entire process and all the ingredients he'd need and what they do in the recipe. At the end of the conversation, he said,

"I think I've got everything I need to do this now, but tell me, where in the grocery store can I find the scalded milk?" In fact, pasteurization takes care of some of the benefits of scalding milk, but it's still useful to scald milk for recipes where you'd like a head start on thickening, as in custards.

To scald milk, place it in a heavy saucepan and heat over medium heat just until you see tiny bubbles forming around the edges of the pan; don't let the milk come to a boil. To keep a skin from forming on the surface, stir the milk frequently as it heats.

Indian Pudding

YIELD: 8 servings
BAKING TEMPERATURE: 300°F
BAKING TIME: 1 hour

This New England tradition is wonderful with the added complexity of whole grain cornmeal, and sublime served warm with vanilla ice cream! When we began testing recipes, we found an enormous range of milk to cornmeal ratios—from 4:1 to 12:1. We like a fairly firm pudding, so we're using a ratio of 6:1, and this texture seems just right. It's soft when it's warm and gets quite firm as it cools. Using half maple syrup instead of all molasses makes for a milder flavor, and the combination of ginger and cinnamon is just spicy enough. Remember that whole grain cornmeal is very susceptible to rancidity, so be sure your supply is stored airtight in the freezer.

½ cup (2⅜ ounces) whole yellow cornmeal
3 cups (24 ounces) milk
¼ cup (2¾ ounces) maple syrup
¼ cup (3 ounces) molasses
¼ cup (1⅞ ounces) packed light or dark brown sugar
2 tablespoons (1 ounce) unsalted butter
1 teaspoon ground ginger
½ teaspoon ground cinnamon
¼ teaspoon salt

Preheat the oven to 300°F. Butter a 1½-quart ceramic baking dish.

Measure the cornmeal into a heavy saucepan and very gradually whisk in the milk, being careful to keep the mixture free of lumps. Place the pan over medium heat and cook the mixture, whisking frequently to keep lumps from forming at the bottom of the pan. As the liquid begins to heat up, whisk in the maple syrup, molasses, brown sugar, butter, spices and salt. Continue stirring the mixture until it thickens a bit, 12 to 15 minutes total cooking time. Pour the mixture into the prepared baking dish.

Bake the pudding for about 1 hour. The mixture will still look pretty jiggly, but take it out anyway. As it cools, it will thicken considerably. Let the pudding cool for 10 to 15 minutes before serving, but serve it warm—with vanilla ice cream, of course!

NUTRITION INFORMATION PER SERVING (1 SERVING, 131G): 8g whole grains, 181 cal, 4g fat, 4g protein, 11g complex carbohydrates, 22g sugar, 1g dietary fiber, 13mg cholesterol, 128mg sodium, 258mg potassium, 79RE vitamin A, 1mg iron, 136mg calcium, 114mg phosphorus.

Tropical Quinoa Custard

YIELD: 8 servings

BAKING TEMPERATURE: 300°F

BAKING TIME: 40 to 45 minutes

If you're a tapioca fan, this rich custard is for you. The lime, ginger and rum make for an exotic flavor, faintly reminiscent of Thai food. If you want something tamer, eliminate the ginger, or try lemon or orange zest instead. Be sure to rinse the quinoa well as stated in the instructions—otherwise it will taste soapy or musty.

½ cup (3⅛ ounces) quinoa

1 cup (8 ounces) boiling water

1 cup (8 ounces) milk

¾ cup (6 ounces) heavy cream

3 large eggs

¾ cup (5⅝ ounces) packed light or dark brown sugar

2 tablespoons (1 ounce) dark rum

¼ teaspoon salt

¼ teaspoon ground nutmeg

½ cup (2¼ ounces) dried mango, chopped

2 to 4 tablespoons (¾ to 1⅝ ounces) crystallized ginger, minced

Grated zest of 1 lime

Rinse the quinoa well (see sidebar, below). Place in a small bowl, pour the boiling water over it, and let the quinoa soak for 1 hour. Drain the quinoa and rinse it again with cold water.

RINSING QUINOA

We found a wide range of quality in the quinoa purchased on our shopping trips, and as a result we varied the way we handled it. Most packaged quinoa comes with instructions to rinse it well in cold water before cooking it. Quinoa grows with a resin on its surface called saponin that protects the plant but tastes awful—like soap. Quinoa is usually treated with an alkaline agent to remove the saponin as part of its processing, but it's such potent stuff that there's often a bit of residue left, and even that little bit can affect the flavor. Without rinsing, whatever you make with quinoa runs the risk of taking on that soapy flavor. We found that quinoa sold in bulk often seemed to need a little more rinsing, while prepackaged quinoa was more apt to need just a quick rinse. To rinse the quinoa, place it in a fine sieve and run cold water over it until the water runs clear out the bottom. Taste one of the grains to see if it still has a soapy flavor. If it does, rinse it a bit longer.

Preheat the oven to 300°F. Butter a 1½-quart baking dish.

Place the quinoa in a saucepan with the milk and cook over medium heat, stirring constantly, until it's thickened, about 15 minutes. Stir in the heavy cream and heat through.

Beat the eggs, brown sugar, rum, salt and nutmeg in a medium bowl with a wire whisk. Gradually whisk in the hot quinoa mixture. Stir in the dried mango, crystallized ginger to taste and lime zest. Turn the custard into the buttered dish.

Bake until the sides of the custard are set, about 40 minutes. The center will still be wobbly—that's OK. Remove the custard from the oven and let cool for 20 minutes before serving.

NUTRITION INFORMATION PER SERVING (1 SERVING, 135G): 11g whole grains, 287 cal, 12g fat, 6g protein, 15g complex carbohydrates, 24g sugar, 2g dietary fiber, 113mg cholesterol, 129mg sodium, 350mg potassium, 253RE vitamin A, 1mg vitamin C, 2mg iron, 95mg calcium, 137mg phosphorus.

BREAD PUDDINGS

When the winter wind is wild outside, it's wonderful to warm up the kitchen and infuse the house with the tempting scents of just-baked bread pudding. These hearty, homey desserts are so versatile—and a simple way to slip whole grains into your diet. They're a baker's best friend, using up bits of leftover bread, yet open to endless variation. Using whole grain bread in place of the traditional white was a bit of a challenge, but we overcame it by increasing the liquid and giving the bread a long period of time to absorb the custard. If you want to make it a speedier process, heat the liquid in the recipe, whisk it into the eggs, and pour the warm custard over the bread to soak while the oven preheats. Because there's a broad range of whole grain bread types, you may need to adjust the liquid in the recipes up or down; in general, you're better off using bread with a somewhat softer crumb, such as a squishy sandwich bread. You'll especially love the ease of these do-ahead dishes; it's gratifying to bake and serve a dish without any frantic, last-minute assembly.

Cranberry-Orange Bread Pudding

YIELD: **16 servings**

BAKING TEMPERATURE: **325°F**

BAKING TIME: **45 to 50 minutes**

One of our favorite flavor combinations, orange and cranberry brighten the flavor of this cozy comfort food. You may certainly vary the fruit and flavor to suit your taste; just remember the dried fruit absorbs some of the liquid, and fresh or frozen fruit is apt to release liquid instead. If you're lucky enough to have any leftover cinnamon raisin bread, it would be delicious in this dessert—you'd want to cut back on the cinnamon in the recipe and change the cranberries to raisins.

2 cups (16 ounces) milk

2 cups (16 ounces) half-and-half

4 tablespoons (½ stick, 2 ounces) unsalted butter

1 cup (7½ ounces) packed light or dark brown sugar

½ teaspoon salt

4 large eggs

¼ cup (2 ounces) orange juice

2 teaspoons ground cinnamon

½ teaspoon ground nutmeg

2 teaspoons vanilla extract

Grated zest of 1 orange

10 cups (about 1 pound) cubed, slightly stale whole wheat bread

1 cup (4 ounces) dried cranberries

In a 2-quart saucepan, heat the milk, half-and-half, butter, brown sugar and salt over medium heat until the milk is steaming hot and the butter is almost all melted. Whisk the eggs in a large bowl. Whisk the orange juice, cinnamon and nutmeg into the eggs; this will help keep the eggs from cooking when the hot milk is added. Whisk in the hot milk mixture, a little at a time, and then stir in the vanilla and orange zest. Add the bread cubes and cranberries; stir well to be sure all the bread is moistened. Let sit for 20 minutes, stirring occasionally.

While the pudding is resting, preheat the oven to 325°F. Butter a 9-inch-square pan. Turn the bread mixture into the buttered pan. Bake until the pudding is puffed up and set, and the edges are pulling away from the sides of the pan, 45

LEFTOVER BREAD

Whenever your bread is beginning to stale, cut it into cubes, pop the cubes in a plastic bag, and save it in the freezer. Each time you're nearing the end of a loaf, you can add to the bag. Store savory breads like rye and rosemary in one bag, and sweet or plain breads in another; that way you'll always have bread on hand for stratas, bread puddings or croutons, and nothing goes to waste.

to 50 minutes. A knife inserted in the center will come out mostly clean. Remove the pan from the oven and let the bread pudding cool for 15 minutes before cutting and serving. Serve warm with ice cream or whipped cream.

NUTRITION INFORMATION PER SERVING (1 SERVING, 131G): **14g whole grains,** 245 calories, 10g fat, 6g protein, 19g complex carbohydrates, 15g sugar, 2g dietary fiber, 78mg cholesterol, 229mg sodium, 293mg potassium, 104RE vitamin A, 3mg vitamin C, 1mg iron, 114mg calcium, 152mg phosphorus.

Pineapple Upside-Down Bread Pudding

YIELD: 16 servings
BAKING TEMPERATURE: 325°F
BAKING TIME: 40 to 45 minutes

Dreaming of Hawaii in the middle of January? Here is comfort food with a tropical twist, guaranteed to take the sting out of winter. In this version, the pineapple is both on the top and in the filling, and the shredded coconut extends the theme. If you want a piña colada bread pudding, add a little dark rum. Use a softer whole wheat bread with no flavorings or additions (such as our bread recipes on pages 180 and 182) to detract from the flavors.

Topping
4 tablespoons (½ stick, 2 ounces) unsalted butter
½ cup (3¾ ounces) packed light or dark brown sugar
2 tablespoons (½ ounce) toasted coconut (see sidebar, below)
1 can (20 ounces) pineapple slices or chunks, well drained

TOASTING COCONUT

Toasting coconut substantially enhances its flavor, but it's important to keep in mind that it can scorch easily at high temperatures. Or if you have too thick a layer on the pan as you're toasting, you can end up with a completely untoasted bottom layer and a top layer that's way too dark. To toast coconut evenly, preheat the oven to 300°F to 325°F. Spread the coconut very thinly across an ungreased baking sheet. Toast for 15 to 18 minutes, but give it a stir at least twice in that time to be sure it toasts evenly. And remember, sweetened coconut toasts more quickly than unsweetened.

WELCOME!

Pineapple came to be a symbol of hospitality in Colonial America, when food displays were a highlight of any social occasion. Hostesses would hide the food-laden table behind closed doors and open them at the height of the evening for added excitement. A fresh pineapple on a pedestal to top the arrangement was an indication of how far a hostess would go to delight her guests. From there, pineapples began to appear in carvings, stencils and statuary as an indication of the warm hospitality associated with them. Even today, the juicy, sweet, sunny fruit denotes warmth with a hint of extravagance, giving a generous touch to the most humble dishes.

Pudding

3 cups (24 ounces) whole milk

$1/2$ cup ($3^3/4$ ounces) packed light or dark brown sugar

2 tablespoons (1 ounce) unsalted butter

$1/2$ teaspoon salt

4 large eggs

2 tablespoons (1 ounce) dark rum (optional)

2 teaspoons vanilla extract

8 generous cups (about 12 ounces) cubed, slightly stale whole wheat bread

1 can (20 ounces) crushed pineapple, well drained

1 cup (3 ounces) sweetened shredded coconut

Preheat the oven to 325°F.

TO PREPARE THE TOPPING: Melt the butter and pour it into a 9-inch-square pan. Sprinkle the brown sugar evenly over the butter in the pan, and sprinkle with toasted coconut. If you're using rings of pineapple, arrange them across the bottom of the pan; if you're using chunks, spread them evenly across the pan. Set aside the pan while you make the pudding.

TO MAKE AND BAKE THE PUDDING: Heat the milk in a saucepan with the brown sugar, butter and salt until the milk is steaming hot, and the butter is mostly melted. Whisk the eggs in a large bowl with the rum, if using, and vanilla. Whisk in the milk mixture gradually, being careful not to cook the eggs by adding the hot liquid too quickly. Add the bread, drained crushed pineapple and shredded coconut to the warm eggs and milk and toss to coat the bread thoroughly. Let the mixture sit for at least 20 minutes, or until the bread has absorbed much of the liquid.

Turn the pudding mixture into the prepared pan, and gently spread it across the pineapple.

Place the pan in the oven and bake until the pudding is puffed up and pulling away from the edges of the pan, 40 to 45 minutes. It will appear set, and a sharp knife inserted in the center of the pudding will come out mostly clean. Remove the pan from the oven, and set it on the counter. Run a knife around the edges of the pan, and place a serving platter upside down over the pan. Using oven pads or mitts, carefully flip the plate and pan together, so now the pan is upside down on top of the plate. The pudding will drop from the pan onto the plate. Cut and serve immediately. Ice cream makes a perfect accompaniment.

NUTRITION INFORMATION PER SERVING (1 SERVING, 155G): 11g whole grains, 241 cal, 10g fat, 5g protein, 17g complex carbohydrates, 15g sugar, 3g dietary fiber, 69mg cholesterol, 224mg sodium, 260mg potassium, 67RE vitamin A, 6mg vitamin C, 1mg iron, 71mg calcium, 130mg phosphorus.

Cherry-Almond Bread Pudding

YIELD: 16 servings
BAKING TEMPERATURE: 325°F
BAKING TIME: 45 to 50 minutes

Sweet and tart and studded with cherries, this pudding is moist without being soggy. Cherry and almond are perfectly suited to each other—one of those flavor combinations that becomes its own unique flavor. If you can, use a slightly sweet, soft whole wheat bread (such as the ones on pages 180 and 182) unless you plan to let the bread soak overnight before baking.

Pudding
3 cups (12 ounces) frozen sour cherries or 2 (15-ounce cans), drained
1 cup (7 ounces) sugar
1 teaspoon ground cinnamon
6 cups (9 ounces) cubed, fresh whole wheat bread
3 large eggs
2 cups (16 ounces) milk
1 teaspoon vanilla extract
½ teaspoon almond extract
½ teaspoon salt

Topping
2 tablespoons (1 ounce) unsalted butter
¼ cup (1⅞ ounces) packed light or dark brown sugar
1 cup (3 ounces) sliced almonds

TO MAKE THE PUDDING: Place the cherries, sugar and cinnamon in a large mixing bowl. Stir to coat the cherries. Add the bread cubes. In a separate bowl, whisk together the eggs, milk, extracts and salt. Pour the egg mixture over the bread cubes in the bowl and stir to coat the bread thoroughly. Let the mixture sit for 30 minutes so the bread can soak up the egg mixture.

While the bread is soaking, preheat the oven to 325°F and butter a 9-inch-square pan.

TO MAKE THE TOPPING: Melt the butter in a medium saucepan. Stir in the brown sugar and cook until the sugar melts and the mixture is bubbly. Remove from the heat and stir in the almonds; set aside.

Pour the pudding mixture into the prepared pan. Bake for 20 minutes; remove from the oven and sprinkle the topping evenly over the pudding. Return to the oven and bake until the pudding is puffed and set, and the sides are pulling away from the edges of the pan, 25 to 30 minutes. A clean knife inserted in the center will come out almost clean. Remove the pudding from the oven and let cool for 10 minutes before serving. Serve warm with ice cream.

NUTRITION INFORMATION PER SERVING (1 SERVING, 101G): 7g whole grains, 189 cal, 5g fat, 7g protein, 11g complex carbohydrates, 17g sugar, 2g dietary fiber, 49mg cholesterol, 158mg sodium, 180mg potassium, 52RE vitamin A, 1mg vitamin C, 1mg iron, 72mg calcium, 111mg phosphorus.

IN A HURRY?

If you want to make a quick bread pudding, take the time to heat the milk separately before you mix it with the eggs. The hot milk mixture will absorb into the bread more quickly, and you can bake the pudding almost immediately. Be aware, though, that the lower the fat content of a milk product, the more prone it is to curdling when you heat it. If you're planning to make and bake a bread pudding on the same day, use whole milk in the recipe. If you're interested in a lower-fat version of bread pudding, plan ahead. You can use lowfat milk, but don't heat it; instead, whisk it with the eggs, and let the bread soak in the custard as long as possible—overnight if you can, but at least an hour or two.

Pumpkin Bread Pudding

YIELD: 16 servings
BAKING TEMPERATURE: 350°F
BAKING TIME: 40 to 45 minutes

The perfect cross between pumpkin pie and bread pudding, this dessert is easy to put together ahead of time and bake just before you need it. Most whole grain breads work well in this recipe, but it's worth trying with cinnamon raisin or pumpkin raisin bread for a truly extraordinary indulgence.

Pudding
6 cups (9 ounces) cubed, slightly stale whole wheat bread
1 cup (5¼ ounces) raisins
1 can (15 ounces) pumpkin purée
2 large eggs
½ cup (3¾ ounces) packed light or dark brown sugar
2 cups (16 ounces) half-and-half
2 tablespoons (1 ounce) dark rum
1 teaspoon ground cinnamon
½ teaspoon ground nutmeg
½ teaspoon ground ginger
¼ teaspoon ground cloves
2 tablespoons (¾ ounce) crystallized ginger (optional)

Topping
¼ cup (1 ounce) white whole wheat flour
¼ cup (1⅞ ounces) packed light or dark brown sugar
2 tablespoons (1 ounce) unsalted butter
¼ cup (⅞ ounce) diced pecans

Toss the bread cubes in a large bowl with the raisins. In a separate bowl, whisk the pumpkin with the eggs and brown sugar. Whisk in the half-and-half, rum and spices and pour the mixture over the bread. Stir the mixture to be sure everything is coated, cover the bowl and let the mixture sit overnight in the refrigerator.

When you are ready to bake the pudding, remove the custard from the refrigerator. To make the topping, combine the flour and sugar with the butter in a small bowl and press together with your fingers until you have a crumbly mixture. Stir in the pecans.

Preheat the oven to 350°F. Grease a 9-inch-square pan. Add the crystallized ginger, if using, to the bread mixture and give it a final stir, then turn it into the greased pan.

Sprinkle the pecan topping evenly over the top of the pudding.

Bake the pudding until it's set, 40 to 45 minutes. Remove the pudding from the oven and let it cool for 10 minutes before serving. Serve warm with whipped cream.

NUTRITION INFORMATION PER SERVING (1 SERVING, 106G): 8g whole grains, 186 cal, 8g fat, 4g protein, 15g complex carbohydrates, 10g sugar, 2g dietary fiber, 44mg cholesterol, 91mg sodium, 237mg potassium, 266RE vitamin A, 2mg vitamin C, 1mg iron, 67mg calcium, 101mg phosphorus.

Lemon-Raspberry Flummery

YIELD: 12 servings
REFRIGERATOR TIME: 6 hours

Imagine the hottest summer day—you're picking raspberries, and they're ripening faster than you can get them in the basket. It's tempting to eat them straight from the bush, but here's a recipe that retains the fresh quality of the fruit, and you don't even need to turn on the oven. This old fashioned dessert may be made with any combination of berries and is lovely with raspberries and peaches. Be sure to use a soft, slightly sweet whole wheat bread, such as the bread recipes on pages 180 and 182.

1¼ pounds (about 5 cups) fresh or frozen unsweetened raspberries
1¼ cups (8¾ ounces) sugar
2 tablespoons (1 ounce) water
1 tablespoon fresh lemon juice
1½ teaspoons grated lemon zest
1 loaf (1 to 1¼ pounds, 12 ounces trimmed) slightly stale whole wheat bread, in thin slices
½ cup (1 stick, 4 ounces) unsalted butter, melted

Lemon cream topping
1 cup (8 ounces) heavy cream
⅓ cup (1⅜ ounces) confectioners' sugar
2 tablespoons (1 ounce) lemon juice
1½ teaspoons lemon zest

TO MAKE THE BERRY MIXTURE: Place 1 cup of the raspberries in a saucepan with the sugar and the water, and stir over medium-high heat until the sugar has melted and the liquid is boiling. Reduce the heat to medium and simmer, stirring occasionally, until the mixture has thickened just a bit, 3 or 4 minutes. Remove from the heat and stir in the rest of the raspberries, lemon juice and lemon zest.

TO ASSEMBLE THE PUDDING: Line a 9-inch-square, nonreactive (glass or ceramic) baking pan with plastic wrap, or line the bottom only with parchment or wax paper. Cut the crusts off the bread slices. Arrange the bread slices across the bottom of the pan, cutting and piecing them together to cover the base completely. Brush the bread with one-third of the melted butter. Ladle about half the berry mixture evenly over the first layer of bread slices. Cover the fruit with another layer of thinly sliced bread and brush the bread with another third of the melted butter. Ladle the remaining fruit over the bread, and cover with one last layer of bread. Brush the top layer of bread with the last of the melted butter. Cover the pudding with plastic wrap, then place another pan of the same or slightly smaller size on top of the pudding. Place cans in the pan to weight the pudding—they should total at least 2 pounds. Put the whole thing in the refrigerator and chill for at least 6 hours—overnight is fine.

TO SERVE THE PUDDING: Make the topping by whipping the cream with the sugar until it is thick but not stiff. Sprinkle the lemon juice and zest over the cream and whip until it is stiff. Take the pudding from the refrigerator and remove the weights. Remove the plastic wrap from the top of the dessert and loosen the edges with a sharp knife. Invert a serving plate over the pudding, and flip the whole thing over to release the pudding. Spread the whipped cream over the top, and serve chilled.

NUTRITION INFORMATION PER SERVING (1 SERVING, 141G): 14g whole grains, 329 cal, 17g fat, 3g protein, 17g complex carbohydrates, 26g sugar, 5g dietary fiber, 51mg cholesterol, 121mg sodium, 179mg potassium, 159RE vitamin A, 16mg vitamin C, 1mg iron, 47mg calcium, 88mg phosphorus.

FLATBREADS
& crackers

Flatbreads and crackers are among the earliest breads known to civilization, with strong roots in peasant culture, so of course they're a natural for whole grains; they've been around a lot longer than white flour. For centuries before bakeries and commercial yeast, women knelt by the fire, patting dough made from indigenous grains and baking it quickly over intense heat, just as the meal was ready to serve. These breads, made from whole grains, truly were the staff of life; from pizza to pita, from crackers to tortillas, flatbreads are the ideal accompaniment to rustic meals, often serving as the plates and forks for hearty fare.

The surprise is how easy these breads are to work with—they roll out easily, without the resistance you find with white flour. And because there's no need for the lofty rise of most yeast breads, you can concentrate instead on flavor and nutrition, playing with new combinations of grains, to come up with the textures and tastes you love. The rich flavors and aromas of these grains take us back centuries to the time of the first bakers, who used the few ingredients available to them to create nourishing meals for themselves and their families.

PIZZA

Of all the flatbreads, pizza must be the most universally adored food—at least in this country, and most likely in Europe as well. A few years back, when our Baking Education Center was new, we even had a student make the trek from Beirut to learn how to make pizza; he was sure a chain of pizza parlors would be all the rage back home! No doubt you can now find pizza on every continent. And when pizza-lovers everywhere discuss pizza, what do they talk about? The sauce? No. The crust! Here's where whole grain crusts can be the stars—they are thinner than white-flour crusts, but the full flavor of the grains keeps the crust in a prominent role.

As you try these recipes, you'll encounter wetter dough than you may be accustomed to, and the challenge in rolling it out will be how to stretch without tearing, not the battle with tight gluten you find in a white-flour crust. Be patient, and remember parchment paper is a great tool for pizza success, both for getting the pie in and out of the oven and in shaping the crust. Above all, enjoy the fruits of your labor, freshly made pizza, topped with your favorite ingredients and filled with the added fiber and flavor of whole grains.

THE ART OF THE PIZZAIOLO

What's a pizzaiolo? Why, if you're running the oven and topping the pizzas, you are! There's a certain rhythm to making pizza for a crowd (even a crowd of two, if you have different tastes in toppings). The key is to assemble your ingredients and tools ahead of time. Be sure you have enough toppings prepared that you don't have to pause in the middle of topping to grate more cheese or roast more peppers. You can roast your vegetables up to a day ahead of time, or while the oven is heating up for the pizza, but once your oven and baking stone are hot and ready to go, you'll want to have everything laid out for quick work. Roll out and top your first pizza, and use your peel (parchment paper makes it even easier) to load it into the oven. Now, while that first pizza is baking, roll out and top the next pie. Be sure you've cleared some space on your counter for the just-baked pizza. Remove the baked pizza and load the next one. Call in help to cut and serve the baked pizza, while you begin to roll and top the third one. The rhythm is established, and before you know it, you're ready to open a pizzeria!

Pizza with Overnight Crust

YIELD: 2 thin-crust pizzas, 12-inch rounds or 10 x 12-inch rectangles, 8 servings
BAKING TEMPERATURE: 500°F
BAKING TIME: 9 to 11 minutes

Whole grains benefit from an overnight rest period, making them ideal for this do-ahead pizza crust, one of our favorites. Using bread flour instead of all-purpose flour helps hold this crust together. The crust is satisfyingly crisp, with a chewy interior. Smoked mozzarella makes for a wood-fired flavor that stands up to the hearty flavor of the crust and adds a terrific nuance to the pizza.

Crust
1 cup (4 ounces) traditional whole wheat flour
1 cup (4$\frac{1}{4}$ ounces) unbleached bread flour
1 cup (5$\frac{3}{4}$ ounces) semolina flour
1$\frac{1}{2}$ teaspoons salt
$\frac{3}{4}$ teaspoon instant yeast
2 tablespoons ($\frac{7}{8}$ ounce) olive oil
1$\frac{1}{4}$ cups (10 ounces) cool water

Topping
$\frac{1}{2}$ cup (4 ounces) tomato sauce
$\frac{1}{2}$ cup (2$\frac{1}{2}$ ounces) kalamata olives, pitted and halved
2 tablespoons ($\frac{3}{4}$ ounce) sun-dried tomatoes
1 cup (4 ounces) shredded smoked mozzarella
$\frac{1}{2}$ cup (2 ounces) shredded mozzarella

TO MAKE THE CRUST: This dough is much slacker than most; it's so wet, you can't really knead it by hand, and you'll be tempted to add way too much flour. We suggest using an electric mixer, fitted with a dough hook. Combine the flours, salt and yeast in your mixer bowl. With the mixer running on its lowest speed, add the olive oil, then pour in the water. After you've added all the water, increase the speed to medium and knead the dough for 2 minutes. Cover the dough and let it rise for 45 minutes.

Turn the dough out onto a heavily floured surface and give it a fold. This will be a very messy process, so be sure your hands and work surface are well-floured; you will find it helpful to use a baker's bench knife. Use the scraper to gently fold the dough over itself, as you would a business letter, brushing away any excess flour as you fold to keep from incorporating raw flour into the middle of the dough. Next, fold the dough in a similar fashion, this time from the long ends, to make a packet.

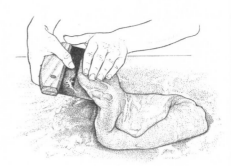

Use a baker's bench knife to fold the dough like a business letter.

Then fold the edges in to make a packet.

Return the dough to the bowl, cover it tightly, and place it in the refrigerator overnight. The dough will be too loose to use until it's had an overnight rest.

TO SHAPE AND TOP THE PIZZA: About 30 minutes before you're ready to make the pizza, put your baking stone on the bottom rack of the oven, and heat the oven (and stone) to 500°F.

Remove the dough from the refrigerator, and divide it in half. It will still be very wet; work with one half at a time on a generously floured surface, and try to keep from poking the surface of the dough as you work. With floured hands, flip the dough a couple of times to be sure it's floured on both sides, and then roll or stretch it to a large round or rectangular shape. A 13 x 18-inch half-sheet pan works well if you're making a rectangular pizza. You'll want to finish the stretching on a piece of parchment paper. Keep flouring your hands and gently press the dough out to the edges of the parchment; the dough will be quite thin.

Flour your fingers and gently stretch the dough directly on a piece of parchment paper.

If you wind up with holes, don't worry; just pinch the edges of the hole together and keep going.

For the first pizza, spread half of the tomato sauce in a thin layer over the dough, top with half the olives and sun-dried tomatoes. Reserve the cheese.

TO BAKE THE PIZZA: When your pizza is topped, and your stone and oven are piping hot, use a pizza peel to deposit the pizza, parchment paper and all, onto the hot baking stone. If you don't have a peel, put the parchment on your thinnest baking sheet, and place the sheet directly on the stone. Bake the pizza until the crust is set and starting to color around the edges, 4 to 5 minutes. Use the peel to remove the pizza, still on the parchment, from the oven. Put the pizza on the counter and top it with half the mozzarella cheeses.

Use the peel to return the pizza to the oven, this time without the parchment, and bake until the crust is crisp and browned, and the cheese is melted and bubbly, 5 to 6 minutes more. Using your peel, remove the pizza from the oven. Cut and serve immediately.

While the first pizza is baking, stretch and top the second pizza according to the above instructions. When you remove the first pizza from the oven, repeat the baking process for the second pizza.

Use a large peel to place pizza on the stone and to remove it from the oven.

NUTRITION INFORMATION PER SERVING (¹/₄ PIZZA, 143G): 14g whole grains, 315 cal, 11g fat, 12g protein, 41g complex carbohydrates, 1g sugar, 4g dietary fiber, 17mg cholesterol, 687mg sodium, 238mg potassium, 66RE vitamin A, 5mg vitamin C, 3mg iron, 131mg calcium, 188mg phosphorus.

Two-Corn Pizza

YIELD: 2 large pizzas, 12-inch rounds or 10 x 12-inch rectangles, 8 servings
BAKING TEMPERATURE: 500°F
BAKING TIME: 8 to 10 minutes

This pizza features corn in two forms: cornmeal in the crust and fresh corn off the cob in the topping. The bread flour holds together the crunchy cornmeal and the tender barley flour and lets you roll the crust quite thin for a crisp, light crust that makes a lovely foil for the fresh flavors of the topping. This pizza uses a pre-ferment, a mixture of flour, water and yeast you make the night before to add extra flavor and extensibility, or stretchiness, to your dough.

Pre-ferment
1 cup (4 ounces) traditional whole wheat flour
Scant pinch of instant yeast
¹/₂ cup (4 ounces) cold water

Crust
All of the pre-ferment
1¹/₄ cups (10 ounces) cool water
1 cup (4¹/₂ ounces) whole cornmeal
1 cup (4 ounces) whole barley flour
1 cup (4¹/₄ ounces) unbleached bread flour
2 teaspoons salt
³/₄ teaspoon instant yeast

WHY WE PREFER PRE-FERMENTS

In many of our recipes for breads we suggest getting your dough started with a pre-ferment or starter. Experienced bakers sometimes use a mixture of flour, water and yeast to jump-start the flavor and the rising power of bread. You'll hear the terms biga, chef, levain, mere, mother, pâte fermentée, poolish, pre-ferment, sour, sponge and starter to describe different methods for fermenting part of the flour in a recipe before you make the final dough, and many of the terms are used interchangeably. Each term represents a technique from a different country or culture, and when the terminology came to America, we put them in our famous melting pot and created lots of confusion. There have been some recent attempts to clarify and codify the different terms according to their origins as well as their baking applications. In this book, we're using "pre-ferment" to describe a starter made with the type of yeast you purchase and the term "levain" to refer to a starter that makes use of wild yeast, as in many sourdough recipes.

Within the classification of pre-ferment you could have a poolish, which is commonly accepted to indicate a combination of equal weights of flour and water with a very small amount of added yeast. Poolish is believed to have come from Poland to France and appears frequently in recipes from that heritage.

The term biga is of Italian origin and is also a combination of flour and water with a bit of yeast added, but it usually refers to a starter that is stiffer (dryer) than a poolish.

A sponge is when some of the flour from the recipe is mixed with some of the liquid and at least half the yeast. Because sponges have so much more yeast, they usually work for a shorter time than either a biga or a poolish, and can be used in the recipe from a few minutes to a few hours after preparing them. Pâte fermentée is a small piece of dough you save from the bread you are making to mix into the next batch of bread you bake. It contains all the ingredients of the bread instead of just flour, water and yeast.

Chef, levain, *mère*, mother and sour all refer to the starter used in sourdough baking, which makes use of wild yeast, or yeast that exists in your kitchen and in flour.

We hope you'll make use of the pre-ferments in our recipes because they improve the flavor, texture and longevity of baked bread. The long fermentation time gives the loaf a fuller, more complex flavor. It also develops acids that help strengthen the gluten in bread dough and enhance both rise and internal structure. And last, but not least, the increased acidity of a pre-ferment slows the staling process, so your delicious loaf will last longer.

IT'S COOL, MAN.

You may notice that many of our bread recipes call for cool water, not the warm 100°F–110°F water called for in most traditional bread recipes. Why cool? Well, warm water does speed the fermentation process of the bread dough, but in doing so, there's a sacrifice in both flavor and structure. Professional bakers take the temperatures of all their ingredients and adjust the water temperature to control the temperature of the dough. Unless it's the dead of winter and you're baking in a cold kitchen, chances are a cool water temperature and a long, cool rise will enhance the flavor of the finished bread, so for the best results, try to stay cool.

Topping

2 ears fresh corn, husked

1 tablespoon olive oil

½ cup (2½ ounces) chopped onion

1 clove garlic, minced

3 (about 10 ounces) ripe plum tomatoes, chopped

2 tablespoons chopped fresh basil

2 tablespoons chopped fresh oregano

¼ cup (2⅛ ounces) pesto (homemade is great, but use store-bought in a pinch)

1 cup (4 ounces) Monterey Jack cheese, grated

TO MAKE THE PRE-FERMENT: The night before you want to serve the pizza, measure the flour into a medium mixing bowl, and toss it with a scant pinch of yeast. Stir in the cold water to thoroughly moisten the flour. Cover the bowl with plastic wrap and set aside at room temperature for 12 to 15 hours. This pre-ferment won't have the same bubbly appearance as one made with white flour, but it will have puffed up a bit and changed its appearance. We consider it "ripe" at this point and ready to use.

TO MAKE THE DOUGH: The next morning, loosen the ripe pre-ferment by adding the cool water, then add the cornmeal, flours, salt and yeast. This will be a wet dough; it's best to mix it in a mixer, so you won't be tempted to knead in too much flour. Mix the dough at medium speed for about 5 minutes, cover the bowl with plastic wrap, and set aside the dough to rise for 30 minutes.

When the dough starts to look noticeably puffy, it's time to fold it to build its strength. Turn the dough out onto a heavily floured surface and give it a fold. This will be a very messy process, so be sure your hands and work surface are well-floured; you will find it helpful to use a bench knife. Use the scraper to gently fold the dough over itself, as you would a business letter, brushing any excess flour away as you fold, to keep from incorporating raw flour into the middle of the dough. Next, fold the dough in a similar fashion, this time from the long ends, to make a packet. (See illustration, p. 130.) Return the dough to the bowl, cover, and let it rest for another 30 minutes. Repeat this fold every 30 minutes for 2 hours, for a total of 4 folds.

Divide the dough in half and form each piece into a round. Cover the pieces well with plastic wrap, and let them rest for 30 minutes to 1 hour.

TO MAKE THE CORN TOPPING: Cook the corn on the cob in boiling water just until it's tender, 3 to 5 minutes. After it cools, use a sharp knife to cut the kernels from the cob. Heat the olive oil in a medium skillet and sauté the onion and garlic briefly, until the onion is translucent. Remove the pan from the heat, and add the corn kernels, tomatoes, basil and oregano.

TO MAKE THE PIZZA: About 30 minutes before you bake the pizza, preheat your oven and a baking stone, if you have one, to 500°F.

Sprinkle your work surface lightly with flour, and pat a piece of dough flat on the flour, being careful not to poke through the surface of the dough. Using well-floured hands or a well-floured rolling pin, stretch or roll the pizza into a 12-inch round or 10 x 18-inch rectangular shape. You may want to finish the shaping on a piece of parchment paper. Keep flouring your hands and gently press the dough out to the edges of the parchment; the dough will be quite thin. If you wind up with holes, don't worry; just pinch the edges of the hole together and keep going.

For the first pizza, spread 2 tablespoons of the pesto over the surface of the stretched dough. Sprinkle half of the corn mixture over the pesto and top with half of the grated Monterey Jack. Use your peel to deposit the pizza, parchment paper and all, on the hot baking stone. The parchment can stay in the oven for the entire baking time, or you may reach in and slide it out after the crust has started to set, about 3 minutes. Bake the pizza until the cheese is bubbly and beginning to brown, 8 to 10 minutes. Use your peel to remove the baked pizza from the oven. Place it on a flat cutting surface, cut into 8 to 10 slices, and serve immediately.

While the pizza bakes, shape and top the remaining piece of dough. When the first pizza comes out of the oven, the second one will be ready to bake.

NUTRITION INFORMATION PER SERVING (¼ PIZZA, 213G): 43g whole grains, 349 cal, 12g fat, 12g protein, 52g complex carbohydrates, 7g dietary fiber, 14mg cholesterol, 678mg sodium, 318mg potassium, 83RE vitamin A, 8mg vitamin C, 3mg iron, 148mg calcium, 225mg phosphorus.

Herbed Whole Wheat Pizza with Mushrooms and Spinach

YIELD: 2 pizzas, 12-inch rounds or 10 x 12-inch rectangles, 8 servings
BAKING TEMPERATURE: 425°F
BAKING TIME: 20 to 22 minutes

This pizza crust is 100 percent whole wheat, but you'd never guess it from the flavor and texture; it manages to be both light and crunchy. The lower baking temperature makes for a somewhat breadlike effect, different from thin-crust versions. We recommend mild toppings for this one, so the herbs in the crust really shine through.

Crust
3¾ cups (15 ounces) white whole wheat flour
1 tablespoon plus 1½ teaspoons instant yeast

1½ cups (12 ounces) cool water

1 tablespoon honey

1 tablespoon olive oil

2 teaspoons salt

1 tablespoon dried oregano

1 tablespoon dried basil

½ teaspoon cayenne pepper

Topping

4 to 5 tablespoons (1¾ to 2⅛ ounces) olive oil

1 pound mushrooms, sliced

8 ounces (about 6½ cups) fresh spinach leaves, washed and dried

5 ounces (about 1¼ cups) fontina cheese, grated

TO MAKE THE CRUST: Measure 2 cups of the flour into a medium mixing bowl, and stir in the yeast. Combine the water and honey, add to the flour mixture and stir to mix well. Cover with plastic and let rest for 1 hour.

Stir in the olive oil, salt, herbs and cayenne, and then add the remaining 1¾ cups flour. Turn the dough out onto a very lightly floured surface and knead for about 5 minutes, until it is shiny and elastic, but still quite soft. Resist the temptation to keep adding flour—this should be softer than a bread dough. Return the dough to the bowl, cover, and let it rise until doubled in bulk, about 1½ hours.

Turn the dough out onto a lightly floured surface and divide it in half. Lightly form each half into a loose round, cover and let the halves rest for about 20 minutes.

TO MAKE THE TOPPING: Heat the olive oil in a large sauté pan over medium-high heat. Add the mushrooms and sauté until they are just lightly browned. Add the spinach, stir just to wilt, and remove from the heat. Set aside.

TO SHAPE AND BAKE THE CRUST: Place your baking stone on the bottom rack of your oven and preheat the oven and stone to 375°F. Use a well-floured rolling pin to roll out half the dough on a lightly floured surface into a 12-inch round or 10 x 12-inch rectangular shape. Place the dough on a pizza pan, a baking sheet or a piece of parchment paper. Repeat with the second piece of dough. Roll the edges of the dough up to make a small rim around each piece. Prick each piece all over with a fork. Bake the crusts on the stone, one at a time, for 10 minutes each. After the second piece comes out of the oven, increase the oven temperature to 425°F.

TO TOP AND BAKE THE PIZZA: Divide the mushroom-spinach mixture between the two crusts, and sprinkle each with half the fontina. Use a peel to deposit the pizza on the baking stone. Bake the pizza until the cheese is melted and bubbly, 10 to 12 minutes. Remove the pizza from the oven, cut into 8 wedges, and serve immediately. While the first pizza is baking, top the second pizza, and when you remove the first pizza from the oven, the second one will be ready to load.

NUTRITION INFORMATION PER SERVING (¼ PIZZA, 218G): 53g whole grains, 368 cal, 15g fat, 15g protein, 46g complex carbohydrates, 2g sugar, 9g dietary fiber, 20mg cholesterol, 703mg sodium, 653mg potassium, 241RE vitamin A, 10mg vitamin C, 4mg iron, 149mg calcium, 357mg phosphorus.

LESS IS MORE

It's long been the American way to pack your pizza with as much sauce and as many toppings as you possibly can. Extra cheese, three kinds of meat, slather on the sauce, please. Problem is, too many toppings can make for a soggy pizza, especially with the thin-crust variety, and a big load of salty, cheesy toppings will dominate the overall flavor, so you miss the taste of the crust or the herbs in the sauce. In Italy, the toppings tend to be spare and carefully chosen for their intensity of flavor, and we're starting to see this trend in the small artisan pizzerias springing up around the country. Some of their menus suggest that patrons limit the number of topping selections to assure a peak pizza experience. We're not going to monitor your kitchen, but we suggest you try scaling back to just two or three toppings, with a light coating of sauce and a gentle hand with the cheese, and see if you don't appreciate more the interplay of ingredients and the delicious flavor of your perfectly crisped crust.

ROLLING, ROLLING, ROLLING...

There's an ongoing debate about whether it's best to roll or to stretch pizza crust. The stretchers (and those professional tossers are part of this group) believe you get a better result if you gently stretch or toss the dough into its final shape. The rollers claim there's just no way to get a thin, even circle without a rolling pin. Who's right? In a way, they both are. A rolling pin does a great job of flattening and shaping the dough into an even crust, without risk of the tearing that can occur as you stretch a tender dough across your knuckles. A rolled crust, however, tends to have a more crisp, cracker-like texture. If your dough is strong and extensible, stretching the dough is a good skill to learn, so by all means give it a try and see if you like the results. If, however, your dough is tender and susceptible to shredding, as are many whole grain crusts, you're probably better off with a well-floured pin.

Thai Chicken Pizza

YIELD: 2 large pizzas, 12-inch rounds or 10 x 12-inch rectangles, 8 servings
BAKING TEMPERATURE: 500°F
BAKING TIME: 8 to 10 minutes

The newest wave of pizza toppings is really pushing boundaries, literally. If Thailand and Italy don't have a common border, well, that's OK. In the culinary world, we can make that happen. Even in small-town Vermont, the local pizzeria offers Thai pizza, although its version is a little on the tame side, in an attempt to cater to our northern taste buds. We find the whole wheat crust on this pizza stands up to the strong, spicy flavors of peanut sauce and chili paste, so feel free to make it as spicy as you please. Start the pre-ferment the night before you bake, put the dough together early in the day, and give it plenty of time to ripen before you bake.

Pre-ferment
1 cup (4 ounces) traditional whole wheat flour
Scant pinch of instant yeast
½ cup (4 ounces) cold water

Dough
All of the pre-ferment
1¼ cups (10 ounces) cool water
2 cups (8 ounces) white whole wheat flour
1 cup (4¼ ounces) unbleached bread flour
1½ teaspoons salt
¾ teaspoon yeast

Thai chicken topping
2 large (about 12 ounces) bone-in chicken breasts
½ cup (4 ounces) Thai fish sauce
1 lime, juiced
¼ cup (1⅞ ounces) packed light or dark brown sugar
1 teaspoon chili-garlic paste
½ cup (4 ounces) Thai spicy peanut sauce
1 bunch (2 ounces) scallions, trimmed and chopped
1 cup (4 ounces) shredded mozzarella
¼ cup (¼ ounce) chopped fresh cilantro

TO MAKE THE PRE-FERMENT: The night before you want to make the pizza, measure the flour into a medium mixing bowl, and toss it with a scant pinch of yeast. Stir in the cold water to thoroughly moisten the flour. Cover the bowl with plastic wrap and set aside at room temperature for 12 to 15 hours. This pre-ferment won't have the same bubbly appearance as one made with white flour, but it will have puffed up a bit and changed its appearance. We consider it "ripe" at this point and ready to use.

TO MAKE THE DOUGH: The next morning, stir the cool water into the bowl with the ripe pre-ferment, and add the remaining flours, salt and yeast. This will be a wet dough; it's best to mix it in a mixer so you won't be tempted to knead in too much flour. Mix the dough for about 5 minutes, cover the bowl with plastic wrap, and set it aside to rise.

After about 30 minutes, when the dough starts to look noticeably puffy, it's time to fold the dough to build its strength. Turn the dough out onto a heavily floured surface and give it a fold. This will be a very messy process, so be sure your hands and work surface are well floured; you will find it helpful to use a bench knife or dough scraper. Use the scraper to gently fold the dough over itself, as you would a business letter, brushing any excess flour away as you fold, to keep from incorporating raw flour into the middle of the dough. Next, fold the dough in a similar fashion, this time from the long ends, to make a packet. (See illustration, p. 130.) Return the dough to the bowl, cover, and let it rise for another 30 minutes. Repeat this fold every 30 minutes for 2 hours, for a total of 4 folds.

Divide the dough in half and form each piece into a round. Cover them well with plastic wrap, and let them rest for 30 minutes to 1 hour.

To prepare the chicken, place the chicken breasts in a small baking dish. Combine the fish sauce, lime juice, sugar and chili-garlic paste, and pour over the chicken. Marinate the chicken for at least 2 hours, or overnight.

Preheat the oven to 350°F. Bake the chicken until cooked through, about 30 minutes. Remove the chicken from the oven and let cool completely. Strip the meat from the bones, chop and toss with a tablespoon or two of the cooking juices.

About 30 minutes before you bake your pizza, preheat your oven and a baking stone, if you have one, to 500°F.

Sprinkle your work surface lightly with flour and pat a piece of dough flat on the flour, being careful not to break through the surface of the dough. Using well-floured hands or a well-floured rolling pin, stretch or roll the pizza into a large round or rectangular shape. You may want to finish the shaping on a piece of parchment paper. Keep flouring your hands and gently press the dough out to the edges of the parchment; the dough will be quite thin. If you wind up with holes, don't worry; just pinch the edges of the hole together and keep going.

For the first pizza, spread ¼ cup of the peanut sauce over the dough. Sprinkle half the chopped chicken and half the scallions over the peanut sauce. Top with half the mozzarella. Use your peel to deposit the pizza, parchment paper and all, on the hot baking stone. The parchment can stay in the oven for the entire baking time, or you may reach in and slide it out after the crust has started to set, about 3 minutes. Bake the pizza until the cheese is bubbly and beginning to brown, 8 to 10 minutes. Use your peel to remove the baked pizza from the oven. Place it on a flat cutting surface, top with half the chopped cilantro, cut into 8 to 10 slices, and serve immediately.

While the pizza bakes, shape and top the remaining piece of dough. When the first pizza comes out of the oven, the second one will be ready to bake.

NUTRITION INFORMATION PER SERVING ($\frac{1}{4}$ PIZZA, 165G): **43g whole grains,** 294 cal, 5g fat, 19g protein, 44g complex carbohydrates, 1g sugar, 6g dietary fiber, 30mg cholesterol, 652mg sodium, 299mg potassium, 32RE vitamin A, 2mg vitamin C, 3mg iron, 139mg calcium, 291mg phosphorus.

TOOL TIME

The quest for great pizza can quickly become an obsession, especially when it comes to the equipment you need. Do you really need a stone? How about a pizza peel? Parchment paper? How about a wood-fired oven? When have you gone too far? No doubt the intense heat of a wood-fired oven makes great pizza, but if you're not yet ready to start laying brick, what can you do to improve the quality of the pizza coming from your kitchen? We'd say the first crucial tool is some sort of baking stone. Having a stone in the oven significantly improves the ability to retain and intensify the heat, which in turn helps to bake a crisp and delicious pizza. Once you have a stone, you need a way to load the pizza onto it. If you plan to bake the pizza directly on the stone a peel is crucial to getting it on and off without searing your forearms. And getting it on and off the peel? We've tried flour, cornmeal, rice flour, semolina, and we have to say the truly surefire method is to use a piece of parchment paper. The parchment paper will brown in a 500°F oven, but it won't burn, and it will ensure a smooth ride in and out of the oven for your precious pizza cargo. As for the outdoor wood-fired oven, we'll let your finances and leisure time determine whether you want to tackle one of those!

Focaccia

YIELD: 1 large focaccia, 12 servings
BAKING TEMPERATURE: 425°F
BAKING TIME: 18 to 20 minutes

When we first thought about a whole grain focaccia, it seemed impossible to imagine a version that would be as lush and lofty as those that grace the breadbaskets of Italian tables. This version, which is more than half whole wheat flour, may not reach the same heights as the fluffiest focaccia, but its creamy, chewy texture and fragrant flavor make it one of our favorites. The secret is making a pre-ferment the night before with whole wheat flour, water and a pinch of yeast.

Pre-ferment
1 cup (4 ounces) traditional whole wheat flour
½ cup (4 ounces) water
Scant pinch of instant yeast

Dough
All of the pre-ferment
1 cup plus 2 tablespoons (9 ounces) water
1¼ cups (5 ounces) traditional whole wheat flour
1⅞ cups (8 ounces) unbleached all-purpose flour
2 teaspoons salt
¾ teaspoon instant yeast

Topping
1 onion, thinly sliced
2 tablespoons olive oil
1 tablespoon chopped fresh rosemary

TO MAKE THE PRE-FERMENT: The night before you want to bake the bread, in the bowl of your mixer combine the flour, water and pinch of yeast until well blended. Cover the bowl and let it stand at room temperature for 12 to 16 hours. The mixture will puff up and look bubbly. At this point it's ripe and ready to use.

TO MAKE THE DOUGH: To the bowl with the ripe pre-ferment, add all the remaining dough ingredients, beginning with the water. Mix the dough on the lowest speed of your mixer until it begins to hold together. The dough should be very wet and slack. You may need to add 1 or 2 tablespoons more water if conditions are dry. Mix on the slowest speed for 2 minutes, then increase the mixer speed to medium and mix for about 4 minutes. The dough will still be quite soft. Cover the dough tightly and let it rise for 30 minutes.

After 30 minutes, it's time to fold the dough to build its strength. Generously flour a flat surface and scrape the dough out onto it. Give the dough a fold. This will be a very messy process, so be sure your hands and work surface are well-floured; you will find it helpful to use a bench knife or dough scraper. Use the scraper to gently fold the dough over itself, as you would a business letter, brushing any excess flour away as you fold, to keep from incorporating raw flour into the middle of the dough.

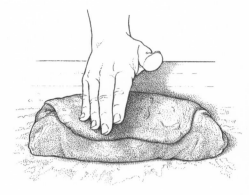

Gently brush the excess flour from the surface of the dough to prevent dried-out areas inside the bread.

Next, fold the dough in a similar fashion, this time from the long ends, to make a packet. Place the dough back in the bowl, cover with plastic, and let rise for another 30 minutes. Repeat the folding process and let the dough rise for another 30 minutes. With each fold, the dough should gain strength and elasticity. Fold one more time, and turn out the dough into a sheet pan that has been oiled generously with olive oil. Spread the dough into the edges of the pan. Cover the dough and let it rise for another 30 minutes.

As the dough is rising for its final 30 minutes, preheat your oven and a baking stone, if you have one, to 500°F. Allow the oven and stone to heat for at least 30 minutes.

TO MAKE THE TOPPING: Toss the onion slices with the olive oil in a small bowl and spread them on a baking sheet with a rim. Place the baking sheet in the oven and roast the onions until they're golden brown, 15 to 20 minutes. You may do this step while the oven is preheating for the pizza. Remove the onions from the oven and toss in the rosemary.

TO TOP AND BAKE THE FOCACCIA: Spread the roasted onions across the surface of the risen focaccia dough. You may lightly dimple the dough as you top it.

Place the pan onto the stone and lower the oven temperature to 425°F. Bake the focaccia until it is a deep golden color, 18 to 20 minutes. Remove the focaccia from the oven and let cool for at least 10 minutes before serving.

As you sprinkle the onions and rosemary across the dough, dip your oiled fingertips lightly into the dough to dimple it a bit.

NUTRITION INFORMATION PER SERVING ($^1/_{12}$ FOCACCIA, 91G): 21g whole grains, 175 cal, 4g fat, 5g protein, 31g complex carbohydrates, 4g dietary fiber, 358mg sodium, 144mg potassium, 1mg vitamin C, 2mg iron, 13mg calcium, 104mg phosphorus.

VARIATION: GARLIC-STEEPED FLATBREAD *Mince 2 or 3 cloves of garlic and stir them, along with the rosemary, into $^1/_2$ cup olive oil in a large bowl. For the third rise, slip the dough into the garlic olive oil and let it rise, immersed in the oil, for 30 minutes. Slide the dough from the bowl to a large rimmed baking sheet and spread it into the edges of the pan. Let the dough rise for 30 minutes, then bake as above. Use baking shears to cut into irregular pieces and serve as soon as it's cool enough to handle.*

When it came time to change some of our favorite flatbread recipes to incorporate whole grains, we weren't quite sure what to do about the pre-ferments. We did some experiments and found our breads were better when we pre-fermented the whole grain flour in a recipe instead of the white flour. Often the white flour pre-ferment would look better—wetter and more bubbly—but when the dough was mixed, the whole wheat pre-ferments would rise higher, have a smoother flavor and better mouthfeel. According to our master baker, Jeffrey Hamelman, saving the white flour for the final dough gives a better result because you've expended some of the whole wheat in the pre-ferment, and saved the flour with the best capacity for rising to do its work in the final dough. In addition, the overnight rest for the whole wheat helps with its digestibility—a win/win for the bread and for you.

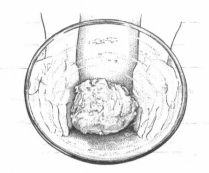
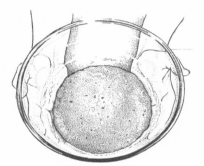

It may look too dry when you first mix it together, but the next day it's moist and aerated.

Fougasse with Two Fillings

YIELD: 2 loaves, 8 servings each
BAKING TEMPERATURE: 425°F
BAKING TIME: 20 to 25 minutes

The intricate shaping of this crusty French peasant bread makes a beautiful presentation for the dinner table. A loaf is lovely as a gift or to bring to a potluck. There's lots of surface area for crunchy-crust fans, and the rye in the recipe is the perfect foil for any number of flavorful fillings; we've outlined some of our favorites here—even a couple of dessert fougasses—but let your imagination run wild! The pre-ferment in this recipe has more water than usual; that's because the whole rye flour absorbs so much—pre-fermenting the rye smoothes the flavor of the grain and makes for a more toothsome interior too.

Pre-ferment

1 cup (3¾ ounces) whole rye (pumpernickel) flour
¾ cup (6 ounces) cool water
Scant pinch of instant yeast

Dough

All of the pre-ferment
½ cup (4 ounces) water
⅔ cup (2¼ ounces) whole rye (pumpernickel) flour
2 cups (8½ ounces) unbleached all-purpose flour
1½ teaspoons salt
1 teaspoon yeast
2 tablespoons (⅞ ounce) olive oil

Olive-rosemary filling

½ cup (2½ ounces) kalamata olives, pitted and coarsely chopped
1 tablespoon chopped fresh rosemary

Blue cheese and walnut filling

½ cup (2 ounces) crumbled blue cheese
¼ cup (1 ounce) chopped walnuts

TO MAKE THE PRE-FERMENT: The night before you want to bake the bread, stir together the flour, water and yeast in your mixing bowl until well combined. Cover the bowl with plastic wrap, and set it aside to rest at room temperature for 15 hours or so, until the mixture is bubbly and domed.

TO MAKE THE DOUGH: To the bowl with the pre-ferment, add all the remaining dough ingredients, beginning with the water. Mix the ingredients on the mixer's slowest speed or until the dough just comes together, about 2 minutes. This is the best time to check the dough for water—you want a dough that is quite sticky, so you may need to add 1 or 2 tablespoons water, depending on how much the flour absorbs. Once you've adjusted the water, turn the mixer up to medium speed and knead for 3 minutes. The dough will pull away from the sides of the bowl and smooth out significantly. There may still be some dough sticking around the bottom of the bowl—that's OK. Cover the bowl with plastic wrap and let rise until the dough is puffy, 1 hour.

After an hour, it's time to fold the dough to build its strength. Generously flour a flat surface and scrape the dough onto it. Gently fold the dough as you would a business letter, brushing any excess flour away to keep from incorporating raw flour into the middle of the dough. Fold the dough again in a similar fashion, this time from the long ends, to make a firm packet. (See illustration, p. 130.) Place the dough back in the bowl, cover with plastic, and let it rise for another hour.

TO MAKE THE FILLINGS: Combine the olives and rosemary in one small bowl and the blue cheese and walnuts in another small bowl.

TO SHAPE THE LOAVES: Lightly flour your work surface and place the dough on it. Divide the dough into 2 equal pieces. Work with one piece at a time, covering the other one to keep it from drying out. Flour your hands and pat the dough into a rectangular shape. Spread the first filling down one side of the rectangle. Fold the dough over the filling and pinch the edges to seal.

Using a lightly floured rolling pin, gently roll the dough into an oval shape about 10 inches long. Place the loaf on a piece of parchment paper and cover it with plastic wrap. Shape and fill the second piece to the same point, using the second filling. Allow the loaves to rise, covered, for about 40 minutes.

Keep your hands well floured as you fold and seal the fougasse.

Adjust the racks to divide the oven into thirds, and place your baking stone on the bottom rack. Preheat your oven and baking stone to 425°F.

TO SLASH AND BAKE THE LOAVES: When the loaves are puffy, it's time for the final shaping. Take a sharp knife and cut three parallel slashes across and all the way through to the center of the dough. Pull the dough apart to form a ladder shape. (See illustrations below.)

Mist the surface of the loaf with water and use a peel to deposit the loaf, parchment and all, onto the baking stone. While the first loaf bakes, slash the second loaf, this time in the shape of a leaf.

Pick up the end of the oval closest to you and stretch it toward you while pulling your hands apart to form a long triangle. Cut one long slash along the center of the triangle,

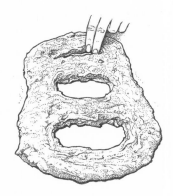

Cut three parallel slashes all the way through the partially risen dough. Stretch open these slashes to form a ladder shape.

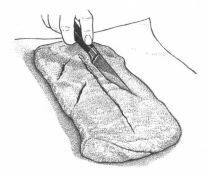

Use a sharp knife to cut a long slash down the center of the rectangle and diagonally up the edges, like the veins of a leaf.

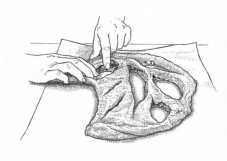

Flour your fingers and gently pull the cuts apart to complete the leaf shape.

There was a time not too long ago when people baked and cooked using their intuition and their experience as guides, rather than recipes. Many of our grandmothers passed along recipes that called for a pinch of this or a handful of that, but as our society has gotten more scientific, so have our recipes. Many cookbooks translate a pinch as $1/8$ teaspoon, and that has slowly become standard. With pre-ferments, however, there are times when $1/8$ teaspoon is too much yeast, especially since whole grain pre-ferments tend to ripen quickly. Since $1/8$ teaspoon weighs barely 1 gram, how can you weigh something any smaller using a standard kitchen scale? Well, it may be that in this case the old-fashioned way is the best. When it's midsummer, and even our Vermont kitchens are getting pretty steamy, less than $1/32$ of a teaspoon should be enough yeast to move your pre-ferment along. In the middle of the winter, your pinch may well approach a gram. You'll want to pay close attention to how quickly the pre-ferments reach their peak and scale back or forward according to how they're responding to your kitchen's climate. In other words, practice using your intuition and experience to guide you!

There's a big difference between $1/8$ teaspoon, a winter pinch and a summer pinch.

and then cut diagonal slashes up from the center line, as veins on a leaf. Gently pull the slashes apart to spread the loaf into a broad leaf shape.

Mist the surface of the loaf lightly with water.

When the first loaf has been in the oven for about 5 minutes, open the oven partway and mist the interior with a quick spray of water. After the loaf has baked for 10 to 15 minutes and is firm enough to move—and the second loaf is shaped and ready to load—use your peel to move the first loaf, parchment and all, to the higher rack. Now place the second loaf on the stone. The loaves will need a total of about 20 minutes to finish baking, or until they're crusty and golden brown. After you remove the first loaf, you may quickly mist the interior of the oven one last time—it should be about 5 minutes into the baking of the second loaf. Cool the loaves on a rack before serving.

NUTRITION INFORMATION PER SERVING ($1/8$ LOAF, 56G): 11g whole grains, 122 cal, 3g fat, 4g protein, 20g complex carbohydrates, 3g dietary fiber, 3mg cholesterol, 298mg sodium, 132mg potassium, 12RE vitamin A, 2mg iron, 36mg calcium, 114mg phosphorus.

VARIATION: DESSERT FOUGASSE *In place of the olive oil in the dough, use 2 tablespoons butter and add 1 tablespoon honey. For the fillings, use $1/4$ cup walnuts and $1/2$ cup chopped dried apricots for one, and $1/2$ cup bittersweet chocolate chips and $1/4$ cup mini marshmallows for the other. The marshmallows will melt in the hot oven, leaving only their lightly caramelized vanilla flavor and slightly sticky texture.*

Whole Wheat Pretzels

YIELD: 8 soft pretzels
BAKING TEMPERATURE: 450°F
BAKING TIME: 12 to 15 minutes

The whole wheat flour in these pretzels adds a hearty note to a traditional favorite. Giving the whole wheat flour time to absorb the water before adding the other ingredients helps the texture and rise of the finished pretzels.

Dough
1¾ cups (7 ounces) whole wheat flour, traditional or white whole wheat
1 cup (8 ounces) water, at room temperature
1 tablespoon soft butter
1½ cups (6⅜ ounces) unbleached bread flour
1½ teaspoons salt
1 teaspoon instant yeast
1 teaspoon barley malt extract, syrup or dried

Water bath
8 cups (64 ounces) water
2 tablespoons baking soda

Glaze
1 egg beaten with 1 tablespoon water and a pinch of salt
Kosher salt and/or seeds for topping

TO MAKE THE DOUGH: Mix the whole wheat flour and water. Cover and let it sit for 20 minutes. Stir in the soft butter, bread flour, salt, yeast and barley malt extract (or malt powder) and mix well. You may mix this dough by hand or with a mixer, but if you're mixing by hand, try to use as little additional flour as possible. The dough should be a little tacky at first, but will smooth out as you knead it. Knead the dough until it's smooth and elastic, about 4 minutes in the mixer, 6 minutes by hand. Cover the bowl, and let the dough rise until doubled in bulk, about 1½ hours.

Preheat the oven to 450°F. Grease 2 baking sheets or line them with parchment paper. To make the water bath, pour the water into a wide pot and place it over heat to boil.

TO SHAPE AND BAKE THE PRETZELS: Turn the dough out onto a very lightly floured work surface. Divide it in half and divide each half into fourths, so that you have 8 equal pieces. Roll each piece into a rope about ½ inch thick. You may need to flour your hands a bit, but keep the work surface slightly tacky, so you have friction for rolling. You may need to let the ropes rest halfway through rolling—be careful not to tear the dough.

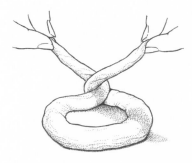

Form the rope of dough into a circle, leaving 4 inches free on each end of the rope. Twist these ends around each other, and fold the twist down the middle of the circle. Press the ends of the dough to the outside of the ring to make the pretzel shape.

Take each rope and make a loop with fairly short ends. Give the ends an extra twist and fold them down to the bottom of the loop to form the traditional pretzel shape.

By the time all the pretzels are formed, the water should be boiling. Turn it down to a simmer and add the baking soda. Carefully pick up the pretzels and add them to the water. Cook about 3 at a time, making sure there is plenty of room. The pretzels will expand quickly and dramatically. Cook for about 1 minute. Use a slotted spatula or spoon to transfer the pretzels to the prepared baking sheets.

When all the pretzels have been boiled, brush them with the egg wash and sprinkle with seeds and/or kosher salt. Bake the pretzels until well browned, 12 to 15 minutes. Remove them from the oven and serve warm.

NUTRITION INFORMATION PER SERVING (1 PRETZEL, 81 G): 25g whole grains, 168 cal, 1g fat, 6g protein, 36g complex carbohydrates, 4g dietary fiber, 802mg salt, 146mg potassium, 2mg iron, 10 mg calcium, 118mg phosphorus.

ROLLING FIRMLY, BUT GENTLY

When rolling dough into a long rope or snake shape, our tendency is to go at it hard; our fingers spring up and the palms of our hands bear down, as though it were Play-Doh we were pressing into shape. When you exert pressure on the dough this way, it tears, and when it's time to bake the bread, that tear becomes a weak spot in the crust, resulting in a "blowout." Instead, when you're rolling, try to curve the palms of your hands and let up a bit on the dough.

You want a firm hand, but be patient and give the dough a rest if it's resisting you. In the end, you'll have an even strand for shaping and a smooth crust as it comes out of the oven.

Try not to press too hard on the dough as you roll. Instead curve your hands firmly over the strand.

Golden Sesame Breadsticks

YIELD: 5 dozen (10-inch) breadsticks
BAKING TEMPERATURE: 350°F
BAKING TIME: 25 minutes

These crunchy, golden breadsticks are so light and great-tasting you'll find it hard to believe they're more than half whole wheat. The bran in the flour makes them a snap to roll out, and they stretch even longer as you shape them, for a crisp and elegant beginning to any meal.

Pre-ferment
1 cup (4 ounces) traditional whole wheat flour
1/2 cup (4 ounces) cool water
Scant pinch of instant yeast

Dough
All of the pre-ferment
1/2 cup (2 ounces) traditional whole wheat flour
1 cup (4 1/4 ounces) unbleached all-purpose flour
1 1/2 teaspoons instant yeast
1 teaspoon salt
1/2 cup (4 ounces) water
3 tablespoons (1 1/4 ounces) olive oil
Toasted sesame seeds, or seeds of your choice, for topping

TO MAKE THE PRE-FERMENT: The night before you want to bake the breadsticks, combine the whole wheat flour, water and a pinch of yeast in a medium mixing bowl. Stir to blend, cover with plastic wrap, and set aside to rise at cool room temperature for 12 to 14 hours. The dough will puff up, but won't be as bubbly as a white-flour poolish.

TO MAKE THE DOUGH: Add the flours, yeast, salt, water and olive oil to the pre-ferment and knead them together —by hand or mixer—till you've made a smooth, very soft dough. Place the dough in a greased bowl, and allow it to rise, covered, for 1 to 1 1/2 hours; it'll become puffy, though not necessarily doubled in bulk.

TO SHAPE THE BREADSTICKS: Lightly grease baking sheets or line with parchment paper. Lightly oil your work surface with olive oil and turn out the dough onto it. Using an oiled rolling pin, roll the dough into a 10 x 20-inch rectangle. Cut the rectangle lengthwise into two 5 x 20-inch strips. Sprinkle the dough with seeds, and roll the dough lightly to press in the seeds. Use a pizza wheel or sharp knife to cut the dough (the short way) into 1/2-inch x 5-inch strips. Twist the ends of each strip in opposite directions (as you might to wring out a wet towel) to make a spiral, and place them on the prepared baking sheets.

The dough is soft, so the breadsticks will stretch as you work with them—that's why it's easier to begin with a 5-inch-wide strip of dough. Let the breadsticks rest, covered, for 1 hour; they won't appear to rise much, but they will in fact be getting lighter.

While the breadsticks are resting, preheat the oven to 350°F. Bake the breadsticks, rotating the pans top to bottom halfway through, for about 25 minutes. They'll be golden-brown when they're done; watch them closely toward the end, as they'll begin to brown quickly. Remove from the oven and let cool on a rack.

NUTRITION INFORMATION PER SERVING (5 BREADSTICKS, 52G): 14g whole grains, 133 cal, 5g fat, 4g protein, 19g complex carbohydrates, 3g dietary fiber, 180mg sodium, 98mg potassium, 2mg iron, 37mg calcium, 87mg phosphorus.

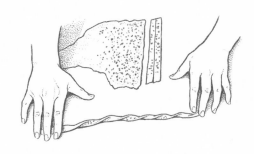

After cutting the dough into $\frac{1}{2}$-inch strips, twist the ends of each strip in opposite directions to form a spiral. Transfer the twisted dough to a baking sheet.

Whole Wheat Pita

YIELD: 8 large pitas
BAKING TEMPERATURE: 450°F
BAKING TIME: 5 minutes

Have you ever bought whole wheat pita bread in the grocery store? It's a little reminiscent of cardboard, in both taste and texture. Not so this version, which makes a fluffy, beautifully ballooned bread, just right for stuffing with fresh vegetables, salad or whatever you happen to have on hand.

> $1\frac{3}{4}$ cups (7 ounces) traditional whole wheat flour
> $1\frac{1}{2}$ cups ($6\frac{3}{8}$ ounces) bread flour
> $1\frac{1}{2}$ teaspoons salt
> $1\frac{1}{2}$ teaspoons instant yeast
> $1\frac{1}{4}$ cups (10 ounces) warm water
> 2 tablespoons ($\frac{7}{8}$ ounce) olive oil

Combine all the ingredients and mix and knead them together—by hand or mixer—until you have a soft, supple dough, about 8 minutes by hand or 5 minutes in the mixer. You may need a bit more flour, but remember whole grain dough starts out a bit stickier and absorbs liquid as it develops, so don't add too much at the beginning of the process; you'll regret it later. You want a soft dough that feels tacky to the touch. Cover the bowl tightly and let the dough rise until doubled in bulk, about $1\frac{1}{2}$ hours.

Place a baking stone on the bottom rack of your oven and preheat the oven to 450°F.

After it's risen, turn the dough out onto a lightly floured surface and cut it in half. Divide one half into 4 equal portions and form each into a rough ball. Let the balls rest for 10 minutes, covered, while dividing the second half of dough in the same way. This rest makes the dough easier to roll out.

The breads will balloon from the steam as the dough hits the hot oven.

Using a rolling pin, roll out each ball to a circle about 6 inches in diameter and less than ¼ inch thick. Use only enough flour to keep the dough from sticking to the pin and the work surface. Too much flour allows the dough to skid around. Keep the waiting balls of dough covered as you work.

Flour a baker's peel and load 2 pitas at a time directly on the hot baking stone. It should take 3 to 4 minutes for the pitas to go into a full "balloon."

Turn them once while they're baking to assure a speckled, brown crust on each side. Remove the pitas from the oven and repeat with the remaining pieces. Stack the warm pitas together in a kitchen towel to keep them from crisping as they cool.

NUTRITION INFORMATION PER SERVING (1 PITA, 90G): 25g whole grains, 196 cal, 4g fat, 6g protein, 35g complex carbohydrates, 4g dietary fiber, 402mg sodium, 148mg potassium, 2mg iron, 10mg calcium, 120mg phosphorus.

Spelt Pita

YIELD: 8 pitas
BAKING TEMPERATURE: 500°F
BAKING TIME: 3 to 5 minutes

The chewy sweetness of spelt shines through in this recipe for spelt pita, developed for The King Arthur Flour Baking Education Center by instructor Rosemary Hubbard. These pitas are surprisingly simple to make and pack so much more flavor than any you can buy.

1 cup (4¼ ounces) unbleached all-purpose flour
½ teaspoon instant yeast
1 cup (8 ounces) warm water
¾ teaspoon salt
1½ teaspoons olive oil
1½ cups (5¼ ounces) whole spelt flour

TO MAKE THE SPONGE: Combine the all-purpose flour and yeast in a medium bowl. Add the water and stir to create a smooth batter. Cover the bowl with plastic wrap and let the sponge rest for at least 10 minutes or as long as 2 hours.

TO MAKE THE DOUGH: Sprinkle the salt over the sponge, stir in the olive oil and mix well. Add 1 cup of the spelt flour and stir to create a shaggy mass, or a dough that sort of gathers up on the spoon. You may need to add more spelt at this point, but try not to create a dry dough. Turn out the dough onto a lightly floured surface and knead it until it's smooth and elastic, about 8 minutes. Handle the dough gently, and use only enough flour to keep it from sticking. Lightly grease the bowl, place the dough in it, cover and let it rise until it has at least doubled in bulk, about 1 hour.

TO SHAPE AND BAKE THE PITAS: Place a baking stone in the oven, and preheat both oven and stone to 500°F.

Fold the dough to remove the bubbles from it, and divide it into 8 pieces. Lightly flour your hands and flatten each piece. Using a floured rolling pin, roll out each piece on a lightly floured surface to a circle about 6 inches in diameter and less than ¼ inch thick. Use only enough flour to keep the dough from sticking to the pin and the work surface. Too much flour allows the dough to skid around. Keep the waiting balls of dough covered as you work.

Flour a baker's peel and use it to load 2 pitas at a time directly onto the hot baking stone. It should take 3 to 4 minutes for the pitas to go into a full "balloon." Turn them once while they're baking to assure a speckled, brown crust on each side. Remove the pitas from the oven and repeat with the remaining pieces. Stack the warm pitas together in a kitchen towel to keep them from crisping as they cool.

NUTRITION INFORMATION PER SERVING (1 PITA, 72G): **19g whole grains,** 133 cal, 1g fat, 5g protein, 29g complex carbohydrates, 4g dietary fiber, 201mg sodium, 135mg potassium, 2mg iron, 1mg calcium, 107mg phosphorus.

Scallion Pancakes

YIELD: 6 (8-inch) pancakes, 8 pieces each, 12 servings
COOKING METHOD/TEMPERATURE: Stovetop, medium-low heat
COOKING TIME: 6 to 7 minutes

This Chinese-restaurant staple is really very easy to make at home; if you like cooking because of the tactile reinforcement (sometimes called "the mud pie factor"), you'll have fun with this recipe. Every time we make them they disappear in record time.

Dough
2 cups (6¾ ounces) whole wheat pastry flour
2¼ cups (9½ ounces) unbleached bread flour
2 cups (16 ounces) water
½ cup (3½ ounces) peanut oil

Filling
2 bunches (about 2 cups, or 8 ounces) scallions, green tops only
¼ cup (1¾ ounces) peanut oil, plus more for rolling and frying
1 tablespoon kosher salt

TO MAKE THE DOUGH: Combine the flours in the bowl of an electric mixer fitted with a paddle. With the mixer on low speed, gradually pour in the water. Let the mixer run on low until a sticky, stretchy batter forms, 6 minutes. The batter will stick to the bottom and sides of the bowl; it's supposed to.

Remove the bowl from the mixer and remove the paddle from the bowl. Pour the peanut oil over the dough to keep the top from drying out; cover and refrigerate while you prepare the filling.

TO MAKE THE FILLING: Cut the scallions on the bias in ¼-inch slices. Place in a bowl, add the ¼ cup peanut oil and salt. Stir to combine.

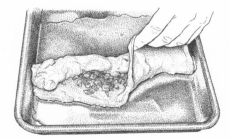

Keeping your fingers and the dough oiled makes it easier to roll the pancake into a long tube shape.

Wind the rolled dough like a snail to make a flat coil.

TO ASSEMBLE: Divide the dough into 6 pieces (each piece will weigh about 6 ounces, and be about ¾ cup). Try to keep each piece coated with peanut oil as you do this. Using a rimmed baking sheet greased with more peanut oil, pat each piece of dough out to an 8-inch circle. Sprinkle ¼ cup of the filling mixture over each dough circle.

Starting from one edge, roll each circle up to make a long tube. Holding one end of the tube in place, wind the rest of the dough around it like a snail. Wrap each scallion pancake in plastic wrap (a foldover sandwich bag is also good for this), and store in a covered container until you're ready to cook. The pancakes can be held this way, refrigerated, for up to 2 days.

TO COOK THE PANCAKES: Place a 10-inch skillet over medium-low heat. Put enough peanut oil in the pan to cover the bottom. When the pan is hot enough, the oil will show ripples on its surface.

On a small plate, also greased with peanut oil, pat out one of the scallion pancakes to an 8-inch circle. Use the plate or your hand to transfer the pancake to the skillet.

The peanut oil makes it easy to slip the pancake into the pan.

Fry the pancake until the bottom is golden brown and crispy, 3 to 4 minutes. Turn the pancake over and continue cooking until the second side is also golden brown, 3 minutes more. The center of the dough will stay chewy—that's as it should be. Remove the pancake from the skillet and drain on paper towels. Repeat with the remaining dough. Slice each pancake into eighths, like a pie, and serve with dipping sauce (see recipe below).

NUTRITION INFORMATION PER SERVING (½ PANCAKE, 4 PIECES, 92G): 12g whole grains, 246 cal, 10g fat, 6g protein, 34g complex carbohydrates, 4g dietary fiber, 493mg sodium, 151mg potassium, 6RE vitamin A, 3mg vitamin C, 2mg iron, 23mg calcium, 100 mg phosphorus.

VARIATION: TO MAKE THESE WITH BROWN RICE FLOUR, *increase the bread flour to 3¼ cups (13⅞ ounces) and substitute 1½ cups (6¾ ounces) brown rice flour for the whole wheat pastry flour.*

Dipping Sauce for Scallion Pancakes

YIELD: 3½ cups

This dipping sauce has everything—it's sweet, salty, sour and spicy! This makes more dipping sauce than you'll use for the scallion pancakes, but it lasts forever. It's also good as a marinade for chicken wings.

2 cups (16 ounces) soy sauce

½ cup (4 ounces) rice wine vinegar

½ cup (4 ounces) mirin (sweet rice wine) or simple syrup

1 tablespoon sesame oil

2 teaspoons chili-garlic paste

1½ cups (3⅜ ounces) scallions, sliced very thin

½ cup (4 ounces) grated fresh ginger

¼ cup (2 ounces) minced garlic

2 tablespoons (⅝ ounce) sesame seeds

Combine the liquid ingredients with the chili-garlic paste, and stir in the remaining ingredients. Let the mixture sit for 1 hour before using. Store in a covered container in the refrigerator.

Whole Wheat Flour Tortillas

YIELD: 10 to 12 tortillas

COOKING METHOD/TEMPERATURE: Stovetop, medium-high heat

COOKING TIME: 2 to 3 minutes per tortilla

We made flour tortillas from all kinds of wheat, and other grains too. Our favorites were tortillas made with white whole wheat flour. The amount of water varied a bit from grain to grain, so if you're using a flour different from King Arthur White Whole Wheat, add the water cautiously. These are a little thicker than white-flour tortillas, and they need to rest a little longer to give the flour a chance to absorb the water, but they have a hearty, complex flavor that goes nicely with spicy food.

2 cups (8 ounces) white whole wheat flour

½ teaspoon salt

3 tablespoons (1¼ ounces) vegetable oil

⅔ cup (5⅜ ounces) warm water

TO MAKE THE DOUGH: Combine the flour and salt in a medium mixing bowl or a food processor and mix together. Add the oil and mix into the flour thoroughly. Mix in the warm water (with the machine running, if you're using a food processor). Because the protein content and absorption of different flours can vary, you may need to use more or less water. You'll want a dough that's a bit softer than ones you make with white flour; the whole wheat will absorb some of the liquid as it sits. Once you've mixed the dough, let it sit, covered, for 20 minutes.

TO SHAPE AND BAKE THE TORTILLAS: Turn out the dough onto a lightly floured surface, knead it a couple of times, and pat it into an even disk. Cut the dough into 10 to 12 pieces, and roll each piece into a ball. Cover the balls and let them rest for 20 minutes. If you have a tortilla press, use it to flatten each ball. If you're rolling the tortillas by hand, take one of the balls and flatten it into a small disk. Using a floured rolling pin on a lightly floured work surface, roll the tortilla into a very thin, flat round about 6 to 8 inches in diameter.

Heat a heavy, ungreased griddle over medium-high heat. Toss a tortilla onto the griddle and let it heat on one side for about 1 minute, then use tongs to lift and flip the tortilla to bake it on the other side. Bake the tortilla until each side begins to brown in spots, about 1 minute to a side. While the first tortilla is baking, roll the second one. Transfer the baked tortilla to a plate and toss on the next tortilla. Repeat until all the tortillas are rolled and baked. You may stack the tortillas and cover them with a towel to keep them soft and warm until you're ready to use them.

NUTRITION INFORMATION PER SERVING (1 TORTILLA, 37G): 19g whole grains, 99 cal, 4g fat, 3g protein, 15g complex carbohydrates, 2g dietary fiber, 90mg sodium, 81mg potassium, 1mg iron, 7mg calcium, 69mg phosphorus.

VARIATION: WHOLE SPELT FLOUR TORTILLAS *Substitute whole spelt flour for the whole wheat flour and use a little less water—4 to 5 ounces should be enough to get a texture that will roll thin enough for tortillas.*

FRESH WHOLE WHEAT FLOUR

We tried tortillas with four kinds of whole wheat flour, spelt, cornmeal, rice flour, oat flour and whole barley flour. The oat, barley and rice flour tortillas shredded as they rolled, and cornmeal doesn't work unless you use limed corn, otherwise known as masa harina. The spelt flour and all the whole wheat flours turned out smooth and tasty tortillas. We were especially delighted by the freshly milled whole wheat flour. It had a sweet, fresh flavor without a hint of the bitterness you often find with whole wheat. We did need to give it a bit more water to get a comparable dough, and it tended to absorb even more as it sat. The baked tortillas, though, were wonderful—sweet, soft, chewy and very, very flavorful.

CRACKERS

Crackers were most likely the first bread ever, crisp and unleavened, baked on hot stone. Is it any wonder we love them so much? They're surely part of our DNA—just ask any mother of a teething toddler or a hungry adolescent nosing around the kitchen before dinner's ready. Nothing fits our nibbly appetites quite like a cracker, so it's great to have some whole grain crackers in your snack arsenal. These crackers were a revelation to us: so easy to roll out because of the whole grain, so richly flavored, and they help to fill that little, hungry gap quickly and healthfully.

Whole Wheat Lavash

YIELD: **4 large lavash, 24 servings**
BAKING TEMPERATURE: **450°F**
BAKING TIME: **8 minutes**

The recipe for this large, ultrathin cracker comes from Jeffrey Hamelman, director of the King Arthur Flour Bakery. The cayenne pepper intensifies the crisp texture with a vibrant snap of flavor—the terrific accompaniment for creamy dips and cool cocktails on the deck. Though the dough must be rolled extremely thin, it's extensible enough to roll out by hand with just a bit of patience.

> 1 cup (4 ounces) traditional whole wheat flour
> 1 cup (4¼ ounces) unbleached all-purpose flour
> 1 cup (3¾ ounces) unbleached pastry flour
> 2 teaspoons sugar
> 1½ teaspoons salt
> 1½ teaspoons instant yeast
> ½ teaspoon cayenne pepper
> 4 tablespoons (½ stick, 2 ounces) unsalted butter, softened
> ⅔ to ¾ cup (5⅜ to 6 ounces) water
> Seeds and/or coarse salt for topping

TO MAKE THE DOUGH: Combine the dry ingredients and softened butter in the bowl of an electric mixer fitted with a dough hook. With the mixer set to the slowest speed, add only enough water to bring the dry ingredients together into a very stiff dough. Mix for 2 minutes on the slowest speed, and then mix for 2 minutes more at the next higher speed. At this point the dough will still be stiff, but it'll have smoothed out considerably. Remove the dough from the mixer and divide it into fourths; cover with plastic wrap and chill for 1 to 2 hours.

GET OUT YOUR PASTA MACHINE

The original instructions for lavash included using a mechanical sheeter to roll the dough to a thickness of 1 millimeter; a sheeter is a handy tool in the bakery, but one that simply doesn't exist in the home kitchen. The sheeter in our bakery quickly rolls large quantities of dough for a variety of purposes, from croissants to piecrust to sugar cookies. Is there anything in a home kitchen that might accomplish the same task of getting a dough super thin? We decided to try the pasta machine, and with very little effort, we had thin, even sheets of crackers. You'll want to have some flour on hand to help the dough through the machine initially. Once you begin rolling it thinner, you'll have to cut the pieces of dough to lengths that will fit your baking sheets, and of course the finished crackers won't be nearly as wide as the hand-rolled crackers. Still, it's a great shortcut for the right cracker doughs—look for doughs that aren't too soft, and get rolling!

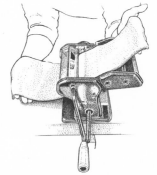

The sheeter in a bakery rolls large amounts of dough to an even width. At home, a pasta machine does the same, in miniature.

Preheat the oven to 450°F.

TO SHAPE THE CRACKERS: When you're ready to roll, lightly dust your work surface with flour. Unwrap one piece of dough and place it on the floured surface. Lightly dust your rolling pin with flour and roll the dough into a piece approximately 11 x 17 inches. The dough will be very thin, but you'll need very little flour to roll it out, as it's not at all sticky. In fact, a bit of stick on the surface will really help you get the piece large and thin enough to fit a half-sheet pan. (If you have too much flour on the surface, the dough will skid across it, rather than expanding as you roll.) If the dough shrinks back while you're rolling, set the pin down for a few minutes before returning to it. You want to aim for a smooth sheet of dough that is very thin—imagine 1 millimeter, even if you don't quite make it that far.

TO BAKE THE CRACKERS: Once the dough is thin enough, and approximately the shape of your baking sheet, place it on the ungreased, parchment-lined pan. Lightly brush the surface of the dough with water, but not all the way out to the edges, or they may crisp too quickly in the oven. Sprinkle the dough with a mix of seeds and/or herbs (sesame, caraway and poppy are nice), and coarse salt if you like, and lightly press them into the surface with your hands.

Press the seeds into the dough so they don't fall off when you take the crackers out of the oven.

Bake the lavash until it begins to brown, 8 minutes. It's best to bake the lavash one sheet at a time—if you place one above the other in the oven, the lower one doesn't brown evenly. While one sheet is baking, you'll have enough time to roll out another piece of dough.

Remove the lavash from the oven and let cool completely before serving. The large sheets make a dramatic presentation, but you may also break them into pieces for storage. Store in airtight containers.

NUTRITION INFORMATION PER SERVING ($1/6$ CRACKER, 26G): 5g whole grains, 70 cal, 2g fat, 2g protein, 11g complex carbohydrates, 1g dietary fiber, 5mg cholesterol, 134mg sodium, 39mg potassium, 20RE vitamin A, 3mg calcium, 30mg phosphorus.

Rosemary Flatbread

YIELD: 8 large pieces, 32 servings
BAKING TEMPERATURE: 475°F
BAKING TIME: 4 to 6 minutes

This crisp, unleavened flatbread makes a beautiful, bubbly cracker fragrant with olive oil and fresh rosemary. Our bakery director, Jeffrey Hamelman, developed the recipe especially for this book, and when he brought the large, dramatic crackers down, we couldn't stop eating them! It takes a bit of patience to roll them thin, but it's well worth the effort.

1 cup plus 2 tablespoons (4$1/2$ ounces) traditional whole wheat flour
1$1/4$ cups (5$5/8$ ounces) durum flour
1$1/3$ cups (5$1/2$ ounces) unbleached all-purpose flour
1$1/2$ to 2 tablespoons chopped fresh rosemary
2 teaspoons salt
1 cup (8 ounces) water
3 tablespoons (1$1/4$ ounces) olive oil

TO MIX THE DOUGH: Attach the dough hook to your mixer. Combine the flours, rosemary and salt in a large mixer bowl. Add the water and olive oil and knead until you have a stiff, smooth dough, about 5 minutes—just long enough to bring it together. You may need to finish the kneading by hand to get the dough completely smooth. Wrap the dough in plastic and chill for 1 hour.

Preheat the oven and a baking stone to 475°F.

TO ROLL THE DOUGH: Unwrap the chilled dough, and divide it into 8 equal pieces. As you roll out each piece, keep the remaining pieces covered with plastic so they don't dry out. Working with one piece at a time, place the dough on a very lightly floured surface. You should only need a couple teaspoons of flour to roll out all 8 pieces; too much flour will make the dough skid across the surface. Lightly flour your rolling pin, and roll the piece until it's as thin as you can get it, to a rough circle 10 to 12 inches in diameter. Flip the dough frequently to keep it from sticking. You may need to let it rest part way through to get the circle large enough.

TO BAKE THE CRACKERS: When you've finished rolling the dough, place it on a piece of parchment paper and mist the surface lightly with water. Sprinkle with coarse salt and seeds, if desired, and slide the flatbread, parchment and all, onto the baking stone. Bake until the flatbread has bubbled and lightly browned, 4 to 6 minutes. Be sure the bread is browned. If it's not, it isn't fully baked, and the crackers won't be crisp. Remove the flatbread from the oven, and repeat the process with the other pieces. You can get a good rhythm going, rolling one piece while another one bakes.

Let the crackers cool completely before serving, and store leftovers airtight to keep them crisp.

NUTRITION INFORMATION PER SERVING (26G): 4g whole grains, 68 cal, 2g fat, 2g protein, 12g complex carbohydrates, 1g dietary fiber, 134mg sodium, 56mg potassium, 1mg iron, 5mg calcium, 57mg phosphorus.

Multi-Seed Crackerbread

YIELD: 8 crackers, about 24 servings
BAKING TEMPERATURE: 450°F
BAKING TIME: 7 to 10 minutes

This recipe comes from our dear friend Lora Brody, author of numerous cookbooks, one of our favorite teachers at The Baking Education Center and baker extraordinaire. Crackerbread is extremely quick and easy to make, and packs a punch of aromatic flavor from the seed blend that gets rolled right into the dough. A little sturdier than the lavash (p. 156), it's great with your chunkiest dips!

1 cup (4 ounces) traditional whole wheat flour
1 cup (4¼ ounces) unbleached all-purpose flour
½ cup (1⅞ ounces) whole rye (pumpernickel) flour
½ cup (2⅜ ounces) whole yellow cornmeal
2 teaspoons salt
2 tablespoons (⅞ ounce) olive oil
1 cup (8 ounces) water
½ cup (2½ ounces) assorted seeds, such as sesame, poppy, fennel, caraway and anise
2 tablespoons assorted dried herbs, such as rosemary, basil, dill, tarragon and thyme

1 teaspoon freshly ground black pepper

1 tablespoon coarse salt (optional; use it if you like a salty, crunchy cracker)

Preheat the oven to 450°F, with the rack in the center position. Line a baking sheet with parchment paper.

TO MAKE THE DOUGH: Combine the flours, cornmeal and salt in a medium bowl or your food processor fitted with the metal blade. Mix in the olive oil thoroughly, then add the water. You may not need the entire cup of water, so hold back a couple tablespoons and check the texture. It should be stiff, not crumbly. Turn the dough out onto a floured board and knead it until it's a stiff yet supple ball of dough. You can feel it get supple as you're kneading. Add more all-purpose flour if the dough is too wet. This dough does not require a long kneading period—just enough time to get it to hold together well. Combine the seeds, herbs, pepper and coarse salt, if using, in a small bowl.

TO SHAPE AND BAKE THE CRACKERBREAD: Divide the dough into 8 equal pieces and cover them with plastic wrap. Working with one piece at a time, scatter about 1 tablespoon of the seed mixture on the work surface. Press the dough onto the seed mixture, and begin to roll it out with a rolling pin. If the dough sticks, flip it over, apply more seeds and continue rolling.

The goal is to get the dough as thin as possible and impregnated with lots of seeds. Once you have the dough as thin as you can get it, place it on a prepared baking sheet. You may find it easier to finish the rolling right on the baking sheet.

Bake the crackerbread until the top is medium brown, 7 to 10 minutes. Cool completely on wire racks before serving.

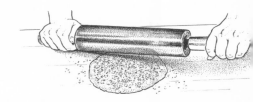

Rolling the dough directly on the seeds assures they'll bake right into the cracker.

NUTRITION INFORMATION PER SERVING (30G): 10g whole grains, 74 cal, 2g fat, 2g protein, 12g complex carbohydrates, 2g dietary fiber, 269mg sodium, 84mg potassium, 3RE vitamin A, 1mg iron, 28mg calcium, 63mg phosphorus.

Crispy Rye Crackers

YIELD: 6 dozen crackers
BAKING TEMPERATURE: 325°F
BAKING TIME: 18 to 23 minutes

These quick, easy to make crackers are bold in flavor, but have a remarkably light texture. They make great open-faced sandwiches—a little cream cheese and smoked salmon, some corned beef and Swiss, or maybe garlicky hummus and sliced tomato, and you're set for a hearty snack or a light meal.

> 1 cup (3¾ ounces) whole rye (pumpernickel) flour
> 1 cup (4¼ ounces) unbleached all-purpose flour
> 1 tablespoon cocoa powder
> 1 teaspoon salt
> 4 tablespoons (½ stick, 2 ounces) butter
> 3 tablespoons (⅞ ounce) caraway seeds
> ½ cup (4 ounces) water
> 1 tablespoon molasses
> Additional salt for sprinkling (optional)

Preheat the oven to 325°F. Lightly grease baking sheets or line with parchment paper.

TO MAKE THE DOUGH: Combine the flours, cocoa and salt in a large bowl. Cut in the butter until the mixture is crumbly, using your fingers, a pastry blender or fork or a mixer. Add the caraway seeds and toss to mix.

Combine the water and molasses in a measuring cup and stir to mix. Gradually add the liquid to the dry ingredients, mixing till you can gather the dough into a cohesive ball.

TO SHAPE AND BAKE THE CRACKERS: Divide the dough into 3 pieces; roll it out, one piece at a time, till it's 1/16 inch thick, being sure to flour underneath when necessary so the dough doesn't stick to the work surface.

Use a baker's bench knife, a sharp knife, a pizza wheel or a square cookie cutter to cut the dough into 2-inch squares. Transfer the squares to prepared baking sheets.

Bake the crackers until they begin to brown and smell toasty, 18 to 23 minutes. Remove the crackers from the oven, transfer to a rack and cool completely before serving. Store in airtight containers.

NUTRITION INFORMATION PER SERVING (4 CRACKERS, 30G): 6g whole grains, 77 cal, 3g fat, 2g protein, 10g complex carbohydrates, 1g sugar, 2g dietary fiber, 7mg cholesterol, 121mg sodium, 88mg potassium, 26RE vitamin A, 1mg iron, 14mg calcium, 60mg phosphorus.

Steel-Cut Oat Crackers

YIELD: **About 5 dozen crackers**
BAKING TEMPERATURE: **350°F**
BAKING TIME: **12 to 15 minutes**

This is a delightfully simple cracker with a nice nubbly quality from the steel-cut oats. Oat flour and rolled oats make for crackers that just won't crisp, but the steel-cut variety lends the flavor of oats without sacrificing the crackery texture. These are very easy to make and a delicious way to use up leftover cereal!

½ cup (2 ounces) whole wheat flour, traditional or white whole wheat
½ cup (1⅔ ounces) whole wheat pastry flour
½ cup (2 ounces) whole barley flour
½ cup (2⅛ ounces) unbleached all-purpose flour
1 teaspoon baking powder
1 teaspoon salt
3 tablespoons (1½ ounces) unsalted butter, cut into bits
½ cup (4½ ounces) cooked steel-cut oats
4 to 6 tablespoons (2 to 3 ounces) water

Preheat the oven to 350°F. Lightly grease baking sheets or line with parchment paper.

TO MAKE THE CRACKER DOUGH: Combine the flours with the baking powder and salt in a medium bowl. Cut in the butter as you would for piecrust, mixing until the mixture is crumbly. Next cut in the cooked oats and mix until they're well distributed. Begin adding the water, mixing until the dough begins to hold together. You may need more or less water, depending on the density of your oat porridge. Gather and squeeze the dough into a ball, and divide it in half. Cover the half you're not using with plastic wrap to keep it from drying out.

TO SHAPE THE CRACKERS: Roll half the dough into a rectangle ¹⁄₁₆-inch thick. Use a baker's bench knife, a sharp knife, a pizza wheel or a square cookie cutter to cut the dough into 2-inch squares. Transfer the squares to prepared baking sheets, placing them quite close together; they won't expand. Repeat with the remaining dough. You may reroll the scraps for these crackers one time to make another sheet. If you reroll more than once, your crackers will be tough.

TO BAKE THE CRACKERS: As soon as you've filled a baking sheet with crackers, begin baking them. These crackers brown more evenly if you bake them one sheet at a time. Bake until they're a deep, golden brown, 12 to 15 minutes. Remove the crackers from the oven and transfer them to a wire rack to cool completely.

NUTRITION INFORMATION PER SERVING (4 CRACKERS, 34G): 11g whole grains, 81 cal, 3g fat, 2g protein, 12g complex carbohydrates, 2g dietary fiber, 7mg cholesterol, 167mg sodium, 49mg potassium, 23RE vitamin A, 1mg iron, 28mg calcium, 772mg phosphorus.

Cheese Crackers

YIELD: 200 crackers

BAKING TEMPERATURE: 325°F

BAKING TIME: 8 to 10 minutes

These crackers are a toned-down, multi-grain version of the crackers you buy in the box. If you crave the neon orange, or if you can't find Vermont Cheddar powder, use two cheese-powder packets from boxed macaroni and cheese and omit the dry milk and salt from the recipe.

$\frac{1}{3}$ cup (1$\frac{1}{8}$ ounces) whole wheat pastry flour

$\frac{1}{3}$ cup (1$\frac{3}{8}$ ounces) whole barley flour

$\frac{1}{2}$ cup (2 ounces) unbleached bread flour

1 tablespoon dry milk

1 teaspoon baking powder

$\frac{1}{2}$ teaspoon baking soda

$\frac{1}{4}$ teaspoon salt

$\frac{1}{8}$ teaspoon paprika

$\frac{1}{2}$ cup (2 ounces) Vermont Cheddar powder

6 tablespoons ($\frac{3}{4}$ stick, 3 ounces) unsalted butter, chilled

$\frac{1}{4}$ cup (2 ounces) buttermilk

$\frac{1}{4}$ teaspoon salt mixed with 1 tablespoon cheese powder for topping (optional)

TO MAKE THE DOUGH: Sift together the flours, dry milk, baking powder, baking soda, salt, paprika and cheese powder in a large bowl or a food processor. Cut in the butter, using a pastry blender or the metal blade of the food processor, until the mixture is a fine meal. Add the buttermilk and mix until the dough comes together—it'll be very moist and sticky. Turn out the dough onto a floured board and knead lightly for a minute or two, incorporating extra flour as needed to keep the dough from sticking to the surface. Pat the dough into 2 flat rounds, wrap in plastic and chill for 30 minutes.

Preheat the oven to 325°F.

TO SHAPE THE CRACKERS: Remove one piece of dough from the refrigerator and place it on a generously floured surface. Using a floured rolling pin, roll the dough into a large square. You'll want to make this very thin—no more than $\frac{1}{16}$ inch thick. As you roll, be sure to lift, turn and reflour frequently. The dough will be very tender and sticky, but be sure to roll it thin enough. Trim the edges using a pizza cutter or sharp knife and cut the dough into 1-inch squares.

TO BAKE THE CRACKERS: Place the squares close together on a baking sheet lined with parchment paper. Use a cake tester to poke a small hole in the center of each cracker.

Bake the crackers until they begin to brown around the edges, 8 to 10 minutes. Remove the crackers from the oven and cool on racks. Repeat the rolling and baking process with the remaining dough.

After the crackers have cooled completely, toss them in the salt and cheese powder to coat them lightly, if desired.

NUTRITION INFORMATION PER SERVING (20 CRACKERS, 29G): 7g whole grains, 117 cal, 9g fat, 3g protein, 8g complex carbohydrates, 1g dietary fiber, 22mg cholesterol, 397mg sodium, 78mg potassium, 63RE vitamin A, 1mg iron, 98mg calcium, 117mg phosphorus.

A cake tester or a darning needle works well for poking holes into the center of each cracker.

Wheat Thins

YIELD: About 13 dozen crackers
BAKING TEMPERATURE: 400°F
BAKING TIME: 5 to 7 minutes

These crisp little wheat crackers with a hint of vanilla sweetness shatter the myth of "heavy" whole wheat. They're so light, it's impossible to stop eating them. Every time we made them, they disappeared—we had to hide some to test how long they'd stay crisp!

1¼ cups (5 ounces) whole wheat flour, traditional or white whole wheat
1½ tablespoons sugar
½ teaspoon salt
¼ teaspoon paprika
4 tablespoons (½ stick, 2 ounces) butter
¼ cup (2 ounces) water
¼ teaspoon vanilla
Additional salt for topping (optional)

TO MAKE THE DOUGH: Combine the flour, sugar, salt and paprika in a medium bowl. Cut the butter into small pieces and mix it in thoroughly, using your fingers, a pastry blender, a mixer or a food processor. Combine the water and vanilla, and add to the flour mixture, mixing until smooth.

Preheat the oven to 400°F. Lightly grease baking sheets or line with parchment paper.

TO ROLL AND CUT THE DOUGH: Divide the dough into 4 pieces; keep the other pieces covered while you work with one at a time. Lightly flour your work surface and your rolling pin and roll the piece of dough into a large rectangle, which should be at least 12 inches square when trimmed. Keep your pin and the surface of your dough evenly floured. Flip the dough frequently to keep it from sticking, but too much flour will make it difficult to roll. Keep rolling until the dough is as thin as you can get it without tearing, at least $\frac{1}{16}$ inch thick. Trim the dough to even the edges and use a pizza cutter or a sharp knife to cut the piece into squares approximately $1\frac{1}{2}$ inches wide. Transfer the squares to a prepared baking sheet; you can crowd them together, as they don't expand while baking. Sprinkle the squares lightly with salt, if desired. Repeat with the remaining pieces of dough. Save the scraps under plastic wrap and reroll them all at once just one time.

TO BAKE THE CRACKERS: Bake the crackers, one sheet at a time, until crisp and browned, 5 to 7 minutes. If some of the thinner crackers brown too quickly, remove them and return the remaining crackers to the oven to finish baking. These crackers bake quickly, so watch them closely—even 30 seconds can turn them from golden brown to toast! Remove the crackers from the oven and cool on the pan or on a plate; they cool quickly. These crackers will stay crisp for several days, but are best stored in airtight containers.

NUTRITION INFORMATION PER SERVING (20 CRACKERS, 29G): 18g whole grains, 101 cal, 5g fat, 2g protein, 11g complex carbohydrates, 2g sugar, 2g dietary fiber, 13mg cholesterol, 108mg sodium, 64mg potassium, 48RE vitamin A, 1mg iron, 7mg calcium, 53mg phosphorus.

Sesame Crackers

YIELD: About 4 dozen (2-inch-square) crackers
BAKING TEMPERATURE: 325°F
BAKING TIME: 15 to 18 minutes

These crisp, nutty crackers came to us from Richard Miscovich, who worked in our bakery and Baking Education Center and is an instructor at Johnson & Wales University. He developed these for a class he taught on artisan baking, and he agreed to let us fiddle with the recipe a bit to come up with this tasty whole grain version.

1 cup (4 ounces) white whole wheat flour
$\frac{1}{2}$ cup (1$\frac{5}{8}$ ounces) whole wheat pastry flour
1 tablespoon sugar
1 teaspoon baking powder
$\frac{1}{2}$ teaspoon salt
3 tablespoons (1$\frac{1}{2}$ ounces) unsalted butter, chilled
5 tablespoons (1$\frac{1}{2}$ ounces) toasted sesame seeds
$\frac{1}{3}$ cup (2$\frac{5}{8}$ ounces) milk
1 teaspoon hot sesame oil (optional)

Preheat the oven to 325°F. Line baking sheets with parchment paper.

TO MAKE THE DOUGH: Combine the flours, sugar, baking powder and salt in a medium bowl. Cut in the butter using a pastry blender until the mixture is the texture of cornmeal. Add the sesame seeds and toss to combine. Combine the milk and sesame oil, if using, and add to the flour mixture, mixing just until the dough comes together.

TO ROLL OUT THE CRACKERS: Working with one half at a time, roll out the dough on a lightly floured surface until it is 1/16 inch thick. If you use too much flour, the dough will slip across the surface. Using a pastry wheel, cut the crackers into 1-inch squares, or cut them into shapes using decorative cutters. You may reroll the scraps once—after that, the cracker dough is too tough to get thin enough. Place the crackers on prepared baking sheets.

TO BAKE THE CRACKERS: Bake until the crackers are golden brown—darker is more flavorful but don't let them get too dark—15 to 18 minutes. Remove them from the oven, and let them cool completely before serving so they'll be crisp. Store in airtight containers.

NUTRITION INFORMATION PER SERVING (4 CRACKERS, 31G): **13g whole grains,** 107 cal, 5g fat, 3g protein, 12g complex carbohydrates, 1g sugar, 3g dietary fiber, 8mg cholesterol, 125mg sodium, 88mg potassium, 33RE vitamin A, 1mg iron, 48mg calcium, 128mg phosphorus.

VARIATION: *These are also wonderful made with barley flour in place of some of the whole wheat flour. Simply substitute 1/3 cup whole barley flour for 1/2 cup of the whole wheat pastry flour. The barley flour adds a mild sweetness and a slightly sandy texture.*

A CRACKER'S BEST FRIEND

If you own a food processor, get it on your counter when it's time to make crackers or any dough where you're cutting fat into flour. With a quick press of your finger, that laborious task is done! Pour in the liquid, and your dough is finished and ready to roll and cut. The same is true for tortillas, piecrust, even scones. The key to success is not to over-process the dough. Process the fat and flour for just a few seconds and check to see the size of the chunks; stop processing a little sooner than you would if you were doing it by hand, since the fat will be cut some more when you add the liquid. Pay close attention the first few times you use the food processor, and you'll soon have a sense of how long it takes—never more than a minute or two to have a perfectly mixed dough. In these days of tight schedules and multitasking, the speed and simplicity of a food processor can really make the difference between making homemade or being forced to accept store-bought.

Graham Crackers

YIELD: 6 dozen (3-inch) crackers
BAKING TEMPERATURE: 350°F
BAKING TIME: 12 to 15 minutes

No book on whole grains would be complete without a recipe for graham crackers, an invention of Sylvester Graham, one of the early proponents of whole wheat flour. The graham crackers we find in the grocery store today have very little whole grain flour left in them. This version, using barley flour to add crispness, is mostly whole grain.

> 1 cup (4 ounces) whole wheat flour, traditional or white whole wheat
> ½ cup (2 ounces) whole barley flour
> ½ cup (2⅛ ounces) unbleached all-purpose flour
> ¼ cup (1⅞ ounces) packed light or dark brown sugar
> ¼ cup (1¾ ounces) granulated sugar
> 1 teaspoon baking powder
> 1 teaspoon ground cinnamon
> ½ teaspoon salt
> ¼ teaspoon ground cloves
> ½ cup (1 stick, 4 ounces) unsalted butter, chilled
> ¼ cup (2 ounces) milk
> Cinnamon-sugar (optional)

Combine flours, sugars, baking powder, cinnamon, salt and cloves in a mixing bowl. Cut the chilled butter into the dry ingredients until very crumbly. Add the milk and combine until you have a stiff dough—you may need to add a bit more or less milk. If using white whole wheat, use a little less milk because the flour will absorb less. Knead the dough lightly to be sure it's smooth, cut it into 2 pieces and flatten each into a rectangle. Wrap the pieces in plastic wrap and chill until firm, about 1 hour (or overnight, if it's more convenient).

Preheat the oven to 350°F. Lightly grease baking sheets or line with parchment paper.

Working with one piece of dough at a time, turn it out onto a floured surface and roll it till it's about ¹⁄₁₆ inch thick; the thinner you can roll it, the crispier the crackers. Be sure your rolling surface and pin are well floured; you may want to roll this dough directly onto a piece of parchment paper, as it's difficult to transfer it to your baking sheet. When you're done rolling, and you've trimmed the edges, you should have a piece of dough about 9 x 12 inches. The scraps may be rerolled into a third rectangle.

Cut the dough into 3-inch squares, then cut each square in half. Prick the crackers several times with a fork, or a dough docker and place the crackers on prepared baking sheets.

If you've rolled onto parchment paper, this step will be a breeze. If you like, sprinkle the tops of the crackers with cinnamon-sugar.

Bake the crackers until they're lightly browned (they'll brown more quickly with the cinnamon sugar on top!), 12 to 15 minutes. Remove the crackers from the oven, transfer to a rack, and let cool completely before serving.

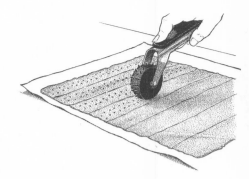

A dough docker makes even holes and does the job much more quickly than a fork.

NUTRITION INFORMATION PER SERVING (4 CRACKERS, 29G): 9g whole grains, 116 cal, 6g fat, 2g protein, 10g complex carbohydrates, 6g sugar, 2g dietary fiber, 15mg cholesterol, 84mg sodium, 55mg potassium, 52RE vitamin A, 1mg iron, 32mg calcium, 60mg phosphorus.

VARIATION: ANIMAL GRAHAMS *These crackers may be cut into animal shapes for children. Roll out the dough to ⅛ inch thick, and cut the shapes directly on a piece of parchment paper. You may bake the animals without docking as long as the crackers are less than 4 inches in length or width. The larger crackers may take a minute or two longer to bake.*

CRUST OR CRACKER?

Some cracker recipes bear a striking similarity to piecrust recipes. They call for flour, fat and water, and often the instructions include cutting the fat into the flour as you might for a piecrust. It's really no accident: there's a distinct connection. Piecrusts used to be quite a bit tougher than they are now—they were originally a breadlike case for meat, fruit or vegetables. They had much less fat in them, and the focus was really on the filling. Most likely the first pies used leftover dough, leavened or unleavened, to enclose the filling. With a bit more fat, many of these crackers could serve as a crust, and you often see crumbled crackers held together by melted butter masquerading as piecrust. Keep the link in mind while you make your crackers; though they don't need to be as light and tender as a piecrust, the same principles apply—cold fat, a light hand and a quick bake will turn out tender bits of crustlike crackers.

Chocolate Graham Crackers

YIELD: **About 4 dozen (3-inch-square) crackers**
BAKING TEMPERATURE: **350°F**
BAKING TIME: **12 to 14 minutes**

It's fun to re-create these childhood favorites, because you can make them as chocolaty as you like. We found the addition of barley flour made for perfectly crisp grahams. The sugar on top makes a pretty presentation—get out the milk and start dunking!

1 cup (4 ounces) whole barley flour
1 cup (4¼ ounces) unbleached all-purpose flour
½ cup (2 ounces) traditional whole wheat flour
1 cup (3 ounces) Dutch-process cocoa
1 cup (7½ ounces) packed light or dark brown sugar
1 teaspoon baking powder
½ teaspoon salt
½ cup (1 stick, 4 ounces) unsalted butter, chilled
⅓ cup (2⅝ ounces) milk
¼ cup (3 ounces) honey
1 tablespoon vanilla
Granulated sugar for topping (optional)

TO MAKE THE DOUGH: Combine the flours, cocoa, brown sugar, baking powder and salt in a food processor fitted with a metal blade or a mixing bowl using the paddle attachment. Cut the butter into chunks and cut into the dry ingredients, using the metal blade of your processor or the paddle attachment of your mixer. Stir together the milk, honey and vanilla and stir into the flour mixture. If necessary, knead the dough gently (without any additional flour) until it is smooth. It will still be quite sticky. Divide the dough into 2 pieces and shape into flat, square disks. Wrap the disks in plastic wrap and chill for 1 hour.

Preheat the oven to 350°F. Line baking sheets with parchment paper.

TO SHAPE THE CRACKERS: On a lightly floured surface, using one piece of dough at a time, roll out the dough to a large rectangle approximately the size of your baking pan. You'll need to flour the pin and the surface generously, and turn the dough frequently to keep it from sticking. This is a very tender dough, and you may want to roll it out directly onto a sheet of parchment paper. Once it's rolled to a piece approximately 12 x 15 inches, it should be between ⅛ and 1/16 inch thick. Using a pizza cutter or a very sharp knife, cut the dough into 3-inch squares, then cut each square in half. Prick the crackers with the tines of a fork or with a dough docker if you have one. Place the crackers on prepared baking sheets, and sprinkle them with granulated sugar, if you wish.

TO BAKE THE CRACKERS: Bake the crackers until the edges are firm, 12 to 14 minutes. Let cool completely before serving. Store in airtight containers. You may recrisp the crackers by placing them in a hot oven for 5 minutes.

NUTRITION INFORMATION PER SERVING (3 CRACKERS, 27G): 11g whole grains, 97 cal, 3g fat, 2g protein, 8g complex carbohydrates, 9g sugar, 2g dietary fiber, 8mg cholesterol, 48mg sodium, 112mg potassium, 29RE vitamin A, 1mg iron, 24mg calcium, 50mg phosphorus, 2mg caffeine.

YEAST BREADS

Of all the baked goods you might consider making with whole grains, yeast bread is probably the first that comes to mind. Bread does have that history: the first leavened loaves baked, purportedly almost 10,000 years ago, were nothing but whole grains and water. It wasn't until Greek and Roman times that "white flour" (flour with some of its bran sifted out) became a status symbol, available only to the elite. The battle pitting health against flavor has raged ever since. We know whole grain flour is more nutritious, but we still crave the taste of refined white flour.

We crave it because that's what we're used to; that's what most of us grew up with. Along the way we may have tried whole grain breads that were dense, dry and strong-flavored, baked at home or at a corner bakery as an attempt at more healthful nutrition. On the other end of the spectrum, now we have available to us, on grocery store shelves, artificially colored, additive-loaded, squishy whole grain sandwich loaves. We're here to show you that there's lots of fertile ground in between, and it yields wonderful whole grain bread: moist loaves with great texture and, most important, complex, rich flavor.

So rid your mind of the concept of "doorstop loaves." Everything from soft sandwich bread to artisan hearth loaves to the stickiest sticky buns ever can be successfully (and deliciously) made with whole grains. Try these breads. You might just find the mild flavor of white flour boring in comparison!

How to make a loaf of bread

There are numerous paths to a great loaf of whole grain yeast bread. The basic ingredients—whole grain flour, yeast, salt and the liquid to bring them to life—can take all manner of incarnations. Choose from a wide array of flours and different types of yeast; add water or beer, juice, milk or heavy cream... just the combinations of those three ingredients alone are limitless. Add a sweetener, spices, fruit, nuts, cheese, vegetables... well, you can see where this is heading. Baking bread allows you incredible leeway in choosing ingredients.

You'll also find that the techniques you use—for mixing, kneading, rising and baking—can take many forms. We're here to explain both ingredients and techniques and to point out some things you should stop and notice along the way.

Flour

If yeast is the soul and inspiration of bread, flour is its body. Without flour, there is no bread—it's that simple. You may choose rye flour or barley flour or freshly ground whole wheat, but whatever your choice, flour makes up the greatest part of any loaf.

Flour is made by milling (grinding) whole grains, then either removing the bran and germ (to make all-purpose or bread flour) or leaving them in (to make whole grain flour). At the heart of each single grain is the vitamin and oil-rich germ, birthplace of the new plant. The germ is surrounded by the starchy endosperm, which provides food for the growing seedling. And the whole package is enclosed in a thin, tough layer of bran, which protects the seed as it's working its internal magic. It's the endosperm that makes up the great majority of any flour, and in the endosperm of some grains are the elements that create gluten, strands of protein that form when you mix flour and liquid, and become elastic when you knead dough. It's gluten, this elastic-strand network, that gives bread the structure and strength it needs to rise.

Whole grain breads have earned a reputation for being low-rising and dense. That's unfair. It's true that 100 percent whole grain bread will not be as light, or rise as high, as bread made from white flour. Of all the grains, only wheat has enough gluten to produce a high-rising bread. Bread made from 100 percent barley or oats or rye or any other whole grain simply won't rise much, if at all; most grains other than wheat have very little ability to form gluten, and some grains simply have no capacity to make it at all. These grains must be combined with some form of wheat flour in order to rise.

Thus it would stand to reason, if you're baking with whole grains, that you would add whole wheat flour to these other grains to make a nice, light loaf. Or, even more effective, use whole wheat flour on its own. But anyone who's tried to bake a light, high-rising 100 percent whole wheat loaf knows that it isn't that simple. While whole wheat contains all the protein it needs to effectively form gluten, it also includes bran, which, in bread dough, is a destructive little culprit. Bran, when milled, breaks into many tiny, tough, sharp-sided pieces. As you knead bread dough, and the elastic network of gluten forms, these sharp bran pieces cut the strands. What wants to become a structure is continually cut into individual pieces. Think of blowing up a balloon made of a single sheet of latex; now think of blowing up a balloon made of 1-inch-square pieces, all haphazardly patched together. Which balloon will inflate faster? Which will be stronger? Bread is the same way.

Since wheat has, by far, the greatest amount of gluten-producing protein, bread made from 100 percent whole wheat flour will still rise fairly well; there isn't enough bran to completely destroy the gluten network. And when you add all-purpose or bread flour—with its gluten-producing capabilities, and no bran to harm it—to a whole grain loaf, you add a great deal of strength. Bread made with some white flour and some whole grain flour will have the wonderful rise of white bread and most of the flavor and nutrition of a whole grain loaf. Bread made with some whole wheat flour and some other whole grain flour will be more dense—which isn't necessarily a bad thing. We sometimes equate "dense" with a loaf that takes on the appearance and flavor of a brick. But dense bread can and should be pleasing in flavor and texture: think raisin rye bread. On the other hand, bread made with 100 percent whole grain flour other than wheat, except in rare instances, will be unpleasantly dense, wet and crumbly.

Many of the recipes in this chapter include some bread flour or all-purpose flour, to lighten the bread's texture. Some with a very high percentage of gluten-poor whole grains include vital wheat gluten, which is gluten that's been developed, dried and ground; it's gluten in its purest form, and gives a much-needed boost to whole grains with little or no gluten-forming capabilities of their own. In addition, some recipes use

---

FLOUR: BRAND MATTERS

All the recipes in this book using all-purpose, bread, or whole wheat flour were developed with King Arthur Flour. If you choose another brand, the recipes may not yield the desired result; this is especially true with bread, where flour is the major component.

Flours are typically compared via their protein level; King Arthur bread flour has a protein level of 12.7%, its all-purpose flour is 11.7% protein and its whole-wheat flour ranges from 13 to 14.2% protein. If you use another brand of flour, use one with those protein levels, give or take one or two tenths of a point. Other national brands of all-purpose flour check in at about 10.5% protein for all-purpose and 11.7% protein for bread flour. The higher the protein, the more liquid the flour will absorb. If you use a lower-protein all-purpose or bread flour, you should decrease the amount of liquid in the recipe slightly, by approximately 1 to 2 tablespoons.

King Arthur produces four whole wheat flours: all natural traditional whole wheat (red wheat), 100% organic whole wheat (red wheat), all natural white whole wheat and 100% organic white whole wheat. White wheat, a different strain than red wheat, is lighter in color and slightly lower in protein; it also has a milder flavor. The recipes in this chapter that call for whole wheat flour were developed using King Arthur All Natural Traditional Whole Wheat Flour, as that's the type most widely available across the country. However, any of the other King Arthur whole wheat flours can be substituted 1:1 by volume.

whole wheat pastry flour in combination with a bit of bread flour. While not appropriate for any loaf that has to rise very high—soft whole wheat pastry flour has much less gluten than hard whole wheat flour—it's appropriate for rolls and buns, where it produces a very tender crumb.

We encourage you to experiment with the amount of all-purpose flour, whole wheat flour and other whole grain flours in your dough, to come up with a ratio that pleases you. We've structured these recipes to allow you to follow them word for word and ingredient for ingredient. In addition, as you work your way through a few of them, we hope you'll feel confident enough to develop your own recipe to create a bread that has the rise, texture, nutritional value and flavor that please you and your family.

Yeast

While flour provides bread with structure and some flavor, it's yeast—a living organism—that builds on that structure and gives the bread depth and complexity of flavor impossible with just flour alone. When you mix yeast with liquid and flour, it awakens and begins to grow. As it grows and multiplies, it gives off both carbon dioxide, which makes bread rise, and alcohol and organic acids, which add to its flavor. Yeast reacts very happily with whole grain flour; the nutrients in the germ feed it as it grows, as does the starch in the endosperm. So whole grain flour is actually a plus, as far as yeast is concerned.

There are two types of yeast you may choose. The first, traditional active dry yeast (picture those yellow packets at the supermarket), must be dissolved in liquid ("proofed") before it's added to the remaining ingredients in the dough. The second, instant yeast, can be added to the dough along with the other dry ingredients, no dissolving necessary. (A third type of yeast, rapid rise, is inappropriate for these recipes, as is old-fashioned compressed or fresh yeast, a clay like form of yeast that also must be dissolved before using.) We call exclusively for instant yeast in this book, simply because it's so easy to use. If you want to use active dry yeast, dissolve it in some of the liquid in the recipe before adding to the dough.

Salt

Salt, as we all know, is a flavor enhancer. Bread made without salt will taste very flat: "cardboardy" is a term we've often heard used. Salt also controls yeast, forcing it to grow more slowly than it would like, which is a good thing. The longer and more slowly the yeast grows, the more flavor it produces in your bread.

Some people try to avoid added salt in their diet. You may certainly make bread without salt, but we don't advise it. The recipes in this chapter are written assuming the specified amount of salt will be used, so if you stray from that amount, there's no guarantee the bread will succeed.

Liquid

Flour needs liquid to form gluten. Liquid can take the form of water, juice, wine, beer or milk (and its various liquid incarnations); eggs, butter or oil; or even a liquid sweetener, e.g., honey or maple syrup.

Water is the all-purpose, foolproof liquid; it brings nothing to the loaf other than itself, where other liquids can bring extra protein, fat, sugar and alcohol, all of which can affect bread's texture and flavor. In general terms, for each cup of flour in a bread recipe, you'll need between ⅓ and ½ cup of liquid to attain a loaf with the proper structure. This is a good ratio to keep in mind, particularly when you're planning to try a new recipe from an unfamiliar book and you want to assess whether it its ingredients sound sensible.

What temperature should the water be? If you do your kneading with the aid of a bread machine, cool tap water is preferable; the machine will heat the dough up as it kneads, and starting with warm water will overheat the dough. If you're kneading with your hands, or with an electric mixer, choose water that's lukewarm and feels like tepid bath water when you test it with your finger.

Sugar

Does yeast need sugar to grow? Yes, it does. But that doesn't mean you have to add sugar to your bread dough. Yeast very efficiently converts flour's starch into sugar. Feel free to add a couple teaspoons of sugar to your dough to give the yeast a jump-start, but it's not necessary.

Fat

Fat—in the form of butter, oil, egg yolks, cheese or ground nuts—tends to give bread a finer crumb, richer mouthfeel, and better keeping qualities. Whole grain flours already include some oil (from the germ), so if you're converting a white-flour bread recipe to whole grain, cut back on the fat by about 1 tablespoon.

And the rest...

Spices and herbs, fruits and nuts, cheese and vegetables—what's your pleasure? Here are some tips for using bread "add-ins":

Spices and herbs: Use to taste. A couple of caveats: Yeast is slowed down by ground cinnamon and by fresh garlic. Add either with a light hand. When making a typical 3-cup-of-flour recipe, use up to about 2½ teaspoons ground cinnamon, or up to 6 medium cloves of garlic, crushed or minced. More than that, and you'll see a noticeable decrease (or slowing down) in the bread's rise.

Fruits: Use dried fruits as is; no presoaking is necessary. Add them after the dough's first rise, and before shaping. Fresh fruit (whole berries, or cut pieces of any fruit) is problematic, due to the liquid it will exude during baking. The best way to use fresh fruit is puréed, as part of the dough, in which case you'll have to account for both the liquid and sugar it adds. You may also choose to top a sweet dough with slices of fresh fruit before baking, as the direct oven heat will evaporate their excess moisture.

Cheese: Grated cheese adds both fat and flavor to bread dough; add it to the other dough ingredients, cutting back on the fat in the recipe (if the recipe isn't written with cheese as an ingredient).

WANT TO ENHANCE YOUR LOAF? ADD MILK AND POTATOES

Nonfat dry milk adds extra protein (but no fat) to your loaf, which will enhance its structure; it's especially helpful in high-rising sandwich loaves. Why not use regular liquid milk? Because with dry milk you get just the milk solids, not the liquid, so you don't upset the recipe's liquid-to-flour ratio when you introduce it. Also, unlike liquid milk, dry milk won't start to turn sour during extra-long rises in warm conditions.

When purchasing dry milk, buy the type that's fine and powdery, and looks like flour, rather than the coarser, granular type; all the weights and volume measurements for nonfat dry milk in this book are based on the finely ground type.

Potato flour—dried ground potatoes—adds starch to your loaf, starch that will attract and hold water, thus making the bread moister, and keeping it fresh longer. Since potato flour can be difficult to find (see a mail-order source, p. 588), the recipes in this chapter call for potato flour or dried potato flakes. If you have potato flour, note that, by volume, 3 tablespoons potato flour equals approximately a heaping $1/2$ cup potato flakes. If measuring by weight, simply substitute potato flour 1:1 for potato flakes. When purchasing potato flakes, buy flakes, not buds or granules. They dissolve easily in your bread, and all the weights and volume measurements for potato flakes in this book are based on flakes, not buds.

Mixing and kneading

OK, let's get started. First, select the tool you'll use for mixing and kneading bread dough: your hands, an electric mixer or a bread machine set on the dough cycle. Some folks choose to use a food processor; we don't include directions for it here, as they can vary so much from machine to machine. If you want to use a processor, follow the manufacturer's directions for mixing and kneading bread dough. Here in the test kitchen we test all three methods continually, and consistently find that bread dough kneaded in a bread machine yields the highest-rising bread with the most pleasing texture. The electric mixer comes in second, and your hands—unless you're very energetic and an experienced kneader—come in third. That's not to say that you can't choose any of the three methods; just that a bread machine set on the dough cycle (which doesn't include baking) probably gives you the most consistently satisfactory loaf.

Normally you will combine all the dough ingredients; the recipe will tell you which, if any, to leave out. Chunks of cheese or nuts, for instance, may be added later, as they might otherwise be broken up during kneading. And fruits are often added later, as their sugar might leach out into the dough, slowing down its development (yeast slows down when faced with an overabundance of sugar). Here are some tips for using each of the main mixing and kneading methods:

To mix and knead dough in the bread machine: Place all the ingredients in the bucket of the machine. Usually the liquids go in first, but check your owner's manual for specific instructions. Program the machine for the dough cycle, and press the start button.

Check the dough after 15 to 20 minutes, to make sure it's looking fairly smooth and elastic; if it isn't, add additional water or flour to adjust its consistency. Let the machine finish kneading the dough and allow the dough to rise in the bread machine; it offers the optimal and consistent temperature for bread-rising.

To mix and knead dough using an electric stand (or hand) mixer: Place all the ingredients in the bowl. Mix, using the flat beater paddle, *just* until the flour and liquid are combined. Turn off the mixer, cover the bowl, and wait 45 minutes. This gives the flour a chance to absorb the liquid; it also gives the yeast a jump-start. After 45 minutes, uncover the bowl switch to the dough hook, and knead the dough for 15 minutes at low speed, stopping to scrape down the bowl and the dough hook midway through. The dough will be quite smooth and satiny, much smoother than if you'd simply mixed and kneaded everything together without a rest.

To make dough by hand: Use a spoon or a dough whisk to mix the ingredients in a large bowl. Give the dough a 45-minute rest, as directed above. Transfer the dough to a lightly floured or lightly oiled work surface or a nonstick kneading mat, and knead till it's smooth and springy, giving it (and yourself) a rest midway through; the amount of time will depend on your kneading technique and your energy.

The first rise

Once the dough is smooth, transfer it to a lightly greased bowl or leave it in the pan of your bread machine. Cover the bowl with plastic wrap, and allow the dough to rise until it has expanded as much as the recipe directs. Some doughs will double in bulk; others will become only slightly puffy. We provide some time guidelines, but the heat of your rising place, the way you kneaded the dough, even the weather (dough rises faster when the barometric pressure drops) affect how fast dough will rise. We've found that dough kneaded in a bread machine will rise just about twice as fast as one kneaded in an electric mixer or by hand. Use the recipe's guidance on what the dough should look like rather than a strict time measurement.

Shaping

Pick the dough up out of the bowl and squeeze it gently to deflate it. Forget what you might have heard about punching the dough or slamming it onto the counter. Yeast is a living thing; it doesn't take well to punching or slamming. All this rough treatment does is a) excite the gluten so that it becomes tough and resistant to shaping, and b) drive the air out of the dough, those same gases you're counting on to make a tall, light loaf. So treat it gently!

Now it's up to you (and the recipe) to decide what shape your bread will take. Sandwich bread? A free-form loaf? A batch of rolls? Work on a lightly greased work surface to divide and/or shape the dough. Transfer the shaped loaf or rolls to the appropriate pan, making sure you've greased the pan or lined it with parchment paper.

The second rise

Once bread dough is shaped, it needs to rise again. Cover the shaped dough with thoroughly greased plastic wrap or a homemade proof cover, which can be anything clear and tall. You can use a large glass or clear plastic bowl, turned upside down over your shaped loaf: finally, here's the perfect use for that tall, clear plastic cover of a large takeout party platter.

Your recipe will tell you how the dough should look at the end of its second rise. Sometimes dough needs to double; sometimes, it'll just become moderately puffy. And sometimes it needs to rise just a bit before going into the oven to complete its rise. Follow your recipe.

A large glass or plastic bowl makes a good proof cover, as does the clear plastic top of a takeout party platter. Use your imagination; you want something clear, so you can check the dough's progress easily, and tall enough that the dough doesn't bump against it as it rises.

Baking

Crusty hearth breads bake for a short amount of time at a high (425°F to 450°F or hotter) temperature. Soft sandwich loaves or sweet breads bake at a lower temperature (350°F to 375°F) for a longer amount of time. A hot, fast bake produces a crisp crust; a slower, cooler bake yields a more tender crust. An exception to this is large breads without much fat or sugar, such as round country loaves or boules. These breads need a lower tempera-

---

THE PERFECTLY BAKED LOAF

What should you do if your bread appears to be perfectly browned, but it's nowhere near ready to come out of the oven, according to the times given in the recipe? This sometimes happens with breads that are high in sugar (especially honey) or fat. It also happens with whole grain loaves, as they're naturally higher in fat, due to the inclusion of germ in the flour. If this seems to be an issue, tent the bread midway through its baking time with a sheet of foil. This will slow down its browning and give the center a chance to bake without the crust burning.

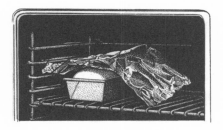

Lay a sheet of foil gently over your baking bread, making sure it covers the entire top surface, but doesn't touch the pan. You don't want to anchor the foil anywhere; that would inhibit the bread's rise in the oven. It needs to sit atop the loaf just as gently as a feather sits on water.

ture and longer time in the oven to bake all the way through; in the process, their crust tends to become thick and chewy, rather than tender.

Your bread is done when its interior temperature registers between 190°F (for most loaves) and 210°F (for heavier, denser country-type loaves). You'll only know that if you use an instant-read thermometer, available at most kitchen stores. You plunge the small tip into the bread and the thermometer registers the internal temperature, without making a huge dent in the top of the loaf. Once the bread reaches that temperature, remove it from the oven and transfer it from its pan to a cooling rack as soon as possible. Cooling bread left in a pan will steam, making the crust rubbery. For sandwich bread, wait a couple of minutes after taking it out of the oven, then turn the loaf out of the pan and run a stick of butter over the top of the hot loaf, if desired. This will give it a soft, buttery crust. To preserve the crisp crust of crunchy hearth loaves, turn off the oven, remove the bread from the pan and set the loaf on the oven rack. Prop the door open a couple of inches and allow the bread to cool in the oven. This prevents steam from migrating from the bread's center and condensing on its crust, which tends to soften the crust.

Enjoy!

Warning! Tempting though it may be, it's better to wait at least 30 minutes before cutting into your bread. Until it has a chance to "set" as it cools a bit, it's very tender. Cutting into bread at this point tends to mar its shape, as well as allow too much moisture to escape, which can result in it becoming stale more quickly. Waiting 30 to 60 minutes allows you to cut a slice of bread, while it's still warm, without compromising the quality of the entire loaf.

Storage

Bread becomes stale when the moisture inside gradually migrates out to the surface of the loaf and evaporates. This process happens most quickly at temperatures between approximately 25°F and 50°F: refrigerator-temperature, more or less. So bread stored in the refrigerator will become stale much more quickly than bread stored on the counter. Bread stays freshest when it's wrapped in plastic after it's completely cool, and stored at room temperature.

When the weather is hot and humid, bread has a tendency to mold; if you're experiencing such weather, your best alternative is the refrigerator, if the bread's going to be around longer than a day. For long-term storage, the freezer is a great option: wrap bread in plastic wrap, then seal it in a zip-top plastic bag, sucking the air out of the bag with a drinking straw before sealing. Or wrap bread in plastic, then wrap tightly in foil. Bread stored like this will last several months in the freezer. To serve, unwrap it and thaw at room temperature. Wrap loosely in foil and bake in a preheated 350°F oven for 6 to 10 minutes; the larger the piece of bread, the longer you'll need to bake it. Serve immediately; as soon as it cools, it'll become stale.

The Easiest 100% Whole Wheat Bread Ever

YIELD: **One 8½ x 4½-inch loaf, 16 servings**

BAKING TEMPERATURE: **350°F**

BAKING TIME: **45 minutes**

If you've never baked yeast bread, but want to dip your toe into the (lukewarm) water, this is the loaf to start with. Unlike most yeast breads, this one isn't kneaded; instead, the very fluid dough is simply beaten in a bowl for several minutes, then spooned into a bread pan. An hour later, it's ready to pop into the oven. The result: a coarse-grained, moist, easy-to-slice loaf a lot like a quick bread. Spread thin slices with flavored cream cheese; the extra fiber in the bread will assuage any guilt you feel about the richness of the cheese!

1¼ **cups (10 ounces) lukewarm water**
¼ **cup (2 ounces) orange juice**
3 **tablespoons (2¼ ounces) molasses**
3 **cups (12 ounces) traditional whole wheat flour**
¼ **cup (1 ounce) nonfat dry milk**
1¼ **teaspoons salt**
2 **teaspoons instant yeast**

Thoroughly grease an 8½ x 4½-inch pan. It's important to grease the pan well, as this bread tends to stick if you don't.

Combine all the ingredients in a large bowl. Beat the mixture vigorously for about 3 minutes; an electric mixer on medium-high speed works well here. Scoop the batter into the prepared pan.

Cover the pan with lightly greased plastic wrap or a proof cover, and let the dough rise for 1 hour; it won't fill the pan. It also won't dome as it rises, but will remain flat across the top. While the batter is rising, preheat the oven to 350°F.

Uncover and bake the bread for about 45 minutes, tenting it with foil after 20 minutes. The bread is done when it's golden brown on top and an instant-read thermometer inserted in the center registers 190°F. Remove it from the oven, and after 5 minutes use a table knife to loosen the edges, then turn it out onto a rack. Brush with melted butter, if desired; this will keep the crust soft. Cool the bread for 30 minutes before slicing.

NUTRITION INFORMATION PER SERVING (1 SLICE, 49G): **21g whole grains,** 95 cal, 4g protein, 17g complex carbohydrates, 3g sugar, 3g dietary fiber, 183mg sodium, 154mg potassium, 2mg vitamin C, 1mg iron, 35mg calcium, 100mg phosphorus.

BEAUTY IS MORE THAN SKIN DEEP

The interior of this moist, tender loaf is the deep orange-gold color of carrot cake or pumpkin bread, a very different color than the typical brown of other whole wheat breads. Because the dough isn't kneaded, and is only mixed briefly, the whole wheat flour doesn't oxidize; i.e., it isn't infused with oxygen. Oxidation changes flour's natural color, so whole wheat bread prepared in this quick, noknead manner is a deeper, richer, more natural color than its kneaded siblings.

SANDWICH LOAVES

The sandwich loaf (a.k.a. pan bread) is the traditional darling of American home bakers. Our rectangular, square-cornered loaf is much less ubiquitous in Europe; only English and Dutch bakers use bread pans on a regular basis, with the rest of the Continent fashioning free-form loaves. France's *pain de mie,* used almost exclusively for toast and stuffing, was actually developed to imitate English pan breads.

Sandwich loaves are ideal for sandwiches (of course), toast, French toast, croutons, bread pudding and various other desserts calling for sliced or cubed bread. These high-rising loaves do, however, present something of a challenge for the whole grain baker: most loaves with a high percentage of whole grains simply aren't able to rise that high. An exception to this is whole wheat, which contains enough gluten to produce a typical tall sandwich loaf. Thus, most of the recipes in this section include at least some whole wheat flour, and many are based entirely on whole wheat. We found the other grains better suited to rolls, flatbreads and other shapes that don't require a significant rise.

So, if you're searching for a great loaf of bread for your favorite sandwich or your stuffed French toast, you've turned to the right section. Break out the peanut butter, get out the jelly, and let's get started!

100% Whole Wheat Sandwich Bread

YIELD: One 8¹/₂ x 4¹/₂-inch loaf, 16 slices
BAKING TEMPERATURE: 350°F
BAKING TIME: 35 minutes

Tender, moist and light yet close-grained, this is the Holy Grail of 100 percent whole wheat breads. This is the loaf you'll find yourself making over and over again—for sandwiches and toast, French toast and bread pudding, any time you want a bread with the texture of a typical white sandwich loaf, and the dark, wheaty color and added fiber and nutrition of whole wheat.

2 tablespoons (1 ounce) orange juice
1 cup (8 ounces) lukewarm water
4 tablespoons (¹/₂ stick, 2 ounces) unsalted butter, cut into 6 pieces
3 cups (12 ounces) traditional whole wheat flour
3 tablespoons (1¹/₄ ounces) sugar
Heaping ¹/₂ cup (1¹/₄ ounces) dried potato flakes or 3 tablespoons (1¹/₄ ounces) potato flour
¹/₄ cup (1 ounce) nonfat dry milk
1¹/₄ teaspoons salt
2¹/₂ teaspoons instant yeast

Combine all the ingredients, and mix and knead them—by hand, mixer or bread machine—until you have a soft, smooth dough. Cover and allow the dough to rise until it's puffy and nearly doubled in bulk, 1 to 2 hours.

Lightly grease an 8¹/₂ x 4¹/₂-inch loaf pan. Gently deflate the dough, and shape it into an 8-inch log. Place it in the prepared pan.

To make a loaf with a braided top, cut off about one-third of the dough. Form the large piece into a loaf, and divide the smaller piece into three equal sections. Roll each section

---

ORANGE JUICE AND WHOLE WHEAT: A HAPPY MARRIAGE

You'll notice that nearly all the recipes in this chapter using whole wheat call for orange juice as part of the liquid. We've discovered that the flavor of orange juice tempers the somewhat tannic flavor (some perceive it as bitter) of whole wheat, without adding any orange flavor of its own. If you don't want to use orange juice, substitute water, but we do think it makes a positive improvement in the taste of the bread.

into a long strand, and braid them together. Lay the braid lengthwise along the top of the loaf before placing it in the pan.

Cover the loaf gently with lightly greased plastic wrap or a proof cover and allow it to rise till it's crowned about 1½ inches over the rim of the pan, 1¼ to 2½ hours. Near the end of the bread's rising time, preheat the oven to 350°F.

Place the log in the pan, tucking the ends underneath, and smoothing the top gently.

Uncover and bake the bread for about 35 minutes, tenting it with foil after 15 minutes. The bread is done when it's golden brown and an instant-read thermometer inserted in the center registers 190°F. Remove it from the oven, and after a minute or so turn it out onto a rack. Brush with melted butter, if desired; this will keep the crust soft. Cool the bread for 30 minutes before slicing.

NUTRITION INFORMATION PER SERVING (1 SLICE, 49G): 21g whole grains, 124 cal, 3g fat, 4g protein, 17g complex carbohydrates, 2g sugar, 3g dietary fiber, 8mg cholesterol, 193mg sodium, 137mg potassium, 26RE vitamin A, 1mg vitamin C, 1mg iron, 33mg calcium, 33mg phosphorus.

Grab the dough in both hands and squeeze it gently to deflate it.

To make a loaf with a braided top, cut off about ⅓ of the dough. Form the large piece into a loaf, and divide the smaller piece into three equal sections.

Roll each section into a long strand, and braid them together. Lay the braid lengthwise along the top of the loaf before placing it into the pan. Tuck the ends of the braid under the loaf before you place it into the loaf pan.

Golden Malted Wheat Bread

YIELD: One 8½ x 4½-inch loaf, 16 servings
BAKING TEMPERATURE: 350°F
BAKING TIME: 35 minutes

This mild-flavored, light-textured loaf is a lovely golden color; malted milk powder and malted wheat give it a rich, slightly sweet flavor. We think you'll enjoy it for peanut butter and jam sandwiches, French toast and grilled cheese, where the sweetness contrasts nicely with sharp cheese, much as it does when you serve Cheddar cheese with hot apple pie.

¾ cup plus 2 tablespoons (7 ounces) lukewarm water

2 tablespoons (1 ounce) orange juice

2 tablespoons (⅞ ounce) vegetable oil

1¾ cups (7 ounces) traditional whole wheat flour

1 cup (4¼ ounces) unbleached all-purpose flour

½ cup (2 ounces) malted wheat flakes or dry Maltex® cereal

2 tablespoons (1 ounce) packed light or dark brown sugar

1¼ teaspoons salt

¼ cup (1¼ ounces) malted milk powder

2 teaspoons instant yeast

Combine all the ingredients, and mix and knead them—by hand, mixer or bread machine—until you have a soft, smooth dough. Cover and allow the dough to rise until it's puffy and nearly doubled in bulk, 1 to 2 hours.

Lightly grease an 8½ x 4½-inch loaf pan. Transfer the dough to a lightly oiled work surface and shape it into an 8-inch log. Place the log in the pan. Cover the pan loosely with greased plastic wrap or a proof cover, and allow the bread to rise until it's crowned about 1½ inches above the edge of the pan, about 1 hour.

Near the end of the bread's rise, preheat the oven to 350°F.

Uncover and bake the bread for about 35 minutes, tenting it with foil after 15 minutes. The bread is done when it's golden brown and an instant-read thermometer inserted in the center registers 190°F. Remove it from the oven, and after a minute or so turn it out onto a rack. Brush with melted butter, if desired; this will keep the crust soft. Cool the bread for 30 minutes before slicing.

NUTRITION INFORMATION PER SERVING (1 SLICE, 44G): 15g whole grains, 111 cal, 2g fat, 4g protein, 20g complex carbohydrates, 2g dietary fiber, 179mg sodium, 95mg potassium, 2RE vitamin A, 1mg vitamin C, 3mg iron, 14mg calcium, 73mg phosphorus.

WHY DOESN'T MY FAVORITE BREAD RECIPE ALWAYS TAKE THE SAME AMOUNT OF LIQUID?

Flour is like a sponge: it absorbs moisture from the air when it's warm and humid. When it's cool and dry in your kitchen, the flour dries out too. So the bread recipe with a perfect balance of liquid and flour during humid months will probably require more liquid in dry months. When making a yeast bread recipe in humid weather, you'll want to keep your eye on the liquid, perhaps start-ing with a tablespoon or so less, to account for flour that's "wet-ter" than it is during the dry season.

 # Sprouted Wheat Sandwich Bread

YIELD: One 9 x 5-inch loaf, 18 servings

BAKING TEMPERATURE: 350°F

BAKING TIME: 40 minutes

This big, high-rising loaf is perfect for oversized sandwiches. Its light texture and mild flavor make it a good match for any kind of filling, from egg salad or ham and cheese to the fanciest Dagwood your imagination can produce! Sprouting the wheat takes some time (see directions and timeline, p. 186) so plan ahead. This bread is well worth the time.

¼ cup (1¾ ounces) wheat berries, sprouted (see sidebar, p. 186) or about ¾ cup
    (3¼ ounces) sprouted wheat berries
1 cup (8 ounces) lukewarm water
3 tablespoons (1½ ounces) orange juice
4 tablespoons (½ stick, 2 ounces) unsalted butter, cut into 6 pieces
2 tablespoons (1½ ounces) honey
2½ cups (10 ounces) traditional whole wheat flour
⅔ cup (2¾ ounces) unbleached bread flour
½ cup (1¾ ounces) old-fashioned rolled oats
1¼ teaspoons salt
2 teaspoons instant yeast

Process the sprouts, water and orange juice in a blender or food processor until the sprouts are finely chopped and the mixture is milky white. Don't be tempted to leave the sprouts whole; though they're soft when you put them into the dough, baking turns them unpleasantly hard and crunchy.

Combine all the ingredients, including the water-sprout mixture, and mix and knead them—by hand, mixer or bread machine—until you have a soft, smooth dough. Cover and allow the dough to rise until it's puffy and nearly doubled in bulk, 1 to 2 hours.

Lightly grease a 9 x 5-inch loaf pan. Gently deflate the dough, and shape it into a 9-inch log. Place it in the prepared pan. Cover it gently with lightly greased plastic wrap or a proof cover, and allow it to rise till it's crowned about 1 inch over the rim of the pan, 1 to 2 hours. Near the end of the bread's rise, preheat the oven to 350°F.

Uncover and bake the bread for about 40 minutes, tenting it with foil after 20 minutes. The bread is done when it's golden brown and an instant-read thermometer inserted in the center registers 190°F. Remove it from the oven, and after a minute or so turn it out onto a rack. Brush with melted butter, if desired; this will keep the crust soft. Cool the bread for 30 minutes before slicing.

NUTRITION INFORMATION PER SERVING (1 SLICE, 51G): **21g whole grains,** 123 cal, 3g fat, 4g protein, 19g complex carbohydrates, 2g sugar, 2g dietary fiber, 7mg cholesterol, 121mg sodium, 104mg potassium, 22RE vitamin A, 12mg vitamin C, 1mg iron, 11mg calcium, 90mg phosphorus.

SPROUTING WHEAT BERRIES

You may have seen sprouted wheat bread at the grocery store. But what is it, exactly? It's simply bread that includes sprouted wheat berries, seeds of the wheat plant that have just begun to germinate. When a seed starts to germinate and prepares for growth, its nutrient level increases; sprouted wheat is an excellent source of magnesium, manganese and selenium, which stimulates the immune system and helps keep us healthy.

You don't have to be an aging hippie to sprout wheat berries. Neither do you need any special equipment. Here's what you do:

Wheat seeds (wheat berries) increase in volume about three-fold when sprouted; for 3 cups of wheat sprouts (enough for about 4 loaves of bread), begin with 1 cup wheat berries. (See Where to Buy, p. 588.). Place the berries in a screwtop jar whose capacity is at least 7 cups; a 2-quart Mason jar is ideal. Add 4 cups cool (60°F to 70°F) water (four times the amount of the berries), and shake well. Soak berries, at room temperature, for 12 hours.

Drain the water, and rinse the berries thoroughly in cool (60°F to 70°F) water. Use lots of water, and high pressure; think of washing your car. You're trying not only to rinse the berries thoroughly, but to infuse them with oxygen and keep them from becoming packed down. Drain the berries as thoroughly as possible; place them in a strainer and toss and shake them till no more water drips out.

Return the drained berries to the jar, set it on its side with the cap set on loosely (don't screw it down at all), and let the berries rest at room temperature, not in direct sunlight, for 8 to 12 hours. After 8 to 12 hours, rinse and drain again; you may see tiny white roots starting to sprout from the ends of the berries. Rinse, drain and let the berries rest one more time for another 8 to 12 hours. Berries are ready to use when the white roots are about as long as the seed itself, about 1/4 inch.

Use sprouts right away or store them in the refrigerator for a day or so. If you plan to store them, gently pat them as dry as possible, to prevent mold, and store in a covered container in the fridge. Enjoy any leftover sprouted wheat in salads.

NOTE: For weekend bread-bakers, here's a sample schedule for sprouting wheat berries:

8 a.m. Friday: Put berries in a jar with water to soak.

8 p.m. Friday: Rinse and drain.

8 a.m. Saturday: Rinse and drain

8 p.m. Saturday: Rinse and drain.

8 a.m. Sunday: Sprouted berries are ready to use.

Honey Sprouted Wheat Bread

YIELD: One 8½ x 4½-inch loaf, 16 servings
BAKING TEMPERATURE: 350°F
BAKING TIME: 40 minutes

This golden loaf, subtly sweetened with a bit more honey than the previous loaf, also features the faint but distinct flavor of sprouted wheat, a fresh, "grassy" taste. Soft and moist, this bread is great toasted, with peanut butter or jam (or both), made into French toast or simply spread with sweet butter.

¼ cup (1¾ ounces) wheat berries, sprouted, or about ¾ cup (3¼ ounces) sprouted
　　wheat berries (see sidebar, p. 186)
⅔ cup (5⅜ ounces) lukewarm water
2 tablespoons (1 ounce) orange juice
¼ cup (3 ounces) honey
2 tablespoons (1 ounce) unsalted butter, cut into 3 pieces
1½ cups (6 ounces) traditional whole wheat flour
1½ cups (6⅜ ounces) unbleached all-purpose flour
1¼ teaspoons salt
2 teaspoons instant yeast

Process the sprouts, water and orange juice in a blender or food processor until the sprouts are chopped and the mixture is milky white. Don't be tempted to leave the sprouts whole; though they're soft when you put them into the dough, baking turns them unpleasantly hard and crunchy.

Combine all the ingredients, including the water-sprout mixture, and mix and knead them—by hand, mixer or bread machine—until you have a soft, smooth dough. Cover and allow the dough to rise until it's puffy and nearly doubled in bulk, 1 to 2 hours.

Lightly grease an 8½ x 4½-inch loaf pan. Gently deflate the dough and shape it into an 8-inch log. Place it in the prepared pan. Cover it gently with lightly greased plastic wrap or a proof cover, and allow it to rise till it's crowned about 1 inch over the rim of the pan, 1 to 1½ hours. Near the end of the bread's rising time, preheat the oven to 350°F.

Uncover and bake the bread for about 40 minutes, tenting it with foil after 20 minutes. The bread is done when it's golden brown and an instant-read thermometer inserted in the center registers 190°F. Remove it from the oven, and after a minute or so turn it out onto a rack. Brush with melted butter, if desired; this will keep the crust soft. Cool the bread for 30 minutes before slicing.

NUTRITION INFORMATION PER SERVING (1 SLICE, 50G): 15g whole grains, 125 cal, 2g fat, 4g protein, 20g complex carbohydrates, 2g sugar, 2g dietary fiber, 4mg cholesterol, 170mg sodium, 87mg potassium, 12RE vitamin A, 1mg vitamin C, 1mg iron, 9mg calcium, 74mg phosphorus.

Walnut Whole Wheat Bread

YIELD: One 8½ x 4½-inch loaf, 16 servings

BAKING TEMPERATURE: 350°F

BAKING TIME: 40 minutes

This 100 percent whole wheat bread features the nutty taste of both the wheat itself, and walnuts or pecans. The fat in the nuts also helps keep the bread tender and fresh. It's great for sandwiches, or try it toasted and spread with jam at breakfast.

3 tablespoons (1½ ounces) orange juice

1 cup (8 ounces) lukewarm water

2 tablespoons (⅞ ounce) vegetable oil

3 cups (12 ounces) traditional whole wheat flour

2 tablespoons (1 ounce) firmly packed light or dark brown sugar

1¼ teaspoons salt

¾ cup (3 ounces) walnuts or pecans, finely chopped or crushed

2½ teaspoons instant yeast

Combine all the ingredients, and mix and knead them—by hand, mixer or bread machine—until you have a soft, smooth dough. Cover and allow the dough to rise until it's puffy and nearly doubled in bulk, 1 to 2 hours.

Lightly grease an 8½ x 4½-inch loaf pan. Gently deflate the dough, and shape it into an 8-inch log. Place it in the prepared pan. Cover it gently with lightly greased plastic wrap or a proof cover, and allow it to rise till it's crowned about 1 inch over the rim of the pan, 1½ to 2½ hours. Near the end of the bread's rising time, preheat the oven to 350°F.

Uncover and bake the bread for about 40 minutes, tenting it with foil after 15 minutes. The bread is done when it's golden brown and an instant-read thermometer inserted into the center registers 190°F. Remove it from the oven, and after a minute or so turn it out onto a rack. Brush with melted butter, if desired; this will keep the crust soft. Cool the bread for 30 minutes before slicing.

> **DON'T TRY TO "FIX THE STICKIES"**
>
> Don't add extra flour to whole grain yeast bread dough in an attempt to make it as smooth and supple as white bread dough. The bran and germ in the whole grain will keep the dough somewhat sticky. If you're having difficulty handling it, lightly oil your hands, rather than adding more flour; additional flour will make your bread dry and heavy.

NUTRITION INFORMATION PER SERVING (1 SLICE, 48G): 21g whole grains, 134 cal, 6g fat, 4g protein, 17g complex carbohydrates, 2g sugar, 3g dietary fiber, 169mg sodium, 132mg potassium, 1mg vitamin C, 1mg iron, 14mg calcium, 97mg phosphorus.

VARIATION: *For a lighter-colored loaf, substitute 2 cups whole spelt flour for 2 cups of the whole wheat flour.*

Micro-Brewery Honey-Wheat Bread

YIELD: One 8½ x 4½-inch loaf, 16 servings
BAKING TEMPERATURE: 350°F
BAKING TIME: 30 to 35 minutes

A pleasant yeasty aroma, reminiscent of the local pub, is the only clue you have to this bread's main liquid ingredient: beer. This moist, light-textured wheat-and-oat bread is lightly sweetened with honey, successfully walking the line between sandwich loaf and sweet bread. It makes marvelous toast and does equally well in a sharp Cheddar grilled cheese sandwich.

¾ cup (6 ounces) amber ale or mild-flavored beer
¼ cup (2 ounces) orange juice
3 tablespoons (2¼ ounces) honey
4 tablespoons (½ stick, 2 ounces) unsalted butter, cut into 6 pieces
1¾ cups (7 ounces) traditional whole wheat flour
½ cup (1¾ ounces) old-fashioned rolled oats
1 cup (4¼ ounces) unbleached all-purpose flour
1¼ teaspoons salt
2¼ teaspoons instant yeast

Combine all the ingredients, and mix and knead them—by hand, mixer or bread machine—until you have a soft, smooth dough. Cover and allow the dough to rise until it's puffy and nearly doubled in bulk, 1 to 2 hours.

Lightly grease an 8½ x 4½-inch loaf pan. Gently deflate the dough, and shape it into an 8-inch log. Place it in the prepared pan. Cover it gently with lightly greased plastic wrap or a proof cover, and allow it to rise till it's crowned about 1½ inches over the rim of the pan, 1½ to 2½ hours. Near the end of the bread's rising time, preheat the oven to 350°F.

Uncover and bake the bread for 30 to 35 minutes, tenting it with foil after 15 minutes. The bread is done when it's golden brown and an instant-read thermometer inserted in the center registers 190°F. Remove it from the oven, and after a minute or so turn it out onto a rack. Brush with melted butter, if desired; this will keep the crust soft. Cool the bread for 30 minutes before slicing.

NUTRITION INFORMATION PER SERVING (1 SLICE, 48G): 17g whole grains, 134 cal, 3g fat, 4g protein, 19g complex carbohydrates, 3g sugar, 2g dietary fiber, 8mg cholesterol, 169mg sodium, 102mg potassium, 25RE vitamin A, 2mg vitamin C, 1mg iron, 10mg calcium, 85mg phosphorus.

Naturally Sweet Wheat Bread

YIELD: **One 8$^{1}/_{2}$ x 4$^{1}/_{2}$-inch loaf, 16 servings**

BAKING TEMPERATURE: **350°F**

BAKING TIME: **35 to 40 minutes**

This bread is tender, sweet, and a delicate beige color. Ground raisins give it extra flavor, and a pretty, flecked color. Rye adds to its taste.

2 tablespoons (1 ounce) orange juice

2 tablespoons (1 ounce) water

2 tablespoons ($^{7}/_{8}$ ounce) vegetable oil

1 tablespoon ($^{3}/_{4}$ ounce) honey

$^{1}/_{4}$ cup (1$^{1}/_{2}$ ounces) raisins, packed

2 tablespoons (1 ounce) firmly packed dark brown sugar

$^{3}/_{4}$ cup (6 ounces) milk, heated to lukewarm

1$^{1}/_{4}$ cups (5 ounces) traditional whole wheat flour

$^{3}/_{4}$ cup (2$^{3}/_{4}$ ounces) medium or white rye flour

1$^{1}/_{2}$ cups (6$^{3}/_{8}$ ounces) unbleached bread flour

1$^{1}/_{2}$ teaspoons salt

2 teaspoons instant yeast

Blend together the orange juice, water, oil, honey, raisins and sugar in a blender or small food processor, processing until the raisins are finely ground. Combine the liquid mixture with the remaining ingredients, and mix and knead them—by hand, mixer or bread machine—until you have a soft, smooth dough. Cover and allow the dough to rise until it's puffy and nearly doubled in bulk, 1 to 2 hours.

Lightly grease an 8$^{1}/_{2}$ x 4$^{1}/_{2}$-inch loaf pan. Gently deflate the dough, and shape it into an 8-inch log. Place it in the prepared pan. Cover it gently with lightly greased plastic wrap or a proof cover, and allow it to rise till it's crowned about 1$^{1}/_{2}$ inches over the rim of the pan, 1 to 2 hours. Near the end of the bread's rise, preheat the oven to 350°F.

Uncover and bake the bread for 35 to 40 minutes, tenting it with foil after 20 minutes. The bread is done when it's golden brown and an instant-read thermometer inserted in the center registers 190°F. Remove it from the oven, and after a minute or so turn it out onto a rack. Brush with melted butter, if desired; this will keep the crust soft. Cool the bread for 30 minutes before cutting it.

NUTRITION INFORMATION PER SERVING (1 SLICE, 48G): **9g whole grains,** 129 cal, 2g fat, 4g protein, 22g complex carbohydrates, 3g sugar, 2g dietary fiber, 1mg cholesterol, 207mg sodium, 121mg potassium, 6RE vitamin A, 1mg vitamin C, 1mg iron, 22mg calcium, 73mg phosphorus.

VARIATION: *Substitute $^{3}/_{4}$ cup pumpernickel flour for the medium or white rye flour. The loaf will be denser and will have more fiber, and it'll take longer to rise and slightly longer to bake.*

Maple-Walnut Oat Bread

YIELD: **One 9 x 5-inch loaf, 18 servings**

BAKING TEMPERATURE: **350°F**

BAKING TIME: **40 to 45 minutes**

Whole wheat and oats are the featured whole grains in this soft, high-rising loaf. Maple sugar and syrup add a hint of sweetness, and the nuttiness of the walnuts is a nice counterpoint. If you don't happily consume the entire loaf before it starts to get stale, use it to make a tasty bread pudding.

Though maple is a flavor beloved by many, it's a hard read in yeast bread; in order for any maple taste at all to come through, it's necessary to add maple flavor. In addition, brushing the top crust with butter and maple syrup as soon as the loaf comes out of the oven helps put that maple flavor right out front.

Dough

1 cup plus 2 tablespoons (9 ounces) lukewarm water

2 tablespoons (1³⁄₈ ounces) maple syrup

4 tablespoons (¹⁄₂ stick, 2 ounces) unsalted butter, cut into 6 pieces

1¹⁄₂ cups (5¹⁄₄ ounces) old-fashioned rolled oats, ground for 30 seconds in a food processor

³⁄₄ cup (3 ounces) traditional whole wheat flour

2 cups (8¹⁄₂ ounces) unbleached all-purpose flour

3 tablespoons (1 ounce) maple sugar or brown sugar (1³⁄₈ ounces)

¹⁄₄ to ¹⁄₂ teaspoon maple flavor, to taste (optional)

1¹⁄₄ teaspoons salt

2¹⁄₂ teaspoons instant yeast

1 cup (4 ounces) chopped walnuts

Glaze

1 tablespoon maple syrup

2 teaspoons unsalted butter, melted

Combine all the dough ingredients, and mix and knead them—by hand, mixer or bread machine—until you have a soft, smooth dough. Cover and allow the dough to rise until it's puffy and nearly doubled in bulk, 1 to 2 hours.

Lightly grease a 9 x 5-inch loaf pan. Gently deflate the dough, and shape it into a 9-inch log. Place it in the prepared pan. Cover it gently with lightly greased plastic wrap or a proof cover, and allow it to rise till it's crowned about 1¹⁄₂ inches over the rim of the pan, 1¹⁄₂ to 2¹⁄₂ hours. Near the end of the bread's rising time, preheat the oven to 350°F.

NO PROOF NECESSARY

Instant yeast doesn't have to be dissolved in water before you use it. Just add it to the mixing bowl along with the rest of your bread ingredients.

Uncover and bake the bread for 40 to 45 minutes, tenting it with foil after 15 minutes. The bread is done when it's golden brown and an instant-read thermometer inserted in the center registers 190°F. To make the glaze, stir together the maple syrup and melted butter. Remove the bread from the oven, and after a minute or so turn it out onto a rack. Brush it with the maple glaze. Cool the bread for 30 minutes before cutting it.

NUTRITION INFORMATION PER SERVING (1 SLICE, 13G): 13g whole grains, 181 cal, 8g fat, 5g protein, 21g complex carbohydrates, 4g sugar, 2g dietary fiber, 8mg cholesterol, 151mg sodium, 114mg potassium, 25RE vitamin A, 2mg iron, 19mg calcium, 100mg phosphorus.

PICK THE RIGHT PAN

For the nicest-looking, tallest-rising yeast loaves, pay attention to what size loaf pan you use: choose the size pan specified in the recipe. If the recipe doesn't say what size pan to use, use these guidelines: a 9 x 5-inch pan is appropriate for recipes calling for 3½ to 4 cups flour (or flour and grains, e.g., rolled oats). For a recipe using less than 3½ cups of flour, grab an 8½ x 4½-inch loaf pan.

Toasted Sesame and Sunflower Loaf

YIELD: **One 9 x 5-inch loaf, 18 slices**
BAKING TEMPERATURE: **350°F**
BAKING TIME: **45 to 50 minutes**

While wheat and oats are the most common whole grains found in yeast breads, pumpernickel (whole rye, the rye equivalent of whole wheat flour) and cornmeal also make frequent appearances. Here their flavor joins the nutty taste of sesame and sunflower seeds in a soft sandwich loaf. A touch of sesame oil highlights this bread's "nuttiness" and gives the loaf an enticing aroma as well. If you're a secret peanut-butter-and-jelly aficionado, but embarrassed to admit to such juvenile cravings, this bread makes a nice grown-up version of that sandwich.

Pumpernickel and whole cornmeal, unlike whole wheat and oats, aren't available at most supermarkets. (The familiar cornmeal in the round cardboard box doesn't qualify as whole grain, since it's had its germ removed.) The natural-foods section of some supermarkets (and natural-foods and health-food stores) may carry these flours; or find a mail-order source, p. 588.

½ cup (2½ ounces) hulled sunflower seeds
½ cup (2½ ounces) sesame seeds
4 tablespoons (½ stick, 2 ounces) unsalted butter, cut in 6 pieces
1¼ cups (10 ounces) milk, heated to lukewarm
2 teaspoons dark sesame oil
½ cup (2 ounces) traditional whole wheat flour
½ cup (1¾ ounces) old-fashioned rolled oats
¼ cup (1⅛ ounces) whole yellow cornmeal
¼ cup (1 ounce) whole rye (pumpernickel) flour
2 cups (8½ ounces) unbleached all-purpose flour
¼ cup (1⅞ ounces) firmly packed light or dark brown sugar
1¼ teaspoons salt
2¼ teaspoons instant yeast

Place the sunflower and sesame seeds in an ungreased 9 x 13-inch pan. Bake them in a preheated 350°F oven until the sesame seeds are beginning to brown, 10 to 12 minutes. Remove them from the oven.

Combine all the ingredients, including the seeds, and mix and knead them—by hand, mixer or bread machine—until you have a soft, smooth dough. Cover and allow the dough to rise until it's puffy and nearly doubled in bulk, 1 to 2 hours.

Lightly grease a 9 x 5-inch loaf pan. Gently deflate the dough, and shape it into a 9-inch log. Place it in the prepared pan. Cover it gently with lightly greased plastic wrap or a proof cover, and allow it to rise till it's crowned about 1 inch over the rim of the pan, 1 to 2 hours. Near the end of the bread's rise, preheat the oven to 350°F.

Uncover and bake the bread for 45 to 50 minutes, tenting it with foil after 15 minutes. The bread is done when it's golden brown and an instant-read thermometer inserted in the center registers 190°F. Remove it from the oven, and after a minute or so turn it out onto a rack. Brush with melted butter, if desired; this will keep the crust soft. Cool the bread for 30 minutes before slicing.

NUTRITION INFORMATION PER SERVING (1 SLICE, 50G): 9g whole grains, 147 cal, 5g fat, 5g protein, 19g complex carbohydrates, 3g sugar, 2g dietary fiber, 1mg cholesterol, 159mg sodium, 138mg potassium, 10RE vitamin A, 2mg iron, 36mg calcium, 127mg phosphorus.

KEEP A CLOSE EYE ON RISING BREAD

When you're making a loaf of pan bread (a sandwich loaf), and it's rising nicely, it's tempting to let it keep rising till it towers over the rim of the pan. The more rise the better, right? Wrong. Most bread will continue to rise once it's in the oven, so the loaf that looks perfect going in may come out mushroom-shaped, due to the inability of the baking loaf to support itself outside the confines of the pan. In addition, bread that's overrisen will have a coarse, crumbly texture. Bread rising in the pan should crown about 1 inch over the rim of the pan. Your recipe will tell you if that's not the case.

If the recipe tells you to let the bread rise for 1 hour, until it's crowned 1 inch over the rim of the pan, but it's only been rising for 45 minutes, and it's already reached its full height, what do you do? Put it in the oven. Pay more attention to the height of the bread than to how long it's "supposed" to rise. Rising times, due to a tremendous number of variables, will always be an approximation.

DOES IT MAKE A DIFFERENCE WHICH LIQUID SWEETENER I USE?

Most liquid sweeteners can be used interchangeably in yeast breads. Honey and molasses weigh the same, and maple syrup and corn syrup (dark, light or brown sugar syrup) weigh almost the same, just fractionally less than honey or molasses. Be aware that molasses will give your bread a deeper, richer color than any of the other syrups, and that honey, especially when used in fairly high amounts, can make bread brown very quickly.

Irish Porridge Bread

YIELD: One 8½ x 4½-inch loaf, 16 servings

BAKING TEMPERATURE: 350°F

BAKING TIME: 35 to 40 minutes

Irish (or Scottish) oats are simply the berry of the oat plant, coarsely chopped; they're the oat equivalent of cracked wheat. They make wonderful, stick-to-your-ribs porridge (see recipe, p. 29). Instead of the smooth, soft breakfast oatmeal you might be used to, these oats make a heartier version with a pleasant "bite," equivalent to that you get from al dente pasta.

This chewy-yet-soft loaf makes absolutely delightful toast. And it's perfect for sandwiches; pick something mild, like egg salad or sliced turkey, to avoid masking the bread's delicate oat flavor. It's the perfect way to use leftover porridge.

Note that vital wheat gluten is listed in the ingredients; while you may choose not to use it, bread made without it may be more crumbly than you like.

1¾ cups (14 ounces) water

⅔ cup (3¾ ounces) Irish oats (steel-cut oats)

¼ cup (1⅞ ounces) packed light or dark brown sugar

4 tablespoons (½ stick, 2 ounces) unsalted butter, cut into 6 pieces

1¼ teaspoons salt

1 cup (3½ ounces) old-fashioned rolled oats

¼ cup (1 ounce) wheat germ

2 tablespoons (⅝ ounce) vital wheat gluten

2 cups (8½ ounces) unbleached bread flour

¼ cup (1 ounce) nonfat dry milk

2 teaspoons instant yeast

TO PREPARE THE OATS: The night before you plan to make the bread, stir together the water and Irish (steel-cut) oats, cover, and refrigerate.

Next day, transfer the oats and water to a small saucepan, and simmer until the oats are tender but "toothsome," all the water is absorbed and the mixture is thick, 15 to 20 minutes. (Note: If you have any leftover porridge such as the recipe on p. 29, this recipe makes great use of it.). Add the brown sugar, butter and salt, stirring until the butter melts. Transfer the mixture to a large bowl (or the bucket of your bread machine), and allow it to rest at room temperature, covered, for 1 hour. This will allow time for the oats to totally absorb their cooking liquid and soften.

TO PREPARE THE DOUGH: Combine the remaining ingredients with the oat mixture, and mix and knead them—by hand, mixer or bread machine—until you have a soft, smooth dough. Cover and allow the dough to rise until it's puffy and nearly doubled in bulk, 1 to 2 hours.

Lightly grease an 8½ x 4½-inch loaf pan. Gently deflate the dough, and shape it into an 8-inch log. Place it in the prepared pan. Cover it gently with lightly greased plastic wrap or a proof cover, and allow it to rise till it's crowned about 1½ inches over the rim of the pan, 45 minutes to 1 hour. Near the end of the bread's rise, preheat the oven to 350°F.

TO BAKE THE BREAD: Uncover and bake the bread for 35 to 40 minutes, tenting it with foil after 15 minutes. The bread is done when it's golden brown and an instant-read thermometer inserted in the center registers 190°F. Remove it from the oven, and after a minute or so turn it out onto a rack. Brush with melted butter, if desired; this will keep the crust soft. Cool the bread for 30 minutes before slicing.

NOTE: If you've already got some prepared Irish oatmeal on hand, substitute 1½ cups (13½ ounces) cooked oatmeal for the 1¾ cups water and ⅔ cup Irish oats. If the oatmeal has been seasoned with salt, cut the salt in the recipe back to account for the salt in the oats. If it's been sitting for awhile (over an hour), there's no need to let it rest for an hour before combining with the remaining ingredients.

NUTRITION INFORMATION PER SERVING (1 SLICE, 62G): 13g whole grains, 149 cal, 4g fat, 4g protein, 21g complex carbohydrates, 3g sugar, 2g dietary fiber, 8mg cholesterol, 179mg sodium, 116mg potassium, 23RE vitamin A, 1mg iron, 36mg calcium, 100mg phosphorus.

ADDING COOKED GRAINS TO YEAST BREAD

We encourage you to add those leftover bits of porridge, cooked brown rice or other cooked grains to your bread dough; they give bread wonderful flavor and texture. The challenge is that cooked grains contain a lot of liquid. It's not readily apparent when you look at them, but add them to your dough, knead, and before you know it the dough is looking *way* too wet. The solution? Mix all the dough ingredients till they're combined (using a few tablespoons less liquid, if you're using more than ¼ cup or so cooked grains), knead briefly (a couple of minutes should do it), cover the bowl, and let the dough rest for 45 minutes before kneading to completion. This will give the flour a chance to draw some of the moisture out of those cooked grains, making it less likely you'll have to make major flour/liquid adjustments during the final knead.

Honey-Oatmeal Sandwich Bread

YIELD: One 9 x 5-inch loaf, 18 servings
BAKING TEMPERATURE: 350°F
BAKING TIME: 35 to 45 minutes

Oats have a natural sweetness that makes them almost everyone's favorite whole grain. Their mild, naturally nutty flavor marries well with other whole grains and with just about any sandwich filling you can think of, from sweet to savory. This loaf is moist and relatively close-textured, perfect for sandwiches. Add a delicate inner swirl (and shiny topping) of vanilla-cinnamon, and it's everyone's favorite breakfast toast (see variation, next page).

1¼ cups (10 ounces) boiling water
1 cup (3½ ounces) old-fashioned rolled oats
2 tablespoons (1 ounce) unsalted butter, cut into 3 pieces
1½ teaspoons salt
¼ cup (3 ounces) honey
1 cup (4 ounces) traditional whole wheat flour
1⅔ cups (7 ounces) unbleached all-purpose flour
¼ cup (1 ounce) nonfat dry milk
½ cup (1⅞ ounces) finely chopped pecans or walnuts (optional)
2 teaspoons instant yeast

Place the boiling water, oats, butter, salt and honey into a medium bowl, stir, and let the mixture cool to lukewarm.

Mix the remaining dough ingredients with the oat mixture, and knead—by hand, mixer or bread machine—until you've made a soft, smooth dough. Place the dough in a lightly greased bowl, cover it, and let it rise for 1 hour; the dough should be doubled in bulk.

Lightly grease a 9 x 5-inch loaf pan. Gently deflate the dough—it'll be sticky, so oil your hands—and shape it into a 9-inch log. Place it in the prepared pan. Cover it gently with lightly greased plastic wrap or a proof cover, and allow it to rise till it's crowned 1 ½ inches over the rim of the pan, about 1 to 1½ hours. Near the end of the bread's rising time, preheat the oven to 350°F.

Uncover and bake the bread for about 45 minutes, tenting it with foil after 20 minutes to prevent over-browning. The bread is done when it's golden brown and an instant-read thermometer inserted in the center registers 190°F. Remove it from the oven, and after a minute or so turn it out onto a rack. Brush with melted butter, if desired; this will keep the crust soft. Cool the bread completely before cutting it.

NUTRITION INFORMATION PER SERVING (1 SLICE, 46G): 12g whole grains, 126 cal, 4g fat, 4g protein, 15g complex carbohydrates, 4g sugar, 2g dietary fiber, 4mg cholesterol, 190mg sodium, 113mg potassium, 12RE vitamin A, 1mg iron, 34mg calcium, 90mg phosphorus.

VARIATION: CINNAMON-SWIRL OATMEAL TOASTING BREAD *Hints of brown sugar, vanilla and cinnamon add lively flavor to this loaf and turn it into a delightful toasting bread.*

Prepare the bread dough as directed on the previous page, adding 1 large egg yolk to the dough. Allow the dough to rise once.

Filling
1 large egg white
⅔ cup (5 ounces) packed light brown sugar
2 tablespoons (⅝ ounce) unbleached all-purpose flour
1 tablespoon ground cinnamon
1 teaspoon vanilla extract

Lightly grease a 9 x 5-inch loaf pan. Gently deflate the dough, transfer it to a lightly greased work surface, and pat and roll it into a long 8 x 24-inch rectangle. The dough is fairly soft and it's easy to shape.

TO PREPARE THE FILLING: Combine the egg white, brown sugar, flour, cinnamon and vanilla. Spread the filling over the rolled-out dough. Starting at a short end, roll the dough up, gently tucking in the edges (to contain the filling) as you go along. Seal the seam, and pat and smooth the roll into a 9-inch log. Place it in the prepared pan.

Cover the pan with lightly greased plastic wrap or a proof cover, and let the loaf rise till it's crowned about 1 inch over the rim of the pan, 1¼ to 2 hours. Near the end of the bread's rising time, preheat the oven to 350°F.

TO BAKE THE BREAD: Set the bread pan on a parchment-lined baking pan, to catch any potential filling overflow. Bake the bread for 50 to 55 minutes, tenting it loosely with foil after 20 minutes to prevent overbrowning. The bread is done when it's golden brown and an instant-read thermometer inserted in the center registers 190°F. Remove it from the oven, and after 5 minutes loosen the edges and turn it out onto a rack. Cool the bread completely before slicing.

Granola Bread

YIELD: One 8½ x 4½-inch loaf, 16 servings
BAKING TEMPERATURE: 350°F
BAKING TIME: 35 to 40 minutes

This whole grain loaf bears the mildly sweet, chewy-crunchy imprint of whatever granola you choose to add to it. It makes great sandwiches and is also super at breakfast, toasted and spread with butter, or peanut butter and fruit preserves.

1 cup (8 ounces) lukewarm water
¼ cup (2 ounces) orange juice
4 tablespoons (½ stick, 2 ounces) unsalted butter, cut into 6 pieces,
    or vegetable oil (1¾ ounces)
1 cup (4 ounces) traditional whole wheat flour
⅔ cup (2¼ ounces) old-fashioned rolled oats, ground for 30 seconds
    in a food processor
1 cup (4 ounces) prepared granola
1 cup (4¼ounces) unbleached all-purpose flour
1¼ teaspoons salt
3 tablespoons (1⅜ ounces) packed light or dark brown sugar
¼ cup (1 ounce) nonfat dry milk
Heaping ½ cup (1¼ ounces) instant potato flakes;
    or 3 tablespoons (1¼ ounces) potato flour
1 teaspoon ground cinnamon (optional)
2 teaspoons instant yeast

Combine all the ingredients, and mix and knead them—by hand, mixer or bread machine—until you have a soft, smooth dough. Cover and allow the dough to rise until it's quite puffy, but not necessarily doubled in bulk, 1½ to 2 hours.

Lightly grease an 8½ x 4½-inch loaf pan. Gently deflate the dough, and shape it into an 8-inch log. Place it in the prepared pan. Cover it gently with lightly greased plastic wrap or a proof cover, and allow it to rise till it's crowned about 1½ to 2 inches over the rim of the pan, about 1 hour. Near the end of the bread's rise, preheat the oven to 350°F.

Uncover and bake the bread for 35 to 40 minutes, tenting it with foil after 15 minutes. The bread is done when it's golden brown and an instant-read thermometer inserted in the center registers 190°F. Remove it from the oven, and after a

HOW SWEET IS YOUR GRANOLA?

Remember that yeast loves sugar, but it doesn't love too much sugar. If you're using extra-sweet granola in a yeast bread recipe, cut back any sweetener in the recipe by a tablespoon.

minute or so turn it out onto a rack. Brush with melted butter, if desired; this will keep the crust soft. Cool the bread for 30 minutes before cutting it.

NUTRITION INFORMATION PER SERVING (1 SLICE, 55G): 16g whole grains, 153 cal, 5g fat, 4g protein, 19g complex carbohydrates, 3g sugar, 2g dietary fiber, 8mg cholesterol, 185mg sodium, 149mg potassium, 32RE vitamin A, 2mg vitamin C, 1mg iron, 39mg calcium, 104mg phosphorus.

Fruits of the Earth Loaf

YIELD: One 8½ x 4½-inch loaf, 16 servings

BAKING TEMPERATURE: 350°F

BAKING TIME: 45 minutes

This honey-sweetened loaf gets its moist texture and golden color from mashed yam, which also contributes the starch that helps keep the bread fresh. A typical potato bread, it's wonderful fresh, lovely for toast and ideal for sandwiches—especially turkey with cranberry sauce.

⅓ cup (2⅝ ounces) milk, heated to lukewarm

½ cup (4 ounces) lukewarm water

3 tablespoons (2¼ ounces) honey

4 tablespoons (½ stick, 2 ounces) unsalted butter, cut into 6 pieces

½ cup (4 ounces) mashed cooked yam or sweet potato

1½ cups (6 ounces) traditional whole wheat flour

½ cup (1¾ ounces) old-fashioned rolled oats

1½ cups (6⅜ ounces) unbleached bread flour

1½ teaspoons salt

½ teaspoon ground cinnamon

¼ teaspoon ground nutmeg

¼ teaspoon ground ginger

2 teaspoons instant yeast

½ cup (3 ounces) raisins

½ cup (1⅞ ounces) chopped pecans or walnuts

Combine all of the ingredients except the raisins and nuts, and mix and knead them—by hand, mixer, or bread machine—until you have a soft, smooth dough. Cover and allow the dough to rise until it's puffy and nearly doubled in bulk, 1 to 2 hours.

Lightly grease an 8½ x 4½-inch loaf pan. Gently deflate the dough, and knead the raisins and nuts into it.

Shape it into an 8-inch log, and place it in the prepared pan. Cover it gently with lightly greased plastic wrap or a proof cover, and allow it to rise till it's crowned about 1½ inches over the rim of the pan, 1¼ to 2½ hours. Near the end of the bread's rise, preheat the oven to 350°F.

Uncover and bake the bread for about 45 minutes, tenting it with foil after 15 minutes. The bread is done when it's golden brown and an instant-read thermometer inserted in the center registers 190°F. Remove it from the oven, and after a minute or so turn it out onto a rack. Brush with melted butter, if desired; this will keep the crust soft. Cool the bread for 30 minutes before slicing it.

NUTRITION INFORMATION PER SERVING (1 SLICE, 61G): 14g whole grains, 176 cal, 6g fat, 4g protein, 25g complex carbohydrates, 3g sugar, 3g dietary fiber, 8mg cholesterol, 208mg sodium, 155mg potassium, 27RE vitamin A, 1mg vitamin C, 2mg iron, 22mg calcium, 94mg phosphorus.

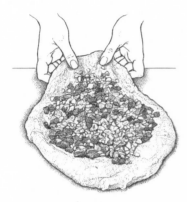

When adding fruit and/or nuts to risen dough, first flatten the dough into a rough oval. Sprinkle the fruit evenly over the dough, pressing it in.

Fold the dough in half, and knead it until everything is well dispersed, adding back any stray pieces that fall out along the way.

Millet-Sunflower Bread

YIELD: One 9 x 5-inch loaf, 18 servings.
BAKING TEMPERATURE: 350°F
BAKING TIME: 40 to 45 minutes

Millet is a grain that adds an elusive flavor and a pleasingly moist texture to a loaf of bread. It turns from bright yellow to cream-colored when cooked and is porridgelike in consistency. Though it's possible to make bread with uncooked millet, you have to be quite fond of crunch in your loaf; the tiny gold seeds don't soften as they bake. Here we pair it with sunflower seeds, which add their nutty taste and refined crunch.

Our thanks to Marti Mikels of Louisa, Virginia, for her assistance in nailing down the final recipe for this bread. Under her capable hands, it went from craggy and misshapen to a smooth, domed, picture-perfect loaf.

1 ⅔ cups (8 ounces) cooked millet (see instructions, next page), very lightly packed, refrigerated overnight before using

¼ cup (2 ounces) orange juice

½ cup (4 ounces) lukewarm water

3 tablespoons (1¼ ounces) olive oil

1 tablespoon (¾ ounce) honey

1 teaspoon dark sesame oil

¾ cup (3 ounces) traditional whole wheat flour

⅔ cup (2¼ ounces) old-fashioned rolled oats, ground for 30 seconds in a food processor

2 cups (8½ ounces) unbleached bread flour

2 tablespoons (⅝ ounce) vital wheat gluten

⅓ cup (1⅝ ounces) hulled sunflower seeds, coarsely chopped

1¼ teaspoons salt

1 teaspoon instant yeast

Combine all the ingredients and mix just till thoroughly combined. Let the mixture rest for 45 minutes; this gives the flour a chance to absorb some of the moisture from the millet. Knead the mixture—by hand, mixer or bread machine—until you have a soft, smooth dough. Cover and allow the dough to rise until it's puffy and nearly doubled in bulk, 1 to 2 hours.

Lightly grease a 9 x 5-inch loaf pan. Gently deflate the dough, and shape it into a 9-inch log. Place it in the prepared pan. Cover it gently with lightly greased plastic wrap or a proof cover, and allow it to rise till it's crowned about 1 to 1½ inches over the rim of the pan, 1½ to 2½ hours. Near the end of the bread's rising time, preheat the oven to 350°F.

Uncover and bake the bread until it's golden brown and an instant-read thermometer inserted in the center registers 190°F, 40 to 45 minutes. This bread browns slowly; there's no need to tent it with foil. Remove the bread from the oven, and after a minute or so turn it out onto a rack. Brush with melted butter, if desired; this will keep the crust soft. Cool the bread for 30 minutes before slicing.

NOTE: The longer you store cooked millet in the refrigerator, the drier it becomes, and the more water you'll need to add to the dough. The amount of water in the recipe is for millet stored overnight in the refrigerator; increase the water by 2 tablespoons if the millet's been stored for up to 4 days. After 4 days, enjoy the millet in the fridge as a side dish, and cook some new millet to use in this bread recipe.

NUTRITION INFORMATION PER SERVING (1 SLICE, 50G): 8g whole grains, 131 cal, 4g fat, 4g protein, 20g complex carbohydrates, 1g sugar, 2g dietary fiber, 149mg sodium, 81mg potassium, 1mg vitamin C, 1mg iron, 9mg calcium, 79mg phosphorus.

Cooked Millet

YIELD: About 4½ cups cooked millet

Enjoy cooked millet as a side dish, breakfast cereal or in bread. If you're using it for bread, it's better to let it rest overnight, refrigerated, before using. This gives it a chance to fully absorb the liquid in which it's been cooked.

Place 1 cup (7¼ ounces) millet in a strainer, and rinse it under cool water for about 1 minute. Drain by shaking the strainer.

Heat a large skillet over medium heat, add the drained millet, and stir it in the pan until it's dry and you can smell its fragrance, 2 to 3 minutes. Remove it from the heat.

Bring 3 cups water to a boil in a medium saucepan; add the roasted millet. Return the water to a boil, reduce heat to a simmer and cover. Cook the millet, stirring occasionally, until all the liquid is absorbed, 25 to 27 minutes. Remove it from the heat and let it stand, covered, for a few minutes. Serve immediately or refrigerate.

Hummus Bread

YIELD: One 8½ x 4½-inch loaf, 16 servings

BAKING TEMPERATURE: 350°F

BAKING TIME: 35 to 40 minutes

This moist, savory bread is great for sandwiches and also perfect alongside your breakfast eggs. Toast and spread with butter—or with a thin layer of hummus, for added punch!

½ cup (4 ounces) milk, heated to lukewarm

¼ cup (2 ounces) orange juice

1 cup (8 ounces) prepared hummus (recipe follows)

¼ cup (1¾ ounces) olive oil

1 large egg

2 cups (8 ounces) traditional whole wheat flour

1 cup (4¼ ounces) unbleached all-purpose flour

1 teaspoon sugar

1¼ teaspoons salt

⅓ cup (1⅝ ounces) toasted sesame seeds

2 teaspoons instant yeast

Combine all the ingredients and mix and knead them—by hand, mixer or bread machine—until you have a soft, smooth dough. Cover and allow the dough to rise until it's puffy and nearly doubled in bulk, 1 hour.

Lightly grease an 8½ x 4½-inch loaf pan. Gently deflate the dough, and shape it into an 8-inch log. Place it in the prepared pan. Cover it gently with lightly greased plastic wrap or a proof cover, and allow it to rise till it's crowned about 1½ inches over the rim of the pan. While the bread is rising, preheat the oven to 350°F.

Uncover and bake the bread for 35 to 40 minutes, tenting it with foil after 20 minutes. The bread is done when it's golden brown and an instant-read thermometer inserted in the center registers 190°F. Remove it from the oven, and after a couple of minutes turn it out onto a rack. Brush with melted butter, if desired; this will keep the crust soft. Cool the bread for 30 minutes before slicing.

NUTRITION INFORMATION PER SERVING (1 SLICE, 57G): 14g whole grains, 155 cal, 6g fat, 5g protein, 21g complex carbohydrates, 3g dietary fiber, 14mg cholesterol, 242mg sodium, 139mg potassium, 9RE vitamin A, 3mg vitamin C, 2mg iron, 32mg calcium, 123mg phosphorus.

VARIATION: *For a crispier crust, shape the bread dough into an 8-inch disk, and press it into a 9 x 2-inch round cake pan. Cover the pan, and allow the dough to rise until the dome in the center is nearly level with the top of the pan, and the sides are about ½ inch below the rim, about 1½ hours.*

. Bake the bread in a preheated 350°F oven for 35 minutes, tenting it with foil after 20 minutes. Remove the bread from the oven, brush it with olive oil, remove it from the pan, and place it directly on the oven rack. Bake for 5 minutes more, to crisp the crust. Remove from the oven, and cool for 30 minutes before slicing.

For an even crunchier crust, turn off the oven, prop open the door, and allow the bread to cool completely in the cooling oven.

Hummus

YIELD: About 3¼ cups

This makes enough for three loaves of hummus bread, but don't save it just for that. It's a great dip or sandwich filling on its own.

> ½ cup (2½ ounces) tahini (sesame paste)
> 2 tablespoons (1 ounce) fresh lemon juice
> 1 teaspoon salt
> 2 teaspoons ground cumin
> 4 to 12 medium garlic cloves, peeled, to taste
> 2 (15-ounce) cans chickpeas (garbanzo beans), drained, ¾ cup of the liquid reserved

Put all the ingredients except the chickpea liquid into a food processor. Add ½ cup of the reserved chickpea liquid. Blend until smooth; if the mixture doesn't become smooth, add up to ¼ cup additional liquid. Refrigerate until ready to use.

NOTE: Using 4 cloves of garlic produces mild garlic taste; 12 cloves is very assertive. "To taste" means just that; keep adding garlic cloves until the hummus is as garlicky as you like. One caution: The more garlic you add, the less your bread will rise; yeast doesn't like raw garlic. Twelve cloves produces a noticeable, but not unacceptable reduction in height; more than that, you're on your own.

Sauerkraut-Rye Bread

YIELD: One 8½ x 4½-inch loaf, 16 servings

BAKING TEMPERATURE: 350°F

BAKING TIME: 45 minutes

This moist, easy-to-slice bread fairly sings with "deli rye" flavor. And don't worry—no one will ever guess that sauerkraut's the secret ingredient that makes this bread so delightfully moist and tangy. This is a low-rising, fairly dense loaf. It's moist enough to slice easily, holds together well, and makes flavorful corned beef and Swiss, pastrami or grilled Reuben sandwiches.

1 can (8 ounces) sauerkraut, drained and wrung dry, juice discarded
(about 5 ounces sauerkraut, drained; about 1⅓ cups, very lightly packed)

⅔ cup (5⅜ ounces) lukewarm water

¼ cup (2 ounces) dill pickle juice or sour pickle juice

¼ cup (1¾ ounces) vegetable oil

1⅓ cups (5 ounces) whole rye (pumpernickel) flour

1 cup (4 ounces) traditional whole wheat flour

1 cup (4¼ ounces) unbleached bread flour

Heaping ½ cup (1¼ ounces) dried potato flakes or 3 tablespoons (1¼ ounces) potato flour

2 tablespoons (⅝ ounce) vital wheat gluten

1 tablespoon caraway seeds

1 tablespoon whole mustard seeds

1 tablespoon dried minced onion

1 teaspoon salt

1 tablespoon sugar

2½ teaspoons instant yeast

Lightly grease an 8½ x 4½-inch loaf pan.

Combine the sauerkraut, water and pickle juice in a blender or food processor, and process until the kraut is finely chopped.

Combine the chopped sauerkraut and its liquid with the remaining ingredients, stirring vigorously to make a crumbly mixture; it won't hold together. Allow the mixture to rest, covered, for 45 minutes; this will give the flour a chance to absorb some of the sauerkraut's liquid. After the dough's resting period, knead it—by hand, mixer or bread machine—until you have a cohesive, very stiff dough. This dough won't be very elastic; that's OK. Let the dough rise in a lightly greased bowl for 1 to 1½ hours; it won't rise much at all.

Turn the dough out onto a lightly oiled or lightly floured surface, and shape it into a log. Place the log in the prepared pan, cover the pan with a proof cover or greased plastic wrap, and allow the loaf to rise till it's crested about 1 inch over the edge of the pan. This will take 1½ to 2½ hours. Be aware that this bread has very little oven spring, so what you see when you put it in the oven is pretty much what you'll get coming out of the oven. During the last part of the rise, preheat the oven to 350°F.

Uncover and bake the bread for 20 minutes. Tent it lightly with foil and bake until its internal temperature registers 190°F on an instant-read thermometer, 25 minutes more. Remove it from the oven, and after a minute or so turn it out onto a rack. Cool the bread for 30 minutes before slicing.

NUTRITION INFORMATION PER SERVING (1 SLICE, 58G): 16g whole grains, 134 cal, 4g fat, 5g protein, 20g complex carbohydrates, 1g sugar, 5g dietary fiber, 222mg sodium, 233mg potassium, 1RE vitamin A, 3mg vitamin C, 2mg iron, 24mg calcium, 159mg phosphorus.

ROLLS

Like basic black, rolls are always in fashion. Focaccia may come, five-seed semolina boules may go, but the dinner roll lives on forever. And for good reason: rolls are simply your favorite bread, baked in handy single-serving size. Pretty in the bread basket, a perfect fit on the bread plate at dinner, and just as much at home with a simple pat of butter as your craziest sandwich concoction, yeast rolls are the equivalent of the second baseman on a baseball team: they stay in the background, but we'd be lost without them.

A Quartet of Dinner Rolls

"Squishy white rolls" would seem to have no place in a whole grain baking book, but if you're a fan of these classic, soft dinner rolls—and after all, who isn't?—we encourage you to make a variety of tasty clones using whole grains. In fact, we think you may even prefer these soft rolls to the original white version; their texture is heartier and their flavor more complex.

Oat Rolls

YIELD: 16 rolls
BAKING TEMPERATURE: 350°F
BAKING TIME: 25 minutes

These warm-beige rolls look a bit craggy from the oats, which also give them marvelous flavor.

Dough
1 cup plus 2 tablespoons (9 ounces) lukewarm water
2 tablespoons (1 ounce) orange juice
4 tablespoons (½ stick, 2 ounces) unsalted butter, cut into 6 pieces
3 tablespoons (2¼ ounces) honey
1 cup (3½ ounces) old-fashioned rolled oats
½ cup (2 ounces) traditional whole wheat flour
¼ cup (1⅛ ounces) wheat germ
¼ cup (⅞ ounce) oat bran
2 cups (8½ ounces) unbleached all-purpose flour
1 ¼ teaspoons salt
Heaping ½ cup (1¼ ounces) dried potato flakes or 3 tablespoons (1 ¼ ounces) potato flour
¼ cup (1 ounce) nonfat dry milk
2¼ teaspoons instant yeast

Topping
2 to 3 tablespoons (1 to 1½ ounces) unsalted butter, melted

TO PREPARE THE DOUGH: Combine all of the dough ingredients, and mix and knead them—by hand, mixer, or bread machine—until you have a medium-soft, smooth dough. Cover and allow the dough to rise until it's quite puffy, though probably not doubled in bulk, 1 to 2 hours.

Lightly grease a 9 x 13-inch, 11-inch square, 12-inch round, or similar-size pan.

TO SHAPE THE ROLLS: Gently deflate the dough, and transfer it to a lightly greased work surface. Divide it into 16 pieces. Shape each piece into a rough ball by pulling the dough into a very small knot at the bottom, then rolling it under the palm of your hand into a smooth ball.

Place the rolls in the prepared pan, spacing them evenly; they won't touch one another. Cover the pan with lightly greased plastic wrap or a proof cover, and allow the rolls to rise for 1 to 1¼ hours. They won't double in size, but will become about half again as large as they were originally. They should barely touch each other. Near the end of the second rise, preheat the oven to 350°F.

TO BAKE THE ROLLS: Uncover and bake the rolls until they're golden brown on top but still light-colored on the sides, 25 minutes. Remove them from the oven, and after 2 or 3 minutes, carefully transfer them to a rack. They'll be hot and delicate, so be careful. Brush the hot rolls with the melted butter (twice, if you're using 3 tablespoons of butter); this will give them a soft, satiny crust. Serve warm or at room temperature.

NUTRITION INFORMATION PER SERVING (1 ROLL, 60G): 13g whole grains, 164 cal, 5g fat, 5g protein, 22g complex carbohydrates, 3g sugar, 2g dietary fiber, 12mg cholesterol, 182mg sodium, 136mg potassium, 38RE vitamin A, 1mg vitamin C, 1mg iron, 33mg calcium, 120mg phosphorus.

Smooth the rough ball of dough by pulling it downward all around its top surface, gathering it at the bottom. Place all the balls smooth-side up on an unfloured work surface.

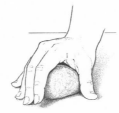

Cup your fingers over the dough, and roll it quickly and gently in a circular motion, using the very top of your palm (at the base of your fingers) and applying the barest amount of downward pressure.

The ball on the left, shown before rolling, has a shaggy, rough surface. The rolled ball on the right is very smooth.

Wheat Rolls

YIELD: 16 rolls
BAKING TEMPERATURE: 350°F
BAKING TIME: 23 to 25 minutes

These deep-brown rolls are tender and moist, the perfect accompaniment to a roast, stew or other meat-based main dish. They make delicious sandwiches too.

Dough
1 cup (8 ounces) lukewarm water
¼ cup (2 ounces) orange juice
4 tablespoons (½ stick, 2 ounces) unsalted butter, cut into 6 pieces
3 tablespoons (2¼ ounces) honey
2 cups (8 ounces) traditional whole wheat flour
1 cup (4¼ ounces) unbleached all-purpose flour
1¼ teaspoons salt
Heaping ½ cup (1¼ ounces) dried potato flakes or 3 tablespoons (1¼ ounces)
    potato flour
¼ cup (1 ounce) nonfat dry milk
2¼ teaspoons instant yeast

Topping
2 to 3 tablespoons (1 to 1½ ounces) unsalted butter, melted

TO PREPARE THE DOUGH: Combine all the dough ingredients, and mix and knead them—by hand, mixer or bread machine—until you have a medium-soft, smooth dough. Cover and allow the dough to rise until it's quite puffy, though probably not doubled in bulk, 1 to 2 hours.

Lightly grease a 9 x 13-inch, 11-inch square, 12-inch round or similar-size pan.

TO SHAPE THE ROLLS: Gently deflate the dough, and transfer it to a lightly greased work surface. Divide it into 16 pieces. Shape each piece into a rough ball by pulling the dough into a very small knot at the bottom, then rolling it under the palm of your hand into a smooth ball. (See illustrations, p. 209.)

Place the rolls in the prepared pan, spacing them evenly; they won't touch one another. Cover the pan with lightly greased plastic wrap or a proof cover, and allow the rolls to rise for 1½ to 2 hours. They'll become very puffy and will reach out and touch one another. While the rolls are rising, preheat the oven to 350°F.

TO BAKE THE ROLLS: Uncover and bake the rolls until they're mahogany-brown on top but lighter colored on the sides, 23 to 25 minutes. Remove them from the oven, and after 2 or 3 minutes, carefully transfer them to a rack. They'll be hot and delicate, so be careful.

Brush the hot rolls with the melted butter (twice, if you're using 3 tablespoons of butter); this will give them a soft, satiny crust. Serve warm or at room temperature.

NUTRITION INFORMATION PER SERVING (1 ROLL, 55G): 13g whole grains, 144 cal, 4g fat, 5g protein, 18g complex carbohydrates, 3g sugar, 2g dietary fiber, 12mg cholesterol, 180mg sodium, 119mg potassium, 37RE vitamin A, 2mg vitamin C, 1mg iron, 31mg calcium, 84mg phosphorus.

Corn Rolls

YIELD: **16 rolls**
BAKING TEMPERATURE: **350°F**
BAKING TIME: **25 to 27 minutes**

It can be difficult to find fresh whole grain (with the germ) cornmeal but there are some brands available (see Where to Buy, p. 588). The cornmeal you see in the grocery store most often has been degerminated, meaning it's no longer considered a whole grain. Whole cornmeal is harder to keep fresh, so grocery stores stock less of it. When you find it, plop it into the freezer right away; cornmeal that has started to turn rancid can taste bitter. In this recipe we worked around that problem by using fresh-frozen corn in place of much of the cornmeal, adding cornmeal for its crunch but not its flavor. These gold-tinted, light brown rolls are dense and moist, perfect with soup or stew.

Dough
$\frac{1}{2}$ **cup (4 ounces) water**
1 cup (4 ounces) frozen corn
$\frac{1}{4}$ **cup (2 ounces) orange juice**
1 teaspoon vanilla extract
6 tablespoons ($\frac{3}{4}$ stick, 3 ounces) unsalted butter, cut into 9 pieces
3 tablespoons (2 ounces) light corn syrup
$\frac{1}{2}$ **cup ($2\frac{3}{8}$ ounces) whole yellow cornmeal**
$\frac{1}{4}$ **cup (1 ounce) wheat germ**
$\frac{1}{2}$ **cup (2 ounces) traditional whole wheat flour**
2 cups ($8\frac{1}{2}$ ounces) unbleached bread flour
$1\frac{1}{4}$ **teaspoons salt**
Heaping $\frac{1}{2}$ cup ($1\frac{1}{4}$ ounces) dried potato flakes or 3 tablespoons ($1\frac{1}{4}$ ounces) potato flour
$\frac{1}{4}$ **cup (1 ounce) nonfat dry milk**
$2\frac{1}{4}$ **teaspoons instant yeast**

Topping
2 to 3 tablespoons (1 to 1½ ounces) unsalted butter, melted

TO PREPARE THE CORN: Combine the water and frozen corn in a small microwave-safe dish. Microwave until the corn is thawed; then grind the mixture in a food processor for 30 seconds, or until it's fairly smooth. Be careful; it may be hot. Allow it to cool to lukewarm before preparing the dough.

TO PREPARE THE DOUGH: Combine all the dough ingredients including the corn and mix and knead them—by hand, mixer or bread machine—until you have a medium-soft, smooth dough. Cover and allow the dough to rise until it's quite puffy, though it may not have doubled in bulk, 1 to 2 hours.

Lightly grease a 9 x 13-inch pan, 11-inch square pan, 12-inch round pan, or similar-size pan.

TO SHAPE THE ROLLS: Gently deflate the dough, and transfer it to a lightly greased work surface. Divide it into 16 pieces. Shape each piece into a rough ball by pulling the dough into a very small knot at the bottom, then rolling it under the palm of your hand into a smooth ball (see illustration, p. 209).

Place the rolls in the prepared pan, spacing them evenly; they won't touch one another. Cover the pan with lightly greased plastic wrap or a proof cover, and allow the rolls to rise for 1½ to 2 hours. They'll become quite puffy, and will reach out and (barely) touch one another. While the rolls are rising, preheat the oven to 350°F.

TO BAKE THE ROLLS: Uncover and bake the rolls until they're light brown all over, 25 to 27 minutes. Remove them from the oven, and after 2 or 3 minutes, carefully transfer them to a rack. They'll be hot and delicate, so be careful. Brush the hot rolls with the melted butter (twice, if you're using 3 table-spoons of butter); this will give them a soft, satiny crust. Serve warm, or at room temperature.

> **FRESHENING DAY-OLD ROLLS**
>
> Rolls and other "small" breads (e.g., a chunk of baguette, a leftover hunk of a round artisan loaf) tend to become stale more quickly than pan (sandwich) breads. But they're easily "refreshed" by wrapping them loosely in foil and baking in a preheated 350°F oven for 6 to 10 minutes (the smaller the roll or piece of bread, the shorter the time in the oven).

NUTRITION INFORMATION PER SERVING (1 ROLL, 51G): 9g whole grains, 146 cal, 6g fat, 5g protein, 14g complex carbohydrates, 3g sugar, 2g dietary fiber, 16mg cholesterol, 187mg sodium, 194mg potassium, 51RE vitamin A, 2mg vitamin C, 1mg iron, 30mg calcium, 127mg phosphorus.

Buttermilk-Rye Rolls

YIELD: 16 rolls

BAKING TEMPERATURE: 350°F

BAKING TIME: 25 minutes

These beige-gold rolls feature the very mild tang of buttermilk, and the more assertive flavor of caraway. Serve them with pork or beef or a hearty stew. They also make lovely deli-style sandwiches (think corned beef, liverwurst or pastrami); don't forget the dill pickle (half-sour, please) on the side.

Dough
1¼ cups (10 ounces) buttermilk, heated to lukewarm
4 tablespoons (½ stick, 2 ounces) butter, cut into 6 pieces
2 tablespoons (1½ ounces) molasses
½ cup (2 ounces) traditional whole wheat flour
1 cup (3¾ ounces) whole rye (pumpernickel) flour
1½ cups (6⅜ ounces) unbleached all-purpose flour
2 teaspoons caraway seeds
1¼ teaspoons salt
Heaping ½ cup (1¼ ounces) dried potato flakes or 3 tablespoons (1¼ ounces)
    potato flour
2¼ teaspoons instant yeast

Topping
2 to 3 tablespoons (1 to 1½ ounces) unsalted butter, melted

TO PREPARE THE DOUGH: Combine all the dough ingredients, and mix and knead them—by hand, mixer or bread machine—until you have a medium-soft, smooth dough. Cover and allow the dough to rise until it's quite puffy, though it may not have doubled in bulk, 1 to 2 hours.

Lightly grease a 9 x 13-inch, 11-inch square, 12-inch round, or similar-size pan.

TO SHAPE THE ROLLS: Gently deflate the dough, and transfer it to a lightly greased work surface. Divide it into 16 pieces. Shape each piece into a rough ball by pulling the dough into a very small knot at the bottom, then rolling it under the palm of your hand into a smooth ball. (See illustration, p. 209.)

Place the rolls in the prepared pan, spacing them evenly; they won't touch one another. Cover the pan with lightly greased plastic wrap or a proof cover, and allow the rolls to rise for 1¾ to 2½ hours. They'll become quite puffy, and will reach out and touch one another. Toward the end of the rise, preheat the oven to 350°F.

TO BAKE THE ROLLS: Uncover and bake the rolls until they're an even light brown all over, 25 minutes. Remove them from the oven, and after 2 or 3 minutes, transfer them to a rack. They'll be hot and delicate, so be careful. Brush the hot rolls with the melted butter (twice, if you're using 3 tablespoons of butter); this will give them a soft, satiny crust. Serve warm or at room temperature.

NUTRITION INFORMATION PER SERVING (1 ROLL, 50G): 10g whole grains, 137 cal, 5g fat, 4g protein, 17g complex carbohydrates, 2g sugar, 2g dietary fiber, 12mg cholesterol, 192mg sodium, 127mg potassium, 38RE vitamin A, 1mg vitamin C, 1mg iron, 33mg calcium, 91mg phosphorus.

> ### THE SMALLER THE ROLL, THE SOONER YOU SHOULD EAT IT
>
> Bread becomes stale as moisture migrates from its interior out through the crust. The smaller the roll, the more crust area it has in proportion to the interior, and thus the more quickly it'll go stale. Eat small rolls the same day you bake them, or plan on reheating them if they're a day old.

Dark & Soft Restaurant Dinner Rolls

YIELD: 10 large rolls, 20 servings
BAKING TEMPERATURE: 350°F
BAKING TIME: 25 to 30 minutes

These dinner rolls replicate the soft, mildly sweet, deep chocolate-colored rolls served at various chain restaurants (particularly steakhouses) around the country. The taste-testers here at King Arthur Flour raved about these, so even if they're not an exact match for those restaurant rolls, we're sure you'll find them tasty.

We make these rolls about twice as large as the typical dinner roll, shaping them into little logs before baking. Now, close your eyes and imagine each roll on its own serving board, complete with a tiny ramekin of whipped butter. Conjure up a salad bar. There! You're dining out without ever leaving the house.

1 cup (8 ounces) lukewarm water
⅓ cup (2⅝ ounces) orange juice
4 tablespoons (½ stick, 2 ounces) unsalted butter, cut into 6 pieces
⅓ cup (4 ounces) honey
2¼ cups (9 ounces) traditional whole wheat flour
2¼ cups (9½ ounces) unbleached bread flour
1¾ teaspoons salt
3 tablespoons (1¼ ounces) sugar
2 tablespoons (⅜ ounce) Dutch-process cocoa
2½ teaspoons instant yeast

TO PREPARE THE DOUGH: Combine all the dough ingredients, and mix and knead them—by hand, mixer or bread machine—until you have a medium-soft, smooth dough. Cover and allow the dough until it's quite puffy, though probably not doubled in bulk, 1 to 2 hours.

Lightly grease a baking sheet or line with parchment paper.

TO SHAPE THE ROLLS: Gently deflate the dough, and transfer it to a lightly greased work surface. Divide the dough into 10 even pieces (about 4 ounces each), and shape the pieces into 5 x 2-inch oval rolls. Place the rolls on the prepared baking sheet, and allow them to rise, covered, for 1½ to 2 hours. They won't have doubled in size, but will appear puffy; when you gently press your finger into one, the indentation will rebound quite slowly. Toward the end of the rise, preheat the oven to 350°F.

TO BAKE THE ROLLS: Uncover and bake the rolls until the bottoms appear slightly browned (you'll have to carefully pick one up to look) or until an instant-read thermometer inserted in the center of a roll reads about 200°F, 25 to 30 minutes. Remove the rolls from the oven, and cool them on a rack.

NUTRITION INFORMATION PER SERVING (1/2 ROLL, 52G): 13g whole grains, 141 cal, 3g fat, 4g protein, 20g complex carbohydrates, 6g sugar, 2g dietary fiber, 6mg cholesterol, 189mg sodium, 99mg potassium, 20RE vitamin A, 1mg vitamin C, 1mg iron, 9mg calcium, 71mg phosphorus.

DIVIDING DOUGH INTO EVEN PIECES

Most roll recipes call for dividing the dough into either 12 or 16 pieces, then rolling the pieces into balls to make rolls. What's the best way to divide dough?

First, make sure you have a clean, lightly greased work surface to work on. Use a baker's bench knife or a plastic bowl scraper to cut the dough in half; second choice would be a sharp knife. If you want your rolls to be perfectly even, weigh the dough, then use the reading to cut two equal pieces. If you're not fussy, just eyeball it.

For 16 rolls, continue dividing each piece in half three more times (using a scale, if you like); first you'll have 2 pieces of dough; then 4; then 8 and, finally, 16 pieces of dough.

To make 12 larger rolls, divide each of the dough halves in half again. Then divide those 4 pieces into 3 pieces each.

Cheddar-Scallion Rolls

YIELD: 16 rolls

BAKING TEMPERATURE: 350°F

BAKING TIME: 25 to 28 minutes

Robin Rice, a passionate baker and founding contributor to King Arthur Flour's baking newsletter, The Baking Sheet, *came up with this recipe for soft sandwich-type rolls. Says Robin, "These zippy rolls are best when served hot, a perfect accompaniment to vegetable soups and spinach salads." With their distinct cheese flavor set off by bright green bits of scallion, they're a treat unto themselves, simply served warm and spread with sweet butter.*

³⁄₄ cup (6 ounces) lukewarm water

¹⁄₄ cup (2 ounces) orange juice

2 tablespoons (1¹⁄₂ ounces) honey

1 cup (4 ounces) grated Cheddar cheese

2 cups (8 ounces) traditional whole wheat flour

1 cup (4¹⁄₄ ounces) unbleached all-purpose flour

1¹⁄₄ teaspoons salt

¹⁄₄ cup (1 ounce) nonfat dry milk powder

1¹⁄₂ teaspoons dill weed

2¹⁄₄ teaspoons instant yeast

1 cup (2¹⁄₄ ounces) minced scallions

TO PREPARE THE DOUGH: Combine all the ingredients except the scallions, and mix and knead them—by hand, mixer or bread machine—until you have a medium-soft, smooth dough. Cover and let the dough rise until it's quite puffy, though probably not doubled in bulk, 1 to 2 hours.

Lightly grease a 9 x 13-inch pan.

While the dough is rising, prepare the scallions by trimming the ends and snipping both white and green parts into small pieces (¹⁄₄ inch or so). For 1 cup of snipped scallions, you'll need nearly all of a typical 4 ounce bunch of scallions.

TO SHAPE THE ROLLS: Gently deflate the dough and knead in the scallions. Transfer the dough to a lightly greased work surface. Divide it into 16 pieces, and roll each piece into a round ball. Place the balls in the prepared pan. Let the rolls rise, covered, in a warm place, until they're puffy but not doubled in size, 2 to 2¹⁄₂ hours. Near the end of the rise, preheat the oven to 350°F.

TO BAKE THE ROLLS: Uncover and bake the rolls in the oven, tenting them with foil after 20 minutes, until they're a deep golden brown on top, 25 to 28 minutes. Remove them from the oven, and brush them with melted butter, if desired; this will keep their crust soft.

NUTRITION INFORMATION PER SERVING (1 ROLL, 53G): **14g whole grains,** 124 cal, 3g fat, 5g protein, 18g complex carbohydrates, 2g sugar, 2g dietary fiber, 8mg cholesterol, 223mg sodium, 140mg potassium, 22RE vitamin A, 3mg vitamin C, 1mg iron, 86mg calcium, 121mg phosphorus.

FOR THE DARKEST ROLLS AND BREAD, USE CARAMEL COLORING

Restaurant and other professional bakers rely on caramel coloring, either dry or liquid, for their signature dark breads, such as pumpernickel. Home bakers don't have easy access to this ingredient, although it's available via mail order. If you do have a source for caramel coloring, use about ¾ teaspoon per cup of flour to make bread that's the rich, deep color of dark chocolate.

CLEANING STUBBORN DOUGH FROM YOUR MIXING BOWL

Do you find yourself battling to scrape a barnacle-like layer of sticky yeast dough out of the mixing bowl when you're cleaning up? Wash bowls in which you've prepared yeast dough first in cool water, to remove the dough; then in hot water, to finish the job. Beginning with hot water actually "cooks" the dough onto the bowl, making it cling more stubbornly than ever. For seriously crusty, stuck-on dough, soak the bowl for 15 minutes in cool water before washing.

Pull-Apart Cranberry-Pecan Buns

YIELD: 16 buns

BAKING TEMPERATURE: 350°F

BAKING TIME: 25 to 30 minutes

Whole wheat gives these buns their lovely, rich, whole grain color. And they're as moist, tender and perhaps even tastier—heartier, more complex—than white-flour buns. Serve them warm, with melting butter, at any holiday feast. Or split them open, layer with cooked chicken or turkey, anoint with mayo and cranberry relish, and enjoy a delightful little sandwich.

Pre-ferment

1 cup (4 ounces) traditional whole wheat flour

½ cup (4 ounces) cool water

Pinch of instant yeast

Dough

All of the pre-ferment

¼ cup (2 ounces) orange juice

¼ cup (2 ounces) lukewarm water

⅓ cup (2⅝ ounces) applesauce, sweetened or unsweetened

4 tablespoons (½ stick, 2 ounces) unsalted butter, cut into 6 pieces

1½ cups (6 ounces) traditional whole wheat flour

1 cup (4¼ ounces) unbleached all-purpose flour

1½ teaspoons salt

3 tablespoons (1⅜ ounces) packed light or dark brown sugar

2½ teaspoons instant yeast

1 cup (4 ounces) dried cranberries

½ cup (1⅞ ounces) chopped pecans

TO PREPARE THE PRE-FERMENT: Combine all the pre-ferment ingredients in a small (2- to 3-cup) bowl. Cover the bowl, and let the pre-ferment rest overnight at room temperature.

TO PREPARE THE DOUGH: Combine the pre-ferment with the remaining dough ingredients, except the cranberries and pecans, and mix and knead them—by hand, mixer or bread machine—until you have a medium-soft, smooth dough. Cover and allow the dough to rise until it's quite puffy, though probably not doubled in bulk, 1 to 2 hours.

Lightly grease a 9 x 13-inch pan.

TO SHAPE THE BUNS: Gently deflate the dough, transfer it to a lightly greased work surface, and knead the cranberries and pecans into it. Divide it into 16 pieces, rounding each piece into a ball. Evenly space the balls in the prepared pan. Cover and let the buns rise in a warm place until they're crowding against one another, 1½ to 2½ hours. Toward the end of the rise, preheat the oven to 350°F.

TO BAKE THE BUNS: Uncover and bake the buns until they're a light golden brown, 25 to 30 minutes. Remove them from the oven, and after several minutes transfer them to a rack. Brush them with melted butter, if desired; this will keep their crust soft. Serve warm or at room temperature.

NUTRITION INFORMATION PER SERVING (1 BUN, 62G): 18g whole grains, 172 cal, 6g fat, 4g protein, 26g complex carbohydrates, 2g sugar, 3g dietary fiber, 8mg cholesterol, 204mg sodium, 180mg potassium, 25RE vitamin A, 2mg vitamin C, 1mg iron, 17mg calcium, 96mg phosphorus.

JUMP-STARTING YOUR YEAST

We love to use a pre-ferment— a starter—when baking yeast bread or rolls. It's a very simple matter of combining 1 cup of the flour and ½ cup of water called for in the recipe with a tiny pinch—less than 1/16 teaspoon—of instant yeast, and letting it rest overnight (12 to 16 hours). Combine the risen pre-ferment with the remainder of the ingredients, and proceed. The yeast gets a wonderful head start, and as it develops it produces lots of flavor, flavor that will permeate your baked bread.

Honey-Sesame Crescents

YIELD: **1½ dozen crescent rolls**

BAKING TEMPERATURE: **350°F**

BAKING TIME: **20 to 25 minutes**

The snap of sesame, both inside and out, gives these golden rolls super flavor and texture. The crunch of the seeds is especially nice set against the soft texture of the bread, which comes from soft whole wheat pastry flour.

Dough

¾ cup plus 2 tablespoons (7 ounces) lukewarm water

¼ cup (3 ounces) honey

3 tablespoons (1½ ounces) unsalted butter, cut into 4 pieces

1 large egg, separated (white reserved)

1½ teaspoons dark sesame oil

2 cups (6¾ ounces) whole wheat pastry flour

1½ cups (6⅜ ounces) unbleached all-purpose flour

1¼ teaspoons salt

Heaping ½ cup (1¼ ounces) dried potato flakes, or 3 tablespoons (1¼ ounces) potato flour

2½ teaspoons instant yeast

Topping

1 large egg white lightly beaten with 1 tablespoon water

⅓ cup (1⅝ ounces) sesame seeds

3 tablespoons (1½ ounces) melted butter (optional)

TO PREPARE THE DOUGH: Combine all the dough ingredients, using the egg yolk and setting the white aside to use in the topping. Mix and knead—by hand, mixer or bread machine—until you have a fairly stiff dough. Cover and allow the dough to rise until it's quite puffy, though probably not doubled in bulk, 1 to 2 hours.

Lightly grease (or line with parchment) 2 baking sheets or line with parchment paper.

TO SHAPE THE ROLLS: Gently deflate the dough, and transfer it to a lightly greased work surface. Divide the dough into 3 pieces. Roll each piece into a 9-inch round, about ½ inch thick. Brush the rounds with the egg white mixture, then sprinkle each round with a generous 1 tablespoon of the sesame seeds. Cut each round like a pie into 6 wedges. Roll

Bend the rolls into a gentle crescent shape.

up each wedge, beginning at the wide end, and then curve the ends in to form a crescent-shaped roll.

Place the rolls on the prepared baking sheets. Brush them with more beaten egg white, and sprinkle with the remaining sesame seeds. Cover and let the rolls rise in a warm place until they've puffed a bit but are definitely not doubled in size, 1¼ to 1½ hours. Don't let them rise too long; if they do, they'll uncurl in the oven. Toward the end of the rise, preheat the oven to 350°F.

TO BAKE THE ROLLS: Uncover and bake the rolls until they're a light golden brown, 20 to 25 minutes. Remove them from the oven, and brush them with melted butter, if desired, for added flavor. Serve warm or at room temperature.

NUTRITION INFORMATION PER SERVING (1 ROLL, 47G): 11g whole grains, 132 cal, 5g fat, 4g protein, 15g complex carbohydrates, 4g sugar, 2g dietary fiber, 17mg cholesterol, 157mg sodium, 82mg potassium, 21RE vitamin A, 1mg iron, 8mg calcium, 82mg phosphorus.

SHAPED LOAVES

From fat rounds and skinny baguettes to wreaths and fancy braids, bread can take many shapes. In fact, only in North America, England and Holland is bread dough regularly confined to a rectangular pan; the rest of the world gives yeast dough some guidance, then lets it find its own perfect shape as it rises and bakes.

Many of the breads in this section rise and bake in a round cake pan. Whole grain loaves need support to keep their shape, and we've found that using a cake pan for breads with a high percentage of whole grains allows them to approximate the size and shape of free-form rounds made with all-purpose or bread flour.

The majority of these breads also employ a starter, which is a wonderful way to add flavor to your bread. A starter is a bit of flour, a bit of water and a pinch of yeast mixed together the night before you plan to bake the bread. The trio percolates nicely at room temperature, creating a heavenly flavor and a lush texture in your bread. We found traditional whole wheat flour creates a great starter.

Wheat Baguettes

YIELD: 3 (16-inch) baguettes, 8 servings each

BAKING TEMPERATURE: 425°F

BAKING TIME: 18 to 23 minutes

While any self-respecting resident of Paris would scoff at this version of France's beloved signature bread, there are those who appreciate the rich, wheaty taste and heartiness of these baguettes. While they won't be as light and crisp-crusted as the classic all-white-flour version, they'll still have lovely texture, full of the baguette's signature irregular-size holes.

Pre-ferment

1 cup (4 ounces) traditional whole wheat flour

½ cup (4 ounces) cool water

Pinch of instant yeast

Dough

All of the pre-ferment

¾ cup plus 2 tablespoons (7 ounces) cool water

¼ cup (2 ounces) orange juice

1¼ cups (5 ounces) traditional whole wheat flour

2¼ cups (9½ ounces) unbleached bread flour

1½ teaspoons salt

¼ teaspoon instant yeast

TO PREPARE THE PRE-FERMENT: Mix the pre-ferment ingredients in a small (2- to 3-cup) bowl, cover the bowl, and let rest overnight at room temperature.

TO PREPARE THE DOUGH: Combine all the ingredients, and mix and knead them—by hand, mixer or bread machine—until you have a dough that's cohesive, but whose surface is still a bit rough. If you're using a bread machine, cancel the machine after about 7 minutes of kneading. Cover with lightly greased plastic wrap and allow the dough to rise for 3 to 4 hours, gently deflating it and turning it over once each hour.

Turn the dough out onto a lightly greased or floured work surface. Divide the dough into 3 pieces. Shape each piece into a rough, slightly flattened oval, cover with greased plastic wrap or a proof cover, and let them rest for 15 minutes. Lightly grease a large (13 x 18-inch) baking sheet or line with parchment paper.

Working with one piece of dough at a time, fold the dough in half lengthwise, and seal the edges with the heel of your hand. Flatten it slightly, and fold and seal again. With the seam side down, cup your fingers and gently roll the dough into a 16-inch log.

HOW DO I GET MORE OF THOSE NICE BIG HOLES INSIDE MY BAGUETTE?

A hallmark of the baguette is its open texture, featuring lots of big holes to catch melting butter or olive oil. You can affect the size and number of these holes by the hydration of the dough: the amount of water in the recipe compared to the amount of flour. The more water (up to a point), the larger and more irregular the holes. Clearly, too much water will give you dough that's so slack it can't hold its shape while it's rising; the trick is to hit the hydration just right. The preceding baguette recipe is written with a hydration that will yield a moderate number of irregular holes, making a dough that's fairly easy to work with, and that holds its shape well while rising. For more and larger holes, increase the water by 2 tablespoons. This will yield a stickier dough that's harder to work with, and a slightly flatter baguette, but one with a craggier, more hole-filled interior, if that's your goal. One final note: This recipe was developed in cool, dry weather conditions. If you're baking baguettes where it's hot and humid, you may need to reduce the amount of water by 2 tablespoons to obtain a dough that's easy to work with.

Place the logs on the prepared pan, spacing them evenly. Cover them with a proof cover or lightly greased plastic wrap, and allow them to rise for 30 minutes. Drape them gently with heavily greased plastic wrap (don't anchor the wrap to the edges of the pan), and refrigerate them overnight. The next day, let the loaves rest at room temperature for about 1½ hours, covered with a proof cover or lightly greased plastic wrap, before baking.

About 30 minutes before you're ready to bake the baguettes, preheat your oven to 425°F. If you're using a baking stone, place it on the lowest shelf.

TO BAKE THE BAGUETTES: Uncover the baguettes. If you're baking on a stone, lift the baguettes (including the parchment) onto a peel, and then transfer them to the stone. If you're baking on a baking sheet, simply place the sheet on the middle rack of the oven. Bake the baguettes for 18 minutes, tent them lightly with foil, and bake for an additional 5 minutes, until they're a deep, golden brown. For the crispest crust, turn off the oven, crack it open about 2 inches, transfer the baguettes from the pan onto the oven rack, and allow them to cool completely in the oven. These are best served the same day they're

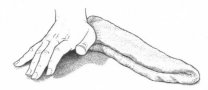

Fold the dough in half lengthwise and seal the edge with the heel of your hand.

Cup your hands and roll the dough, applying very gentle pressure with the palms of your hands right where they meet your fingers.

Roll from the center outward along the length of the dough.

made. After that, refresh them by wrapping lightly in foil and baking in a preheated 350°F oven for 8 to 10 minutes.

NUTRITION INFORMATION PER SERVING (1/8 LOAF, 38G): 11g whole grains, 78 cal, 3g protein, 17g complex carbohydrates, 2g dietary fiber, 134mg sodium, 61mg potassium, 1mg vitamin C, 1mg iron, 6mg calcium, 50mg phosphorus.

# Ciabatta Integrale

YIELD: 2 (12-inch) loaves, 12 servings each
BAKING TEMPERATURE: 425°F
BAKING TIME: 20 to 25 minutes

Ciabatta, a rough-hewn, light-textured Italian bread, makes wonderful sandwiches. In Italy, ciabatta is the basis for panini, those grilled sandwiches that have become so popular in America in recent years. Slice the loaf around its equator to make a top and a bottom, fill the bottom with your favorite sandwich fixings, add the top, and grill in a panini press or hinged grill. Ecco! You've made a panino. Slice crosswise for individual panini. Even if you're not making grilled sandwiches, the bread is delightfully full of air pockets, which serve as great little collection points for olive oil or the juice from your Italian stuffed-sandwich filling.

Classic ciabatta is made of all-purpose or bread flour. When made with whole wheat flour, as this one is, the bread is called ciabatta integrale (literally translated "entire," and meaning whole grain).

Pre-ferment
1 cup (4 ounces) traditional whole wheat flour
1/2 cup (4 ounces) cool water
Pinch of instant yeast

Dough
All of the pre-ferment
1 1/4 cups (5 ounces) traditional whole wheat flour
2 1/4 cups (9 1/2 ounces) unbleached bread flour
1 1/4 cups (10 ounces) cool water
1/4 cup (1 3/4 ounces) olive oil
1/4 cup (1 ounce) nonfat dry milk
1 1/2 teaspoons salt
1/4 teaspoon instant yeast

TO PREPARE THE PRE-FERMENT: Mix the pre-ferment ingredients in a small (2- to 3-cup) bowl, cover the bowl, and let rest overnight at room temperature.

At 1-hour intervals during the dough's 3-hour rise, grease your hands and lift it out of the bowl deflating it gently.

Return the dough to the bowl, tucking what was on top underneath. Re-cover the bowl.

TO PREPARE THE DOUGH: This very slack (wet) dough is developed somewhat differently than normal yeast dough. It's impossible to knead thoroughly by hand, so choose an electric mixer or bread machine.

If you're using an electric mixer, combine all the dough ingredients, stop the mixer, cover the bowl, and let them rest for 45 minutes. Switch to the dough hook, and knead at low speed for 10 minutes; the dough will never form a ball. Lightly grease a large bowl, and use a bowl scraper or spatula to scrape the dough into the greased bowl. Cover the bowl.

If you're using a bread machine, allow the machine to knead the dough until it's thoroughly combined and fairly smooth, 10 minutes. Cancel the machine, and use a spatula to scrape the dough into a lightly greased large bowl. Cover the bowl.

Allow the dough to rise for 3 hours, gently deflating it and turning it over after 1 hour, then again after 2 hours, and again after 3 hours.

Let the dough rest in the bowl for 10 minutes while you lightly grease 2 baking sheets or line them with parchment paper. If you plan to bake the ciabatta on a baking stone, line the baking sheets with parchment.

Grease your hands, and grasp the dough, breaking it into 2 fairly even pieces. Leave one piece in the bowl. Gently stretch the other piece into a log about 10 inches long, and lay it on one of the prepared baking sheets. Stretch and pat

> **A SHORTER KNEAD, A LONGER REST**
>
> There's a correlation between how long you knead yeast dough, and how long it rises. In general, the shorter the amount of time you knead (and thus, the less "developed" the dough is), the longer you should let it rise. The gluten in the dough will continue to strengthen as the dough rises.

it till it's about 12 inches long and 3 to 4 inches wide. Repeat with the remaining piece of dough. Cover both baking sheets with proof covers, or heavily greased plastic wrap, laid gently over the loaves. Allow the loaves to rise until they're very puffy, about 2 hours. Near the end of their rise, preheat the oven to 425°F. If you're using a baking stone (and this is a great place to use one), place it on the lowest shelf.

TO BAKE THE CIABATTA: If you're baking on a stone, uncover and transfer the ciabatta, parchment and all, to the stone. Otherwise, uncover the bread and place the pans on the lower and middle racks of your oven. Bake the ciabatta, rotating them halfway through the baking time, until they're a deep, golden brown and a thermometer inserted in the center registers 205°F or more, 20 to 25 minutes. Turn off the oven, crack it open about 2 inches, remove the ciabatta from the pans and place them directly on the oven racks, and allow them to cool in the oven. Ciabatta will be crisp for awhile, but will gradually soften over the course of the day, or overnight. To refresh and recrisp, wrap them lightly in foil, and reheat in a preheated 350°F oven for about 10 minutes.

NUTRITION INFORMATION PER SERVING (1/12 LOAF, 42G): 11g whole grains, 99 cal, 2g fat, 3g protein, 17g complex carbohydrates, 2g dietary fiber, 141mg sodium, 78mg potassium, 1mg iron, 21mg calcium, 61mg phosphorus.

Going With the Grain Wreath

YIELD: 1 (10-inch) wreath, 16 servings
BAKING TEMPERATURE: 375°F
BAKING TIME: 35 minutes

A good way to use a number of different grains in your bread, without having to buy a supply of each one separately, can be found in your supermarket's cereal aisle. Five-grain cereal (or 7-, 9-, 10-, or whatever number of grains the manufacturer decides to throw together) is usually a mix of flattened, sliced whole grains, sometimes including cracked grains or seeds as well. This fiber-rich mixture is a great way to add both texture and flavor to whole grain breads.

The chief flour in this bread is spelt, a mild-flavored variety of wheat. Spelt—along with einkorn and emmer—is one of the "ancient wheats," the three varieties of wheat from which all other hybrids have sprung. Mainly found in Europe—it's commonly used in both bread and cake in Germany and Italy—spelt can be more difficult to find in this country. But it's worth the search: though spelt's gluten is somewhat delicate, and it won't produce as high-rising a loaf as whole wheat flour, its flavor is superb.

Dough
1 cup (8 ounces) lukewarm water
¼ cup (2 ounces) orange juice
2 tablespoons (⅞ ounce) olive oil
1 large egg, separated (white reserved)
½ teaspoon dark sesame oil (optional)
2¼ cups (7⅞ ounces) whole spelt flour
1 cup (4¼ ounces) unbleached all-purpose flour
2 tablespoons (1 ounce) packed light or dark brown sugar
1½ teaspoons salt
¾ cup (3 ounces) 5-grain cereal or the grain blend of your choice
2 teaspoons instant yeast

Topping
1 large egg white
1 tablespoon cold water
¼ cup (1 ounce) 5-grain cereal or the grain blend of your choice

TO PREPARE THE DOUGH: Combine all the dough ingredients, using the egg yolk and setting the white aside to use in the topping. Mix and knead—by hand, mixer or bread machine—until you have a soft, smooth dough. Cover and allow the dough to rise until it's puffy though not doubled in bulk, 1 to 2 hours.

TO SHAPE THE WREATH: Lightly grease a baking sheet or line with parchment paper. Gently deflate the dough, and transfer it to a lightly greased work surface. Divide it into 3 equal pieces, and roll each piece into a 24-inch log. Braid the logs together, then lift the braid onto the prepared pan, coiling it into a 9-inch wreath and pinching the ends together.

Prepare the topping by whisking the egg white and water together till frothy; brush the loaf with this mixture. Sprinkle with the cereal. Cover the loaf gently with lightly greased plastic wrap or a proof cover, and allow it to rise until it's puffy but not doubled

Roll each piece of dough into a smooth 24-inch rope.

Anchor one end of each of the three ropes and braid them; try not to pull and stretch the dough as you gently braid. Pinch the ends together.

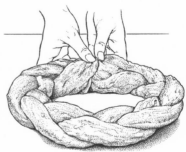

Shape the braid into a wreath, pinching the two ends together as neatly as possible.

in bulk, 1 hour. Don't let this bread overrise; spelt isn't as strong as wheat, and it might collapse in the oven. Near the end of the bread's rise, preheat the oven to 375°F.

TO BAKE THE WREATH: Uncover and bake the bread for about 35 minutes, tenting it with foil after 20 minutes. The bread is done when it's golden brown and an instant-read thermometer inserted in the center registers 195°F. Remove it from the oven, and after a minute or so turn it out onto a rack. Cool the bread for 30 minutes before serving.

NUTRITION INFORMATION PER SERVING (1/16 OF WREATH, 54G): 21g whole grains, 124 cal, 3g fat, 5g protein, 21g complex carbohydrates, 2g sugar, 3g dietary fiber, 13mg cholesterol, 206mg sodium, 121mg potassium, 5RE vitamin A, 2mg vitamin C, 2mg iron, 9mg calcium, 104mg phosphorus.

CRACKED GRAINS? DON'T CRACK YOUR TEETH!

The multi-grain cereals that are appropriate for bread are made from flaked grains, grains that look like rolled oats. Cereal, in this case, refers to the grain itself, not to the box of crunchy breakfast food you pour your milk over every morning. Any kind of flaked grain or seed is a good addition to bread dough. But watch out for cracked grains; they can sometimes be so hard that they'll give your loaf an unpleasantly tough crunch. Read the label on the cereal you're buying. If it contains flaked grains and seeds, it should be fine. If it includes cracked grains, you might still want to try it, as the cracked grains might have been precooked by the manufacturer. Try experimenting by kneading some of the cereal into a single roll, next time you make a batch. If it bakes up satisfactorily in the roll it's good to go for your next loaf of bread.

Whole Wheat Challah

YIELD: One (15- to 16-inch) braid, 16 servings
BAKING TEMPERATURE: 375°F
BAKING TIME: 30 minutes

This recipe for high-rising challah comes from Lora Brody, author, photographer, and longtime King Arthur friend. The loaf was inspired by Lora's mother, Millie, who long ago discovered the virtue of using whole wheat pastry flour to make this light-textured golden braid, traditionally served on the Jewish Sabbath and other holidays. Whole wheat gives the challah deeper color and more complex flavor, and using whole wheat pastry flour, ground from softer wheat than traditional whole wheat flour, allows it to retain its feather-light texture.

½ cup (4 ounces) lukewarm water

6 tablespoons (2½ ounces) vegetable oil

¼ cup (3 ounces) honey

2 large eggs

2 cups (6¾ ounces) whole wheat pastry flour

2 cups (8½ ounces) unbleached bread flour

1½ teaspoons salt

2½ teaspoons instant yeast

TO PREPARE THE DOUGH: Combine all the ingredients and mix and knead them—by hand, mixer, or bread machine—until you have a soft, smooth dough. Cover and allow the dough to rise until it's puffy and nearly doubled in bulk, 1 to 2 hours.

Lightly grease a baking sheet or line with parchment paper.

TO SHAPE THE CHALLAH: Gently deflate the dough, and transfer it to a lightly greased work surface. Divide it into 3 equal pieces, shape each piece into a rough log, cover the pieces, and let them rest for 10 minutes.

Roll each piece of dough into an 18-inch rope. Place the 3 pieces of dough side by side on the prepared pan, and braid them, squeezing the ends together then tucking them neatly underneath. Cover the braid gently with lightly greased plastic wrap or a proof cover, and allow it to rise until it's puffy, but not doubled in bulk, about 1 hour. Near the end of the rise, preheat the oven to 375°F.

TO BAKE THE CHALLAH: Uncover and bake the bread for 20 minutes; tent it with foil and bake until it's a deep, golden brown and an instant-read thermometer inserted in the center registers 190°F, 10 minutes more. Remove it from the oven, and after a minute or so carefully transfer it to a rack. Cool the bread to lukewarm before cutting it.

NUTRITION INFORMATION PER SERVING (1 SLICE, 52G): 12g whole grains, 165 cal, 6g fat, 4g protein, 20g complex carbohydrates, 4g sugar, 2g dietary fiber, 26mg cholesterol, 210mg sodium, 84mg potassium, 9RE vitamin A, 1mg iron, 7mg calcium, 79mg phosphorus.

VARIATION: SESAME SEED CHALLAH: *Reserve about 2 teaspoons egg white from the eggs in the dough. Combine it with 2 teaspoons water, and whisk until smooth. Gently brush this mixture on the risen challah just before baking, and sprinkle with sesame seeds.*

BREAD-BAKING: SCIENCE AND ART

Of all the baking you might do with whole grains, yeast-leavened breads (including sourdough) are probably the least straightforward. They're made up mainly of flour, and flour varies wildly from brand to brand, as well as undergoing slighter seasonal variations in your kitchen. Its grind may range from extra-fine to coarse, its absorption can vary, its protein level will be higher or lower, brand to brand... all of these factors will affect bread dough. In addition, yeast is a living organism, and thus unpredictable. As it grows, it responds to heat, weather, liquid and the food it's consuming. Variations in any of those will produce changes in your bread dough.

So what's a bread baker to do? Relax. Watch your dough, and make slight adjustments as you go along. If you've carefully measured all the ingredients and produced dough wetter than what the instructions indicate, add more flour. If your dough consistently rises too slowly, up the yeast a bit each time you bake, until the dough is moving along as quickly as the recipe says it should. Above all, don't get discouraged. Yeast bread, while it can be fickle, is also extremely forgiving. Unlike a cake that, once the batter is mixed, is pretty much a *fait accompli,* bread dough can be played around with. Adjust its flour-to-liquid ratio as you go; refrigerate it along the way, if your schedule dictates; make a braid instead of a loaf. Once you understand yeast bread's quirky disposition, it'll become a fast friend.

YEAST, KNEADING AND RISING: A FINE BALANCE

When making yeast breads, there's a balance between how much yeast you use, how long you knead the dough and how long you let it rise. In general, the longer you let dough rise, the more flavor it develops, due to the greater amount of organic acids and alcohol produced by yeast as it grows. And, as bread dough rises, its gluten also develops and tightens. Thus, dough in which the gluten has been fully developed during kneading shouldn't be allowed to rise for an extended time, as the gluten will actually become overdeveloped, producing dough that's tightly elastic and hard to work with.

How does this theory translate to practice? Try this: Cut the amount of yeast in your recipe in half. Knead the dough half as long as you normally would, till it's cohesive but still fairly rough on the surface. Let it rise 2 to 3 times as long as you normally would, deflating it and turning it over every 1½ hours or so along the way, to redistribute the yeast. We think you'll be pleased with the bread's improved flavor and texture. And the more casual schedule is a plus too. If, at any point during its rise, you need to go do something else, simply refrigerate the dough (for up to 24 hours; no need to turn it during this rest), and come back to it later. Once you get used to making bread this way, you'll discover how flexible and user-friendly the process really is!

Whole Wheat Cranberry-Orange Country Loaf

YIELD: 1 (8-inch) round loaf, 16 servings
BAKING TEMPERATURE: 350°F
BAKING TIME: 45 to 55 minutes

Not every holiday bread is sweet, despite the evidence produced by endless variations on egg and sugar-rich fruit breads. The following dense, chewy country loaf, studded with pecans and cranberries and scented with orange, features the toasty, nutty flavor of whole wheat, and the tang of orange and cranberry tempered by a touch of honey.

Pre-ferment
1 cup (4 ounces) traditional whole wheat flour
⅓ cup (2⅝ ounces) cool water
Pinch of instant yeast

Dough
All of the pre-ferment
½ cup (4 ounces) lukewarm water
3 tablespoons (1¼ ounces) vegetable oil
¼ cup (3 ounces) honey
⅓ cup (2⅝ ounces) orange juice
2½ cups (10 ounces) traditional whole wheat flour
1½ teaspoons salt
Grated zest of 1 orange
2½ teaspoons instant yeast
1 cup (3¾ ounces) chopped toasted pecans
1 cup (4 ounces) dried cranberries

TO PREPARE THE PRE-FERMENT: Mix the pre-ferment ingredients in a small (2- to 3-cup) bowl; it'll be very stiff. Knead gently with your fingers to incorporate all the flour. Cover the bowl, and let the pre-ferment rest overnight at room temperature.

TO PREPARE THE DOUGH: Combine the pre-ferment and all the dough ingredients except the pecans and cranberries. Mix and knead—by hand, mixer or bread machine—until smooth. Cover and allow the dough to rise until it's puffy though probably not doubled in bulk, 1 to 2 hours.

TO BAKE THE BREAD: Lightly grease a baking sheet or line with parchment paper. Gently deflate the dough, and knead the pecans and cranberries into it. Shape the dough into a ball, and place it on the prepared pan. Cover the pan with a proof cover or lightly greased plastic wrap, and allow the dough to rise until it's noticeably expanded, though not doubled in bulk, 2 hours. While the dough is rising, preheat the oven to 350°F.

Uncover and bake the bread for 45 to 55 minutes, tenting it lightly with foil after about 20 minutes. The internal temperature will register between 200°F and 210°F when the bread is done. Remove the bread from the oven, and transfer it to a rack to cool. Cool the bread for 30 minutes before slicing.

NUTRITION INFORMATION PER SERVING (1 SLICE, 64G): 25g whole grains, 190 cal, 8g fat, 5g protein, 26g complex carbohydrates, 4g sugar, 4g dietary fiber, 203mg sodium, 206mg potassium, 1RE vitamin A, 3mg vitamin C, 1mg iron, 18mg calcium, 121mg phosphorus.

Golden Raisin Hearth Bread

YIELD: 2 round loaves, 8 servings each
BAKING TEMPERATURE: 350°F
BAKING TIME: 40 to 45 minutes

This round country-style loaf is an interesting combination of flavors and textures. The bread itself is mildly savory, with the heartiness of whole grains. Fennel seeds add a subtle hint of licorice and golden raisins bring their own sweetness and enhance the bread's moist texture. Serve this bread with goulash or another hearty stew or with a mildly sauced pasta, such as spaghetti aglio e olio.

Pre-ferment
1 cup (4 ounces) traditional whole wheat flour
1/2 cup (4 ounces) cool water
Pinch of instant yeast

Dough
All of the pre-ferment
1/2 cup (4 ounces) lukewarm water
1/4 cup (2 ounces) orange juice
3 tablespoons (1 1/4 ounces) olive oil
1/2 cup (2 ounces) traditional whole wheat flour
1/2 cup (2 3/8 ounces) yellow cornmeal or semolina (2 7/8 ounces)
1 cup (4 1/4 ounces) unbleached all-purpose flour
1/4 cup (1 ounce) wheat germ
1/4 cup (1 ounce) oat bran
1 1/4 teaspoons salt
1 tablespoon fennel seeds
2 teaspoons instant yeast
2 cups (12 ounces) golden raisins, firmly packed

TO PREPARE THE PRE-FERMENT: Mix the pre-ferment ingredients in a small (2- to 3-cup) bowl and let rest overnight at room temperature.

TO PREPARE THE DOUGH: Combine the pre-ferment and all the dough ingredients except the raisins, and mix and knead—by hand, mixer or bread machine—till you have a smooth, elastic dough. Cover and allow the dough to rise until it's puffy and nearly doubled in bulk, 1 to 2 hours.

Lightly grease a baking sheet or line with parchment paper. Gently deflate the dough, and knead the raisins into it. Divide the dough in half, and shape each half into a ball.

Place them on the prepared pan, leaving several inches between them. Cover the pan with a proof cover or lightly greased plastic wrap, and allow the loaves to rise until they're very puffy, 1 to 1½ hours. While the bread is rising, preheat the oven to 350°F.

TO BAKE THE BREADS: Uncover and bake the breads for 40 to 45 minutes, tenting them lightly with foil after 15 minutes; this will preserve their light-gold color. The internal temperature will register between 200°F and 210°F when the bread is done. Remove the loaves from the oven, and transfer them to a rack to cool. Cool for 30 minutes before slicing.

NUTRITION INFORMATION PER SERVING (1 SLICE, 65G): 11g whole grains, 169 cal, 3g fat, 4g protein, 34g complex carbohydrates, 3g dietary fiber, 171mg sodium, 246mg potassium, 1RE vitamin A, 2mg vitamin C, 2mg iron, 22mg calcium, 112mg phosphorus.

 # Pain aux Noix

YIELD: 2 round loaves, 12 servings each
BAKING TEMPERATURE: 425°F
BAKING TIME: 25 to 27 minutes

Nut bread is the simple translation of pain aux noix, *one of France's delightful whole grain loaves. This dark, tender bread is fairly simple to make, but the texture and flavor are complex: oven heat brings out the walnuts' flavor, as well as the deep, rich taste of whole wheat. Serve this bread, thinly sliced, with a nice goat cheese, Roquefort, Brie or Camembert. Sliced pears on the side are a tasty addition.*

Pre-ferment
1½ cups (6 ounces) traditional whole wheat flour
⅔ cup (5⅜ ounces) cool water
Pinch of instant yeast

Dough
All of the pre-ferment
¾ cup (6 ounces) milk, heated to lukewarm
¼ cup (2 ounces) orange juice
4 tablespoons (½ stick, 2 ounces) unsalted butter, cut into 6 pieces
1½ cups (6 ounces) traditional whole wheat flour
1½ cups (6⅜ ounces) unbleached all-purpose flour
1 tablespoon brown sugar
1¼ teaspoons salt
2 teaspoons instant yeast
2 cups (8 ounces) chopped walnuts

TO PREPARE THE PRE-FERMENT: Mix the pre-ferment ingredients in a medium bowl, cover and let rest overnight at room temperature.

TO PREPARE THE DOUGH: Combine all the ingredients except the walnuts, and mix and knead—by hand, mixer or bread machine—until you have a soft, smooth dough. Cover and allow the dough to rise until it's puffy and nearly doubled in bulk, 1 to 2 hours.

TO PREPARE THE NUTS: Preheat the oven to 350°F. Spread the nuts in an ungreased 9 x 13-inch pan. Bake them for 10 minutes; they should smell faintly toasty, and just barely be beginning to brown. Remove them from the oven, and let cool.

Lightly grease a baking sheet or line with parchment paper. Gently deflate the dough, and knead the nuts into it (see illustration, p. 201). Divide the dough in half, and shape each half into a ball. Place the balls on the prepared baking sheet, cover, and let them rise until they're quite puffy, though not necessarily doubled in bulk, 45 minutes. Toward the end of the rise, preheat the oven to 425°F.

TO BAKE THE LOAVES: Uncover and bake the loaves until they're golden brown and an instant-read thermometer inserted in the center reads approximately 190°F, 25 to 27 minutes. Remove the loaves from the oven, and cool them for 30 minutes before slicing.

NUTRITION INFORMATION PER SERVING (1 SLICE, 50G): 14g whole grains, 161 cal, 9g fat, 5g protein, 18g complex carbohydrates, 3g dietary fiber, 5mg cholesterol, 116mg sodium, 131mg potassium, 21RE vitamin A, 1mg vitamin C, 1mg iron, 25mg calcium, 102mg phosphorus.

GRINDING YOUR OWN WHEAT

Freshly ground wheat makes a lovely, mild-tasting, bran-flecked loaf of whole grain bread. If you have a grain mill gathering dust in a closet, haul it out and put it to use. To grind enough flour for one standard (8^1/$_2$ x 4^1/$_2$-inch) loaf of bread, begin with 1^3/$_4$ cups (12 ounces) hard red or white wheat berries. (Soft wheat berries will yield whole wheat pastry flour.) Once milled, this will yield roughly 3 cups of flour.

For best-tasting results, use this fresh flour right away. Its absorption capabilities may vary from what you're used to; a lot will depend on the age of the wheat berries. Usually, freshly ground wheat requires a bit more liquid than wheat flour from a bag.

Sesame-Barley Bread

YIELD: **1 (9-inch) round loaf, 16 servings**

BAKING TEMPERATURE: **350°F**

BAKING TIME: **45 minutes**

John Dyall, a longtime baker who's lived all over the world, shared this homemade recipe with us while he was in Pakistan. Says John, "This is a very nice, chewy loaf. I don't think I have used barley flour much before and it seems to give a flavor a bit like rye, but it is easier to use. I like this loaf quite a lot, and it goes very well indeed with cheese (and would be good with ham or salami, except these aren't available here)."

Barley makes a deep brown loaf and, because of its very limited gluten content, does best in flatter rather than taller loaves, as it has difficulty holding its shape. We added a topping of sesame seeds (and some inside, too) to John's suggested recipe, and the seeds not only lend nutty flavor, but a sunny, golden look to the loaf's top.

Dough
1³⁄₄ cups (14 ounces) lukewarm water
2 tablespoons (⁷⁄₈ ounce) olive oil
1 teaspoon dark sesame oil
1³⁄₄ cups (7 ounces) whole barley flour
³⁄₄ cup (3 ounces) malted wheat flakes or Maltex dry cereal
1³⁄₄ cups (7³⁄₈ ounces) unbleached all-purpose flour
¹⁄₄ cup (1¹⁄₄ ounces) sesame seeds
3 tablespoons (⁷⁄₈ ounce) vital wheat gluten
1¹⁄₂ teaspoons salt
1 tablespoon sugar
2 teaspoons instant yeast

Topping
1 large egg white beaten with 1 tablespoon cold water
3 tablespoons (1 ounce) sesame seeds

Combine all the dough ingredients, and mix and knead—by hand, mixer or bread machine—until you have a soft, smooth dough. Cover and allow the dough to rise until it's puffy and nearly doubled in bulk, 1 to 2 hours.

Lightly grease a 9-inch round cake pan.

Gently deflate the dough, shape it into a slightly flattened ball, and place it in the prepared pan; pat it out till it nearly reaches the sides of the pan.

Brush the surface of the bread all over with the beaten egg white, and sprinkle heavily with sesame seeds. Dab with egg white again, and sprinkle with additional seeds. Cover the pan with a proof cover or lightly greased plastic wrap, and allow the bread to rise until it's crested just even with the rim of the pan, 1 to 1½ hours. The crust may crack a bit; that's OK. Near the end of the bread's rise, preheat the oven to 350°F.

Uncover and bake the bread for about 45 minutes. It won't rise much; it may even fall a bit. The bread is done when it's golden brown and an instant-read thermometer inserted in the center registers 190°F. Remove it from the oven, and after a minute or so turn it out onto a rack.

NUTRITION INFORMATION PER SERVING (1 SLICE, 66G): 19g whole grains, 156 cal, 4g fat, 5g protein, 24g complex carbohydrates, 1g sugar, 3g dietary fiber, 206mg sodium, 105mg potassium, 2mg iron, 29mg calcium, 104mg phosphorus.

A NIFTY SECRET INGREDIENT

Maltex, a hot cereal that may be found in your grocery store's cereal aisle alongside the oatmeal, is a great substitute for hard-to-find malted wheat flakes. Malted wheat flakes are crushed, thin-sliced wheat berries that have been sweetened with malt syrup. They lend a bit of texture, and a hint of caramelized sugar flavor to your yeast breads. In Maltex the berries are chopped into fine pieces rather than sliced, but their flavor is the same. Use them 1:1 as you would malted wheat flakes.

Greek Olive and Onion Bread

YIELD: **2 loaves, 10 servings each**
BAKING TEMPERATURE: **425°F**
BAKING TIME: **40 to 45 minutes**

Many Greek breads are associated with specific religious holidays: the most famous of these are Tsoureki, a golden braid enclosing colorful dyed hardboiled eggs, at Easter; and citrus and spice Christopsomo, at Christmas. Elioti, an olive-studded loaf, was originally a Lenten bread, but is now commonly available year-round. The following is our take on that classic.

Barley and wheat, the main grain crops of ancient Greece, give this round loaf its rich color. We use spelt, an old European variety of wheat, in place of the more familiar whole wheat flour in this aromatic loaf; spelt has milder flavor, allowing the taste of olive and onion to shine through.

This savory bread is softer than a typical hearth loaf, though it's quite chewy. We like to serve it plain, toasted and drizzled with olive oil, or sliced for sandwiches (fresh tomato and feta cheese is a favorite).

1 cup (5 ounces) lightly packed pitted drained kalamata olives (about 8 ounces undrained)

Pre-ferment
1 cup (4 ounces) whole barley flour
1 cup (3½ ounces) whole spelt flour
1 cup (8 ounces) cool water
Pinch of instant yeast

Dough
All of the pre-ferment
¼ cup (2 ounces) lukewarm water
2 tablespoons (1 ounce) orange juice
3 tablespoons (1¼ ounces) olive oil
⅓ cup (1 ⅜ ounces) wheat germ
2 cups (8½ ounces) unbleached all-purpose flour
1½ teaspoons salt
2 teaspoons instant yeast
2.8-ounce can French-fried onions

TO PREPARE THE OLIVES: Preheat the oven to 350°F. Lightly grease a 9-inch round cake pan. Place the drained olives in the prepared pan. Bake for 30 minutes; they'll lose half their weight (in liquid), but will still be soft and pliable. Remove them from the oven and, when they're cool enough, snip each olive in half. Place in a bowl, cover, and refrigerate overnight, while the pre-ferment is working.

TO PREPARE THE PRE-FERMENT: Mix the pre-ferment ingredients in a medium bowl, cover the bowl, and let rest overnight at room temperature.

TO PREPARE THE DOUGH: Combine all the ingredients except the olives and onions, and mix and knead them—by hand, mixer or bread machine—until you have a soft, smooth dough. Cover and allow the dough to rise until it's puffy and nearly doubled in bulk, 1 to 2 hours.

Lightly grease a 13 x 18-inch baking sheet (or similar-size cookie sheet) or line with parchment paper. Gently deflate the dough, and knead the olives and onions into it.

Turn the dough out onto a lightly greased work surface. Divide it in half and form each half into a ball. Place the balls on the prepared pan. Cover the loaves with a proof cover or lightly greased plastic wrap, and allow them to rise until they're very puffy, about 1½ hours. Note: If desired, refrigerate the risen loaves for 4 to 18 hours before baking. This will give them their best flavor and will contribute to a nice, open texture. Before baking refrigerated loaves, let them sit at room temperature for about 3½ hours, until they're thoroughly warmed.

TO BAKE THE LOAVES: Preheat your oven to 425°F. Just before placing the loaves in the oven, uncover and spritz them lightly with water. Bake the bread for 40 to 45 minutes, tenting it with foil after 15 minutes. The bread is done when an instant-read thermometer inserted in the center registers 200°F to 210°F. Remove the loaves from the oven, and cool on a rack for 30 minutes before cutting.

NUTRITION INFORMATION PER SERVING (1 SLICE, 54G): 11g whole grains, 135 cal, 5g fat, 4g protein, 20g complex carbohydrates, 2g dietary fiber, 248mg sodium, 96mg potassium, 3RE vitamin A, 1mg vitamin C, 1mg iron, 14mg calcium, 79mg phosphorus.

HOW CAN I TELL IF MY BREAD IS DONE?

Is my bread done when it's golden brown? Not necessarily. Is it done when I thump it on the bottom and it sounds hollow? Probably, but the resonance of the thump is subjective; and besides, you have to be pretty nimble to juggle a loaf of hot bread while you get it out of the pan to thump its bottom. So what's the best way to tell if your bread's done?

The easiest and most reliable method by far is to measure the loaf's temperature, at the center, with an instant-read thermometer. Sandwich or pan bread (the typical rectangular loaf) should be about 190°F. A large, dense free-form loaf—e.g., a whole grain artisan hearth loaf—will be about 200°F to 210°F at its center when it's fully baked.

Rosemary-Asiago Chop Bread

YIELD: 1 (8-inch) round loaf, 16 servings
BAKING TEMPERATURE: 350°F
BAKING TIME: 35 minutes

The assertive flavors of dried rosemary and Asiago cheese blend together very happily in this round loaf. Since it's not a high-riser, we're able to add some barley flour, to temper the wheat's taste, without affecting the loaf's texture. Cut it in wedges and serve with pasta or soup. Or cut it in long, ¼-inch-thick slices, and toast in the oven till crisp, to make delicious "dip sticks."

Why the moniker "chop bread"? Because you actually chop the top of the loaf into pieces while adding the toppings, and it then "heals" itself and becomes a cohesive round as it rises and bakes.

1 cup (8 ounces) lukewarm water
2 tablespoons (⅞ ounce) olive oil
1½ cups (6 ounces) traditional whole wheat flour
1 cup (4 ounces) whole barley flour
½ cup (2⅛ ounces) unbleached bread flour
2 teaspoons dried rosemary
1¼ teaspoons salt
1 tablespoon brown sugar
2 teaspoons instant yeast
1 cup (4 ounces) Asiago cheese, cut into ½-inch cubes

Combine all the ingredients except the cheese, and mix and knead—by hand, mixer or bread machine—until you have a soft, smooth dough. Cover and allow the dough to rise until it's puffy and nearly doubled in bulk, 1 to 2 hours.

Lightly grease an 8-inch round cake pan. Gently deflate the dough, and shape it into a ball. Flatten the ball till it's a 9 x 12-inch oval. Spread the cheese cubes over half the dough, and fold the other half over it. Shape the dough into a rough 7-inch circle, and place it in the prepared pan.

Using a baker's bench knife or a metal spatula, chop into the top of the dough randomly, cutting into (but not through) the bottom layer. The top of the loaf will look very ragged and pieces of cheese will show through.

Cover the loaf with lightly greased plastic wrap or a proof cover, and allow it to rise for 1½ hours, till puffy. Toward the end of the bread's rise, preheat the oven to 350°F.

Make random cuts all over the surface of the dough, cutting down to (but not through) the bottom layer.

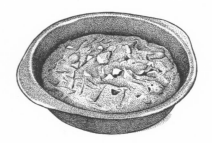

When you're done, the top of the bread will look ragged, with pieces of cheese showing through.

Uncover and bake the bread until it's golden brown and the cheese is melted, about 35 minutes. Remove it from the oven, and transfer it to a rack to cool for 30 minutes before slicing.

NUTRITION INFORMATION PER SERVING (1 SLICE, 47G): 18g whole grains, 122 cal, 4g fat, 5g protein, 16g complex carbohydrates, 1g sugar, 2g dietary fiber, 5mg cholesterol, 282mg sodium, 90mg potassium, 8RE vitamin A, 1mg iron, 94mg calcium, 118mg phosphorus.

Stromboli

YIELD: 2 (12-inch) loaves, 6 servings each
BAKING TEMPERATURE: 350°F
BAKING TIME: 35 to 40 minutes

Stromboli, kissing cousin to a calzone, in its classic version is made from pizza dough spread with pizza-type ingredients (pepperoni and mozzarella are a typical combination), then rolled like a jelly roll and baked. The result is a "pizza log" that's sliced into serving-size pieces and enjoyed hot or at room temperature. In recent years, however, "stromboli" has come to mean any type of sandwich made in stromboli fashion: dough that's rolled out, spread with filling, rolled up and baked.

The following stromboli dough, made with soft whole wheat pastry flour, makes a golden, tender casing for your favorite sandwich fillings, whatever they may be. We give several suggestions, but this is somewhere you can allow your imagination free rein. Try roasted vegetables with Monterey Jack cheese. Or go ahead and make what is purportedly America's favorite sandwich combo—ham and cheese. Some things just can't be beat!

Dough

1 cup plus 2 tablespoons (9 ounces) lukewarm water

¼ cup (2 ounces) orange juice

1 tablespoon honey

4 tablespoons (½ stick, 2 ounces) unsalted butter, cut into 6 pieces

3 cups (10⅛ ounces) whole wheat pastry flour

1 cup (4¼ ounces) unbleached bread flour

Heaping ½ cup (1¼ ounces) dried potato flakes or 3 tablespoons (1¼ ounces)
    potato flour

¼ cup (1 ounce) nonfat dry milk

1½ teaspoons salt

2 teaspoons instant yeast

Spinach and cheese filling

3 tablespoons (1¼ ounces) olive oil

2 cloves garlic (about ½ ounce), peeled and minced

10 ounces mushrooms, washed and chopped or sliced (4 to 5 cups)

10 ounces fresh spinach (about 8 cups, stemmed, cleaned and torn) or two 10-ounce
    packages frozen chopped spinach, thawed and thoroughly squeezed dry

½ teaspoon salt

1 teaspoon coarsely ground black pepper

5 ounces feta cheese, crumbled (about 1¼ cups)

½ cup (2½ ounces) pitted and sliced kalamata olives (optional)

TO PREPARE THE DOUGH: Combine all the ingredients, and mix and knead them—by hand, mixer, or bread machine—until you have a soft, smooth dough. Cover and allow the dough to rise until it's puffy and nearly doubled in bulk, 1 to 2 hours.

TO PREPARE THE FILLING: Heat a large skillet until hot, add the oil and garlic, then immediately add the mushrooms. Stir with a heatproof spatula; the mushrooms will begin to give off their juice. After about 2 minutes, add the spinach, salt and pepper. Cook just enough to wilt the spinach. Remove the pan from the heat, and transfer the contents to a bowl. Stir in the cheese and olives, if using, and set aside.

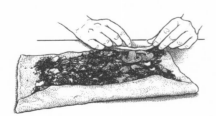

Folding the two long edges over the filling will help keep it from leaking out as the stromboli bakes.

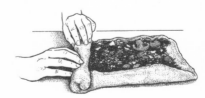

Carefully roll the dough into a log, beginning with the short edge.

Pat the log to even it out, and cut 4 diagonal slashes in the top.

STROMBOLI, AS IN THE VOLCANO?

Where does the name for this rolled sandwich come from? Like the names of many dishes, its origin isn't certain, though most sources agree it's probably not named after the lava-spouting Italian volcano off the coast of Sicily. It's known that so-called stromboli sandwiches first appeared in Philadelphia early in the 20th century, and it's surmised that this Italian sandwich may have been named after a character in one of the popular fairy tales of that time, *The Adventures of Pinocchio*—which was written by an Italian, Carlo Lorenzini (whose pen name was Collodi, for those of you who can picture the cover of that book from your childhood).

Lightly grease a large baking sheet or line with parchment paper.

TO ASSEMBLE THE STROMBOLI: Transfer the dough to a lightly greased work surface, gently deflate it, and divide it in half. Working with one half at a time, roll and pat the dough to a 10 x 12-inch rectangle. It'll be very soft; be careful not to tear it.

Layer half the filling on the dough, leaving a 1-inch margin clear on all sides. Fold the two long edges over the filling; this will help keep it from leaking out as it bakes. Starting with a short edge, gently (and fairly loosely) roll the dough into a 10- to 12-inch log. Place the log on the prepared baking sheet. Repeat with the other piece of dough and the remaining filling.

With a sharp knife, cut 4 diagonal slashes in each log, to allow steam to escape while baking. Cover the logs with a proof cover or lightly greased plastic wrap, and allow them to rest for 30 minutes, while you preheat your oven to 350°F.

TO BAKE THE STROMBOLI: Bake the stromboli until they're a light, golden brown, and the filling is bubbling, 35 to 40 minutes; if they appear to be browning too quickly, tent them lightly with foil for the final 10 minutes of baking. Remove the loaves from the oven, and allow them to cool on the pan for 15 minutes. They may settle and flatten a bit as they cool; don't worry, they'll taste just fine. To serve, slice each loaf into 6 pieces. Refrigerate any leftovers.

NUTRITION INFORMATION PER SERVING (1 SLICE, 147G): 31g whole grains, 271 cal, 11g fat, 10g protein, 30g complex carbohydrates, 2g sugar, 5g dietary fiber, 22mg cholesterol, 584mg sodium, 346mg potassium, 194RE vitamin A, 5mg vitamin C, 3mg iron, 137mg calcium, 219mg phosphorus.

VARIATIONS: REUBEN STROMBOLI *Remember, no one said stromboli had to be strictly Italian! This version features classic Reuben sandwich ingredients. To enhance the "deli" effect even more, add 2 teaspoons crushed caraway seeds to the dough.*

Filling
½ **pound thinly sliced corned beef**
1 to 1½ **cups (4 to 6 ounces) coleslaw, very well drained**
1½ **cups (6 ounces) shredded Swiss cheese**

Prepare the stromboli dough, divide it in half and roll it out as directed in the basic recipe (see p. 242).

Layer half the thinly sliced corned beef on one piece of the dough, leaving a 1-inch margin clear on all sides. Spread the corned beef evenly with half the coleslaw, then with half the cheese. Repeat with the other piece of dough and the remaining filling. Finish and bake the stromboli as directed. Serve with Thousand Island or Russian dressing, if desired.

TUNA MELT STROMBOLI *This is the ultimate comfort lunch for tuna-salad lovers. Warm bread, warm tuna, and melting cheese... it just doesn't get any better than this!*

> *Filling*
> **2 (6-ounce) cans tuna in water, drained and pressed dry**
> **½ cup (2 ounces) finely diced celery**
> **3 tablespoons (1½ ounces) mayonnaise**
> **½ teaspoon salt**
> **¼ teaspoon black pepper**
> **2 cups (8 ounces) grated Cheddar cheese**

Prepare the stromboli dough, divide it in half and roll it out as directed in the basic recipe (see p. 242).

Combine all the filling ingredients, and spread half the filling on each piece of rolled-out dough. Finish and bake the stromboli as directed.

Swedish Dipping Bread

YIELD: 1 10-inch loaf, 20 slices
BAKING TEMPERATURE: 375°F
BAKING TIME: 35 minutes

The following recipe for doppbröd, *a special "dipping bread" served in Sweden at Christmas, yields a light-colored, light-textured rye with a chewy crust and spongy interior. It's perfect for soaking up broth from the stockpot in which traditional smörgåsbord meats have been cooked. Redolent of the fennel and anise seeds that perfume it, it also has an elusive tang, which comes from the ale and buttermilk that bind together the dry ingredients.*

½ cup (4 ounces) beer or ale, room temperature
½ cup (4 ounces) buttermilk, heated to lukewarm
¼ cup (2 ounces) orange juice
2 tablespoons (1 ounce) butter, melted
1 cup (3¾ ounces) whole rye (pumpernickel) flour
1 cup (4 ounces) traditional whole wheat flour
2 cups (8½ ounces) unbleached all-purpose flour
2 tablespoons (1 ounce) packed light or dark brown sugar
1½ teaspoons fennel seed, crushed or ground
1½ teaspoons anise seeds, crushed or ground
1¼ teaspoons salt
2½ teaspoons instant yeast

Combine all the ingredients and mix and knead them—by hand, mixer or bread machine—until you have a soft, smooth dough. Cover and allow the dough to rise until it's puffy and nearly doubled in bulk, 1 to 2 hours.

Lightly grease a large baking sheet or line with parchment paper. Gently deflate the dough, and shape it into a fat 9-inch log. Place it on the prepared pan. Cover it gently with lightly greased plastic wrap or a proof cover, and allow it to rise till it's very puffy, 1 to 1½ hours. Near the end of the bread's rise, preheat the oven to 375°F.

Uncover and bake the bread for 35 minutes; it's done when it's golden brown and an instant-read thermometer inserted in the center registers 190°F. This loaf browns fairly slowly, so there's no need to tent it with foil as it bakes. Remove it from the oven, and after a minute or so turn it out onto a rack. Cool the bread completely before slicing it.

NOTE: For an extra-crisp crust, turn off the oven, transfer the bread from the pan to the oven rack, crack open the oven door about 2 inches, and cool the loaf entirely in the turned-off oven.

NUTRITION INFORMATION PER SERVING (1 SLICE, 42G): 11g whole grains, 105 cal, 2g fat, 3g protein, 18g complex carbohydrates, 1g sugar, 2g dietary fiber, 3mg cholesterol, 141mg sodium, 111mg potassium, 11RE vitamin A, 2mg vitamin C, 1mg iron, 19mg calcium, 83mg phosphorus.

# Limpa

YIELD: **1 (8-inch) round loaf, 16 servings**
BAKING TEMPERATURE: **350°F**
BAKING TIME: **35 to 40 minutes**

This light-textured, orange and spice-scented rye loaf is a favorite among Scandinavians. It's especially delightful toasted and spread with sweet butter, or butter and orange marmalade.

Pre-ferment
1 cup (4 ounces) traditional whole wheat flour
½ cup (4 ounces) cool water
Pinch of instant yeast

Dough
All of the pre-ferment
⅓ cup (2⅝ ounces) orange juice, room temperature
2 tablespoons (1 ounce) lukewarm water
¼ cup (3 ounces) molasses
2 tablespoons (1 ounce) unsalted butter, cut into 3 pieces
1 cup (3¾ ounces) whole rye (pumpernickel) flour
1 cup (4¼ ounces) unbleached all-purpose flour
¼ cup (1 ounce) nonfat dry milk
1½ teaspoons each caraway seeds, fennel seeds and anise seeds
Grated zest of 1 medium orange (about 2½ teaspoons)
1¼ teaspoons salt
1 tablespoon instant yeast

TO PREPARE THE PRE-FERMENT: Mix the pre-ferment ingredients in a small (2- to 3-cup) bowl, cover the bowl, and let rest overnight at room temperature.

TO PREPARE THE DOUGH: Combine all the ingredients including the pre-ferment and mix and knead them—by hand, mixer or bread machine—until you have a soft, smooth dough. Cover and allow the dough to rise until it's puffy, though not doubled in bulk, 1 to 2 hours. Lightly grease an 8-inch round cake pan.

Shape the dough into a ball, flatten it slightly, and center it in the prepared pan. Cover with a proof cover or lightly greased plastic wrap, and allow it to rise until it's nearly filled the pan, edge to edge, and has domed to about 1 inch higher than the rim of the pan in the center, 1¼ to 1½ hours. Toward the end of the rise, preheat the oven to 350°F.

TO BAKE THE BREAD: Uncover and bake the bread for 35 to 40 minutes, tenting it with foil after 20 minutes. The bread is done when an instant-read thermometer inserted in the center registers 190°F. Remove it from the oven, and after a minute or so turn it out onto a rack. Cool the bread for 30 minutes before slicing.

NUTRITION INFORMATION PER SERVING (1 SLICE, 45G): 14g whole grains, 239 cal, 2g fat, 4g protein, 17g complex carbohydrates, 4g sugar, 3g dietary fiber, 4mg cholesterol, 185mg sodium, 176mg potassium, 13RE vitamin A, 3mg vitamin C, 2mg iron, 42mg calcium, 108mg phosphorus.

Raisin-Pecan Rye Bread

YIELD: 1 (9-inch) round loaf, 16 servings
BAKING TEMPERATURE: 350°F
BAKING TIME: 40 minutes

A generous helping of pecans and raisins stud this soft-textured wheat-and-pumpernickel loaf. Because it has a relatively high percentage of pumpernickel, which contains no gluten and thus doesn't help the bread's rise, we bake it in a round, shallow pan, allowing it to expand outward rather than up. The result: A round loaf that's 3 to 4 inches high at its center, ideal for slicing thin and serving with sweet butter or a spread. Try cream cheese with fig jam, for a special treat.

Pre-ferment
1 cup (4 ounces) traditional whole wheat flour
½ cup (4 ounces) cool water
Pinch of instant yeast

Dough
All of the pre-ferment
½ cup (4 ounces) lukewarm water
2 tablespoons (1 ounce) unsalted butter, cut into 3 pieces
¾ cup (2¾ ounces) whole rye (pumpernickel) flour
1¼ cups (5¼ ounces) unbleached bread flour
1¼ teaspoons salt
3 tablespoons (1⅜ ounces) packed light or dark brown sugar
2½ teaspoons instant yeast
1 cup (5¼ ounces) lightly packed currants or raisins
½ cup (1⅞ ounces) chopped pecans

TO PREPARE THE PRE-FERMENT: Mix the pre-ferment ingredients in a small (2- to 3-cup) bowl, cover the bowl, and let rest overnight at room temperature.

TO PREPARE THE DOUGH: Combine the pre-ferment with all the ingredients, except the dried fruit and nuts, and mix and knead—by hand, mixer or bread machine—until you have a soft, smooth dough. Cover and allow the dough to rise until it's quite puffy, 1 to 2 hours.

Lightly grease a 9-inch round cake pan.

Gently deflate the dough, transfer it to a lightly greased work surface, and knead the fruit and nuts into it (see illustration, p. 201). Shape the dough into a ball, and place it in the prepared pan. Cover it gently with lightly greased plastic wrap or a proof cover, and allow it to rise till it's spread out to reach the sides of the pan, 1½ to 2 hours. Its center will have domed about 1 inch over the rim of the pan.

Preheat the oven to 350°F.

TO BAKE THE BREAD: Uncover and bake the bread for 40 minutes, tenting it with foil after 15 minutes. The bread is done when it's golden brown and an instant-read thermometer inserted in the center registers 190°F. Remove it from the oven, and after a minute or so turn it out onto a rack. Brush with melted butter, if desired; this will keep the crust soft. Cool the bread for 30 minutes before cutting it.

NUTRITION INFORMATION PER SERVING (1 SLICE, 53G): 12g whole grains, 147 cal, 4g fat, 4g protein, 23g complex carbohydrates, 2g sugar, 3g dietary fiber, 4mg cholesterol, 170mg sodium, 193mg potassium, 13RE vitamin A, 2mg iron, 20mg calcium, 95mg phosphorus.

VARIATION: DARK AND DENSE RAISIN-PECAN RYE *This version is darker, denser and moister than the original, the flavor of the raisins and nuts concentrated into a loaf that's just about 2 inches high. Combine the ingredients as directed in the basic recipe, increasing the pumpernickel to 1½ cups (5⅛ ounces) and decreasing the bread flour to ½ cup (2⅛ ounces). Prepare the dough, allow it to rise, and shape the bread as directed; let it rise in the pan until it has come nearly to the height of the rim, and the dough is starting to shred a bit on top. Uncover and bake the bread for 35 to 40 minutes, tenting it with foil after 15 minutes. The bread is done when it's golden brown and an instant-read thermometer inserted in the center registers about 200°F. Remove it from the oven, and after about 5 minutes turn it out of the pan onto a rack. Brush with melted butter, if desired; this will keep the crust soft. Cool the bread for 30 minutes before cutting it.*

Westphalian Rye Bread

YIELD: 2 loaves, 48 slices each

BAKING TEMPERATURE: 225°F

BAKING TIME: 4 hours

Westphalia, a state in northwestern Germany, is famous for both its unctuous, lightly smoked ham, and its dense, dark pumpernickel. Both are sliced ultrathin, then served with one another in a perfect marriage of bread and meat. Accompanied by sweet butter, perhaps some smoked sausage, and a stein of beer or glass of schnapps, this is a standard Westphalian repast.

The following rye bread mimics Westphalian rye, but is prepared in a less time-consuming manner. In other words, it's been Americanized. Don't be discouraged while preparing the dough; it's very heavy and sticky, more like mortar than bread dough. The resulting loaf is dense and moist, your own homemade version of those very heavy, dark, thin-sliced German breads ("cocktail loaves") you'll find at the supermarket. Serve it in scant ¼-inch thick slices with Westphalian ham, of course, or smoked salmon, liverwurst, butter, cheese or prosciutto, which is a ham similar to Westphalian.

1 cup (5¼ ounces) cracked wheat
½ cup (2 ounces) malted wheat flakes or dry Maltex cereal
⅓ cup (2⅜ ounces) sugar
3 cups (24 ounces) boiling water
4 cups (15 ounces) whole rye (pumpernickel) flour
1 cup (4 ounces) traditional whole wheat flour
2½ teaspoons salt
2 tablespoons (⅞ ounce) vegetable oil
¼ teaspoon instant yeast

Put the cracked wheat and malted wheat flakes (or cereal) in a large bowl. Set aside.

Place the sugar in a 1-quart saucepan. Heat over medium heat, stirring occasionally, until the sugar melts. Continue cooking the sugar until it turns a medium mahogany brown. Note: Take the sugar off the heat just before you think it's the right color, as it'll continue to cook in the pan. And don't let it get too dark; even a hint of black means it'll be bitter. Think of a horse chestnut: it should be a tiny bit lighter in color than that.

Remove the sugar from the heat and allow it to cool for 2 minutes. Add 3 cups boiling water and stir until the sugar is mostly dissolved. Return to the heat, and bring to a boil, stirring till the sugar is completely dissolved.

Pour the boiling sugar water over the cracked wheat and malted wheat in the bowl. Allow the mixture to cool to lukewarm, stirring occasionally. Stir in the pumpernickel flour, whole wheat flour, salt, oil and yeast. This is not your typical yeast dough; the mixture will be sticky and have about as much life as a lump of clay. Place the dough in a greased bowl, cover it with a damp towel, and let it sit in a warm place (70°F to 75°F) for at least 18 hours and up to 24 hours. Six to 8 hours into the dough's resting period, fold it over once or twice, then cover it again and allow it to continue to mellow. (We hesitate to use the word "rise" here. Though there is in fact a bit of yeast in the dough, it'll rise very little. It'll be more like the effect of letting your belt out a couple of notches after a big dinner; it's not that you've really gotten very much bigger, just that you've expanded comfortably.)

After the mellowing period is complete, grease two 8½ x 4½ -inch pans. The dough may have cracked a bit; that's OK. Turn it out onto a floured or lightly greased work surface, knead until it holds together, then divide it in half. Press each half into a prepared pan, smoothing the surface with wet hands.

Let the loaves sit, covered, for 1½ hours; they'll rise just slightly. Near the end of the rise, preheat the oven to 225°F. Grease 2 pieces of foil, and cover the pans tightly with the foil, greased-side down.

Place the covered pans in the oven. Bake the bread for 4 hours. After 4 hours, remove the foil from the pans, and check to see that the bread is firm and looks set. It should be dark brown, and an instant-read thermometer inserted in the center of a loaf should register about 210°F.

Remove the bread from the oven. Let it cool in the pans for 15 minutes to firm. Remove it from the pans and allow it to cool to lukewarm before wrapping in plastic wrap. Let it rest in its wrapping for 8 hours or more before slicing.

NUTRITION INFORMATION PER SERVING (1 SLICE, 16G): 8g whole grains, 31 cal, 1g protein, 5g complex carbohydrates, 1g sugar, 1g dietary fiber, 57mg sodium, 43mg potassium, 3mg calcium, 40mg phosphorus.

SWEET BREADS

What do sticky buns, cinnamon rolls, panettone and hot cross buns have in common? First, they're all sweet breads that start with yeast dough. And second, we'd be bereft without them!

Sweet breads (as opposed to sweetbreads, a type of meat) are in some ways the most challenging yeast breads to bake, aside from sourdough. Yeast loves sugar; in fact, it loves sugar so much that it can easily overeat, effectively putting itself to sleep and bringing your rising bread to a standstill. The challenge is to add just enough sugar to the dough to make bread sweet, but not so much that it slows the yeast.

A partial solution, particularly apropos to whole grain breads, is to add sugar in the form of dried fruit. Another way to add sweet flavor is to gild the barely sweetened bread with frosting or stuff it with a sugar-based filling. Either way, you've added sugar to the outside (not inside) of the dough, and the yeast in your rising bread will happily toil on.

Continental Coffee Bread

YIELD: 1 (9-inch) round loaf, 16 servings

BAKING TEMPERATURE: 350°F

BAKING TIME: 50 to 55 minutes.

This light-textured, European-style coffee bread is surprisingly tender. The sugar topping drizzled on top before baking gives it a pretty, crunchy sugar glaze. And, unlike American-style coffeecakes, this isn't super-sweet; the glaze on top and the fruit inside are a wonderful complement to the bread itself, which truly isn't sweet at all. Serve it with butter, cream cheese or jam, for breakfast; or with coffee or tea later in the day.

Pre-ferment

1 cup (4 ounces) traditional whole wheat flour

½ cup (4 ounces) cool water

Pinch of instant yeast

Dough

All of the pre-ferment

⅓ cup (2⅝ ounces) lukewarm water

⅓ cup (2⅝ ounces) orange juice, room temperature

1 large egg

4 tablespoons (½ stick, 2 ounces) unsalted butter, cut into 6 pieces

1⅓ cups (4⅝ ounces) old-fashioned rolled oats, ground for 30 seconds in a food processor

1¾ cups (7⅜ ounces) unbleached all-purpose flour

1¼ teaspoons salt

2 tablespoons (1 ounce) packed light or dark brown sugar

2 teaspoons instant yeast

1 cup (4 ounces) toasted walnuts, very coarsely chopped

¾ cup (4 ounces) chopped dates

¾ cup (4 ounces) raisins, preferably golden

Topping

2 tablespoons (⅞ ounce) packed light or dark brown sugar

1 teaspoon water

½ teaspoon vanilla extract

TO PREPARE THE PRE-FERMENT: Mix the pre-ferment ingredients in a small (2- to 3-cup) bowl, cover the bowl, and let rest overnight at room temperature.

TO PREPARE THE DOUGH: Combine the pre-ferment and all the dough ingredients except the walnuts, dates and raisins. Mix and knead—by mixer or bread machine—until you have a very soft, smooth dough. (This dough is too soft to knead by hand.) Cover and allow the dough to rise until it's puffy and nearly doubled in bulk, 1 to 2 hours. Lightly grease a 9-inch round cake pan.

Gently deflate the dough, and knead the nuts and fruit into it, either by machine or by hand. Shape the dough into a flat ball, and place it in the prepared pan, patting to reach the edges of the pan. Cover the pan with a proof cover or lightly greased plastic wrap, and allow the dough to rise until its center just reaches the height of the pan, 1 hour. While the dough is rising, preheat the oven to 350°F.

TO BAKE THE BREAD: Combine the sugar, water and vanilla, stirring until the sugar is suspended in the liquid, even if it hasn't dissolved. Drizzle this mixture over the top of the risen bread. Bake it for 35 minutes, tent it lightly with foil to prevent overbrowning, and bake until it's a deep golden brown and the internal temperature registers 190°F, 15 to 20 minutes more. Remove it from the oven, and after 5 minutes, carefully turn it out of the pan and transfer it to a rack to cool. Cool the bread for 30 minutes before cutting it.

NOTE: This bread may settle in the center somewhat as it bakes. Don't worry; once you slice it, no one will be the wiser!

NUTRITION INFORMATION PER SERVING (1 SLICE, 77G): 15g whole grains, 237 cal, 9g fat, 6g protein, 33g complex carbohydrates, 3g sugar, 3g dietary fiber, 21mg cholesterol, 175mg sodium, 239mg potassium, 29RE vitamin A, 3mg vitamin C, 2mg iron, 29mg calcium, 129mg phosphorus.

> **LET BREAD DOUGH RISE BEFORE ADDING DRIED FRUIT**
>
> When you're adding raisins or other dried fruits to yeast-bread dough, it's better to knead them in after the first rise, just before shaping the loaf. If you knead them in before the bread rises, their natural sugars leach out into the dough, slowing down the yeast's growth and making for a slower rise.

Cinnamon Spiral Bread

YIELD: 1 (9-inch) round loaf, 16 servings
BAKING TEMPERATURE: 350°F
BAKING TIME: 33 to 35 minutes

This dark-brown, spiraled loaf resembles nothing so much as a giant cinnamon bun. Made from wheat and oats and very lightly sweetened with honey, it'll bring your family into the kitchen as it bakes, their noses twitching like bloodhounds on the trail.

Since cinnamon in bread dough slows down rising (cinnamon and yeast don't play well together), much of the cinnamon flavor here is on the outside—in the coating and the topping—where it can make an immediate impact on your taste buds.

Pre-ferment
1 cup (4 ounces) traditional whole wheat flour
½ cup (4 ounces) cool water
Pinch of instant yeast

Dough
All of the pre-ferment
½ cup (4 ounces) milk, heated to lukewarm
3 tablespoons (1½ ounces) orange juice
3 tablespoons (2¼ ounces) honey
4 tablespoons (½ stick, 2 ounces) unsalted butter, cut into 6 pieces
¾ cup (3 ounces) traditional whole wheat flour
⅔ cup (2¼ ounces) old-fashioned rolled oats, ground for 30 seconds in a food processor
⅔ cup (4¼ ounces) old-fashioned rolled oats, left whole
1 cup (2¼ ounces) unbleached all-purpose flour
1¼ teaspoons salt
1 to 1½ teaspoons ground cinnamon, to taste
2¼ teaspoons instant yeast

Coating
¼ cup (1 ounce) confectioners' sugar
½ to 2 teaspoons ground cinnamon

Topping
2 tablespoons (⅞ ounce) packed light or dark brown sugar
1 teaspoon water
½ teaspoon vanilla extract
¼ to ½ teaspoon ground cinnamon

Icing
1 cup (4 ounces) confectioners' sugar
1 teaspoon vanilla extract
Pinch of salt
Drop of almond extract
3 to 4 tablespoons (1½ to 2 ounces) cream or milk

TO PREPARE THE PRE-FERMENT: Mix the pre-ferment ingredients in a small (2- to 3-cup) bowl, and let rest overnight at room temperature.

TO PREPARE THE DOUGH: Combine the pre-ferment and all of the dough ingredients, and mix and knead them—by hand, mixer or bread machine—until you have a soft, smooth dough. Cover and allow the dough to rise until it's puffy and nearly doubled in bulk, 1 to 2 hours.

Lightly grease a 9-inch round cake pan. Prepare the coating by whisking together the confectioners' sugar and cinnamon to taste.

Gently deflate the dough, and roll it into a 40-inch-long snake. The dough is soft, and very easy to work with. Sprinkle the length of the snake generously with the coating mixture, turning to coat it with sugar.

Coil the dough into the prepared pan. Scrape any remaining cinnamon-sugar off the work surface, and sprinkle it over the dough in the pan. Cover it gently with lightly greased plastic wrap or a proof cover, and allow it to rise till its center is just about level with the rim of the pan, 1¼ to 1¾ hours. Near the end of the bread's rise, preheat the oven to 350°F. Make the topping by stirring together the sugar, water, vanilla and cinnamon to taste.

Coil the dough around itself in a neat spiral, starting at the center of the pan and finishing at the edge.

TO BAKE THE BREAD: Drizzle the topping over the risen loaf. Bake the bread for 33 to 35 minutes, tenting it with foil after 15 minutes. The bread is done when it's dark brown, and an instant-read thermometer inserted in the center registers 190°F. Remove it from the oven, and after a minute or so turn it out onto a rack. Allow it to cool completely before drizzling with the icing.

TO PREPARE THE ICING: Mix together the sugar, vanilla, salt, almond extract and enough milk (or cream) to make a thick (but pourable) icing. Drizzle the icing over the cooled bread. Allow the bread to rest for several hours, so that the icing can set. Or not; if you don't mind sticky icing, cut it in wedges and serve immediately.

NOTE: The ranges of cinnamon indicated in the ingredients reflect differences of opinion our taste-testers had about how much cinnamon was just right. If you love cinnamon, go for the greatest amount; if you're lukewarm toward it, cut back.

NUTRITION INFORMATION PER SERVING (1 SLICE, 92G): 20g whole grains, 277 cal, 4g fat, 7g protein, 53g complex carbohydrates, 12g sugar, 3g dietary fiber, 9mg cholesterol, 175mg sodium, 156mg potassium, 32RE vitamin A, 1mg vitamin C, 3mg iron, 33mg calcium, 136mg phosphorus.

SWEET BREAD MADE WITH A PRE-FERMENT?

The use of a pre-ferment, or starter—a mixture of flour, water and a tiny pinch of yeast, left to rest overnight before using in bread dough—gives bread added flavor and keeping qualities. We often use a pre-ferment in savory yeast breads; we feel it helps bring out the wheat flavor in loaves that might otherwise seem a bit plain. But in a sweet bread, loaded with sugar, butter and fruit—who needs a pre-ferment?

As it turns out, true Italian panettone is traditionally made with a pre-ferment (see recipe, p. 257). It gives the bread a finer texture than loaves made without a pre-ferment and helps the dough rise better than anything with that amount of sugar and fat has a right to. Though the dough still needs a big kick of instant yeast, the pre-ferment gives it the strength to take off and rise, despite the sugar and fat doing their best to retard the whole process.

Tender Ginger Bread

YIELD: 1 (9-inch) round loaf, 16 servings
BAKING TEMPERATURE: 350°F
BAKING TIME: 45 to 50 minutes

That's ginger bread, not gingerbread. This light-gold loaf is moist and spicy, with a sweet-hot ginger glaze. Try a wedge spread with butter, cream cheese or a bit of lemon curd. Want to gild the lily? Spread with that ginger marmalade you bought on a whim at the farmer's market.

Dough

1 cup (8 ounces) lukewarm water
2 tablespoons (1 ounce) orange juice
4 tablespoons (½ stick, 2 ounces) unsalted butter, cut into 6 pieces
2 tablespoons (1½ ounces) molasses
2 tablespoons (1¼ ounces) ginger syrup (see recipe, next page) or water
1 cup (4 ounces) traditional whole wheat flour
½ cup (1½ ounces) quick-cooking oats
1¾ cups (7⅜ ounces) unbleached all-purpose flour
1¼ teaspoons salt
¾ teaspoon ground cinnamon
½ teaspoon ground ginger
⅛ teaspoon ground cloves
Heaping ½ cup (1¼ ounces) dried potato flakes or 3 tablespoons (1¼ ounces) potato flour
¼ cup (1 ounce) nonfat dry milk
2¾ teaspoons instant yeast
½ cup (3¼ ounces) finely diced crystallized ginger

Topping

3 tablespoons (1⅜ ounces) packed light or dark brown sugar
2 to 2½ tablespoons (1¼ to 1⅜ ounces) ginger syrup or 1½ to 2 tablespoons water

TO PREPARE THE DOUGH: Combine all the dough ingredients except the crystallized ginger, and mix and knead them—by hand, mixer or bread machine—until you have a medium-soft, smooth dough. Cover and allow the dough to rise until it's quite puffy, though probably not doubled in bulk, 1 to 2 hours. Lightly grease a 9-inch round cake pan.

Gently deflate the dough, transfer it to a lightly greased work surface, and knead the crystallized ginger into it. Shape the dough into a flattened ball, and place it in the prepared pan. Cover the pan with a proof cover or lightly greased plastic wrap, and allow the bread to rise until it's just about doubled in bulk, 1 hour; it'll crest about ½ inch below the rim of a 2-inch tall pan. Toward the end of the bread's rise, preheat the oven to 350°F.

TO PREPARE THE TOPPING: Combine the sugar and ginger syrup (or water), stirring until the mixture is smooth.

Drizzle the topping over the top of the risen bread. Bake the bread for 20 minutes, tent it lightly with foil to prevent overbrowning, and bake until it's golden brown and the internal temperature at the center registers 190°F, 25 to 30 minutes. Remove it from the oven, and after 5 minutes, carefully turn it out of the pan and transfer it to a rack to cool. Cool the bread for 30 minutes before slicing.

NOTE: We highly recommend using ginger syrup (recipe follows) where it's called for. It's simple to make, and keeps indefinitely in the refrigerator, ready to drizzle on cake or scones or mix into seltzer for homemade ginger ale.

NUTRITION INFORMATION PER SERVING (1 SLICE, 61G): 10g whole grains, 160 cal, 3g fat, 4g protein, 17g complex carbohydrates, 10g sugar, 2g dietary fiber, 8mg cholesterol, 188mg sodium, 128mg potassium, 25RE vitamin A, 3mg vitamin C, 1mg iron, 39mg calcium, 79mg phosphorus.

Ginger Syrup

YIELD: 3½ cups syrup

Sweet and with a good, hot bite, this syrup is a ginger lover's dream. It's so tasty and so easy to make, you'll wonder why no one told you about it before now!

> 4 cups (about 13 ounces) fresh ginger root, unpeeled, cut into ⅛- to ¼-inch thick slices (a food processor makes short work of this task)
> 3½ cups (1½ pounds) sugar
> 3½ cups (28 ounces) water

In a large, heavy saucepan, bring the ginger, sugar and water to a boil. Boil the mixture gently until it registers 216°F to 220°F on an instant-read thermometer, 1¼ to 1½ hours. The lower temperature will give you a thinner syrup, one that's easy to stir into drinks; the higher temperature will yield a thicker syrup, more the consistency of corn syrup. You can't tell how thick the syrup will be while it's still hot; you have to go by its temperature, as it'll thicken as it cools.

Remove the pan from the burner, and carefully strain the syrup into a nonreactive container, such as a glass jar. Store indefinitely in the refrigerator.

Christmas Panettone

YIELD: 1 (9- to 10-inch) round loaf, 16 servings
BAKING TEMPERATURE: 350°F
BAKING TIME: 35 to 40 minutes

Panettone, a classic Italian Christmas bread, is loaded with eggs and butter and fruit. Given that information, you might assume it's a dense, moist bread. Panettone is actually quite dry and somewhat austere, perfect for enjoying with a glass of wine or a cup of espresso. Dried fruit gives panettone most of its flavor, and that fruit also provides a welcome touch of moistness.

For those of you who turn up your nose at the traditional candied fruits of Christmas— citron, lemon peel, orange peel—we offer this Americanized version of panettone, using the dried fruits of your choice. And for those who don't have a traditional panettone pan (a tall, round loaf pan), or who've encountered difficulties using such a pan (raw center, burned crust), we break with tradition again and suggest using a tube or angel-food pan.

Pre-ferment
1½ cups (6 ounces) traditional whole wheat flour
½ cup (4 ounces) cool water
Pinch of instant yeast

Dough
All of the pre-ferment
¼ cup (2 ounces) orange juice
3 large eggs
2 tablespoons (1½ ounces) honey
½ cup (1 stick, 4 ounces) unsalted butter, cut into 12 pieces
1⅓ cups (4⅝ ounces) old-fashioned rolled oats, ground for 30 seconds in a food processor
1⅔ cups (7 ounces) unbleached all-purpose flour
¼ cup (1⅞ ounces) packed light or dark brown sugar
1¼ teaspoons salt
1 tablespoon vanilla extract
1 scant tablespoon grated lemon zest (rind of ½ lemon)
1 tablespoon instant yeast
2 cups (10 to 12 ounces) dried fruit

Topping
2 tablespoons (1 ounce) unsalted butter, melted
3 tablespoons (¾ ounce) confectioners' sugar

TO PREPARE THE PRE-FERMENT: Mix the pre-ferment ingredients in a small (2- to 3-cup) bowl, cover the bowl, and let rest overnight at room temperature.

TO PREPARE THE DOUGH: Combine the pre-ferment with all the ingredients except the dried fruit, and mix and knead by mixer or bread machine (the dough is too soft to knead by hand) until you have a very soft but cohesive dough. Cover and allow the dough to rise until it's puffy, 1 to 2 hours.

Lightly grease a 9 to 10-inch tube pan, Bundt pan or angel-food pan. Gently deflate the dough, and knead the fruit into it. Shape the dough into a log about 24 inches long. Place the log into the prepared pan. Cover it gently with lightly greased plastic wrap or a proof cover, and allow it to rise till it's quite puffy but not doubled in bulk, 2 to 3 hours. Near the end of the bread's rise, preheat the oven to 350°F.

TO BAKE THE BREAD: Uncover and bake the bread for 35 to 40 minutes, tenting it with foil after 20 minutes. The bread is done when it's golden brown and an instant-read thermometer inserted in the center registers 190°F. Remove it from the oven, and after a minute or so turn it out onto a rack. Brush with melted butter; this will keep the crust soft. When the bread is nearly cool, sprinkle it heavily with confectioners' sugar. Cool the bread completely, then sprinkle it with sugar again before cutting it.

NOTE: We like to use a mixture of dried apricots, pineapple and golden raisins in panettone; while not traditional, these fruits give it a sunny, cheerful look and feel. Chopped dates, dark raisins and toasted walnuts would also seem appropriate, as would dried cranberries and cherries.

NUTRITION INFORMATION PER SERVING (1 SLICE, 87G): 19g whole grains, 265 cal, 8g fat, 6g protein, 39g complex carbohydrates, 6g sugar, 4g dietary fiber, 55mg cholesterol, 189mg sodium, 298mg potassium, 62RE vitamin A, 3mg vitamin C, 2mg iron, 26mg calcium, 135mg phosphorus.

VARIATION: *To make a traditional round panettone (without the hole in the center), shape the dough into a ball, and place it in a lightly greased 2-quart panettone pan, or a 2-quart casserole pan with tall, straight sides (at least 4 inches tall). Cover it gently with lightly greased plastic wrap or a proof cover, and allow it to rise till it's quite puffy but not doubled in bulk, 2 to 3 hours. Near the end of the bread's rise, preheat the oven to 400°F (375°F for a glass pan).*

Uncover and bake the bread for 15 minutes. Reduce the oven temperature to 350°F (325°F for a glass pan), tent the bread lightly with foil, and bake for an additional 35 to 45 minutes. The bread is done when it's golden brown and an instant-read thermometer inserted in the center registers 190°F. Remove it from the oven, and after a minute or so turn it out onto a rack. Brush with melted butter; this will keep the crust soft. When the bread is nearly cool, sprinkle it heavily with confectioners' sugar. Cool the bread completely, then sprinkle it with sugar again before cutting it.

Chocolate Loves Vanilla Bread

YIELD: 1 (9-inch) round loaf, 16 servings
BAKING TEMPERATURE: 350°F
BAKING TIME: 50 to 55 minutes.

Here they are, two of America's favorite complementary flavors, happily married in a tender loaf that's rich enough to be served as is—no butter, no jam, no spread of any kind necessary. Though, come to think of it, a spoonful of raspberry preserves wouldn't be amiss... By chopping the chocolate chips before adding them to the vanilla-scented dough, you'll create a fair amount of chocolate "dust," which swirls itself throughout the loaf to give it a nicely marbled appearance.

Dough
1½ cups (9 ounces) semisweet chocolate chips
1 cup (8 ounces) milk, heated to lukewarm
1 large egg
2 tablespoons (1 ounce) orange juice
4 tablespoons (½ stick, 2 ounces) unsalted butter, cut into 6 pieces
2 cups (8 ounces) traditional whole wheat flour
1½ cups (6⅜ ounces) unbleached all-purpose flour
1¼ teaspoons salt
⅓ cup (2½ ounces) packed light or dark brown sugar
1 tablespoon vanilla extract
¼ teaspoon almond extract
1 teaspoon espresso powder (optional)
2½ teaspoons instant yeast

Topping
3 tablespoons (1⅜ ounces) packed light or dark brown sugar
2 teaspoons water
1 teaspoon vanilla extract

Place the chocolate chips in the bowl of a food processor. Process until the chips are coarsely chopped and covered with a coating of ground chocolate. Set aside.

TO PREPARE THE DOUGH: Combine all the ingredients except the chopped chocolate, and mix and knead—by hand, mixer or bread machine—until you have a soft, smooth dough. Cover and allow the dough to rise until it's puffy and nearly doubled in bulk, 1 to 2 hours. Lightly grease a 9-inch round cake pan.

Gently deflate the dough, and knead the reserved chips into it. Shape the dough into a flat ball, and place it in the prepared pan, flattening to reach the edges of the pan. Cover the pan with a proof cover or lightly greased plastic wrap, and allow the dough to rise until its center just reaches the height of the pan, 1¼ to 2½ hours. Preheat the oven to 350°F.

TO PREPARE THE TOPPING: Combine the sugar, water and vanilla, stirring until the sugar is suspended in the liquid, even if it hasn't dissolved. Drizzle this mixture over the top of the risen bread.

To slice a round loaf, cut the loaf in half and turn one half so it's cut-side-down on the counter. You can now cut the bread into even slices, starting at one end of the piece.

TO BAKE THE BREAD: Bake the bread for 35 minutes, tent it lightly with foil to prevent overbrowning, and continue baking until it's a deep golden brown and the internal temperature registers 190°F, 15 to 20 minutes more. Remove it from the oven, and after 5 minutes, carefully turn it out of the pan and transfer it to a rack to cool. Cool the bread for 30 minutes before slicing.

NUTRITION INFORMATION PER SERVING (1 SLICE, 77G): **14g whole grains,** 245 cal, 9g fat, 6g protein, 22g complex carbohydrates, 15g sugar, 3g dietary fiber, 22mg cholesterol, 184mg sodium, 280mg potassium, 37RE vitamin A, 1mg vitamin C, 2mg iron, 41mg calcium, 150mg phosphorus, 15mg caffeine.

USING UP THE LEFTOVERS

If you have yeast bread that's become stale, congratulations: it's a prime candidate for transformation into delicious crispbread! Slice any leftover bread between ¼ and ³⁄₈ inch thick, and lay the slices on an ungreased baking sheet. If it's savory bread, you may apply olive oil spray, if desired; this will add extra flavor and crispness. Bake the bread in a preheated oven—anywhere from 275°F to 350°—with sweet breads preferring the lower temperature—until it's dry, crisp and just barely beginning to brown. This will take anywhere from 30 minutes to 1½ hours, depending on a number of factors, including how thin you slice the bread, the temperature of your oven, the type of bread and how stale it is. Turn the bread over approximately midway through the baking period. Remove the bread from the oven, and allow it to cool on the pan; it'll become crispier as it cools. Serve sweet or savory breads as is; savory breads can also be spread with soft cheese or served with dip. Store leftovers in an airtight container, where they'll stay good for at least 1 week.

Hot Cross Buns

YIELD: 2 dozen buns
BAKING TEMPERATURE: 350°F
BAKING TIME: 25 minutes

Served at the end of Lent, these sweet, rich buns are topped with a cross of thick white icing. Though they're traditional on Good Friday, we see no need to limit them to that day; they go great with a cup of tea or coffee any time of the year. As with so many old-style sweet breads, these buns originally featured chopped, candied citrus peel and/or candied fruit; feel free to use rum-soaked raisins (as we do here), or another favorite dried fruit (cherries, apricots, cranberries...) However, if you're a real traditionalist, be sure to substitute candied peel for up to ⅓ cup of whatever fruit you choose.

Dough
1 cup (5¼ to 6 ounces) currants, raisins or golden raisins, moistened in 1 tablespoon water or rum
⅔ cup (5⅜ ounces) lukewarm water
⅓ cup (2⅝ ounces) orange juice
2 large eggs
½ cup (1 stick, 4 ounces) unsalted butter, cut into 12 pieces
2¼ cups (9 ounces) traditional whole wheat flour
2½ cups (10⅝ ounces) unbleached all-purpose flour
⅓ cup (2½ ounces) packed light or dark brown sugar
¼ cup (1 ounce) nonfat dry milk
1½ teaspoons salt
2 teaspoons vanilla extract
¼ teaspoon ground nutmeg
¼ teaspoon ground cinnamon
2 teaspoons baking powder
2¼ teaspoons instant yeast

Icing
1½ cups (6 ounces) confectioners' sugar
1 teaspoon vanilla extract
Pinch of salt
4 to 5 teaspoons milk or cream

In a small, nonreactive bowl, combine the currants (or raisins) with the water (or rum). Stir to coat, then set aside.

TO PREPARE THE DOUGH: Combine all dough ingredients except the raisins or currants, and mix and knead—by hand, mixer, or bread machine—until you have a medium-soft, smooth dough. Cover and allow the dough to rise until it's quite puffy, though probably not doubled in bulk, 1 to 2 hours.

TO SHAPE THE BUNS: Lightly grease two 9 x 2-inch cake pans. Gently deflate the dough, and transfer it to a lightly greased work surface. Knead in the raisins or currants. Divide the dough into 24 equal pieces. Roll each piece into a round ball.

Place 12 balls, smooth side up and about ¾-inch apart, in each of the prepared pans. Cover and let the buns rise in a warm place until they're nicely puffy and touching one another, 1 to 1½ hours. Toward the end of the rise, preheat your oven to 350°F.

TO BAKE THE BUNS: Uncover and bake the buns until they're a light golden brown on top, 25 minutes. Remove them from the oven.

TO FINISH THE BUNS: To make the icing, combine the confectioners' sugar with the vanilla, salt, and enough milk (or cream) to make a smooth icing.

Let the buns cool for 15 minutes or so before icing. If they're very hot, the icing will melt; if they're completely cool, it won't stick well. Pipe icing over the slightly warm rolls in the traditional cross pattern. You can do this with a pastry bag or, more simply, by spooning the icing into a plastic bag, snipping off a corner, and squeezing it out onto the buns.

NUTRITION INFORMATION PER SERVING (1 BUN, 55G): **11g whole grains,** 162 cal, 5g fat, 4g protein, 23g complex carbohydrates, 3g sugar, 2g dietary fiber, 28mg cholesterol, 179mg sodium, 169mg potassium, 39RE vitamin A, 2mg vitamin C, 1mg iron, 62mg calcium, 124mg phosphorus.

Dark and Dangerous Cinnamon Buns

YIELD: 16 buns
BAKING TEMPERATURE: 350°F
BAKING TIME: 25 to 28 minutes

Dark with whole wheat—dangerous if you're dieting, because these buns are simply irresistible. Loaded with rich cinnamon filling and glazed with creamy white icing, this is the quintessential 100 percent whole grain (AND delicious) cinnamon bun. The honey in the dough makes them good keepers too. Unlike some cinnamon buns, these will stay fresh and moist for several days, covered and stored at room temperature.

Author Jodi Picoult, a King Arthur neighbor in nearby Hanover, New Hampshire and a passionate baker, came up with this recipe after feeling guilt pangs about her family's diet. Now husband Tim van Leer, and kids Kyle, Jake and Sammy are enjoying fiber-rich breakfast buns (and until now, they didn't even know it)!

Dough
³⁄₄ cup plus 2 tablespoons (7 ounces) lukewarm water
¹⁄₄ cup (2 ounces) orange juice
5 tablespoons (3³⁄₄ ounces) honey
1 large egg, separated (reserve the white)
4 tablespoons (¹⁄₂ stick, 2 ounces) unsalted butter, cut into 6 pieces
3¹⁄₂ cups (14 ounces) traditional whole wheat flour
¹⁄₂ cup (1³⁄₄ ounces) old-fashioned rolled oats
Heaping ¹⁄₂ cup (1¹⁄₄ ounces) dried potato flakes or 3 tablespoons (1¹⁄₄ ounces)
    potato flour
¹⁄₄ cup (1 ounce) nonfat dry milk
1¹⁄₂ teaspoons salt
2 teaspoons instant yeast

Filling
1 cup (7¹⁄₂ ounces) packed light or dark brown sugar
1 large egg white
2 tablespoons (¹⁄₂ ounce) ground cinnamon
Pinch of salt

Icing
2 cups (8 ounces) confectioners' sugar
2 teaspoons vanilla extract
2 tablespoons (1 ounce) unsalted butter, melted
Pinch of salt
2 or 3 tablespoons (1 to 1¹⁄₂ ounces) milk or cream, enough to make a spreadable
    icing

TO PREPARE THE DOUGH: Combine all the dough ingredients, using the egg yolk and setting the white aside to use in the filling. Mix and knead—by hand, mixer or bread machine—until you have a medium-soft, smooth dough. Cover and allow the dough to rise until it's quite puffy, though probably not doubled in bulk, 1 to 2 hours. While the dough is rising, make the filling.

TO PREPARE THE FILLING: Combine the filling ingredients in a small bowl, stirring until smooth.

Lightly grease a 9 x 13-inch, 11-inch-square, 12-inch round or similar-size pan.

TO SHAPE THE BUNS: Gently deflate the dough, and transfer it to a lightly greased work surface. Roll and pat it into a 12 x 16-inch rectangle. Spread the filling over the dough, leaving a 1inch margin along one long edge. If the filling seems too sticky to spread easily, wet your fingers and smear it over the dough as best you can.

Starting with the filling-covered long edge, roll the dough into a log, turning it so the seam is flat against the work surface. Using a serrated knife or dental floss (see illustrations, p. 264), gently cut it into 16 pieces.

Place the buns in the prepared pan, spacing them evenly; they won't touch one another. Cover the pan with lightly greased plastic wrap or a proof cover, and allow the buns to rise for 1 to 1¼ hours. They won't double in size, but will become about half again as large as they were originally. They should barely touch each other. Near the end of the buns' rise, preheat the oven to 350°F.

TO BAKE THE BUNS: Bake the buns, until they're a deep golden brown on top, 25 to 28 minutes. Remove them from the oven, and after 3 minutes, carefully turn them out, upside-down, onto a rack. Place another rack, feet side up, on the buns, and invert them once again, so their tops are up. They'll be hot and delicate, so be careful. While the buns are cooling a bit, make the icing.

TO FINISH THE BUNS: Beat together the sugar, vanilla, butter, salt and 2 tablespoons of the milk (or cream) in a medium mixing bowl. Beat in additional milk or cream if the icing is too stiff to spread. Spread the icing on the lukewarm buns. Serve immediately, or cool completely, cover, and store at room temperature. Buns will keep well, covered, for several days.

NUTRITION INFORMATION PER SERVING (1 BUN, 96G): 28g whole grains, 288 cal, 5g fat, 6g protein, 22g complex carbohydrates, 33g sugar, 4g dietary fiber, 25mg cholesterol, 225mg sodium, 225mg potassium, 43RE vitamin A, 3mg vitamin C, 2mg iron, 62mg calcium, 139mg phosphorus.

VARIATION: *We like to spread icing on the buns while they're warm, as it seeps down into the cracks and infuses the entire bun with sweetness. However, if you prefer a thicker icing, one that stays on the surface, wait until the buns are entirely cool before icing them.*

> ### TAKE IT EASY
>
> Isn't it aggravating to put a beautifully risen batch of sticky buns or cinnamon rolls into the oven, and 30 minutes later pull out buns that have "exploded," their center spiral popping up above the edges? The secret is to roll the filled dough into a log loosely. If you roll it tightly, it has so little room for expansion as it bakes that it pops out the top. So don't make a nice, neat, tight log, when rolling dough for filled buns; take it easy, and you'll be much more pleased with the results.

1. After spreading the dough with filling, roll it into a log, starting with a long edge. Don't roll the dough too tightly, as this will make the center of the buns pop up when they bake.

2. Use a serrated knife to cut the log into buns, first dividing it in half, then each half in half again, and so on. Use a gentle sawing motion to keep the dough from flattening out as you cut it.

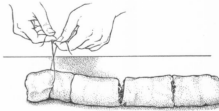

You may also cut your sticky buns using dental floss (nonminted, please!). Cut a strand of floss about 12 inches long and slide it under the roll dough to the width you want the buns to be. This technique slices through the buns without compressing them as much as a knife does.

Classic Sticky Buns

YIELD: **16 sticky buns**

BAKING TEMPERATURE: **350°F**

BAKING TIME: **28 minutes**

Sticky buns, those luscious spirals of cinnamon-stuffed yeast dough topped with a thick layer of dark syrup and nuts, are often associated with Philadelphia. Legend has it that 18th-century German and English immigrants to Philadelphia brought with them the original sticky bun recipe; but even that was preceded by schnecken, a similar though simpler bun popular in and around Philadelphia as early as the late 1600s. Whatever its provenance, the sticky bun has become one of America's most popular sweet breakfast treats. This dough is the same as the dough in the preceding recipe, but the filling and toppings create a totally different experience.

Dough

¾ cup plus 2 tablespoons (7 ounces) lukewarm water

¼ cup (2 ounces) orange juice

5 tablespoons (3¾ ounces) honey

1 large egg, separated (reserve the white)

4 tablespoons (½ stick, 2 ounces) unsalted butter, cut into 6 pieces

3½ cups (14 ounces) traditional whole wheat flour

½ cup (1¾ ounces) old-fashioned rolled oats

Heaping ½ cup (1¼ ounces) dried potato flakes or 3 tablespoons (1¼ ounces) potato flour

¼ cup (1 ounce) nonfat dry milk

1½ teaspoons salt

2 teaspoons instant yeast

Filling

1 cup (7½ ounces) packed light or dark brown sugar

1 large egg white

2 tablespoons (½ ounce) ground cinnamon

Pinch of salt

⅔ cup (3½ ounces) currants (optional)

Topping

⅔ cup (5 ounces) packed light or dark brown sugar

1 teaspoon ground cinnamon

1 teaspoon unbleached all-purpose flour

Pinch of salt

4 tablespoons (½ stick, 2 ounces) unsalted butter, melted

2 tablespoons (1⅜ ounces) light corn syrup

1 cup (3¾ ounces) chopped pecans

TO PREPARE THE DOUGH: Combine all the dough ingredients, using the egg yolk and setting aside the white to use in the filling. Mix and knead—by hand, mixer or bread machine—until you have a medium-soft, smooth dough. Cover and allow the dough to rise until it's quite puffy, though probably not doubled in bulk, 1 to 2 hours. While the dough is rising, make the filling and topping.

TO PREPARE THE FILLING AND TOPPING: Combine all the filling ingredients except the currants in a small bowl, stirring until smooth. Combine all the topping ingredients except the pecans in another small bowl, stirring until smooth.

Lightly grease a 9 x 13-inch, 11-inch-square, 12-inch round, or similar-size pan.

TO SHAPE THE BUNS: Gently deflate the dough, and transfer it to a lightly greased work surface. Roll and pat it into a 12 x 16-inch rectangle. Spread the filling over the dough, leaving a 1inch margin along one long edge. If the filling seems too sticky to spread easily, wet your fingers and smear it over the dough as best you can. Spread the currants evenly over the filling, if using.

Starting with the filling-covered long edge, roll the dough into a log, turning it so the seam is flat against the work surface. Using a serrated knife (or dental floss; see illustrations, p. 264) gently cut the log into 16 pieces.

Spread the topping in a thin layer in the prepared pan. Sprinkle the pecans over the topping. Lay the buns on top, spacing them evenly. Cover the pan with lightly greased plastic wrap or a proof cover, and allow the buns to rise for 1 to 1¼ hours. They won't double in size, but will become about half again as large as they were originally. They should barely touch each other. Near the end of the buns' rise, preheat the oven to 350°F.

TO BAKE THE BUNS: Uncover and bake the buns for 28 minutes; they should be a light golden brown. While the buns are baking, set a rectangular cooling rack, large enough to hold the pan of buns in one piece, over a sheet of parchment or wax paper. Remove the baked buns from the oven, and turn them out onto the rack, letting the paper catch the inevitable drips. Immediately scrape any topping remaining in the pan onto the buns. Allow the buns to cool a bit before serving.

If you're using a 9 x 13-inch pan, space 12 of the buns in four staggered rows of three buns each, reserving the two buns from the ends of the log. Using the two end buns, which are a bit smaller, squeeze four buns into the fifth and final row.

NUTRITION INFORMATION PER SERVING (1 BUN, 99G): 28g whole grains, 334 cal, 12g fat, 6g protein, 23g complex carbohydrates, 30g sugar, 4g dietary fiber, 29mg cholesterol, 262mg sodium, 288mg potassium, 54RE vitamin A, 2mg vitamin C, 2mg iron, 69mg calcium, 157mg phosphorus.

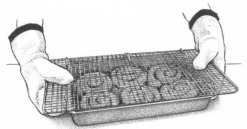

Place the cooling rack, feet side up on a pan of buns, grasping both the rack and the pan at either end.

Quickly turn the pan and rack upside down, so that the cooling rack is on the bottom with the buns on top.

Lift off the pan, and quickly scrape any remaining topping out of the pan, smearing it onto the buns.

STICKY BUNS VS. CINNAMON ROLLS—WHAT'S THE DIFFERENCE?

Both of these rolls are characterized by sweet filling rolled inside yeast dough, which is then sliced, baked and the resulting rolls topped with a sweet glaze or icing. Cinnamon rolls are filled with strongly cinnamon-flavored brown sugar, and baked untopped; after baking, they're spread with thick white icing. Sticky buns, filled with the same filling as cinnamon rolls, may add currants to that filling, according to the whim of the baker. They're baked in a pool of brown sugar, butter, cinnamon, syrup and nuts, which becomes their topping when the pan is turned over after baking. Interestingly, there's no such thing as a sticky bun in Philadelphia, the legendary home of those buns; in Philly, they're simply called cinnamon buns.

New York Crumb Buns

YIELD: 1 dozen buns

BAKING TEMPERATURE: 350°F

BAKING TIME: 35 to 40 minutes

New Yorkers who've left the Big Apple often wax nostalgic over many treats they can't find outside the city. New York bagels, cheesecake and deli sandwiches simply can't be replicated anywhere else, if you believe what these city-dwellers say. Another "only in New York" treat is crumb buns, tender, golden buns filled and covered, top and sides, with cinnamon-scented butter-and-sugar crumbs. This whole wheat version is our attempt to bring New York's classic sweet buns to the rest of the country, in somewhat more nutritious (but still authentic) form.

Dough

1 cup plus 2 tablespoons (9 ounces) lukewarm water

¼ cup (2 ounces) orange juice

2 tablespoons (1½ ounces) honey

4 tablespoons (½ stick, 2 ounces) butter, cut into 6 pieces

3¼ cups (11 ounces) whole wheat pastry flour

¾ cup (3⅛ ounces) unbleached bread flour

Heaping ½ cup (1¼ ounces) dried potato flakes or 3 tablespoons (1¼ ounces) potato flour

¼ cup (1 ounce) nonfat dry milk

1½ teaspoons salt

2 teaspoons instant yeast

Filling and topping

10 tablespoons (1¼ sticks, 5 ounces) unsalted butter, cut into 15 pieces

1 cup plus 2 tablespoons (8½ ounces) firmly packed light or dark brown sugar

1 teaspoon ground cinnamon

Heaping ¼ teaspoon salt

1 teaspoon vanilla extract

2 cups (6¾ ounces) whole wheat pastry flour

Glaze

2 to 3 tablespoons (1 to 1½ ounces) milk or cream

Confectioners' sugar, for sprinkling (optional)

TO PREPARE THE DOUGH: Combine all the ingredients and mix and knead them—by hand, mixer or bread machine—until you have a soft, smooth dough. Cover and allow the dough to rise until it's quite puffy, 1 to 2 hours.

TO PREPARE THE FILLING AND TOPPING: Beat together the butter, sugar, cinnamon, salt and vanilla in a large mixing bowl until they're thoroughly combined. Add the flour, and mix until uneven crumbs form. Don't over-mix or the crumbs will become a solid mass. Set aside.

Lightly grease a 9 x 13-inch pan.

TO ASSEMBLE THE BUNS: Transfer the dough to a lightly greased work surface, and gently deflate it. Divide it in half. Working with one half at a time, roll the dough into a 10 x 12-inch rectangle. Brush with milk or cream. Sprinkle 1 cup of the crumb mixture over the dough. Grasp one of the long edges, and fold it into the center, letter-fashion. Brush the folded-over piece with milk or cream. Then grasp the other long edge, and fold it over the first; again, this is just like folding a letter. Brush with milk or cream. Press the edge and ends to seal. Repeat with the remaining dough and filling. Pat and stretch each piece of dough into a 12 x 2-inch rectangle (approximately). Cut each piece into 6 even slices; they should be fairly square.

Space the slices evenly in the prepared pan. Sprinkle them with the remaining topping. Much of it will fall off into the pan; that's OK. Cover the pan with a proof cover or lightly greased plastic wrap, and allow the buns to rise for 1 hour. They won't rise much; that's fine. Preheat the oven to 350°F.

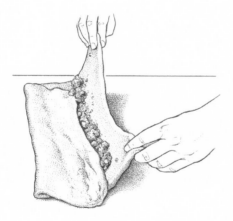

Grasp one of the long edges, and bring it two-thirds of the way over the dough, as though you're folding a letter. Brush the bare dough with milk and fold the other edge over it, again like a letter.

Cut the dough into six 2-inch pieces.

TO BAKE THE BUNS: Uncover and bake the buns until their crust and the crumbs are golden brown and the crumbs in the bottom of the pan are bubbly, 35 to 40 minutes. Remove them from the oven and allow them to cool in the pan for 10 minutes. Then carefully separate them, and transfer them to a rack to cool completely. Sprinkle the buns with confectioners' sugar just before serving, if desired.

NOTE: Unless you're a New York native, you're probably unfamiliar with this type of crumb topping, sometimes known as "blonde streusel." Instead of the typical cinnamon-infused streusel, this one is just faintly spiced with cinnamon and vanilla; the main flavor is that of sugar and butter. If desired, triple the amount of cinnamon in the crumbs, from 1 teaspoon to 1 tablespoon, for a more typical cinnamon crumb topping flavor.

NUTRITION INFORMATION PER SERVING (1 BUN, 120G): 42g whole grains, 382 cal, 14g fat, 8g protein, 38g complex carbohydrates, 18g sugar, 6g dietary fiber, 36mg cholesterol, 338mg sodium, 307mg potassium, 115RE vitamin A, 3mg vitamin C, 2mg iron, 69mg calcium, 195mg phosphorus.

SOURDOUGH

Sourdough, levain, mother, starter, chef, barm, leaven, desem—all these terms are names for the process by which flour is naturally fermented and leavened into bread. The names themselves suggest the mystery that surrounds the topic of wild yeast. Little wonder it's mysterious to so many—it does seem almost magical to mix together flour, water, a pinch of salt and conjure up a loaf of bread without any visible rising agent— no packet of yeast, no baking soda, no beaten eggs. How does that bread rise? Where does all that flavor come from? There are scores of self-proclaimed sourdough technicians each willing to share with you the one perfect answer to those questions. Many of those perfect answers are, however, completely contradictory. Sourdough is an area of enormous controversy and stongly held beliefs.

Such wild swings between science and superstition make for interesting lore. We know that it's yeast and lactobacilli doing the work of leavening and flavoring our bread, not magic. At the same time, intuition and experience are essential to success. We see the same precise weights of flour behaving differently from one time of year to another or even from day to day, and our experience with the dough will be helpful in knowing how to adapt.

A combination of understanding and experience will bring success in baking with wild yeast, and the same is true when we introduce yet another variable: whole grains.

Whole grains are both more hospitable and more hostile to the process of sourdough baking. Most whole grain flours have more wild yeast present in the flour because they include more of the whole berry on which the yeast has settled as the grains grow. They capture and sustain fermentation more quickly than their white counterparts. At the same time, they're more susceptible to rancidity than white flours. In a warm environment, rancidity can quickly become a concern, especially when working with whole wheat. We noticed a tendency for liquid whole wheat levains to develop a pronounced tang. While this may not be true in your kitchen, we found that cooler temperatures and/or a stiffer texture helped to keep the flavor from being overwhelmingly acidic. By far the greatest challenge, though, was that whole grains simply don't rise the way white flour does. If you really want a good rise with a chewy, palatable texture, the stark truth is that white flour works best. In whole grain sourdough breads, by the time the yeast has raised the bread, the acidity in the dough is pronounced, and the already tenuous gluten in the flour has begun to degrade, further inhibiting the rise.

Still, we were committed to incorporating whole grains into these breads. We used them in the levain, saving the white flour for the final dough so it could do its work in supporting the bread. Because we were trying to restrain the acidity, we used smaller amounts of levain, both in the levain maintenance and in the bread dough. The breads we present here are the result of countless recipes we tested and rejected. We simply didn't include anything here that we didn't love. We've included a range of breads from those that are half whole grain to breads that are 100 percent whole grain, in the belief that as your palate adjusts, you'll welcome increasing amounts of whole grains. By the time we were done with the chapter, plain old yeast bread made from 100 percent white flour tasted insipid to us, and we craved the complexity of flavor and texture found in sourdough breads made with whole grains.

Capturing wild yeast

Where to begin? We tried a variety of techniques and ingredients to capture and bake with wild yeast. At one point there were 14 little bowls on our kitchen counter, each with its own set of instructions for care. We tried fermenting apples and burying starters in flour; feeding twice a day and twice a week; using freshly ground organic wheat and unbleached white flour. And after about a week of observation and experimentation, we began to see what did and didn't work in our kitchen. Techniques that emphasize long periods of time with no feedings tended to develop a cheesy aroma that wound up giving the finished bread an "off" flavor. The stiffer the levain, the more slowly it developed; so stiff levains didn't need to be fed as frequently as liquid levains. The key to consistent success was close attention at the beginning of the process, followed by more close attention as the levains developed.

But what's happening in this process? Those little bowls of flour and water are simply providing a friendly home for the wild yeast and lactobacilli to inhabit. You can see yeast settled on the skins of fresh fruit, and realize that it's all around us, and it settles where it finds food. Flour and water make an ideal environment for yeast to inhabit—like putting out a dish of cream to attract a stray cat. Some flours work better than others at attracting and sustaining yeast. Whole grain rye and wheat were by far the quickest to become active. Spelt, too, was quick to ferment and developed a healthy appetite for frequent feeding.

The method below is for starting a rye, whole wheat, or spelt levain, and is similar to the method in our earlier cookbook, *The King Arthur Flour Baker's Companion*. It takes 5 to 7 days to develop a levain that's strong enough to use for bread baking. If you're making a whole wheat levain, it will likely be more liquid than a whole rye levain. The rye levains are so stiff that it can be hard to tell if they're really developing into a culture. So make sure to smell and even taste the levain each time you feed it. Within a few days it will begin to acquire a sour but still "fresh" aroma and a tangy flavor. Whether you're making a whole wheat, rye or spelt levain, you'll need to use that type of flour throughout the entire process of creating and maintaining the levain. In other words, you don't switch back and forth from rye to whole wheat to spelt in a single starter.

To start your own whole wheat, rye or spelt sourdough levain, using your chosen flour throughout the process:

Day 1

4 ounces (1 to 1⅛ cups) whole wheat, whole rye (pumpernickel) or whole spelt flour

4 ounces (½ cup) cool nonchlorinated water

Combine the flour and water in a nonreactive container. Glass, crockery, stainless steel or food-grade plastic all work fine for this. Cover the container and let the mixture sit at room temperature (65°F to 75°F) for 24 hours.

WATERWORLD

One of the most frequent questions we get about sourdough is what kind of water to use. We're lucky to have great well water at our bakery and school site, and that's what we use in our sourdough baking there, both for refreshing the levains and for making the doughs for bread. In our test kitchen, though, our tap water is heavily chlorinated, and we ran into trouble trying to maintain levains with water straight from the tap. One solution is to turn to filtered water or bottled spring water, but with twice-daily feedings, that can quickly become pretty expensive. Frugal Vermonters that we are, we decided to find another way!

Each night we'd fill a pitcher of water and set it out, uncovered on the counter. The next morning, the chlorine would have evaporated out, leaving a supply of cool, nonchlorinated water perfect for feeding levains and making dough.

Day 2

You may see no activity at all in the first 24 hours or you may see a bit of growth or bubbling. Either way, discard half the levain from yesterday, and add to the remainder:

4 ounces (1 to 1⅛ cups) whole wheat, whole rye (pumpernickel) or whole spelt flour

4 ounces (½ cup) cool nonchlorinated water

Mix well, cover and let the mixture sit at room temperature for 24 hours.

Days 3, 4 & 5

By the third day, you will likely be seeing evidence of activity. For whole wheat and whole spelt levains, this will be bubbling, a fresh, fruity aroma and some evidence of expansion. For rye levains, the activity is harder to see, but there will begin to be signs of aeration, and the smell of the levain begins to become distinctively fresh and tangy. It's now time to begin two feedings a day, as evenly spaced as your schedule allows.

For each feeding discard all but 4 ounces of the levain. To that 4 ounces add:

4 ounces (1 to 1 ⅛ cups) whole wheat, whole rye (pumpernickel), or whole spelt flour

4 ounces (½ cup) cool nonchlorinated water

Mix well, cover and let the mixture sit at room temperature for approximately 12 hours before repeating.

After 5 days of consistent feeding, your levain should be ready to use in a sourdough bread recipe. If not, don't lose heart; keep feeding it regularly, and it will gain strength—really! Be patient. The conditions in your kitchen may be more or less conducive to building a levain depending on the season, humidity, or how much you've been baking. On occasion, some bakers have problems with the pH of their levains and develop a very sluggish, very sour levain. This can be helped by including a small amount of ascorbic acid in the water at the beginning of the process until the levain has a chance to establish itself.

Care and feeding

The pet analogy continues into maintenance for the levain. If you offer just one dish of cream, the cat won't stay—you have to continue to feed it to keep it and keep it healthy. Likewise with levains. One of the recipes we read suggested stirring the levain every day for a week, but without adding any flour. Needless to say, that levain never really did much. Your levain requires regular feeding, (also known as "refreshment") and comfortable temperatures to thrive. Consistency is key to continued success.

We strongly recommend spending some weeks feeding your levain 2 or 3 times a day, and baking with it regularly. As you work with your levain, keep a record of your observations, both of the levain itself and of the bread you make with it. How does it smell? Taste? How is it rising? Does it seem active enough for your needs? Can you spot the levain's characteristics in the finished bread? It doesn't need to be an elaborate journal, just a few notes to help you spot trends or trouble areas.

To maintain a levain at room temperature:

Cool room temperature (about 65°F) is the perfect environment for most whole grain levains. It keeps them from developing so quickly they have to be fed 3 times a day to stay fresh, and it helps to slow rancidity. Maintaining your levain at room temperature will give you a sense of how it should be working and tasting in your breads. If your room temperature is warmer or cooler, you may need to adjust the feeding schedule to keep the levain fresh. Notice what happens if you miss a feeding, and pay attention to how the levain changes over time.

Feed the levain twice a day, and space the feedings 12 hours apart if possible. Feed the levain as you did when you were building it:

4 ounces of ripe levain

4 ounces (1 to 1⅛ cups) whole wheat, rye (pumpernickel) or spelt flour

4 ounces (½ cup) cool nonchlorinated water

Mix the ingredients well, cover the levain and let it sit until the next feeding. If you're not baking regularly with your levain, this can start to seem like a lot of flour you're using and discarding in maintenance. You may cut the feeding quantities in half without a problem and build them back up as you get ready to bake. If you're baking daily, simply use the 8 ounces of ripe levain for baking and discard what you don't use for baking or maintenance.

To refrigerate a levain:

If you plan to refrigerate your levain, you'll need to continue feeding it on a weekly basis and go through the process of resuscitating it each time you want to bake with it. To feed it weekly, remove the levain from the refrigerator and discard all but 2 ounces (about ¼ cup). Add 4 ounces of water and 4 ounces of flour to the levain. Stir it well, cover it and let it sit for at least 2 hours before returning it to the refrigerator.

To bake with a refrigerated levain:

Two or three days before you want to bake, pull your levain from the refrigerator and begin to feed it on a regular basis at room temperature. It's important to check on the characteristics of the levain at the beginning of this refreshment period. How does it smell and taste? Are you getting increased volume as the flour ferments? We found that the levains became pretty acidic in the refrigerator, and so we'd begin the refreshment cycle by taking only a tablespoon or so of the original levain and feeding it with 4 ounces each of flour and water to restore balance to the levain. You may want to try that if you encounter excess acidity at any point in the process.

WATER TEMPERATURE FORMULA

(Water Temperature = (4 x Desired Dough Temperature) –
(Flour Temperature + Room Temperature + Levain Temperature + Friction)
(degrees are Fahrenheit)

SUMMER EXAMPLE:

Desired Dough Temperature	75°
Flour Temperature	80°
Room Temperature	85°
Levain Temperature	75°
Friction (Using a mixer)	26°

TO CALCULATE:

Water Temperature = (4 x 75) – (80 + 85 + 75 + 26)
= 300 – 266
= 34°

WINTER EXAMPLE

Desired Dough Temperature	75°
Flour Temperature	65°
Room Temperature	65°
Levain Temperature	68°
Friction (By hand)	12°

TO CALCULATE:

Water Temperature = (4 x 75) – (65 + 65 + 68 + 12)
= 300 – 210
= 90°

STAYING OUT OF HOT WATER

Most breads in this section call for cool water. That's because we're aiming for bread dough that's around 75°F. Sourdough breads do best at temperatures right around 75°F, which, coincidentally, is a common kitchen temperature. If you're aiming for a temperature of about 75°F, and most of your ingredients are in that temperature range, your dough will be close to that range if your water is a little cooler, because you're adding heat to the dough through friction as you mix and knead it. Mixing and kneading can add anywhere from 10 to 30 degrees to a dough, depending on how long you're kneading, whether or not you're using a mixer, or even whether you have cold or hot hands.

The temperatures of the flour, levain and friction are harder to manipulate than the water temperature, so professional bakers (and passionate home bakers, too) use a formula to figure their water temperature precisely. You can use the formula above to figure the water temperature that will yield the dough temperature you want, or you can use your instincts. If it's 95°F in your kitchen, then your flour and levain are probably close to that and you'll probably want cold water in the dough. If, on the other hand, you're pulling flour right from your freezer, which may well be the case with whole grain flours, the water should be warmer to compensate for the cold flour. Remember, though, that hot water will kill the yeast, and sourdough has fewer yeast cells to start with, so to play it safe, don't go above 100°F.

HOOCH!

What's that layer of liquid that separates out of your levain? Should you throw it away? This is a topic rife with controversy. After one of our instructors suggested you simply stir that layer of alcohol back into the levain, we received a three-page hand-written letter from an angry student elaborating why you *must* discard that liquid! In fact, there are proponents of both and we've had success with both. We're more apt to stir it back in to maintain the appropriate balance of liquid and flour, but if it's offensive to you, simply pour it off, and feed the remaining levain according to your usual schedule. The best solution is to feed your levain frequently enough to avoid developing that layer of fermented liquid.

WHY WEIGH?

It may seem like a lot of trouble to get a scale and weigh your ingredients, but it'll make a tremendous difference to the end result, especially in the realm of sourdough. When you see a recipe that calls for 1 cup of sourdough, what does that really mean? How much flour and how much water are in that cup: 1/2 cup of each? 4 ounces of each? (That would be 1 cup of flour and 1/2 cup of water.) How much does that cup of sourdough weigh? Do you measure 1 cup using levain that's fully expanded, or do you stir it down first? Does that make a difference? How do you get your expanded culture into the cup measure without having it deflate?

Our instinct with baking is that volume is so much easier to work with, but in fact it's so much simpler when you put away the cup measures and pull out a scale. Now you know you need 9 ounces of ripe levain, and it does-n't matter if the levain collapses a bit as you measure it into your bowl. An added bonus is that you cut your dishwashing considerably when you're weighing directly from your levain storage into your mixing bowl—no gluey cups and spoons to wash!

We also find it's easier to maintain a levain if you're weighing the flour. It's especially important to be precise with whole grain flours, because they tend to absorb much more liquid to begin with. If you add a little too much flour, it can really slow the fermentation process to a crawl. If you weigh the flour and water, you can be sure the levain will be ready to use when you need it.

One cup of expanded starter weighs 4 1/2 ounces and equals 1/2 cup of stirred down starter.

Four ounces each of white, whole wheat and rye flour, each mixed with four ounces of water, before and after ripening.

WHAT WENT WRONG?

Because yeast and lactobacilli live in a delicate balance, it's possible for things to go wrong. Sometimes you don't notice it until you bake the bread. Sometimes you can tell with a glance at the levain. It could be that you've overheated the levain and killed the yeast (microwaving will do this). It may be that you're using chlorinated water in the feedings. But by far the most frequent problem we encounter is irregular or insufficient feeding. Most of the questions we get about what's gone wrong with a levain are answered by simply pulling the levain from the refrigerator, feeding it more frequently and attending to the result. Troubleshooting an ailing levain is where keeping notes on your sourdough levain can be especially useful. If the levain has become very acidic, you can combat the acidity by using a small amount of levain relative to the overall feeding. This will also slow the fermentation if you're going to be away from the levain for a longer period of time than usual. If your levain doesn't seem sour enough, it's possible you're not letting it ripen sufficiently before feeding, or it may be that your area isn't conducive to an aggressively sour culture. Most of the time, though, more frequent and more regular feedings will cure what ails your levain. One caveat: If you see mold growing on your levain, toss it out and start the process again.

CONVERTING REGULAR (WHITE) SOURDOUGH TO WHOLE WHEAT CULTURE

It can be pretty time and space consuming to maintain different cultures for each different kind of bread you want to bake. It's not hard for professional bakers to keep a variety of levains going, as they can easily build the feeding schedules into their workday. For home bakers, though, it may be more convenient to keep one levain on hand and convert it to coincide with the bread you're planning to make. If you have a healthy, active white flour levain, you can use that to make a whole wheat levain. To convert a liquid, white flour levain to whole wheat, simply continue your feeding schedule, but instead of feeding with white flour, substitute an equal weight of whole wheat flour. After 3 or 4 feedings, your levain will be predominantly whole wheat.

Pain au Levain with Whole Wheat

YIELD: 2 small loaves, 20 slices
BAKING TEMPERATURE: 450°F, then 425°F
BAKING TIME: 40 to 45 minutes

This is a great recipe to learn how to work with whole wheat, both in your levain, and in the dough. It has a wonderful wheaty flavor, and it gets a nice rise in the oven. This also is an ideal recipe to use as a base for flavored loaves, since the white flour helps to carry the addition of other ingredients. After you're comfortable with all the steps in the process, and you're familiar with the flavor of the finished loaves, you can add other ingredients, such as olives, nuts, fruits or herbs.

> 1 cup (9 ounces) ripe whole wheat levain
> 1^2/₃ cup (6⁵/₈ ounces) whole wheat flour
> 2²/₃ cups (11¼ ounces) unbleached bread flour
> 1½ cups (12 ounces) cool water
> 1 tablespoon honey
> 2 teaspoons salt

The night before you're ready to bake, feed your levain, so that it'll be ripe when you're ready to bake. This will likely take 6 to 8 hours, depending on the conditions in your kitchen. If you've been keeping track of how quickly it ripens, you'll know what time to feed it to have it ready for baking.

The next morning, check your levain. It should be bubbly, with a fresh, fruity aroma, and not yet receding.

Place all of the levain in your mixer bowl and mix in the flours and water. Mix together the ingredients at the slowest possible speed just until they're well combined and the flour is thoroughly moistened. Cover the bowl, and let it rest for 20 minutes. This resting period is called an autolyse.

After 20 minutes, stir in the honey and salt on the slowest speed. Once the salt is incorporated, turn up the mixer speed, and knead the dough for 2 to 3 minutes. If you prefer to knead by hand, see suggestions on page 282. The dough will not be completely kneaded, and will still be quite sticky, but that's OK. Cover the bowl, and let the dough rise for 45 minutes.

After 45 minutes even if the dough doesn't look risen, use a dough scraper to take it from the bowl, and place it on a well-floured surface. It's time to fold the dough. Folding the dough is comparable to "punching" the dough, but it's a much gentler process, and it helps to build the dough strength, as well as redistribute the carbon dioxide produced by the yeast. With well-floured hands, pat the dough out to a rough rectangle. Use a metal bench knife to fold the dough in thirds, as you would a business letter. Use your hands to pat away any excess flour from the dough as you're folding it. You'll now have a horizontal strip of dough. Again, use your bench knife and fold the dough, this time from the opposite direction. You'll be left with a packet of dough to return to the bowl.

To fold the dough, first fold it in thirds like a business letter. Brush any excess flour off the dough.

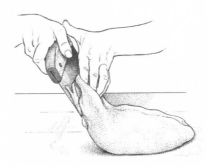

Next, fold the dough in thirds again, this time from the opposite side, patting away excess flour as necessary.

The remaining packet of dough is flipped back into the bowl. This completes a double fold.

Cover the bowl, and let the dough rise for another 45 minutes. Scrape the dough out onto a well-floured surface and repeat the double fold described above. Return the dough to the bowl for a final 45-minute rise. As the dough is finishing its rise, heavily flour two bannetons or brotforms.

If you don't have a banneton or brotform, make your own by lining bowls, colanders or round baskets with linen tea towels. It's important to choose a smooth-textured fabric, or your bread dough will get stuck in the material. Linen or smooth cotton work best.

After a total of 2¼ to 2½ hours of rising time, the dough is ready to shape. Flour your work surface lightly but thoroughly, and flour your hands well. Use a dough scraper to scrape the dough out of the bowl onto the work surface, and divide it in half. Pull the edges of each half into the center to form a rough round. This is called a preshape. Let the dough rest,

These proofing baskets are the perfect place for your sourdough loaf to finish its rise. We love how the dough rises in a French-linen banneton (top) or a German brotform (left), but you can make your own proofing basket by lining a bowl with a linen tea towel (at right). The shaped loaf is placed bottom up in the basket for its final rise, then turned out of the basket onto a baking pan or stone.

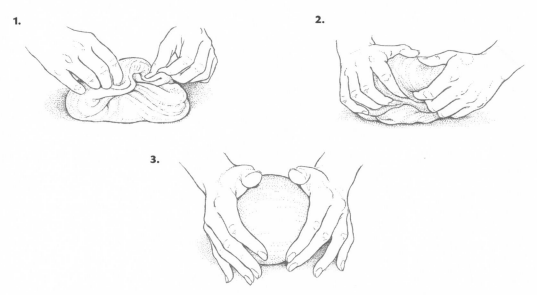

SHAPING THE DOUGH: *1. Pull the edges of the dough into the center. The point where all of the edges come together will be the bottom seam of the shaped loaf. 2. Turn the dough over so that point is on the bottom. Begin tightening the surface by pulling the loaf toward you repeatedly on the work surface. Use your little fingers to tuck the loose edges into the bottom of the ball. Roll the loaf sideways as you work to create an evenly round boule. The goal is equal tension over the loaf's surface. 3. To further tighten and round the loaf, drag it across the work surface with cupped hands. Repeat this step until you're satisfied that the boule is sufficiently tight.*

rough side up, on a floured surface for 15 to 20 minutes. This rest will allow you to shape the dough more firmly.

After 20 minutes, it's time to make the final shape. If your dough is sticky, you may flour your work surface very lightly, but remember you'll need some friction on the surface to help you shape the loaf. Instead of loading the surface with flour, keep your hands floured and the surface as clear as possible.

Remember that whole grain breads are a bit more prone to tearing, so be careful not to tighten the boules too much. If you see little stretch marks start to appear across the surface of the boule, it's time to stop. After you've shaped the boules as illustrated above, turn them upside down, pinch the bottoms to seal them shut, and put them into the floured bannetons or proof baskets. Cover them well with plastic wrap, or better yet, turn a large bowl over each one to let it rest. The bread will take from 2 to 2½ hours before it's ready to bake, depending on the conditions in your kitchen. Check the dough frequently with floured fingers. Poke it gently to see how quickly the depressions your fingers make fill back in—at first it'll be pretty quick, but will slow as the bread proofs.

About half an hour before you're ready to bake, preheat your oven and baking stone to 450°F. Prepare the oven for steam, see sidebar on page 284.

KNEADING A STICKY DOUGH BY HAND

For many of these breads it's much easier to knead the dough in a mixer, so you won't be tempted to incorporate too much flour. If you don't have the luxury of a mixer that can handle bread dough, you can of course knead the dough by hand, as long as you resist the temptation to keep adding flour. Adding flour to the point that the dough is no longer sticky will result in a dense, heavy loaf that simply can't rise in the oven.

There are several techniques for handling sticky doughs. The easiest one for many is just to grit your teeth and knead it as you would an ordinary loaf, acknowledging that you and your work surface will become a sticky mess in the process.

Lift the dough from the side and give it a quarter turn in the air. Slap it gently onto the work surface and fold it over itself. After a few turns with this method, the dough will become cohesive enough to manage entirely by hand.

A traditional technique is to stretch the dough into a lengthwise rectangle, and pierce the

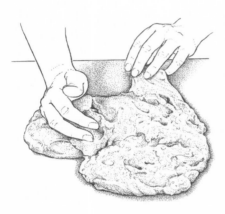

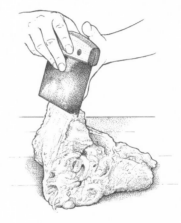

Using traditional kneading methods for sticky dough is very messy. Nonetheless, the dough will eventually become smoother and more elastic. Another technique is to use a metal bench knife as one of your hands to help lift the dough cleanly from the work surface.

Using a bench knife keeps at least one of your hands clean, and helps to form a cohesive dough mass. The dough will get a quarter turn in the air as you lift it and set it back down and will keep the kneading process even.

When the dough is ready to bake, it will feel very bubbly to your floured fingers—even slack. It will seem quite sluggish when you press it. Turn the boules out of the bannetons onto a piece of parchment paper, and slash them. If there's a lot of excess flour on the loaves, gently brush it away with a very soft, dry pastry brush before you slash them. Use a peel to transfer the bread, parchment and all, to the baking stone. Steam the oven, (see box, p. 284) and let the bread bake for 5 minutes. Crack the oven door to check the steam. If all the water's evaporated, spray the loaves again quickly, and let the bread bake for another 10 minutes. Reduce the temperature to 425°F, and bake the loaves for 25 to 30 minutes longer. When the bread is done, it'll be golden brown, and when you squeeze it dough with both hands along its length.

Then fold the dough over itself, flip it 90 degrees, and repeat the process. After a few rounds of this, the dough will pull together for finishing the kneading.

One novel, but effective technique, is to use a baker's bench knife to cut the dough into small chunks.

Once they're cut, gather them together again with the bench knife and repeat.

Try different methods and see what works best for you. You're likely to settle on a combination of one or two techniques you find most comfortable. Whichever technique you use, remember that using an autolyse will reduce the amount of time you have to spend with your hands in the sticky dough mass. Once you think the dough is ready, rub the dough from your hands and flour them lightly. Poke the dough with a floured finger to see if it springs back— that's a sign the gluten is sufficiently developed. Use your floured hands to form the dough into a neat ball to return to its bowl for rising.

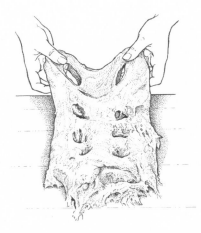

Use your hands to press through the dough and make a series of holes along its length.

Cutting the dough into pieces at the beginning of the kneading process brings it together quickly.

gently it will feel quite firm. We find the customary internal temperature of 190° to 195°F is not nearly done enough for these breads; they're often 210°F before they're done.

When the bread is done, use the peel to slide it out of the oven and let the loaves cool on a rack before slicing.

NUTRITION INFORMATION PER SERVING (1 SLICE, 57G): 16g whole grains, 115 cal, 4g protein, 24g complex carbohydrates, 1g sugar, 2g dietary fiber, 215mg sodium, 82mg potassium, 1mg iron, 8mg calcium, 72mg phosphorus.

SLASHING

Slashing the dough just before it goes in the oven may have started as a signature for the baker, but it serves an important structural purpose. By slashing the dough in the appropriate spot, you're telling the bread just where you want it to expand. Loaves that aren't slashed have less overall volume and a denser internal structure. An unslashed loaf will be apt to find whatever weak spot you may have created in shaping the dough and explode out asymmetrically, making for an ugly loaf and an uneven texture.

When you're slashing the loaf, be sure to use a very sharp blade so you don't drag the dough as you cut. Many bakers use a lame, a razor blade set on a small handle, but you can simply use the sharpest knife you own. Don't be tentative. Think about where you want to slash the loaf before you set the blade to the dough. You want to use a single, bold, smooth stroke for each cut, and you want the cuts to be about 1/4-inch deep. Pay attention to how different slashes open differently as the bread bakes. Remember, practice makes better, if not perfect. If you think of slashing as a signature, you'll approach the task with confidence and panache, and the loaf will expand beautifully in the oven.

ALL STEAMED UP!

Our bakery has a beautiful 6-ton steam-injected oven that came to us from France, complete with a wonderful Frenchman to help us assemble it. The breads that come out of that oven are simply spectacular—high-rising, crusty, and filled with holes. Of course, most of that is due to the skill of the bakers, but the oven certainly doesn't hurt! For those of us who don't have access to baking in an oven like that, there are some methods that'll give us similar results from our humble home ovens.

The two most important characteristics of that bakery oven are its thermal mass, and the ability to get steam into it without losing heat. Keeping these two things in mind while you adapt your home oven will help in your quest for crusty bread.

To get more mass into your oven, use some kind of baking stone. You can purchase a variety of stones specifically made for a home oven, or you can make your own with firebrick. Using a stone means that your oven will hold heat better, even when you're opening and closing the door to load and steam the bread. It also drives the bread to rise up (instead of pancake out) when you place the dough directly on it. When you use a stone, it's important to preheat it along with the oven. This usually takes considerably longer than it takes to heat the air in your oven, so be sure to allow at least half an hour for preheating the stone.

Once you've got a hot stone ready to go, you need to get steam in the oven so that as the bread rises up off the hot stone, it's not constricted by the dry air in the oven. We've found the best technique is to place a cast-iron pan on the bottom rack of the oven and heat it up along with the baking stone. This has the added advantage of increasing the thermal mass inside the oven. While the oven is heating up, let a small pan of water heat on top of the stove. Just as you slide the bread into the oven, pour a small amount of hot water into the cast-iron pan to create a burst of steam. This is very effective, so be sure to stand back from the oven door and wear oven mitts for the pouring job, or you can burn your hands from the hot steam. You don't need a lot of water, just enough to create steam for the first 5 to 15 minutes of the baking time—maybe 1/2 cup. Use water that's almost ready to boil, so it'll create steam quickly, without introducing something cold into the hot environment you've worked to create. As soon as you have the bread and steam in the oven, close the door. Home ovens lose heat very quickly when the door is open.

For sourdough bread, you may want to check the oven about 5 minutes into the baking time. If the steam has dissipated, have a mister on hand to spray water quickly into the chamber, right around the bread, then close the door again and let the bread bake undisturbed until the crust has formed. No need to keep spraying past this point; steaming past the first 15 minutes of baking will give you a heavy, dense crust, rather than the crisp, caramelized crust that crunches so pleasingly in your mouth.

Whole Wheat Multigrain Sourdough Bread

YIELD: 1 loaf, 16 servings
BAKING TEMPERATURE: 425°F
BAKING TIME: 35 to 40 minutes

We love the sunflower seeds in this loaf, and the cracked wheat adds a subtle chewy texture. This loaf has enough white flour in it to allow you to retard it overnight in the refrigerator to increase the sour flavor, if it's not sour enough to suit your taste.

¼ cup (1¼ ounces) cracked wheat
¼ cup (2 ounces) cool water
1 cup (9 ounces) ripe whole wheat levain
½ cup (2 ounces) traditional whole wheat flour
1½ cups (6⅜ ounces) unbleached bread flour
1 cup (8 ounces) water
1½ teaspoons salt
¼ cup (1¼ ounces) sunflower seeds

The night before you're ready to bake, combine the cracked wheat and cool water in a small bowl. Cover and set aside to soak at room temperature until morning. The next day, when your levain is ripe, mix together the levain, cracked wheat and all its liquid, the flours, water and salt in a large bowl. Once the ingredients are thoroughly combined, knead the dough, by hand or in a mixer until the dough is springy and elastic, about 4 minutes. If you're kneading by hand, be sure not to incorporate more flour into the dough. Use one of the techniques for kneading sticky doughs described on page 282. When the dough is soft and elastic, add the sunflower seeds and knead them into the dough. Return the dough to its bowl, cover it and set it aside to rise for 1 hour.

After an hour, the dough will be somewhat puffy, though not doubled in bulk. Turn it from the bowl onto a well-floured work surface, and give it a double fold, as described on page 280. Return the dough to its bowl, and let it rise for another hour.

While the dough is rising, heavily flour a banneton or a bowl or colander lined with a linen towel (see p. 280 for illustrations). Remove the dough from the bowl and place it on a very lightly floured surface. Flour your hands well and shape the dough into a round. Place it upside down in the floured banneton, cover it and set it aside to proof for 2½ hours.

About half an hour before you're ready to bake, preheat your oven and baking stone to 425°F. Prepare the oven for steam (see p. 284).

When the dough is ready to bake, it will be very soft and feel bubbly and full, and it will be slow to recover when you press it gently with floured fingers. Flip it from the banneton onto a piece of parchment paper, and gently brush away any excess flour with a soft, dry pastry brush. Slash the loaf with a very sharp blade. Use a peel to load the bread, parchment paper and all, onto the hot baking stone. Steam the oven, and bake the bread for 35 to 40 minutes, or until it's browned and stays firm if you give it a gentle squeeze. Remove the bread from the oven, place it on a rack and let it cool completely before slicing.

NUTRITION INFORMATION PER SERVING (1 SLICE, 54G): 14g whole grains, 104 cal, 2g fat, 4g protein, 19g complex carbohydrates, 2g dietary fiber, 201mg sodium, 86mg potassium, 1mg iron, 10mg calcium, 80mg phosphorus.

MY BREAD'S TOO SOUR/NOT SOUR ENOUGH

Sourdough bread has to be one of the most subjective areas in all of baking. What's divine to one is revolting to another. It's fun to watch a roomful of people sampling sourdough. The responses to a single loaf can range from "way too mild" to "way too sour," along with every stop in between, including "just right!" Yeast and lactobacilli native to different areas have different flavor characteristics, so the bread will have different degrees of sour, as well. With regular sourdough bread, one of the simplest ways to increase the sour flavor is to retard the loaves. This means to cover the shaped dough and put it in the refrigerator for a period of time as it proofs. With whole grains, the relationship between increased acidity and decreased volume is more pronounced, though, so this retarding may results in loaves that are more acidic or "sour", but that same increased acidity can make for loaves that simply don't rise as well. Instead, you might try varying the amount of levain you use in the dough. Again, though, be aware that you may come up against problems with the rise, as the increased acidity degrades the gluten.

If, on the other hand, the bread is too sour for your taste, you can reduce its acidity by using less levain in the recipe (remember to increase the flour and water to compensate for the reduced levain). Or, use a small amount of levain to ferment the flour, much like a yeasted preferment, which uses a small amount of commercial yeast to inoculate flour and water. For instance, if your recipe calls for 1 cup (or 9 ounces) of levain, add 2 tablespoons of levain to 4 ounces of flour and 4 ounces of water the night before you bake. The resulting levain will be less acidic and your bread will be, too.

Walnut-Currant Sourdough Bread

YIELD: 1 loaf, 16 slices

BAKING TEMPERATURE: 450°F, then 400°F

BAKING TIME: 45 to 50 minutes

This bread is so good; it has a complex combination of flavors and a deep sourdough aroma, sweet with currants and rich with walnuts. It's great toasted first thing in the morning, and even better in the late afternoon with fresh cream cheese. Because it's nearly 75 percent whole wheat, the bread is dense and chewy and studded with nuts and fruit. Feel free to substitute your favorite dried fruits and nuts for the currants and walnuts.

Levain
½ **cup (2 ounces) traditional whole wheat flour**
¼ **cup (2 ounces) cool, nonchlorinated water**
1 tablespoon ripe whole wheat levain

Dough
All of the levain
1½ cups (6 ounces) traditional whole wheat flour
1 cup (4¼ ounces) unbleached bread flour
1 cup (8 ounces) cool water
2 tablespoons (1½ ounces) honey
1 teaspoon salt
¼ **cup (1¼ ounces) currants**
¼ **cup (1 ounce) walnuts, chopped fine**

Make the levain the night before you bake. Combine the whole wheat flour, cool water and ripe sourdough levain in a bowl. Mix these together thoroughly, cover and set aside to ferment at room temperature for 12 hours, or overnight.

The next morning, check the levain; it should be bubbly and expanded and not yet receding. In the bowl of your mixer, combine all of the levain with the remaining 1½ cups whole wheat flour, bread flour and the cool water. Using the paddle attachment, mix at the lowest possible speed just until the flour is thoroughly moistened. Turn off the mixer, cover the bowl, and let the mixture autolyse, or rest, for 20 minutes. After 20 minutes, add the honey and salt and mix at low speed until they're incorporated. Then turn the mixer up a notch, to kneading speed, and knead for 2 minutes. Cover the bowl and let the dough rest for 30 minutes.

After 30 minutes, turn the dough out onto a well-floured surface. Flour your hands well and lightly pat the dough out into a rough rectangle, about 6 x 9 inches. Sprinkle the currants over the dough, and use a metal bench knife to fold the dough in thirds over the currants, patting the dough lightly to remove any excess flour as you fold. Now pat the dough out into a rough rectangle again, sealing in the currants, and sprinkle the dough with the walnuts. Use the bench knife to fold the dough in thirds in the opposite direction.

Incorporate the additions into the dough as you fold it, first the currants in one direction . . .

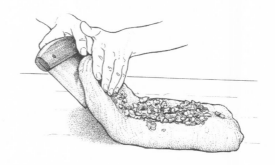

. . . and then the walnuts in the other. Keep the work surface well floured, but be sure to brush away the excess flour as you fold, so as not to incorporate extra flour into the dough.

This will be a very sticky dough at this stage; that's OK. It'll smooth out as it rises and is folded repeatedly. Return the dough to the bowl, cover it and let it rise for another 30 minutes. After 30 minutes, remove the dough from the bowl and give it another double fold on a well-floured surface. A metal bench knife comes in handy here, as the dough is still fairly sticky. Return the dough to the bowl, and repeat the rising and folding twice more. After 4 folds and 2½ hours of rising time, it's time to shape the dough. Heavily flour a banneton or a bowl or colander lined with a linen towel. Turn the dough from the bowl onto a lightly floured surface. By now the dough should be quite smooth, puffy and soft. Flour your hands well and shape the dough into a round as directed on page 281. Be careful not to tighten the round too much or the currants and walnuts will tear the surface of the loaf. Turn the loaf upside down into the floured banneton, cover it well, and let it rise for 2 to 2½ hours.

Check the dough frequently to see if it's ready to bake. About half an hour before you think it'll be ready for the oven, preheat your oven and baking stone to 450°F. Prepare the oven for steam. When the dough is ready to bake, it will be very puffy and will feel full and bubbly. When you touch it with floured fingers, the depressions your fingers leave will be slow to refill. Flip the loaf out of the banneton onto a piece of parchment paper. Use a dry pastry brush to gently brush any excess flour from the surface of the dough. Slash the dough to a depth of about ¼ inch. Use a peel to load the loaf into the oven, parchment and all. Steam the oven, and let the bread bake for 15 minutes. After 15 minutes, reduce the heat to 400°F, and let the bread continue to bake until the crust is golden brown and remains firm when you gently squeeze the loaf, 30 to 35 minutes longer. Use a peel to unload the bread, and place it on a rack to cool thoroughly before slicing.

NUTRITION INFORMATION PER SERVING (1 SLICE, 51G): 14g whole grains, 104 cal, 2g fat, 3g protein, 18g complex carbohydrates, 2g sugar, 2g dietary fiber, 135mg sodium, 96mg potassium, 1mg iron, 61mg calcium, 68mg phosphorus.

AUTOLYSE

Autolyse (pronounced *auto-leeze*) refers to the technique of letting the flour and water in a recipe rest together before kneading. It's a very simple step to take, yet it gives enormous advantages. In a sourdough recipe, it means combining all of the levain, flour and water for a recipe, stirring them together until the flour is thoroughly moistened, and letting the mixture sit for at least 20 minutes. Doing this gives the gluten in the recipe a jump start, meaning you have to spend less time kneading the finished dough. It also helps to counteract the negative impact sourdough acids can have on gluten, adding extensibility, or stretchiness, to the dough. This translates to easier shaping for the dough and increased volume for the finished loaf. When you use the autolyse technique, be sure to set the salt, sweeteners and any other additions aside to add after the rest period. Salt and yeast, in particular, interfere with the gluten's ability to sort itself out during the autolyse. If you have them waiting by the bowl, you won't forget to add them when the autolyse is finished.

DESEM

We'd heard a lot about the legendary Desem bread, a 100 percent whole wheat, 100 percent naturally leavened bread that rose spectacularly and wasn't sour. We decided we had to try it for ourselves, so we ground fresh flour from organic wheat berries to feed the levain, and we used only Vermont spring water in the feedings. We hunted for cool (as in low temperature, not hip) corners of our building—not easy to find places in the 50- to 60-degree range in an office building! The information technology folks a couple rooms over thought it was odd to see us slipping in with our container of flour-encased levain, and chortling with delight when it erupted, volcano-like from below the flour surface. (Turns out that computers like a cool temperature too.)

After a week of careful attention, we were able to bake a loaf of bread that was really extraordinary: relatively light, with a buttery texture, and not especially sour. Is it worth maintaining a separate levain with such finicky requirements? That's up to you to decide. It was a pretty arduous process to manage at work, where cool temperatures are hard to come by, but it might be easier to make at home, where you may have a corner that stays cool, but not cold, 24 hours a day. If you're interested, there are very detailed instructions for building, maintaining and baking with a desem levain in *The Laurel's Kitchen Bread Book* (Random House, 2003).

Instead, we played with converting our liquid whole wheat levain to a stiff one by doubling the weight of the flour in the feedings for a couple days. As long as the flour was really fresh, we had good results baking a loaf that was similar to the traditional desem, getting a nice rise and an even texture, but with a slightly more sour flavor. If you want to give it a try, convert a portion of your levain by feeding it with twice the weight of flour to water for two or three days and give the 100% Whole Wheat Sourdough recipe on page 290 a try.

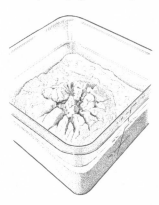

You can really sense the power of this levain when you see it driving the flour up from underneath.

100% Whole Wheat Sourdough Bread

YIELD: 1 small loaf, 12 slices

BAKING TEMPERATURE: 450°F, then 400°F

BAKING TIME: 45 to 50 minutes

This bread is made with a very stiff levain, modeled after the Desem bread from Belgium. If you want to convert your liquid levain to a stiff one, feed your levain with twice the weight of flour to water for two or three days. This levain has the bonus of needing less frequent feeding and will keep well in the refrigerator. If it's been refrigerated, feed it twice before baking with it. You'll need a cool place (about 60°F) for the first rise, and a warmer place (at least 75°F) for the final proof. This was our hands-down favorite 100 percent whole wheat sourdough.

²/₃ cup (6 ounces) stiff whole wheat levain
1 cup (8 ounces) cool water
2½ cups (10 ounces) whole wheat flour
1 teaspoon salt

Break the levain up with your fingers and let it soak in the water to soften it. After 5 or 10 minutes of soaking, stir in the flour and salt and knead the dough very well, about 10 minutes by hand or 8 minutes in the mixer. Place the dough in a bowl, cover it, and let it rise in a cool place for about 3 hours. The dough will look like it's doing absolutely nothing for the first couple of hours—that's fine. In the last hour, you start to see some movement, and after 3 hours, the dough will feel soft and aerated when you take it from the bowl.

While the dough is rising, heavily flour a banneton or a bowl lined with a linen towel.

After 3 hours take the dough from the bowl, handling it gently. If you're rough with it, it will resist shaping. Shape it into a loose round, and let it rest for 20 minutes before making the final shape. Shape the dough into a round, as directed on page 281, and place it upside down in the floured banneton. Cover the loaf and let it proof in a warm place for 2 to 3 hours. If you're lucky enough to have a really warm proofing area, this will take less time, maybe 1½ to 2 hours. Check the dough. It should feel very soft and aerated.

About half an hour before you're ready to bake, preheat your oven and baking stone to 450°F. Prepare the oven for steam (see p. 284).

When the dough is very soft and puffy, turn it out onto a piece of parchment paper, and gently brush away any excess flour. Slash the loaf. Use a peel to load the loaf onto the baking stone, parchment paper and all. Steam the bread, and let it bake for 15 minutes.

Reduce the heat to 400°F, and bake for 30 to 35 minutes more. The bread will be golden brown and will remain firm when you squeeze it gently.

Remove the bread from the oven and let it cool on a rack before slicing.

NUTRITION INFORMATION PER SERVING (1 SLICE, 57G): **33g whole grains,** 112 cal, 1g fat, 5g protein, 24g complex carbohydrates, 4g dietary fiber, 180mg sodium, 134mg potassium, 1mg iron, 12mg calcium, 115mg phosphorus.

Maple-Oat Sourdough Bread

YIELD: 1 large loaf, 20 slices
BAKING TEMPERATURE: 450°F, then 400°F
BAKING TIME: 45 to 50 minutes

Looking for a high-rising loaf with a mild tang? The addition of soaked oats to this bread increases the whole grain content without detracting from the volume. It has a softer texture than many sourdough loaves, making it perfect for sandwiches or toast or as an accompaniment to a creamy soup.

Soaker
1 cup (3½ ounces) old-fashioned rolled oats
¾ cup (6 ounces) cool water

Levain
1 tablespoon ripe whole wheat levain
1 cup (4 ounces) traditional whole wheat flour
½ cup (4 ounces) cool nonchlorinated water

Dough
All of the soaker
All of the levain
1 cup (4 ounces) traditional whole wheat flour
2 cups (8½ ounces) unbleached bread flour
¾ cup (6 ounces) cool water
2 tablespoons (1⅜ ounces) maple syrup
1½ teaspoons salt

The night before you plan to bake, combine the oatmeal with the ¾ cup cool water. Cover and let sit at room temperature overnight. In a separate bowl, combine the levain, whole wheat flour and the ½ cup cool water. Mix the ingredients well, cover, and set aside at room temperature for 12 hours or overnight.

The next day, check the levain. It should be expanded and very bubbly, but not yet receding. Combine all of the levain with all of the soaker, the additional flours, cool water, maple syrup and salt. Mix the ingredients well, and knead them by hand or in a mixer for at least 5 minutes. The dough will be somewhat rough from the oats, but the gluten will develop and become very elastic. If you've kneaded the dough in the mixer, remove it from the bowl and give it a few turns on a very lightly floured surface to be sure the dough is supple. Return the dough to the bowl, cover it and let it rise at room temperature for 1 hour.

After an hour, turn the dough from the bowl onto a well-floured surface, and give it a double fold, as directed on page 280. Return the dough to the bowl, cover it and let it rise for another hour. While the dough is rising, heavily flour a banneton or a bowl lined with a linen towel. After an hour, gently remove the dough from the bowl and place it on a well-floured surface. This time, when you take the dough from the bowl, it will feel quite soft and risen. Shape the dough into a round, as directed on page 281, and place it upside down into the floured banneton. Cover the banneton with plastic wrap or an upside-down bowl, and let it rise until the dough feels very puffy, 1½ to 2½ hours.

Check the dough every half hour or so to see if it's ready to bake. About half an hour before it's ready, preheat your oven and baking stone to 450°F. Get the oven ready for steam. When the dough is ready to bake, flip it out of the banneton onto a piece of parchment paper. Use a dry pastry brush to gently brush any excess flour from the surface of the dough. Slash the dough to a depth of about ¼ inch. Use a peel to load the loaf into the oven, parchment and all. Steam the oven, and let the bread bake for 15 minutes. Reduce the heat to 400°F, and let the bread continue to bake until the crust is golden brown and remains firm and crisp when you gently squeeze the loaf, 30 to 35 minutes longer. Use a peel to unload the bread, and place it on a rack to cool thoroughly before slicing.

NUTRITION INFORMATION PER SERVING (1 SLICE, 55G): 17g whole grains, 111 cal, 1g fat, 4g protein, 22g complex carbohydrates, 1g sugar, 2g dietary fiber, 162mg sodium, 83mg potassium, 1mg iron, 10mg calcium, 78mg phosphorus.

The imaginative combination of whole wheat pastry flour and bread flour yields croissants and Danish pastries that are tender, buttery and just as tasty as their white-flour counterparts.

Take your pick: oats or wheat? The pastry shell for Caramel Éclairs, left (p. 528) can be made with either kind of flour, and both make a light-gold, tender-crisp case for the sumptuous caramel cream within.

Whole wheat Chocolate–Chocolate Chip Waffles, right (p. 301), topped with ice cream, fudge sauce and nuts, were a grand-slam favorite among our King Arthur taste-testers. This dessert waffle is a nice change from the usual chocolate cake or cookies.

The imaginative combination of whole wheat pastry flour and bread flour yields croissants and Danish pastries that are tender, buttery and just as tasty as their white-flour counterparts.

Imagine the aroma of warm bread and cinnamon wafting out of the kitchen on a lazy weekend morning. Whole wheat is the major player in all of these breakfast treats, though oats play a supporting role, as well.

Clockwise from bottom left: Cinnamon Spiral Bread, p. 252; Chocolate Loves Vanilla Bread, p. 259; Blueberry Buckle Coffeecake, p. 68; Classic Sticky Buns, p. 265.

Orange Cloud Pancakes (p. 7) made with white whole wheat showcase that flour's light-gold color. Their airy texture puts to rest any notion that whole wheat pancakes must be dense.

Sour Cream Muffins (p. 33) are the perfect vehicle for fresh berries or dried fruit. Just a touch of all-purpose flour gives their main ingredient, whole wheat flour, a nice boost.

Top to bottom: Buttermilk-Rye Bread (p. 59), Corn Sticks (p. 557) and Parmesan–Pine Nut Biscuits (p. 77) are a savory accompaniment to soup and stew, or even your breakfast eggs. All three are quick breads, meaning they go from mixing bowl to serving plate in under an hour, more quickly than yeast breads.

Breakfast, coffee break, anytime is right for scones and muffins. Great Britain's traditional teatime treat, scones are basically sweetened biscuits, usually enhanced with fruit, nuts or chocolate, and often glazed with icing. Scones take well to a variety of whole grains. Muffins, those all-American treats, also can be baked in a loaf pan, where they become quick bread. To attain the airy texture of traditional muffins, these recipes include whole wheat flour, which has enough gluten to support a lovely rise in the oven.

Clockwise, from bottom: Morning Glory Muffins, p. 35; Coconut Scones, p. 96; Macadamia-Oat Scones with Orange Glaze, p. 97; Peach-Oatmeal Bread, p. 57.

High-rising yeast breads and rolls take
their substance and soul from flour.
The wonderful flavor of oats, wheat,
barley, rye and other whole grains come
through loud and clear in yeast breads,
where there are few competing ingredients.

To give whole grain breads sufficient
rise, wheat flour must be part of the
equation. Whole wheat flour is all you
need, if you enjoy close-textured, hearty
loaves. But if you're looking for a higher
rise and lighter texture, all-purpose
flour (or bread flour) can be substituted
for part of the whole wheat.

Clockwise from bottom left: Whole
Wheat Challah, p. 228; Ciabatta
Integrale, p. 224; Christmas
Panettone, p. 257; Oat Rolls, p. 208;
Buttermilk-Rye Rolls, p. 213;
Cinnamon-Swirl Oatmeal Toasting
Bread, p. 198; Dark & Soft
Restaurant Dinner Rolls, p. 214;
sliced ciabatta. Center: Pain aux
Noix, p. 234.

Cookies—drop, rollout or shaped, baked on a baking sheet or made into bars—are a natural showcase for whole grains. Cookies aren't required to rise very high, so many whole grains that wouldn't be appropriate for yeast breads, muffins or other high-rising treats are perfect for cookies. Barley and oat flour, as well as whole wheat, are important elements in the cookies pictured above.

Left to right: Triple Cinnamon–Pecan Biscotti, p. 339; Russian Teacakes, p. 324; Thin & Crisp Wheat Cookies, p. 329.

There's just nothing like a warm-from-the-oven chocolate chip cookie, is there? Old favorites like chocolate chip cookies, oatmeal cookies, and brownies are easily made with 100 percent whole grains. In fact, we found the flavor of these classic cookies is enriched by the likes of barley, oats and whole wheat.

Clockwise from bottom left: Classic Crunchy Chocolate Chip Cookies, p. 305; Crunchy Cinnamon-Oat Drops, p. 317; Chocolate Crinkles, p. 328; Iced Orange Cookies, p. 320; Double Fudge Brownies, p. 341.

Many cakes rely on whole wheat pastry flour for their beautiful texture. A lower-protein flour than traditional whole wheat, whole wheat pastry flour is suitable for cake, piecrust, cookies, and other tender treats.

Black Forest Cake, left (p. 398) is a classic cherry-filled chocolate cake.

Elegant Devil's Food Cupcakes, above (p. 371) are a perfect take-me-along gourmet treat. Ice them in contrasting colors for the prettiest presentation.

Peach Melba Jelly Roll (left, p. 409) pairs raspberry jam and creamy peach filling with genoise (a moist sponge cake). The cake's light-gold color belies the fact that the flour it's made with is 100 percent whole wheat. Toasted Almond–Mocha Cake, right (p. 395) features a moist crumb, and buttercream frosting. With whole grains comprising over 80 percent of the flour in the cake, it's a whole grain lover's dream.

Classic Apple Pie (p. 444) features a hearty 100 percent whole wheat crust cradling cinnamon-scented apples.

The filling for Golden Pumpkin Pie (p. 471) is lightly spiced, sweetened with honey, and nestles in a wheat- and oat-flour crust.

Nectarine Galette (p. 510) is a beautiful, fresh-tasting, open-faced rustic French tart. Bread flour gives the galette its structure; barley flour gives it light, nutty flavor.

The crust for Cran-Apricot Surprise Pie, below (p. 476) combines a little bread flour with whole wheat pastry flour, giving it the strength to hold the pie's cream-cheese-and-fruit filling securely without being tough.

Individual Peach-Blueberry Cobblers, front (p. 105), and Apple-Raspberry Oat Crumble, back (p. 100), are a wonderful way to bake with fresh fruit and berries. Served bubbly-hot from the oven, they're both a natural with ice cream. The cobblers feature whole wheat-based star-shaped biscuits on top; the crisp, a classic topping of sweet, crunchy oats.

Sourdough baking is a natural for whole grain flours. The rich, assertive taste of sourdough, created by growing yeast during the dough's long fermentation, pairs wonderfully well with the complex flavor of whole wheat.

Clockwise from bottom: Walnut-Currant Sourdough Bread, p. 287; Whole Wheat Sourdough Waffles, p. 300; Pain au Levain with Whole Wheat, p. 279; sliced Walnut-Currant Sourdough Bread, and a beaker of sourdough starter.

Pizza crust and crackers are a great place to begin your whole grain baking. Since they rise very little (if at all), they're a wonderful way to try all kinds of whole grains. Barley, whole wheat and rye flours, as well as whole cornmeal, give the pizza and crackers pictured above crisp texture and tantalizing flavor.

Clockwise from left: Pizza with Overnight Crust, p. 129; Multi-Seed Crackerbread, p. 159; Cheese Crackers, p. 163.

Take your pick: oats or wheat? The pastry shell for Caramel Éclairs, left (p. 528) can be made with either kind of flour, and both make a light-gold, tender-crisp case for the sumptuous caramel cream within.

Whole wheat Chocolate–Chocolate Chip Waffles, right (p. 301), topped with ice cream, fudge sauce and nuts, were a grand-slam favorite among our King Arthur taste-testers. This dessert waffle is a nice change from the usual chocolate cake or cookies.

Rye with Whole Wheat Levain

YIELD: 2 loaves, 16 slices each

BAKING TEMPERATURE: 425°F, then 375°F

BAKING TIME: 50 to 55 minutes

Here's a fragrant rye bread that doesn't require a special rye levain to make. Diluting the levain the night before with a little more water gives the yeast an opportunity to develop and increases the overall volume a bit. Although the bread is time consuming from start to finish, there's not actually a lot of hands-on time. Most of the time is spent fermenting, rising and proofing, and the results are spectacular!

Levain

¾ cup (6¾ ounces) ripe whole wheat levain

¾ cup (6 ounces) cool, nonchlorinated water

¾ cup (3 ounces) whole wheat flour

Dough

All of the levain

4¼ cups (1 pound) whole rye (pumpernickel) flour

3¾ cups (1 pound) unbleached all-purpose flour

3 cups (24 ounces) cool water

¼ cup (1¼ ounces) caraway seeds

1 tablespoon salt

TO MAKE THE LEVAIN: The night before you plan to bake, combine the ripe whole wheat levain with the water and whole wheat flour. Mix well, cover, and set aside to ripen for 8 hours or overnight.

After 8 hours, check the levain. It should be bubbly and expanded but not yet receding.

TO MAKE THE DOUGH: Add the rye and all-purpose flours, water, caraway seeds and salt to the levain. Mix well, and turn out onto a well-floured surface to knead briefly, incorporating very little additional flour, until the dough is smooth and somewhat elastic. The rye flour will make the dough less elastic than a wheat flour dough—that's OK. Return the dough to the bowl, cover it, and let it rise until it's puffed up considerably, 3 to 4 hours. As it's finishing its rise, heavily flour two bannetons or bowls lined with linen towels.

Turn the dough out onto a lightly floured surface and divide it in half. Flour your hands well, and form each half into a round. Place the rounds upside down in the floured bannetons, cover them and let them proof for 2 hours.

About half an hour before you're ready to bake, preheat your oven and baking stone to 425°F. Prepare the oven for steam.

When the oven is hot, and the loaves are nearly doubled in bulk, flip the loaves out of the bannetons onto a piece of parchment paper. Slash the loaves. Use a peel to load the loaves, parchment paper and all, onto the preheated baking stone. Steam the oven and let the breads bake for 15 minutes. Reduce the temperature to 375°F and bake until the loaves are browned and the crust stays firm when you give it a gentle squeeze, 35 to 40 minutes more. Use the peel to unload the loaves, and let them cool on a rack before slicing. Rye breads tend to be gummy if you slice them while they're still warm.

NUTRITION INFORMATION PER SERVING (1 SLICE, 65G): 20g whole grains, 119 cal, 1g fat, 4g protein, 25g complex carbohydrates, 5g dietary fiber, 201mg sodium, 156mg potassium, 2mg iron, 20mg calcium, 130mg phosphorus.

CAN I BAKE SOURDOUGH BREAD IN MY BREAD MACHINE?

We get so many questions at King Arthur Flour about baking sourdough in a bread machine, most of them prefaced by the failures people have already experienced. The truth is it's very difficult to make a true sourdough (no yeast added) bread in a preprogrammed bread machine. First of all, they almost all have a preheat cycle that raises the temperature to a point that the bread is rushed through its fermentation. The other problem that arises is that the proofing, or final rise, stage is too short for most sourdough breads. There are now machines that allow you to program the different stages of the cycle, and even machines that have a specific sourdough cycle, and you'd likely have more success with those. Remember, though, that an important part of the sourdough process is checking the dough to be sure it's ready for the next stage, and sourdough is less apt to be perfectly consistent in its activity. You'll need to check the dough at various stages to make sure it's proceeding as you need it to for your recipe. By the time you've done the reprogramming and the checking on the bread rising, proofing and baking, you may feel it would be easier to make it outside the machine!

One workable solution is to use the machine's dough cycle to knead your dough, and let the shaping, rising and baking happen outside the machine. Another possibility is to make sourdough bread using packaged yeast to control the rise times. In this way, the sourdough is adding flavor to the bread but isn't responsible for its rise. If you have a bread machine, refer to the sourdough recipe in the booklet that came with the machine.

BREADS MADE WITH RYE LEVAINS

Light Sourdough Rye Bread

YIELD: 1 loaf, 16 servings
BAKING TEMPERATURE: 450°F
BAKING TIME: 35 to 40 minutes

This loaf has a full sour aroma and flavor, yet gets great spring from the bread flour. It's impressive that such a small amount of levain can power such a large amount of flour. You might like to use caraway or fennel and make this more of a deli rye, but first try it without, so you can really taste the complex flavors of the bread without having them masked by the aromatic seeds.

Levain
2 tablespoons (1 ounce) ripe rye levain (see p. 273 for recipe)
2⅛ cups (8 ounces) whole rye (pumpernickel) flour
1 cup (8 ounces) cold water

Dough
All of the levain
2 cups (8½ ounces) unbleached bread flour
1¼ teaspoons salt
½ cup (4 ounces) cool water

The night before you're ready to bake, combine the ripe rye levain with the whole rye flour and 1 cup cold water. Mix well, cover, and let the mixture rest overnight at room temperature.

The next morning, combine the levain with the bread flour, salt and cool water. This is easiest to mix together in an electric mixer, but you may also do it by hand. Once the ingredients are thoroughly incorporated, increase the mixer speed to knead the dough for 3 minutes. The dough will not be as springy as a wheat-flour dough, but it will smooth out quite a bit and become somewhat elastic. Turn the dough out of the bowl onto a lightly floured counter and give the dough a few turns by hand to finish the kneading and smooth the ball of dough. Place the dough in a bowl, cover it tightly, and let it rest for 1 hour. As the bread rests, lightly flour a banneton or a bowl lined with a linen towel.

After 1 hour, the dough won't have doubled in bulk, but if you poke it lightly with your finger, you'll be able to tell that it's puffier than it was right after kneading. Turn the dough onto a barely floured board, flour your hands well, and shape the dough into a round loaf. Be careful not to tighten the loaf too much, as the rye dough is prone to tearing. Place the shaped loaf, upside down, into the floured banneton. Let the loaf rise for no more than 1 hour more before baking. When you press a finger gently into the side of the dough, it should have a very slow return, and the loaf will feel "full" to your fingers when you touch it.

About half an hour before you're ready to bake, place your baking stone on the bottom rack of your oven, and preheat the oven to 450°F. Prepare the oven for steam.

When the bread is ready to bake, swiftly turn it out of the banneton onto a piece of parchment paper. Use a pastry brush to brush away any excess flour, and slash it in a pattern that pleases you. Slide a peel under the loaf, parchment paper and all, and place it on the hot stone. Fill the oven with steam as directed on page 284. Bake the bread until the loaf is nicely browned, 35 to 40 minutes. Remove the bread from the oven and let it cool completely before slicing. REALLY! It's hard to resist the scent of warm bread, but if you slice the bread while it's still warm, the texture is very gummy because of the rye flour. It's best served the next day.

NUTRITION INFORMATION PER SERVING (1 SLICE, 52G): 14g whole grains, 104 cal, 1g fat, 4g protein, 22g complex carbohydrates, 4g dietary fiber, 53mg cholesterol, 167mg sodium, 126mg potassium, 2mg iron, 11mg calcium, 112mg phosphorus.

VARIATION: SALT-CARAWAY STICKS *These fragrant rolls are incredible. Jeffrey Hamelman, King Arthur Flour's master baker and author of* Bread: A Baker's Book of Techniques and Recipes *(John Wiley & Sons, Inc., 2004) teaches them to his advanced professional students, and you'll see a gaggle of employees hanging around the bakery on Salt Caraway day, waiting to bite into one of these salty aromatic treats.*

> **Light Sourdough Rye dough (see recipe, previous page), ready to shape**
> **½ cup (2½ ounces) caraway seed and coarse salt combined to your taste**

Divide the dough into 10 (3-ounce) pieces, and shape each one into a roll 4 to 5 inches long. Spread the seed/salt mixture onto a plate; wet a towel and wring it out well. Roll the top of each stick onto the wet towel, and then dip it into the seeds. Place the seeded rolls, seed side up, on a baking sheet to rise for 1 hour, before baking according to the instructions above. These sticks will take only about 15 minutes to bake. It's impossible to wait for them to cool completely before eating.

Sourdough Dark Rye

YIELD: 1 large or 2 small loaves, about 24 servings
BAKING TEMPERATURE: 400°F or 375°F
BAKING TIME: 35 to 50 minutes, depending on loaf size

This bread is on its way to pumpernickel—a great sandwich rye, with a darker flavor than its color would suggest. The oil gives it a soft texture that reminded our tasters of "store-bought" rye, and the black coffee and molasses lend subtle notes to the sourdough flavor. You may make it in two small loaves, perfect for sandwiches, or one large, spectacular loaf, perfect to serve with strong cheese and pickles.

Levain
1 tablespoon (½ ounce) ripe rye levain (see p. 273 for recipe)
1 cup (8 ounces) cold black coffee (or water if you don't have any coffee around)
2 cups (7½ ounces) whole rye (pumpernickel) flour

Dough
All of the levain
1 cup (8 ounces) room-temperature water
2 cups (8 ounces) traditional whole wheat flour
2 cups (8½ ounces) unbleached bread or all-purpose flour
¼ cup (3 ounces) dark molasses
2 tablespoons (⅞ ounce) vegetable oil
2 teaspoons salt

The night before you want to bake, stir together your levain, the cold coffee (or water) and the pumpernickel flour. Cover the bowl tightly and let it rest 12 hours or overnight.

The next morning, check the levain—it probably won't look much different, but it should have a pronounced aroma from the sour levain. Stir the water into the rye sour to loosen it, and then add the flours, molasses, oil and salt and mix well. This will make a very sticky dough. You may knead it in a mixer or by hand, but be careful not to incorporate extra flour into the mix. Knead until the dough is smooth and elastic; it will still be quite tacky to the touch—that's OK. Put the dough back in the bowl, cover it well and let it rise at room temperature for 50 minutes.

After 50 minutes, it still won't look like it's risen much, but don't worry. Turn the dough from the bowl onto a lightly floured surface, and give it a double fold, as directed on page 280. Return the dough to the bowl, cover it, and let it rise for another 50 minutes. This time the dough will look a little more active. Turn it from the bowl onto a lightly floured surface, and give it another double fold. Return the dough to the bowl for a final 50 minutes—about 2½ hours total rising time.

At the end of the 2½ hours, the dough will be quite active. Flour your work surface lightly. Take the dough out of the bowl, and shape it. If you're making one loaf, make a large round; be careful not to over-tighten the loaf or it will tear as it rises. If you're making two loaves, divide the dough in half, and form two small rounds, or two loaves for loaf pans. Cover the shaped loaves well with plastic wrap, and set them aside to rise until almost doubled in bulk. This may take as long as 3 hours if the room is cool or as little as 1 hour if the room is warm. Flour your fingers and press the loaf or loaves gently to see how they feel. The risen loaves will feel full and bubbly under the surface.

After about 1 hour of rise time, preheat your oven, and your baking stone if you have one, to 375°F for 1 large loaf or 400°F for 2 smaller loaves. When the bread is ready for the oven, slash it lightly. Use a peel to slide the bread onto the stone, if using. Steam the oven as you load the bread (see directions on p. 284). Let it bake for 50 minutes for a large loaf, 35 minutes for smaller loaves. The bread will be well browned. Cool the bread completely before serving—rye breads can be gummy if you cut them when they are warm.

NUTRITION INFORMATION PER SERVING (1 SLICE, 53G): 19g whole grains, 116 cal, 2g fat, 4g protein, 21g complex carbohydrates, 2g sugar, 4g dietary fiber, 181mg sodium, 209mg potassium, 2mg iron, 41mg calcium, 103mg phosphorus, 4mg caffeine.

A FEW WORDS ABOUT SPELT

We were thrilled with how quickly spelt picked up yeast and lactobacillus activity. We were able to build a levain in a matter of a few days. Our spelt levain was very quick to ferment, and it had a lovely, almost frothy texture. We found it was very quick to revive after time in the refrigerator. We could easily manufacture large quantities of levain from a very small amount of active levain, and this was the best way to maintain the levain. A teaspoon of levain was enough to liven 4 ounces of flour (and 4 ounces of water) in 12 hours. Because it was so active, we found it worked best if we used a very small amount of levain to inoculate the bread. We had a little more trouble when we tried to make a 100 percent whole spelt sourdough loaf. Spelt has a fairly delicate gluten structure—it activates pretty well, but if you overmix it, the gluten begins to quickly degrade. When we made 100 percent spelt bread with our spelt levain, it seemed that by the time the yeast had developed enough to make the bread rise, the acidity that goes hand in hand with the yeast had interfered with the gluten enough that the bread wouldn't rise, and remained dense and gummy. As soon as we added some wheat flour to the mix, the bread rose beautifully, yielding a soft, moist, slightly sour loaf.

BREAD FROM A SPELT LEVAIN

Sweet Spelt Sourdough Bread

YIELD: One 8½ x 4½-inch loaf, 16 servings
BAKING TEMPERATURE: 425°F, then 400°F
BAKING TIME: 40 to 45 minutes

What's a sweet recipe doing in the sourdough chapter? Spelt is such a sweet grain, and it responds so well to sourdough activity, we just had to include it. The natural sweetness of spelt and the tart acidity of sourdough are an ineffable combination. The sour in this loaf is very mild, made more so by the addition of just a little honey. This makes a high-rising, even-textured loaf, and it has a natural, nutty sweetness that makes it perfect for toasting. You may substitute white spelt flour for the unbleached all-purpose flour to make it 100 percent spelt, but the resulting loaf is much denser, unless you also incorporate ½ teaspoon of instant yeast. If you haven't built a spelt levain from scratch, see instructions on page 278 for converting a white levain to whole grain.

Levain
1 tablespoon ripe spelt levain (see recipe on p. 273)
1 cup (3½ ounces) whole spelt flour
½ cup (4 ounces) cold, nonchlorinated water

Dough
All of the levain
3 cups (10½ ounces) whole spelt flour
1 to 1½ cups (4¼ to 6⅜ ounces) unbleached all-purpose flour
1 cup (8 ounces) cool water
2 tablespoons (1 ounce) unsalted butter, melted
2 tablespoons (1½ ounces) honey
1¼ teaspoons salt

The night before you're going to bake, make the levain by combining the spelt levain, the spelt flour and the cold water. Mix the ingredients well, cover, and set aside at room temperature for 12 hours, or overnight.

The next day, the levain should be expanded and very bubbly, but not yet receding. Combine all of the levain, the remaining spelt flour and 1 cup of all-purpose flour, water, melted butter, honey and salt in a medium bowl. Stir the ingredients well until you have a soft, shaggy dough. Turn the dough out onto a well-floured surface, and knead the dough by hand, incorporating only as much of the remaining ½ cup all-purpose flour as you need to keep from sticking to the dough. Be careful not to add too much flour to the dough. It should remain soft and will quickly become smooth and elastic. Put the kneaded dough back in the bowl, and let it rise for about an hour. It won't double in that time, but it will start to get puffy and expanded.

While the bread is rising, grease an 8½ x 4½-inch loaf pan. This bread needs the support of a pan as it proofs and bakes. After an hour, remove the dough from the bowl and roll it into a loaf shape. Place the loaf in the pan, cover it, and let it rise for 1½ hours.

About 30 minutes before you're ready to bake, preheat your oven to 425°F, and prepare it for steaming as directed on page 284. After an hour, check the dough. It should be rising at this point, though it won't reach the tops of the pan. You want it to be within ½ inch of the top—this may take anywhere from 1 to 1¾ hours, depending on the temperature in your kitchen. Don't let it go longer than 2 hours or the loaf will be very sour and dense. Use a very sharp blade to slash the loaf down the center. Put the bread in the oven and steam it. After 10 minutes, reduce the heat to 400°F and continue to bake until the loaf is golden brown, 30 to 35 minutes more. Remove the bread from the oven, turn it out of the pan immediately and cool thoroughly before slicing.

NUTRITION INFORMATION PER SERVING (1 SLICE, 62G): 25g **whole grains,** 131 cal, 2g fat, 5g protein, 25g complex carbohydrates, 2g sugar, 4g dietary fiber, 4mg cholesterol, 134mg sodium, 120mg potassium, 12RE vitamin A, 2mg iron, 3mg calcium, 98mg phosphorus.

 # Whole Wheat Sourdough Waffles

YIELD: 12 (4-inch) waffles

BAKING TIME: 4 to 5 minutes

This recipe uses the acidity of sourdough in reaction with baking soda for leavening. It makes light, crispy waffles with a flavor you won't find anywhere else. We love it with the light flavor of white whole wheat, but you could use whatever whole wheat you have on hand—these are especially delicate with whole wheat pastry flour.

Levain

1 tablespoon active sourdough levain

1½ cups (6 ounces) white whole wheat flour

1 cup (8 ounces) buttermilk

Batter

2 eggs
¼ cup (2 ounces) orange juice
¼ cup (2 ounces) milk
¼ cup (½ stick, 2 ounces) unsalted butter, melted, or vegetable oil
2 tablespoons sugar
1 teaspoon baking soda
½ teaspoon salt

TO MAKE THE LEVAIN: The night before you make the waffles, or early in the morning if you're planning to have them for dinner, combine the levain, whole wheat flour and buttermilk in a medium bowl. Mix until thoroughly combined, then cover the bowl and set it aside for at least 8 hours.

TO MAKE THE BATTER: When you're ready to make the waffles, beat the eggs, orange juice, milk and melted butter together and stir them into the sponge. Blend the sugar together with the baking soda and salt in a small bowl. With a wire whisk, stir these dry ingredients into the sponge. You'll see the sponge (now officially a waffle batter) begin to swell and bubble quite dramatically as the baking soda begins to react with the acidic sourdough.

TO BAKE THE WAFFLES: Bake the waffles in a preheated iron until the steam stops coming out of the sides, 4 to 5 minutes.

NUTRITION INFORMATION PER SERVING (1 WAFFLE, 55G): 14g whole grains, 117 cal, 5g fat, 4g protein, 11g complex carbohydrates, 2g sugar, 2g dietary fiber, 46mg cholesterol, 228mg sodium, 109mg potassium, 48RE vitamin A, 2mg vitamin C, 1mg iron, 34mg calcium, 89mg phosphorus.

Chocolate–Chocolate Chip Waffles

YIELD: 14 (4-inch square) Belgian waffles
BAKING TIME: 3 to 5 minutes per waffle

These decadent dessert waffles are so light and crispy it's hard to believe they're made with sourdough and whole wheat. The inspiration came from the Fudge Waffles in The King Arthur Flour Baker's Companion, *and it's a bonus to use up some of the sourdough starter that can quickly take over the kitchen when you're keeping a starter. We love the waffles with heaps of whipped cream and fresh raspberries, but try them with your favorite chocolate accoutrements: coffee ice cream, hot fudge, brandied cherries—in fact, what doesn't go with chocolate?*

Levain

4 ounces (about ½ cup) ripe, bubbly sourdough levain (made with equal weights of water and flour; see p. 273 for how to create a levain)

1 cup (8 ounces) buttermilk

1 cup (4 ounces) white whole wheat flour

Batter

½ cup (1½ ounces) Dutch-process cocoa

1 teaspoon baking soda

½ teaspoon salt

Pinch of ground cinnamon

2 eggs

4 tablespoons (½ stick, 2 ounces) unsalted butter, melted

¾ cup (5¼ ounces) sugar

2 teaspoons vanilla extract

¾ cup (4½ ounces) chocolate chips, semisweet or bittersweet

TO MAKE THE LEVAIN: The night before you make the waffles, or early in the morning if you're planning to have them for dinner, weigh 4 ounces of sourdough starter into a medium bowl. Stir in the buttermilk and whole wheat flour, and mix until thoroughly combined. Cover the bowl and set it aside for at least 8 hours.

TO MAKE THE BATTER: When you're ready to make the waffles, stir the cocoa, baking soda, salt and cinnamon in a small bowl; you may need to sift it if your cocoa is lumpy. In a separate bowl, whisk the eggs with the melted butter, sugar and vanilla. Add the cocoa mixture to the egg mixture and stir well; then add the cocoa-egg mixture to the sourdough mixture all at once. Stir the batter thoroughly; you don't want any streaks of unmixed sourdough in your batter. When the mixture is completely homogenous, stir in the chocolate chips.

TO BAKE THE WAFFLES: Bake the waffles in a preheated iron until the steam stops coming out the sides, 3 to 5 minutes. The waffles will feel a little flabby coming out of the iron, but they will crisp up quickly after you remove them. These are especially nice made in a Belgian waffle iron—light and lacy, but with a dark, rich flavor.

NUTRITION INFORMATION PER SERVING (1 WAFFLE, 69G): 4g whole grains, 186 cal, 8g fat, 4g protein, 12g complex carbohydrates, 15g sugar, 2g dietary fiber, 40mg cholesterol, 201mg sodium, 176mg potassium, 28RE vitamin A, 1mg iron, 31mg calcium, 94mg phosphorus, 9mg caffeine.

COOKIES & BARS

Once you've made the decision to add whole grains to your diet, the very easiest place to start is with cookies. After all, who doesn't indulge in cookies? From the time we're toddlers, we're bribed with cookies; we're supplied with cookies in our lunchboxes, fed them after school, given them on the sidelines when the basketball game or soccer match is over. As adults, we turn the tables and bake cookies: for our kids, our friends, our coworkers... and ourselves. Studies show that when American bakers turn on the oven, they're more likely to bake cookies than anything else.

Cookies (and bar cookies) are sweet and flavorful, full of chips and nuts, candy and dried fruit. And that's why they're so easy to convert to a whole grain version. Think about it: when you're eating an oatmeal cookie, or any of its myriad variations, you're already enjoying a whole grain cookie. Exchange whole wheat flour for all-purpose flour in a cookie laden with dark brown sugar, butter, toasted pecans and chocolate chips, and no one will be the wiser. Add barley flour to a soft sugar-cookie recipe, and you get a sugar cookie with the golden color of that grain... *and* the great taste of a classic sugar cookie. Cookies are not really about the flour, they're about the butter, sugar, eggs, vanilla and chocolate. The flour is just there to bind it all together—and if it's a whole grain flour, so much the better.

As you read this chapter, you'll find some familiar favorites and some interesting newcomers. We've stayed true to the spirit of whole grains by concentrating on cookies featuring wholesome fresh fruits, dried fruits and nuts (though chocolate makes an appearance, too, of course). We've also tried to use dark sweeteners—molasses, dark corn syrup, brown sugar—in place of white sugar, when possible.

Pick out a recipe and let's get started—whole grain cookies are about to become your new best friends.

Chewy Chocolate Chip Cookies

YIELD: 4 dozen cookies
BAKING TEMPERATURE: 375°F
BAKING TIME: 12 to 13 minutes

This is it: the quintessential soft, chewy chocolate chip cookie. A deep, rich brown from whole wheat flour and brown sugar, it's positively packed with chips. There's no question: this will be one of the most popular whole grain baked treats you'll ever make!

¾ cup (1½ sticks, 6 ounces) unsalted butter
1 cup (7½ ounces) packed light or dark brown sugar
2 teaspoons vanilla extract
½ teaspoon salt
½ teaspoon baking soda
½ teaspoon espresso powder (optional)
¼ teaspoon baking powder
⅓ cup (3⅝ ounces) light corn syrup or brown sugar corn syrup
1 tablespoon cider vinegar
2 large eggs
2¼ cups (9 ounces) traditional whole wheat flour
3 cups (18 ounces) semisweet or bittersweet chocolate chips

In a saucepan or microwave-safe bowl, melt the butter, then stir in the sugar. Heat until the mixture is just beginning to bubble. Remove it from the burner or microwave, transfer it to a medium bowl and allow it to cool to lukewarm.

Stir in the vanilla, salt, baking soda, espresso powder (if using), baking powder, corn syrup and vinegar. Add the eggs, beating well after each addition, then the flour, stirring to combine, and finally mix in the chips. Refrigerate the dough, covered, overnight.

Preheat the oven to 375°F. Lightly grease 2 baking sheets or line with parchment paper.

Drop the dough by tablespoonfuls onto the prepared baking sheets. Bake the cookies, reversing the pans midway through (top to bottom, bottom to top), until they're just beginning to brown around the edges, 12 to 13 minutes. Remove the cookies from the oven and allow them to cool completely on the pan, using a turner to loosen them after 5 minutes.

NUTRITION INFORMATION PER SERVING (1 COOKIE, 29G): 6g whole grains, 128 cal, 6g fat, 2g protein, 5g complex carbohydrates, 12g sugar, 1g dietary fiber, 16mg cholesterol, 48mg sodium, 75mg potassium, 27RE vitamin A, 1mg iron, 13mg calcium, 42mg phosphorus, 10mg caffeine.

FOR COOKIES WITH PERFECT TEXTURE

Uncertain about how long to bake your cookies? Experiment. Preheat the oven, place two cookies in the center of a baking sheet, and bake for the minimum amount of time called for in the recipe. Remove the sheet from the oven, transfer one cookie to a cooling rack, and bake the remaining cookie for the maximum amount of time called for in the recipe. Allow the cookies to cool, then sample. Which has the texture you like? That's how long you should bake your cookies.

Classic Crunchy Chocolate Chip Cookies

YIELD: 43 cookies
BAKING TEMPERATURE: 350°F
BAKING TIME: 14 to 16 minutes

Light and crisp, absolutely packed with chocolate chips, this is our favorite crunchy chocolate chip cookie. The addition of barley flour to the dough gives the cookies a pleasant taste, milder than a cookie made with 100 percent traditional whole wheat. To ensure crunchiness, be sure to bake these cookies thoroughly; they should be golden brown all over, without any hint of softness in the center.

4 tablespoons ($\frac{1}{2}$ stick, 2 ounces) unsalted butter

$\frac{1}{2}$ cup ($3\frac{1}{2}$ ounces) vegetable oil

$\frac{3}{4}$ cup ($5\frac{1}{4}$ ounces) granulated sugar

$\frac{3}{4}$ cup ($5\frac{5}{8}$ ounces) packed light or dark brown sugar

2 teaspoons vanilla extract

$\frac{3}{4}$ teaspoon salt

$\frac{1}{2}$ teaspoon espresso powder (optional)

1 tablespoon cider vinegar

1 large egg

$\frac{1}{2}$ teaspoon baking soda

$\frac{1}{2}$ teaspoon baking powder

1 cup (4 ounces) whole barley flour

1 cup (4 ounces) traditional whole wheat flour

$2\frac{2}{3}$ cups (16-ounce bag) semisweet chocolate chips

Preheat the oven to 350°F. Lightly grease 2 baking sheets or line with parchment paper.

Beat the butter, oil, sugars, vanilla, salt and espresso powder in a large bowl till smooth. Beat in the vinegar, egg, baking soda and baking powder. Stir in the barley flour and whole wheat flour, then the chocolate chips. The dough will appear oily and, because of the quantity of chocolate chips, it won't be completely cohesive; that's OK. Drop the dough by tablespoonfuls onto the prepared baking sheets.

Bake the cookies, reversing the pans midway through (top to bottom, bottom to top), until they're golden brown, 14 to 16 minutes. Remove the cookies from the oven and allow them to cool for 5 minutes before transferring them to a rack to cool completely.

VARIATION: *Use 2 cups (8 ounces) whole wheat flour instead of 1 cup each barley and whole wheat.*

NUTRITION INFORMATION PER SERVING (1 COOKIE, 30G): 5g whole grains, 139 cal, 7g fat, 1g protein, 5g complex carbohydrates, 14g sugar, 1g dietary fiber, 8mg cholesterol, 59mg sodium, 66mg potassium, 11RE vitamin A, 1mg iron, 12mg calcium, 33mg phosphorus, 10mg caffeine.

PRESSED FOR TIME?

If you're baking drop cookies and find yourself running out of time, simply cover the bowl of dough and refrigerate it overnight. When you come back to it the next day, the dough will be stiffer; if it's so stiff you can't scoop it, just let it rest at room temperature for an hour or so. If you scoop and bake cookies right from the fridge, they'll probably need 2 or 3 additional minutes of baking time to make up for the cold temperature of the dough.

Salted Cashew–Crunch Cookies

YIELD: 2½ dozen cookies

BAKING TEMPERATURE: 350°F

BAKING TIME: 12 to 14 minutes

The salty-sweet combination is increasingly popular: think caramel corn or chocolate-dipped pretzels. These crunchy oatmeal treats are filled with chopped salted cashews; a very light drift of extrafine salt on top makes them extra-special.

½ cup (1 stick, 4 ounces) unsalted butter

¾ cup (5¼ ounces) sugar

½ teaspoon salt

¼ teaspoon baking powder

1 teaspoon vanilla extract

1 large egg

2 cups (7 ounces) old-fashioned rolled oats, ground for 30 seconds in a food processor

2 cups (8 ounces) salted cashew pieces or coarsely chopped cashews

extrafine salt for topping

Preheat the oven to 350°F. Lightly grease 2 baking sheets or line with parchment paper.

Beat the butter, sugar, salt, baking powder, vanilla and egg in a medium bowl. Beat in the ground oats, then the cashews.

Drop the dough by tablespoonfuls onto the prepared baking sheets. Sprinkle them with a very light coating of salt, preferably extrafine (such as Diamond Crystal brand). Using your fingers or the flat bottom of a drinking glass or measuring cup, press the cookies to about ⅜ inch thick.

Bake the cookies, reversing the pans midway through (top to bottom, bottom to top), until they're light golden brown, 12 to 14 minutes. Remove the cookies from the oven and allow them to cool right on the pan.

> **COOKIE DOUGH STICKING TO THE SCOOP?**
>
> When using a cookie scoop, keep a glass of cold water on the counter beside you as you scoop and deposit. If dough begins to stick in the scoop, simply dip it in the water, shake off any excess, and continue.

NUTRITION INFORMATION PER SERVING (1 COOKIE, 26G): **7g whole grains,** 125 cal, 8g fat, 3g protein, 7g complex carbohydrates, 5g sugar, 1g dietary fiber, 15mg cholesterol, 98mg sodium, 76mg potassium, 28RE vitamin A, 1mg iron, 12mg calcium, 82mg phosphorus.

Multigrain Snickerdoodles

YIELD: 38 cookies
BAKING TEMPERATURE: 350°F
BAKING TIME: 12 to 14 minutes

These traditional cinnamon cookies get an interesting facelift with oats for texture, barley for flavor and whole wheat for body. A bit softer than the classic crunchy Snickerdoodle (which derives much of its crunchiness from nutritionally suspect vegetable shortening), flavor-wise they're a close match—albeit with greater depth, due to the whole grains.

Dough
¾ cup (1½ sticks, 6 ounces) unsalted butter
1½ cups (10½ ounces) sugar
2 teaspoons baking powder
¾ teaspoon salt
1 teaspoon vanilla extract
1 tablespoon orange juice
2 large eggs
1⅓ cups (4⅝ ounces) old-fashioned rolled oats, ground for 30 seconds
    in a food processor
1 cup (4 ounces) whole barley flour
¾ cup (3 ounces) traditional whole wheat flour

Coating
⅓ cup (2⅜ ounces) sugar
1 tablespoon ground cinnamon

Preheat the oven to 350°F. Lightly grease 2 baking sheets or line with parchment paper.

Cream the butter, sugar, baking powder, salt and vanilla in a large bowl. Beat in the orange juice and eggs, scraping the bowl, then add the oats, barley flour and whole wheat flour, beating until well combined. Refrigerate the dough, covered, overnight.

To prepare the coating, combine the sugar and cinnamon in a large plastic bag.

Drop the dough by the tablespoonful, 6 pieces or so at a time, into the bag. Gather the bag closed at the top, trapping some air inside. Shake gently to coat the balls with the sugar (see illustration, p. 328). Place them on the prepared baking sheets and flatten to about ½ inch thick, using the flat bottom of a measuring cup or drinking glass. Repeat till you've used all the dough.

Bake the cookies, reversing the pans midway through (top to bottom, bottom to top), until they're beginning to brown around the edges, 12 to 14 minutes. Remove the cookies from the oven and transfer them to a rack to cool. For soft Snickerdoodles, place them in an airtight container or plastic bag once they're cool. For crisper cookies, allow them to remain uncovered overnight before transferring to a storage container.

NUTRITION INFORMATION PER SERVING (1 COOKIE, 27G): 9g whole grains, 109 cal, 4g fat, 2g protein, 6g complex carbohydrates, 11g sugar, 1g dietary fiber, 21mg cholesterol, 66mg sodium, 33mg potassium, 34RE vitamin A, 26mg calcium, 57mg phosphorus.

Frosted Ginger-Apple Cookies

YIELD: 41 cookies

BAKING TEMPERATURE: 350°F

BAKING TIME: 12 minutes

Tender, light and soft, these cookies are reminiscent of iced spice cake. Golden raisins lend their own distinct flavor and add interest to the cookies' texture. Tangy-sweet apple-flavored frosting completes the picture. We call for brown sugar corn syrup in the ingredients; if your store doesn't carry it, use dark corn syrup. Brown sugar corn syrup is worth searching for, though; it has lovely flavor, somewhere between the bland sweetness of light corn syrup and the molasses-like tang of dark.

Dough
¾ **cup (1½ sticks, 6 ounces) unsalted butter**
¾ **cup (5⅝ ounces) packed light or dark brown sugar**
½ **teaspoon salt**
½ **teaspoon baking soda**
¼ **teaspoon baking powder**
¼ **teaspoon ground allspice**
¼ **teaspoon ground ginger**
¼ **teaspoon ground nutmeg**
¼ **teaspoon ground cinnamon**
¼ **cup (2 ounces) orange juice**
1 large egg
2 tablespoons (1⅜ ounces) brown sugar corn syrup or dark corn syrup
2 tablespoons (1½ ounces) molasses
1 cup (6 ounces) firmly packed golden raisins
1 medium-small apple, peeled, cored and diced very fine (about ⅔ cup, 3 ounces)
⅓ **cup (2¼ ounces) minced crystallized ginger**
2¼ **cups (9 ounces) traditional whole wheat flour**

Frosting

2½ **cups (10 ounces) confectioners' sugar**

2 **tablespoons (1 ounce) unsalted butter, melted**

½ **teaspoon vanilla extract**

½ **teaspoon ground cinnamon**

⅛ **teaspoon salt**

4 to 5 **tablespoons (2 to 2½ ounces) apple juice concentrate, thawed (enough to make a spreadable icing)**

Preheat the oven to 350°F. Lightly grease 2 baking sheets or line with parchment paper.

TO PREPARE THE DOUGH: Beat the butter, brown sugar, salt, baking soda, baking powder and spices in a medium bowl until smooth. Beat in the orange juice, scraping the bowl, then the egg, corn syrup and molasses. Add the raisins, apple and crystallized ginger, beating until well combined. Then add the flour, again beating until well combined. Drop the dough by tablespoonfuls onto the prepared baking sheets.

TO BAKE THE COOKIES: Bake the cookies, reversing the pans midway through (top to bottom, bottom to top), until they're just barely beginning to brown around the edges and still appear soft in the middle, 12 minutes. Remove the cookies from the oven and allow them to cool completely on the pan (or transfer them to a rack, if you need the baking sheet for another batch).

TO PREPARE THE FROSTING: Whisk all the frosting ingredients in a small bowl, adding additional apple juice concentrate, if necessary, to make a spreadable frosting. Spread the cooled cookies with frosting, using about 1 generous teaspoon of frosting on each.

NUTRITION INFORMATION PER SERVING (1 COOKIE, 35G): 6g whole grains, 124 cal, 4g fat, 1g protein, 9g complex carbohydrates, 13g sugar, 1g dietary fiber, 16mg cholesterol, 59mg sodium, 85mg potassium, 35RE vitamin A, 1mg vitamin C, 14mg calcium, 35mg phosphorus.

WHEN ADDING FRUIT, BE GENTLE

When adding soft fruit to cookie dough, be aware that beating the fruit in—rather than gently mixing it in—may result in fruit bits, not whole fruit pieces. This is fine, if that's what you're after; but if you want your raisins, currants, apricot chunks or other fruits to remain whole or chunky, mix them in gently.

Peanut Chews

YIELD: 28 cookies

BAKING TEMPERATURE: 350°F

BAKING TIME: 11 to 12 minutes

These craggy, deep-brown cookies are chewy and moist. Though they contain lots of peanut butter, as well as dry-roasted peanuts, they're not overwhelmingly peanutty. Instead, the flavors of peanut and brown sugar meld into a smooth-tasting cookie that'll be a hit with anyone partial to one of childhood's favorite comfort foods.

1 cup (9½ ounces) smooth peanut butter

½ cup (3¾ ounces) packed dark brown sugar

½ cup (3½ ounces) granulated sugar

1 large egg

¼ cup (2 ounces) water

2 tablespoons (1⅜ ounces) dark corn syrup or honey (1½ ounces)

1 teaspoon vanilla extract

1 teaspoon baking soda

½ teaspoon salt

1½ cups (6 ounces) traditional whole wheat flour

½ cup (2½ ounces) lightly salted dry-roasted peanuts, finely ground in a food processor

Preheat the oven to 350°F. Lightly grease 2 baking sheets or line with parchment paper.

Cream the peanut butter, sugars, egg, water, corn syrup, vanilla, baking soda and salt in a medium bowl, beating until smooth. Add the flour and ground peanuts, beating until the mixture is well combined. The dough will be very stiff; an electric stand mixer is the best bet here.

Drop the dough by tablespoonfuls onto the prepared baking sheets. Press the top of each cookie with a fork to make a crisscross design, flattening the cookies to about ½ inch thick. Dip the fork in cold water if it starts to stick.

Bake the cookies, reversing the pans midway through (top to bottom, bottom to top), until they're very lightly browned, 11 to 12 minutes. Remove the cookies from the oven and transfer them to a rack to cool. Repeat with the remaining dough.

Use a fork to flatten and make a crisscross design on the unbaked cookies.

NOTE: This recipe was developed using traditional smooth peanut butter, not all-natural or homemade peanut butter. Because the recipe's sugar and salt are balanced for traditional peanut butter, we suggest you use that.

NUTRITION INFORMATION PER SERVING (1 COOKIE, 31G): 6g whole grains, 123 cal, 6g fat, 4g protein, 6g complex carbohydrates, 9g sugar, 2g dietary fiber, 8mg cholesterol, 150mg sodium, 116mg potassium, 3RE vitamin A, 1mg iron, 8mg calcium, 63mg phosphorus.

Soft Barley-Sugar Cookies

YIELD: 10 large (4-inch) cookies
BAKING TEMPERATURE: 450°F
BAKING TIME: 8 minutes

"These taste just like my grandma's!" This comment was heard over and over again when our taste-testers were sampling this soft, mild-tasting, palm-size sugar cookie. Cakey rather than crisp or chewy, the combination of vanilla, nutmeg and lemon does indeed give it old-fashioned "grandma-style" flavor.

½ **cup (1 stick, 4 ounces) unsalted butter**
¾ **cup plus 2 tablespoons (6⅛ ounces) sugar**
½ **teaspoon baking powder**
½ **teaspoon baking soda**
½ **teaspoon salt**
¾ **teaspoon ground nutmeg**
1 tablespoon vanilla extract
1 tablespoon lemon juice, preferably fresh squeezed
1 large egg
1½ **cups (6 ounces) whole barley flour**
½ **cup (2⅛ ounces) unbleached all-purpose flour**
⅓ **cup (2⅝ ounces) sour cream**
Coarse white or granulated sugar for topping

Cream the butter, sugar, baking powder, baking soda, salt, nutmeg, vanilla and lemon juice in a medium bowl. Add the egg, beating until smooth.

Whisk the barley flour and all-purpose flour in another bowl. Add half the flour mixture to the butter mixture, beating to combine. Beat in the sour cream, then the remaining flour. Refrigerate the dough overnight.

Preheat the oven to 450°F. Lightly grease 2 baking sheets or line with parchment paper. Remove the dough from the refrigerator. Place the coarse sugar (or regular granulated sugar, if you don't have coarse) into a small bowl.

Scoop out ¼-cupfuls of dough; a muffin scoop or large ice cream scoop makes short work of this task. Pick up each ball of dough and dip its top in the sugar, pressing down and rolling it around a bit so the sugar sticks and coats the top third of the cookie. Place dough balls onto the prepared baking sheets. Cookies will spread to about 4 inches in diameter, so leave plenty of room between them. Using the flat bottom of a measuring cup or drinking glass, dipped in sugar, flatten cookies to about ⅜ inch thick. Sprinkle cookies with additional sugar, if desired, gently pressing it in with your fingers.

Use the flat bottom of a drinking glass or measuring cup to flatten the cookies to about ⅜ inch thick.

Bake the cookies, reversing the pans midway through (top to bottom, bottom to top), until they're barely beginning to brown around the edges but still look soft in the center, 8 minutes. Remove the cookies from the oven and allow them to cool on the pan for 10 minutes before transferring them to a rack to cool completely. To keep the cookies soft, store them in an airtight container.

NUTRITION INFORMATION PER SERVING (1 COOKIE, 68G): 17g whole grains, 259 cal, 12g fat, 4g protein, 18g complex carbohydrates, 18g sugar, 3g dietary fiber, 49mg cholesterol, 200mg sodium, 58mg potassium, 97RE vitamin A, 1mg vitamin C, 1mg iron, 35mg calcium, 63mg phosphorus.

FLATTENING COOKIES WITH FLARE

Some drop-cookie recipes call for you to flatten the ball of cookie dough after dropping it onto the baking sheet. You can do this with the flat bottom of a drinking glass or with the tines of a fork, making a crisscross pattern. But if you have a food processor, check out the pusher that forces food down through the lid onto the slicing disk. Many pushers are round, about 1¾ to 2 inches in diameter—the ideal size for flattening dough—and some sport a circular pattern of ridges on the business end, a pattern that will make a lovely spiral imprint on top of your cookies.

CHILLING DOUGH: YES, THERE'S A REASON

If your cookie recipe directs you to chill the dough before shaping—do it! Chilling accomplishes four things in whole grain cookies. First, it gives any gluten in the cookies time to relax, resulting in a more tender cookie. Second, it gives the fat time to harden, yielding a lighter-textured cookie. Third, it gives the whole grains a chance to absorb the liquid in the dough; because of their coarse grind, whole grains absorb liquid more slowly than all-purpose flour. And fourth, this rest in the fridge prevents the cookies from spreading too much as they bake.

Chewy Oatmeal Cookies

YIELD: **50 cookies**

BAKING TEMPERATURE: **350°F**

BAKING TIME: **13 to 17 minutes (see Variations)**

This recipe makes a flat, chewy, golden-brown cookie that stays moist and soft for days, making it great for shipping off to the kids at college. Feel free to adjust the spices to taste; if you're a fan of ginger or nutmeg, up the ante!

¾ cup (1½ sticks, 6 ounces) unsalted butter

1¼ cups (9⅜ ounces) packed light or dark brown sugar

3 tablespoons (2 ounces) dark corn syrup

¾ teaspoon baking soda

½ teaspoon baking powder

½ teaspoon salt

2 teaspoons ground cinnamon

¼ teaspoon ground ginger

¼ teaspoon ground nutmeg

1 tablespoon cider vinegar

1 tablespoon vanilla extract

1 large egg

1⅓ cups (4⅝ ounces) old-fashioned rolled oats

1¼ cups (5 ounces) traditional whole wheat flour

2 cups (9 to 12 ounces) dried fruit: diced dried apples, chopped dates, dried cranberries, raisins, chopped dried apricots or the dried fruits of your choice

1 cup (3¾ ounces) chopped pecans or walnuts

Preheat the oven to 350°F. Lightly grease 2 baking sheets or line with parchment paper.

Cream the butter, sugar, corn syrup, baking soda, baking powder, salt, spices, vinegar and vanilla. Beat in the egg. Add the oats, flour, dried fruit and nuts, and stir to combine. Drop the dough by heaping tablespoonfuls onto the prepared baking sheets.

Bake the cookies, reversing the pans midway through (top to bottom, bottom to top), until they're beginning to brown around the edges but are still soft in the center, 14 minutes. Remove them from the oven and transfer them to a rack to cool.

NUTRITION INFORMATION PER SERVING (1 COOKIE, 26G): 5g whole grains, 104 cal, 5g fat, 1g protein, 10g complex carbohydrates, 6g sugar, 1g dietary fiber, 12mg cholesterol, 50mg sodium, 100mg potassium, 25RE vitamin A, 1mg iron, 18mg calcium, 44mg phosphorus.

VARIATIONS: *For a soft, puffy (rather than flat and chewy) cookie, grind $\frac{1}{3}$ cup of the oats in a food processor before adding to the dough.*

Baking time makes a difference: 14 minutes in the oven yields a cookie that's crisp at the edges and soft in the center. A minute or so less in the oven makes a cookie that's soft from edge to edge; 2 to 3 minutes more, a cookie that's more crisp than chewy.

To make 16 bake-sale-size (4-inch) jumbo cookies, drop the dough by $\frac{1}{4}$-cupfuls onto the baking sheets. Bake in a preheated 350°F oven for 20 to 22 minutes.

ENSURING CHEWY COOKIES

Not sure just how long to bake those chewy cookies? If you're after a chewy, soft cookie, it behooves you to bake a single cookie first, and let it cool. Does it have the exact degree of chewiness you're after? If it's too crisp or crunchy, reduce the baking time by 30 seconds to 1 minute, and try again. Nail down the exact time before you bake the whole batch; this may seem time consuming, but it's better than baking an entire batch of crunchy cookies that were supposed to be soft and chewy.

Soft Currant Drops

YIELD: **2½ dozen cookies**

BAKING TEMPERATURE: **350°F**

BAKING TIME: **15 to 17 minutes**

The world seems to be divided into two camps: raisin lovers and raisin haters. Seldom do you find anyone indifferent to this most ubiquitous of dried fruits. If you number yourself in the first camp, you'll appreciate these simple cookies. They're chewy, vanilla-scented and packed with currants (baby raisins), which give them wonderful flavor as well as enhancing their moist texture.

½ **cup (1 stick, 4 ounces) unsalted butter**

¾ **cup (5⅝ ounces) packed light or dark brown sugar**

2 **teaspoons vanilla extract**

½ **teaspoon salt**

¼ **teaspoon baking powder**

1 **large egg**

1 **tablespoon white or cider vinegar**

1½ **cups (5¼ ounces) whole spelt flour**

2 **cups (10 ounces) dried currants, not packed**

SPELT: GIVE IT A REST

When baking cookies with whole spelt flour, we found that an overnight rest in the refrigerator is a critical step in preparing the dough. Spelt is slower than most whole grains to absorb liquid, and without this rest, cookies tend to flatten out drastically as they bake, due to the "free" water in the dough. Giving the dough a slow, cool rest, however, yields a cookie that holds its shape beautifully as it bakes.

Cream the butter, sugar, vanilla, salt and baking powder in a medium bowl. Beat in the egg and vinegar. Add the spelt flour, beating to combine. Stir in the currants. Cover the bowl and refrigerate the dough overnight.

Preheat the oven to 350°F. Lightly grease 2 baking sheets or line with parchment paper. Drop the dough by tablespoonfuls onto the prepared baking sheets.

Bake the cookies, reversing the pans midway through (top to bottom, bottom to top), until they're beginning to brown around the bottom edges but are still fairly tender in the middle, 15 to 17 minutes. Remove the cookies from the oven and transfer them to a rack to cool.

NUTRITION INFORMATION PER SERVING (1 COOKIE, 25G): **5g whole grains,** 90 cal, 3g fat, 1g protein, 10g complex carbohydrates, 5g sugar, 1g dietary fiber, 15mg cholesterol, 42mg sodium, 103mg potassium, 29RE vitamin A, 1mg iron, 12mg calcium, 37mg phosphorus.

Crunchy Cinnamon-Oat Drops

YIELD: 2 dozen cookies

BAKING TEMPERATURE: 350°F

BAKING TIME: 20 minutes

"Crunchy" is the key word in the name of these cookies. Oats and toasted walnuts lend nutty taste and crisp texture, while cinnamon—both the spice and cinnamon chips—add their signature flavor. A warm summer day is the perfect setting for these cookies, and lemonade the perfect accompaniment.

1 cup (4 ounces) chopped walnuts

$1/4$ teaspoon salt, preferably extrafine

$1/2$ cup (1 stick, 4 ounces) unsalted butter

$3/4$ cup ($5 1/4$ ounces) sugar

2 teaspoons vanilla extract

$1/2$ teaspoon ground cinnamon

$1/2$ teaspoon salt

$1/4$ teaspoon baking powder

1 large egg

$1 1/3$ cups ($4 5/8$ ounces) old-fashioned rolled oats, ground for 30 seconds in a food processor

1 cup (6 ounces) cinnamon chips

Preheat the oven to 350°F. Lightly grease 2 baking sheets or line with parchment paper.

TO PREPARE THE WALNUTS: Toss the walnuts with the $1/4$ teaspoon salt and spread them in a 9-inch round cake pan or similar-size pan. Bake them until they're beginning to brown, 8 minutes. Remove them from the oven and set them aside to cool.

TO PREPARE THE DOUGH: Cream the butter, sugar, vanilla, cinnamon, $1/2$ teaspoon salt and baking powder in a medium bowl. Beat in the egg, then the oats. Stir in the chips and toasted walnuts. Drop the dough by tablespoonfuls onto the prepared baking sheets.

TO BAKE THE COOKIES: Bake the cookies, reversing the pans midway through (top to bottom, bottom to top), until they're golden brown around the edges, though still quite light in the center, 20 minutes. Remove them from the oven and transfer them to a rack to cool.

NUTRITION INFORMATION PER SERVING (1 COOKIE, 31G): 11g whole grains, 156 cal, 10g fat, 2g protein, 5g complex carbohydrates, 10g sugar, 1g dietary fiber, 20mg cholesterol, 85mg sodium, 60mg potassium, 37RE vitamin A, 28mg calcium, 60mg phosphorus.

Nutty for Oats Cookies

YIELD: 38 cookies

BAKING TEMPERATURE: 350°F

BAKING TIME: 11 to 13 minutes

Peanut butter cookies. Oatmeal cookies. Chocolate chip cookies. Put 'em all together, and what do you have? This chewy, peanutty, chocolate chip–laden cookie, made with two kinds of oats: rolled and ground.

⅔ cup (6¼ ounces) smooth peanut butter

4 tablespoons (½ stick, 2 ounces) unsalted butter

¾ cup (5⅝ ounces) packed light or dark brown sugar

1 teaspoon vanilla extract

½ teaspoon salt

¼ teaspoon baking soda

2 large eggs

1 cup (3½ ounces) old-fashioned rolled oats, ground
   for 30 seconds in a food processor

1½ cups (5¼ ounces) old-fashioned rolled oats

2 cups (12 ounces) chocolate chips

Preheat the oven to 350°F. Lightly grease 2 baking sheets or line with parchment paper.

Cream the peanut butter, butter, sugar, vanilla, salt and baking soda in a medium bowl. Beat in the eggs, scraping the bowl once they're incorporated, then the ground oats, old-fashioned rolled oats and chocolate chips. Drop the dough by tablespoonfuls onto the prepared baking sheets.

Bake the cookies, reversing the pans midway through (top to bottom, bottom to top), until they're barely set and just beginning to brown around the edges, 11 to 13 minutes. Remove the cookies from the oven and let them cool completely on the pans.

NUTRITION INFORMATION PER SERVING (1 COOKIE, 29G): 7g whole grains, 131 cal, 7g fat, 3g protein, 5g complex carbohydrates, 10g sugar, 1g dietary fiber, 14mg cholesterol, 64mg sodium, 99mg potassium, 14RE vitamin A, 1mg iron, 11mg calcium, 62mg phosphorus, 7mg caffeine.

ROTATING PANS FOR EVEN BAKING

The majority of cookie recipes direct you to reverse the pans midway through the baking time. What does this mean?

As cookies bake, the ones on the oven's upper rack will become browner than those below, while those on the lower rack will brown more on the bottom. In addition, due to fluctuations in your oven's heat, the cookies toward the front of the oven may bake differently than those toward the back. Thus it's a good idea to switch the position of the pans in the oven midway through the baking time: take the bottom pan and put it on top, and vice versa. In addition, as you switch the pans, turn them around so the cookies that were in the back of the oven are now in the front. Yes, it's another step, but one well worth taking to ensure success.

All Oats, All the Time

YIELD: 42 cookies
BAKING TEMPERATURE: 375°F
BAKING TIME: 14 minutes

A cookie without flour? Oats and nuts step in to provide the structure (and wonderful flavor) in these ultra-chewy cookies. They're perfect to offer to family members or friends trying to avoid wheat in their diet.

2 cups (6¼ ounces) quick-cooking oats (see Note)
¾ cup (2¾ ounces) coarsely chopped pecans or walnuts
1½ teaspoons ground cinnamon
1 teaspoon baking powder
¼ teaspoon salt
4 tablespoons (½ stick, 2 ounces) unsalted butter
¾ cup (5⅝ ounces) packed light or dark brown sugar
¼ cup (1¾ ounces) granulated sugar
2 large eggs
1 tablespoon cider vinegar
2 teaspoons vanilla extract

Preheat the oven to 375°F. Lightly grease 2 baking sheets or line with parchment paper.

Combine the oats, nuts, cinnamon, baking powder and salt in a food processor. Pulse until the nuts are finely chopped and evenly distributed.

Beat the butter and sugars in a large bowl until smooth. Add the eggs, scraping the bowl and again beating until smooth. Stir in the vinegar and vanilla, then the oat mixture. Drop the dough by teaspoonfuls onto the prepared baking sheets.

Bake the cookies, reversing the pans midway through (top to bottom, bottom to top), until the edges are barely browned, 14 minutes. Remove them from the oven and let them cool on the pans for about 5 minutes. Transfer to a rack to cool completely.

NOTE: Substitute old-fashioned rolled oats for quick-cooking oats, if you like. Pulse them in the food processor several times before adding the nuts and remaining ingredients, and then pulse again.

NUTRITION INFORMATION PER SERVING (1 COOKIE, 16G): 4g whole grains, 62 cal, 3g fat, 1g protein, 3g complex carbohydrates, 5g sugar, 1g dietary fiber, 13mg cholesterol, 27mg sodium, 40mg potassium, 13RE vitamin A, 17mg calcium, 42mg phosphorus.

Iced Orange Cookies

YIELD: 2½ dozen cookies

BAKING TEMPERATURE: 350°F

BAKING TIME: 10 minutes

While most of us associate Christmas with chocolate, ginger and peppermint, these citrus-scented cookies are a holiday must-have for Kelly Mousley, head of our customer service department at King Arthur Flour. The flavor of these soft, cakey cookies comes mainly from orange zest, both in the cookie itself and in the creamy frosting.

Dough

11 tablespoons (5½ ounces) unsalted butter

¾ cup (5¼ ounces) sugar

1 teaspoon vanilla extract

½ teaspoon baking powder

½ teaspoon baking soda

½ teaspoon salt

1 large egg

½ cup (4 ounces) freshly squeezed orange juice (grate the fruit's zest before juicing)

2 tablespoons grated orange zest (the rind of 1 large or 2 small oranges)

2 cups (8 ounces) traditional whole wheat flour

Icing

2 cups (8 ounces) confectioners' sugar

2 tablespoons (1 ounce) unsalted butter, softened

1 tablespoon grated orange zest (the rind of 1 small orange)

¼ teaspoon vanilla extract

⅛ teaspoon salt

2 tablespoons (1 ounce) freshly squeezed orange juice

Preheat the oven to 350°F. Lightly grease 2 baking sheets or line with parchment paper.

TO PREPARE THE DOUGH: Cream the butter, sugar, vanilla, baking powder, baking soda and salt in a medium bowl. Beat in the egg, then the orange juice and orange zest, scraping the bowl. The mixture will look curdled; that's OK. Add the flour, beating until smooth. Drop the dough by tablespoonfuls onto the prepared baking sheets.

TO BAKE THE COOKIES: Bake the cookies, reversing the pans midway through (top to bottom, bottom to top), until they're just barely beginning to brown around the edges, 10 minutes. Remove the cookies from the oven and let them cool on the pans for 10 minutes before transferring them to a rack to cool.

TO PREPARE THE ICING: Beat the sugar, butter, orange zest, vanilla and salt in a medium bowl till well combined. Beat in the orange juice till the mixture is spreadable. Spread icing on the cookies when they're completely cool, using a generous 1 teaspoon icing for each.

NUTRITION INFORMATION PER SERVING (1 COOKIE, 26G): **8g whole grains,** 124 cal, 5g fat, 1g protein, 6g complex carbohydrates, 13g sugar, 1g dietary fiber, 20mg cholesterol, 75mg sodium, 44mg potassium, 45RE vitamin A, 2mg vitamin C, 11mg calcium, 39mg phosphorus.

USE A LIGHT HAND WHEN GREASING BAKING SHEETS

Does it matter how heavily you grease your baking sheets? Yes! Most cookies, with their high ratio of both fat and sugar, spread as they bake. A heavily greased pan exacerbates this spreading: instead of picking up resistance from the pan as the cookie bakes, it glides right over that grease and spreads too far. The result? Thin edges, with a tendency to burn. So when the directions say *not* to grease the pan—don't.

To grease the pan lightly, use an easy hand with the vegetable shortening or nonstick vegetable oil spray. And remember, the best solution of all is parchment paper; it doesn't add extra fat to your cookies, helps protect their bottoms from burning and allows them to slide right off the pan onto the cooling rack.

WANT TO MAKE YOUR FAVORITE COOKIE RECIPES USING WHOLE GRAINS?

Exchanging the unbleached all-purpose flour in cookie dough for whole wheat flour is one of the simplest ways to make your cookies more nutritious. In very plain-textured (e.g., rollout gingerbread) and/or light-colored (e.g., sugar) cookies, the change is noticeable, though not at all unpleasant. To temper the some-times "tannic" flavor of whole wheat in these plain cookies, where it's more likely to stand out, add 2 tablespoons orange juice per cup of flour. If the recipe calls for liquid (milk or water), simply substitute the orange juice for some of that liquid. If the recipe doesn't call for liquid, adding juice may change the cookie's structure a bit, making it flatter and/or harder. Give it a try.

In "craggier" cookies (e.g., oatmeal, chocolate chip, bar cookies), substituting up to 50 percent whole wheat for the unbleached all-purpose flour is virtually unnoticeable. If you're willing to experiment, try using 100 percent whole wheat, with no all-purpose flour; this often works just fine, though we can't guarantee it for every recipe. (For instance, we don't recommend it for shaped cookies, such as date pinwheels; the dough can be tricky to work with.)

One more hint: let the baked cookies or bars rest for 24 hours before serving. This rest gives the bran a chance to soften, which tempers the somewhat "gritty" mouth-feel some folks get from whole wheat.

Cranberry-Apricot Chocolate Chews

YIELD: **2½ dozen cookies**

BAKING TEMPERATURE: **350°F**

BAKING TIME: **14 to 15 minutes**

This takeoff on a chewy chocolate chip cookie is packed with dried fruit and nuts. The combination of tangy-sweet fruit and dark chocolate in a brown sugar cookie is first unexpected, then delightful.

½ cup (1 stick, 4 ounces) unsalted butter

¾ cup (5⅝ ounces) packed light or dark brown sugar

2 tablespoons (1 ounce) orange juice

1 teaspoon vanilla extract

½ teaspoon baking powder

¼ teaspoon baking soda

¼ teaspoon salt

1 large egg

1¼ cups (5 ounces) traditional whole wheat flour

⅔ cup (4 ounces) semisweet chocolate chips or chunks

⅔ cup (2⅝ ounces) dried cranberries

⅔ cup (3 ounces) dried apricots, snipped into 4 to 6 pieces each

⅔ cup (2½ ounces) chopped pecans

Preheat the oven to 350°F. Lightly grease 2 baking sheets or line with parchment paper.

Cream the butter, sugar, orange juice, vanilla, baking powder, baking soda and salt in a medium mixing bowl. Beat in the egg, scraping the bowl. The mixture will look curdled; that's OK. Add the flour, beating until smooth. Stir in the chocolate chips or chunks, cranberries, apricots and pecans. Drop the dough by tablespoonfuls onto the prepared baking sheets.

> **COOKIES SPREADING TOO MUCH?**
>
> Be sure your baking sheet is cool before scooping the next batch of cookie dough onto it. Also, try scooping onto a parchment-lined sheet, rather than onto a greased baking sheet.

Bake the cookies, reversing the pans midway through (top to bottom, bottom to top), until they're barely beginning to brown around the edges, 14 to 15 minutes. They won't look set in the center. Remove the cookies from the oven and let them cool on the pan.

NUTRITION INFORMATION PER SERVING (1 COOKIE, 28G): 5g whole grains, 115 cal, 6g fat, 1g protein, 8g complex carbohydrates, 7g sugar, 1g dietary fiber, 15mg cholesterol, 40mg sodium, 129mg potassium, 88RE vitamin A, 1mg vitamin C, 1mg iron, 21mg calcium, 45mg phosphorus, 2mg caffeine.

VARIATIONS: *Feel free to substitute your own favorite dried fruits or to exchange walnuts or almonds for the pecans; just be sure you add a total of 2 cups of whatever fruits/nuts you choose.*

If you're a fan of white chocolate, substitute white chocolate chips or chunks for the semisweet chocolate. A nice complement to the white chocolate is 1 cup dried cranberries and 1 cup shelled pistachio nuts.

THE FASTEST WAY TO SHAPE DROP COOKIES

Depositing cookie dough onto the baking sheet with a cookie scoop or ice cream scoop ensures that all the cookies will be the same size when you're done, and speeds the task dramatically. Why use a cookie scoop, rather than an ice cream scoop? Because cookie scoops are sized to match your recipe's instructions: they deposit the dough "by the tablespoonful" or "by the teaspoonful," depending on which size scoop you use. For where to find these types of scoops, see "Where to Buy" on page 588.

And by the way: The teaspoonful and tablespoonful called for in the instructions for depositing drop-cookie dough are different than a measuring teaspoon or tablespoon. A teaspoonful measures about 3/4 of a tablespoon ($2\frac{1}{4}$ teaspoons), while a tablespoonful measures about 4 teaspoons. These measurements are a reflection of the teaspoons and tablespoons you use on your table, rather than in your measuring.

Russian Teacakes

YIELD: 41 cookies
BAKING TEMPERATURE: 325°F
BAKING TIME: 15 minutes

Russian Teacakes, Mexican Wedding Cakes, Greek Kourabiedes, Spanish Polvorones... they're basically all one and the same: a mound-shaped, tender, nut-filled cookie heavily coated with confectioners' sugar. Though considered a special-occasion cookie in most cultures, in this country you'll find them served year-round.

1⅓ cups (4⅝ ounces) old-fashioned rolled oats
1 cup (4 ounces) whole barley flour
⅔ cup (2⅝ ounces) chopped walnuts
11 tablespoons (5½ ounces) unsalted butter
½ cup (2 ounces) confectioners' sugar
½ teaspoon salt
1 tablespoon vanilla extract
1 teaspoon almond extract
Grated zest of 1 lemon
1 cup confectioners' sugar for coating

Preheat the oven to 325°F. Line 2 baking sheets with parchment paper (or use them without parchment, ungreased). Place the oats, barley flour and walnuts in a food processor. Process for 30 seconds, or until everything is finely ground.

Beat the butter, sugar and salt in a medium bowl until smooth. Beat in the extracts and lemon zest, then the oat mixture. Roll the dough into teaspoon-size balls (a teaspoon cookie scoop works well here). Place the balls on the prepared baking sheets, leaving about 1½ inches between them.

Bake the cookies, reversing the pans midway through (top to bottom, bottom to top), for 15 minutes; they won't have begun to brown, except perhaps very slightly around the bottom edge. While they're baking, spoon about 1 cup confectioners' sugar into a plastic bag with a plain (not zip) top.

Remove the cookies from the oven and allow them to cool for 5 minutes. Place the warm cookies in the bag and shake gently to coat with sugar. Allow them to cool completely, then shake them in the sugar again, adding more sugar to the bag if necessary. Place the cookies on the rack once more, to allow time for the sugar to adhere, before serving or storing.

NUTRITION INFORMATION PER SERVING (1 COOKIE, 14G): 6g whole grains, 69 cal, 5g fat, 1g protein, 5g complex carbohydrates, 2g sugar, 1g dietary fiber, 8mg cholesterol, 27mg sodium, 26mg potassium, 26RE vitamin A, 5mg calcium, 25mg phosphorus.

COATING WITH SUGAR—TWICE

Some cookie recipes call for you to coat the baked cookies with confectioners' sugar twice or even three times. If you've ever made stollen, you know you do the same thing with that holiday bread. The reason? Coating a cookie with sugar while it's warm allows some of the sugar to be absorbed into its very outer layer, giving it a softer, sweeter crust. However, as the sugar is absorbed, it disappears. So, more for looks than any other reason, the recipe may direct you to coat the cookies with sugar again. This second coating remains on the surface, giving the cookies a beautiful, snowy white appearance.

Sugar and Spice Drops

YIELD: 53 cookies

BAKING TEMPERATURE: 350°F

BAKING TIME: 11 to 12 minutes

These molasses-spice cookies should please everyone: they're crunchy around the edges, chewy in the center. Spiced with ginger, cinnamon and allspice (a complex spice with a mild clove undertone), they're a wonderful holiday cookie.

¾ cup (1½ sticks, 6 ounces) unsalted butter
1 cup (7 ounces) sugar
1 teaspoon baking soda
½ teaspoon salt
1¼ teaspoons ground cinnamon
¾ teaspoon ground allspice
½ teaspoon ground ginger
¼ cup (3 ounces) molasses
1 large egg
2 cups (8 ounces) traditional whole wheat flour

Beat the butter, sugar, baking soda, salt and spices in a medium bowl until smooth. Beat in the molasses, then the egg, scraping the sides and bottom of the bowl. Beat in the flour. Refrigerate the dough, covered, for 30 minutes (or overnight).

Preheat the oven to 350°F. Lightly grease 2 baking sheets or line with parchment paper. Remove the dough from the refrigerator, and drop it by teaspoonfuls onto the prepared baking sheets.

Bake the cookies, reversing the pans midway through (top to bottom, bottom to top), until they've flattened out and started to brown, 11 to 12 minutes. Remove the cookies from the oven and transfer them to a rack to cool.

NUTRITION INFORMATION PER SERVING (1 COOKIE, 14G): 5g whole grains, 60 cal, 3g fat, 1g protein, 3g complex carbohydrates, 5g sugar, 1g dietary fiber, 11mg cholesterol, 48mg sodium, 29mg potassium, 23RE vitamin A, 5mg calcium, 19mg phosphorus.

BRINGING CRISP COOKIES BACK TO LIFE

To keep cookies crisp, store them in an airtight container, adding a cracker crisper if it's particularly humid out. To re-crisp cookies that have gone soft, bake them in a preheated 300°F oven for 3 to 5 minutes; remove them from the oven, allow them to cool, and they should be crisp again.

Molasses-Rye Snaps

YIELD: 46 cookies
BAKING TEMPERATURE: 350°F
BAKING TIME: 14 to 16 minutes

Molasses and rye have a natural affinity, and they join forces here in a thin, dark brown cookie that straddles the line between crisp and chewy: while its edges are crisp, it still has just the slightest "bend" at the center. These are a great accompaniment to homemade applesauce.

½ cup (1 stick, 4 ounces) unsalted butter
¾ cup (5⅝ ounces) packed light or dark brown sugar
½ teaspoon baking soda
½ teaspoon salt
1 teaspoon ground ginger
1 teaspoon ground cinnamon
¼ teaspoon ground allspice
1 large egg
2 tablespoons (1½ ounces) molasses
1 cup (3½ ounces) whole spelt flour
¼ cup (1¾ ounces) diced crystallized ginger (optional)
⅔ cup (2½ ounces) white rye or medium rye (not pumpernickel) flour

Cream the butter, sugar, baking soda, salt and spices in a medium mixing bowl. Beat in the egg and molasses, scraping the bowl. The mixture will look curdled; that's OK.

Combine ½ cup of the spelt flour with the crystallized ginger, if using, in a mini food processor, and process until the ginger is finely ground. Add this mixture to the bowl, along with the remaining spelt flour and the rye flour, beating until smooth. Cover the bowl, and refrigerate the dough for 1 hour or overnight.

Preheat the oven to 350°F. Lightly grease 2 baking sheets or line with parchment paper.

Drop the dough by teaspoonfuls onto the prepared sheets. Bake the cookies, reversing the pans midway through (top to bottom, bottom to top), until they're an even, deep-golden brown, 14 to 16 minutes. At 14 minutes, they'll still have some significant chewiness; at 16 minutes, they'll be almost entirely crisp. Remove the cookies from the oven and allow them to cool for 5 minutes on the pan before transferring them to a rack to cool completely.

NUTRITION INFORMATION PER SERVING (1 COOKIE, 13G): 2g whole grains, 50 cal, 2g fat, 1g protein, 3g complex carbohydrates, 5g sugar, 1g dietary fiber, 10mg cholesterol, 42mg sodium, 35mg potassium, 18RE vitamin A, 7mg calcium, 183mg phosphorus.

VARIATION: LIGHT AS AIR RYE SNAPS *Divide the dough in half before chilling. Working with one half at a time, roll the dough ⅛ inch thick. Use a 2-inch cutter to cut rounds (or the shapes of your choice), and transfer them to the prepared baking sheets. Bake the cookies, reversing the pans midway through (top to bottom, bottom to top), and watching them carefully, 7 to 8 minutes. At 7 minutes, they'll be crisp with just the slightest bit of "bend"; at 8 minutes, they'll be totally crisp, with just the slightest bit of caramelized sugar flavor, a flavor some enjoy and some don't. Try to catch them right in between those two points. Remove them from the oven and cool them on the pan for 5 minutes before transferring to a rack to cool completely. Because these cookies are so thin, you'll get twice as many from the recipe.*

STORING COOKIES

Want to keep soft cookies soft? Store them in a cookie jar or plastic container, including a sugar softener (a small chunk of terra cotta, which you soak in water before adding to your brown sugar container) or a slice of apple. Want to keep crisp cookies crunchy? Store them in an airtight container. To freeze cookies for long-term storage (up to 3 months), wrap in a zip-top plastic bag, expelling as much air from the bag as possible before sealing.

Chocolate Crinkles

YIELD: 34 cookies

BAKING TEMPERATURE: 400°F

BAKING TIME: 11 minutes

These soft, moist, fudgy cookies are striking in appearance, with their dark chocolate base and Appaloosa-like coating of confectioners' sugar. They're delicate enough that they don't travel well, so enjoy them at home, with a glass of cold milk.

5$\frac{1}{2}$ tablespoons (2$\frac{3}{4}$ ounces) unsalted butter

1 cup (7 ounces) sugar

1 teaspoon vanilla extract

$\frac{1}{2}$ teaspoon baking soda

$\frac{1}{2}$ teaspoon salt

1 large egg

$\frac{1}{3}$ cup (2$\frac{5}{8}$ ounces) brewed coffee, cooled

1$\frac{3}{4}$ cups (6$\frac{1}{8}$ ounces) whole spelt flour

$\frac{1}{3}$ cup (1 ounce) Dutch-process cocoa

2 cups (12 ounces) semisweet chocolate chips

$\frac{2}{3}$ cup (2$\frac{5}{8}$ ounces) confectioners' sugar for coating

Cream the butter, sugar, vanilla, baking soda and salt in a medium bowl until smooth. Beat in the egg and coffee, scraping the bowl, then stir in the flour, cocoa and chips. Refrigerate the dough, covered, overnight.

Remove the dough from the refrigerator. Preheat the oven to 400°F. Lightly grease 2 baking sheets or line with parchment paper. Place the confectioners' sugar in a large plastic bag.

Drop the dough by tablespoonfuls into the sugar in the bag, about 6 pieces at a time. Twist the bag closed, trapping air inside, and gently shake, coating the balls with sugar. Place them on the prepared sheets. Repeat with the remaining dough.

Grab the bag at the top and twist it closed, to trap the maximum amount of air inside.

Turn the bag sideways and gently shake to coat the balls of dough with sugar.

Bake the cookies, reversing the pans midway through (top to bottom, bottom to top), until they're set around the edges but still soft in the middle, 11 minutes. Remove the cookies from the oven and let them cool completely on the pan, loosening (but not lifting) them after about 10 minutes.

NUTRITION INFORMATION PER SERVING (1 COOKIE, 30G): 5g whole grains, 118 cal, 5g fat, 2g protein, 18g complex carbohydrates, 5g sugar, 1g dietary fiber, 11mg cholesterol, 52mg sodium, 77mg potassium, 18RE vitamin A, 1mg iron, 5mg calcium, 38mg phosphorus, 9mg caffeine.

COFFEE AND CHOCOLATE: BEST FRIENDS

Bakers know that chocolate is a flavor whose richness is enhanced by the clean, flowery flavor of vanilla. What many don't know is that coffee performs the same function: it complements and enhances the flavor of chocolate, without contributing any discernible taste of its own. Use a touch of espresso powder in your chocolate recipes or, if the recipe includes water, substitute cold brewed coffee. You'll be pleasantly surprised by the difference in flavor coffee makes.

Thin & Crisp Wheat Cookies

YIELD: 6½ dozen (2½-inch) cookies
BAKING TEMPERATURE: 350°F
BAKING TIME: 14 to 15 minutes

These 100 percent whole wheat cookies roll out beautifully and bake up sweet and crisp. An added bonus: they're sturdy enough for easy decorating, with no crumbling. Bring on the kids!

¾ cup (1½ sticks, 6 ounces) unsalted butter
¾ cup plus 2 tablespoons (6¼ ounces) sugar
¾ teaspoon salt
¼ cup (2 ounces) orange juice
2 teaspoons vanilla extract
2 cups (8 ounces) traditional whole wheat flour
½ teaspoon baking powder

Beat the butter, sugar and salt in a medium bowl, then add the orange juice, vanilla, flour and baking powder.

Divide the dough into 2 pieces, wrap each piece in plastic wrap, and refrigerate for about 30 minutes.

Preheat the oven to 350°F. Lightly grease 2 baking sheets or line with parchment paper.

Working with one piece of dough at a time, roll it into a circle about 14 inches in diameter. Use your favorite cutters to cut out cookies, re-rolling and cutting the scraps. Place the cutout cookies on the prepared baking sheets; they can be fairly close together, as they don't spread much.

Bake the cookies, reversing the pans midway through (top to bottom, bottom to top), till they're brown around the edges, 14 to 15 minutes. Remove the cookies from the oven and transfer them to a rack to cool. Repeat with the remaining dough. Decorate as desired.

NUTRITION INFORMATION PER SERVING (1 COOKIE, 8G): **3g whole grains,** 35 cal, 2g fat, 1g protein, 2g complex carbohydrates, 2g sugar, 5g cholesterol, 25mg sodium, 14mg potassium, 15RE vitamin A, 4mg calcium, 14mg phosphorus.

VARIATION: TO MAKE A DIFFERENT *kind of cookie, roll out, cut and bake just half the dough (as directed above). Roll the other half into a 14-inch circle, and transfer it to a 12-inch pizza pan, rolling the edge under to make a rim. (Alternatively, roll it to approximately 9 x 13 inches, and transfer to a 9 x 13-inch pan.) Sprinkle 1 cup chopped pecans or walnuts on the dough, and bake in a preheated 350°F oven for 10 minutes. Remove from the oven, sprinkle with 1 cup chocolate chips, and return to the oven till the edges of the cookie are brown, 5 to 7 minutes more. Remove from the oven and drizzle with melted caramel, if desired. While still warm, cut the giant cookie into wedges or squares.*

ROLL A PERFECT CIRCLE OF DOUGH

Don't you hate it when your roll-out-cookie dough develops big, ragged cracks all around the edge? Head off the problem by starting with a smooth edge. Once cookie dough is thoroughly mixed, gather it into a ball and transfer it to a lightly floured work surface. Flatten the ball to about 1 inch thick and roll it on its edge along the work surface, as though you were rolling a wheel or a hoop along the street. Flatten the dough again and roll the edges again. Repeat until you have a round, hockey puck-like disk with smooth edges. Wrap in plastic and refrigerate until ready to roll out.

ROLLING DOUGH FOR TENDER COOKIES

When rolling dough for cutout cookies, roll from the center outward, giving the dough a quarter turn on the floured surface with each stroke of the pin. This will produce a more tender cookie than rolling back and forth over the dough.

Chewy Oatmeal Decorating Cookies

YIELD: 6½ dozen (2½-inch) cookies
BAKING TEMPERATURE: 350°F
BAKING TIME: 12 to 15 minutes

Who says cutout cookies for decorating need to be either A) sugar cookies, or B) gingerbread? These chewy oatmeal cookies, with a hint of whole wheat and lots of flavor, are easy to roll and cut out with your favorite shaped cutters.

1 cup (2 sticks, 8 ounces) unsalted butter
¾ cup (5⅝ ounces) packed light or dark brown sugar
1 large egg
2 teaspoons vanilla extract
¾ teaspoon salt
½ teaspoon baking powder
1 teaspoon ground cinnamon
½ teaspoon ground ginger
1 cup (3½ ounces) old-fashioned rolled oats
½ cup (2 ounces) traditional whole wheat flour
2 cups (8½ ounces) unbleached all-purpose flour
Cinnamon sugar (optional)

Beat the butter and sugar in a medium bowl, then add the egg, vanilla, salt, baking powder, cinnamon and ginger, beating until smooth. Scrape the bottom and sides of the bowl. Beat in the oats and flours; the mixture may look dry at first, but don't worry, it'll come together. Divide the dough into 2 pieces, wrap each piece in plastic wrap, and refrigerate for about 30 minutes.

Preheat the oven to 350°F. Lightly grease 2 baking sheets or line with parchment paper.

Working with one piece of dough at a time, roll it into a circle about 14 inches in diameter. Use your favorite cutters to cut out cookies, re-rolling and cutting the scraps. Place the cutout cookies on the baking sheets; set them fairly close together, as they don't spread.

Bake the cookies, reversing the pans midway through (top to bottom, bottom to top), 12 to 15 minutes. The shorter amount of time will make softer cookies, the longer amount of time crisper cookies. Remove the cookies from the oven, sprinkle with cinnamon sugar, if desired, and transfer to a rack to cool. Repeat with the remaining dough. Decorate as desired.

NUTRITION INFORMATION PER SERVING (1 COOKIE, 13G): 2g whole grains, 48 cal, 3g fat, 1g protein, 4g complex carbohydrates, 2g sugar, 9mg cholesterol, 25mg sodium, 20mg potassium, 21RE vitamin A, 7mg calcium, 17mg phosphorus.

Scottish Shortbread

YIELD: 24 wedges

BAKING TEMPERATURE: 300°F

BAKING TIME: 40 minutes

Shortbread, a combination of flour, sugar and butter, with a bit of salt for seasoning, is about the simplest cookie dough you can make. Normally made with all-purpose flour, we make it here with oats, formerly the staple cereal crop of Scotland, the birthplace of shortbread. Oats and butter, the two major ingredients in this recipe, were so common in medieval Scotland that they were considered food for the poor. Thus, oat shortbread was a ubiquitous dish throughout the country, where it was typically baked in celebration of the winter solstice: Its round shape was thought to mimic the sun. We've updated this version with more sugar and a touch of vanilla, but it's still a tasty, centuries-old throwback.

1 cup (2 sticks, 8 ounces) unsalted butter
¾ cup plus 2 tablespoons (6¼ ounces) sugar
1 teaspoon salt
1 teaspoon vanilla extract
2⅔ cups (9¼ ounces) old-fashioned rolled oats, ground for 30 seconds in a food processor
½ cup (2⅛ ounces) unbleached all-purpose flour

Preheat the oven to 300°F. Lightly grease two 9-inch round cake pans.

Cream the butter, sugar, salt and vanilla in a medium bowl until smooth. Add the ground oats and flour. Mix until the dough is smooth; it'll be quite stiff.

Divide the dough in half; each half will weigh about 12¼ ounces. Place half the dough in each of the prepared pans, patting it till it covers the bottom of the pan. Smooth it out with your fingers as best you can, though you don't need to be overly particular; it'll smooth itself out as it bakes. Prick the shortbread all over with a fork; you can do this randomly or in a neat pattern, your choice.

Bake the shortbread until it's light golden brown and slightly browner around the edges, 40 minutes. Remove the shortbread from the oven and set it on a rack to cool for about 1 minute. Run a table knife around the edge of the shortbread to loosen it, then set a flat plate or small cookie sheet on the pan. (You're going to turn the shortbread out onto this plate or sheet, so it needs to be flat.) Using potholders or mitts, grasp the edges of the plate or cookie sheet and the edges of the pan, and quickly flip them over so the pan is on top. Give it a sharp rap on the bottom, to coax the shortbread onto the plate or cookie sheet. Lift off the pan. Repeat with the other pan.

Use a pizza wheel, a baker's bench knife or other sharp knife to immediately cut each shortbread into 12 wedges. Allow them to cool on the plate or cookie sheet for several minutes, then carefully transfer the wedges to a rack to cool completely.

NUTRITION INFORMATION PER SERVING (1 WEDGE, 32G): 12g whole grains, 151 cal, 8g fat, 2g protein, 10g complex carbohydrates, 7g sugar, 1g dietary fiber, 20mg cholesterol, 90mg sodium, 47mg potassium, 65RE vitamin A, 1mg iron, 9mg calcium, 61mg phosphorus.

NOTE: Reduce the butter to ¾ cup (1½ sticks, 6 ounces) if you're counting fat grams or calories. The shortbread will be marginally less crisp and buttery, but will still bake up fine.

VARIATIONS: LIGHT AND CRUNCHY OAT SHORTBREAD: *For a lighter-textured, more delicate shortbread, grind just half the oats (1⅓ cups) and leave the other half as is. Prepare and bake as directed above.*

CINNAMON-PECAN SHORTBREAD: *Add 2 to 3 teaspoons cinnamon (to taste) to the dough along with the flour. Once the dough is patted into the pans, sprinkle each shortbread with ¼ cup sugar mixed with ¼ teaspoon cinnamon. Top each with ½ cup chopped pecans. Bake as directed above.*

LETTING OFF STEAM

While you might think that the holes poked in shortbread dough are for decorative purposes only, they actually have another use: they keep the shortbread from ballooning as it bakes. As short-bread bakes, steam forms between the dough and the pan, and without the vents you've made by pricking the dough, the steam's actually powerful enough to buckle the dough. So, whether or not you're into precise, decorative patterns, be sure to poke sufficient holes in the dough to keep it flat as it bakes.

Molletes with Chocolate

YIELD: 22 cookies

BAKING TEMPERATURE: 350°F

BAKING TIME: 15 minutes

This traditional Mexican cornmeal cookie is often coated with pine nuts, rather than pecans, and the chocolate we've added is our own North American touch. But the crunch of cornmeal, paired with the cookie's soft center, keeps it firmly anchored to its origins. These golden treats are as attractive—with their chocolate candy center—as they are tasty. The recipe calls for whole-germ cornmeal. See sidebar on next page for where to find it.

Dough
½ cup (2⅜ ounces) whole yellow cornmeal
2 tablespoons (1 ounce) water
2 tablespoons (1 ounce) orange juice
½ cup (1 stick, 4 ounces) unsalted butter
¾ cup (5¼ ounces) sugar
1 teaspoon baking powder
½ teaspoon salt
1 large egg plus 1 egg yolk (save the extra white for the topping)
1 teaspoon vanilla extract
1⅓ cups (5⅜ ounces) traditional whole wheat flour

Topping
1½ cups (5⅝ ounces) finely chopped pecans
22 chocolate kisses or 22 chocolate nonpareils

Combine the cornmeal, water and orange juice, and allow the mixture to rest for 1 hour to soften the cornmeal.

TO PREPARE THE DOUGH: Cream the butter, sugar, baking powder and salt in a medium bowl. Beat in the egg, egg yolk, vanilla and the softened cornmeal, beating until smooth and scraping the bowl. Add the flour, mixing until well combined. Cover the bowl, and refrigerate the dough overnight.

Preheat the oven to 350°F. Lightly grease 2 baking sheets or line with parchment paper.

TO PREPARE THE TOPPING: Lightly beat the reserved egg white with 1 tablespoon water in a small bowl until frothy. Place the pecans in a shallow pan or bowl.

Scoop out tablespoon-size pieces of the dough one at a time, dip in the egg white and roll in the diced pecans, turning to coat. Place the balls on the prepared baking sheets.

TO BAKE THE COOKIES: Bake the cookies, reversing the pans midway through (top to bottom, bottom to top), until they're a light golden brown, 15 minutes. Remove the cookies from the oven and immediately press a chocolate into the center of each cookie; be gentle, so you don't crack the cookies. Allow them to cool completely on the pan.

NUTRITION INFORMATION PER SERVING (1 COOKIE, 39G): **9g whole grains,** 178 cal, 12g fat, 3g protein, 9g complex carbohydrates, 9g sugar, 2g dietary fiber, 31mg cholesterol, 26mg sodium, 92mg potassium, 42RE vitamin A, 1mg vitamin C, 1mg iron, 37mg calcium, 94mg phosphorus, 1mg caffeine.

FINDING WHOLE CORNMEAL

If you're looking to add whole grains to your diet, it's tempting to add corn in the form of cornmeal—after all, there are already plenty of recipes in your repertoire using cornmeal, right? But be aware that the cornmeal you buy in the supermarket's baking aisle probably isn't *whole* cornmeal, and therefore doesn't deliver the nutritional punch of a whole grain.

Whole cornmeal, usually found at health-food stores or in the bulk or specialty section of your supermarket, includes the oil-rich germ of the corn kernel as well as the ground endosperm. It's this germ that tends to go rancid quickly, making whole cornmeal a storage challenge. If you purchase whole cornmeal, be sure to store it in your freezer, where it'll stay good for several months.

How can you tell whole cornmeal from refined cornmeal? Whole cornmeal is generally a coarser grind and will contain darker flecks—golden, brown, even dark brown—amid the typically light yellow meal. For mail-order sources, see page 588.

Bizcochuelos

YIELD: 88 cookies

BAKING TEMPERATURE: 350°F

BAKING TIME: 10 minutes

These light-and-crunchy, licorice-flavored cookies will be a huge hit with those who like that flavor. Even our taste-testers who profess to not being licorice fans enjoyed these treats, which hail from Mexico.

1 cup (2 sticks, 8 ounces) unsalted butter
¾ cup (5¼ ounces) sugar
1 large egg
2 tablespoons (1 ounce) orange juice
1 teaspoon salt
1 tablespoon anise seeds
½ teaspoon anise extract
2 cups (6¾ ounces) whole wheat pastry flour
¼ cup (1 ounce) unbleached all-purpose flour

Cream the butter and sugar in a medium mixing bowl. Beat in the egg, orange juice, salt, seeds and anise extract. Scrape the bowl, then beat in the flours. Cover the bowl and refrigerate the dough till it's firm, about 1 hour, or refrigerate overnight.

Remove the dough from the refrigerator. Preheat the oven to 350°F. Lightly grease 2 baking sheets or line with parchment paper. You'll be shaping the dough, so prepare a work surface by lightly flouring it.

Break off a chestnut-size piece of dough (about 1-inch diameter, about ½ ounce). Roll it into a rope 8 to 10 inches long. Cut the rope in half, and loop each piece so its ends cross: it'll look like a handwritten letter "l." Place the shaped cookies on the prepared sheets. They can go fairly close together; they won't spread much as they bake.

Bake the cookies, reversing the pans midway through (top to bottom, bottom to top), until they're lightly browned around the edges, 10 minutes. They'll flatten out as they bake; that's OK. Remove the cookies from the oven and transfer them to a rack to cool.

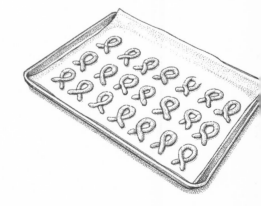

A baking sheet of shaped bizcochuelos will look like a series of thin loops or handwritten letter l's.

NUTRITION INFORMATION PER SERVING (1 COOKIE, 8G): 2g whole grains, 35 cal, 2g fat, 2g complex carbohydrates, 2g sugar, 8mg cholesterol, 25mg sodium, 11mg potassium, 18RE vitamin A, 1mg calcium, 10mg phosphorus.

VARIATION: *If you don't have time to shape cookies in the traditional loops, simply place the balls of dough on the prepared baking sheets and use a glass dipped in sugar, or your fingers, to press them to ¼ inch thick. Bake the cookies for 12 minutes. This will yield about 44 cookies.*

Butter Brickle Biscotti

YIELD: 21 biscotti
BAKING TEMPERATURE: 350°F, then 325°F
BAKING TIME: 55 minutes to 1 hour

Italian biscotti—literally, "twice baked," referring to their method of preparation—are ultra-hard cookies, originally served with sweet wine, now more often found alongside a latte or cup of espresso. This cookie with a long history translates well to a whole grain recipe. The following takeoff on biscotti is tender and crunchy, rather than hard. We call these American-style biscotti, as they're much more in line with what Americans think of as cookies—sweet, crisp—than the more austere European version.

> 6 tablespoons (¾ stick, 3 ounces) unsalted butter
> ⅔ cup (4¾ ounces) sugar
> 1½ teaspoons baking powder
> ¼ teaspoon salt
> 1 teaspoon vanilla extract
> 2 large eggs
> 2 cups (8 ounces) traditional whole wheat flour
> 1 cup (5½ ounces) toffee bits, such as Heath English Toffee Bits

Preheat the oven to 350°F. Lightly grease (or line with parchment paper) a baking sheet that's at least 16 inches long.

TO PREPARE THE DOUGH: Beat the butter and sugar in a medium bowl until smooth. Beat in the baking powder, salt and vanilla. Add the eggs one at a time, beating well after each addition and scraping the bowl. Add the flour and toffee bits, beating gently until the dough is well mixed. The dough will be soft and sticky, but will hold its shape when you drop it from a spoon.

TO SHAPE THE DOUGH: Scrape the dough onto the prepared baking sheet. Wet your fingers, and pat and smooth the dough into a log about 14 inches long, 2½ inches wide and ¾ inch thick. Make it as smooth and even as possible: this will yield the most uniform cookies.

TO BAKE THE BISCOTTI: Bake the log for 25 minutes, and remove it from the oven. Reduce the oven temperature to 325°F. After 15 minutes, spritz the log lightly with water. Let it rest for 5 minutes, then use a serrated knife to cut it into crosswise slices, ¾ inch thick. For longer biscotti, cut diagonal slices. The log has a tendency to crumble, so use the serrated knife to carefully cut it as slowly and gently as necessary, beginning the cut at the edge farthest from you (rather than on the top) and drawing the knife toward you as you gently saw.

Arrange the slices, upright, on the baking sheet. Return the baking sheet to the oven, and bake until biscotti are a very light, golden brown, 30 to 35 minutes. Remove them from the oven and let cool right on the pan.

NUTRITION INFORMATION PER SERVING (1 BISCOTTI, 34G): 11g whole grains, 137 cal, 6g fat, 2g protein, 9g complex carbohydrates, 10g sugar, 1g dietary fiber, 32mg cholesterol, 186mg sodium, 65mg potassium, 34RE vitamin A, 1mg iron, 35mg calcium, 87mg phosphorus, 1mg caffeine.

VARIATION: FOR A CLASSIC *Italian-flavored biscotti, substitute 2 teaspoons almond extract for the vanilla, add 1 tablespoon anise seeds, and substitute 1 cup toasted slivered almonds for the toffee bits.*

Triple Cinnamon–Pecan Biscotti

YIELD: 38 mini biscotti
BAKING TEMPERATURE: 350°F, then 325°F
BAKING TIME: 1 hour

It's interesting to watch someone take a bite of one of these biscotti. Invariably, an "Aha!" expression is followed by a comment noting the biscotti's flavor similarity to cinnamon-streusel coffeecake. Not surprising: cinnamon, sugar and butter play a starring role in each of these seemingly dissimilar treats.

6 tablespoons (¾ stick, 3 ounces) unsalted butter
⅔ cup (4¾ ounces) sugar
1½ teaspoons baking powder
1 teaspoon ground cinnamon
¼ teaspoon salt
1 teaspoon vanilla extract
2 large eggs
1¾ cups (7 ounces) traditional whole wheat flour
½ cup (1¾ ounces) old-fashioned rolled oats
½ cup (3 ounces) cinnamon chips
½ cup (1⅞ ounces) chopped toasted pecans
Cinnamon sugar for topping

Preheat the oven to 350°F. Lightly grease (or line with parchment paper) a baking sheet that's at least 16 inches long.

TO PREPARE THE DOUGH: Beat the butter and sugar in a medium bowl until smooth. Beat in the baking powder, cinnamon, salt and vanilla. Add the eggs one at a time, beating well after each addition and scraping the bowl. Add the flour and oats to the batter. Stir in the cinnamon chips and toasted nuts.

TO SHAPE THE DOUGH: Scrape half the dough onto the prepared baking sheet. Wet your fingers, and pat the dough into a smooth log about 12 inches long, 2 inches wide and 1 inch thick. Repeat with the other half of the dough. Make the logs as smooth and even as possible: this will yield the most uniform cookies. Spritz the top of each log with water, and sprinkle heavily with cinnamon sugar.

A NOTE ON OATS

Oat flour can be substituted, cup for cup, for ground old-fashioned rolled oats. Surprisingly, 1 cup old-fashioned rolled oats measures virtually the same before grinding as after. So 1 cup old-fashioned rolled oats = 1 cup old-fashioned oats, ground = 1 cup oat flour. You can find oat flour at health-food stores, food co-ops and via mail order (see p. 588).

TO BAKE THE BISCOTTI: Bake the logs for 35 minutes, and remove them from the oven. Reduce the oven temperature to 325°F. After 10 minutes, spritz the logs lightly with water. Let them rest for 10 minutes, then use a serrated knife to cut them into crosswise slices, ¾ inch thick. This will yield mini biscotti about 2½ to 3 inches long. Cut on the diagonal, if desired, to make longer biscotti. The logs have a tendency to crumble, particularly at the edges. Use the serrated knife to carefully cut them as slowly and gently as necessary. Starting at the far edge, rather than on the top of the log, seems to be most effective.

Arrange the slices, upright, on the baking sheet. Return the baking sheet to the oven, and bake until the biscotti are golden brown, 25 minutes. Remove them from the oven and let cool right on the pan.

NOTE: To toast pecans, spread them in a shallow, ungreased pan, and bake in a preheated 350°F oven until they're light golden brown and smell toasty, 8 to 10 minutes.

NUTRITION INFORMATION PER SERVING (1 BISCOTTI, 19G): 7g whole grains, 81 cal, 4g fat, 2g protein, 5g complex carbohydrates, 5g sugar, 1g dietary fiber, 16mg cholesterol, 36mg sodium, 43mg potassium, 19RE vitamin A, 25mg calcium, 56mg phosphorus.

Cut the log crosswise into ¼-inch slices. Cutting it this way will yield mini biscotti.

Cutting the log on the diagonal will yield longer biscotti.

BAR COOKIES

What could be easier than beating ingredients in a bowl, pouring the batter into a pan and baking? And what could be more delicious than fudge brownies, butterscotch blondies or pumpkin bars? One-step bars are fast, easy to make and quickly provide you with as many servings as a typical batch of cookies—with much less effort. The surprise is that these bar cookies actually benefit from the use of whole grain flours. We dare you to put out a plate of the double fudge brownies (below) and see if anyone even suspects that they contain a serious amount of whole grain goodness.

Two-step bars—bars that include a pre-baked bottom crust that's then filled, or filled and topped—take a bit more time, but are also a step up the ladder beauty-wise. Where brownies are humble, lemon squares are elegant. Many get better with an overnight rest, so make these bar cookies a day ahead, then hide them. You'll be ready for that potluck or dinner party well ahead of time.

Double Fudge Brownies

YIELD: 2 dozen (2-inch-square) brownies
BAKING TEMPERATURE: 350°F
BAKING TIME: 30 minutes

These brownies walk the line between too fudgy and perfectly moist. The balanced flavor, achieved by the use of both unsweetened cocoa and semisweet chocolate chips, earned us lots of "brownie points" with our taste-testers.

We discovered something interesting when making these whole wheat brownies. Their texture is greatly improved if you wait 24 hours before cutting them. The wait gives the wheat bran a chance to soften, making it much less evident.

1 cup (2 sticks, 8 ounces) unsalted butter
2 cups (15 ounces) packed light or dark brown sugar
¾ cup (2¼ ounces) Dutch-process cocoa
1 teaspoon baking powder
1 teaspoon salt
1 teaspoon espresso powder (optional)
1 tablespoon vanilla extract
4 large eggs
1½ cups (6 ounces) traditional whole wheat flour
2 cups (12 ounces) semisweet chocolate chips

Preheat the oven to 350°F. Lightly grease a 9 x 13-inch pan.

Melt the butter in a medium microwave-safe bowl or in a saucepan set over low heat. Add the sugar and stir to combine. Return the mixture to the microwave (or heat) briefly, until it's hot and starting to bubble. Heating this mixture a second time will dissolve more of the sugar, which will yield a shiny top crust on your brownies.

Stir in the cocoa, baking powder, salt, espresso powder (if using) and vanilla. Cool the mixture until you can test it with your finger: it should feel like comfortably hot bath water. Whisk in the eggs, stirring until smooth, then add the flour and chips, again stirring until smooth. Spoon the batter into the prepared pan.

Bake the brownies until a cake tester or sharp knife poked into the center reveals wet crumbs but not raw batter, 30 minutes. The brownies should feel set on the edges and in the center. Remove them from the oven and cool on a rack; cover when cool. Let sit overnight before serving; this gives the bran a chance to soften, giving the brownies a more pleasing texture.

NUTRITION INFORMATION PER SERVING (1 BROWNIE, 61G): **7g whole grains,** 252 cal, 13g fat, 3g protein, 8g complex carbohydrates, 25g sugar, 2g dietary fiber, 56mg cholesterol, 125mg sodium, 216mg potassium, 76RE vitamin A, 2mg iron, 46mg calcium, 100mg phosphorus, 15mg caffeine.

VARIATIONS: LOWER-FAT BROWNIES *Cut the fat in these brownies by substituting* $1/2$ *cup unsweetened applesauce for* $1/2$ *cup of the butter; add it after the vanilla. The brownies will have a slightly milder chocolate flavor and slightly less fudgy texture.*

ROCKY ROAD BROWNIES *Rocky Road—chocolate with marshmallow and nuts—has been a favorite ice cream flavor for years. Here it's translated into brownies.*

> **1 batch Double Fudge Brownies batter (p. 341)**
> **1 cup (5 ounces) roasted salted whole almonds, coarsely chopped**
> **2 cups (3½ ounces) miniature marshmallows**

Prepare the brownie batter as directed in the recipe, folding the chopped almonds into the batter along with the chocolate chips. Bake the brownies in a preheated 350°F oven for 25 minutes. Remove them from the oven, sprinkle evenly with the marshmallows, and return to the oven until the marshmallows have softened but aren't beginning to brown, 5 to 7 minutes more. Remove the brownies from the oven and let cool overnight before cutting and serving.

PEANUT BUTTER MARSHMALLOW-CRUNCH BROWNIES *Peanut butter fans will love this rich topping; it takes plain fudge brownies over the top!*

> **1 batch Double Fudge Brownies batter (p. 341)**
> **3 cups (4½ ounces) miniature marshmallows**
> **1 cup (6 ounces) semisweet chocolate chips**

1 cup (9½ ounces) smooth peanut butter
1½ cups (5 ounces) bran buds cereal

Prepare the brownie batter as directed in the recipe. Bake the brownies in a preheated 350°F oven for 25 minutes. Remove them from the oven, sprinkle the marshmallows evenly over the top, and return to the oven for 5 minutes more. Remove the brownies from the oven—the marshmallows will have puffed and softened, but they won't be brown. Place the pan on a rack to cool.

Heat the chocolate chips and peanut butter in a small saucepan set over low heat, or in the microwave, stirring frequently, until the chips have melted and the mixture is smooth. Stir in the bran buds. Dollop the mixture over the marshmallow-topped brownies. Allow to cool overnight before cutting and serving.

COCOA MAKES THE BEST-TASTING BROWNIES

Here in the King Arthur Flour test kitchen, we all agree that making brownies with Dutch-process cocoa instead of unsweetened baking chocolate is a good choice. Cocoa is easy to use; you don't have to fuss with melting it (and thus worry about scorching it). Since it's pure chocolate, with very little cocoa butter to temper it, its flavor is intense and rich. And Dutch-process cocoa, treated to reduce the acidic bite that often mars the flavor of baking chocolate, is also darker in color; people naturally tend to "eat with their eyes," and associate dark color with rich chocolate flavor.

BLACK FOREST BROWNIES *German Black Forest Cake marries cherry liqueur-brushed chocolate cake, pitted tart cherries and a garnish of whipped cream. These brownies mimic that flavor combination, adding dried cherries to the brownie batter and substituting white chocolate for the whipped cream.*

1 batch Double Fudge Brownies batter (p. 341)
1 teaspoon cherry flavor, or to taste (use less if you're using an extra-strong flavor)
1 cup (5 ounces) dried cherries
1 cup (6 ounces) white chocolate chips

Prepare the brownie batter as directed in the recipe, except: reduce the vanilla extract to 1 teaspoon, substitute the cherry flavor for the espresso powder, and fold the dried cherries into the batter along with the chocolate chips. Bake the brownies in a preheated 350°F oven for 25 minutes. Remove them from the oven, sprinkle evenly with the white chocolate chips, and return to the oven until the chips have softened but haven't melted, 5 to 7 minutes more. Remove the brownies from the oven and let cool overnight before cutting and serving.

Banana-Chocolate Chip Squares

YIELD: 2 dozen (2-inch) squares

BAKING TEMPERATURE: 350°F

BAKING TIME: 35 to 40 minutes

The tropical sweetness of ripe bananas is balanced here by dark chocolate, which adds its own distinctive flavor. There are those of us who anxiously await the day each spring when the ice cream stand reopens, making available our favorite treat: chocolate-covered frozen bananas. If you're in that camp, here's a welcome stand-in. This recipe takes full advantage of spelt, a light and mild ancient grain; it lets the flavor of the bananas take center stage.

³/₄ cup (1¹/₂ sticks, 6 ounces) unsalted butter

1¹/₄ cups (9³/₈ ounces) packed light or dark brown sugar

3 very ripe medium bananas (about 8 ounces, peeled; about 1 cup, mashed)

1 tablespoon lemon juice

1 teaspoon vanilla extract

³/₄ teaspoon baking powder

¹/₂ teaspoon salt

2 teaspoons ground cinnamon

¹/₄ teaspoon ground nutmeg

1 large egg

1³/₄ cups (6¹/₈ ounces) whole spelt flour

1 cup (6 ounces) semisweet chocolate chips

1 cup (4 ounces) chopped walnuts

Preheat the oven to 350°F. Lightly grease a 9 x 13-inch pan.

Cream the butter and sugar in a medium bowl till smooth. Beat in the bananas, lemon juice, vanilla, baking powder, salt and spices, scraping the bowl. Add the egg, beating until smooth and scraping the sides and bottom of the bowl again. Stir in the flour, mixing thoroughly. Spoon the batter into the prepared pan. Allow the batter to rest for 15 minutes; it'll thicken a bit as it stands. Sprinkle the chips and nuts on top.

DON'T DITCH THOSE BLACK BANANAS!

If you have bananas that have gone past ripe to black, don't throw them away. Bananas at this point are perfect for baking, their flavor intense and rich. Use them right away in muffins, bars or quick breads, or place them, unpeeled, in a plastic bag and freeze till you need them. When you're ready to use them, thaw overnight in the fridge, then peel and mash. They'll be soft and messy, but their flavor will be great.

Bake the squares until the center is moist but not liquid, 35 to 40 minutes. Remove them from the oven and let cool on a rack. For best texture, allow them to rest overnight, covered, before cutting and serving.

NUTRITION INFORMATION PER SERVING (1 SQUARE, 53G): 8g whole grains, 198 cal, 11g fat, 3g protein, 10g complex carbohydrates, 15g sugar, 2g dietary fiber, 24mg cholesterol, 68mg sodium, 171mg potassium, 53RE vitamin A, 2mg vitamin C, 1mg iron, 33mg calcium, 75mg phosphorus, 6mg caffeine.

Cinnamon-Apple Bars with Peanut Butter Glaze

YIELD: 2 dozen (2-inch) bars

BAKING TEMPERATURE: 350°F

BAKING TIME: 35 to 40 minutes

Cinnamon, apples and peanut butter are a delightful flavor combination. These soft, moist apple bars, studded with cinnamon chips, are spread with a simple glaze of peanut butter and honey. The result is a bar that should please just about every age group, from elementary school kid to senior citizen. And a nutritional plus for both groups: in addition to whole wheat flour, this recipes also calls for oats.

Batter

¾ **cup (1½ sticks, 6 ounces) unsalted butter**

1⅓ **cups (10 ounces) packed light or dark brown sugar**

1 cup (8 ounces) applesauce, natural or sweetened

1 teaspoon vanilla extract

¾ **teaspoon baking powder**

1½ **teaspoons salt**

2 teaspoons ground cinnamon

½ **teaspoon ground nutmeg**

¼ **teaspoon each ground ginger and ground allspice**

1 large egg

1¼ **cups (5 ounces) traditional whole wheat flour**

⅔ **cup (2⅜ ounces) old-fashioned rolled oats, ground for 30 seconds in a food processor**

1 cup (6 ounces) cinnamon chips

Glaze

1 cup (9½ ounces) smooth peanut butter

6 tablespoons (4½ ounces) honey

Preheat the oven to 350°F. Lightly grease a 9 x 13-inch pan.

TO PREPARE THE BATTER: Cream the butter and sugar in a medium bowl. Beat in the applesauce, vanilla, baking powder, salt and spices. The mixture will look curdled; that's OK.

Add the egg, beating until smooth and scraping the sides and bottom of the bowl. Stir in the flour, oats and chips, mixing thoroughly. Spoon the batter into the prepared pan.

TO BAKE THE BARS: Bake the bars until the center is moist but not liquid, 35 to 40 minutes. Remove from the oven and let cool completely before spreading with glaze.

TO GLAZE THE BARS: Place the peanut butter and honey in a microwave-safe bowl and heat in the microwave until the peanut butter softens. Stir the mixture until smooth, and spread it on the cooled bars.

NUTRITION INFORMATION PER SERVING (1 BAR, 63G): 9g whole grains, 265 cal, 14g fat, 5g protein, 9g complex carbohydrates, 21g sugar, 2g dietary fiber, 24mg cholesterol, 128mg sodium, 178mg potassium, 52RE vitamin A, 1mg iron, 46mg calcium, 98mg phosphorus.

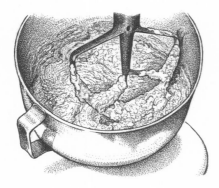 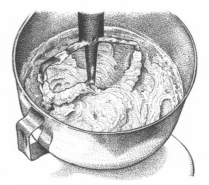

When beating liquid into a mixture of creamed butter and sugar, the batter will suddenly become curdled-looking. Don't panic!

Flour absorbs liquid, so as soon as you add the flour, the batter smoothes out beautifully.

Soft 'n' Chewy Date Squares

YIELD: 2 dozen (2-inch) squares
BAKING TEMPERATURE: 350°F
BAKING TIME: 22 minutes

When you think "date squares," do you imagine bars with a cookie-like bottom, crumbly top and a swath of dark-brown date filling in between? Think again. These one-step bars (just mix up the batter and spoon it into the pan) are more like a brownie in texture: smooth, rich and moist. (For the layered bars, see Classic Date-Nut Bars, p. 357.)

> 4 tablespoons ($\frac{1}{2}$ stick, 2 ounces) unsalted butter
> 1 cup ($7\frac{1}{2}$ ounces) packed light or dark brown sugar
> $\frac{1}{2}$ teaspoon salt
> $\frac{1}{8}$ teaspoon baking soda
> 1 teaspoon vanilla extract
> 2 large eggs
> 1 cup (4 ounces) traditional whole wheat flour
> 1 cup ($5\frac{1}{4}$ ounces) chopped pitted dates
> 1 cup (4 ounces) chopped walnuts
> Confectioners' sugar for topping

Preheat the oven to 350°F. Lightly grease a 9 x 13-inch pan.

Beat the butter, sugar, salt, baking soda and vanilla in a medium bowl until smooth. Beat in the eggs, scraping the bowl to incorporate the butter-sugar mixture.

Beat in the flour, dates and nuts. Scoop the batter into the prepared pan. Wet your fingers and press and smooth the batter into the bottom of the pan. It'll make a very thin layer; that's OK.

Bake the squares until they're golden brown around the edges and a lighter gold in the middle, 22 minutes. Remove them from the oven and let cool for 30 minutes in the pan. After 30 minutes, cut them into 2 dozen squares and transfer the squares to a cooling rack. Using a sifter or shaker, shower the squares with confectioners' sugar. Allow them to cool completely before serving.

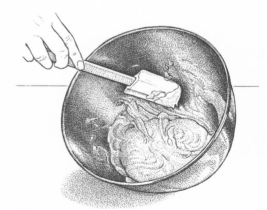

To make sure all the ingredients are thoroughly combined, it's important to scrape the sides and bottom of the bowl after you've beaten in the eggs and before adding the flour.

NUTRITION INFORMATION PER SERVING (1 SQUARE, 31G): 5g whole grains, 122 cal, 6g fat, 2g protein, 9g complex carbohydrates, 9g sugar, 1g dietary fiber, 23mg cholesterol, 61mg sodium, 118mg potassium, 22RE vitamin A, 1mg iron, 19mg calcium, 47mg phosphorus.

Butter-Nut Blondies

YIELD: 2 dozen (2-inch) squares
BAKING TEMPERATURE: 350°F
BAKING TIME: 26 to 28 minutes

Imagine a dense, moist, chewy brownie. Now take chocolate out of the equation and substitute a different childhood favorite, butterscotch. That's Butter-Nut Blondies. These will be popular with those who count the rich, caramelized taste of butterscotch as one of their favorite flavors.

½ cup (1 stick, 4 ounces) unsalted butter
2 cups (15 ounces) packed dark brown sugar
3 large eggs
1 tablespoon vinegar, preferably apple cider vinegar
1 teaspoon vanilla extract
¼ teaspoon butter-rum, butterscotch or butter-pecan flavor (optional, but delicious)
1 teaspoon baking powder
1 teaspoon salt
1½ cups (6 ounces) traditional whole wheat flour
1½ cups (5⅝ ounces) chopped pecans or walnuts

Preheat the oven to 350°F. Lightly grease a 9 x 13-inch pan.

Melt the butter in a microwave-safe bowl or in a saucepan set over low heat. Remove from the heat and add the sugar, mixing until well blended. Transfer the mixture to a mixing bowl and let it cool to lukewarm.

Add the eggs one at a time, beating well after each addition. Beat in the vinegar, vanilla, flavor (if using), baking powder and salt. Stir in the flour and nuts. Spread the batter in the prepared pan.

Bake the blondies until the top looks shiny, 26 to 28 minutes. Don't overbrake; bake just until the edges start to pull away from the sides of the pan and a sharp knife tip poked into the very center reveals sticky crumbs but not wet batter. Remove from the oven and run a knife all around the edge of the pan; this will help keep the blondies flat as they cool, by allowing the edges to settle in the pan along with the middle. Cool completely before cutting. If you prefer squares with a very smooth texture, wait 24 hours before cutting; this waiting period gives the bran in the whole wheat time to soften up.

NUTRITION INFORMATION PER SERVING (1 BAR, 43G): 7g whole grains, 178 cal, 9g fat, 3g protein, 7g complex carbohydrates, 16g sugar, 1g dietary fiber, 34mg cholesterol, 120mg sodium, 129mg potassium, 41RE vitamin A, 1mg iron, 61mg calcium, 86mg phosphorus.

Harvest Fruitcake Bars

YIELD: 32 (1 x 2-inch) bars

BAKING TEMPERATURE: 350°F

BAKING TIME: 45 minutes

These moist bars are packed with dried fruit, similar to the way a fruitcake is chock-full of dried fruit—but without the surrounding ultra-sweet cake. Instead, these light-gold bars are thoroughly dredged with superfine sugar, which gives them a lovely frosted appearance.

¾ cup (1½ sticks, 6 ounces) unsalted butter

1 cup (7½ ounces) packed light or dark brown sugar

½ teaspoon salt

1⅓ cups (4⅝ ounces) old-fashioned rolled oats, ground for 30 seconds in a food processor

¾ cup (3 ounces) whole wheat flour, traditional or white whole wheat

¾ teaspoon baking powder

1 cup (6 ounces) packed golden raisins

1 cup (6 ounces) dried apricots, snipped into 4 to 5 pieces each, packed

1 cup (4 ounces) packed dried cranberries

½ cup (1⅞ ounces) chopped pecans

1 large egg

3 tablespoons (2 ounces) light corn syrup

2 tablespoons (1 ounce) orange juice

2 teaspoons vanilla extract

⅓ cup (2⅜ ounces) superfine or granulated sugar for dusting

EXTRACTS AND FLAVORS: KNOW WHAT YOU'RE USING

The strength of various extracts and flavors on the market varies wildly from brand to brand. Supermarket-type flavors, the kind you'll see arrayed alongside vanilla in the baking aisle, aren't very potent. Use them as you would vanilla, usually by the teaspoonful. On the other hand, flavors you might find in a gourmet store, or a shop dedicated to cake decorating or candymaking, can be extremely strong. These should be used judiciously, drop by drop. The best way to add these flavors is to taste: add a few drops to the batter or dough, mix it in and taste. When the flavor seems strong enough, that's it; don't add any more, at the risk of overpowering all the other flavors in whatever it is you're baking.

Preheat the oven to 350°F. Lightly grease a 9-inch-square pan.

Heat the butter with the sugar and salt in a large saucepan set over medium heat or in a large bowl in the microwave, stirring until the butter melts. Remove from the heat and stir in the remaining ingredients, except for the superfine (or granulated) sugar. Spread the mixture in the prepared pan.

Bake the bars until they appear set all the way through, 45 minutes. Use the tip of a sharp knife to peek into the center: they should look moist but not wet or doughy. Remove the bars from the oven and set the pan on a rack to cool completely. Slice into 16 squares, then slice each square in half to make 32 rectangular bars.

Place the superfine (or granulated) sugar in a large plastic bag. Add the bars, 6 or so at a time, to the sugar in the bag. Close the bag at the top, trapping some air inside, and gently shake it to coat the bars with sugar. Transfer them to a rack and repeat with the remaining bars.

NUTRITION INFORMATION PER SERVING (1 BAR, 43G): 7g whole grains, 162 cal, 6g fat, 2g protein, 17g complex carbohydrates, 10g sugar, 2g dietary fiber, 18mg cholesterol, 52mg sodium, 211mg potassium, 123RE vitamin A, 1mg vitamin C, 1mg iron, 31mg calcium, 67mg phosphorus.

Granola Bars

YIELD: 2 dozen (3-inch) bars
BAKING TEMPERATURE: 375°F
BAKING TIME: 25 minutes

Do you like your granola bars crunchy or chewy? With this recipe, you can have both! You'll find that, once baked, the bars around the outside of the pan are crunchy, while those away from the edge are chewy. Now how convenient is that?

Customize these bars by making your own homemade granola; you'll find some of our favorite granola recipes on pages 25 to 27. Or use prepared granola. Don't like nuts? Leave 'em out. Ditto fruit. Just be sure to use 5 cups of whatever you like, be it plain oat granola or an exotic blend of oats, dried papaya and pineapple, and macadamia nuts.

¾ **cup (1½ sticks, 6 ounces) unsalted butter**
⅓ **cup (2½ ounces) packed light or dark brown sugar**
2 **tablespoons (1⅜ ounces) light corn syrup or brown sugar corn syrup**
½ **teaspoon salt**
1 **large egg**
2 **teaspoons vanilla extract**

5 cups (20 ounces) prepared granola with fruit and nuts (or 3 cups prepared granola without fruit and nuts plus 1 cup dried fruit and 1 cup nuts or any combination that equals 5 cups of granola)

Preheat the oven to 375°F. Lightly grease a 9 x 13-inch pan.

Melt the butter with the brown sugar, corn syrup and salt in a saucepan set over medium heat or in the microwave, stirring until the butter is melted and the mixture is smooth. Set it aside to cool to lukewarm. Stir it again to mix in any butter that has separated out.

Add the egg and vanilla to the butter mixture, stirring until well combined. Stir in the granola (plus fruit and nuts, if you're adding them). Spread the mixture in the prepared pan.

Bake the bars until they're golden brown, 25 minutes. If you bake the bars 3 to 5 minutes longer, you'll have a greater quantity of crunchy bars; bake 3 to 5 minutes less, and you'll have more bars that are chewy. Remove the bars from the oven and let cool in the pan for 10 minutes. Loosen the bars in the pan by running a baker's bench knife or table knife all around the edge. Cut the bars into rectangles, making sure to cut all the way through to the bottom of the pan. They're easiest to cut while they're warm, so do the job before they cool. Cool the bars completely in the pan before removing.

NUTRITION INFORMATION PER SERVING (1 BAR, 38G): 6g whole grains, 172 cal, 11g fat, 3g protein, 10g complex carbohydrates, 7g sugar, 2g dietary fiber, 24mg cholesterol, 68mg sodium, 135mg potassium, 76RE vitamin A, 1mg iron, 22mg calcium, 81mg phosphorus.

Glazed Raisin Bars

YIELD: 35 (2-inch) squares
BAKING TEMPERATURE: 350°F
BAKING TIME: 25 minutes

If you like hermit bars, you'll appreciate the tender-chewy texture and spicy flavor of this close cousin. The thin glaze of sugar on top helps keep these bars moist.

Batter
3 cups (18 ounces) packed raisins
4 cups (1 pound) tradtional whole wheat flour
1⅓ cups (9⅜ ounces) sugar
¾ cup (1½ sticks, 6 ounces) unsalted butter
¼ cup (3 ounces) molasses
1¾ teaspoons baking soda
¾ teaspoon salt
¾ teaspoon ground cinnamon
¾ teaspoon ground allspice
½ teaspoon ground ginger
2 large eggs
⅓ cup (2⅝ ounces) water

Glaze
1 cup (4 ounces) confectioners' sugar
3 tablespoons (1½ ounces) milk

Preheat the oven to 350°F. Lightly grease a 10 x 15-inch jelly roll pan, a 14-inch deep-dish pizza pan or similar-size pan.

Place the raisins and 2 cups of the flour in a food processor. Process until the raisins are coarsely chopped. Imagine each raisin having been chopped into about 4 pieces: that's the size you want.

TO PREPARE THE BATTER: Beat the sugar and butter in a large mixing bowl until smooth. Add the molasses, baking soda, salt and spices, beating until well combined. Beat in the eggs, scraping the bowl, then add the water and the flour-raisin mixture, beating gently until everything is combined. Stir in the remaining 2 cups flour.

Spread the stiff batter in the prepared pan. Wet your fingers and smooth out the surface as much as possible.

TO BAKE THE BARS: Bake the bars until the edges are beginning to brown, 25 minutes. Poke the sharp tip of a knife into the center of the dough; it should reveal an interior that's very moist but not wet or unbaked-looking. Remove the bars from the oven and let them cool in the pan.

TO GLAZE THE BARS: Stir together the confectioners' sugar and milk. When the bars are cool, use a pastry brush to paint them with glaze. When the glaze has hardened, cut pieces approximately 2 inches square.

NUTRITION INFORMATION PER SERVING (1 SQUARE, 52G): 4g whole grains, 178 cal, 4g fat, 3g protein, 22g complex carbohydrates, 13g sugar, 2g dietary fiber, 17mg cholesterol, 117mg sodium, 183mg potassium, 36RE vitamin A, 1mg vitamin C, 1mg iron, 19mg calcium, 68mg phosphorus.

VARIATION: *For a delightful lemon glaze, substitute 3 tablespoons freshly squeezed lemon juice (the juice of 1 medium lemon) for the milk.*

Place a bowl of cold water next to the pan. Dip your fingers in the water, then use your wet fingers to smooth the surface. Don't worry about getting the surface of the bars wet; any water will evaporate quickly in the hot oven.

Golden Cinnamon-Pumpkin Bars

YIELD: 2 dozen (2-inch) bars
BAKING TEMPERATURE: 350°F
BAKING TIME: 40 to 45 minutes

These moist, spicy bars are the deep gold color of burnished copper and look lovely on a dessert buffet. They're similar to brownies in texture, but are a nice change from that ubiquitous chocolate treat, particularly in the fall, when the flavor of pumpkin seems especially apropos.

¾ cup (1½ sticks, 6 ounces) unsalted butter
1⅓ cups (10 ounces) packed light or dark brown sugar
1 teaspoon vanilla extract
¾ teaspoon baking powder
½ teaspoon salt
2 teaspoons ground cinnamon
¾ teaspoon ground ginger
¼ teaspoon ground cloves
¼ teaspoon ground allspice
1 large egg
1 cup (9½ ounces) canned pumpkin (not pumpkin pie filling)
1½ cups (6 ounces) traditional whole wheat flour
1 cup (6 ounces) cinnamon chips
1 cup (5¼ ounces) loosely packed golden raisins or dried cranberries

Preheat the oven to 350°F. Lightly grease a 9 x 13-inch pan.

Melt the butter in a medium microwave-safe bowl or in a saucepan set over low heat, then add the sugar and stir to combine. Return the mixture to the microwave (or heat) briefly, until it's hot and starting to bubble. Transfer the mixture to a medium bowl and allow it to cool till you can comfortably test it with your finger.

Beat in the vanilla, baking powder, salt and spices. Add the egg, beating until smooth and scraping the sides and bottom of the bowl. Stir in the pumpkin, flour, chips and dried fruit, mixing thoroughly. Spoon the batter into the prepared pan.

Bake the bars until a sharp knife inserted into the center reveals moist crumbs, 40 to 45 minutes. Remove from the oven and let cool on a rack.

NUTRITION INFORMATION PER SERVING (1 BAR, 52G): **7g whole grains,** 186 cal, 9g fat, 2g protein, 12g complex carbohydrates, 15g sugar, 2g dietary fiber, 24mg cholesterol, 77mg sodium, 159mg potassium, 131RE vitamin A, 1mg vitamin C, 1mg iron, 51mg calcium, 66mg phosphorus.

CUTTING STICKY BARS

When cutting fudgy brownies or other gooey bars, use a baker's bench knife, a rectangular sheet of stainless steel set into a handle along one long edge. Move the knife from one end of the pan to the other by making a series of vertical cuts. Rinse the knife off in hot water every few cuts, to prevent the bars from sticking to the knife. Another solution is to use a plastic knife, which not only is friendly to your nonstick pan, but also slides through gooey brownies more easily than a conventional metal knife.

When using a baker's bench knife, make a series of vertical cuts, rather than dragging the knife through the bars from end to end. This will prevent the bars from sticking to the knife and tearing.

Caramel-Rum Squares

YIELD: 16 (2-inch) squares

BAKING TEMPERATURE: 350°F

BAKING TIME: 10 minutes for the crust, 12 minutes for the squares

When winter winds blow, treat yourself to a trip to the Caribbean—well, a culinary trip, at any rate. These caramel-almond squares are heavily scented with rum and topped with dark chocolate. Serve with Jamaican Blue Mountain coffee and you'll swear you hear the roar of the surf!

Crust
1 cup (3⅛ ounces) quick-cooking oats
1 cup (4 ounces) traditional whole wheat flour
¾ cup (5⅝ ounces) packed light or dark brown sugar
½ teaspoon baking soda
½ teaspoon salt
A few drops strong butter-rum flavor (optional)
2 tablespoons (1 ounce) orange juice
½ cup (1 stick, 4 ounces) unsalted butter, melted

Filling
⅔ cup (6⅝ ounces) caramel (from a block, or about 21 individual candies)
2 tablespoons (1 ounce) milk
2 tablespoons (1 ounce) rum
⅔ cup (2 ounces) sliced almonds, toasted

Topping
½ cup (3 ounces) semisweet chocolate chips

Preheat the oven to 350°F. Lightly grease a 9-inch-square pan.

TO PREPARE THE CRUST: Whisk the oats, flour, brown sugar, baking soda and salt in a medium bowl. Stir in the butter-rum flavor (if using) and orange juice, then the melted butter, stirring till thoroughly combined.

Measure out 1¾ cups (10 ounces) of the crust mixture, and spread it in the prepared pan, gently patting it down. Bake the crust for 10 minutes, then remove it from the oven and set it aside to cool while you prepare the filling.

TO PREPARE THE FILLING: Melt the caramel, milk and rum in a small saucepan or in the microwave, stirring till smooth. It'll look very gloppy at first, and you'll despair of having it come together, but just keep stirring: it will. Pour the thin caramel mixture evenly over the baked crust. Sprinkle with the almonds, then spread the remaining crust mixture over the almonds.

TO FINISH THE SQUARES: Return the pan to the oven to bake the squares for 12 minutes more. Remove them from the oven and immediately sprinkle them with the chocolate chips. After about 30 minutes, use a bench knife or table knife to loosen the squares from the sides of the pan. Gently press toward the center as you do this, loosening the entire block in the pan so that any caramel that may have seeped through won't glue the squares in place when they're totally cool. Allow the squares to cool completely before cutting; make sure the chocolate has set and hardened. If you try to cut these squares while the chocolate is still soft, it'll cling to the knife and when you're done cutting, all the chocolate will be on the knife, with none of it remaining on the squares. So be patient!

NUTRITION INFORMATION PER SERVING (1 SQUARE, 60G): 9g whole grains, 251 cal, 11g fat, 3g protein, 11g complex carbohydrates, 25g sugar, 2g dietary fiber, 16mg cholesterol, 143mg sodium, 176mg potassium, 50RE vitamin A, 1mg vitamin C, 2mg iron, 50mg calcium, 98mg phosphorus, 4mg caffeine.

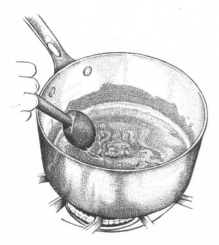

When you first start stirring, it'll seem like the gloppy caramel-milk mixture will never come together.

Just keep stirring; like chocolate ganache, the caramel mixture will finally emulsify and become beautifully smooth.

Classic Date-Nut Bars

YIELD: 2 dozen (2-inch) bars

BAKING TEMPERATURE: 300°F for the crust, 350°F for the bars

BAKING TIME: 30 minutes for the crust, 25 to 30 minutes for the bars

Remember going to the local bakery on Sunday morning and seeing the cupcakes, cookies, lemon squares and date bars all lined up in rows in the glass-front display case? With their tender bottom crust, rich layer of deep-brown date filling and a crumbly top crust, these date bars are a delicious and nostalgic treat.

Crust
¾ cup (1½ sticks, 6 ounces) unsalted butter

¾ cup plus 2 tablespoons (6¼ ounces) sugar

1 teaspoon salt

1 teaspoon vanilla extract

1⅓ cups (4⅝ ounces) old-fashioned rolled oats, ground for 30 seconds in a food processor

1⅓ cups (4⅝ ounces) old-fashioned rolled oats

½ cup (2⅛ ounces) unbleached all-purpose flour

Filling
1 pound (about 3 cups) pitted, chopped dried dates

½ cup (3¾ ounces) packed light or dark brown sugar

½ cup (4 ounces) water

1 tablespoon unsalted butter

2 teaspoons lemon juice

⅛ teaspoon salt

Topping
¾ cup (2⅝ ounces) old-fashioned rolled oats, ground for 30 seconds in a food processor

¾ cup (2⅝ ounces) old-fashioned rolled oats

½ cup (3¾ ounces) packed light or dark brown sugar

⅓ cup (1⅜ ounces) chopped walnuts (optional)

¼ teaspoon baking soda

⅛ teaspoon salt

6 tablespoons (¾ stick, 3 ounces) unsalted butter

Preheat the oven to 300°F. Lightly grease a 9 x 13-inch pan.

TO PREPARE THE CRUST: Cream the butter, sugar, salt and vanilla in a medium bowl until smooth. Add the ground oats, old-fashioned rolled oats and flour. Mix until the dough is smooth; it'll be quite stiff. Press the dough into the bottom of the prepared pan, wetting your fingers if it proves sticky. Prick the crust all over with a fork.

Bake the crust for 30 minutes. Remove the crust from the oven and set it aside to cool while you're preparing the filling. Increase the oven temperature to 350°F.

TO PREPARE THE FILLING: Combine the dates, sugar and water in a medium saucepan. Set the pan over medium heat and bring the mixture to a simmer. Cook, stirring frequently, until the liquid is syrupy and nearly evaporated and the mixture has thickened and become sticky, about 3 minutes. Remove it from the heat and stir in the butter, lemon juice and salt. Allow the filling to cool for about 10 minutes.

Dollop the filling onto the baked crust. The best way to do this is to wet your fingers, pinch off pieces of the sticky filling, and drop them onto the crust. The crust is fragile at this point; you won't be able to spread the filling without tearing the crust, so just try to cover as much of the crust's surface as possible. Don't worry, it'll spread to cover any empty spots as it bakes.

TO PREPARE THE TOPPING: Whisk the ground oats, old-fashioned rolled oats, sugar, nuts (if using), baking soda and salt in a small bowl. Work in the butter until the mixture is crumbly; don't mix too much or it'll become a cohesive dough. If this happens, you can still break it into pieces and spread it over the filling; it's just easier to do if it's crumbs.

TO ASSEMBLE AND BAKE: Sprinkle the topping evenly over the filling. Bake the bars until the dates are bubbly and the topping is beginning to brown, 25 minutes. Remove from the oven and let cool on a rack. When lukewarm, cut into bars.

NUTRITION INFORMATION PER SERVING (1 BAR, 75G): **19g whole grains,** 290 cal, 12g fat, 4g protein, 29g complex carbohydrates, 16g sugar, 4g dietary fiber, 24mg cholesterol, 130mg sodium, 235mg potassium, 77RE vitamin A, 1mg iron, 30mg calcium, 115mg phosphorus.

Soft Raspberry Crumble Bars

YIELD: 3 dozen small bars

BAKING TEMPERATURE: 300°F for the crust, 350°F for the bars

BAKING TIME: 40 minutes for the crust, 35 minutes for the bars

Old-fashioned date bars, with their cookie base and streusel topping, are a classic New England treat. We've changed the original date-bar filling to one based on quick-frozen raspberries to create a brand-new treat—one destined to become a classic. Moister than the familiar date bar, these are best left to rest overnight before you cut and serve them. This extra time gives the bottom crust a chance to set completely and the top crust time to soften a bit.

Because these bars are thick and rich, they're best cut in smaller-than-normal pieces. We recommend cutting them into 6 strips both horizontally and vertically, to yield 3 dozen rectangular bars.

Crust
¾ cup (1½ sticks, 6 ounces) unsalted butter
¾ cup plus 2 tablespoons (6½ ounces) packed light or dark brown sugar
¾ teaspoon salt
2 cups (8 ounces) traditional whole wheat flour
⅓ cup (1⅜ ounces) unbleached all-purpose flour
½ teaspoon baking powder
¼ cup (2 ounces) orange juice
2 teaspoons vanilla extract

Filling
6 cups (two 12-ounce bags) quick-frozen raspberries
1¼ cups (9⅜ ounces) packed light or dark brown sugar
6 tablespoons (1½ ounces) cornstarch
⅛ teaspoon salt
1 tablespoon unsalted butter
1 tablespoon freshly squeezed lemon juice
1 teaspoon vanilla extract
¼ teaspoon ground cinnamon

Topping
¾ cup (3 ounces) traditional whole wheat flour
⅔ cup (2¼ ounces) old-fashioned rolled oats
½ cup (3¾ ounces) packed light or dark brown sugar
¼ teaspoon baking powder
¼ teaspoon salt
1 tablespoon orange juice
¼ cup (½ stick, 2 ounces) cold unsalted butter

Several hours before you plan to make the bars, empty the raspberries into a large saucepan and allow them to thaw.

Preheat the oven to 300°F. Lightly grease a 9 x 13-inch pan.

TO PREPARE THE CRUST: Beat the butter, sugar and salt in a medium bowl, then add the flours, baking powder, orange juice and vanilla. Place the dough in the prepared pan, patting it till it covers the bottom. Smooth it out with your fingers as best you can, though you don't need to be overly particular; it'll smooth itself out as it bakes. Prick the dough all over with a fork.

Bake the crust until it's barely beginning to brown, 40 minutes. Remove it from the oven and set it on a rack to cool for about 1 minute. Run a knife around the edge to loosen the crust in the pan. Increase the oven temperature to 350°F.

TO PREPARE THE FILLING: Stir the sugar, cornstarch and salt into the raspberries in the saucepan. Place the pan over medium heat and bring the mixture to a simmer. Cook, stirring constantly, until the mixture thickens and loses its cloudiness. Remove the pan from the heat. Stir in the butter, lemon juice, vanilla and cinnamon.

TO PREPARE THE TOPPING: Whisk the flour, oats, sugar, baking powder and salt in a medium bowl. Stir in the orange juice, then work in the butter until the mixture is evenly crumbly.

TO ASSEMBLE AND BAKE THE BARS: Spoon the raspberry filling over the baked crust. Sprinkle the topping over the filling. Bake the bars till the raspberry filling is bubbly and the topping is golden brown, 35 minutes. Remove the bars from the oven and let cool for 30 minutes, then use a baker's bench knife or table knife to loosen the edges of the bars from the sides of the pan. Allow the bars to cool overnight before cutting.

NUTRITION INFORMATION PER SERVING (1 BAR, 59G): 10g whole grains, 164 cal, 6g fat, 2g protein, 12g complex carbohydrates, 15g sugar, 2g dietary fiber, 14mg cholesterol, 82mg sodium, 129mg potassium, 48RE vitamin A, 4mg vitamin C, 1mg iron, 30mg calcium, 57mg phosphorus.

Your Favorite Chewy Fruit Bars

YIELD: 3 dozen (1½-inch) bars
BAKING TEMPERATURE: 375°F
BAKING TIME: 23 minutes

Yes, your favorite, because it's up to you to select your favorite dried fruit(s). With their chewy-crunchy oat crust and butter-and-cream-enhanced topping, these fruit bars are incredibly rich, but not overly sweet. They're the perfect finale to a dinner party, served in small slices with a cup of cappuccino on the side.

Crust
6 tablespoons (¾ stick, 3 ounces) unsalted butter
½ cup (2 ounces) confectioners' sugar
¼ teaspoon salt
2 teaspoons vanilla extract
1⅓ cups (4⅝ ounces) old-fashioned rolled oats, ground for 30 seconds in a food processor
½ cup (2⅛ ounces) unbleached all-purpose flour
1 tablespoon whipping cream

Filling
½ cup (1 stick, 4 ounces) unsalted butter
½ cup (3½ ounces) granulated sugar
¼ cup (2 ounces) whipping cream
¼ teaspoon salt
1½ cups (7 to 9 ounces) dried fruit, cut into ½-inch pieces if large (cranberries, apricots, golden or regular raisins, cherries, dates, currants, pineapple, mango, papaya and apple are all good)
¼ teaspoon almond extract

Topping
1 cup (3¾ ounces) chopped pecans

Preheat the oven to 375°F. Lightly grease a 9-inch-square pan.

TO PREPARE THE CRUST: Cream the butter, sugar, salt and vanilla in a medium bowl. Add the oats and flour, scraping the bowl and mixing until everything is well combined. Add the cream and beat until the mixture starts to clump and become cohesive. Press the crust into the bottom of the prepared pan, and place it in the refrigerator while you prepare the filling.

TO PREPARE THE FILLING: Melt the butter with the sugar, cream and salt in a medium saucepan set over medium heat. Bring the mixture to a boil, stirring frequently. Boil for 2 minutes, stirring constantly. Stir in the fruit and almond extract. Spread the filling over the chilled crust.

TO BAKE AND TOP THE BARS: Bake the bars for 10 minutes. Remove from the oven, sprinkle the pecans on top, and return to the oven until the crust is starting to brown (you should be able to see just the edge of it) and the fruit mixture is bubbly, 13 minutes more. Remove the bars from the oven. Let cool for 45 minutes, then use a baker's bench knife or table knife to loosen the edges of the bars from the pan. Don't wait too long or they will have cemented themselves to the sides of the pan.

Let the bars rest overnight, covered, before cutting into small squares. This overnight rest is important; without it, the crust is very crumbly.

NUTRITION INFORMATION PER SERVING (1 BAR, 24G): 3g whole grains, 108 cal, 7g fat, 1g protein, 8g complex carbohydrates, 4g sugar, 1g dietary fiber, 13mg cholesterol, 33mg sodium, 53mg potassium, 42RE vitamin A, 7mg calcium, 29mg phosphorus.

Insert the blade of the baker's bench knife between the crust and the side of the pan and gently push inward, loosening the edges of the bars from the side. Repeat on all four sides.

WHEN THE RECIPE SAYS TO LET THE BARS REST OVERNIGHT...

Please do so! As bars cool, their texture can change radically. A bottom crust that's too crumbly to hold together firms up nicely; bars that seem cakey and dry will collapse and become chewy. Difficult as it might be, show some patience; your reward will be a bar with the best possible texture.

Sunny Citrus Squares

YIELD: 16 (2-inch) squares

BAKING TEMPERATURE: 350°F

BAKING TIME: 20 minutes for the crust, 25 minutes for the squares

The bright flavors of different citrus fruits blend together in this tart-sweet bar cookie that uses spelt flour in the crust. A clone of the traditional bright-yellow lemon square, this version sports a somewhat more complex flavor, and pale, yellow-green filling.

Crust

1½ cups (5¼ ounces) whole spelt flour

¼ cup (1 ounce) confectioners' sugar

¼ teaspoon salt

6 tablespoons (¾ stick, 3 ounces) unsalted butter

3 tablespoons (1½ ounces) orange juice

Filling

4 large eggs

1¼ cups (8¾ ounces) sugar

½ cup (4 ounces) citrus juice (lemon, lime or a combination; grate the fruit's zest before juicing)

¼ cup (1 ounce) unbleached all-purpose flour

2 tablespoons grated citrus zest (the rinds of 1 large lemon and 2 medium limes)

½ teaspoon salt

Confectioners' sugar for topping

Preheat the oven to 350°F. Lightly grease a 9-inch-square pan.

TO PREPARE THE CRUST: Whisk the flour, sugar and salt in a medium mixing bowl. Cut the butter into pats and work it into the dry ingredients until the mixture is evenly crumbly. Add the orange juice and mix until large clumps form, then stop mixing. Press the mixture into the prepared pan, covering the bottom completely.

Bake the crust until it's beginning to brown, 20 minutes. Remove it from the oven.

> **DON'T WALK AWAY!**
>
> When mixing a crumb crust, it's just a matter of seconds between "just right" and "too much." When the fat and liquid appear to be evenly distributed among the dry ingredients, and you can see marble-size chunks beginning to form, stop the mixer—your crumb crust is ready. Another 5 to 10 seconds, though, and it may become a solid mass, impossible to sprinkle into the bottom of the pan or on top of the filling. Our advice? Don't walk away when mixing up a crumb crust or you may end up with a result you didn't bargain for.

TO PREPARE THE FILLING AND BAKE THE BARS: Beat the eggs, sugar and juice in a medium bowl. Whisk in the flour, zest and salt. Pour the filling over the baked crust.

Return the bars to the oven and bake until they look set all over, 25 minutes. Remove from the oven and let cool to room temperature. Cover and refrigerate overnight.

One hour before serving, remove the bars from the refrigerator, allowing them to rest at room temperature. Just before serving, cover them with a drift of confectioners' sugar, shaken through a sieve. Cut into squares and serve immediately. Refrigerate any leftovers; don't worry when the sugar disappears—it has simply melted into the filling. Sift more sugar over the top, if desired.

NUTRITION INFORMATION PER SERVING (1 SQUARE, 57G): 10g whole grains, 162 cal, 6g fat, 3g protein, 9g complex carbohydrates, 17g sugar, 2g dietary fiber, 64mg cholesterol, 118mg sodium, 77mg potassium, 54RE vitamin A, 4mg vitamin C, 1mg iron, 9mg calcium, 63mg phosphorus.

Lemon-Oat Squares

YIELD: 2 dozen (2-inch) squares

BAKING TEMPERATURE: 350°F

BAKING TIME: 35 to 40 minutes

These rich, tender squares blend the complementary flavors of tart lemon and sweet, nutty oats. Unlike classic lemon squares, with their bright yellow, egg-and-lemon filling, this recipe pairs lemon juice and condensed milk for a creamier, slightly more subtle lemon flavor.

Crust

½ cup (1 stick, 4 ounces) unsalted butter

1 cup (7½ ounces) packed light or dark brown sugar

1 teaspoon baking powder

½ teaspoon salt

1 cup (3½ ounces) old-fashioned rolled oats

⅔ cup (2¼ ounces) old-fashioned rolled oats, ground for 30 seconds in a food processor

¾ cup (3 ounces) traditional whole wheat flour

2 tablespoons (1 ounce) orange juice

Filling

1 can (14 or 15 ounces) sweetened condensed milk

1 to 2 tablespoons finely grated zest (from 1 to 2 lemons)

½ cup (4 ounces) freshly squeezed lemon juice (from about 2½ lemons)

Preheat the oven to 350°F. Lightly grease a 9 x 13-inch pan.

TO PREPARE THE CRUST: Beat the butter, sugar, baking powder and salt in a medium mixing bowl till smooth. Add the old-fashioned rolled oats, ground oats, flour and orange juice, mixing

---

THE VERY BEST TOOL FOR GRATING CITRUS ZEST

If you're still using one of those raspy old punched-hole box graters to grate citrus zest, do yourself a favor and purchase one of the new, ultra-sharp handheld graters, one whose design is based on the old-fashioned wood rasp. You'll shred the skin off a lemon or lime in under a minute. Grace Manufacturing's Microplane® was the first grater of this type to be heavily marketed, and various models of it are available via mail order (see p. 588) and in specialty shops and department stores.

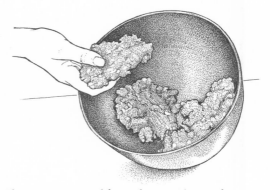

This crust is crumbly and easy to sprinkle in the pan. It's been mixed for just the right amount of time.

This crust was mixed for too long, so it's turned into a solid, cohesive mass, impossible to sprinkle.

to combine. The mixture will start to clump; as soon as it starts to look cohesive, stop mixing.

Sprinkle half the mixture (about 2 generous cups) into the prepared pan. Press it into the bottom of the pan, patting the crumbs firmly to make a smooth layer.

TO PREPARE THE FILLING: Whisk the condensed milk, lemon zest and juice in a small bowl, stirring until smooth and thickened. Spread the filling over the crust in the pan. Sprinkle the remaining crust mixture on top, shaking the pan to distribute it evenly.

TO BAKE THE SQUARES: Bake the squares until they're a light, golden brown, 35 to 40 minutes. Remove them from the oven and set them on a rack to cool. After about 10 minutes, loosen the edges of the squares with a table knife or baker's bench knife. Refrigerate overnight, covered, before cutting and serving.

NUTRITION INFORMATION PER SERVING (1 SQUARE, 41G): 4g whole grains, 140 cal, 6g fat, 2g protein, 5g complex carbohydrates, 16g sugar, 18mg cholesterol, 82mg sodium, 113mg potassium, 38RE vitamin A, 3mg vitamin C, 69mg calcium, 71mg phosphorus.

CAKES

When bakers want to reach deep down, to that place where the sincerest expression of care resides, they turn to cakes. Cakes mean joy and celebration, revelry and recognition, memorable events, big and small. The spectrum of cakes is almost as broad as the range of emotions they represent: from the simple, sincere, stir-together apple cake to welcome a new neighbor, to a majestic, formal, multilayer affair, they're all suffused with the generosity of the baker's spirit.

Until now, most people wouldn't think of reaching for a bag of whole grain flour when baking a cake. Prepare to be surprised, because many of our most beloved cake techniques work beautifully with whole grain flour. Once the balance of liquid and sweetener is properly adjusted, whole grain flour is perfectly at home. You and your family may find yourselves preferring the new, whole grain incarnation of some of your favorite standbys. Many of your guests will have no idea they're feasting on whole grains; we'll leave it to you to enjoy their surprise when you tell them (after they've cleaned their plates).

The cake category encompasses a number of distinct mixing techniques. Each mixing method creates a different type of texture in the cake itself. Butter cakes, such as Devil's Food (p. 370) and Classic Butter Cake (p. 368) count on the thorough creaming of butter and sugar for a moist, pick-up-with-one-finger crumb. Sponge (sometimes called foam) cakes, such as Whole Wheat Genoise (p. 391) and Peach Melba Jelly Roll (p. 409), rely on whipped eggs for their characteristic textures. Stir-together cakes (carrot, apple, zucchini) often use fruit or vegetables and oil for flavor and moisture. Then there are some long-time favorites like pudding cake, cherished from childhood, that can't be left behind. We've grouped the cakes in this chapter by their mixing techniques, to help you find just the right recipe for your next occasion.

BUTTER CAKES

This was probably your first "made from scratch" cake. Even if you've never made one, the steps are familiar. Butter and sugar are creamed together until light and fluffy. Sound like making a cookie so far? You're right. This creaming action creates most of the structure of the cake. As the sugar is beaten into the butter, it forms lots of little air pockets. Eggs are added for tenderness, moisture and structure, then flour, leavening and liquid. In the oven, the little air pockets that were created by creaming are expanded ever so slightly, when the oven's heat and the batter's moisture activate the leavening. The cake rises, and then the flour and egg proteins set, capturing and holding the air pockets to make a wonderfully soft and tender treat.

Whole grains fit nicely into this process, softening as they absorb the batter's moisture and lending their subtle character to the butter/sugar/eggs/flour matrix. Some recipes with stronger flavors, such as chocolate, are an excellent match for traditional whole wheat flour. Some flavors (lemon in particular) paired well with whole yellow cornmeal. Whole wheat pastry flour is the magician of the bunch. It stands in for most of the white flour in many of the following recipes, producing cakes that are practically indistinguishable from their classic progenitors. Whole wheat pastry flour is ground from a softer wheat, and often to a finer texture, than traditional whole wheat flour. These two characteristics give cakes made with whole wheat pastry flour a moist, tender mouthfeel that faithfully reproduces the textures we expect in a cake.

Butter-cake recipes are the ones you turn to when it's time to make cupcakes for school or a take-along dessert for a party. We're pleased to present this collection of memorable delights for any occasion.

Classic Butter Cake

YIELD: One 8- or 9-inch layer cake, 16 servings, 2 dozen cupcakes or one 9 x 13-inch sheet cake, 24 servings
BAKING TEMPERATURE: 350°F
BAKING TIME: 25 to 27 minutes for layers or cupcakes, 30 to 34 for sheet cake

Golden and moist, butter cakes are comfortable being the center of attention on any table. The addition of whole wheat pastry flour assures a tender cake, with just the right balance of flavor and sweetness. This cake is the most versatile canvas a baker can employ, ready and willing to match up with any flavor of icing. Caramel, orange, chocolate or vanilla, all are perfect complements to this cake.

2¼ cups (7⅝ ounces) whole wheat pastry flour (see Where to Buy, p. 588)

1 cup (4¼ ounces) unbleached all-purpose flour

1½ teaspoons baking powder

½ teaspoon baking soda

1 cup (2 sticks, 8 ounces) unsalted butter

1½ cups (10½ ounces) sugar

1 teaspoon salt

4 large eggs

2 teaspoons vanilla extract

1 cup (8 ounces) low-fat plain yogurt

Preheat the oven to 350°F. Grease and flour the pan or pans of your choice or line with parchment paper. For cupcakes, lightly grease 2 muffin tins or line with papers and coat the papers with nonstick spray.

Whisk together the flours, baking powder and baking soda in a medium bowl.

Cream together the butter, sugar and salt in a large mixing bowl with an electric mixer until light and fluffy. Add the eggs, one at a time, beating well after each addition and stopping to scrape the sides and bottom of the mixing bowl once or twice. Add one-third of the flour mixture, mixing until incorporated.

Whisk together the vanilla and yogurt in a separate bowl or cup and add half of this mixture to the large bowl, again beating until the mixture is very fluffy, and scraping the sides and bottom of the bowl. With the mixer running on low speed, add another third of the flour mixture, the remaining yogurt mixture, then the remaining flour, mixing well after each addition and stopping once or twice to scrape the sides and bottom of the bowl.

Pour the batter into the prepared pans. Bake the cake the appropriate time for the size of pan (above). Remove from the oven and cool for 15 minutes before removing from the pan. Place the cake layers or cupcakes on a rack to cool completely before frosting.

> ### PARCHMENT CIRCLES: THE CAKE BAKER'S FRIEND
>
> ....
>
> All bakers have favorite tools (some would say toys) that, once discovered, cannot be done without. If you like to bake layer cakes, precut parchment paper circles are an indispensable aid. You can find them in packages of 8-, 9- or 10-inch rounds, ready to pop into the bottom of your round layer cake pans. They save a lot of time (parchment paper is slippery, and tracing circles and cutting them by hand can be tricky), and they can be the difference between patching potholes in your cake layers and having the cake make a clean getaway from its pan. (See Where to Buy, p. 588.)

NUTRITION INFORMATION PER SERVING (1/12 OF ONE LAYER OR 1 CUPCAKE, UNFROSTED, 61G): 9g whole grains, 220 cal, 10g fat, 5g protein, 16g complex carbohydrates, 121g sugar, 76mg cholesterol, 136mg sodium, 86mg potassium, 101RE vitamin A, 1mg iron, 53mg calcium, 90mg phosphorus.

VARIATION: *You can use white whole wheat flour to make this cake instead of the whole wheat pastry flour, but the texture will be just a little bit sturdier. If you do so, decrease the amount of whole wheat flour from to 2¼ cups to 2 cups.*

Devil's Food Cake

YIELD: Two 9-inch or three 8-inch rounds, 16 servings each, 2 dozen cupcakes (see Variation, below) or one 9 x 13-inch sheet cake, 24 servings

BAKING TEMPERATURE: 350°F

BAKING TIME: 30 to 35 minutes for layers, 35 to 40 for sheet cake

If you're looking for the right disguise for getting whole grains into the fussiest eater, this is the place to start. No one among our veteran tasters had any idea there were whole grains in this cake. We've heard a lot about the antioxidant properties of chocolate, not that we need a reason to indulge. But isn't it nice to know that chocolate can now be even better for you?

¾ cup (1½ sticks, 6 ounces) unsalted butter

1 cup (7½ ounces) packed light or dark brown sugar

¾ cup (5¼ ounces) superfine or granulated sugar

½ teaspoon salt

1½ cups (5 ounces) whole wheat pastry flour

1 cup (4¼ ounces) unbleached all-purpose flour

1 cup (3 ounces) unsweetened natural cocoa powder (see sidebar, p. 417)

1½ teaspoons baking soda

4 large eggs

2 teaspoons vanilla extract

1 cup (8 ounces) plain low-fat or whole-milk yogurt

¾ cup (6 ounces) water

Preheat the oven to 350°F. Grease and flour the pan or pans of your choice or line with parchment paper. For cupcakes, lightly grease 2 muffin tins or line with papers and coat the papers with nonstick spray.

Cream together the butter, sugars and salt in a large mixing bowl till fluffy and light, at least 5 minutes. Stop to scrape the sides and bottom of the bowl at least once during that time. In a separate bowl, whisk together the flours, cocoa and baking soda. If lumps remain, sift or strain the mixture.

Add the eggs to the butter mixture one at a time, beating well (at least a full minute) after each addition, and stopping to scrape the sides and bottom of the bowl before adding the next egg. Mix in the vanilla. Add half the flour mixture and mix until evenly combined. Add the yogurt and water, and mix again. Add the remaining flour, mix, and stop to scrape the sides and bottom of the bowl once more, to make sure the batter is evenly moistened. Pour the batter into the prepared pan(s).

Bake the cakes for the amount of time appropriate to the pan size (above). The cake is done when it begins to pull away from the side of the pan, and a cake tester inserted into the center comes out clean. Remove from the oven and cool for 15 minutes before removing from the pan. Place on a rack to cool completely before frosting.

NUTRITION INFORMATION PER SERVING (1/12 OF ONE LAYER OR 1 CUPCAKE, UNFROSTED,57G): 6g whole grains, 179 cal, 7g fat, 4g protein, 10g complex carbohydrates, 15g sugar, 2g dietary fiber, 52mg cholesterol, 148mg sodium, 155mg potassium, 71RE vitamin A, 1mg iron, 36mg calcium, 84mg phosphorus, 9mg caffeine.

VARIATIONS: DEVIL'S FOOD CUPCAKES *Line two 12-cup muffin pans with cupcake papers. Coat the insides of the papers with nonstick spray (see sidebar at right). Preheat the oven and prepare the batter as directed above. Scoop the batter into the prepared pans, using ¼ cup for each cupcake (a muffin scoop is a great help with this). Bake until a cake tester inserted into the center of one of the cupcakes in the middle of the pan comes out clean, 22 to 24 minutes. Remove the cupcakes from the oven and cool in the pan on a rack for 10 minutes, before removing the cupcakes from the pan and returning to the rack to cool completely.*

CHOCOLATE WHOOPIE PIES *Lightly grease 2 baking sheets, or line them with parchment paper. Preheat the oven as directed above and prepare the batter, reducing the amount of water to ¼ cup. Scoop the batter onto the baking sheets, leaving at least 3 inches between each mound of batter. You should be able to fit 5 scoops of batter on each large baking sheet. Bake until the tops leave no indentation when lightly touched with your finger, 12 to 13 minutes. Remove from the oven and cool completely on a rack. When the cakes are cool, scoop ¼ cup of marshmallow crème (or marshmallow Fluff) onto the flat bottom of one of the cakes. Place another cake, flat side down, on top of the filling. Repeat until all the whoopie pies are filled.*

CHOCOLATE–PEANUT BUTTER WHOOPIE PIES *Combine 2 cups smooth peanut butter with 1 cup marshmallow crème (or Fluff), mixing until smooth. Use this mixture to fill the Whoopie Pies.*

TAKING CARE OF CUPCAKES

Cupcakes are, by nature, meant to be carried around: that's why paper liners for cupcakes are found in the baking aisle of any grocery store. They make it possible to eat cakes out-of-hand, as well as making pan cleanup much easier. To help your cupcake hold itself together when the paper is peeled off, spray the inside of the paper liners with a nonstick spray after placing them in the muffin pan. It only takes a moment, but it makes a world of difference when it's time to partake of each small, delicious cake.

WHEN IS A WHOLE GRAIN CAKE DONE?

Veteran cake bakers have become accustomed to knowing when their cakes are done by recognizing a certain look and feel before they take them out of the oven. In many recipes, cakes are described as done when they "spring back when lightly touched in the center with your finger."

This particular indicator doesn't apply to many whole grain cakes, because the bran in the flour keeps the gluten strands from getting long enough to form a domed top. Luckily, most of the other tests for doneness still apply. The cake will still shrink back ever so slightly from the edge of the pan, just like you're

used to seeing. A cake tester or toothpick inserted in the center will still come out clean. The top of the cake will be golden brown if it's a yellow cake; if it's chocolate you should be able to smell the chocolate aroma before you open the oven door.

Legacy Apple Cake
with Brown Sugar Frosting

YIELD: One 9-inch round 2-layer cake or one 9 x 13-inch sheet cake, 16 servings

BAKING TEMPERATURE: 325°F

BAKING TIME: 35 to 40 for layers, 45 minutes for sheet cake

This moist, semi-chunky cake, spread with the frosting equivalent of brown sugar fudge, is perfect served with a cup of coffee or, better still, a glass of ice-cold milk. Even after its second day on the taste-testing table, it was generating a buzz. One e-mail said, "That's so good, you can make it at my funeral!"

Cake

2½ cups (10 ounces) whole wheat flour, traditional or white whole wheat

½ teaspoon baking soda

½ teaspoon baking powder

1 teaspoon salt

1 teaspoon ground cinnamon

½ teaspoon ground nutmeg

½ teaspoon ground allspice, or 2 teaspoons apple pie spice

1 cup (2 sticks, 8 ounces) unsalted butter

1 cup (7½ ounces) packed light or dark brown sugar

1 cup (7 ounces) granulated sugar

3 large eggs

¼ cup (2 ounces) boiled cider or apple juice concentrate

1 teaspoon vanilla extract

4 cups peeled, chopped apples (about 3 large apples, 1 pound)

1 cup (4 ounces) walnuts, chopped

Brown sugar frosting

5 tablespoons (2½ ounces) unsalted butter

½ cup (3¾ ounces) firmly packed light or dark brown sugar

¼ teaspoon salt

3 tablespoons (1½ ounces) milk

1½ cups (6 ounces) confectioners' sugar

½ teaspoon vanilla extract

Preheat the oven to 325°F. Grease and flour the pan or pans of your choice or line with parchment paper.

TO MAKE THE CAKE: Whisk together the flour, baking soda, baking powder, salt and spices in a medium bowl; set aside. Cream together the butter and sugars in a large mixing bowl until light and fluffy. Beat in the eggs, one at a time, stopping in between to scrape the sides and bottom of the bowl. Mix in the boiled cider (or apple juice concentrate) and vanilla. Mix in the dry ingredients, stirring until evenly moistened. Fold in the apples and walnuts.

Transfer the batter to the prepared pan(s). Bake until a cake tester inserted in the center comes out clean, 30 to 35 minutes for the layers, or 45 minutes for the sheet cake. Remove the cake to a wire rack and cool completely.

TO MAKE THE FROSTING: Melt the butter in a small pan over medium heat. Stir in the brown sugar and salt and cook, stirring, until the sugar melts. Add the milk, bring to a boil and pour into a mixing bowl to cool for 10 minutes.

After 10 minutes, stir in the confectioners' sugar and vanilla. Beat well; if the mixture appears too thin, add more confectioners' sugar. Spread on the cake while the frosting is still warm; it will firm up and be more difficult to spread once it cools.

NUTRITION INFORMATION PER SERVING (1/16 FROSTED LAYER CAKE, 135G): 30g whole grains, 459 cal, 22g fat, 5g protein, 21g complex carbohydrates, 43g sugar, 3g dietary fiber, 83mg cholesterol, 244mg sodium, 259mg potassium, 170RE vitamin A, 2mg vitamin C, 2mg iron, 59mg calcium, 135mg phosphorus.

Coconut Cake

YIELD: One 8-inch 3-layer cake or 9-inch 2-layer cake, 16 servings each, 2 dozen cupcakes or one 9 x 13-inch sheet cake, 24 servings
BAKING TEMPERATURE: 350°F
BAKING TIME: 21 to 23 minutes for layers or cupcakes, 30 to 33 minutes for sheet cake

"Have a piece of cake," she said. After it disappeared, he asked, "Isn't that something you made for the book?" "Yes," she answered. "But I thought the book was whole grain baking?" he asked. She just smiled. You will too.

    This moist white cake is amazing. No one will know it actually has nutritious whole grains in it. We recommend you make the frosting first; while not difficult to do, it does take a little extra time. If you're a fan of the coconut-and-chocolate combination, you could frost this cake with Easy Chocolate Frosting, page 436.

Coconut frosting

1 can (14 ounces) unsweetened coconut milk

½ cup (1 stick, 4 ounces) unsalted butter

5½ cups (22 ounces) confectioners' sugar, divided

½ teaspoon salt

1 teaspoon vanilla or coconut extract

Cake

1 cup (3 ounces) sweetened shredded coconut

1 cup (4¼ ounces) unbleached all-purpose flour

¾ cup (1½ sticks, 6 ounces) unsalted butter, softened

1¼ cups (8¾ ounces) superfine or granulated sugar

1½ teaspoons baking powder

¾ teaspoon salt

1 teaspoon vanilla extract

1 teaspoon coconut extract or ¼ teaspoon coconut flavor

5 large egg whites (6¼ to 7½ ounces)

2 cups (6¾ ounces) whole wheat pastry flour

1 cup (8 ounces) plain yogurt

1 cup (3 ounces) sweetened (shredded) coconut (optional)

TO MAKE THE FROSTING: Set a fine-mesh strainer or colander over a bowl and line it with a clean linen towel. Pour the coconut milk into the lined strainer and let the coconut water drain for up to 2 hours, until you have a thick lump of coconut cream. After the coconut milk has drained, cream the butter with 2 cups confectioners' sugar in a large mixing bowl. Beat in the salt and vanilla (or coconut extract) until the mixture is smooth. Add the coconut cream and mix, scraping the bottom and sides of the bowl. Add the remaining confectioners' sugar until you have a smooth, spreadable frosting. Cover and hold at room temperature until ready to use.

Preheat the oven to 350°F. Grease and flour the pan or pans of your choice or line with parchment paper.

TO MAKE THE CAKE: Place the coconut and all-purpose flour in the bowl of your food processor; process for 30 seconds and set it aside.

Cream together the butter, baking powder, sugar, salt and extracts in a large mixing bowl until fluffy and light, at least 5 minutes. Add the egg whites to the butter mixture one at a time, beating well after each addition. Stir one-third of the whole wheat pastry flour into the creamed mixture, then half the yogurt, another third of the flour, the remaining yogurt, and the remaining flour. Be sure to scrape the sides and bottom of the bowl occasionally throughout this process, so you don't have a puddle of wet batter at the bottom. Add the coconut-flour mixture, and stir until the batter is evenly mixed. Transfer it to the prepared pan(s).

Bake for the amount of time appropriate to the pan size until the cake begins to pull away from the edge of the pan. Remove from the oven and cool on a rack for 15 minutes before removing from the pans and cooling completely. Freeze the layers for 30 minutes before frosting, to make assembly easier.

TO ASSEMBLE: If making a layer cake, trim the top of the cake layers if necessary to make them flat. Turn one of them upside down on a serving plate, cover the top with about ⅔ cup coconut frosting. Repeat with the second layer, covering the top and sides with the remaining frosting. Sprinkle the outside of the cake with more shredded coconut, if desired. For a sheet cake, either frost in the pan or turn the cooled cake out onto a platter and frost.

NUTRITION INFORMATION PER SERVING (1/16 FROSTED LAYER CAKE, 162G): 15g whole grains, 555 cal, 25g fat, 5g protein, 18g complex carbohydrates, 63g sugar, 2g dietary fiber, 50mg cholesterol, 252mg sodium, 192mg potassium, 179RE vitamin A, 1mg iron, 73mg calcium, 166mg phosphorus.

Lemon-Raspberry Cake

YIELD: Three 8-inch or two 9-inch rounds or one 9 x 13-inch sheet cake, 16 servings
BAKING TEMPERATURE: 350°F
BAKING TIME: 20 to 22 minutes for 8-inch layers
27 to 30 minutes for 9-inch layers
35 to 38 minutes for sheet cake

If your favorite part of summer involves a hammock, some lemonade and the sweet luxury of fresh, juicy raspberries, this cake will give you the chance to capture all of those flavors, any time of the year. This is the cake pictured on our cover, made with three 8-inch layers.

2¼ cups (7⅝ ounces) whole wheat pastry flour
1 cup (4¼ ounces) unbleached all-purpose flour
1½ teaspoons baking powder
¼ teaspoon baking soda
1 cup (2 sticks, 8 ounces) unsalted butter
1¾ cups (12¼ ounces) superfine or granulated sugar
¾ teaspoon salt
5 large egg whites (6¼ to 7½ ounces)
1 teaspoon vanilla extract
2 tablespoons lemon zest, or 1 teaspoon lemon extract
¼ cup (2 ounces) fresh lemon juice
¾ cup (6 ounces) milk
¼ cup (3 ounces) seedless raspberry jam
fresh raspberries for garnish

Preheat the oven to 350°F. Grease and flour the pan or pans of your choice or line with parchment paper.

FOR THE BATTER: Whisk together the flours, baking powder and baking soda in a medium bowl. Cream together the butter, sugar and salt in a large mixing bowl until light and fluffy; stop to scrape the sides and bottom of the bowl at least once. This should take at least 5 minutes, and the color of the butter should go from yellow to white. Add the egg whites one at a time, beating well after each addition and scraping the bowl before adding the next. Beat in the vanilla and lemon zest (or extract). Mix in half the flour mixture at slow speed, then mix in the lemon juice and milk. Add the remaining flour mixture, and mix until the batter is evenly combined. Scrape the sides and bottom of the bowl to make sure there are not dry or wet spots in the batter before you finish mixing.

Pour the batter into the prepared pan(s). Level the top of the batter with an offset spatula or the back of a spoon. Bake the cakes for the amount of time appropriate to the pan size (above). The cake is done when it begins to pull back from the edges of the pan and is an even golden brown color on top. The center won't spring back when you touch it lightly, but neither will it let your finger leave a dent. Remove the cake from the oven and cool on a rack for 20 minutes before removing the layers from the pans. Place the cake back on the rack to cool completely before frosting.

TO ASSEMBLE: Chill or freeze the cake layers before assembling the cake; this will make them easier to handle and mean fewer crumbs in your frosting. Place the frozen layers, bottom side up, on plates. Spread the tops with a thin layer of raspberry jam. Return the layers to the freezer for 15 minutes before filling with frosting, placing the second layer on top, and frosting with Lemon Buttercream, page 431, or Easy Lemon Buttercream, page 435.

NUTRITION INFORMATION PER SERVING (1 SLICE, 1/16 OF A FROSTED LAYER CAKE, 138G): 17g whole grains, 500 cal, 21g fat, 5g protein, 19g complex carbohydrates, 57g sugar, 3g dietary fiber, 44mg cholesterol, 198mg sodium, 130mg potassium, 158RE vitamin A, 3mg vitamin C, 1mg iron, 62mg calcium, 128mg phosphorus.

SHAPED BUTTER CAKES

Lots of butter cakes make their appearance wearing the simplest of adornments: perhaps they've been brushed with a simple glaze; sometimes they're glistening with fruit after being turned upside down. Many of these cakes sport majestic silhouettes from being baked in a fancy, decorative tube pan. All of them are beautiful to look at, and if you're uneasy about getting out the frosting and spatula and wrestling with assembling layers, these cakes are the answer.

Brown Sugar–Spice Cake

YIELD: One (9- or 10-cup) Bundt® cake, 16 servings
BAKING TEMPERATURE: 350°F
BAKING TIME: 45 to 50 minutes

Once in a while a cake comes along that's just right for every occasion. Whether for breakfast, lunch, tea, dinner, hostess gift or bake sale, this tender spice cake with a hint of apple in the background will be a memorable addition to any gathering. We don't think you'll have it around for long, but just in case, you should also know that it keeps (or ships) well.

Cake

1 cup (2 sticks, 8 ounces) unsalted butter, softened
2 cups (16 ounces) packed light or dark brown sugar
1½ teaspoons baking powder
½ teaspoon salt
1 teaspoon ground cinnamon
½ teaspoon ground nutmeg
½ teaspoon ground allspice
½ teaspoon ginger
4 large eggs
2½ cups (10 ounces) whole wheat flour, traditional or white whole wheat
½ cup (4 ounces) apple juice
⅔ cup (3 ounces) walnuts or pecans, toasted (see "Toasting Nuts" in the Glossary) and chopped
⅓ cup (2¼ ounces) minced crystallized ginger

Glaze

2 tablespoons (1 ounce) unsalted butter
½ cup (3½ ounces) granulated sugar
⅓ cup (2⅝ ounces) apple juice
1 tablespoon lemon juice
¼ teaspoon ginger

Preheat the oven to 350°F. Grease and flour a 9- or 10-cup Bundt pan.

Beat together the butter, sugar, baking powder, salt and spices in a large mixing bowl. Add one egg and beat until smooth. Scrape the sides and bottom of the bowl, and add the remaining eggs, one at a time, beating until the mixture is smooth and fluffy after each addition. Add the flour, one-third at a time, alternately with the apple juice. Be sure to scrape the bottom and sides of the bowl after each addition. Blend in the nuts and ginger.

Scoop the batter into the pan and level the top with the back of a spoon or a spatula. Bake the cake until a tester inserted in the center comes out clean, 45 to 50 minutes.

Remove the cake from the oven, and let it cool in the pan for 15 minutes.

While the cake is cooling, make the glaze. Heat together the butter, sugar, apple juice, lemon juice and ginger in a small saucepan set over low heat. Stir until the butter is melted and the sugar dissolves, then bring the mixture to a boil.

Turn the cake out of the pan, and poke the top all over with a cake tester or a toothpick. Brush the top of the warm cake with the warm glaze. Repeat until all the glaze has been soaked up.

NUTRITION INFORMATION PER SERVING (1/16 CAKE, WITH GLAZE, 103G): 18g whole grains, 374 cal, 18g fat, 5g protein, 16g complex carbohydrates, 35g sugar, 3g dietary fiber, 90mg cholesterol, 133mg sodium, 231mg potassium, 152RE vitamin A, 1mg vitamin C, 2mg iron, 81mg calcium, 153mg phosphorus.

Cranberry-Cornmeal Cake

YIELD: One 9-inch cake, 10 servings
BAKING TEMPERATURE: 350°F
BAKING TIME: 45 to 50 minutes

These two ingredients, known to our forebears during the earliest Colonial times, are indeed something to be thankful for, especially when baked together. The berries are baked on the bottom of the pan, then the cake is inverted to reveal the jewel-like morsels crowning the top. This cake is best served warm, perhaps with a bit of vanilla ice cream.

Topping
4 tablespoons (½ stick, 2 ounces) unsalted butter
½ cup (3¾ ounces) packed light or dark brown sugar
1½ cups (5½ ounces) fresh or frozen cranberries, thawed if frozen
½ cup (3 ounces) golden raisins

Batter
⅓ cup (5⅜ ounces) buttermilk
1 cup (4⅞ ounces) whole yellow cornmeal
½ cup (2⅛ ounces) unbleached all-purpose flour
½ teaspoon salt
1½ teaspoons baking powder
½ cup (1 stick, 4 ounces) unsalted butter
¾ cup (5⅝ ounces) packed light or dark brown sugar
2 large eggs
1 tablespoon vanilla extract
2 teaspoons orange zest (optional)

Combine the buttermilk and cornmeal in a small bowl; let the mixture soak for 30 minutes. Preheat the oven to 350°F.

TO MAKE THE TOPPING: Melt the butter and pour it into an ungreased 9-inch round cake pan. Tilt to grease the sides of the pan. Sprinkle with the brown sugar and top with the cranberries and raisins; set aside.

TO BAKE THE CAKE: Whisk together the flour, baking powder and salt in a small bowl. Cream together the butter and brown sugar in a large bowl until light and fluffy. Add the eggs, one at a time, beating well after each addition and stopping to scrape the sides and bottom of the bowl. Beat in the vanilla and orange zest (if using). Add the flour mixture alternately with the moistened cornmeal, stirring until batter is evenly combined. Carefully spread the batter over the cranberries and raisins in the prepared pan.

Bake until a toothpick inserted near the center of the cake comes out clean, 45 to 50 minutes. Cool for 10 minutes before inverting onto a serving platter.

NUTRITION INFORMATION PER SERVING (1/10 CAKE, 100G): **12g whole grains,** 345 cal, 16g fat, 4g protein, 21g complex carbohydrates, 27g sugar, 1g dietary fiber, 82mg cholesterol, 208mg sodium, 240mg potassium, 162RE vitamin A, 2mg iron, 107mg calcium, 154mg phosphorus.

Orange Cake

YIELD: **One 9- or 10-cup Bundt cake, 16 servings**
BAKING TEMPERATURE: **350°F**
BAKING TIME: **55 minutes to 1 hour**

The tangy-sweet flavor of oranges and whole wheat have a natural affinity for each other. This cake highlights that happy coincidence, getting an orange glaze while still warm that gives it a crunchy, irresistible texture outside. The inside is tender, moist and smooth.

Batter
2½ cups (8⅜ ounces) whole wheat pastry flour
1 cup (4¼ ounces) unbleached all-purpose flour
2 teaspoons baking powder
½ teaspoon salt
1 cup (2 sticks, 8 ounces) unsalted butter, softened
1¾ cups (12¼ ounces) sugar
4 large eggs
1 cup (8 ounces) milk
1 tablespoon grated orange zest

Glaze
½ **cup (4 ounces) orange juice**
2 **teaspoons orange zest**
¾ **cup (5¼ ounces) sugar**

Place an oven rack a third up from the bottom and preheat the oven to 350°F. Grease and flour a 9- or 10-cup Bundt pan.

TO MAKE THE CAKE: Mix together the flours, baking powder and salt in a medium bowl. Cream together the butter and sugar in a large bowl until light and fluffy; this should take about 5 minutes. Add the eggs one at a time, beating after each addition; scrape the sides and bottom of the bowl after adding each egg. Reduce the mixer's speed to low; add the flour mixture one-third at a time, alternating with the milk. Stir in the orange zest.

Transfer the batter to the prepared pan; level the batter with the back of a spoon. Bake until a cake tester inserted in the center comes out clean, 55 to 60 minutes. Remove from the oven and cool in the pan for 5 minutes, then cover with a rack and invert. Remove the pan and leave the cake upside down on a rack; place the rack over a large tray or piece of wax paper.

TO MAKE THE GLAZE: Mix the orange juice, zest and sugar together in a heatproof bowl. Heat in the microwave at medium power for 1 minute and stir to dissolve the sugar. Brush the glaze all over the hot cake, letting it sink in. Cool the cake completely before transferring to a serving plate.

NUTRITION INFORMATION PER SERVING (1/16 CAKE. GLAZED, 108G): 19g whole grains, 341 cal, 14g fat, 6g protein, 21g complex carbohydrates, 30g sugar, 3g dietary fiber, 87mg cholesterol, 138mg sodium, 146mg potassium, 148RE vitamin A, 6mg vitamin C, 1mg iron, 80mg calcium, 171mg phosphorus.

Nectarine Upside-Down Cake

YIELD: One 8-inch-square cake, 9 servings
BAKING TEMPERATURE: 375°F
BAKING TIME: 45 minutes

When upside-down cakes made their first splash in the 1950s, they wore pineapple rings on top with maraschino cherries in the middle, the fruit bathed in glistening, buttery brown sugar syrup. We've updated that classic with sliced nectarines here. We think their tartness is a perfect foil for the butter-and-sugar combination. The spelt flour in this recipe creates a very tender, very satisfying cake. But if you've a hankering for peaches, or the pineapple rings you grew up with, by all means use those.

Topping

3 tablespoons (1½ ounces) unsalted butter, melted

½ cup (3¾ ounces) packed light brown sugar

¼ teaspoon grated nutmeg

¼ teaspoon ground cinnamon

2 large ripe nectarines (12 to 14 ounces)

2 teaspoons lemon juice

Batter

1¾ cups (6⅛ ounces) whole spelt flour or whole wheat pastry flour

1¾ teaspoons baking powder

¼ teaspoon salt

4 tablespoons (½ stick, 2 ounces) unsalted butter

¾ cup (5⅝ ounces) packed light brown sugar

2 large eggs

1 teaspoon vanilla extract or almond extract

½ cup (4 ounces) milk

Preheat the oven to 375°F.

TO MAKE THE TOPPING: Place the melted butter in an ungreased 8-inch-square baking pan, tilting it to evenly coat the bottom. Mix together the brown sugar and spices, and sprinkle evenly over the melted butter. Slice the nectarines ¼ thick (don't peel them: the skin will look beautiful and help the slices stay together). Lay the slices into the prepared pan, and sprinkle with lemon juice. Set aside.

TO MAKE THE BATTER: Whisk together the flour, baking powder and salt in a small bowl.

Cream together the butter and sugar in a large mixing bowl until light in color and fluffy. Beat in the eggs, one at a time, and the vanilla (or almond) extract; scrape the sides and bottom of the bowl to make sure everything is evenly combined. Stir in half the flour mixture, then the milk. Add the remaining flour mixture, stirring until the batter is evenly moistened and there are no dry or wet patches in it. Gently pour the batter over the fruit in the pan.

Bake until the cake begins to pull away from sides of pan and a cake tester inserted in the center comes out clean, 45 minutes. Remove from the oven, and cool for 5 minutes in the pan. Invert the pan onto a serving platter, and let sit for 1 minute before removing the pan. If any fruit sticks to the pan, use a spatula to carefully scrape it off and replace it on the cake. Serve warm, with whipped cream or ice cream, if desired.

NUTRITION INFORMATION PER SERVING (1/9 CAKE, 113G): 25g whole grains, 273 cal, 10g fat, 6g protein, 21g complex carbohydrates, 25g sugar, 4g dietary fiber, 65mg cholesterol, 200mg sodium, 289mg potassium, 122RE vitamin A, 2mg vitamin C, 2mg iron, 105mg calcium, 207mg phosphorus.

Fruitcake

YIELD: 5½ cups of batter, enough for 3 mini cakes or one 9 x 5-inch fruitcake
BAKING TEMPERATURE: 300°F
BAKING TIME: 1 hour 30 minutes to 2 hours, depending on size of cake

Fruitcake is one of the more polarizing recipes in the baking world: you either love it or not. It's certainly one of the most versatile, easy-to-customize desserts out there. In many cases, the batter for a fruitcake doesn't do much besides hold things together, but the addition of whole grains brings more flavor and a nice round nuttiness to it that's better able to support the kaleidoscope of fruits and nuts within.

Some people who claim not to like fruitcake have fallen in love with it when made without candied peel. If you'd like to convert a skeptic in your circle, try skipping the peel, and substituting some (gasp!) chocolate chips or candied ginger instead. For a darker version, use coffee or molasses instead of the buttermilk. Brushing the cakes with syrup will help them keep longer and give richer flavor as they age and mellow. If you want to make extra for gift giving, this recipe can be doubled.

Dried-fruit mixture
½ cup (2⅝ ounces) currants or raisins
½ cup (2½ ounces) dried cherries or cranberries
½ cup (3 ounces) dried apricots or apple chunks
½ cup (2⅝ ounces) chopped dates or prunes
½ cup (4 ounces) orange juice
2 tablespoons (1 ounce) bourbon, rum or brandy

Batter
2 cups (8 ounces) white whole wheat flour
½ teaspoon baking powder
½ teaspoon salt
½ teaspoon ground cinnamon
½ teaspoon ground nutmeg
¼ teaspoon ground allspice
½ cup (1 stick, 4 ounces) unsalted butter
1 cup (7½ ounces) packed light brown sugar
3 large eggs
1 teaspoon vanilla extract
Reserved liquid from dried fruit mixture, plus enough buttermilk, coffee, or molasses to make ½ cup (4 ounces)
1 cup (4 ounces) chopped walnuts or pecans, plus a few nut halves for garnish
¾ cup (4½ ounces) candied mixed peel: orange, citron, lemon or any of the three
¼ cup (1¼ ounces) candied pineapple or cherries

Syrup (optional)
½ **cup (3½ ounces) granulated sugar**
½ **cup (4 ounces) water**
¼ **cup (2 ounces) brandy, sherry or fruit juice**

TO SOAK THE DRIED FRUITS: Combine the dried fruits in a heatproof bowl. Pour the orange juice over the fruit, stir, and cover loosely. Heat over simmering water or in the microwave for 2 minutes. Remove from the heat and stir in the liquor; set the mixture aside to soak for at least 30 minutes. After the fruit is plump, drain and reserve the excess liquid.

Preheat the oven to 300°F. Grease 3 mini loaf pans (3⅛ x 5⅝-inch) or one 9 x 5-inch pan.

TO MAKE THE BATTER: Whisk together the flour, baking powder, salt and spices in a medium bowl; set aside. Cream together the butter and brown sugar in a large mixing bowl until light and fluffy; stop to scrape the sides and bottom of the mixing bowl at least once during this process. Add the eggs, one at a time, beating well and scraping the bowl between additions. Beat in the vanilla. Stir in half the flour mixture. Add the ½ cup liquid. Add the remaining flour mixture, and stir until evenly combined. Stir in the soaked fruits, the nuts, candied peel and candied pineapple (or cherries).

Transfer the batter to the prepared pan(s), leveling the top. Place some nut halves or candied cherries on top for decoration, if you like. Bake small loaves for 1½ hours or large loaf for 2 hours. Remove from the oven and cool on a rack for 30 minutes before removing from the pans and cooling completely.

TO MAKE THE SYRUP (IF USING): Combine the sugar and water in a small saucepan. Bring to a boil, stirring occasionally, until the sugar dissolves. Remove from the heat and stir in the brandy (or sherry or juice).

TO SOAK AND STORE THE CAKES: After the cakes are cool, brush the tops with the syrup (if using) and store in a large zip-top plastic bag or wrap in plastic wrap. Hold at room temperature, unwrapping to brush with syrup once a day for the next two days. After the cakes have been brushed with syrup the third time, place in an airtight storage tin or wrap in decorative plastic wrap and place in a gift box or container.

NUTRITION INFORMATION PER SERVING (1 3-OUNCE SLICE, 87G): 13g whole grains, 265 cal, 11g fat, 5g protein, 23g complex carbohydrates, 16g sugar, 3g dietary fiber, 50mg cholesterol, 109mg sodium, 309mg potassium, 103RE vitamin A, 4mg vitamin C, 2mg iron, 55mg calcium, 118mg phosphorus.

POUND CAKES

The richest of the rich, pound cakes defy most cake conventions with their ability to proudly stand alone, without benefit of frosting. They wear only the merest hint of a glaze to accent their inherent delectable qualities. When baked with whole grains, the depth of flavor in these majestic creations only increases. They're the perfect cake to bake in decoratively embossed tube pans, needing little more than a plate underneath them and a dusting of powdered sugar to garner oohs and aahs from the baker's audience. Whether for bake sale, potluck or bridge club, these cakes will have diners asking for your recipe, and doing double takes when they find out which type of flour you used.

Vanilla Pound Cake

YIELD: Two 8½ x 4½-inch loaf cakes (ten ¾-inch slices each), one 10-inch tube cake or one 12-cup Bundt cake (20 servings)
BAKING TEMPERATURE: 350°F
BAKING TIME: 55 minutes to 1 hour

Pound cake is a familiar, comforting, reliable dessert that's as versatile as you'd expect of any classic. From the simple slice you dunk in your tea to the dressed-to-the-nines version that wears strawberries, whipped cream and chocolate sauce, there's no substitute for a moist, delicious slice of this golden cake. Whole wheat pastry flour keeps this loaf moist, and the perfume of vanilla throughout ensures that this is a cake for any occasion.

Cake
2½ cups (8⅜ ounces) whole wheat pastry flour
1 cup (4¼ ounces) unbleached bread flour
1 teaspoon salt
1 cup (2 sticks, 8 ounces) unsalted butter
1 cup (4 ounces) confectioners' sugar
1¼ cups (8¾ ounces) granulated sugar
1 teaspoon baking powder
4 large eggs
1 cup (8 ounces) sour cream
1 tablespoon vanilla extract
1 teaspoon grated lemon zest or ½ teaspoon almond extract (optional)

Crunchy sugar glaze (optional)
3 tablespoons (1¼ ounces) granulated sugar
1 teaspoon vanilla extract
2 teaspoons water

Preheat the oven to 350°F. Lightly grease the pan or pans of your choice.

Whisk together the flours and salt in a medium bowl. Cream together the butter, sugars and baking powder in a large mixing bowl until light and fluffy, about 5 minutes. Add the eggs, one at a time, beating well after each addition and stopping to scrape the sides and bottom of the bowl occasionally. Lower the mixer's speed, and add the flour mixture alternately with the sour cream, beginning and ending with the flour. Stir in the vanilla and lemon zest (or almond extract), if using.

Transfer the batter to the prepared pan(s). Bake for 40 to 45 minutes. While the cake is baking, mix together the glaze ingredients, if using.

Remove the cake from the oven and brush the glaze over the top of the cake(s). Return to the oven and continue baking until a cake tester inserted in the center comes out clean, and the cake begins to pull back from the edges of the pan, 15 minutes more. Remove from the oven and place on a rack to cool for 15 minutes. After 15 minutes, carefully remove the cake from the pan and return to the rack to finish cooling completely.

NUTRITION INFORMATION PER SERVING (1 SERVING, 75G): **15g whole grains,** 277 cal, 13g fat, 5g protein, 16g complex carbohydrates, 21g sugar, 2g dietary fiber, 73mg cholesterol, 145mg sodium, 97mg potassium, 128RE vitamin A, 1mg iron, 42mg calcium, 110mg phosphorus.

VARIATION: MARBLE POUND CAKE *When preparing the batter, use almond extract instead of the lemon zest. After the batter is made, measure out 2 cups into a medium bowl. Melt 4 ounces of semisweet chocolate. When the chocolate is cool, stir it into the batter with ½ teaspoon espresso powder.*

TO ASSEMBLE THE CAKE: *Spoon the vanilla batter into the prepared pan(s). Place dollops of the chocolate batter over the vanilla in a random pattern. With a kitchen knife or a rubber spatula, draw the chocolate batter down and through the vanilla, creating a swirl pattern. Bake as directed for Vanilla Pound Cake.*

Lemon-Cornmeal Pound Cake

YIELD: Two 8½ by 4-inch loaves, 10 servings each, or one 12-cup Bundt cake, 20 servings
BAKING TEMPERATURE: 350°F
BAKING TIME: 55 minutes to 1 hour

The sunny flavor and golden color of this pound cake make it a natural to pair with fresh fruit. The lemon glaze that's brushed on the warm cake gives the top a nice crunch that hints at the toothsome treat beneath. Make sure the eggs, butter and buttermilk are all at room temperature before you begin.

Cake

1¼ cups (6 ounces) whole yellow cornmeal
1 cup (3⅜ ounces) whole wheat pastry flour
1 cup (4¼ ounces) unbleached bread flour
1 teaspoon salt
1 cup (2 sticks, 8 ounces) unsalted butter, softened
1½ cups (10½ ounces) granulated sugar
1 cup (4 ounces) confectioners' sugar
1½ teaspoons baking powder
5 large eggs (at room temperature)
1 cup (8 ounces) buttermilk, at room temperature
3 tablespoons (1½ ounces) fresh lemon juice
1 tablespoon grated lemon zest

Glaze

¾ cup (5¼ ounces) granulated sugar
½ cup (4 ounces) fresh lemon juice

Preheat the oven to 350°F. Lightly grease the pan or pans of your choice.

TO MAKE THE CAKE: Whisk together the cornmeal, flours and salt in a medium bowl. Cream together the butter, sugars and baking powder in a large bowl until light and fluffy. Add the eggs, one at a time, stopping to scrape the sides and bottom of the bowl after each addition. With the mixer on slow speed, alternately add the flour mixture and the buttermilk, beginning and ending with the flour. Stir in the lemon juice and zest. Transfer the batter to the prepared pan(s).

Bake until a cake tester inserted in the center comes out clean and the cake pulls slightly away from the edge of the pan, 55 minutes to 1 hour. Remove from the oven, and cool in the pan on a rack for 15 minutes. After 15 minutes, turn the cake out on to the rack; place a baking sheet or wax paper under the rack.

TO GLAZE THE CAKE: Mix the granulated sugar and lemon juice together; heat in the microwave for 30 seconds at medium power and stir to melt the sugar. Brush the mixture over the warm cake until all of it is absorbed.

NUTRITION INFORMATION PER SERVING (1/20 CAKE, GLAZED, 115G): 15g whole grains, 360 cal, 15g fat, 5g protein, 19g complex carbohydrates, 34g sugar, 2g dietary fiber, 100mg cholesterol, 197mg sodium, 117mg potassium, 149RE vitamin A, 5mg vitamin C, 1mg iron, 54mg calcium, 127mg phosphorus.

Chocolate Pound Cake

YIELD: Two 8$^{1}/_{2}$ x 4$^{1}/_{2}$ -inch loaf cakes (10 servings each), one 10-inch tube cake, or one 12-cup Bundt cake (20 servings each)

BAKING TEMPERATURE: 325°F

BAKING TIME: 55 minutes to 1 hour

Dark, moist and full of flavor, there's no competing with the simple glory of a chocolate pound cake. This cake stands well all on its own, but there's nothing to say it won't be just as luscious when it includes the grace note of your choice, be it chocolate chips, dried fruit or chopped nuts. A drizzle of melted chocolate or caramel on top is always nice. We proudly present this cake as your personal chocolate canvas, to enhance in any way you desire.

> 1 cup (3 ounces) unsweetened Dutch-process cocoa powder
> 1$^{3}/_{4}$ cups (6 ounces) whole wheat pastry flour
> $^{3}/_{4}$ cup (3$^{1}/_{8}$ ounces) unbleached bread flour
> $^{1}/_{2}$ teaspoon baking powder
> $^{1}/_{2}$ teaspoon baking soda
> 1 teaspoon salt
> 1 cup (2 sticks, 8 ounces) unsalted butter
> 2 cups (14 ounces) sugar
> 2 teaspoons vanilla extract
> 5 large eggs
> 2 teaspoons espresso powder or 1 tablespoon instant coffee crystals
> $^{1}/_{4}$ cup (2 ounces) warm water
> $^{3}/_{4}$ cup (6 ounces) buttermilk
> 1 cup (6 ounces) chocolate chips (optional)
> 1 cup (5 ounces) dried cherries or chopped nuts (optional)

Preheat the oven to 325°F. Lightly grease the pan or pans of your choice.

Whisk together the cocoa, flours, baking powder, baking soda and salt in a medium bowl. Cream together the butter in a large bowl until light and fluffy, and continue beating while gradually adding the sugar. Beat the mixture on high speed for 2 to 3 minutes, then lower the speed and add the vanilla. Add the eggs one at a time, beating well after each addition and stopping to scrape the sides and bottom of the bowl occasionally.

Dissolve the espresso powder (or instant coffee) in the warm water and combine with the buttermilk. Add the flour mixture to the batter alternately with the coffee mixture, beginning and ending with the flour. Stir in the chocolate chips and dried cherries (or nuts), if using. Blend well and pour into the prepared pan(s).

Bake the cake until a cake tester inserted in the center comes out clean, about 1 hour. Remove the cake from the oven and place it, in the pan, on a wire rack to cool for at least 15 minutes. Unmold the cake onto the rack and let it cool completely.

NUTRITION INFORMATION PER SERVING (1/20 CAKE, WITHOUT "MIX-INS", 48G): 11g whole grains, 252 cal, 12g fat, 5g protein, 13g complex carbohydrates, 20g sugar, 3g dietary fiber, 80mg cholesterol, 177mg sodium, 307mg potassium, 115RE vitamin A, 2mg iron, 39mg calcium, 123mg phosphorus, 16mg caffeine.

Harvest Apple Pound Cake

YIELD: One 10-inch tube or 12-cup Bundt cake, 20 servings
BAKING TEMPERATURE: 350°F
BAKING TIME: 1 hour to 1 hour 10 minutes

When it's time to gather and bake with the bounty of the growing season, this cake is the perfect choice. Big enough to feed a crowd, moist and flavorful enough to taste even better the second day, it's sure to become a household favorite. Whole cornmeal gives the cake some textural pizzazz, while whole wheat pastry flour provides a tender crumb and slightly nutty flavor.

Cake
1¼ cups (6 ounces) whole yellow cornmeal
1 cup (3⅜ ounces) whole wheat pastry flour
1 cup (4¼ ounces) unbleached bread flour
1 teaspoon baking powder
1 teaspoon ground cinnamon
½ teaspoon salt
½ cup (1 stick, 4 ounces) unsalted butter
1 package (8 ounces) cream cheese
1½ cups (10½ ounces) sugar
2 large eggs
1 cup (9½ ounces) spiced apple butter
1 tablespoon bourbon or 1 teaspoon rum flavoring
1 cup (3¾ ounces) chopped pecans

Glaze
1 cup (4 ounces) confectioners' sugar
1 to 2 tablespoons milk
1½ teaspoons corn syrup
½ teaspoon vanilla extract or bourbon

Preheat the oven to 350°F. Lightly grease the pan or pans of your choice.

TO MAKE THE CAKE: Whisk together the cornmeal, flours, baking powder, cinnamon and salt in a medium bowl. Beat together the butter and cream cheese in a large mixer until no lumps remain. Add the sugar gradually, beating until the mixture is light and fluffy. Add the eggs, one at a time, scraping the sides and bottom of the bowl after each addition. Add the dry ingredients, alternating with the apple butter, beginning and ending with the flour mixture. Stir in the bourbon (or rum flavoring) and pecans. Pour the batter into the prepared pan.

Bake until a cake tester inserted in the center comes out clean, 1 hour to 1 hour 10 minutes. Remove from the oven and place the cake, in the pan, on a rack; cool for 10 minutes. After 10 minutes, invert the cake out of its pan onto the rack, and cool completely before glazing. Place the rack over a piece of wax paper or parchment paper.

TO MAKE THE GLAZE: Combine the glaze ingredients until the mixture is smooth; pour the glaze over the cake.

NUTRITION INFORMATION PER SERVING (1/20 CAKE, 85G): 12g whole grains, 309 cal, 14g fat, 4g protein, 19g complex carbohydrates, 25g sugar, 2g dietary fiber, 47mg cholesterol, 117mg sodium, 128mg potassium, 107RE vitamin A, 1mg iron, 38mg calcium, 104mg phosphorus.

SPONGE CAKES: BUILDING BLOCKS OF THE BAKER'S ART

This entire family of cakes is built on the unique ability of eggs to capture and retain air when beaten. These egg foams, as they're known in the professional world, create cakes with a fine crumb and sturdy texture, which is similar to that of a sponge; hence the name. Sponge cakes can be made with little fat, such as a classic genoise, which has only a little butter added for flavor and moistness. Jelly rolls use vegetable oil to keep the cake flexible enough to roll up. Then there's the Blitz Torte (p. 413), which takes a buttery cake base and crowns it with a drift of meringue.

Since sponge cakes rely more on eggs than flour for their structure, introducing whole grains is a matter of finding the right amount to balance and stabilize the liquid in the recipe. How much flour does the cake need to hold itself up? Is the batter moist enough to soften the whole grain's bran, so there's no gritty mouthfeel? Does the cake need to be soaked with a flavored syrup and held overnight before serving, to ensure that it's evenly moist? Hundreds of layers later, we found the answers. Come with us now and discover how amazing these cakes can be when built with whole grains.

GENOISE CAKES

Genoise, sometimes called "genoise sponge" in the bakery trade, is traditionally used as a base to build layered pastry case masterpieces that can take on all kinds of flavors. From the Toasted Almond Mocha Cake (p. 395), to the classic Black Forest Cake (p. 398) topped with whipped cream, chocolate shavings and cherries, these are the kinds of cakes to bake when you want to pull out all the stops. Genoise-based cakes have the added advantage of being excellent keepers. Since they use much less fat than butter cakes do, they're brushed with flavored simple syrup before being frosted. This step ensures moist cake layers without relying on lots of butter and is particularly effective for whole grains. The extra moisture from the syrup serves to soften the bran. The bran then disappears as an element of the cake's texture, allowing the whole grain's richer color and intriguing flavor to come through. The possibilities for cake flavor combinations are limited only by your imagination. Genoise can be filled with buttercream, pie filling, jam or preserves, lemon or raspberry curd, pastry cream or stabilized whipped cream before being frosted and decorated.

SIMPLE SYRUP: ONE STEP, MANY FLAVOR POSSIBILITIES

Simple syrup is in fact simple to make, but its inclusion in a recipe opens up a world of flavor possibilities. The most basic, can't-go-wrong simple syrup is flavored with a hint of vanilla and perhaps a note of citrus.

From there it's easy to branch out, using any number of flavors, depending on the kind of cake you want to make. Most professionals use fruit- or nut-flavored liqueurs to flavor their syrups, but strong flavors or extracts can also be used if you don't want to add any alcohol. Fruit purées are usually avoided, because their colors can make the genoise look muddy, and their textures would interfere with the liquid soaking in evenly. Some fruit juices (lemon, orange, or apple) can stand in for half the water when making the simple syrup.

Whole Wheat Genoise

YIELD: Two 9-inch or three 8-inch round layers or one 13 x 18-inch sheet cake, 16 servings
BAKING TEMPERATURE: 325°F
BAKING TIME: 25 to 27 minutes for layers, 21 to 23 minutes for a sheet cake

This recipe yields 8 cups of batter, suitable for special-occasion cakes that are big enough to feed 16 people at a time. We recommend using at least a 4½-quart mixing bowl and a stand mixer, since the eggs must be beaten for 5 to 8 minutes to achieve the proper volume. If you're baking for a crowd, you can make the recipe twice and have two 13 x 18-inch layers to stack on top of each other. This will make a full, bakery-size half-sheet cake that will yield 48 (1 x 4-inch) slices.

> ½ cup (1 stick, 4 ounces) unsalted butter
> 1¾ cups (6 ounces) whole wheat pastry flour
> ⅓ cup (1⅜ ounces) unbleached all-purpose flour
> 7 large eggs
> 3 large egg yolks
> ¼ teaspoon salt
> 1 teaspoon vanilla extract
> 1¼ cups (8¾ ounces) granulated sugar

Grease and lightly flour two 9-inch or three 8-inch round pans or a 13 x 18-inch half-sheet pan. Or, coat lightly with nonstick spray and line with parchment paper.

Melt the butter over low heat, and set it aside to cool to room temperature. Whisk together the flours in a medium bowl.

Combine the eggs, egg yolks, salt, vanilla and sugar in a large mixing bowl. Place the mixing bowl over a larger bowl half filled with hot tap water (see illustration, p. 392). Whisk the mixture until it feels just slightly warm to the touch when you test it in the center with your finger, about 3 to 5 minutes. If you want to be precise, use a thermometer—the egg mixture should be at 100°F and no warmer. Warming the eggs and dissolving the sugar this way will ensure they reach the highest possible volume when beaten.

Place the mixing bowl on your stand mixer and beat with a wire whip until the mixture is tripled in volume and a very pale yellow color. This will take 5 to 8 minutes on high speed, depending on the power of your mixer. When it's done, the egg mixture should fall off the whisk and mound for a moment before disappearing back into the bowl.

Remove the bowl from the mixer and use a whisk to gently fold in the reserved flour mixture by hand, until no streaks of flour remain. Gently fold in the melted, cooled but-

Place the mixing bowl in a larger bowl of hot water; whisk by hand until the sugar dissolves and the mixture is lukewarm to the touch.

Mark the outside of your mixing bowl with a piece of tape, grease pencil or a sticky note to show the volume of the eggs before beating.

Mark the top of the egg mixture after beating for 5 minutes. If the eggs don't get any higher after beating for 2 minutes more, they're ready for you to fold in the flour.

When the eggs and sugar are at full volume, they'll mound when they fall off the beater, before disappearing back into the batter.

ter, a little at a time, taking care not to mix more than necessary to get the butter to disappear. If you pour too much in at once, the butter will collapse the egg foam, then pool on the bottom of the mixing bowl, making it harder to distribute. The volume of the batter will decrease a bit during this process, but a light touch and quick, confident strokes from the bottom of the bowl up through the batter will see you through.

Pour the batter into the prepared pan(s). Bake until the top is light brown and springs back when lightly touched in the center, 25 to 27 minutes for layers or 21 to 23 minutes for sheet cake.

NUTRITION INFORMATION PER SERVING (1/16 OF RECIPE, UNFROSTED: 61G): 11g whole grains, 200 cal, 9g fat, 5g protein, 9g complex carbohydrates, 15g sugar, 1g dietary fiber, 149mg cholesterol, 63mg sodium, 74mg potassium, 114RE vitamin A, 1mg iron, 17mg calcium, 96mg phosphorus.

VARIATIONS: BROWN BUTTER GENOISE *Brown butter has a rich, nutty flavor that's the perfect complement to hazelnut or toasted-almond-flavored frostings. By using brown butter instead of melted butter in the genoise, you'll be creating a more intense, rather grownup flavor for the cake. Melt the butter over medium heat, cooking it until the milk solids in the butter begin to take on some color and a nutty aroma. Remove from the heat, cool to room temperature and use as directed in the recipe.*

CHOCOLATE WHOLE WHEAT GENOISE *Reduce the whole wheat pastry flour to 1½ cups. Whisk the flour with ¾ cup (2¼ ounces) unsweetened cocoa powder before folding into the beaten eggs.*

HOW TO BUILD A LAYER CAKE

The most versatile use of genoise is to bake it in large sheets so you can customize the size, shape and finish of the dessert you want to create. There are four simple steps to assembling your own bakery-style masterpieces: cut, trim and soak, freeze, frost. Follow along with us as we show you some of the techniques the pros use.

You can make traditional versions of any of the following cakes by baking the Whole Wheat Genoise, p. 391) as two round layers, then finishing them by following Steps 2 through 4.

STEP 1: CUT

RECTANGULAR OR SQUARE CAKES: First, trim off any crispy or dry edges from your sheet cake. Using scissors and a ruler, you can cut the sheet cake into 3-inch wide strips or squares of any size you like. If you've baked the cake on parchment paper, the cake will be easier to handle if you cut it into shapes before peeling off the paper. These can be stacked on top of each other to make a rectangular cake of any length you care to build, or a square cake that's small (a 2-inch personal cake), medium (two 9-inch squares from each sheet), or large (stack two full sheets on top of one another).

ROUND AND ODD-SHAPED CAKES: You can cut any size circle by using a large cutter or cake ring and pressing straight down through the cooled cake. A 6-inch-diameter cutter makes a wonderful small layer cake for two or four people. For unusual or large shapes, use an inverted baking pan as a template. You can make silhouettes or heart shapes this way.

TIP: WHAT TO DO WITH THE SCRAPS: Consider the scraps you generate from the cake-building process a bonus. They're quite useful for appeasing little hands that want a quick taste of what you're up to. The bits and pieces of leftover trim are also perfect for making a trifle; layer them with fruit and pudding for a quick, easy and colorful dessert. Or do as a professional baker does: dry them out and crunch them up for cake crumbs, which are used to create fillings for pastries by mixing them with nut pastes. They're also used to sprinkle into greased baking pans before filling with batter for a surefire way to keep cakes from sticking. Crumbs can even serve as a decoration around the base of a frosted cake.

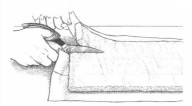

Measure and mark the attached parchment paper, then cut the cake into strips.

Press straight down into the cake with a large cutter to make a small-size cake layer.

You can make special-occasion shapes with extra-large cookie cutters too.

STEP 2: TRIM AND SOAK

For a more evenly moist layer, trim off the very top "skin" of the layers with a serrated knife. This will expose the grain of the cake and allow the syrup to penetrate more quickly and evenly. Brush the syrup (see recipes, p. 432) across the top of one layer, taking care not to saturate it; just make the top evenly moist. Turn the layer over, place it on a cake plate, peel off the parchment paper, and brush that side. Do the same with the other layer or layers.

After soaking one side, turn the layer over and place it on a plate. Peel off the parchment paper by pulling it gently, staying parallel to the cake's surface.

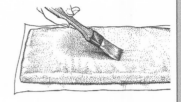

After removing the parchment paper, brush the exposed surface with more simple syrup.

STEP 3: FREEZE

After soaking and assembling the cake layers, freeze the cake for at least 1 hour. This will firm up its texture, making it much easier to frost without crumbs going everywhere and pieces of cake tearing as your spatula goes by.

STEP 4: FROST

Remove one layer at a time from the freezer. Now that the cake is firm, apply the crumb coat. Using a soft-textured frosting (if it's a quick-style buttercream (p. 435), thin some of it with milk if necessary), to cover the cake all over with a very thin layer. It's fine if the crumbs show through and things look a little messy. The purpose of this step is to provide a stable base for the finished frosting layer. Once the cake is covered, top and sides, return it to the freezer for 30 minutes so the frosting can firm up. Repeat with the other layer or layers.

A crumb coat is a very thin layer of frosting that sets the outside surface of the cake. After chilling to firm up, this coat keeps the decorative frosting layer free of crumbs.

Now your cake is ready for the finishing touches. Remove from the freezer, and apply frosting between layers. Apply frosting to the top and sides, and use a pastry bag and tips to form decorative shapes. Any garnish you choose should reflect the flavors inside the cake. Some examples are toasted almond slices for Toasted Almond–Mocha Cake (p. 395), cherries for a Black Forest Cake (p. 398), or fresh strawberries for Strawberry Shortcake Torte (p. 401).

Toasted Almond–Mocha Cake

YIELD: One 8-inch 3-layer cake or 9-inch 2-layer cake, 16 servings each, or two 4 x 8-inch rectangular layer cakes, 8 servings each

BAKING TEMPERATURE: 325°F

BAKING TIME: 25 to 27 minutes for layers, 21 to 23 minutes for a 13 x 18-inch sheet cake

These two flavors complement each other beautifully, while helping to show whole wheat pastry flour to its best advantage. The smaller amount of espresso powder listed in the ingredients yields a frosting that puts the almond taste a little more out front, with the coffee as the supporting cast. If you want the mocha flavor to be a little more prominent, use the larger amount of espresso powder.

If you want to weave some chocolate into this tapestry of flavors, use Easy Chocolate Frosting (p. 436) to fill this cake and as an accent frosting when you decorate the top.

Whole Wheat Genoise
½ cup (1 stick, 4 ounces) unsalted butter
1¾ cups (6 ounces) whole wheat pastry flour
⅓ cup (1⅜ ounces) unbleached all-purpose flour
7 large eggs
3 large (1½ ounces) egg yolks
¼ teaspoon salt
1 teaspoon vanilla extract
1¼ cups (8¾ ounces) granulated sugar

Frangelico simple syrup
½ cup (4 ounces) water
⅓ cup (2⅜ ounces) granulated sugar
½ cup (4 ounces) Frangelico liqueur or hazelnut syrup

Mocha buttercream
⅓ cup (2⅝ ounces) butter
⅓ cup (2⅜ ounces) vegetable shortening
¼ teaspoon salt
4 to 5 cups (1 to 1¼ pounds) glazing or confectioners' sugar
1 teaspoon vanilla extract
½ teaspoon almond extract
1½ to 2½ teaspoons espresso powder or 1 to 2 tablespoons instant coffee crystals
¼ to ⅓ cup (2 to 2⅝ ounces) milk or cream

Garnish
½ to ¾ cup (1½ to 2¼ ounces) sliced almonds, toasted
Chocolate shavings

Preheat the oven to 325°F. Grease and lightly flour the pan or pans of your choice, or coat lightly with nonstick spray and line with parchment paper.

TO MAKE THE CAKE: Melt the butter over low heat, and set it aside to cool to room temperature. Whisk together the flours in a medium bowl; set aside.

Combine the eggs, egg yolks, salt, vanilla and sugar in a large mixing bowl. Place the mixing bowl over a larger bowl half filled with hot tap water (see illustrations, p. 392). Whisk the mixture until it feels just slightly warm to the touch when you test it in the center with your finger, 3 to 5 minutes. If you want to be precise, use a thermometer— the egg mixture should be at 100°F and no warmer. Warming the eggs and dissolving the sugar this way will ensure they reach the highest possible volume when beaten.

Place the mixing bowl on your stand mixer and beat with a wire whip until the mixture is tripled in volume and a very pale yellow color. This will take 5 to 8 minutes on high speed, depending on the power of your mixer. When it's done, the egg mixture should fall off the whisk and mound for a moment before disappearing back into the bowl.

Remove the bowl from the mixer and use a whisk to gently fold in the reserved flour by hand, until no streaks of flour remain. Gently fold in the melted, cooled butter, a little at a time, taking care not to mix more than necessary to get the butter to disappear. If you pour too much in at once, the butter will collapse the egg foam, then pool on the bottom of the mixing bowl, making it harder to distribute. The volume of the batter will decrease a bit during this process, but a light touch and quick, confident strokes from the bottom of the bowl up through the batter will see you through.

Pour the batter into the prepared pan(s). Bake until the top is light brown and springs back when lightly touched in the center, 25 to 27 minutes for layers, 21 to 23 minutes for sheet cake. Remove the cake from the oven and place on a rack to cool completely before assembling.

TO MAKE THE FRANGELICO SIMPLE SYRUP: Bring the water and sugar to a simmer in a small saucepan over medium heat, stirring until the sugar dissolves. Remove from the heat and stir in the liqueur (or hazelnut syrup). Set aside to cool to room temperature.

TO MAKE THE FROSTING: Beat together the butter, shortening and salt in a large mixing bowl with an electric mixer till fluffy. Add about half the sugar, and stir slowly until well blended. Mix in the vanilla and almond extracts. Dissolve the espresso powder (or instant coffee) in ¼ cup of the milk, add to the frosting and beat until fluffy. Continue mixing in the sugar, beating until the frosting is light and fluffy. Add milk as needed, a tablespoon at a time, to achieve the desired spreading consistency.

TO ASSEMBLE THE CAKE: If you've baked a sheet cake, trim the edges, then cut the cooled cake in half across the middle, and in thirds lengthwise to create six 4 x 8-inch strips. Or cut into smaller shapes, as shown on page 393. If you're using 8- or 9-inch layers, remove them from their pans.

Brush the tops of the layers with the Frangelico simple syrup (each layer will need ½ cup of syrup, ¼ cup each for top and bottom). Choose one layer to be the bottom of the cake, and place it, soaked side down, on a serving plate whose edges are covered with wax paper or parchment paper to keep it clean. Soak the other side of the layer with another ¼ cup of syrup, and place it in the freezer for 30 to 45 minutes. After the layer has firmed up in the freezer, spread ⅔ cup of mocha frosting (or Easy Chocolate Frosting, p. 436) over it. Place the next layer, soaked side down, on top of the filling. Brush the top of this layer with syrup, and return the cake to the freezer once more for 30 to 45 minutes, until firm to the touch. If your cake is to have 3 layers, use another ⅔ cup of frosting on the top, place the last layer over the filling, soaked side down, and brush the top with another ¼ cup of syrup. If you're building a 2-layer cake, place the second layer on top of the filling, soaked side down, brush the top with simple syrup, and freeze the cake for another 30 minutes.

FROSTING THE CAKE: Apply a thin layer of mocha frosting to the top and sides of the chilled cake. (See illustration for crumb coat, p. 394.) Return the cake to the refrigerator for 20 minutes to allow the crumb coat to firm up. Once you can touch the crumb coat with your finger without having any frosting stick to it, take it out of the refrigerator and cover the top and sides with more frosting. Decorate the top of the cake with piped frosting, if desired, and garnish with toasted almond slices and chocolate shavings.

NUTRITION INFORMATION PER SERVING (1/16 FROSTED CAKE, 89G): 11g whole grains, 314 cal, 13g fat, 5g protein, 9g complex carbohydrates, 34g sugar, 1g dietary fiber, 155mg cholesterol, 81mg sodium, 80mg potassium, 134RE vitamin A, 1mg iron, 19mg calcium, 98mg phosphorus, 4mg caffeine.

TO HYDROGENATE, OR NOT TO HYDROGENATE

You'll notice that the mocha buttercream recipe for this cake calls for vegetable shortening, something we've avoided wherever possible in this book, because it contains trans fats. If you've taken all trans fats out of your diet, this and any other frosting can be made with all butter, but it won't have the same spreading or shaping characteristics.

When you hold a pastry bag, the heat of your hands will affect the frosting's texture. All-butter frostings will get softer, faster, and decorations made from it may literally melt when a cake is held at room temperature for any length of time, as is often the case at a wedding or on a brunch or buffet table.

Vegetable shortening has a higher melting point than butter, which makes it more stable when it's used in frosting, especially frosting that's piped into shapes.

For that reason, it's included in this recipe. If you choose to use butter instead of shortening, after decorating the cake, keep it in the refrigerator until an hour before you plan to serve it, when it should be placed in a cool room to await slicing.

Black Forest Cake

YIELD: One 8-inch 3-layer cake or 9-inch 2-layer cake, two 6-inch round 3-layer cakes or two 4 x 8-inch rectangular layer cakes, 8 servings each

BAKING TEMPERATURE: 325°F

BAKING TIME: 25 to 27 minutes for layers, 21 to 23 minutes for 13 x 18-inch sheet cake

This cake is a powerful magnet for lovers of the chocolate and cherry flavor combination. The cheery cherries and chocolate curls sitting on top signal the flavor delights beneath. Whole wheat pastry flour blends with unsweetened cocoa to create a rich, tender cake layer that's infused with cherry flavor and filled with the bright snappy flavor of cherry pie filling. The whole thing is dressed in whipped cream with more chocolate and cherries on top; you can see a picture of it on page 400.

Chocolate Whole Wheat Genoise
½ cup (1 stick, 4 ounces) unsalted butter

1½ cups (5 ounces) whole wheat pastry flour

¾ cup (2¼ ounces) unsweetened cocoa, natural or Dutch-process, strained

2 tablespoons (1 ounce) unbleached all-purpose flour

7 large eggs

3 large (1½ ounces) egg yolks

¼ teaspoon salt

1 teaspoon vanilla extract

1¼ cups (8¾ ounces) granulated sugar

Kirsch simple syrup & cherry filling
½ cup (4 ounces) water

⅓ cup (2⅜ ounces) granulated sugar

½ cup (4 ounces) Kirschwasser cherry brandy or ¼ teaspoon strong cherry flavoring

1 to 2 (12-ounce) cans cherry pie filling, depending on size of cake

Stabilized whipped cream
2 tablespoons (1 ounce) cold water

1½ teaspoons unflavored gelatin

2 cups (1 pint, 16 ounces) heavy cream

1 teaspoon vanilla extract

¾ cup (3 ounces) confectioners' sugar

Garnish
16 maraschino or canned cherries, well drained

Chocolate curls or shavings

Preheat the oven to 325°F. Grease and lightly flour the pan or pans of your choice, or coat lightly with nonstick spray and line with parchment paper.

TO MAKE THE CAKE: Melt the butter over low heat, and set it aside to cool to room temperature. Whisk together the whole wheat pastry flour, cocoa and all-purpose flour in a medium bowl; set aside.

Combine the eggs, egg yolks, salt, vanilla and sugar in a large bowl. Place the mixing bowl over a larger bowl half filled with hot tap water (see illustrations, p. 392). Whisk the mixture until it feels just slightly warm to the touch when you test it in the center with your finger (3 to 5 minutes). If you want to be precise, use a thermometer—the egg mixture should be at 100°F and no warmer. Warming the eggs and dissolving the sugar this way will ensure they reach the highest possible volume when beaten.

Place the mixing bowl on your stand mixer and beat with a wire whip until the mixture is tripled in volume and a very pale yellow color. (See illustrations, p. 392.) This will take 5 to 8 minutes on high speed, depending on the power of your mixer. When it's done, the egg mixture should fall off the whisk and mound for a moment before disappearing back into the bowl.

Remove the bowl from the mixer and use a whisk to gently fold in the reserved flour-cocoa mixture by hand, until no streaks of flour remain. Gently fold in the melted, cooled butter, a little at a time, taking care not to mix more than necessary to get the butter to disappear. If you pour too much in at once, the butter will collapse the egg foam, then pool on the bottom of the mixing bowl, making it harder to distribute. The volume of the batter will decrease a bit during this process, but a light touch and quick, confident strokes from the bottom of the bowl up through the batter will see you through.

Pour the batter into the prepared pan(s). Bake until the chocolate is fragrant, and the top springs back when lightly touched in the center, 25 to 27 minutes for layers, 21 to 23 minutes for sheet cake. Remove the cake from the oven and place on a rack to cool completely before assembling the cake. While the cake is cooling, make the simple syrup and whipped cream.

TO MAKE THE SYRUP: Bring the water and sugar to a simmer in a small saucepan over medium heat, stirring until the sugar dissolves. Remove from the heat and stir in the Kirschwasser (or flavoring). Set aside to cool to room temperature. Reserve the cherry pie filling for assembling.

TO MAKE THE WHIPPED CREAM: Place the water in a small heatproof bowl. Sprinkle the gelatin over the water, and let it sit for 5 minutes to absorb the water. Melt the gelatin over simmering water or at low power in the microwave for a very short time (10 to 15 seconds). Let the gelatin cool to room temperature.

Whip the heavy cream with the vanilla in a large mixing bowl until it begins to thicken and the whisk begins to leave tracks as it moves through the cream. With the mixer running on medium speed, pour in the melted gelatin. Once the gelatin is incorporated, stop the mixer and add the confectioners' sugar. Resume beating the cream until it forms medium peaks.

TO ASSEMBLE THE CAKE: If you've baked a sheet cake, cut the cooled cake into six 4 x 8-inch strips or six 6-inch rounds, as desired. If you're using 8- or 9-inch layers, remove them from their pans. Brush the tops of the layers with simple syrup (each layer will need ½ cup of syrup, ¼ cup each for top and bottom). Choose one layer to be the bottom of the cake, and place it, soaked-side down, on a serving plate whose edges are covered with wax paper or parchment paper to keep it clean. Soak the other side of the layer with another ¼ cup of syrup, and place it in the freezer for 30 to 45 minutes. After the layer has firmed up in the freezer, spread ⅔ cup pie filling over it. Place the next layer, soaked side down, on top of the filling. Brush the top of this layer with syrup, and return the cake to the freezer once more for 30 to 45 minutes, until firm to the touch. If your cake is to have 3 layers, use another ⅔ cup of filling on the top, place the last layer over the filling, soaked side down, and brush the top with another ¼ cup of syrup. If you're building a 2-layer cake, place the second layer on top of the filling, soaked side down, brush the top with simple syrup, and freeze the cake for another 30 minutes.

THE SIMPLEST DECORATION

You don't have to be a wizard with an offset spatula to make a beautiful cake. Any cake that includes chocolate can look incredibly elegant with the simple use of a vegetable peeler and a chocolate bar. Take a good-size chunk of chocolate (preferably from a block at least ¾-inch thick; if not, two jumbo candy bars held back to back will do), wrap an end in plastic wrap, so the heat of your hand doesn't melt the chocolate as you hold it, and use your vegetable peeler to take curls of chocolate off the bar. It's best to work over a bowl to catch the shavings as they're created. After your cake is covered with frosting, use a spoon to pile the shavings on top. Voilà, instant masterpiece!

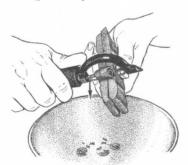

Grasp the chocolate firmly and peel away from you to make shavings.

Use a spoon to place the shavings, so your hands don't melt or break the pieces.

TO FROST THE CAKE: Cover the top and sides with Stabilized Whipped Cream. Pipe rosettes of whipped cream around the top edge of the cake. Place a cherry on top of each rosette, and fill the area in between with chocolate shavings. (See sidebar on previous page.)

NUTRITION INFORMATION PER SERVING (1/16 CAKE, 144G): 9 whole grains, 383 cal, 21g fat, 7g protein, 15g complex carbohydrates, 27g sugar, 3g dietary fiber, 190mg cholesterol, 91mg sodium, 185mg potassium, 240RE vitamin A, 2mg iron, 43mg calcium, 146mg phosphorus, 11mg caffeine.

Strawberry Shortcake Torte

YIELD: One 8-inch 3-layer cake or 9-inch 2-layer cake, 16 servings, or two 6-inch round 3-layer cakes or two 4 x 8-inch rectangular layer cakes, 8 servings each

BAKING TEMPERATURE: 325°F

BAKING TIME: 25 to 27 minutes for layers, 21 to 23 minutes for a 13 x 18-inch sheet cake

This cake is the uptown version of the well-loved backyard and picnic classic. It stands proudly on display, dressed up in its piped whipped cream rosettes, fresh berries sparkling on top. Tender, citrus-infused whole wheat cake layers cradle more berries, layered with vanilla-scented whipped cream.

Whole Wheat Genoise
½ cup (1 stick, 4 ounces) unsalted butter
1¾ cups (6 ounces) whole wheat pastry flour
⅓ cup (1⅜ ounces) unbleached all-purpose flour
7 large eggs
3 large (1½ ounces) egg yolks
¼ teaspoon salt
1 teaspoon vanilla extract
1¼ cups (8¾ ounces) granulated sugar

Filling and garnish
3 pints (2 pounds) fresh strawberries, hulled and sliced

Citrus simple syrup
1 cup (7 ounces) sugar
¾ cup (6 ounces) water
¼ cup (2 ounces) lemon or orange juice
1 tablespoon grated lemon or orange zest

Stabilized whipped cream
2 tablespoons (1 ounce) cold water
1½ teaspoons unflavored gelatin
2 cups (1 pint, 16 ounces) heavy cream
1 teaspoon vanilla extract
½ cup (3 ounces) confectioners' sugar

Preheat the oven to 325°F. Grease and lightly flour the pan or pans of your choice. Or coat lightly with nonstick spray and line with parchment paper.

TO MAKE THE CAKE: Melt the butter over low heat, and set it aside to cool to room temperature. Whisk together the flours in a medium bowl; set aside.

Combine the eggs, egg yolks, salt, vanilla and sugar in a large mixing bowl. Place the mixing bowl over a larger bowl half filled with hot tap water (see illustration, p. 392). Whisk the mixture until it feels just slightly warm to the touch when you test it in the center with your finger, 3 to 5 minutes. If you want to be precise, use a thermometer—the egg mixture should be at 100°F and no warmer. Warming the eggs and dissolving the sugar this way will ensure they reach the highest possible volume when beaten.

Place the mixing bowl on your stand mixer and beat with a wire whip until the mixture is tripled in volume and a very pale yellow color. This will take 5 to 8 minutes on high speed, depending on the power of your mixer. When it's done, the egg mixture should fall off the whisk and mound for a moment before disappearing back into the bowl.

Remove the bowl from the mixer and use a whisk to gently fold in the reserved flour by hand, until no streaks of flour remain. Gently fold in the melted, cooled butter, a little at a time, taking care not to mix more than necessary to get the butter to disappear. If you pour too much in at once, the butter will collapse the egg foam, then pool on the bottom of the mixing bowl, making it harder to distribute. The volume of the batter will decrease a bit during this process, but a light touch and quick, confident strokes from the bottom of the bowl up through the batter will see you through.

Pour the batter into the prepared pan(s). Bake until the top is light brown and springs back when lightly touched in the center, 25 to 27 minutes for layers, 21 to 23 minutes for sheet cake. Remove the cake from the oven and place on a rack to cool completely before assembling.

TO MAKE THE SIMPLE SYRUP: Combine the sugar, water, juice and zest in a small saucepan; bring the mixture to a boil, stirring until the sugar dissolves. Remove from the heat and cool to room temperature.

TO MAKE THE WHIPPED CREAM: Place the water in a small heatproof bowl. Sprinkle the gelatin over the water, and let it sit for 5 minutes to absorb the water. Melt the gelatin over simmering water or at low power in the microwave for a very short time (10 to 15 seconds). Let the gelatin cool to room temperature.

Whip the heavy cream with the vanilla in a large mixing bowl until it begins to thicken and the whisk begins to leave tracks as it moves through the cream. With the mixer running on medium speed, pour in the melted gelatin. Once the gelatin is incorporated, stop the mixer and add the confectioners' sugar. Resume beating the cream until it forms medium peaks.

TO ASSEMBLE THE CAKE: If you've baked a sheet cake, cut the cooled cake into six 4 x 8-inch strips or six 6-inch rounds, as desired. If you're using 8- or 9-inch layers, remove them from their pans. Brush the tops of the layers with simple syrup (each layer will need ½ cup of syrup, ¼ cup each for top and bottom). Choose one layer to be the bottom of the cake, and place it, soaked-side down, on a serving plate whose edges are covered with wax paper or parchment paper to keep it clean. Soak the other side of the layer with another ¼ cup of syrup, and place a layer of strawberry slices on top. Spread ⅔ cup of stabilized whipped cream over the berries. Place the next layer, soaked-side down, on top of the filling. Brush the top of this layer with syrup. If your cake is to have 3 layers, place another layer of sliced strawberries on the cake and cover with another ⅔ cup whipped cream. Place the last layer over the filling, soaked-side down, and brush the top with another ¼ cup of syrup. If you're building a 2-layer cake, place the second layer on top of the filling, soaked-side down, brush the top with simple syrup and refrigerate the cake for another 30 minutes.

After the cake has chilled for 30 minutes, cover the top and sides with the remaining whipped cream. Pipe some rosettes for the berries to sit in, and place a garnish strawberry in the middle of each. Any extra strawberry slices can be placed around the cake's sides, where it meets the plate.

NUTRITION INFORMATION PER SERVING (1/16 2-LAYER CAKE, 140G): 11g whole grains, 344 cal, 20g fat, 6g protein, 13g complex carbohydrates, 22g sugar, 2g dietary fiber, 190mg cholesterol, 75mg sodium, 159mg potassium, 241RE vitamin A, 21mg vitamin C, 1mg iron, 42mg calcium, 122mg phosphorus.

Daffodil Cake

YIELD: One 8-inch 3-layer cake or 9-inch 2-layer cake, 16 servings each; two 6-inch round 3-layer cakes or two 4 x 8-inch rectangular layer cakes, 8 servings each

BAKING TEMPERATURE: 325°F

BAKING TIME: 25 to 27 minutes for layers, 21 to 23 minutes for a sheet cake

This cake will transport you back to those golden, lemon-filled, personalized creations that Mom used to pick up for your birthday at the local bakery.

Whole Wheat Genoise
½ cup (1 stick, 4 ounces) unsalted butter

1¾ cups (6 ounces) whole wheat pastry flour

⅓ cup (1⅜ ounces) unbleached all-purpose flour

7 large eggs

3 large (1½ ounces) egg yolks

¼ teaspoon salt

1 teaspoon vanilla extract

1¼ cups (8¾ ounces) granulated sugar

Lemon cake filling
1 teaspoon unflavored gelatin

2 tablespoons (1 ounce) cold water

4 large (2 ounces) egg yolks

½ cup (4 ounces) fresh lemon juice

Zest of 3 lemons

⅛ teaspoon salt

1½ cups (10½ ounces) sugar

6 tablespoons (¾ stick, 3 ounces) unsalted butter

Citrus simple syrup
1 cup (7 ounces) sugar

¾ cup (6 ounces) water

¼ cup (2 ounces) fresh orange or lemon juice

1 tablespoon grated orange or lemon zest (optional)

1 recipe Stabilized Whipped Cream, page 433, or buttercream, page 430

Garnish
Candied lemon slices or tinted frosting of your choice

Preheat the oven to 325°F. Lightly grease the pan or pans of your choice, or line with parchment paper.

TO MAKE THE CAKE: Melt the butter over low heat, and set it aside to cool to room temperature. Whisk together the flours in a medium bowl; set aside.

Combine the eggs, egg yolks, salt, vanilla and sugar in a large mixing bowl. Place the mixing bowl over a larger bowl half filled with hot tap water (see illustration, p. 392). Whisk the mixture until it feels just slightly warm to the touch when you test it in the center with your finger, 3 to 5 minutes. If you want to be precise, use a thermometer— the egg mixture should be at 100°F and no warmer. Warming the eggs and dissolving the sugar this way will ensure they reach the highest possible volume when beaten. Place the mixing bowl on your stand mixer and beat with a wire whip until the mixture is tripled in volume, and a very pale yellow color. This will take 5 to 8 minutes on high speed, depending on the power of your mixer. When it's done, the egg mixture should fall off the whisk and mound for a moment before disappearing back into the bowl.

Remove the bowl from the mixer and use a whisk to gently fold in the reserved flour by hand, until no streaks of flour remain. Gently fold in the melted, cooled butter, a little at a time, taking care not to mix more than necessary to get the butter to disappear. If you pour too much in at once, the butter will collapse the egg foam, then pool on the bottom of the mixing bowl, making it harder to distribute. The volume of the batter will decrease a bit during this process, but a light touch and quick, confident strokes from the bottom of the bowl up through the batter will see you through.

Pour the batter into the prepared pan(s). Bake until the top is light brown and springs back when lightly touched in the center, 25 to 27 minutes for layers, 21 to 23 minutes for sheet cake. Remove the cake from the oven and place on a rack to cool completely before assembling.

TO MAKE THE LEMON FILLING: Sprinkle the gelatin over the cold water; set it aside to let the gelatin soften. Stir all the remaining ingredients together in the top of a double boiler over simmering water. Whisk or stir constantly, taking care that nothing sticks to the bottom. The sugar will dissolve, then after 10 minutes the mixture will begin to thicken. Cook until the mixture coats the back of a spoon, about 15 minutes in all. Remove from the heat and stir in the softened gelatin until it melts. Cover the filling with plastic wrap, and refrigerate until completely cool and set, 3 to 4 hours.

TO MAKE THE SIMPLE SYRUP: Combine the sugar, water, juice and zest in a small saucepan, bring the mixture to a boil, stirring until the sugar dissolves. Remove from the heat and cool to room temperature.

TO ASSEMBLE: If you've baked a sheet cake, cut the cooled cake into six 4 x 8-inch strips or six 6-inch rounds, as desired. If you're using 8- or 9-inch layers, remove them from their pans. Soak the layers with ¼ cup simple syrup each. Fill the cake with the cooled lemon filling, dividing it evenly among the bottom layers. Frost as described on page 394 with Stabilized Whipped Cream or Buttercream. To decorate, pipe greetings on top with tinted frosting, if applicable, and place candied lemon slices around the bottom and top edges of the cake.

NUTRITION INFORMATION PER SERVING (1/16 OF 2-LAYER CAKE WITH WHIPPED CREAM, 142 G): 11g whole grains, 460 cal, 26g fat, 7g protein, 11g complex carbohydrates, 40g sugar, 2g dietary fiber, 257mg cholesterol, 78mg sodium, 114mg potassium, 308RE vitamin A, 308mg vitamin C, 1mg iron, 46mg calcium, **84**mg phosphorus.

Fresh Berry Tiramisù

YIELD: One 9-inch square cake, 16 servings
BAKING TEMPERATURE: 350°F
BAKING TIME: 20 minutes

No other dessert combines such apparent opposites—light-textured sponge cake, the rich creaminess of mascarpone cheese—as tiramisù. Literally translated as "pick me up", the traditional flavors for this dessert are coffee and chocolate. For a summer alternative, we recommend this version, which uses a touch of citrus for zing and plenty of cheerful fresh berries. The whole grain sponge cake stands in for traditional ladyfingers, while supporting the layers of fruit and cheese.

Cake
4 tablespoons (½ stick, 2 ounces) unsalted butter
1¼ cups (3⅜ ounces) whole wheat pastry flour
1 teaspoon baking powder
½ teaspoon salt
6 large eggs
1 cup (7 ounces) sugar
½ teaspoon almond extract

Simple Syrup
½ cup (3½ ounces) sugar
½ cup (4 ounces) water
2 tablespoons (1 ounce) Grand Marnier or orange juice
¼ cup (2 ounces) fresh lemon juice
Zest of 1 lemon, peeled in strips with a peeler
2 whole cloves

406   KING ARTHUR FLOUR WHOLE GRAIN BAKING

Filling
2 cups (1 pound) mascarpone cheese
2 tablespoons grated orange zest
¾ cup (6 ounces) heavy cream
½ cup (2 ounces) confectioners' sugar
2 quarts berries: raspberries, blueberries, strawberries or any combination you like

Preheat the oven to 350°F. Line a 10 x 15-inch jelly-roll pan with parchment paper.

TO MAKE THE CAKE: Melt the butter in a heatproof bowl over simmering water or at low power in the microwave for a brief time. Set aside. Whisk together the flour, baking powder and salt in a medium bowl, set aside. Combine the eggs, sugar and almond extract in a large mixing bowl. Beat with an electric mixer on high speed until thick and lemon colored, about 5 minutes. Sprinkle one third of the dry ingredients over the egg mixture, and fold them in with a whisk, taking care not to deflate the batter. Repeat twice more with the remaining dry ingredients, then fold in the melted butter. Pour the batter into the prepared pan, leveling the top with an offset spatula. Bake the cake until the top springs back when lightly touched with a finger, 20 minutes. Remove the cake from the oven and run a knife around the edge of the pan while still warm. Place the cake on a rack to cool completely before taking it out of the pan.

TO MAKE THE SYRUP: Combine all the syrup ingredients and bring the mixture to a simmer, stirring occasionally until the sugar dissolves. Once the mixture is clear, remove the syrup from the heat and allow it to cool to room temperature.

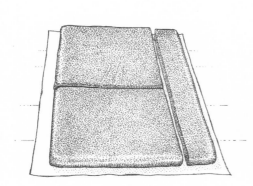

After cutting a 2-inch strip from the layer's long edge, cut the remaining cake into one 8-inch square to fit into the bottom of the pan. The remaining piece will be 7 x 8-inches, and form most of the top.

Use the remaining square of sponge cake and the trim pieces to cover the cake's first layer of berries.

TO MAKE THE FILLING: Place the mascarpone in a mixing bowl and stir the orange zest into it. Add the whipping cream a third at a time, stirring between additions until the mixture is smooth. Mix gently, just until the cream is incorporated, or the mascarpone will become grainy. Stir in the confectioners' sugar.

TO ASSEMBLE THE CAKE: Flip the cooled cake out of its baking pan onto a piece of parchment paper. Peel the parchment paper off the back, pulling the paper straight back and keeping it parallel to the surface of the cake; this will discourage any bits of cake from coming off with the paper (see illustration, p. 394).

Trim a 2-inch strip off the length of the cake. Cut an 8-inch square from the rectangle that's left.

Lightly grease a 9-inch-square pan. Place the 8-inch square of cake in the bottom of the pan. Using a pastry brush, generously soak the cake with ½ cup of the simple syrup. You'll need to dab the syrup on, let it soak in for a few minutes, then repeat the process. After the cake has been soaked, place a single layer of berries over it. Spread half the mascarpone filling over the berries, then place the remaining cake square on top, cutting and using the trim pieces to cover the first layer.

Soak this layer of cake with syrup as you did the first. Spread the remaining filling over the top cake layer, then place the rest of the berries in an attractive design on the top. Refrigerate the tiramisù for at least 1 hour before serving.

NUTRITION INFORMATION PER SERVING (1/16 TIRAMISÙ, 134G): 8g whole grains, 302 cal, 18g fat, 6g protein, 10g complex carbohydrates, 22g sugar, 2g dietary fiber, 131mg cholesterol, 183mg sodium, 162mg potassium, 220RE vitamin A, 25mg vitamin C, 1mg iron, 67mg calcium, 128mg phosphorus.

Peach Melba Jelly Roll

YIELD: One 10-inch jelly roll, 9 servings
BAKING TEMPERATURE: 400°F
BAKING TIME: 12 to 14 minutes

Auguste Escoffier created the combination of peaches and raspberries for dessert in honor of an Australian opera singer named Nellie Melba in the early 1890s. We're sure if Nellie were to have a bite of this cake, she'd be singing its praises too.

The buttermilk and oil in the recipe create a tender cake that won't crack when it's rolled up. For a quicker, more traditional dessert, use only the raspberry jam inside before powdering the top with confectioners' sugar.

Vanilla jelly roll
1 cup (3³⁄₈ ounces) whole wheat pastry flour
1¼ teaspoons baking powder
½ teaspoon salt
4 large eggs
¾ cup (5¼ ounces) sugar
1 teaspoon vanilla extract
¼ cup (1¾ ounces) vegetable oil
¼ cup (2 ounces) buttermilk

Filling
2 tablespoons (1 ounce) cold water
1½ teaspoons unflavored gelatin
1 cup (6 ounces) peeled, diced peaches, thawed if frozen
1 tablespoon fresh lemon juice
½ cup (3½ ounces) sugar
¾ cup (6 ounces) heavy cream
¼ cup (1 ounce) confectioners' sugar
½ cup (6 ounces) seedless raspberry jam
Confectioners' sugar for garnish
Fresh raspberries for garnish (optional)

Preheat your oven to 400°F. Line the bottom of a 10 x 15-inch jelly roll pan with wax paper or parchment paper. Place a linen towel on a flat work surface, and dust generously with confectioners' sugar.

TO MAKE THE CAKE: Whisk together the flour, baking powder and salt in a small bowl. Set aside.

Beat the eggs in a large bowl until light and lemon colored. Sprinkle in the sugar gradually, beating all the while, and continue beating until the batter is very thick and lemon colored. This will take from 3 to 8 minutes, depending on how powerful your mixer is. Just before you finish beating the eggs, add the vanilla.

Gently fold in the reserved flour mixture, using a rubber spatula or whisk. When the flour is almost but not quite uniformly distributed, whisk together the oil and buttermilk and fold them into the mixture. Spread the batter evenly into the prepared pan.

Use the towel to gently roll up the warm cake. Place the wrapped cake on a rack to allow it to cool completely.

Bake the cake until it's golden brown and springy to the touch, 12 to 14 minutes. Remove the cake from the oven, and invert it onto the prepared towel. Peel off the paper, (see illustration, p. 394) and, using scissors or a serrated knife, trim the crusty edges of the cake, if necessary. Use the towel to roll the warm cake up, from one short side of the rectangle to the other. Allow the cake to cool completely.

TO MAKE THE FILLING: Place the water in a small bowl. Sprinkle the gelatin over it, and set it aside to soften. Purée the peach slices in a blender or food processor with the lemon juice. Place the purée in a small saucepan, add the sugar, and heat to a simmer, stirring occasionally, until the sugar melts. Remove the pan from the heat, and stir in the softened gelatin until it melts. Transfer the mixture to a medium bowl, and set aside to cool to room temperature.

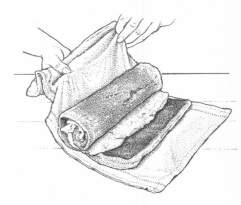

The jam on the outer inches of the cake helps the cake stay neatly rolled up.

Whip the cream with the confectioners' sugar until it forms medium peaks. Fold the cream into the cooled peach purée, then cover and refrigerate until the mixture sets, about an hour.

TO ASSEMBLE THE CAKE: Unroll the cooled cake, and spread the inside with raspberry jam. Starting at the tightest end of the cake's curl, spread the peach filling over the jam, making it ¾ inch thick. Leave the last 4 inches of the cake without peach filling, as shown. This will keep the filling from oozing out when you roll the cake back up. Gently reroll the cake and place it, seam side down, on a serving plate. Dust the top with confectioners' sugar before serving, and garnish with fresh raspberries, if desired.

NUTRITION INFORMATION PER SERVING (1/9 CAKE, 136G): 11g whole grains, 372 cal, 16g fat, 6g protein, 12g complex carbohydrates, 40g sugar, 2g dietary fiber, 122mg cholesterol, 212mg sodium, 148mg potassium, 137RE vitamin A, 2mg vitamin C, 1mg iron, 80mg calcium, 163mg phosphorus.

VARIATION: CHOCOLATE JELLY ROLL *Reduce the whole wheat pastry flour to ¾ cup (2½ ounces), and combine it with ½ cup (1½ ounces) unsweetened cocoa powder before folding it into the batter. Fill with 1½ cups Stabilized Whipped Cream, page 433, and drizzle with Chocolate Glaze, page 413.*

Citrus Surprise Cake

YIELD: One 9-inch round 2-layer cake, 16 servings
BAKING TEMPERATURE: 350°F
BAKING TIME: 20 to 25 minutes

The surprise in this cake is the grapefruit, whose sparkling flavor gives a head-turning zing. This cake got wows, A-pluses and lots of happy exclamation points from our tasters. It's made with the classic chiffon technique, using oil instead of butter. Its light texture comes from folding whipped egg whites into the batter. We've found the combination of whole grain flours and citrus to be a very happy marriage; they bring out the best in each other's flavors.

Cake
2 cups (8 ounces) white whole wheat flour
2 teaspoons baking powder
½ teaspoon salt
5 large (2½ ounces) egg yolks
½ cup (3½ ounces) vegetable oil
1½ cups (10½ ounces) granulated sugar
⅓ cup (2⅝ ounces) water
¼ cup (2 ounces) fresh grapefruit juice
1 tablespoon freshly grated grapefruit zest
5 large (6¼ ounces) egg whites
¼ teaspoon cream of tartar

Cream cheese grapefruit frosting
2 packages (16 ounces) cream cheese, softened
3 cups (12 ounces) sifted confectioners' sugar
2 teaspoons freshly grated grapefruit zest
1 teaspoon freshly grated lemon zest
1 tablespoon fresh grapefruit juice
1 teaspoon fresh lemon juice

1 grapefruit for garnish

Preheat oven to 350°F. Lightly grease two 9-inch cake pans, line with parchment or wax paper, then grease the paper.

TO MAKE THE CAKE: Whisk together the flour, baking powder and salt in a medium bowl; set aside. Combine the egg yolks and oil in a large mixing bowl and mix at low speed while you pour in the sugar. Add the water and grapefruit juice. Beat for 3 minutes on medium speed, then stop to scrape the sides and bottom of the bowl. Mix in the grapefruit zest. Gently fold in the flour mixture, using a rubber spatula or whisk.

In a separate bowl with clean beaters, beat the egg whites until foamy. (Any grease left on the beaters will keep the eggs from whipping to their proper volume, no matter how long you beat them.) Add the cream of tartar, and continue beating until soft peaks form. Carefully fold the beaten egg whites into the cake batter. Divide the batter evenly between the pans. Bake until the top of the cake pulls away from the edge of the pan, and a toothpick inserted in the center comes out clean, 20 to 25 minutes

Remove from the oven, and run a dull knife around the edge of the cake to free the edges (this will allow the cake to contract evenly as it cools, making it easier to frost later). Cool the cake in the pans for 10 minutes. After 10 minutes, remove the layers from their pans, and peel off the parchment paper. Cool completely on wire racks, then refrigerate or freeze before frosting.

Follow the round edge of the fruit with your knife as you cut, moving from top to bottom. Turn the fruit slightly and repeat the process, until you've removed the skin and white pith all the way around.

TO MAKE THE FROSTING: Blend together the cream cheese and confectioners' sugar in a large bowl until smooth. Add the grated zests and juices; beat until smooth.

TO MAKE THE GARNISH: Peel the grapefruit by cutting off the top and bottom to expose the inside. Use your knife to cut under the skin in overlapping strokes as you turn the fruit on its axis (see illustration, above).

Cut the peeled fruit in half from top to bottom. Place cut sides down, then cut into thin halfmoon slices. Place in a strainer or colander to drain.

TO ASSEMBLE THE CAKE: Line the outside edges of a serving plate with wax paper or parchment paper to keep it clean. Place one cake layer on the plate; spread with about ⅔ cup of the frosting. Top with the second cake layer. Frost the top and sides of the cake with the remaining frosting, and garnish the sides and top with the grapefruit slices.

NUTRITION INFORMATION PER SERVING (1/16 FROSTED CAKE, 114G): 15g whole grains, 378 cal, 19g fat, 6g protein, 13g complex carbohydrates, 37g sugar, 2g dietary fiber, 98mg cholesterol, 217mg sodium, 131mg potassium, 154RE vitamin A, 3mg vitamin C, 1mg iron, 80mg calcium, 168mg phosphorus.

Caramel Blitz Torte

YIELD: One 8- or 9-inch layer cake, 16 servings
BAKING TEMPERATURE: 325°F
BAKING TIME: 45 minutes

This fancy-looking-but-oh-so-easy-to-make confection (our favorite kind) features layers of buttery yellow cake made with either traditional whole wheat flour or white whole wheat flour. Traditional whole wheat flour will give this cake a slightly nuttier flavor that serves as a nice counterpoint to the sweetness of the meringue. White whole wheat will allow the denser layers to take more of a background role, letting the meringue and pastry cream take center stage. The cake layer is topped with meringue and a rich filling. Nuts add an intriguing crunch, and of course everything's better with a little chocolate drizzled on top.

Cake
½ cup (1 stick, 4 ounces) unsalted butter
½ cup (3¾ ounces) packed light or dark brown sugar
¼ teaspoon salt
4 large (2 ounces) egg yolks (save the whites for the topping)
1 teaspoon vanilla extract
3 tablespoons (1½ ounces) milk
1 teaspoon baking powder
1 cup (4 ounces) whole wheat flour, traditional or white whole wheat

Topping
4 large (5 ounces) egg whites
¾ cup (5¼ ounces) granulated sugar
½ cup (1⅞ ounces) chopped pecans
1 tablespoon Demerara sugar

Caramel pastry cream filling
½ cup (5 ounces, 14 individual pieces) caramel
1½ cups (12 ounces) whole milk, divided
3 tablespoons (¾ ounce) cornstarch
2 large (1 ounce) egg yolks
¼ cup (1¾ ounces) granulated sugar
¼ teaspoon salt
1 teaspoon vanilla extract

Chocolate glaze (optional)
¼ cup plus 2 tablespoons (3 ounces) heavy cream
⅓ cup (2 ounces) chopped chocolate
1 tablespoon corn syrup

Preheat the oven to 325°F. Lightly grease two 8- or 9-inch round cake pans.

TO MAKE THE CAKE: Cream together the butter, sugar, salt and egg yolks in a medium mixing bowl. Beat in the vanilla, milk, baking powder and flour. The batter will be stiff. Spread the mixture in the prepared pans (the batter will barely cover the bottom of the pans; that's OK).

TO MAKE THE TOPPING: Beat the egg whites in a large, grease-free bowl with clean beaters till light; gradually add the sugar and continue to beat till the meringue is smooth, glossy and forms soft peaks. Spread the meringue on the cake batter in both pans. Choose one pan to be your base layer, and sprinkle the chopped pecans over the meringue. For the top layer, use a spoon or spatula to pull the meringue into decorative points.

A small offset spatula will help you spread the batter evenly in the cake pans.

Use a spoon or the tip of your spatula to pull the meringue into decorative points before baking.

Sprinkle the top layer with the Demerara sugar.

Bake the cakes for 45 minutes, until lightly browned. Remove from the oven, and place on a rack. Run a dull knife around the edge of the cake, so it will contract evenly as it cools. Allow to cool completely in the pan before removing.

TO MAKE THE FILLING: Melt the caramels with ¼ cup of the milk in a small heatproof bowl over simmering water or on low power in the microwave. Stir until smooth; set aside in a warm place. Whisk together ½ cup of the milk with the cornstarch in a medium bowl until no lumps remain. Whisk in the egg yolks. Place the remaining ¾ cup milk, granulated sugar and salt in a medium saucepan. Bring to a simmer over medium heat, stirring constantly. Whisk the hot milk into the egg mixture, then return everything to the saucepan. Bring to a boil, stirring constantly until the mixture thickens. Remove from the heat, and strain into a mixing bowl. Stir in the vanilla and the melted caramel. Cover and refrigerate until completely cool, about 3 hours.

TO ASSEMBLE THE CAKE: Place a plate on top of the base cake layer in its pan, flip everything over to release it, remove the pan, then flip the cake layer right side up again onto a serving

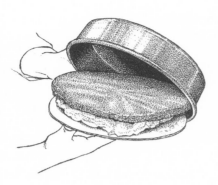

Place a plate over the cake pan, then flip everything over to free the cake layer.

Remove the pan, then place the layer right side up on a serving plate.

plate. Take the top layer out of its pan the same way. Spread the cooled pastry cream over the bottom cake layer. Place the top layer over the pastry cream.

TO MAKE THE GLAZE (IF USING): Bring the heavy cream to a simmer in a small saucepan or the microwave. Pour over the chocolate in a small bowl; add the corn syrup and stir until you have a smooth glaze. Drizzle the glaze over the top of the cake.

NUTRITION INFORMATION PER SERVING (1/16 OF CAKE, WITHOUT CHOCOLATE GLAZE, 83G): 8g whole grains, 271 cal, 14g fat, 5g protein, 10g complex carbohydrates, 24g sugar, 2g dietary fiber, 100mg cholesterol, 129mg sodium, 178mg potassium, 100RE vitamin A, 1mg iron, 79mg calcium, 142mg phosphorus.

VARIATIONS: BANANA SPLIT BLITZ *Slice a banana on top of the pastry cream before putting the second layer on top.*

COCONUT CUSTARD BLITZ *Omit the caramels from the pastry cream. Add ¹/₂ teaspoon coconut extract or ¹/₄ teaspoon strong coconut flavor to the pastry cream after cooking, and fold in 1 cup sweetened shredded coconut into the cooled pastry cream before using it to fill the cake.*

WHAT'S A SOFT PEAK?

When you beat egg whites, they first get foamy, then as more and more air is incorporated, they get higher in volume and more opaque, until they can hold themselves up. When you lift the beater out of the eggs, and the whites come up into a point whose top flops gently over, you've reached the soft peak stage. Adding sugar to the egg whites after the eggs become foamy will have the effect of lengthening the beating time, but it also provides some insurance. The sugar coats the ends of the proteins in the whites, as well as holding on to some of the water in the mixture. This makes it less likely that the meringue can be overbeaten and collapse (see illustrations, p. 468).

PUDDING CAKES

What child hasn't goggled at the alchemy of a cake that starts out with liquid poured on top, goes into the oven, then comes out of the same oven with pudding on the bottom? Such is the magic of pudding cake, made more unforgettable by its preferred method of serving: warm, with a scoop of ice cream or whipped cream sending delicious, slow rivulets over the top.

During our testing, we tried all kinds of techniques and whole grain flour combinations for these loveable desserts. We found that the versions where the moist pudding ingredients travel from the top of the cake to the bottom during baking yielded the best results by far. By now, you know why: the bran from the whole grain is softened in the presence of moisture, yielding a more tender texture to the finished cake. Here are our two favorite recipes from all that we tested.

Fudge Pudding Cake

YIELD: 16 2¼-inch-square servings
BAKING TEMPERATURE: 350°F
BAKING TIME: 45 minutes

Dark and decadent chocolate cake on top, rich fudge sauce underneath—and all in one easy step! Coffee gives the final product an elusive, aromatic, deep-chocolate flavor, without really tasting coffeelike. Our tasters simply commented, "What makes this taste so good?!" We recommend coffee highly, but use water if you're so inclined. No one will ever suspect the whole wheat. Serve this cake warm, with vanilla ice cream gently melting on top.

First layer
1¼ cups (5 ounces) whole wheat flour, traditional or white whole wheat
¾ cup (5¼ ounces) granulated sugar
½ cup (1½ ounces) unsweetened cocoa powder, natural or Dutch-process
2 teaspoons baking powder
½ teaspoon salt
¾ cup (6 ounces) milk
1 large egg
2 teaspoons vanilla extract
½ teaspoon espresso powder
4 tablespoons (½ stick, 2 ounces) unsalted butter, melted
1 cup (4 ounces) chopped nuts (optional)

Second layer
³⁄₄ cup (5⁵⁄₈ ounces) packed light or dark brown sugar
¹⁄₄ cup (³⁄₄ ounce) unsweetened cocoa powder
1¹⁄₂ cups (12 ounces) hot brewed coffee or hot water

Preheat the oven to 350°F. Have a 9-inch square pan on hand.

TO MAKE THE FIRST LAYER: Whisk together the flour, granulated sugar, cocoa, baking powder and salt in a large bowl. Whisk together the milk, egg, vanilla, espresso powder and melted butter in a large measuring cup. Pour this mixture into the dry ingredients, mixing till smooth. Stir in the nuts, if using, and spread the batter evenly in the pan.

TO MAKE THE SECOND LAYER: Mix the brown sugar with the cocoa, and sprinkle this mixture over the batter. Gently drizzle the hot coffee (or water) over the batter; there's no need to mix it in.

TO BAKE THE CAKE: Place the pan in the oven, and bake until it appears set and is bubbly around the edges, 45 minutes. Let the cake cool for at least 15 minutes before serving. The sauce will thicken as it stands, and when totally cooled will be the consistency of medium-thick fudge sauce.

To serve, scoop servings of the warm cake onto individual plates; top with whipped cream or ice cream, if desired. If you can't serve it while it's warm, keep it at room temperature (for 2 or 3 days) and reheat it oh-so-briefly in the microwave just before serving.

NUTRITION INFORMATION PER SERVING (1/16 CAKE, 74G): 9g whole grains, 159 cal, 4g fat, 3g protein, 9g complex carbohydrates, 19g sugar, 2g dietary fiber, 22mg cholesterol, 131mg sodium, 178mg potassium, 41RE vitamin A, 1mg iron, 77mg calcium, 141mg phosphorus, 24mg caffeine.

WHICH KIND OF COCOA?

There are two kinds of unsweetened cocoa powder available for baking. Natural cocoa has a reddish brown color, and is slightly more acidic (more tang) to the taste. Often a recipe that calls for natural cocoa will have baking soda in it, to react with the natural acidity of the cocoa and provide leavening power.

Dutch-process cocoa has been alkalized, making it a darker brown, almost black in color. For the deepest, darkest-looking cakes, Dutch-process cocoa is the way to go. Because it's more alkaline, it's flavor isn't as tangy as natural cocoa.

Maple–Brown Sugar Pudding Cake

YIELD: 16 (2- to 4-inch square) servings
BAKING TEMPERATURE: 350°F
BAKING TIME: 45 minutes

Is anything more magical than a warm dessert that makes its own sauce? Pudding cake is a great way to get kids involved in baking. This cake stirs together quickly and easily, and the scent of warm maple wafting through the house is sure to draw a crowd. The warm water poured over the batter at the beginning of baking combines with the cornstarch and brown sugar as it bakes down to the bottom, moistening the maple-flavored whole grain batter on the way.

First layer
1½ cups (6 ounces) whole wheat flour, traditional or white whole wheat
2 teaspoons baking powder
¼ teaspoon salt
½ cup (3¾ ounces) packed light or dark brown sugar
½ cup (4 ounces) milk
¼ cup (2¾ ounces) grade B or dark amber maple syrup
1 large egg
1 teaspoon vanilla extract
½ teaspoon maple flavor
4 tablespoons (½ stick, 2 ounces) unsalted butter, melted
1 cup (4 ounces) chopped walnuts

Second layer
1 cup (7½ ounces) brown sugar
3 tablespoons (¾ ounce) cornstarch
1¾ cups (14 ounces) hot water

Preheat the oven to 350°F. Have on hand an 8- or 9-inch-square pan.

TO MAKE THE FIRST LAYER: Whisk together the flour, baking powder, salt and brown sugar in a large bowl. Mix together the milk, syrup, egg, vanilla, maple flavor and melted butter in a medium bowl. Pour this mixture into the dry ingredients, stirring until evenly moistened. Stir in the walnuts and spread the batter into the pan.

TO MAKE THE SECOND LAYER: Combine the brown sugar and cornstarch in a bowl until thoroughly mixed. Sprinkle this mixture evenly over the top of the batter. Place the pan on the middle rack of the oven and pour the hot water over the batter.

Bake for 45 minutes. During baking, the cake layer will rise to the top and the pudding layer will settle to the bottom. Remove from the oven and serve warm from the pan, with whipped cream or vanilla ice cream.

NUTRITION INFORMATION PER SERVING (1/16 CAKE, 91G): 11g whole grains, 245 cal, 11g fat, 3g protein, 11g complex carbohydrates, 24g sugar, 2g dietary fiber, 30mg cholesterol, 97mg sodium, 182mg potassium, 68RE vitamin A, 1mg iron, 87mg calcium, 139mg phosphorus.

STIR-TOGETHER CAKES: SIMPLE GOODNESS FOR ANY TIME OF DAY

In these cakes, there's no mechanical action like an egg foam or creaming of butter and sugar to contribute to leavening; they are assisted by chemical leavening to create their tender crumb. The fat in stir-together cakes (usually it's vegetable oil, but occasionally melted butter) is in liquid form. The cakes often rely on the garden or orchard's bounty for their flavor and texture. From all-time favorites, such as Gingerbread and Carrot Cake, to the unusual combination of dark beer and chocolate in our Stout Cake, these whole grain cakes are perfect for a quick snack with afternoon tea. They're also a sneaky, but effective way to get even the most finicky eaters to enjoy their vegetables! Discover what a perfect fit whole grains can be for the riches of the harvest.

Carrot Cake

YIELD: Three 8-inch round layers or two 9-inch round layers, 16 servings, or one 9 x 13-inch sheet cake, 24 servings
BAKING TEMPERATURE: 350°F
BAKING TIME: 30 to 35 minutes for 8-inch layers
  35 to 40 minutes for 9-inch layers
  45 to 50 minutes for sheet cake

This much-beloved cake, with its tweedy texture, is a natural match for whole grains. It's definitely one you could serve without saying anything about the kind of flour you used. After eating a piece, if you speak up, your guest would be astonished to learn the cake was made with whole wheat. This recipe accommodates either of the two distinct carrot cake flavor camps: the combination of coconut and pineapple is one favorite, the version with raisins is the other.

This is a good-size cake; it will generously fill a 9 x 13-inch pan, and is also enough to fill three 8-inch round pans, if you want to make it as a layer cake. The cake is moist and flavorful enough to stand on its own with just a dusting of confectioners' sugar, but we know of no better excuse to have cream cheese frosting than carrot cake!

Cake

4 large eggs

1½ cups (10½ ounces) vegetable oil

2 teaspoons vanilla extract

1½ cups (10½ ounces) granulated sugar

½ cup (3¼ ounces) packed light or dark brown sugar

2 cups (8 ounces) whole wheat flour, traditional or white whole wheat

2 teaspoons baking soda

1½ teaspoons baking powder

1½ teaspoons salt

1 tablespoon ground cinnamon

½ teaspoon ground nutmeg

2½ cups (8¾ ounces) finely grated carrots

1 cup (3¾ ounces) chopped pecans or walnuts

1 cup (3 ounces) shredded or flaked coconut, sweetened or not, according to taste

1 can (8 ounces) crushed pineapple, drained (see Variation, below)

Cream cheese frosting

6 tablespoons (¾ stick, 3 ounces) unsalted butter, at room temperature

1 package (8 ounces) cream cheese, at room temperature

1 teaspoon vanilla extract

4 cups (1 pound) confectioners' sugar, sifted

1 cup (4 ounces) chopped nuts (optional)

½ cup (3¼ ounces) minced candied ginger (optional)

2 to 4 tablespoons (1 to 2 ounces) milk

CARROTS AND CUTTING THE CAKE

When we recently made a carrot cake for a colleague's wedding, we took extra time after grating the carrots in the food processor to chop them even finer by hand. The extra effort had a purpose, though. Having smaller bits of carrot in the cake gave it a finer grain, and made it more certain that the cake would cut cleanly for the big moment in front of the photographer. If you're making a carrot cake for a special occasion or public appearance, it's worth taking the time to chop the carrots a little finer.

Preheat the oven to 350°F. Grease and flour the pan or pans of your choice or line with parchment paper.

TO MAKE THE CAKE: Beat the eggs in a large mixing bowl with an electric mixer, and add the oil while the mixer is running. Add the vanilla, then sprinkle in the sugars. You will have a thick, foamy, lemon-colored mixture. Whisk together the flour, baking soda, baking powder, salt and spices in a medium bowl. Add these dry ingredients to the eggs and oil in your mixing bowl, mixing to make a smooth batter. Add the carrots and nuts, then the coconut and pineapple. Pour the batter into the prepared pan(s).

Bake the cakes for the amount of time appropriate to the pan size (above). The cake is done when a tester inserted in the center comes out clean. Cool completely on a wire rack, then dust with confectioners' sugar or frost with cream cheese frosting.

TO MAKE THE FROSTING: Combine the butter, cream cheese and vanilla in a medium bowl, and beat them together until they are light and fluffy. Add the sugar gradually, beating well. Stir in the nuts and/or ginger if desired, then add the milk a little at a time, until the frosting is a spreadable consistency.

VARIATION: *Substitute 2 cups (12 ounces) raisins for the coconut and pineapple in the cake.*

NUTRITION INFORMATION PER SERVING, COCONUT/PINEAPPLE VERSION (ONE 2-INCH FROSTED SQUARE, WITH COCONUT & PINEAPPLE, 101G): 10g whole grains, 505 cal, 28g fat, 5g protein, 12g complex carbohydrates, 52g sugar, 2g dietary fiber, 61mg cholesterol, 356mg sodium, 172mg potassium, 438RE vitamin A, 2mg vitamin C, 1mg iron, 59mg calcium, 91mg phosphorus.

Honey Cake

YIELD: One 9-inch cake, 16 servings
BAKING TEMPERATURE: 325°F
BAKING TIME: 50 to 55 minutes

This cake is quick to put together and would make a wonderful lunchbox snack cake or afternoon pick-me-up. The unmistakable flavor of honey gives this tender cake a lovely finish. The sliced almonds give their textural counterpoint to the soft grain of the cake. Dress it up for dessert with slices of fruit and a bit of ice cream.

> **1 cup (3 ounces) sliced almonds, divided**
> **1¼ cups (5 ounces) whole wheat flour, traditional or white whole wheat**
> **¾ cup (3⅛ ounces) unbleached all-purpose flour**
> **½ teaspoon baking soda**
> **½ teaspoon salt**
> **¾ cup (1½ ounces, 6 ounces) unsalted butter, at room temperature**
> **1 cup (12 ounces) honey**
> **4 large eggs**
> **1/4 cup (2 ounces) sour cream**
> **Confectioners' sugar for dusting (optional)**

Preheat the oven to 325°F. Lightly grease a 9-inch round cake pan. Sprinkle ¾ cup of the sliced almonds in the bottom of the pan, reserving ¼ cup for the batter.

Whisk together the flours, baking soda and salt in a medium bowl. Mix together the butter, honey and eggs in a large mixing bowl. Stir in the flour mixture, then the sour cream and reserved almonds. Scrape the sides and bottom of the bowl to be sure everything is evenly moistened, then mix for 1 minute more. Gently pour the batter over the almonds in the prepared pan.

Bake until the edge of the cake pulls back from the side of the pan, 50 to 55 minutes. Remove from the oven and place on a rack to cool for 15 minutes. After 15 minutes, invert the cake onto a serving plate and allow it to cool before serving. Decorate the top with confectioners' sugar, if desired.

NUTRITION INFORMATION PER SERVING (1/16 CAKE, 69G): **9g whole grains,** 255 cal, 14g fat, 5g protein, 12g complex carbohydrates, 17g sugar, 2g dietary fiber, 79mg cholesterol, 126mg sodium, 121mg potassium, 115RE vitamin A, 1mg iron, 32mg calcium, 96mg phosphorus.

Chocolate Stout Cake

YIELD: One 9-inch cake, 12 servings
BAKING TEMPERATURE: 350°F
BAKING TIME: 45 to 50 minutes

Stout and other dark beers are often described as having chocolaty overtones, so this combination might not be as farfetched as you might initially think. The deep, dark color of the finished cake comes from the beer, which lends an intriguing background note to the chocolate. For a more intense chocolate experience, add some chocolate chips to the batter before baking.

Soft chocolate ganache frosting
12 ounces bittersweet or semisweet chocolate, chopped
1½ cups (12 ounces) heavy cream
1 teaspoon vanilla extract

Cake
1 cup (8 ounces) stout beer
1 cup (2 sticks, 8 ounces) unsalted butter
¾ cup (2¼ ounces) unsweetened Dutch-process cocoa powder
2 cups (8 ounces) whole wheat flour, traditional or white whole wheat
2 cups (14 ounces) sugar
1½ teaspoons baking soda
¾ teaspoon salt
2 large eggs
6 tablespoons (3 ounces) sour cream
1 cup (6 ounces) bittersweet or semisweet chocolate chips (optional)

TO MAKE THE FROSTING: Make the frosting first, since it needs time to set up in the refrigerator. Place the chopped chocolate in a large heatproof bowl. Bring the cream to a simmer in a heavy medium saucepan. Pour the hot cream over the chocolate, and stir until the mixture is completely smooth. Stir in the vanilla. Refrigerate until the icing is spreadable, stirring occasionally, about 2 hours.

TO MAKE THE CAKE: Preheat the oven to 350°F. Grease and flour a 9-inch round cake pan and line with a parchment paper circle. Place the stout and butter in a large heavy saucepan, and bring to a simmer over medium heat. Remove the pan from the heat, add the cocoa and whisk until the mixture is smooth. Set aside to cool.

Whisk together the flour, sugar, baking soda and salt in a large bowl. Beat together the eggs and sour cream in a large mixing bowl. Add the stout-chocolate mixture, mixing to combine. Add the flour mixture and mix together at slow speed. Scrape the sides and bottom of the mixing bowl, add the chocolate chips, if using, and mix again for 1 minute. Pour the batter into the prepared pan.

Bake the cake until a cake tester inserted in the center comes out clean, 45 to 50 minutes. Remove the cake from the oven and cool on a rack for 10 minutes, then turn it out of its pan onto the rack to cool completely.

TO ASSEMBLE THE CAKE: Trim the cake layer to have a flat top, if necessary (otherwise the layer will crack when you place it upside down on your cake plate). Split it horizontally (see illustration) and place one of the halves on a serving plate. Spread ⅔ cup of icing on this half, then top with the other half of the cake layer, and use the remaining frosting to cover the top and sides of the cake.

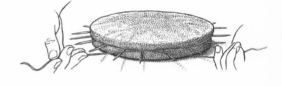

Mark the halfway point on the side of the cake with toothpicks, as shown. Using a piece of unflavored dental floss, wrap it around the cake, resting on the toothpicks, crossing the ends over each other. Gently pull the floss through the cake, keeping your hands level, until it's sliced in half.

NUTRITION INFORMATION PER SERVING (1/12 CAKE, WITH FROSTING, 172G): 15g whole grains, 483 cal, 29g fat, 6g protein, 15g complex carbohydrates, 35g sugar, 4g dietary fiber, 93mg cholesterol, 245mg sodium, 382mg potassium, 230RE vitamin A, 2mg iron, 43mg calcium, 160mg phosphorus, 26mg caffeine.

Pumpkin Cake

YIELD: **One 9 x13-inch sheet cake or 9-inch round 2-layer cake, 16 servings**
BAKING TEMPERATURE: **350°F**
BAKING TIME: **30 to 35 minutes for layers, 35 to 40 minutes for sheet cake**

This cake is simple to make and can wear many hats. You can bake it as two layers or serve as a frost-in-the-pan sheet cake for a crowd. It can comfortably go on its own for a healthy dessert choice, since the barley flour and pumpkin keep it nice and moist. Or you can dress it up with Ginger Cream Cheese frosting on top. We hope the variations below will get you started on the path to customizing this cake to your own tastes. Add some cranberries and chocolate chips for a flavor combination that will keep them coming back for more or go traditional with extra spices and raisins (see variations below). We think dried apples, walnuts or toffee chips would all work too.

Cake

1½ cups (6 ounces) whole wheat flour, traditional or white whole wheat

1 cup (4 ounces) whole barley flour

1 teaspoon baking powder

1 teaspoon baking soda

¾ teaspoon salt

1 teaspoon ground cinnamon

1 teaspoon ground ginger

½ teaspoon ground nutmeg

¼ teaspoon ground allspice

1¾ cups (13⅛ ounces) packed light or dark brown sugar

½ cup (1 stick, 4 ounces) unsalted butter, softened

½ cup (3½ ounces) vegetable oil

4 large eggs

1 can (15-ounces) pumpkin purée

Ginger cream cheese frosting

6 tablespoons (¾ stick, 3 ounces) unsalted butter, at room temperature

1 package (8 ounces) cream cheese, at room temperature

1 teaspoon vanilla extract

4 cups (1 pound) confectioners' sugar, sifted

1 cup (4 ounces) chopped nuts (optional)

½ cup (3¼ ounces) minced crystallized ginger

2 to 4 tablespoons (1 to 2 ounces) milk, if needed, to make frosting spreadable

Preheat the oven to 350°F. Grease and flour the pan or pans of your choice or line with parchment paper.

TO MAKE THE CAKE: Whisk together the flours, baking powder, baking soda, salt and spices in a medium bowl. Mix together the brown sugar, butter and oil in a large bowl until thick and mayonnaise-like in consistency. Beat in the eggs, one at a time, scraping the sides and bottom of the bowl once or twice to be sure everything is evenly combined. Stir in the pumpkin, then the dry ingredients. Mix until evenly moistened. Transfer the batter to the prepared pan(s).

Bake until the top springs back when lightly touched and the edges of the cake pull back from the pan, 30 to 35 minutes for layers, 35 to 40 minutes for the sheet cake. Remove from the oven and cool on a rack before frosting.

TO MAKE THE FROSTING: Combine the butter, cream cheese and vanilla in a medium bowl, and beat them together until they are light and fluffy. Add the sugar gradually, beating well. Stir in the nuts, if desired, and/or ginger, then add the milk a little at a time until the frosting is a spreadable consistency.

NUTRITION INFORMATION PER SERVING (1/16 CAKE, FROSTED, 137G): 18g whole grains, 445 cal, 20g fat, 5g protein, 17g complex carbohydrates, 49g sugar, 4g dietary fiber, 84mg cholesterol, 265mg sodium, 234mg potassium, 725RE vitamin A, 2mg vitamin C, 2mg iron, 77mg calcium, 126mg phosphorus.

VARIATIONS: RAISIN-SPICE PUMPKIN CAKE *Increase the ginger to 2 teaspoons, and add ½ teaspoon ground cloves. Mix in 1½ cups raisins before putting the batter into the pan(s).*

CRANBERRY–CHOCOLATE CHIP PUMPKIN CAKE *Stir in 1 cup each dried cranberries and bittersweet or semisweet chocolate chips before baking. Dust the cooled cake with confectioners' sugar before serving.*

Gingerbread

YIELD: One 9-inch-square cake, 16 servings
BAKING TEMPERATURE: 350°F
BAKING TIME: 45 to 50 minutes

Nothing says home and comfort like a warm square of moist gingerbread, either eaten out of hand or complemented by some whipped cream or fruit. Wholesome enough to suffice for a quick breakfast, this beloved treat goes together in minutes. We tested this cake with traditional whole wheat flour and whole wheat pastry flour, side by side. The traditional whole wheat gave a more cakelike texture, rose higher and was preferred by our testers as being more what they think of as a traditional gingerbread. The whole wheat pastry flour version was more brownielike, if that's the texture you crave.

2¼ cups (9 ounces) traditional whole wheat flour or whole wheat pastry flour

1 teaspoon baking soda

½ teaspoon salt

1 teaspoon ground ginger

1 teaspoon ground cinnamon

½ cup (1 stick, 4 ounces) unsalted butter, melted

¼ cup (1¾ ounces) granulated sugar

2 tablespoons (1⅜ ounces) brown sugar corn syrup

1 large egg

¾ cup (9 ounces) molasses

1 cup (8 ounces) buttermilk

½ cup (3¼ ounces) minced crystallized ginger

Preheat the oven to 350°F. Grease and flour a 9-inch-square pan.

Whisk together the flour, baking soda, salt, ginger and cinnamon in a medium bowl. Stir together the butter, sugar, corn syrup, egg, molasses and buttermilk in a large mixing bowl. Stir in the flour mixture until the batter is evenly moistened. Stir in the crystallized ginger. Pour the batter into the prepared pan. Bake until the center is set, 45 to 50 minutes. Remove from the oven and cool on a rack for 15 minutes. Serve warm, with whipped cream, if desired.

NUTRITION INFORMATION PER SERVING (1/16 CAKE, 71G): 17g whole grains, 211 cal, 7g fat, 3g protein, 14g complex carbohydrates, 22g sugar, 2g dietary fiber, 30mg cholesterol, 195mg sodium, 178mg potassium, 64RE vitamin A, 1mg vitamin C, 1mg iron, 49mg calcium, 87mg phosphorus.

VARIATION: APRICOT GINGERBREAD *Stir in 1 cup diced dried apricots with the crystallized ginger; bake as directed.*

Chocolate Zucchini Cake

YIELD: One (10-cup) Bundt cake or 9 x 13-inch cake, 16 servings
BAKING TEMPERATURE: 350°F
BAKING TIME: 45 to 50 minutes

Chocolate and whole wheat are a very companionable duo, and when you add grated zucchini to the chorus, the result is a moist, delicious cake that includes lots of healthy ingredients. When made with vegetable oil instead of butter, it's even cholesterol-free. We predict you'll be able to get even the most recalcitrant of diners to eat their vegetables when this cake comes to the table. While moist and rich enough to need no frosting at all, if you want to make extra sure your vegetable detectives give it a try, we've included a quick chocolate glaze as insurance.

Cake

2½ cups (10 ounces) traditional whole wheat flour

½ cup (1½ ounces) unsweetened cocoa powder (not Dutch-process)

1 teaspoon baking soda

1 teaspoon baking powder

½ teaspoon salt

1 cup (7½ ounces) packed light or dark brown sugar

½ cup (3½ ounces) granulated sugar

½ cup (1 stick, 4 ounces) unsalted butter, softened, or vegetable oil

½ cup (4 ounces) buttermilk

3 large eggs

1 teaspoon vanilla extract

2 cups (about 1 pound) shredded or chopped zucchini (2 small zucchinis)

1 cup (6 ounces) chocolate chips

Glaze (optional)

½ cup (4 ounces) heavy cream

¾ cup (4½ ounces) chocolate chips

2 teaspoons corn syrup

Preheat the oven to 350°F. Lightly grease and flour the pan or pans of your choice.

TO MAKE THE CAKE: Whisk together the flour, cocoa, baking soda, baking powder and salt in a medium bowl. Stir together the sugars and butter (or oil) in a large mixing bowl until smooth. Add the buttermilk, eggs and vanilla; mix well. Add half the dry ingredients, stirring until evenly moistened. Stir in the zucchini, then the remaining flour mixture. Stir in the chocolate chips. Pour the batter into the prepared pan.

Bake until the top springs back when lightly touched, 45 to 50 minutes. Remove from the oven and cool on a rack for 15 minutes. If you have used a tube pan, lightly loosen the cake around the edges and center tube by pulling it gently away from the pan with your fingers or a running a thin, flexible spatula down the sides, then put the rack on top of the pan and flip everything over. Remove the pan and cool the cake completely. If you've used a 9 x 13-inch pan, you can either serve it from the pan or invert the cake onto a serving platter and drizzle with chocolate glaze, if desired.

TO MAKE THE GLAZE (IF USING): Heat the heavy cream to a simmer, and pour over the chocolate chips in a bowl. Stir in the corn syrup, and keep stirring until there are no more lumps and the mixture is smooth. Drizzle over the cooled cake, if desired.

NUTRITION INFORMATION PER SERVING (1/16 CAKE, UNGLAZED, 94G): 19g whole grains, 278 cal, 11g fat, 5g protein, 17g complex carbohydrates, 25g sugar, 3g dietary fiber, 57mg cholesterol, 198mg sodium, 267mg potassium, 81RE vitamin A, 2mg vitamin C, 2mg iron, 64mg calcium, 159mg phosphorus, 15 mg caffeine.

VARIATION: *Instead of a chocolate glaze, sprinkle confectioners' sugar over the cooled cake.*

Sweet Plum Cake with Rum Frosting

YIELD: One 9-inch 2-layer cake, 16 servings, or one 9 x 13-inch cake, 24 servings

BAKING TEMPERATURE: 350°F

BAKING TIME: 25 minutes for layers, 35 to 40 for sheet cake

The Victorians had a much more attractive name for the worthy fruit we think of as prunes: they called them sugarplums, after rolling them in sugar and making a confection out of them. It's a term we like much better. This cake brings to mind the heady delights of a Victorian-style dessert: redolent with spices, moist and flecked with bits of diced dried plums, it's easy to see why sugarplums were celebrated as a special-occasion food. This cake is best made a day ahead and refrigerated before frosting, to give the flavors time to meld.

Cake

1½ cups (8¼ ounces) prunes

1 to 3 tablespoons boiling water

¾ cup (3⅛ ounces) unbleached all-purpose flour

1¾ cups (7 ounces) whole wheat flour, traditional or white whole wheat

2½ teaspoons baking powder

1 teaspoon baking soda

1 teaspoon salt

1 teaspoon ground cinnamon

1 teaspoon ground nutmeg

1 teaspoon ground allspice

3 large eggs

¾ cup (5¼ ounces) vegetable oil

¾ cup (5⅝ ounces) packed light or dark brown sugar

¾ cup (5¼ ounces) granulated sugar

1 cup (8 ounces) buttermilk

Rum frosting

½ cup (1 stick, 4 ounces) unsalted butter, softened

3½ to 4 cups (14 ounces to 1 pound) confectioners' sugar, divided

1 teaspoon vanilla extract

2 teaspoons dark rum or 1 teaspoon rum extract

2 tablespoons (1 ounce) orange juice, or as needed

Preheat the oven to 350°F. Grease and flour the pan or pans of your choice or line with parchment paper.

FOR THE CAKE: Snip the prunes into ½-inch pieces, using scissors. If they're not soft, place them in a heatproof bowl and sprinkle with 1 to 3 tablespoons boiling water, depending on how dry they are. Cover and set aside for 10 minutes to soften. After 10 minutes, drain off any excess water and spread the prunes out on a plate to dry. Sprinkle the prepared prunes with 1 tablespoon of the all-purpose flour and toss gently. Whisk together the remaining flour, whole wheat flour, baking powder, baking soda, salt and spices.

Beat together the eggs, oil and sugars in a large bowl. Mix in half the dry ingredients, then the buttermilk, then the remaining dry ingredients. Fold the floured prunes into the batter. Pour the batter into the prepared pan(s). Bake until the cake springs back when lightly touched in the center, 25 minutes for layers, 35 to 40 minutes for sheet cake.

TO MAKE THE FROSTING: Cream the butter, gradually adding 2 cups of the confectioners' sugar. Add the vanilla, rum (or rum extract) and orange juice. Add the remaining 1 1/2 to 2 cups confectioners' sugar, beating until the frosting is a fluffy, spreadable consistency. Adjust with more orange juice as necessary.

NUTRITION INFORMATION PER SERVING (1/24 CAKE (2-INCH SQUARE) 85G): 9g whole grains, 292 cal, 12g fat, 3g protein, 16g complex carbohydrates, 29g sugar, 2g dietary fiber, 38mg cholesterol, 247mg sodium, 167mg potassium, 71RE vitamin A, 1mg iron, 80mg calcium, 126mg phosphorus.

FROSTINGS, FILLINGS AND GLAZES

These are the surprise within and the crowning touch, the luxurious flavors that surround and enhance a cake. Lemon and caramel, chocolate and peanut butter, all are here to mix and match with your favorite cakes.

Buttercream

YIELD: 4½ to 5 cups, enough to fill, frost and decorate one 8 or 9-inch layer cake or 9 x 13-inch cake

Our favorite traditional buttercream is based on a cooked meringue. You may use fresh egg whites or meringue powder (See Where to Buy, p. 588) as the base for the meringue. This recipe takes a bit of time to put together, but the results are worth it! It pipes beautifully for decorations and can be flavored or tinted in many different ways. Note: We call for the nutritionally dreaded shortening in some recipes. You may use all butter, but the frosting will be more stable with the vegetable shortening; all-butter frostings can melt or slide if kept in a warm room for too long.

½ cup egg whites (4 ounces, the whites from 3 to 4 large eggs) or ¼ cup (1½ ounces) meringue powder (see Where to Buy, p. 588) dissolved in ½ cup cool water
¼ cup (2¾ ounces) light corn syrup
1 cup (7 ounces) sugar
⅓ cup (2⅝ ounces) water
½ teaspoon cream of tartar (if using fresh egg whites)
½ teaspoon salt
1 cup (2 sticks, 8 ounces) unsalted butter, at room temperature
½ cup (3¼ ounces) vegetable shortening
2 teaspoons vanilla extract
½ teaspoon almond extract (optional)

Place the egg whites (or reconstituted meringue powder) in the bowl of your mixer. Place the corn syrup, sugar and water in a medium saucepan. Stir until combined and the sugar is dissolved. Cover the pan and bring to a boil. Boil for 3 minutes, with the pan covered to wash any sugar crystals down from the sides. Uncover and cook to the soft ball stage, 240°F.

Meanwhile, begin to beat the egg whites on slow speed. When they are foamy, add the cream of tartar, if using fresh egg whites, and salt. Gradually increase the speed and continue beating until soft peaks form.

As soon as the sugar syrup reaches the soft ball stage, remove it from the heat. Turn off the mixer. Very carefully pour about ¼ of the hot syrup down the inside of the mixing bowl. Turn the mixer on high speed, and beat well. Add the syrup in two more additions, stopping the mixer each time, working as quickly as possible. If the sugar is slightly over-cooked and hardens a bit, return it to the heat for a moment to remelt it. Do not pour the sugar syrup into the bowl while the mixer is on: you may splash yourself with hot syrup or the syrup will end up all on the sides of the bowl.

Continue to beat the meringue until it cools to room temperature. This takes about 20 minutes of continuous beating. If you need to hurry it along, place the bowl of your mixer in an ice bath for a few moments while mixing by hand, then return it to the machine. If you attempt to add the butter before the meringue is cool, the butter will melt and the frosting will collapse.

When the meringue is cool, beat in the soft butter a bit at a time. If the frosting starts to separate, continue beating without adding any more butter until the frosting looks fluffy again. Beat in the vegetable shortening. Beat in vanilla and almond extract, if using. Frost cake as desired. If the frosting is very soft, refrigerate before using, or beat in extra vegetable shortening. If you have two mixing bowls, beating the butter and vegetable shortening together before adding will ensure you end up with the lightest, fluffiest frosting.

NUTRITION INFORMATION PER SERVING (2 TABLESPOONS, MADE WITH BUTTER AND SHORTENING, 15G): 76 cal, 8g fat, g protein, 2g sugar, 14mg cholesterol, 37 mg sodium, 13mg potassium, 48RE vitamin A, 2mg calcium, 2mg phosphorus.

VARIATIONS: LEMON BUTTERCREAM *Omit the almond extract. When boiling the sugar, use ¼ cup water plus 2 tablespoons fresh lemon juice. Add 2 more tablespoons of lemon juice and 1 tablespoon of lemon zest when most of the butter and/or shortening has been beaten into the frosting.*

HAZELNUT BUTTERCREAM *Combine ¼ cup hazelnut paste with 2 tablespoons Frangelico liqueur. Mix this into the frosting with the last ½ cup of butter or shortening.*

RASPBERRY BUTTERCREAM *Mix in ¼ cup strained raspberry purée alternately with the last ½ cup of butter or shortening.*

CHOCOLATE BUTTERCREAM *Melt 2 ounces of unsweetened chocolate and cool to room temperature. Add to the frosting at the end.*

Simple Syrups

YIELD: **1 cup, enough for 4 cake layers**

Brushing your cake with a plain or flavored simple syrup, especially a lower-fat cake, such as the Whole Wheat Genoise, page 391, adds extra flavor and depth to the cake, and will ensure it stays moist after being frosted. This is a trick used by professional pastry chefs to keep special-occasion cakes (such as wedding cakes) moist for a couple of days. You didn't think they baked all those layers at 2:00 in the morning, did you? We think simple syrup should be in every home baker's box of tricks.

1 cup (7 ounces) sugar
1 cup (8 ounces) water, or a combination of water, juice and liquor or liqueur
½ vanilla bean

Combine sugar and liquid in a small saucepan with the vanilla bean (or spices, zest, or ginger, if using; see variations below) and bring the mixture to a boil, stirring until the sugar dissolves. Remove from the heat and allow to cool, then strain. Store in the refrigerator until you're ready to use.

NUTRITION INFORMATION PER SERVING: (1 TEASPOON, MADE WITH WATER, 9G): 16 cal, 4g sugar.

VARIATIONS: HAZELNUT SIMPLE SYRUP *Add ½ cup (4 ounces) Frangelico or hazelnut syrup to the mixture after removing it from the heat.*

CITRUS SIMPLE SYRUP *Replace ¼ cup of the water with ¼ cup orange or lemon juice.*

ORANGE SIMPLE SYRUP *Replace ¼ cup of the water with fresh orange juice; simmer the syrup with the zest of one orange; add ¼ cup (2 ounces) Grand Marnier after removing the syrup from the heat.*

CHOCOLATE SIMPLE SYRUP *Add 1 teaspoon chocolate extract and ½ cup (4 ounces) Kahlua to the mixture after removing it from the heat.*

RASPBERRY SIMPLE SYRUP *Add ½ cup (4 ounces) Chambord to the mixture after removing it from the heat.*

Stabilized Whipped Cream

YIELD: 4 cups, enough to fill and frost one 8- or 9-inch layer cake or 9 x 13-inch cake

Adding just the right touch of gelatin to whipped cream will keep it from separating, and if you are using a piping bag and tips, it makes piped shapes more stable. If you like your whipped cream just barely sweet, use the smaller amount of confectioners' sugar.

2 tablespoons (1 ounce) cold water
1 teaspoon unflavored gelatin
2 cups (1 pint, 16 ounces) heavy cream
1 teaspoon vanilla extract
½ to ¾ cup (2 to 3 ounces) confectioners' sugar, to your taste

Place the water in a small heatproof bowl. Sprinkle the gelatin over the water, and let it sit for 5 minutes to absorb the water. Melt the gelatin over simmering water or in the microwave set on low power for a very short time (10 to 15 seconds). Set aside to cool to room temperature.

Whip the cream with the vanilla in a large mixing bowl until it begins to thicken and the whisk begins to leave tracks as it moves through the cream. With the mixer on medium speed, pour in the melted gelatin. Once the gelatin is incorporated, stop the mixer and add the confectioners' sugar. Resume beating the cream until it forms medium peaks. At this point it's ready to use to fill and frost cakes, and for piping.

NUTRITION INFORMATION PER SERVING (2 TABLESPOONS, 18G): 61 cal, 6g fat, 2g sugar, 21mg cholesterol, 6mg sodium, 11mg potassium, 63RE vitamin A, 10mg calcium, 9mg phosphorus.

VARIATION: STABILIZED CHOCOLATE WHIPPED CREAM *Add ½ cup unsweetened natural cocoa powder and ½ teaspoon espresso powder to the cream before beating; cover and chill for 30 minutes to let the cocoa become thoroughly moistened. Proceed with the recipe as directed.*

Chocolate Whipped Cream

YIELD: 4 cups, enough to fill and frost one 8 or 9-inch layer cake

This recipe does not have gelatin in it so is not suitable for piping decorations. You might use it to frost an angel food cake or fill a jelly roll.

2 cups (1 pint, 16 ounces) heavy cream
½ cup (1½ ounces) unsweetened cocoa powder (not Dutch-process)
½ teaspoon espresso powder (optional)
1 cup (4 ounces) confectioners' sugar
1 teaspoon vanilla extract

Combine the cream, cocoa and espresso powder, if using, in a large mixing bowl; cover and chill for 30 minutes to let the cocoa become thoroughly moistened. After this rest, whip the cream until the whisk begins to leave tracks in the bowl as it goes by; add the confectioners' sugar and vanilla extract. Continue whipping until the cream has reached the desired consistency.

NUTRITION INFORMATION PER SERVING (2 TABLESPOONS, 17G): 60 cal, 5g fat, 1g protein, 1g complex carbohydrates, 3g sugar, 17mg cholesterol, 6mg sodium, 29mg potassium, 53RE vitamin A, 10mg calcium, 17mg phosphorus, 3mg caffeine.

Easy Fluffy White Frosting

YIELD: 4½ cups, enough to fill and frost one 8- or 9-inch layer cake or a 9 x 13-inch sheet cake or 2 dozen cupcakes

This buttercream frosting goes together in a snap. It's deliciously smooth and creamy.

> ⅓ cup (2⅝ ounces) unsalted butter
> ⅓ cup (2⅜ ounces) vegetable shortening (not butter-flavored)
> ⅛ teaspoon salt
> 4 to 5 cups (1 to 1¼ pounds) glazing or confectioners' sugar, sifted
> 2 teaspoons vanilla extract
> ¼ to ⅓ cup (2 to 2⅝ ounces) milk or cream

Beat together the butter, shortening and salt in a large mixing bowl till fluffy. Add about half the sugar, and beat slowly until well blended. Add the vanilla and half the milk (or cream), and beat until fluffy. Continue mixing in the remaining sugar and milk alternately until they've been completely incorporated, and beat until the frosting is light and fluffy.

If you want frosting left over to use for decorating, change the ingredient amounts as follows: ½ cup butter, ½ cup vegetable shortening, ¼ teaspoon salt, approximately 6 cups sugar, and up to ½ cup milk or cream.

NUTRITION INFORMATION PER SERVING (2 TABLESPOONS, 43G): 127 cal, 5g fat, 20g sugar, 7mg cholesterol, 16mg sodium, 5mg potassium, 26RE vitamin A, 4mg calcium, 3mg phosphorus.

VARIATION: EASY LEMON BUTTERCREAM *Decrease the vanilla extract to 1 teaspoon; substitute 2 tablespoons fresh lemon juice for 2 tablespoons of the milk in the recipe; beat in 1 tablespoon lemon zest at the end.*

Easy Chocolate Frosting

YIELD: Approximately 4½ cups, enough to enough to fill and frost one 8- or 9-inch layer cake, 2 dozen cupcakes or 9 x 13-inch sheet cake

This is a simple chocolate frosting that's deliciously smooth and creamy. You can customize it for your particular chocolate taste by using unsweetened, bittersweet or semisweet chocolate. We like a combination of unsweetened and bittersweet chocolates, for an intense chocolate taste.

⅔ cup (4 ounces) chopped chocolate, your choice of unsweetened, bittersweet or semisweet

½ cup (1 stick, 4 ounces) unsalted butter

⅛ teaspoon salt

5 to 6 cups (1¼ to 1½ pounds) confectioners' sugar, sifted

2 teaspoons vanilla extract

¼ cup (2 ounces) milk or cream

Place the chocolate in a heatproof bowl or measuring cup. Using the medium power setting on your microwave, or over simmering water, melt the chocolate three-fourths of the way. Remove from the heat or microwave and stir the chocolate until all the lumps are melted. Set aside to cool to room temperature.

Beat together the butter and salt in a large mixing bowl till fluffy. Add about half the sugar, and beat slowly until well blended. Add the vanilla and half the milk (or cream), and beat until fluffy. Add the melted chocolate, and mix until thoroughly blended. Scrape down the sides of the bowl, and continue mixing in the remaining sugar and milk (or cream) alternately until they've been completely incorporated. Beat until the frosting is light and fluffy, adjusting the consistency with more milk or confectioners' sugar as needed.

NUTRITION INFORMATION PER SERVING (2 TABLESPOONS, MADE WITH BITTERSWEET CHOCOLATE AND MILK, 24G): 100 cal, 4g fat, 17g sugar, 7mg cholesterol, 10mg sodium, 16mg potassium, 25RE vitamin A, 5mg calcium, 9mg phosphorus, 2mg caffeine.

CHOCOLATE

When a recipe calls for chopped chocolate, is there any reason not to reach for a bag of chocolate chips? It depends. If the chocolate is to be melted and mixed into a batter or frosting, a good quality (real chocolate, not "chocolate flavored") chip is fine. Most chocolate chips have lecithin in them, which is an emulsifier that helps them hold their distinctive shape when baked. If you're making a ganache or tempering chocolate that needs to harden when cool, it's best to chop chocolate that has no other additives, which can interfere with the hardening process.

Caramel Frosting

YIELD: 3 cups, enough to fill and frost one 8- or 9-inch layer cake or 9 x 13-inch sheet cake

This is an easy frosting to make. When matched with chocolate cake and some crushed peanuts, you can create your favorite candy-bar flavored creation!

½ cup (1 stick, 4 ounces) unsalted butter
1 cup (7½ ounces) packed light or dark brown sugar
¼ teaspoon salt
¼ cup (2 ounces) heavy cream
1 teaspoon vanilla extract
3½ cups (14 ounces) confectioners' sugar, sifted
Milk, as needed, to adjust consistency

Melt the butter in a heavy 2-quart saucepan. Stir in the brown sugar and salt, and heat the mixture to boiling, stirring constantly. Cook over low heat for 2 minutes, until the sugar is thoroughly dissolved. Stir in the cream and return to a boil once more. Remove the pan from the heat and cool to lukewarm. Stir in the vanilla, then gradually stir in the confectioners' sugar. Adjust consistency with a little milk, if necessary.

NUTRITION INFORMATION PER SERVING (3 TABLESPOONS, 34G): 128 cal, 4g fat, 24g sugar, 11mg cholesterol, 29mg sodium, 41mg potassium, 39RE vitamin A, 15mg calcium, 8mg phosphorus.

Peanut Butter Frosting

YIELD: 3 cups frosting, enough to fill and frost one 9-inch layer cake or 9 x 13-inch cake

Who can resist peanut butter with chocolate cake, or banana cake, or any cake?

> ¾ cup (7⅛ ounces) smooth peanut butter
> 1½ teaspoons vanilla extract
> 3½ cups (14 ounces) confectioners' sugar, sifted
> ½ cup to 10 tablespoons (4 to 5 ounces) milk

Combine peanut butter and vanilla in a large mixing bowl. Add the confectioners' sugar in thirds, alternating with the milk, until you have a smooth, spreadable frosting.

NUTRITION INFORMATION PER SERVING (2 TABLESPOONS, 28G): 107 cal, 4g fat, 2g protein, 1g complex carbohydrates, 16g sugar, 1g dietary fiber, 40mg sodium, 60mg potassium, 3RE vitamin A, 6mg calcium, 30mg phosphorus.

PIE & QUICHE

Do you go weak in the knees at the sight of a towering banana cream pie? Do you sigh with delight at the aroma of a hot-from-the-oven, cinnamony apple pie? Join the club. We Americans are brought up on an array of pies unparalleled by any other nation in the world. From apple in September to pumpkin at Thanksgiving, fresh peach at the height of the summer harvest to decadent chocolate pie any old time of the year, pie is the standard-bearer of traditional American desserts.

Converting the national dish to whole grain goodness presented opportunities, as well as challenges. While piecrust is typically made with all-purpose flour, we've found that whole wheat, barley and oats make delicious crusts. And what's more, these whole grains lend texture and flavor to crust that white flour just can't rival.

We must be admit that the ratio of piecrust to filling is necessarily small; pie will seldom yield a significant serving of whole grains. But as you prepare the recipes in this chapter, you will certainly become a much better piecrust-maker; and as you enjoy the fruits (and vegetables) of your labor, you'll add whole grain goodness to your diet as well. One caveat: pie is usually high in calories. Our forebears were able to enjoy pie three times a day because they worked at physically demanding jobs and burned off its calories. With our sedentary lifestyle today, pie is best enjoyed in small slices, on special occasions.

A whole grain crust primer

Baking piecrust with whole grains is a bit different than baking it with all-purpose flour. The crust absorbs more liquid as you're making it, and once baked, tends to have a sturdier, somewhat less flaky texture, and more assertive flavor. Different grains lend crust different attributes, and should be handled differently. Here are the chief ingredients in piecrust, and how each contributes to the whole.

Flour

We tried various whole grain flours in developing the crust recipes in this chapter, and settled on wheat, oats and barley as the three best suited to piecrust. Whole wheat—in the form of whole wheat pastry, red whole wheat and white whole wheat flours—makes a crust with assertive flavor and, in the case of red and white whole wheat, hearty texture due to its relatively coarse grind. Recipes in this chapter using whole wheat were developed with King Arthur Traditional Whole Wheat Flour and King Arthur White Whole Wheat Flour. If you use another brand, watch carefully when adding the liquid; different grinds result in different flour-to-liquid ratios.

Oats, in the form of ground oats (or oat flour, a 1:1 substitute by weight for ground oats), make a very mild, light-colored crust. We love the sweet, nutty flavor oats lend crust, and the tender, nubbly texture they promote.

Barley was a surprise favorite in our search for the whole grain best suited to piecrust. With its mild taste, it allows other flavors to shine through, particularly butter. And its fine grind makes a tender crust that's nearly as flaky as one made with all-purpose flour.

FRESH-GROUND VS. BAGGED WHOLE GRAIN FLOURS

The flavor of fresh-ground whole grain flour is noticeably different than bagged whole grain flour. Why? Because once grains are ground, oxidation of their oil-rich germ begins, and that germ has a flavor profile that most of us associate with whole wheat. The oxidation is actually the germ beginning to go rancid. This rancidity isn't harmful to the flour's performance, nor does it affect food safety; it just adds a touch of bitterness to the flavor. If you think whole wheat has an "off" or bitter taste, the solution is to grind your own. Excellent electric grinders are on the market now (see p. 588). Before you turn to that, though, we hope you'll try the piecrust recipes that follow: we didn't find any bitterness or off flavors in the grains we used, though as we've noted elsewhere, you should store your whole grains in the freezer to keep the oxidation to a minimum.

Fresh-ground whole grain flour will probably vary from store-bought bagged flour both in moisture level and in size of the ground particles. You may have to adjust the liquid-to-flour ratio a bit, but with all the variables, it's impossible to say exactly what, if any, adjustment you'll need to make. When making piecrust with fresh-ground flour, simply drizzle in enough liquid for the dough to hold together, just as you would when using bagged flour.

With any whole grain crust, gluten is a challenge. Oats and barley contain insignificant amounts; the gluten in whole wheat flour is often rendered useless by the bran, which cuts the network the gluten tries to form. The solution? Adding a bit of all-purpose or bread flour. These flours contain gluten in an easily accessible form, and give whole grain crusts enough structure to be easily rolled out and handled.

Salt

Salt plays two roles in piecrust. Most important, it adds flavor; like bread made without salt, piecrust made without salt will taste flat. Salt also strengthens, ever so slightly, whatever gluten may be in the crust, making the dough easier to handle.

Sugar

Sugar may be added to piecrust dough for flavor and browning. The amount is usually 1 teaspoon to 1 tablespoon per cup of flour. Some sources recommend never using sugar in piecrust dough, as it's hygroscopic (water-attracting) and will result in a soggy crust. Other sources recommend adding sugar, as it attracts the water that would otherwise go toward developing gluten, producing a more tender crust. We've made two piecrusts, side by side, using 1 tablespoon of sugar in one and none in the other. Truthfully, there was very little difference, in browning, tenderness or crispness. In our opinion, the amount of sugar used in most piecrust recipes is so small that it doesn't have a significant impact on texture, so use it if you like.

Baking powder

A touch of baking powder in piecrust helps it expand ever so slightly in the oven, giving it a lighter texture. We use it in recipes where the combination of ingredients might otherwise make for a stiff, dense crust.

Eggs

Whole eggs add protein, water and fat to piecrust dough, along with color and flavor. Adding a lightly beaten egg enhances browning and texture, from the protein and fat. Adding just the yolk adds mostly fat, which enhances tenderness and color. If you want to experiment with your own whole grain crusts, and find you're having trouble rolling them out (or that they fall apart once baked), try substituting an egg for some or all of the liquid; 1 large egg can replace approximately 4 tablespoons liquid.

Fat

Fat has a major effect on a piecrust's outcome. With fresh, flavorful lard hard to come by, and hydrogenated shortening having fallen into disfavor because of its trans fats, unsalted butter is currently our fat of choice. Butter is a more brittle fat than lard or vegetable shortening. It's harder when cold and becomes softer when warmed to room temperature, so everything must be kept cool when working with butter. If the butter is over-worked and warm, too much will melt into the flour, resulting in a sandy-textured crust. Butter has a pleasing flavor and contributes to the color and browning of the crust.

All our pie recipes, as well as the other recipes in this book, assume the baker will use unsalted butter. Because salt can mask "off" flavors in butter, grocers like to fill their dairy case with salted butter–it will seem fresher longer. If you buy unsalted butter, you'll have a better chance of getting a product that's fresh. In addition, we prefer to balance the salt-to-flour ratio in piecrust ourselves, rather than have to adjust for the additional salt (¼ teaspoon salt per 4 ounces butter) in salted butter.

Liquid

Water, juice or cream binds the piecrust dough and activates the gluten so it holds together. To keep the fat as cold and solid as possible (for the best flaky crust), we recommend using ice water (water in which you've floated a couple of ice cubes) or ice-cold juice or cream. Vinegar, lemon juice or orange juice are sometimes added to piecrust because acids break down protein in the flour, so they'll help keep the crust tender even if it's overworked a bit. In addition, adding buttermilk (in liquid or powder form) to crust enhances its flavor.

Liquid is another element that needs to be precisely balanced in piecrust dough: too much, and you have a sticky, hard-to-handle mess; too little, and the crust won't hold together or will crack around the edges as you roll it. Time is the great teacher here; the more frequently you make crust, the better you'll be at recognizing exactly what it should look like before rolling. Grab a handful in the palm of your hand and squeeze gently. If it holds together and doesn't seem dry or crumbly, you've added enough liquid.

You'll notice that our crusts relying primarily on whole wheat call for orange juice, rather than water or cream, for their liquid. Why? Because the balance of flavors between orange and whole wheat results in a mild-flavored crust, tasting neither of whole wheat nor orange. Orange juice tempers whole wheat's assertive flavor, without lending any taste of its own.

Let's start with crusts that use traditional whole wheat flour. Using a high percentage of whole wheat creates a simple, old-fashioned crust that pairs well with some of America's most beloved classic pies, including apple, blueberry and pecan, featured here.

Whole Wheat Piecrust

YIELD: Crust for one 9-inch single-crust pie

Here are step-by-step directions to make a whole wheat, single 9-inch piecrust. To make a double-crust pie, double all the ingredients. Use the following techniques to make any crust in this chapter.

1 cup (4 ounces) traditional whole wheat flour
1 tablespoon buttermilk powder (optional)
1 tablespoon confectioners' sugar
¼ teaspoon baking powder
¼ teaspoon salt
6 tablespoons (¾ stick, 3 ounces) cold unsalted butter
2 tablespoons (1 ounce) orange juice
2 to 4 tablespoons (1 to 2 ounces) ice water

Whisk together the flour, buttermilk powder (if using), sugar, baking powder and salt in a medium bowl. Cut the butter into small cubes and work it into the dry ingredients using your fingers, a pastry blender or fork, or a mixer until the dough is unevenly crumbly. This isn't exact science; the goal is a crumbly mixture featuring uneven bits of butter, with the butter being in recognizable pieces.

Sprinkle the orange juice over the dough and toss to moisten. Add ice water a table-spoon at a time, mixing until the dough is cohesive. Grab a handful; if it holds together willingly and doesn't seem at all dry or crumbly, you've added enough liquid.

An easy way to cut butter into small cubes is to use a baker's bench knife or chef's knife. Cut butter lengthwise twice, to make 3 long strips. Turn 90° and cut twice again, to make 9 long strips. Now cut crosswise pats, to make cubes.

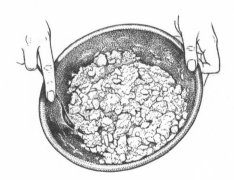

Don't mix the flour and fat too thoroughly; some of the butter should remain in fairly large pieces.

Turn the dough out onto a lightly floured surface, and shape it into a round disk as illustrated at right. Roll on its edge along a floured work surface, as though the disk were a wheel, to smooth the edges out. This will result in a rolled-out crust with smooth, rather than ragged, edges.

Pat the disk till it's evenly round and about 1 inch thick and roll it like a wheel again. Wrap it in plastic wrap and refrigerate overnight or for up to 3 days, depending on the recipe. For optimum results, we found that dough made with predominantly whole grains needs at least an overnight rest in the refrigerator. This rest softens the flour's bran, makes the dough easier to handle, and yields a smoother-textured crust.

Gently grasp the center of the dough disk between your thumb and middle finger, and roll on its edge along a floured work surface.

 Classic Apple Pie

YIELD: One 9-inch pie, 8 to 10 servings
BAKING TEMPERATURE: 375°F
BAKING TIME: 1 hour

What's the most popular pie in America? You guessed it: apple. Despite its ancient history (written recipes for apple pie go back to at least the 1500s), apple pie definitely isn't old-hat. It's a must-have at Thanksgiving, and a favorite restaurant dessert. If there were a comfort food hall of fame, apple pie would be a charter member.

This single-crust pie features a walnut-studded streusel topping, which adds another element to both the texture and taste of the pie. And for those of you who might be a little tentative about your crust-rolling skills, this pie requires you to roll just one crust, instead of the usual two.

Crust
1 cup (4 ounces) traditional whole wheat flour
1 tablespoon buttermilk powder (optional)
1 tablespoon confectioners' sugar
¼ teaspoon baking powder
¼ teaspoon salt
6 tablespoons (¾ stick, 3 ounces) cold unsalted butter
2 tablespoons (1 ounce) orange juice
2 to 4 tablespoons (1 to 2 ounces) ice water

Filling

5 to 6 cups sliced peeled apples, such as Granny Smith or your favorite pie apples (about 4 large or 6 medium apples, about 2 pounds)

1¼ cups (5 ounces) confectioners' sugar

¼ cup (1⅞ ounces) packed light or dark brown sugar

1 teaspoon ground cinnamon

¼ teaspoon ground nutmeg

¼ teaspoon ground allspice

¼ teaspoon salt

1 tablespoon vanilla extract

1 tablespoon lemon juice

2 tablespoons (1 ounce) unsalted butter, melted

3 tablespoons (¾ ounce) unbleached all-purpose flour

Topping

½ cup (2 ounces) traditional whole wheat flour

½ cup (1¾ ounces) old-fashioned rolled oats

½ cup (2 ounces) chopped walnuts

½ cup (3¾ ounces) lightly packed light or dark brown sugar

¾ teaspoon baking powder

½ teaspoon ground cinnamon

⅛ teaspoon salt

1 teaspoon vanilla extract

4 tablespoons (½ stick, 2 ounces) unsalted butter

TO PREPARE THE CRUST: Whisk together the flour, buttermilk powder (if using), sugar, baking powder and salt in a medium bowl. Cut the butter into small cubes and work it into the dry ingredients using your fingers, a pastry blender or fork, or a mixer until the dough is unevenly crumbly.

Sprinkle the orange juice over the dough and toss to moisten. Add ice water a tablespoon at a time, mixing until the dough is cohesive. Grab a handful; if it holds together willingly and doesn't seem at all dry or crumbly, you've added enough liquid.

Turn the dough out onto a lightly floured surface, and shape it into a disk. Roll on its edge along a floured work surface, as though the disk were a wheel, to smooth the edges out. This will result in a rolled-out crust with smooth, rather than ragged, edges. Pat the disk till it's about 1 inch thick and roll it like a wheel again. Wrap it in plastic wrap and refrigerate overnight or for up to 3 days.

About 30 minutes before you're ready to assemble the pie, remove the dough from the refrigerator. Allow it to warm up a bit and become flexible, 15 to 30 minutes.

Flour your work surface, and roll the dough into a 12-inch circle. Transfer the dough to a 9-inch regular (not deep-dish) pie pan that's at least 1¼ inches deep. Trim and crimp the edges, making a tall crimp. Place the crust in the refrigerator to chill while you're preparing the filling.

Preheat the oven to 375°F.

TO PREPARE THE FILLING: Cut the apple slices into halves or thirds; you're looking for apple pieces that are about 1 inch square. Place the apples in a shallow, microwave-safe bowl, and microwave them, uncovered, for 5 to 6 minutes, until they've softened but still retain a bit of "bite." Remove them from the oven, transfer them to a medium mixing bowl, and stir in the sugar, spices, salt, vanilla and lemon juice. As you stir, the mixture will become syrupy. Add the butter and flour, and stir until everything is well blended. Set aside.

TO MAKE THE TOPPING: Whisk together the flour, oats, nuts, sugar, baking powder, cinnamon and salt in a medium bowl. Stir in the vanilla. Cut the butter into small cubes, and work it into the dry ingredients till the mixture is evenly crumbly.

TO ASSEMBLE AND BAKE THE PIE: Spoon the apples into the chilled crust. Spread the topping evenly over the apples. Tent the entire pie lightly with foil.

Bake the pie until the crust and topping are golden brown and the apples are bubbling, 1 hour. Remove the pie from the oven, and allow it to cool for at least 1 hour before serving. Serve warm, with vanilla ice cream, if desired.

NUTRITION INFORMATION PER SERVING (1 SLICE, 1/10 PIE, 158G): 22g whole grains, 412 cal, 18g fat, 5g protein, 29g complex carbohydrates, 31g sugar, 4g dietary fiber, 37mg cholesterol, 184mg sodium, 273mg potassium, 120RE vitamin A, 15mg vitamin C, 2mg iron, 82mg calcium, 169mg phosphorus.

VARIATION: CARAMEL-APPLE PIE *Remember going to the fair as a kid, and begging your mom for one of those gooey caramel apples on a stick? There's nothing quite so fine as the combination of tart, crisp apple and sweet, sticky caramel, enjoyed under a crayon-blue sky on a brisk fall afternoon. This pie brings those complementary flavors together once again.*

Prepare the Classic Apple Pie crust, the filling (omit ¼ cup brown sugar) and the topping.

In a microwave-safe bowl or in a saucepan set over low heat, gently heat ½ cup (4 ounces) half-and-half, light cream or heavy cream and ½ cup (5 ounces) caramel, from a block or unwrapped vanilla-caramel candies. Stir frequently, heating until the mixture is smooth. Remove from the heat.

TO ASSEMBLE AND BAKE THE PIE: *Roll out the crust, transfer it to the pie pan and spoon in the filling. Pour the caramel mixture on top, and spread the topping evenly over the caramel and apples. Bake as directed in the Classic Apple Pie recipe.*

Blueberry Pie

YIELD: One 9-inch pie, 8 to 10 servings
BAKING TEMPERATURE: 375°F
BAKING TIME: 1 hour to 1 hour 10 minutes

If you live in Maine, you know it's August when fresh blueberry pie appears on the menu at the local diner. Maine's tiny, sweet low-bush blueberries, grown chiefly along the state's vast, meandering coastline, make an incredibly tasty pie. For blueberry pie almost any time of the year, you'll have to rely on a more practical solution: frozen berries from the supermarket. That's what we call for in this recipe.

We like to simmer the frozen berries in wine before using them, which allows them to thaw and release some of their liquid. The liquid then evaporates as the berries gently cook. This prevents the finished pie from being watery, and the wine infuses the berries with rich flavor. The alcohol evaporates as the berries simmer. For those of you who don't want to take this extra step, we present a quicker variation at the end. And if you can lay your hands on fresh blueberries, we give directions for that option too.

The buttery whole wheat crust used here is a pleasant counterpoint to the sweet berry filling. Both speak of summer and the harvest, and each is a testament to simplicity.

Crust
1½ cups (6 ounces) traditional whole wheat flour
4 teaspoons buttermilk powder (optional)
1½ tablespoons confectioners' sugar
¼ teaspoon baking powder
¼ teaspoon salt
9 tablespoons (4½ ounces) cold unsalted butter
3 tablespoons (1½ ounces) orange juice
4 to 6 tablespoons (2 to 3 ounces) ice water

Filling
6 cups (1¾ pounds) frozen blueberries
½ cup (4 ounces) fruity red wine; use blueberry wine, if you can find it
1 cup (4 ounces) confectioners' sugar
¼ cup (1⅞ ounces) packed light or dark brown sugar
2 tablespoons (1 ounce) lemon juice
1 teaspoon vanilla extract
¼ teaspoon ground cinnamon
¼ teaspoon ground allspice
¼ teaspoon salt
3 tablespoons (1½ ounces) unsalted butter, melted
¼ cup (1 ounce) unbleached all-purpose flour

TO PREPARE THE CRUST: Whisk together the flour, buttermilk powder (if using), sugar, baking powder and salt in a medium bowl. Cut the butter into small cubes, and work it into the dry ingredients using your fingers, a pastry blender or fork, or a mixer until the dough is unevenly crumbly. Add the orange juice, stirring until it's well integrated. Sprinkle in ice water, continuing to mix until the dough is cohesive. Grab a handful; if it holds together willingly and doesn't seem at all dry or crumbly, you've added enough liquid.

Divide the dough into 2 pieces, making one slightly larger than the other. Shape each piece into a disk. Working with one disk at a time, roll on its edge along a floured work surface, as though the disk were a wheel, to smooth the edges out. Pat the disks till they're about 1 inch thick, wrap them in plastic wrap, and refrigerate overnight or for up to 3 days.

TO PREPARE THE BERRIES: Place the berries in a large sauté pan, preferably 12-inch. Add the wine. Bring to a simmer over medium-low heat. Simmer gently until the liquid in the bottom of the pan is syrupy, about 1 hour. Set aside.

About 30 minutes before you're ready to assemble the pie, remove both pieces of dough from the refrigerator. Let them warm up a bit and become flexible, 15 to 30 minutes.

Flour your work surface, and roll the larger piece of dough into a 12-inch circle. Transfer the dough to a 9-inch regular (not deep-dish) pie pan that's at least 1¼ inches deep; leave the edges of the dough hanging over the rim of the pan.

Preheat the oven to 375°F.

TO PREPARE THE FILLING: Combine the cooked blueberries and their juice, the sugars, lemon juice, vanilla, spices and salt in a medium bowl, stirring to combine. Mix in the butter, then the flour.

TO ASSEMBLE AND BAKE THE PIE: Spoon the filling into the crust. Roll the remaining piece of dough into an 11-inch circle, and lay it over the filling. Roll the hanging edges of the bottom crust up and over the top crust, squeezing them together, then crimping decoratively. Cut three slashes in the top of the pie, to allow steam to escape. Protect the edge of the crust with a crust shield or foil.

Bake the pie for 30 minutes. Remove the crust shield, and lay a sheet of foil gently on top, covering the entire crust. Continue baking until the crust is a deep golden brown and you can see the berries bubbling through the slits, 30 to 40 minutes more. Remove the pie from the oven and allow it to cool to room temperature, at least 5 hours. Serve with vanilla ice cream, if desired.

NUTRITION INFORMATION PER SERVING (1 SLICE, 1/10 PIE, 148G): 17g whole grains, 306 cal, 15g fat, 3g protein, 24g complex carbohydrates, 18g sugar, 4g dietary fiber, 37mg cholesterol, 122mg sodium, 158mg potassium, 118RE vitamin A, 5mg vitamin C, 1mg iron, 32mg calcium, 89mg phosphorus.

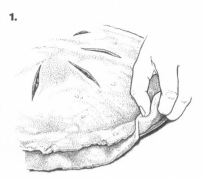
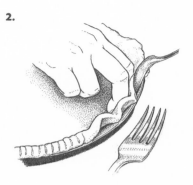
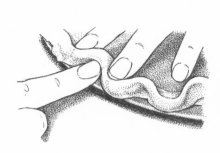

1. *Roll the top crust slightly smaller than the bottom, and trim any odd edges. Bring the bottom crust up and over to seal, and pinch the two crusts together when fluting the edges. Be sure to cut vents in the top crust to allow steam to escape.* **2–3.** *To finish the edge of your pie, fold it under to make it even with the rim of the pan. Then press it flat with the tines of a fork, press the edge against the back of a spoon, or flute it with your fingers.*

VARIATIONS: SIMPLE BLUEBERRY PIE *This pie skips simmering the blueberries in wine. The filling isn't quite as flavorful, but it's quicker to prepare.*

Prepare the crust as directed in the original recipe. Defrost frozen berries for several minutes in the microwave, until they've started to exude some juice when you stir them. They don't need to be fully defrosted. Combine the berries with the remainder of the filling ingredients, increasing the flour to ⅓ cup (1⅜ ounces). Spoon the berries into the prepared crust. Finish and bake as directed above.

FRESH BLUEBERRY PIE *If you've been berry-picking and want something delicious to do with those berries (besides sprinkle them on cereal), try this fresh berry pie.*

Prepare the crust as directed in the original recipe. Rinse the fresh berries, and combine them with the remaining ingredients, reducing the flour to 3 tablespoons (¾ ounce). Spoon the berries into the prepared crust. Finish and bake as directed above.

Pecan Pie

YIELD: One 9-inch pie, 8 to 10 servings

BAKING TEMPERATURE: 350°F

BAKING TIME: 45 minutes

Pecan pie, a specialty of the American South (and Georgia in particular), seems like it would have a long and storied history. Sugar pies were a staple of early American baking, and with all of those pecan trees yielding their bounty, surely some housewife somewhere combined the two... If so, there's no written record of it. The first recipes for pecan pie appeared in the early 20th century, perhaps created by the Karo syrup company, which did much to popularize the pie through marketing its own syrup as the key ingredient. Whatever its provenance, we've been enjoying this super-sweet, nut-filled pie ever since. The whole wheat crust's texture is lightened with a bit of cornstarch, a nice complement to the pie's rich, sweet filling.

Crust

¾ cup (3 ounces) traditional whole wheat flour

2 tablespoons (½ ounce) cornstarch

1 tablespoon confectioners' sugar

¼ teaspoon baking powder

¼ teaspoon salt

6 tablespoons (¾ stick, 3 ounces) cold unsalted butter

2 tablespoons (1 ounce) orange juice

2 to 3 tablespoons (1 to 1½ ounces) ice water

Filling

4 large eggs

1 cup (11 ounces) light corn syrup

1 cup (7½ ounces) firmly packed light or dark brown sugar

Heaping ¼ teaspoon salt

2 teaspoons vanilla extract

1 teaspoon cider vinegar or white vinegar

5 tablespoons (2½ ounces) unsalted butter, melted

1 cup (3¾ ounces) chopped pecans

TO PREPARE THE CRUST: Whisk together the flour, cornstarch, sugar, baking powder and salt in a medium bowl. Cut the butter into small cubes, and work it into the dry ingredients using your fingers, a pastry blender or fork, or a mixer until the dough is unevenly crumbly. Add the orange juice, stirring until it's well integrated. Sprinkle in the ice water one tablespoon at a time, continuing to mix until the dough is cohesive. Grab a handful; if it holds together willingly and doesn't seem at all dry or crumbly, you've added enough liquid.

Shape the dough into a disk. Roll on its edge along a floured work surface, as though the disk were a wheel, to smooth the edges out. Pat the disk till it's about 1 inch thick, wrap it in plastic wrap, and refrigerate overnight or for up to 3 days.

About 30 minutes before you're ready to assemble the pie, remove the dough from the refrigerator. Allow it to warm up a bit and become flexible, 15 to 30 minutes.

Flour your work surface, and roll the dough into a 12-inch circle. Transfer the dough to a 9-inch regular (not deep-dish) pie pan that's at least 1¼ inches deep. Trim and crimp the edges. Place the crust in the refrigerator to chill while you're preparing the filling.

Preheat the oven to 350°F.

TO PREPARE THE FILLING: Mix the eggs, corn syrup, brown sugar, salt, vanilla, vinegar and butter in a medium bowl, beating until smooth. Pour the filling into the prepared crust. Scatter the pecans on top. Cover the edges of the crust with a crust protector or foil.

TO BAKE THE PIE: Bake the pie on the middle rack of the oven until it's puffed and brown, 45 minutes. Remove it from the oven and place it on a rack to cool. Allow the pie to rest overnight before serving; really, trust us on this. The overnight rest gives the pie a chance to set fully before you cut it, and changes the texture of the filling from curdled-looking to ultra-smooth.

NUTRITION INFORMATION PER SERVING (1 SLICE, 1/10 PIE, 139G): 9g whole grains, 433 cal, 23g fat, 5g protein, 10g complex carbohydrates, 46g sugar, 2g dietary fiber, 118mg cholesterol, 193mg sodium, 194mg potassium, 136RE vitamin A, 2mg vitamin C, 1mg iron, 54mg calcium, 120mg phosphorus.

DON'T SCRIMP ON SIZE

Be sure to roll piecrust large enough for the pan you're using. A good rule is the pan's diameter plus twice the pan's height: for example, a 9 x 1½ inch pie pan needs a 12-inch bottom crust.

Why is this important? Because pastry dough that's stretched to fit a pan will try like heck to revert to its original size as it bakes. If you've stretched a too-small round of dough to cover the pan, it'll most likely shrink down the sides of the pan, disappearing into the filling as the pie bakes. If you're making a double-crust pie, the top crust should be 1 inch wider than the top inside diameter of the pan; this should yield just enough overhang to pinch top crust and bottom crust together and make a not-too-bulky crimped edge. An exception to this is "mile-high" fruit pie, where the fruit is mounded in the crust to a significant height. In this case, simply roll your top crust the same size as the bottom crust.

CRUSTS WITH BARLEY FLOUR

The next four pies use virtually the same barley flour piecrust, with minor adjustments depending on the filling. Whole barley flour, with its light color and mild flavor, is a serendipitous choice for piecrust. Its subtle taste is an unobtrusive but pleasant background for any type of pie. We begin with sweet pies here, but if you have a favorite meat or vegetable pie or quiche, this crust will work well there also. We've given you some savory recipes on pages 488 to 498 to help get you into that main-dish mode.

 Buttery Pear Tart

YIELD: One 10-inch tart, 10 to 12 servings
BAKING TEMPERATURE: 400°F
BAKING TIME: 30 minutes

Apples and pears are very similar in texture, and both are pleasingly sweet-tart, yet the words "apple" and "pie" go together like... well, like mom and apple pie, while pears are seldom thought of as potential pie filling. This pear tart features layers of whisper-thin pear slices in a mild golden barley crust, with the piquant flavor of crystallized ginger on top. The result? A delicate, elegant tart, the perfect ending to an autumn dinner party. Note: Anjou pears are generally crisper and harder than Bosc pears. If you want the fruit in the baked tart to be a bit firm, choose Anjou; if you want fruit that's totally soft, choose Bosc.

Crust
¾ cup (3 ounces) whole barley flour
¼ cup (1 ounce) unbleached all-purpose flour
1 tablespoon confectioners' sugar
Heaping ¼ teaspoon salt
½ cup (1 stick, 4 ounces) cold unsalted butter
1 large egg, lightly beaten
1 to 2 teaspoons cold cream or milk

Filling
2 large Bosc or Anjou pears (1¼ pounds), peeled and cored
3 tablespoons (1¼ ounces) sugar
2 tablespoons (¾ ounce) minced crystallized ginger
2 pinches of salt
1 tablespoon lemon juice
3 tablespoons unsalted butter, melted

TO PREPARE THE CRUST: Whisk together the flours, sugar and salt in a medium bowl. Cut the butter into small cubes, and work it into the dry ingredients using your fingers, a pastry blender or fork, or a mixer until the dough is unevenly crumbly. Add the egg, stirring until it's well integrated. Sprinkle in the cream (or milk), continuing to mix until the dough is cohesive. Grab a handful; if it holds together willingly and doesn't seem at all dry or crumbly, you've added enough liquid.

Shape the dough into a disk. Roll on its edge along a floured work surface, as though the disk were a wheel, to smooth the edges out. Pat the disk till it's about 1 inch thick, wrap it in plastic wrap, and refrigerate overnight or for up to 3 days.

Remove the dough from the refrigerator. Allow it to warm up a bit and become flexible, about 15 minutes.

Flour your work surface, and roll the dough into a 13-inch circle. Roll the edges up all the way around, and crimp them decoratively. You should have a flat circle of dough about 10 inches in diameter. Place the crust on a parchment-lined baking sheet, and return it to the refrigerator while you prepare the filling.

TO PREPARE THE FILLING: Cut a small slice off the ends of each peeled, cored pear, just enough to get rid of the stem and woody bottom. Slice pears lengthwise as thin as you can.

Using a food processor (mini, if you have one), process the sugar, crystallized ginger and salt until the ginger is finely ground.

TO ASSEMBLE AND BAKE THE TART: Remove the crust from the refrigerator. Arrange a circle of pear slices around the outside edge.

Sprinkle the pears with some of the lemon juice, then brush lightly with some of the butter. Repeat, arranging another circle of pears within the first; pile any leftover bits and pieces into the center. Sprinkle with lemon juice and brush lightly with butter. Sprinkle the entire tart with about one third of the ginger-sugar.

Make your 13-inch circle of dough into a 10-inch-diameter circle by rolling the edges toward the center.

Arrange the pear slices decoratively around the crust.

Bake the tart for 10 minutes. Remove it from the oven, brush it with butter and sprinkle with another one third of the ginger-sugar. Bake for 10 minutes more; brush with butter and sprinkle with the remaining sugar. Bake until the edge of the crust is brown and the pears are beginning to turn golden, 10 minutes more. Remove the tart from the oven and allow it to cool for 30 minutes before serving.

NUTRITION INFORMATION PER SERVING (1/10 TART, 76G): 9g whole grains, 210 cal, 14g fat, 2g protein, 14g complex carbohydrates, 6g sugar, 3g dietary fiber, 58mg cholesterol, 64mg sodium, 75mg potassium, 135RE vitamin A, 2mg vitamin C, 1mg iron, 15mg calcium, 28mg phosphorus.

VARIATION: *A few dried cranberries (soak them in warm water first, and drain well) or a handful of pomegranate seeds sprinkled over the pears before the last 10 minutes of baking will give the tart an elegant jewel-scattered appearance.*

Vermont Breakfast Maple-Oat Pie

YIELD: One 9-inch pie, 8 to 10 servings
BAKING TEMPERATURE: 400°F, then 350°F
BAKING TIME: 40 to 50 minutes

Oatmeal and maple syrup: what a classic cold-weather combination! The two join forces in this hearty, old-fashioned breakfast pie, a cross between a dish of hot oatmeal and a slice of pecan pie.

We made this pie two ways: once using brown sugar, once using maple sugar. The difference in flavor was amazing, with the maple-sugar version the clear winner among our taste-testers. If you can find maple sugar, use it; you may be able to buy it locally, or see page 588 for a mail-order source. This crust is the same as the crust for the pear tart (p. 452) with the exception of the maple sugar addition.

Crust
¾ cup (3 ounces) whole barley flour
¼ cup (1 ounce) unbleached all-purpose flour
1 tablespoon confectioners' sugar or maple sugar
Heaping ¼ teaspoon salt
½ cup (1 stick, 4 ounces) cold unsalted butter
1 large egg, lightly beaten
1 to 2 teaspoons cold cream or milk

Filling
½ cup (1¾ ounces) old-fashioned rolled oats
1 cup (8 ounces) water

4 large eggs

½ cup (2 ¾ ounces) maple sugar or firmly packed light or dark brown sugar

¾ teaspoon salt

1 tablespoon cider vinegar or white vinegar

1 cup (11 ounces) maple syrup

4 tablespoons (½ stick, 2 ounces) unsalted butter, melted

½ to 1 teaspoon maple flavor

1 cup (4 ounces) chopped walnuts

TO PREPARE THE CRUST: Whisk together the flours, sugar and salt in a medium bowl. Cut the butter into small cubes, and work it into the dry ingredients using your fingers, a pastry blender or fork, or a mixer until the dough is unevenly crumbly. Add the egg, stirring until it's well integrated. Sprinkle in the cream (or milk), continuing to mix until the dough is cohesive. Grab a handful; if it holds together willingly and doesn't seem at all dry or crumbly, you've added enough liquid.

Shape the dough into a disk. Roll on its edge along a floured work surface, as though the disk were a wheel, to smooth the edges out. Pat the disk till it's about 1 inch thick, wrap it in plastic wrap, and refrigerate overnight or for up to 3 days.

About 30 minutes before you're ready to assemble the pie, remove the dough from the refrigerator. Allow it to warm a bit and become flexible, about 30 minutes.

Flour your work surface, and roll the dough into a 12-inch circle. Transfer the dough to a 9-inch regular (not deep-dish) pie pan that's at least 1¼ inches deep. Trim and crimp the edges. Place the crust in the refrigerator to chill while you're preparing the filling.

Preheat the oven to 400°F.

TO PREPARE THE FILLING: In the microwave or over a burner, cook the oats in the water until thickened and creamy; they should be the consistency of breakfast cereal. Remove from the heat, scrape into a mixing bowl, and set aside to cool to lukewarm. Stir frequently to hasten the cooling and to prevent a skin from forming. Make sure the oats are only lukewarm when you add the eggs; you don't want the eggs to cook!

Add the eggs, sugar, salt, vinegar, maple syrup, melted butter and maple flavor to taste to the cooled oats, beating at low speed until well combined. Pour the filling into the prepared crust; sprinkle the nuts on top.

TO BAKE THE PIE: Bake the pie on the bottom rack of the oven for 15 minutes. Lower the oven temperature to 350°F and bake until the center is set, 25 to 35 minutes more. Add a pie shield or cover the pie's edges with foil after 30 minutes. Remove the pie from the oven, remove the shield or foil, and allow it to cool for 30 minutes before serving.

NUTRITION INFORMATION PER SERVING (1/10 PIE, 141G): 13g whole grains, 427 cal, 25g fat, 7g protein, 14g complex carbohydrates, 33g sugar, 3g dietary fiber, 146mg cholesterol, 257mg sodium, 232mg potassium, 186RE vitamin A, 2mg iron, 64mg calcium, 120mg phosphorus.

Thanksgiving Sweet Potato Pie

YIELD: One 9-inch pie, 8 to 10 servings
BAKING TEMPERATURE: 425°F, then 350°F
BAKING TIME: 50 minutes

Come on, admit it: when someone brings one of those sweet potato casseroles to Thanksgiving dinner, you're all over it. You know the one, with pineapple on top, marshmallows, probably some toasted pecans... potatoes never had it so good! This pie mimics that casserole, with the addition of a golden barley and whole wheat crust to keep it contained on your dessert plate. The dried pineapple and crystallized ginger strike a minor, though pleasing, note.

Crust
⅔ cup (2¾ ounces) whole barley flour
⅓ cup (1¼ ounces) traditional whole wheat flour
¼ cup (1 ounce) unbleached all-purpose flour
1 tablespoon buttermilk powder (optional)
¼ teaspoon baking powder
¼ teaspoon salt
6 tablespoons (¾ stick, 3 ounces) cold unsalted butter
4 to 5 tablespoons (2 to 2½ ounces) cold orange juice

Filling
2 medium sweet potatoes or yams (scant 1 pound), peeled and cut into chunks
¼ cup (2 ounces) cranberry or apple juice (optional)
2 large eggs
½ cup (3¾ ounces) firmly packed light or dark brown sugar
¾ cup (6 ounces) half-and-half or light cream
2 teaspoons vanilla extract
1 teaspoon ground cinnamon
½ teaspoon salt
¼ teaspoon ground allspice
½ cup (2½ ounces) dried sweetened pineapple chunks
½ cup (3¼ ounces) crystallized ginger

Topping
2 cups (3 ounces) miniature marshmallows

Garnish
1 cup (3 ounces) pecan halves
2 tablespoons (⅞ ounce) sugar
Scant ¼ teaspoon salt

TO PREPARE THE CRUST: Whisk together the flours, buttermilk powder (if using), baking powder and salt in a medium bowl. Cut the butter into small cubes, and work it into the dry ingredients using your fingers, a pastry blender or fork, or a mixer until the dough is unevenly crumbly. Sprinkle in orange juice a tablespoon at a time, continuing to mix until the dough is cohesive. Grab a handful; if it holds together willingly and doesn't seem at all dry or crumbly, you've added enough liquid.

Shape the dough into a disk. Roll on its edge along a floured work surface, as though the disk were a wheel, to smooth the edges out. Pat the disk till it's about 1 inch thick, wrap it in plastic wrap, and refrigerate overnight or for up to 3 days.

About 30 minutes before you're ready to assemble the pie, remove the dough from the refrigerator. Allow it to warm a bit and become flexible, 15 to 30 minutes.

Flour your work surface, and roll the dough into a 12-inch circle. Transfer the dough to a 9-inch regular (not deep-dish) pie pan that's at least 1¼ inches deep. Trim and crimp the edges, making a tall crimp. Place the crust in the refrigerator to chill while you're preparing the filling.

Preheat the oven to 425°F.

TO PREPARE THE FILLING: Cook the sweet potatoes by boiling them. Or slice them, place them in a single layer in a microwave-safe dish, drizzle with the cranberry (or apple) juice, cover tightly, and cook in the microwave, covered, till soft, 12 to 14 minutes. Mash the sweet potatoes. You should have about 1¼ cups (about 11 ounces).

Mix the mashed sweet potatoes with the eggs, sugar, half-and-half (or cream), vanilla, cinnamon, salt and allspice. For a perfectly smooth pie, process the mixture in a food processor; if you're an aficionado of "chunky" mashed potatoes (rather than perfectly smooth), and don't mind a certain graininess in the filling, skip this step.

Chop the dried pineapple and crystallized ginger into fine pieces; a mini food processor works well here. Spread the pineapple and ginger in the bottom of the crust, then pour the filling over it.

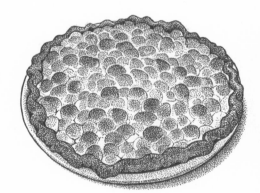

TO BAKE THE PIE: Bake the pie for 15 minutes, reduce the oven temperature to 350°F, cover the edge of the crust with a pie shield or foil and bake for an additional 15 minutes. Remove the pie from the oven, remove the crust shield or foil and sprinkle the top with the mini marshmallows. Return the pie to the oven and bake until a knife inserted 1 inch from the edge comes out clean, 20 minutes more. The

The marshmallows will puff up and become a beautiful light golden brown.

marshmallows will have puffed up and become light golden brown. Remove the pie from the oven and place it on a rack.

While the pie is baking, make the garnish.

TO MAKE THE GARNISH: Place the pecan halves, sugar and salt in a large frying pan. Cook the mixture over medium heat, stirring frequently, until the sugar melts and caramelizes the pecans; watch carefully as the sugar starts to melt, and stir constantly at that point. It can burn easily if you're not paying attention. Once the sugar melts and turns golden brown, remove the pan from the heat, continuing to stir until the nuts are thoroughly coated with the sugar. This whole process should take about 6 to 8 minutes. Transfer the nuts to a piece of parchment paper or foil to cool.

Artfully arrange the caramelized pecans on the pie. The pie is best served 30 minutes to 1 hour after baking; eventually the marshmallows will collapse, and while they taste just as good, the presentation isn't quite as pretty.

NUTRITION INFORMATION PER SERVING (1/10 PIE, 158G): 11g whole grains, 394 cal, 16g fat, 6g protein, 30g complex carbohydrates, 28g sugar, 4g dietary fiber, 69mg cholesterol, 266mg sodium, 384mg potassium, 853RE vitamin A, 10mg vitamin C, 2mg iron, 87mg calcium, 133mg phosphorus.

CRUSTS THAT HIGHLIGHT THE SWEET NUTTINESS OF OATS

When you think about it, the flavor of oats is perfect for piecrust. With their natural nuttiness and faint sweetness, oats provide a subtle taste that nicely complements just about any filling you can imagine. The following crusts take full advantage of this pantry staple. C'mon, open up your cupboard and get started on this delicious piecrust mixed with your favorite (or our favorite) filling.

WHEN TO USE YOUR MINI FOOD PROCESSOR

You know that mini food processor you have at the back of the cabinet, the one you don't use very much? (Or maybe you do.) It's perfect for many of these crusts, because they call for a handful (½ cup or so) of oats to be ground up. In the bowl of a large food processor, that small an amount clings to the sides and doesn't get chopped properly. A large food processor will work, it just takes a little more effort.

Rustic Raspberry Pie

YIELD: One 9-inch pie, 8 to 10 servings
BAKING TEMPERATURE: 425°F, then 375°F
BAKING TIME: 45 minutes

What is so lovely—literally and figuratively—as a golden piecrust brimming with bright red raspberries? With ground oats in the crust (for flavor and whole grain goodness), and a simple filling based on frozen raspberries, this is a pie that's as easy to make as it is to enjoy.

If you're an aficionado of fruit pies, but hate the effort involved in rolling out and patching together top and bottom crusts, try this easy technique: it makes a double-crust pie out of just one piece of rolled-out pastry.

Our thanks to Karen Kayen, a dedicated pie-baker here in our hometown of Norwich, Vermont, for letting us in on the secret ingredient in her special raspberry pie: cinnamon. While you'll perceive just the merest hint of cinnamon flavor, if that, the raspberries are enhanced by its presence, just as chocolate is by vanilla.

Crust
⅔ cup (2¼ ounces) old-fashioned rolled oats
1 cup (4¼ ounces) unbleached all-purpose flour
1 tablespoon buttermilk powder (optional)
¼ teaspoon baking powder
¼ teaspoon salt
½ cup (1 stick, 4 ounces) cold unsalted butter
1 teaspoon white vinegar or cider vinegar
4 to 6 tablespoons (2 to 3 ounces) ice water

Filling
6½ to 7 cups (two 12-ounce bags) frozen raspberries
1¼ cups (8¾ ounces) sugar
½ teaspoon ground cinnamon
2 pinches of salt
4 to 6 tablespoons (1 to 1½ ounces) cornstarch (4 tablespoons will give you filling that oozes when the crust is cut; 6 tablespoons makes a filling that's quite stiff and doesn't ooze at all. Choose either end, or somewhere in between, depending on your preference.)

TO PREPARE THE CRUST: Grind the oats in a food processor (mini, if you have one) for about 30 seconds. Transfer the oats to a medium bowl and stir in the flour, buttermilk powder (if using), baking powder and salt. Cut the butter into small cubes, and work it into the dry ingredients using your fingers, a pastry blender or fork, or a mixer until the dough is unevenly crumbly. Sprinkle in the vinegar, then add the water a tablespoon at a time,

continuing to mix until the dough is cohesive. Grab a handful; if it holds together willingly and doesn't seem at all dry or crumbly, you've added enough liquid.

Gather the dough into a ball, flatten it into a disk about 1 inch thick, and roll it across
the counter like a wheel: this will flatten and smooth any ragged edges that might yield
an uneven crust when it's rolled out. Refrigerate the crust for at least 30 minutes, or
overnight.

Remove the crust from the refrigerator, and let it rest at room temperature for 15 to 30
minutes, until it becomes pliable. If you're using frozen berries, take them out of the
freezer at the same time, and pour them into a bowl to thaw.

Preheat the oven to 425°F. Line a baking sheet with parchment paper.

Roll the crust into a 14- to 16-inch circle, with the edges rolled thinner than the center.
A 14-inch circle will yield a pie with a 3- to 4-inch open circle in the center, with the
berries exposed. A 16-inch (or slightly larger) circle will enclose the berries more thoroughly.

Transfer the dough to a 9-inch regular (not deep-dish) pie pan that's at least 1¼ inches
deep; there'll be lots of overhang. Try to center the crust in the pan as best you can. Set
it aside while you make the filling.

TO PREPARE THE FILLING: Stir together the thawed raspberries, sugar, cinnamon, salt and cornstarch in a large bowl.

TO ASSEMBLE AND BAKE THE PIE: Spoon the raspberry mixture into the crust. Bring the overhanging edges of crust up and over the filling; you can do this catch as catch can, or actually
pleat the crust neatly as you go around. Brush the crust with milk and sprinkle with
sugar, if desired; coarse white sugar makes a lovely presentation.

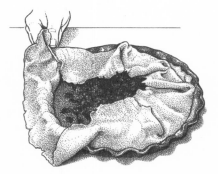

Pick the crust up by one edge and bring it into
the center. Repeat, moving around the circum-
ference of the pie, until the entire edge has been
folded in toward the center. Make even pleats as
you go.

Or, for a more rustic, free-form look, space the
pleats unevenly.

Set the pie on the prepared baking sheet, to catch any spills. Bake it for 15 minutes. Reduce the oven temperature to 375°F, and bake until the filling is bubbling and the crust is golden brown, 30 minutes more. Remove the pie from the oven and allow it to cool for at least 1 hour before serving.

NUTRITION INFORMATION PER SERVING (1/10 PIE, 134G): 6g whole grains, 328 cal, 10g fat, 3g protein, 23g complex carbohydrates, 35g sugar, 4g dietary fiber, 27mg cholesterol, 95mg sodium, 126mg potassium, 95RE vitamin A, 11mg vitamin C, 1mg iron, 34mg calcium, 68mg phosphorus.

MAKE IT NOW, FREEZE IT FOR LATER

Pie is rather labor-intensive, and if you're going to make one crust, you may as well make two (or three, or four...) You can also make and bake a pie, and freeze it; or prepare a pie up to the point of baking, then freeze it. (Neither crust nor baked or unbaked pies should be frozen for longer than 3 months.)

TO FREEZE PIECRUST: Because freezing expands and contracts the liquid in piecrust, which tends to break down its structure, those crusts that freeze most successfully are made with a greater amount of fat, which remains more stable when frozen. A rule of thumb is crust with more fat than water will freeze more successfully than one with more water than fat.

Piecrust can be frozen both unbaked and baked. To freeze a crust unbaked, roll it out as you normally would, place it in a pie pan and freeze. After it's solid, remove it from the pan and seal in an airtight plastic bag. The

crust is fragile, so be careful. We recommend making several crusts at a time and placing them in disposable foil pie pans so that they keep their shape in your freezer; after they're frozen, you can pack them one inside the other to save space, separating them with a piece of wax paper. Place all of them in a large airtight or zip-top plastic bag and remove as much air as you can. Baked crusts also can be frozen the same way unbaked crusts are, in the pan and then removed to an airtight plastic bag. Again, placing them in foil pie pans can help preserve their shape in a crowded freezer.

TO FREEZE A BAKED FRUIT PIE: Cool the pie completely, and wrap it well in plastic wrap, leaving it in the pan. Add an over-wrap of foil, or place it in a zip-top plastic bag, pressing the air out of the bag and sealing it. Place it in the freezer. Thaw, uncovered, at room temperature. If desired, reheat in a preheated

350°F oven, lightly tenting the pie with foil, until it's warm all the way through, about 30 minutes.

TO FREEZE AN UNBAKED FRUIT PIE: Prepare the pie up to the point of baking. Instead of putting it in the oven, wrap it well in plastic wrap, then add an over-wrap of foil or put it in a zip-top plastic bag. Put the pie in the freezer, even if it's just overnight. When you're ready to bake, don't defrost it. Preheat the oven to 425°F, unwrap the pie, and put it on a parchment-lined baking sheet. Bake for 15 minutes, then lower the oven temperature to 350°F and bake until the crust is brown and the filling is bubbly, 45 to 55 minutes more. Freezing the pie, even if just overnight (rather than refrigerating it), gives you much more latitude in your choice of when to bake and serve it.

ONE CAUTIONARY NOTE: Don't freeze cream or custard pies, baked or unbaked; they tend to become watery.

Our Favorite Cherry Pie

YIELD: One 9-inch pie, 8 to 10 servings
BAKING TEMPERATURE: 425°F
BAKING TIME: 40 to 45 minutes

The crust for this classic pie is a slight variation on the one for Rustic Raspberry Pie (p. 459); it includes almond extract to bring out the best in the cherries. Tart cherries, otherwise known as pie cherries or sour cherries, make a wonderfully flavorful pie. While you'll never find fresh ones for sale at the market—the great majority are canned or frozen directly after being harvested—you'll discover that even canned, these are a much better option than gloppy, processed "cherry pie filling." We hope your local store carries pitted tart cherries; they're a tawny red, rather than neon-colored, and while unprepossessing in appearance, they carry a powerful flavor punch.

And while we're on the subject, here's a bit of trivia: on average, a mature tart cherry tree will produce enough cherries, in one growing season, for 28 cherry pies.

Crust
²/₃ cup (2¹/₄ ounces) old-fashioned rolled oats
³/₄ cup (3¹/₈ ounces) unbleached all-purpose flour
1 tablespoon buttermilk powder (optional)
¹/₄ teaspoon baking powder
¹/₄ teaspoon salt
¹/₄ teaspoon almond extract
¹/₂ cup (1 stick, 4 ounces) cold unsalted butter
1 teaspoon white or cider vinegar
4 to 6 tablespoons (2 to 3 ounces) ice water

Filling
5 to 6 cups pitted sour cherries (three 15-ounce cans or jars, packed in water, or 1¹/₄ to 1¹/₂ pounds frozen)
³/₄ cup (5¹/₄ ounces) sugar
¹/₄ cup (1¹/₂ ounces) quick-cooking tapioca
³/₄ teaspoon ground cinnamon
¹/₄ teaspoon almond extract
¹/₂ teaspoon salt
2 tablespoons (1 ounce) unsalted butter

Topping

¾ **cup (2½ ounces) whole wheat pastry flour**

⅔ **cup (2¼ ounces) old-fashioned rolled oats**

½ **cup (3 ¾ ounces) firmly packed light or dark brown sugar**

¼ **teaspoon baking powder**

¼ **teaspoon salt**

¼ **teaspoon almond extract**

½ **cup (1 stick, 4 ounces) cold unsalted butter, cut into small cubes**

IF YOU'RE USING FROZEN CHERRIES: Toss the frozen cherries with the sugar in a large bowl. Allow them to thaw at room temperature; this will take several hours. Stir them occasionally and keep the juice that puddles in the bottom.

TO PREPARE THE CRUST: Grind the oats in a food processor (mini, if you have one) for about 30 seconds. Transfer the oats to a medium bowl and stir in the flour, buttermilk powder (if using), baking powder, salt and almond extract. Cut the butter into small cubes, and work it into the dry ingredients using your fingers, a pastry blender or fork, or a mixer until the dough is unevenly crumbly. Sprinkle in the vinegar, then add the water a table-spoon at a time, continuing to mix until the dough is cohesive. Grab a handful; if it holds together willingly and doesn't seem at all dry or crumbly, you've added enough liquid.

Shape the dough into a disk. Roll on its edge along a floured work surface, as though the disk were a wheel, to smooth the edges out. Pat the disk till it's about 1 inch thick, wrap it in plastic wrap, and refrigerate for at least 1 hour or up to 3 days.

About 30 minutes before you're ready to assemble the pie, remove the dough from the refrigerator. Allow it to warm a bit and become flexible, 15 to 30 minutes.

Preheat the oven to 425°F.

Flour your work surface, and roll the dough into a 12-inch circle. Transfer the dough to a 9-inch regular (not deep-dish) pie pan that's at least 1¼ inches deep. Trim and crimp the edges. Place the crust in the refrigerator to chill while you're preparing the filling.

IF YOU'RE USING CANNED CHERRIES: Drain the cans of cherries, reserving ⅔ cup of liquid from one of them. Place the cherries and reserved liquid in a large mixing bowl.

IF YOU'RE USING FROZEN CHERRIES: By the time they're thawed, there should be between ½ and ⅔ cup juice in the bottom of the bowl. Leave it there; don't drain it off. Add water, if necessary, to total between ½ and ⅔ cup liquid.

Combine the sugar, tapioca and cinnamon. (If using frozen cherries, combine the tapioca and cinnamon.) Stir the tapioca mixture into the cherries until everything is evenly combined. Stir in the almond extract and salt. Reserve the butter. Set the filling aside for 20 minutes, to give the tapioca a chance to start working.

TO MAKE THE TOPPING: Stir together the flour, oats, brown sugar, baking powder, salt and almond extract. Work the cubed butter into the dry ingredients until the mixture is crumbly.

Spoon the filling into the piecrust, and dot with the reserved 2 tablespoons butter. Spread the topping over the filling.

TO ASSEMBLE AND BAKE THE PIE: Bake the pie until the crust and topping are golden brown and the fruit is bubbling, 40 to 45 minutes. Add a crust shield or pieces of foil around the edges of the crust after 20 minutes if it appears to be browning too quickly. Remove the pie from the oven and cool it for at least 1 hour before slicing, so the filling can set up.

NUTRITION INFORMATION PER SERVING (1/10 PIE, 181G): 20g whole grains, 453 cal, 23g fat, 5g protein, 33g complex carbohydrates, 25g sugar, 4g dietary fiber, 60mg cholesterol, 244mg sodium, 249mg potassium, 279RE vitamin A, 2mg vitamin C, 2mg iron, 60mg calcium, 146mg phosphorus.

VARIATION: *Double the crust ingredients to make enough dough for two crusts. Substitute a top crust for the crumb topping. Before baking, brush the crust with milk and sprinkle with coarse sugar.*

A QUICK HISTORY

The expression "American as apple pie" leads one to believe that America was the birthplace of pie. Not so. Pie, defined as a sweet or savory filling encased in a pastry crust, has been a part of the world's culinary landscape for centuries. The very first pies were baked in ancient Greece, at least in their rudimentary form (a flour-and-water dough wrapped around meat). And the first written formula for pie was published in Roman times (it was a goat cheese and honey pie in a rye crust, for the record).

By the 14th century, pie was well known in Europe, particularly in England. English pies of that time were invariably square or rectangular, large and deep, and just as invariably featured a tough crust stuffed with a stew-like combination of meat and

vegetables. Pies were also used as presentation pieces: once baked, the filling was removed, and live birds (or even small people) were put in its place, ready to break open the top crust and make a gala appearance. One such mammoth (and no doubt memorable) pie contained a full coterie of 28 musicians, who began to play as the pie was cut open.

When European settlers came to America in the 17th century, they had to work hard to grow and gather their food, much of it new and strange. With no white flour available, coarsely ground whole grains were used for both bread and piecrust. In order to save precious ingredients, American bakers made their pies round, rather than square, and shallow, rather than deep. Thus England's deep, square pies

segued into the size and shape we know today.

In the 18th and 19th centuries, American pie truly came into its own. Pie was served at every meal, an integral part of breakfast, dinner and supper. The Pennsylvania Dutch, in particular, embraced the practice of enclosing sweetened fruit fillings in a tender crust. Pioneers moved west and brought their recipes with them, adapting them to each new fruit they found along the way. And the plain meat or berry pies of Colonial America soon became Key lime in Florida, blueberry in Maine, peach in Oregon and apple everywhere. American as apple pie? Nearly 400 years of pie-baking lends truth to that analogy.

Blueberry Cream Pie

YIELD: One 9-inch pie, 8 to 10 servings
BAKING TEMPERATURE: 350°F
BAKING TIME: 14 minutes for the crust

All pie bakers look for an easy-to-make, pat-in-the-pan crust. Here it is! And it couldn't be simpler—five ingredients you probably already have on hand. Use it with any pie calling for a traditional graham-cracker crust. The filling is a lovely combination of cooked and fresh blueberries, giving this pie vibrant flavor and a pleasing texture.

Crust
1⅓ cups (4⅝ ounces) old-fashioned or quick-cooking rolled oats (not instant oatmeal)
1 cup (3¾ ounces) diced pecans or walnuts
6 tablespoons (¾ stick, 3 ounces) unsalted butter, melted
⅓ cup (2½ ounces) firmly packed light or dark brown sugar
¼ teaspoon salt

Filling
4 cups (1 quart, 1¼ pounds) blueberries, fresh or frozen, divided
1 cup (7 ounces) granulated sugar
¼ cup (1 ounce) cornstarch
2 tablespoons (1 ounce) lemon juice
1 tablespoon cold water
1 teaspoon vanilla extract

Topping
14 large marshmallows or ¾ cup (3½ ounces) Marshmallow Fluff or 1¼ cups (3¾ ounces) marshmallow crème
½ cup (4 ounces) half-and-half
⅔ cup (5⅜ ounces) whipping or heavy cream
2 tablespoons (1 ounce) bourbon or rum or 1 teaspoon vanilla extract

Preheat the oven to 350°F.

TO PREPARE THE CRUST: Spread the oats in a shallow layer in an ungreased round cake pan. Spread the nuts in a shallow layer in another ungreased cake pan. Bake the nuts until they smell toasty and are beginning to brown, about 8 minutes. Bake the oats until they're starting to brown, 15 to 18 minutes. Watch both the oats and nuts carefully; they go from brown to burned quite quickly. Remove them from the oven and transfer them to a food processor. Add the butter, sugar and salt. Process until the oats and nuts are finely ground and the mixture is cohesive. Remove the mixture from the food processor and press it into the bottom and up the sides of a 9-inch regular (not deep-dish) pie pan that's at least 1¼ inches deep.

Bake the crust until it's just barely beginning to brown, 14 minutes. Remove it from the oven and set it on a rack to cool.

Pat the crust into the pan with your fingers, then use the bottom of a measuring cup or other flat surface to smooth it.

TO PREPARE THE FILLING: Combine 2 cups of the blueberries with the sugar in a large saucepan. Mix the cornstarch with the lemon juice and water, stirring till smooth, and add to the blueberries. Bring to a boil over medium heat, stirring frequently. Cook, stirring frequently, until thickened. Remove from the heat, and add the remaining uncooked berries, stirring to combine. Stir in the vanilla. Refrigerate for 1 hour.

TO PREPARE THE TOPPING: Combine the marshmallow and half-and-half in a saucepan or microwave-safe bowl. Heat over medium heat or in the microwave until melted together. Stir until smooth. Refrigerate till chilled, 1 hour.

Whip the cream in a medium bowl until stiff. Stir in the liquor (or vanilla extract), then the chilled marshmallow cream.

TO ASSEMBLE THE PIE: Spoon the blueberry filling into the baked pie shell. Spoon the cream on top. Refrigerate until ready to serve.

NUTRITION INFORMATION PER SERVING (1/10 PIE, 165G): 13g whole grains, 447 cal, 23g fat, 5g protein, 23g complex carbohydrates, 34g sugar, 4g dietary fiber, 43mg cholesterol, 74mg sodium, 198mg potassium, 134RE vitamin A, 7mg vitamin C, 1mg iron, 49mg calcium, 126mg phosphorus.

FRESH OR FROZEN?

Since the season for fresh berries can be very short, we often substitute frozen. Use IQF (individually quick-frozen) berries, the kind you'll find in a plastic bag in the frozen produce section of the supermarket. Don't use berries packed in syrup and frozen in a tub; they're too sweet and contain too much liquid. Don't thaw the berries before using. Just pour them out and use as you would fresh. Keep in mind that frozen berries may exude a bit more liquid than fresh, so err on the side of more thickener, rather than less.

ALL MARSHMALLOW IS *NOT* CREATED EQUAL!

Marshmallow Fluff, a New England favorite for years, has a counterpart in other areas of the country: marshmallow crème. While similar to Fluff, marshmallow crème isn't quite the same; it's manufactured by a different process, and weighs about 33% less than Fluff, tablespoon for tablespoon. When you melt and stir marshmallow crème to make it spreadable, you may find you have to use more of it to provide the same amount of coverage you get with Marshmallow Fluff.

Tropical Cream Pie

YIELD: One 9-inch pie, 8 to 10 servings
BAKING TEMPERATURE: 350°F
BAKING TIME: 10 minutes for the crust, 15 minutes for the topping

This pie, which sports an impressive golden meringue topping, tastes like the perfect combination of banana cream and coconut custard. And you just can't make an easier pat-in-the-pan crust than this one. With chewy toasted coconut and oats stepping in for the usual crushed graham crackers, we've created a crust that's the perfect match for its filling. It would also make the base for a fabulous chocolate cream pie or anything "tropical" flavored.

Crust
1½ cups (5¼ ounces) old-fashioned rolled oats
⅔ cup (2 ounces) sweetened shredded coconut
¼ cup (1⅞ ounces) firmly packed light or dark brown sugar
2 pinches of salt
5 tablespoons (2½ ounces) unsalted butter, melted

Filling
½ cup (3½ ounces) granulated sugar
3 tablespoons (¾ ounce) cornstarch
2 tablespoons (½ ounce) unbleached all-purpose flour
½ teaspoon salt
2½ cups (20 ounces) milk or cream
3 large egg yolks (reserve the whites for the meringue)
1 tablespoon unsalted butter
1 teaspoon vanilla extract
12 drops strong coconut flavor or 1 teaspoon regular coconut flavor, or to taste
2 medium bananas, cut in ⅜-inch cubes

Meringue topping
¼ cup (1¾ ounces) plus 4½ teaspoons granulated sugar, divided
2¼ teaspoons cornstarch
6 tablespoons (3 ounces) water
3 large egg whites

Preheat the oven to 350°F.

TO PREPARE THE CRUST: Grind the oats and coconut in a food processor for 30 seconds. Add the sugar, salt and butter, pulsing to combine. Pat the crust into the bottom and up the sides of a 9-inch regular (not deep-dish) pie pan that's at least 1¼ inches deep.

Bake the crust until firm, 10 minutes. Remove it from the oven and place it on a rack to cool while you make the filling. Leave the oven on.

TO PREPARE THE FILLING: Whisk together the sugar, cornstarch, flour and salt in a medium saucepan. In a separate saucepan, or in the microwave, heat the milk (or cream) just till small bubbles form around the edge. Pour the milk over the dry ingredients, whisking to combine. Cook over medium heat, stirring frequently, until the custard mixture thickens and becomes smooth.

Whisk the egg yolks in a small bowl, then add about ⅓ cup of the hot custard mixture, stirring to combine. Return this egg yolk mixture to the custard in the saucepan, and cook, stirring almost constantly, for 3 minutes. Remove from the heat and add the butter, vanilla and coconut flavor. Cool to lukewarm while you make the topping.

TO PREPARE THE TOPPING: Combine the ¼ cup sugar, cornstarch and water in a saucepan or microwave, and bring to a boil, stirring occasionally, cooking until thickened. Remove from the heat.

Beat the reserved egg whites and 4½ teaspoons sugar in a large mixing bowl until soft peaks form. Gradually add the hot syrup, and beat on high speed until stiff peaks form.

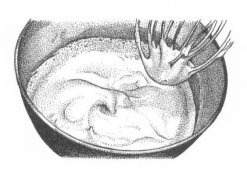 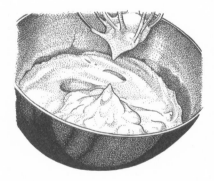

Soft peaks won't stand upright when you lift your beater out of the egg whites; they'll flop over.

Stiff peaks will stand up straight, with perhaps just a slight curl at the very top.

TO ASSEMBLE THE PIE: Peel the bananas and slice them into ⅜-inch pieces. Lay half the slices into the bottom of the cooled crust. Add half the custard filling, then layer the remaining bananas on top and spread on the remaining filling.

Spread the meringue topping over the filling, making sure to spread all the way to the edges of the pie. Bake until very lightly browned, 15 minutes. Cool completely before serving. Refrigerate any leftovers.

NUTRITION INFORMATION PER SERVING (1/10 PIE, 161G): 15g whole grains, 317 cal, 13g fat, 6g protein, 21g complex carbohydrates, 23g sugar, 2g dietary fiber, 92mg cholesterol, 200mg sodium, 283mg potassium, 118RE vitamin A, 3mg vitamin C, 1mg iron, 96mg calcium, 156mg phosphorus.

Light-as-Air Lime Pie

YIELD: One 9-inch pie, 8 to 10 servings
BAKING TEMPERATURE: 350°F
BAKING TIME: 40 minutes

This type of pie was known as a "sponge pie" in days gone by. And once you make it, you'll see why: its intensely lime filling has the same light, "spongy" quality as sponge cake. A thicker layer sinks to the bottom as it bakes, while a frothy top layer develops a delicate, golden-brown crust. It's an interesting, easy-to-make cross between Key lime pie and lime meringue pie, and a real treat for lime-lovers.

Here's a technique that professional pastry bakers employ to good effect: mirroring the flavor of the filling in the crust. This works particularly well with whole grain crusts, where the added flavor serves as yet another element in the crust's complexity, putting it head and shoulders above a blander white-flour crust.

Note the range given for the grated zest and juice of the limes. For a mildly lime-flavored pie, use 1 lime; for a tangy, assertively flavored pie, use 2 limes. If you use just 1 lime, reduce the sugar to ¾ cup.

Crust
⅔ cup (2¼ ounces) old-fashioned rolled oats
¾ cup (3⅛ ounces) unbleached all-purpose flour
1 tablespoon buttermilk powder (optional)
1 tablespoon confectioners' sugar
¼ teaspoon baking powder
¼ teaspoon salt
½ cup (1 stick, 4 ounces) cold unsalted butter
1 to 2 tablespoons (½ to 1 ounce) freshly squeezed lime juice
2 to 4 tablespoons (1 to 2 ounces) ice water

Filling
1 cup (7 ounces) sugar
3 tablespoons (1½ ounces) unsalted butter
2 large eggs, separated
Grated zest of 1 or 2 medium-to-large limes
¼ to ½ cup (2 to 4 ounces) freshly squeezed lime juice (the juice of 1 or 2 medium-to-large limes)
2 pinches of salt
3 tablespoons (¾ ounce) unbleached all-purpose flour
1 cup (8 ounces) milk or half-and-half

TO PREPARE THE CRUST: Grind the oats in a food processor (mini, if you have one) for about 30 seconds. Transfer the oats to a medium bowl and stir in the flour, buttermilk powder (if using), confectioners' sugar, baking powder and salt. Cut the butter into small cubes, and work it into the dry ingredients using your fingers, a pastry blender or fork, or a mixer until the dough is unevenly crumbly. Sprinkle in the lime juice to taste, then the water, continuing to mix until the dough is cohesive. Grab a handful; if it holds together willingly and doesn't seem at all dry or crumbly, you've added enough liquid.

Shape the dough into a disk. Roll on its edge along a floured work surface, as though the disk were a wheel, to smooth the edges out. Pat the disk till it's about 1 inch thick, wrap it in plastic wrap, and refrigerate for at least 30 minutes or overnight.

About 30 minutes before you're ready to assemble the pie, remove the dough from the refrigerator. If it's been chilled longer than 30 minutes, allow it to warm a bit and become flexible, 15 to 30 minutes.

Preheat the oven to 350°F.

Flour your work surface, and roll the dough into a 12-inch circle. Transfer the dough to a 9-inch pie pan that's 1¼ inches deep. Place the crust in the refrigerator to chill while you're preparing the filling.

TO PREPARE THE FILLING: Combine the sugar, butter and egg yolks in a medium mixing bowl, beating until smooth. Add the grated zest, lime juice to taste, and salt; the mixture will look curdled, but that's OK. Stir in the flour and finally the milk (or half-and-half), beating on medium speed until smooth.

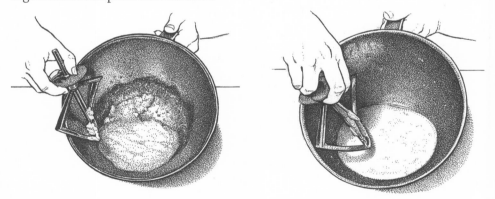

At first the filling will look curdled, but adding the flour and milk will smooth it out nicely.

In a separate bowl, whip the egg whites until they're moderately stiff; a peak will stand up fairly straight when you lift the beater from the bowl (see sidebar, p. 468). The whites shouldn't be at all foamy, like the bubbles in a bubble bath: this means you're starting to over-beat them. Fold the whites into the egg mixture and spoon the filling into the prepared crust.

TO BAKE THE PIE: Bake the pie until the top is golden brown and a knife inserted 1 inch from the edge comes out wet but clean of any filling, 40 minutes. Remove the pie from the oven and cool for at least 1 hour before cutting. Serve with sweetened whipped cream, if desired, or a dollop of marshmallow crème, an easy no-fuss substitute for meringue and a nice counterpoint to the tartness of lime. Refrigerate any leftovers.

NUTRITION INFORMATION PER SERVING (1/10 PIE, 105G): 6g whole grains, 289 cal, 16g fat, 4g protein, 14g complex carbohydrates, 20g sugar, 1g dietary fiber, 82mg cholesterol, 119mg sodium, 110mg potassium, 152RE vitamin A, 4mg vitamin C, 1mg iron, 58mg calcium, 98mg phosphorus.

Golden Pumpkin Pie

YIELD: One 9-inch pie, 8 to 10 servings

BAKING TEMPERATURE: 425°F, then 350°F

BAKING TIME: 50 minutes

If roast turkey is America's signature Thanksgiving entrée, then surely pumpkin pie is that holiday's must-have dessert. Pumpkins are native to the New World and the Pilgrims made good use of them in those early lean years around what is now Plymouth, Massachusetts. In fact, the first Thanksgiving dinner, in 1621, featured pumpkin pudding baked in a hollowed-out pumpkin shell—the precursor of today's pie.

Since pumpkin is such a rich, earthy flavor, we enjoy making this deep-gold pie in a crust to match: one made from whole wheat and oats, with a touch of cinnamon.

Crust
²/₃ cup (2¼ ounces) old-fashioned or quick-cooking rolled oats, ground for 30 seconds in a food processor

⅓ cup (1¼ ounces) traditional whole wheat flour

⅓ cup (1⅜ ounces) unbleached all-purpose flour

2 tablespoons (1 ounce) firmly packed light or dark brown sugar

¾ teaspoon ground cinnamon

¼ teaspoon salt

6 tablespoons (¾ stick, 3 ounces) cold unsalted butter

3 to 4 tablespoons (1½ to 2 ounces) cold milk or half-and-half

Filling
1 ³/₄ cups (15-ounce can) canned pumpkin (not pumpkin pie filling)

3 large eggs

1 cup (8 ounces) half-and-half

³/₄ cup (9 ounces) honey

1 tablespoon unsalted butter, melted

1 teaspoon ground cinnamon

¹/₂ teaspoon ground ginger

¹/₂ teaspoon ground nutmeg

¹/₂ teaspoon salt

2 teaspoons dark or spiced rum (optional)

TO PREPARE THE CRUST: Whisk together the oats, flours, sugar, cinnamon and salt in a medium bowl. Cut the butter into small cubes and work it into the dry ingredients using your fingers, a pastry blender or fork, or a mixer until the dough is unevenly crumbly. Sprinkle in the milk (or half-and-half), continuing to mix until the dough is cohesive. Grab a handful; if it holds together willingly and doesn't seem at all dry or crumbly, you've added enough liquid.

Shape the dough into a disk. Roll on its edge along a floured work surface, as though the disk were a wheel, to smooth the edges out. Pat the disk till it's about 1 inch thick, wrap it in plastic wrap and refrigerate overnight or for up to 3 days.

About 30 minutes before you're ready to assemble the pie, remove the dough from the refrigerator. Allow it to warm a bit and become flexible, 15 to 30 minutes.

Preheat the oven to 425°F.

Flour your work surface, and roll the dough into a 12-inch circle. It may crack a bit around the edge; that's OK. Just patch the crust once it's in the pan. Transfer the dough to a regular (not deep-dish) 9-inch pie pan that's at least 1¼ inches deep. Trim and crimp the edges, making a tall crimp. Place the crust in the refrigerator to chill while you prepare the filling.

TO PREPARE THE FILLING: Mix together all the filling ingredients in a large bowl until smooth.

TO ASSEMBLE AND BAKE THE PIE: Remove the crust from the refrigerator. Pour in the filling. Cover the edge of the crust with a crust shield or foil. Place the pie on the bottom rack of your oven, and bake it for 15 minutes. Reduce the oven temperature to 350°F, move the pie to the middle rack, and bake until the temperature at the center is at least 170°F, and a knife inserted 1 inch from the edge comes out moist but clean, 35 minutes more. Remove the pie from the oven and cool to room temperature (or chill) before serving. Serve with whipped cream, if desired.

NUTRITION INFORMATION PER SERVING (1 SLICE, 1/10 PIE, 138G): 11g whole grains, 285 cal, 13g fat, 5g protein, 16g complex carbohydrates, 24g sugar, 3g dietary fiber, 94mg cholesterol, 198mg sodium, 217mg potassium, 444RE vitamin A, 2mg vitamin C, 2mg iron, 65mg calcium, 123mg phosphorus.

VARIATION: PUMPKIN-PRALINE PIE

Praline filling:

⅓ cup (1¼ ounces) finely chopped pecans

⅓ cup (2½ ounces) firmly packed light or dark brown sugar

2 tablespoons (1 ounce) unsalted butter, melted

Mix together the nuts, sugar and butter in a small bowl. Sprinkle the praline layer in the bottom of the crust before pouring in the pumpkin filling. Bake as directed above.

WHEN TO MAKE A TALL CRIMP

There are many ways to crimp the edge of a piecrust; we show you some on page 449. Does it make a difference which type of crimp you use? Sometimes. When making a pie with a filling that starts out as liquid (e.g., pumpkin, custard), make a tall, fluted crimp. Add the filling; if it falls far short of the top of the crust, feel free to flatten the crimp down with the tines of a fork. But building a tall edge to begin with helps solve the challenge of too much filling and not enough crust to hold it. Even if the filling doesn't come all the way up to the top of the crust, it's nice to have some leeway when you're moving the pie from counter to oven and the filling starts sloshing around.

HOW MUCH CREAM DO I NEED?

Freshly whipped cream is a tasty and elegant touch when serving just about any pie. We all know what a bowl of airy whipped cream looks like, but how much heavy cream do you start with to fill that bowl?

If you're serving an entire pie, and you expect it'll pretty much disappear, count on needing eight servings of whipped cream. For light eaters or dieters, a small dollop—about 3 level tablespoons—is sufficient. You'll need to begin with ¾ cup heavy or whipping cream to make a scant 1½ cups whipped cream, sufficient for eight servings. Sweeten with 2 teaspoons sugar (for very lightly sweetened cream) or increase the sugar to the level you like. Flavor with 1 teaspoon rum or other spirit, or ½ teaspoon vanilla extract, if desired.

For those throwing dietary caution to the wind, twice that amount of whipped cream is perfect. Whip 1½ cups heavy or whipping cream to yield a scant 3 cups whipped cream. Sweeten and flavor as directed above, doubling the amounts of sugar and spirits (or vanilla).

CRUSTS WITH WHOLE WHEAT PASTRY FLOUR

Whole wheat pastry flour is made from a class of wheat known as "soft," typically grown east of the Mississippi River and in the Pacific Northwest. The more common varieties of "hard" wheat, from which most whole wheat flour is milled, are grown in the middle of the country, from Texas to North Dakota. The difference is that soft wheat produces less gluten than hard wheat, making it ideal for tender baked goods, like biscuits, scones and piecrust.

Why not use whole wheat pastry flour for all your piecrust? Because it makes a crust that's harder to work with: more delicate as you roll it, less sturdy once it's filled and baked. With less gluten, it's necessary to add some all-purpose flour or bread flour to ensure the crust will hold together. For those wanting a 100 percent whole grain crust, whole wheat pastry flour isn't an option. But for those willing to trade slightly less fiber, vitamins and minerals for a more tender, milder-flavored crust, whole wheat pastry is the flour of choice.

 All-American Lemon-Blueberry Pie

YIELD: **One 9-inch pie, 8 to 10 servings**
BAKING TEMPERATURE: **350°F**
BAKING TIME: **45 minutes**

The mild flavor of whole wheat pastry flour is ideally suited to fillings with light, sunny flavors. The tart lemon filling in this pie, reminiscent of lemon meringue pie in taste, has the dense, smooth texture of chess pie, an early-American pie based on eggs, butter and sugar, with just a touch of cornmeal for body. Since lemon and blueberry is a popular flavor combination, we decided a scattering of blueberries over the filling wouldn't be amiss. We were right.

Crust
1 cup (3³/₈ ounces) whole wheat pastry flour
3 tablespoons (³/₄ ounce) unbleached bread flour
1 tablespoon buttermilk powder (optional)
¹/₄ teaspoon salt
¹/₄ teaspoon baking powder
6 tablespoons (³/₄ stick, 3 ounces) cold unsalted butter
2 tablespoons (1 ounce) orange juice
3 to 4 tablespoons (1¹/₂ to 2 ounces) ice water

Filling
4 tablespoons (¹/₂ stick, 2 ounces) unsalted butter
1¹/₂ cups (10¹/₂ ounces) sugar

¼ teaspoon salt

4 large eggs

2 teaspoons grated lemon zest (rind of 1 lemon)

½ cup (4 ounces) freshly squeezed lemon juice (juice of 2 to 3 lemons)

1 tablespoon cornmeal, preferably whole grain

1 cup (5 ounces) fresh (not frozen) blueberries

TO PREPARE THE CRUST: Whisk together the flours, buttermilk powder (if using), baking powder and salt in a medium bowl. Cut the butter into small cubes and work it into the dry ingredients using your fingers, a pastry blender or fork, or a mixer until the dough is unevenly crumbly. Sprinkle in the orange juice, then add water a tablespoon at a time, continuing to mix until the dough is cohesive. Grab a handful; if it holds together willingly and doesn't seem at all dry or crumbly, you've added enough liquid.

Shape the dough into a disk. Roll on its edge along a floured work surface, as though the disk were a wheel, to smooth the edges out. Pat the disk till it's about 1 inch thick, wrap it in plastic wrap and refrigerate overnight or for up to 3 days.

About 30 minutes before you're ready to assemble the pie, remove the dough from the refrigerator. Allow it to warm a bit and become flexible, 15 to 30 minutes.

Preheat the oven to 350°F.

Flour your work surface, and roll the dough into a 12-inch circle. Transfer the dough to a 9-inch regular (not deep-dish) pie pan that's at least 1¼ inches deep. Trim and crimp the edges. Place the crust in the refrigerator to chill while you're preparing the filling.

TO PREPARE THE FILLING: Beat together the butter, sugar and salt until smooth. Add the eggs one at a time, beating slowly but thoroughly after each addition; you want to combine them with the butter and sugar, but not beat in a lot of air. Stir in the lemon zest, lemon juice and cornmeal. Pour into the prepared crust. Scatter the blueberries evenly over the top; some will sink and some will float—that's OK.

TO BAKE THE PIE: Bake the pie until the crust is golden brown and a knife inserted 1 inch from the edge comes out wet but clean, 45 minutes. Add a crust shield or foil to the edges of the crust for the final 15 minutes of baking. Remove the pie from the oven and cool it for at least 1 hour before serving.

NUTRITION INFORMATION PER SERVING (1/10 PIE, 111G): 11g whole grains, 308 cal, 14g fat, 5g protein, 13g complex carbohydrates, 30g sugar, 2g dietary fiber, 116mg cholesterol, 150mg sodium, 114mg potassium, 126RE vitamin A, 8mg vitamin C, 1mg iron, 34mg calcium, 101mg phosphorus.

GRATING A LEMON: JUST THE RIND, PLEASE

When a recipe calls for grated lemon peel, grated lemon rind or lemon zest—they're all the same thing—be sure to grate just the yellow rind, not the white pith underneath. The rind holds all the fruit's aromatic oils, while the pith is bitter. Mixing pith in with the rind will lend it an unpleasant flavor. Use a light hand with the grater, stopping and moving on to another part of the lemon once the white part starts to show.

Cran-Apricot Surprise Pie

YIELD: One 9-inch pie, 8 to 10 servings

BAKING TEMPERATURE: 375°F

BAKING TIME: 45 minutes

The crust for this pie is the same one we used in the All-American Lemon-Blueberry Pie on page 474. And the filling features the same type of tart, bright flavors, with an added surprise: a layer of cheesecake filling beneath the fruit and streusel that form the bulk of this tasty pie. Fresh cranberries and dried apricots are simmered together to make a bright-red, tangy-sweet topping for the cheesecake, and the whole is finished with a walnut streusel. Serve this at Thanksgiving, for a total departure from the norm, but one that still stays faithful to that holiday's signature fruit, the cranberry.

Crust

1 cup (3⅜ ounces) whole wheat pastry flour

3 tablespoons (¾ ounce) unbleached bread flour

1 tablespoon buttermilk powder (optional)

¼ teaspoon salt

¼ teaspoon baking powder

6 tablespoons (¾ stick, 3 ounces) cold unsalted butter

2 tablespoons (1 ounce) orange juice

3 to 4 tablespoons (1½ to 2 ounces) ice water

Cream cheese filling

1 cup (8-ounce package) cream cheese

⅓ cup (2⅜ ounces) granulated sugar

2 teaspoons vanilla extract

2 pinches of salt

1 large egg

Fruit filling

Heaping 1 cup (4 ounces) fresh or frozen cranberries

1 cup (4½ ounces) coarsely chopped dried apricots

1 cup (7 ounces) granulated sugar

⅔ cup (5⅜ ounces) water

1 tablespoon lemon juice

1 teaspoon vanilla extract

⅛ teaspoon almond extract

Pinch of salt

1 tablespoon unsalted butter

Topping
1/3 cup (1¼ ounces) traditional whole wheat flour
1/3 cup (1⅛ ounces) old-fashioned rolled oats
1/3 cup (1⅜ ounces) chopped walnuts
1/3 cup (2½ ounces) firmly packed light or dark brown sugar
½ teaspoon baking powder
½ teaspoon ground cinnamon
⅛ teaspoon salt
1 teaspoon vanilla extract
4 tablespoons (½ stick, 2 ounces) cold unsalted butter

TO PREPARE THE CRUST: Whisk together the flours, buttermilk powder (if using), baking powder and salt in a medium bowl. Cut the butter into small cubes and work it into the dry ingredients using your fingers, a pastry blender or fork, or a mixer until the dough is unevenly crumbly. Sprinkle in the orange juice, then add water a tablespoon at a time, continuing to mix until the dough is cohesive. Grab a handful; if it holds together willingly and doesn't seem at all dry or crumbly, you've added enough liquid.

Shape the dough into a disk. Roll on its edge along a floured work surface, as though the disk were a wheel, to smooth the edges out. Pat the disk till it's about 1 inch thick, wrap it in plastic wrap, and refrigerate overnight or for up to 3 days.

About 30 minutes before you're ready to assemble the pie, remove the dough from the refrigerator. Allow it to warm a bit and become flexible, 15 to 30 minutes.

Preheat the oven to 375°F.

Flour your work surface, and roll the dough into a 12-inch circle. Transfer the dough to a 9-inch regular (not deep-dish) pie pan that's at least 1¼ inches deep. Trim and crimp the edges. Place the crust in the refrigerator to chill while you're preparing the filling.

TO PREPARE THE CHEESECAKE FILLING: Combine the cream cheese, sugar, vanilla, salt and egg in a mixing bowl and beat slowly until the mixture is nearly smooth; a few lumps are OK. Set the mixture aside.

TO PREPARE THE FRUIT FILLING: Combine the cranberries, dried apricots, sugar, water and lemon juice in a large saucepan. Bring the mixture to a boil over medium heat, and simmer vigorously until the liquid is syrupy and nearly all absorbed, 18 to 25 minutes. Stir frequently toward the end. Remove from the heat, and stir in the extracts, salt and butter.

TO PREPARE THE TOPPING: Whisk together the flour, oats, nuts, sugar, baking powder, cinnamon and salt in a medium bowl. Stir in the vanilla. Cut the butter into small cubes, and work it into the dry ingredients, till the mixture is evenly crumbly.

TO ASSEMBLE AND BAKE THE PIE: Remove the crust from the refrigerator. Spoon the cream cheese filling into the bottom. Gently dollop the fruit filling on top. Sprinkle with the topping, spreading it evenly over the fruit.

Bake the pie until it's bubbly and the streusel and crust are golden brown, 45 minutes. Remove it from the oven and wait at least 1 hour before cutting. Refrigerate any leftovers.

NUTRITION INFORMATION PER SERVING (1/10 PIE, 160G): 16g whole grains, 487 cal, 25g fat, 7g protein, 28g complex carbohydrates, 33g sugar, 5g dietary fiber, 83mg cholesterol, 378mg sodium, 395mg potassium, 481RE vitamin A, 3mg vitamin C, 2mg iron, 90mg calcium, 184mg phosphorus.

Smooth the cheese filling into the crust, then gently spread the fruit filling on top. The more careful and gentle you are, the more distinctly layered your pie will look.

DON'T STRETCH THAT CRUST!

Stretching piecrust is never, *ever* a good idea. It's bound to rebound and shrink down the sides of the pan as it bakes. Even though you're careful not to develop the gluten in the flour—and some whole grain crusts actually contain very little gluten—any gluten in the crust will still become somewhat elastic.

Be sure to roll your crust plenty wide enough to give you a good overhang once it's laid in the pan. Lay it in the pan, pick up the edges and gently settle the crust so that it's perfectly flush with the bottom and sides of the pan. If you're making a single-crust pie, crimp the edges. As you do, the natural tendency is to pull outward, away from the pan, as you crimp. Do just the opposite: push inward, toward the center of the pan, as you crimp. This will settle the crust even more firmly in the pan, and should prevent the dreaded "crust-shrink."

Classic Peach Pie

YIELD: **One 9-inch pie, 8 to 10 servings**

BAKING TEMPERATURE: **375°F**

BAKING TIME: **50 minutes to 1 hour**

With all the peach pie recipes out there (sour cream peach pie, peach chiffon pie, no-bake peach pie...), it's difficult to find one for just "plain" peach pie: sweetened sliced peaches, mildly scented with spices, baked in a pastry crust. Perhaps it's because simplicity is often the most difficult challenge of all. This recipe for classic peach pie pairs oats and whole wheat pastry flour in a tender crust that marries nicely with it mild-flavored fruit filling, and is sturdy enough to carry that filling. Its nubby texture is a nice counterpoint to the peaches and crunchy topping.

A cautionary note: If you can't find fresh peaches that are perfectly ripe, juicy and flavorful, use frozen. Pie made with rock-hard, tasteless fresh peaches is time and money down the drain.

Crust

¾ cup (2½ ounces) whole wheat pastry flour

⅔ cup (2¼ ounces) old-fashioned rolled oats, ground for 30 seconds in a food processor

1 tablespoon buttermilk powder (optional)

¼ teaspoon baking powder

¼ teaspoon salt

¼ cup (½ stick, 2 ounces) cold unsalted butter

1 tablespoon orange juice

3 to 4 tablespoons (1½ to 2 ounces) ice water

Filling

6 cups (36 ounces) peeled, sliced peaches, fresh or frozen

¾ cup plus 2 tablespoons (6⅛ ounces) sugar

¼ teaspoon salt

¼ teaspoon ground nutmeg

¼ teaspoon ground cinnamon

⅛ teaspoon almond extract

1 tablespoon lemon juice

1 tablespoon unsalted butter, melted

1 teaspoon rum (optional)

1 tablespoon cold water

¼ cup (1 ounce) cornstarch

Topping

²/₃ cup (2¼ ounces) old-fashioned rolled oats, ground for 30 seconds in a food
    processor

½ cup (1¾ ounces) old-fashioned rolled oats, left whole

½ cup (3¾ ounces) packed light or dark brown sugar

4 tablespoons (½ stick, 2 ounces) unsalted butter

1 teaspoon vanilla extract

½ teaspoon ground cinnamon

⅛ teaspoon salt

TO PREPARE THE CRUST: Whisk together the flour, oats, buttermilk powder (if using), baking powder and salt in a medium bowl. Cut the butter into small cubes, and work it into the dry ingredients using your fingers, a pastry blender or fork, or a mixer until the dough is unevenly crumbly. Sprinkle in the orange juice, then add water a tablespoon at a time, continuing to mix until the dough is cohesive. Grab a handful; if it holds together willingly and doesn't seem at all dry or crumbly, you've added enough liquid.

Shape the dough into a disk. Roll on its edge along a floured work surface, as though the disk were a wheel, to smooth the edges out. Pat the disk till it's about 1 inch thick, wrap it in plastic wrap, and refrigerate overnight or for up to 3 days.

About 30 minutes before you're ready to assemble the pie, remove the dough from the refrigerator. Allow it to warm a bit and become flexible, 15 to 30 minutes.

Preheat the oven to 375°F.

Flour your work surface, and roll the dough into a 12-inch circle. Transfer the dough to a regular (not deep-dish) 9-inch pie pan that's at least 1½ inches deep. Trim and crimp the edges. You want to form a high edge to hold the streusel and filling, so do a "stand-up" crimp rather than one you simply flatten with the tines of a fork. Cover the crust with plastic wrap and refrigerate it while you prepare the filling.

TO PREPARE FRESH PEACHES: Combine the thinly sliced peaches, sugar and salt in a medium bowl, stirring to combine. Let the fruit rest for 15 minutes or so, till it's begun to exude its juice.

TO PREPARE FROZEN PEACHES: Combine the peaches, sugar and salt in a large saucepan. Heat over low heat, stirring, until the peaches begin to exude some juice; then raise the heat to medium-low and heat to a simmer. Simmer for 10 minutes, then remove from the heat. Using a potato masher or pastry blender, mash the peaches very coarsely; you just want to break up some of the biggest pieces.

TO PREPARE THE FILLING: Stir the nutmeg, cinnamon and almond extract into the peaches. Combine the lemon juice, melted butter, rum (if using) and cold water in a small bowl. Add the cornstarch, stirring till smooth. Stir the mixture into the fruit.

TO PREPARE THE TOPPING: Stir together all the topping ingredients in a medium bowl, working them together until they're crumbly.

TO ASSEMBLE AND BAKE THE PIE: Remove the crust from the refrigerator. Spoon the filling into it, and sprinkle the topping over the filling. Lay a sheet of foil gently over the pie, without attaching it to the pan.

Bake the pie until the crust and topping are golden brown and the filling is bubbling, 50 minutes to 1 hour. Remove the pie from the oven and allow it to cool to room temperature before cutting, at least 4 hours.

NUTRITION INFORMATION PER SERVING (1 SLICE, 1/10 PIE, 136G): 14g whole grains, 294 cal, 11g fat, 3g protein, 20g complex carbohydrates, 28g sugar, 3g dietary fiber, 28mg cholesterol, 153mg sodium, 237mg potassium, 99RE vitamin A, 6mg vitamin C, 1mg iron, 39mg calcium, 95mg phosphorus.

VARIATION: BLUSHING PEACH PIE *For a rosy-hued, raspberry-scented peach pie, substitute 1 cup (about 4 ounces) raspberries, fresh or frozen, for 1 cup of the sliced peaches.*

DO I REALLY NEED A PIECRUST SHIELD?

Yes, you really need to shield the edges of your crust from over-browning, if that's the question. Whole grain flours have a higher oil content than all-purpose flour, and they tend to brown quickly. A piecrust shield—a ring of light-weight aluminum designed to rest on the perimeter of your pie—is an easy, inexpensive, reusable solution. If you don't use a crust shield, crimp strips of foil to cover just the edges of the crust. Then carefully put them onto the hot crust at the point the recipe directs.

Remove the crust shield as soon as you take the pie out of the oven to cool. If you leave it on, you run the risk of having it stick onto bubbled-out filling. The easiest, safest way to remove a hot crust shield from pie is to grab it with a pair of tongs. Don't try to use a potholder to move the shield; you'll invariably end up crushing either part of the pie's top crust or its edge.

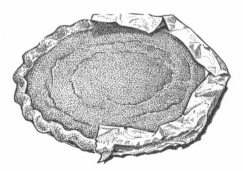 

Use foil or, much easier, a crust shield to keep the edges of crust from overbrowning.

CHOCOLATE AND COFFEE-FLAVORED CRUSTS

No self-respecting pie chapter would be complete without a crust featuring the compelling flavor and rich, dark color of chocolate. Chocolate and whole grains go very well together, as you'll see throughout this book. In addition, the coffee-flavored Café-au-Lait crust on page 486 is one we're certain you'll love. These two crust recipes can be adapted to any favorite pie that calls for a chocolate crust.

Peanut Butter Cream Pie

YIELD: One 9-inch pie, 8 to 10 servings
BAKING TEMPERATURE: 375°F
BAKING TIME: 25 to 30 minutes for the crust

This pie is, yes, over the top. We admit it. Don't go here unless you're willing to get fabulous compliments on the flavor, and a scolding for the calories.

This recipe comes from Robby Kuit, King Arthur test kitchen baker, mother of three and an avid dessert baker. She quoted the recipe for the filling to us from memory, which was our first clue to its status as a family favorite. After we made it, it was obvious why. The creamy filling, flavored with peanut butter, rests in a nicely complementary chocolate crust. Crushed peanut brittle on top lends a final touch.

Chocolate crust
1 cup (3⅜ ounces) whole wheat pastry flour
¼ cup (1 ounce) unbleached bread flour
2 tablespoons (⅜ ounce) Dutch-process cocoa powder
⅓ cup (2 ounces) semisweet chocolate chips
2 tablespoons (⅞ ounce) sugar
¼ teaspoon baking powder
¼ teaspoon salt
¾ teaspoon espresso powder (optional)
1 teaspoon vanilla extract
½ cup (1 stick, 4 ounces) cold unsalted butter
2 tablespoons (1 ounce) orange juice
3 to 4 tablespoons (1½ to 2 ounces) ice water

Filling
⅔ cup (6⅜ ounces) crunchy peanut butter
1 cup (8-ounce package) softened cream cheese

1½ cups (6 ounces) confectioners' sugar
1½ cups (12 ounces) heavy cream
1 teaspoon vanilla extract

Topping
½ cup (3 ounces) semisweet chocolate chips
2 tablespoons (1 ounce) heavy cream
¾ cup (3 ounces) chopped peanut brittle for garnish (optional)

TO PREPARE THE CRUST: Process the flours, cocoa and chocolate chips in a food processor until the chips are finely ground. Transfer the mixture to a medium bowl and whisk in the sugar, baking powder, salt and espresso powder (if using), then stir in the vanilla. Cut the butter into small cubes, and work it into the dry ingredients using your fingers, a pastry blender or fork, or a mixer until the dough is unevenly crumbly. Sprinkle in the orange juice, then add the water a tablespoon at a time, continuing to mix until the dough is cohesive. Grab a handful; if it holds together willingly and doesn't seem at all dry or crumbly, you've added enough liquid.

Shape the dough into a disk. Roll on its edge along a floured work surface, as though the disk were a wheel, to smooth the edges out. Pat the disk till it's about 1 inch thick, wrap it in plastic wrap, and refrigerate overnight. or for up to 3 days.

About 30 minutes before you're ready to assemble the pie, remove the dough from the refrigerator. Allow it to warm a bit and become flexible, 15 to 30 minutes.

Preheat the oven to 375°F.

Flour your work surface, and roll the dough into a 12-inch circle. Transfer the dough to a 9-inch regular (not deep-dish) pie pan that's at least 1¼ inches deep. Trim and crimp the edges, and dock the dough, or prick it with a fork. Line the crust with parchment or foil and fill it with uncooked rice or dried beans.

Bake the crust for 20 minutes. Remove it from the oven, remove the rice or beans and parchment or foil, and bake until you can start to smell the chocolate and the crust appears set, 5 to 10 minutes more. Remove it from the oven and cool it on a rack while you make the filling.

TO PREPARE THE FILLING: Beat together the peanut butter, cream cheese and confectioners' sugar in a medium mixing bowl until smooth. In a separate bowl, whip the heavy cream and vanilla until stiff peaks form; be careful not to go beyond this point, as the cream may separate. Fold a third of the whipped cream into the peanut butter mixture. It will be tough going at first, trying to get the two combined; just keep drawing your spatula through the mixture and turning it over on itself.

Fold in the remaining whipped cream in two batches. As you add more of the cream, folding it in will be easier, and the mixture will become light and fluffy. Be sure to scrape the bottom and sides of the bowl as you go. Pour the filling into the prebaked piecrust.

Chill the pie overnight, until it's firm. This is an important step—don't skip it! The overnight chill allows the flavors to mellow and softens the crust just enough that it's fork-tender.

Use a rubber spatula to gently but thoroughly combine the whipped cream and peanut butter mixture. The goal is to prevent the whipped cream from deflating, in order to keep the filling airy and light.

TO PREPARE THE TOPPING: Next day, combine the chocolate chips and cream in a heat-proof bowl and melt over simmering water or at low power in the microwave; stir until smooth, then drizzle the chocolate over the top of the pie. Sprinkle with chopped peanut brittle, if desired, and cut into wedges to serve.

NUTRITION INFORMATION PER SERVING (1/10 PIE, 157G): 10g whole grains, 640 cal, 46g fat, 11g protein, 19g complex carbohydrates, 31g sugar, 4g dietary fiber, 105mg cholesterol, 231mg sodium, 330mg potassium, 354RE vitamin A, 1mg vitamin C, 2mg iron, 71mg calcium, 197mg phosphorus, 15mg caffeine.

VARIATION: *To intensify the peanut flavor, spread ⅓ cup (3⅛ ounces) peanut butter in the bottom of the baked crust before adding the filling.*

BLIND-BAKING A PIECRUST

Sometimes a recipe calls for you to blind-bake a piecrust—i.e., pre-bake it, without filling, till it's either partially or fully baked. Why do this? Because some pies are filled with fresh, uncooked fruit, and it's impossible to keep fruit uncooked when it's in a hot oven; and some recipes call for a delicate custard filling, or other egg-based filling, that could become curdled or be made rubbery by the long baking needed to fully bake an unbaked crust. In addition, a crust that's blind-baked partway, then filled and finished, has a much better chance of remaining flaky and crisp.

To blind-bake a piecrust, roll it out and place it in the pan. Next, "dock" it, with a pastry docker or fork—prick it all over, to avoid trapping steam underneath.

Use a special docking tool, or a fork, to prick the crust all over.

Then, weigh the crust down; otherwise, steam released below the crust into the pan will cause it to expand like a blown-up balloon. Originally, bakers weighed down their piecrust with dried beans or uncooked rice; if you use this method, first line the crust with parchment paper or foil, to make the beans or rice easier to remove.

Line the piecrust with parchment paper or foil, then fill two-thirds full with dried beans or rice.

You may also choose to use pie weights, which are simply ceramic or aluminum balls about the size of very large peas; again, lining your crust with parchment or foil makes for easier removal of the weights. The pie chain—choose a long, 10-foot version for best utility—is made of a series of connected stainless-steel balls; you simply coil it onto the crust. Its advantage is that it's reusable and it's easy to remove (but watch your fingers—it gets hot!).

If you use a pie chain, for safety's sake be sure to use a pair of tongs to lift it out of the hot crust.

Finally, you may use a set of nesting pie pans: a solid bottom one in which to put the crust, and a perforated one that nests atop that crust as it bakes, holding it down but allowing it to brown. Refrigerate the crust for 20 minutes before baking; this will help prevent it from shrinking in the pan, as the fat (which is providing much of the crust's structure) will have a chance to solidify.

For a fully baked crust, bake it in a preheated 375°F oven for 20 minutes with the weights; then remove the weights, and bake it for an additional 10 to 15 minutes. For a partially baked crust—one that will finish baking with its filling—bake for 15 minutes with the weights, then remove the weights, fill and bake as directed in the recipe.

Midnight Mocha Pie in a Café-au-Lait Crust

YIELD: One 9-inch pie, 8 to 10 servings
BAKING TEMPERATURE: 350°F
BAKING TIME: 45 minutes

The addition of espresso powder to this pie's crust makes all the difference. We only wonder—why did we never think of this before? Instant coffee crystals just aren't the same. Go ahead, treat yourself; you'll find yourself using espresso powder more often than you expect, particularly when you discover the secret flavor boost it gives to chocolate. If espresso powder isn't in your pantry, we give you a mail-order source on page 588.

If you're looking for a deep, dark, dense chocolate pie, one whose filling is so moist it glistens, one that makes its own light, crisp-crackly topping, you've found it. This pie is disturbingly liquid when you pull it out of the oven, but don't panic; an overnight rest in the refrigerator solidifies it and gives all the flavors a chance to mellow.

Café au-lait crust
½ cup (1¾ ounces) old-fashioned rolled oats
½ cup (2 ounces) whole barley flour
⅓ cup (1⅜ ounces) unbleached all-purpose flour
¼ cup (1 ounce) confectioners' sugar
Heaping ¼ teaspoon salt
6 tablespoons (¾ stick, 3 ounces) cold unsalted butter
¼ teaspoon espresso powder
2½ to 3 tablespoons (1¼ to 1½ ounces) milk or cream, divided

Filling
4 tablespoons (½ stick, 2 ounces) unsalted butter
1½ cups (10½ ounces) granulated sugar
¼ teaspoon salt
4 large eggs
¼ cup (¾ ounce) Dutch-process cocoa
2 tablespoons (1 ounce) coffee liqueur (or substitute strong brewed coffee)
1 tablespoon cold milk or cream
2 teaspoons espresso powder
1 teaspoon vanilla extract
2 tablespoons (⅝ ounce) cornmeal
⅔ cup (4 ounces) semisweet chocolate chips

TO PREPARE THE CRUST: Grind the oats in a food processor (mini, if you have one) for about 30 seconds. Transfer the oats to a medium bowl and stir in the flours, sugar and salt. Work the butter into the dry ingredients using your fingers, a pastry blender or fork, or a mixer until the dough is unevenly crumbly. Dissolve the espresso powder in 1 tablespoon of the milk or cream and sprinkle it into the dry ingredients. Then add the remaining milk or cream a tablespoon at a time, continuing to mix until the dough is cohesive. Grab a handful; if it holds together willingly and doesn't seem at all dry or crumbly, you've added enough liquid.

Shape the dough into a disk. Roll on its edge along a floured work surface, as though the disk were a wheel, to smooth the edges out. Pat the disk till it's about 1 inch thick, wrap it in plastic wrap, and refrigerate for at least 1 hour or for up to 3 days.

About 30 minutes before you're ready to assemble the pie, remove the dough from the refrigerator. Allow it to warm a bit and become flexible, 15 to 30 minutes.

Preheat the oven to 350°F.

Flour your work surface, and roll the dough into a 12-inch circle. Transfer the dough to a regular (not deep-dish) 9-inch pie pan that's at least 1¼ inches deep. Trim and crimp the edges. Place the crust in the refrigerator to chill while you're preparing the filling.

TO PREPARE THE FILLING: Beat together the butter, sugar and salt till smooth. Add the eggs one at a time, beating slowly but thoroughly after each addition; you want to combine them with the butter and sugar, but not beat in a lot of air. Stir in the cocoa, liqueur, milk (or cream), espresso powder and vanilla. Use a food processor (mini, if you have one) to grind together the cornmeal and chocolate chips. Add to the batter. Pour the batter into the crust.

TO BAKE THE PIE: Bake the pie for 45 minutes, adding a crust shield or foil around the edges of the crust after 20 minutes. Remove it from the oven, cool to room temperature, then refrigerate overnight before serving.

NUTRITION INFORMATION PER SERVING (1/10 PIE, 105G): 7g whole grains, 392 cal, 18g fat, 6g protein, 14g complex carbohydrates, 38g sugar, 2g dietary fiber, 119mg cholesterol, 32mg sodium, 160mg potassium, 154RE vitamin A, 1mg iron, 30mg calcium, 104mg phosphorus, 11mg caffeine.

> ### ESPRESSO POWDER IS CHOCOLATE'S BEST FRIEND
>
> We've known for years that vanilla enhances the flavor of chocolate. But we just recently discovered that the same is true of espresso powder, roasted coffee beans ground ultrafine so that they dissolve instantly in liquid. Adding just ¼ to ½ teaspoon espresso powder to a brownie or chocolate cake recipe will garner a lot of compliments and have folks asking you how you got the chocolate to taste so "chocolaty." Increasing the espresso powder to the point where you can actually identify coffee flavor in your baked treat is a great way to create mocha flavor. Give it a try.

SAVORY TURNOVERS AND QUICHES

Who says pie has to be just for dessert (or breakfast)? These make perfect entrées. When developing these recipes, we wanted to stay away from those heavy, 1970s whole wheat crusts, so we've used our entire whole grain repertoire to create light yet richly flavored, flaky crusts. In addition, at times we've sneaked in grated cheese, hot sauce or paprika to add pizzazz—let your imagination be your guide. Parsley—sure, go ahead. A little dried basil? You bet. Just don't add something that will make the dough too wet or too dry. Play around with different cheeses first, then some of your favorite spices. Go with understated flavors; the crust is an understudy to the filling, you know!

 # B.L.T. Quiche *(Bacon, Leek and Tomato)*

YIELD: One quiche, 8 to 10 servings
BAKING TEMPERATURE: 425°F, then 350°F
BAKING TIME: 35 minutes

Bacon and tomato, a favorite sandwich combo, joins mild leeks in this creamy quiche. The crust features the tang of Parmesan cheese, while Swiss cheese (or its Dutch cousin, Gouda) adds a mild but pleasant flavor accent to the filling.

Crust
¾ cup (2½ ounces) whole wheat pastry flour
¼ cup (1 ounce) unbleached bread flour
1 teaspoon sugar
¼ teaspoon baking powder
¼ teaspoon salt
⅛ teaspoon paprika
Pinch of cayenne or a few drops of hot sauce
6 tablespoons (1½ ounces) freshly grated Parmesan cheese
4 tablespoons (½ stick, 2 ounces) cold unsalted butter
1 tablespoon orange juice
2 to 3 tablespoons (1 to 1½ ounces) cold half-and-half or cream (light, heavy or whipping)

Filling

10 slices (about 12 ounces) bacon, fried and crumbled (generous ¾ cup), fat drained and reserved

1 large fresh leek, white and most of the green, cleaned, trimmed and sliced ¾ inch thick (about 7½ ounces)

3 medium (about 12 ounces) plum or Roma tomatoes

Salt and sugar to taste

Custard

1 cup (8 ounces) half-and-half

2 large eggs

1 tablespoon unbleached all-purpose flour

Generous ½ teaspoon salt

1 cup (4 ounces) grated Swiss or Gouda cheese

TO PREPARE THE CRUST: Whisk together the flours, sugar, baking powder, salt, paprika, cayenne (or hot sauce) and Parmesan in a medium bowl. Cut the butter into small cubes, and work it into the dry ingredients using your fingers, a pastry blender or fork, or a mixer till the dough is unevenly crumbly. Sprinkle in the orange juice, then add half-and-half (or cream) a tablespoon at a time, continuing to mix till the dough is cohesive. Grab a handful; if it holds together willingly and doesn't seem at all dry or crumbly, you've added enough liquid.

Shape the dough into a disk. Roll on its edge along a floured work surface, as though the disk were a wheel, to smooth the edges out. Pat the disk till it's about 1 inch thick, wrap it in plastic wrap, and refrigerate overnight or for up to 3 days.

About 30 minutes before you're ready to assemble the pie, remove the dough from the refrigerator. Allow it to warm a bit and become flexible, 15 to 30 minutes.

Preheat the oven to 425°F.

Flour your work surface, and roll the dough into a 12-inch circle. Transfer the dough to a 9-inch regular (not deep-dish) pie pan that's at least 1¼ inches deep. Trim and crimp the edges. Place the crust in the refrigerator to chill while you're preparing the filling.

TO PREPARE THE FILLING: Heat 2 tablespoons of the reserved bacon fat in a skillet, and fry the sliced leeks slowly, till they've softened but aren't mushy. Try to keep each slice intact. Remove them from the pan and set them aside.

> ### SUGAR ON TOMATOES?
>
> We often add sugar to tomato-based dishes, including soup, spaghetti sauce, tomato salad and the fried tomatoes in this recipe. Sugar? On a vegetable? Well, first of all, the tomato is a fruit, not a vegetable. And second, it's a fruit with lovely flavor that tends to be hidden by its high acidity. Sugar, like salt, is a flavor enhancer, and it also tames a tomato's acidity, when used judiciously. Just sprinkle and stir and taste till you have tomato flavor that really shines.

Remove the stem end and bottom from each tomato. Slice the tomatoes ½ to ¾ inch thick. Add 2 tablespoons of the reserved bacon fat to the pan and fry the tomatoes over medium heat for 2 minutes on each side. Season with salt and sugar to taste (see sidebar). Remove from the pan and set aside.

TO ASSEMBLE AND BAKE THE QUICHE: Remove the crust from the refrigerator. Carefully set the sliced leeks in the bottom of the crust. Layer the tomatoes over the leeks. Whisk together the half-and-half, eggs, flour, salt, cheese and crumbled bacon in a medium bowl. Pour this mixture over the vegetables.

Bake the quiche for 10 minutes. Reduce the heat to 350°F, add a crust shield or foil around its edges and bake for an additional 25 minutes. When the quiche is done, a knife inserted 1 inch from the edge will come out wet but clean. Remove the quiche from the oven and allow it to cool to lukewarm before serving. Refrigerate any leftovers.

NUTRITION INFORMATION PER SERVING (1/10 QUICHE, 136G): 7g whole grains, 260 cal, 17g fat, 11g protein, 16g complex carbohydrates, 2g dietary fiber, 84mg cholesterol, 389mg sodium, 254mg potassium, 153RE vitamin A, 12mg vitamin C, 2mg iron, 209mg calcium, 218mg phosphorus.

VARIATION: *If you prefer, substitute 1 medium onion, yellow or sweet, for the leek. Peel, slice in ¼-inch rings, and cook as directed for leeks.*

CHANGING WITH THE SEASONS

Flour is like a sponge: it absorbs liquid from the atmosphere. In nondesert climates, flour will be moister in summer, when it's usually humid, and drier in winter, when the air is cold and dry. In low-humidity climes, such as desert areas, flour is usually very dry. What does this mean for your pie baking? There's usually a range of liquid given for the crust; you'll find yourself using the greater amount of liquid during dry months, the lesser amount when the humidity is high. At times you may even need less (or more) liquid than the recipe specifies; that's OK. Enough liquid to make a cohesive dough is the goal, however you get there.

Asparagus and Scallion Quiche

YIELD: One quiche, 8 to 10 servings

BAKING TEMPERATURE: 375°F

BAKING TIME: 40 to 45 minutes

This mild-flavored barley crust really lets the flavors of the filling shine through. In this quiche it's asparagus, one of our favorite harbingers of spring. Asparagus always feels like such an extravagant vegetable: aside from its price, it's also impressive-looking, the bright-green stems with their "flower" tips standing tall and straight on their own special stand in the produce section. This quiche pairs asparagus with scallions in a dish that simply sings of spring.

Crust
¾ cup (3 ounces) whole barley flour

¼ cup (1 ounce) unbleached all-purpose flour

1 tablespoon confectioners' sugar

Heaping ¼ teaspoon salt

½ cup (1 stick, 4 ounces) cold unsalted butter

1 large egg, lightly beaten

1 to 2 teaspoons cold cream or milk

Vegetables
1 pound (before trimming) fresh asparagus, thin stalks

1 bunch (about 4 ounces, untrimmed) scallions

2 tablespoons (1 ounce) unsalted butter

¼ teaspoon salt

½ to ¾ teaspoon dried tarragon, crumbled if coarse

¼ teaspoon dried thyme

2 tablespoons (1 ounce) dry sherry or water

Custard filling
2 large eggs

6 tablespoons (3-ounce package) cream cheese, cut into marble-size bits, softened

¼ teaspoon salt

Dash of pepper

1¼ cups (10 ounces) half-and-half or light cream

¼ cup (2 ounces) goat cheese

TO PREPARE THE CRUST: Whisk together the flours, sugar and salt in a medium bowl. Cut the butter into small cubes, and work it into the dry ingredients using your fingers, a pastry blender or fork, or a mixer till the dough is unevenly crumbly. Add the egg, stirring till it's well integrated. Sprinkle in the cream

---

PREPARING ASPARAGUS

Some recipes call for you to peel asparagus before using. This isn't necessary, and in fact removes some of the vegetable's nutrients. But you may find that, if not thoroughly cooked, the skin can be a bit stringy. This is especially true with large asparagus that may be old and somewhat "woody." The solution? Try to buy thinner stalks, ones that are firm and smooth (not wrinkled) and have tightly closed buds at the tip.

Almost all recipes call for you to cut or snap off the bottom of the stalks. How do you know where to cut? It's easy—the stalk will "tell" you. Simply grasp the lower third of the stalk and break it; it will automatically break at the juncture between tender and tough. Nature is truly amazing.

SCISSORS MAKES SHORT WORK OF CHOPPING VEGETABLES

A plain pair of household scissors is a handy tool to keep in the kitchen. Besides "chopping" meat or vegetables or snipping lettuce or herbs, a pair of scissors is the best tool ever for cutting hot pizza into slices. We also use a scissors to snip down through the top edge of the crust when cutting that first piece of hot pie; it's more maneuverable and precise than a knife and, if your pie pan is nonstick, it's easier to keep a scissors from nicking the pan than it is a knife.

(or milk), continuing to mix till the dough is cohesive. Grab a handful; if it holds together willingly and doesn't seem at all dry or crumbly, you've added enough liquid.

Shape the dough into a disk. Roll on its edge along a floured work surface, as though the disk were a wheel, to smooth the edges out. Pat the disk till it's about 1 inch thick, wrap it in plastic wrap, and refrigerate overnight or for up to 3 days.

About 30 minutes before you're ready to assemble the pie, remove the dough from the refrigerator. Allow it to warm a bit and become flexible, about 10 to 15 minutes.

Preheat the oven to 375°F.

Flour your work surface, and roll the dough into a 12-inch circle. Transfer the dough to a 9-inch regular (not deep-dish) pie pan that's at least 1¼ inches deep. Trim and crimp the edges, making a tall crimp. Place the crust in the refrigerator to chill while you're preparing the filling.

TO PREPARE THE VEGETABLES: Snap the ends off the asparagus. Clean the scallions, trimming off and discarding only the really ragged green parts and leaving the rest intact. Use a knife (or scissors) to snip the asparagus and scallions into bite-size pieces. Melt the butter in a large sauté pan, and fry the vegetables gently till they're lightly browned, about 15 minutes. Add the salt, herbs and sherry or water, stir, cover the pan, and turn off the heat. Let the vegetables rest while you prepare the filling.

TO PREPARE THE CUSTARD FILLING: Whisk together the eggs, cream cheese, salt, pepper and half-and-half or cream in a medium bowl, beating till well combined. There may be a few small lumps of cream cheese remaining; that's OK.

TO ASSEMBLE AND BAKE THE QUICHE: Arrange the vegetables in the bottom of the crust. Crumble the goat cheese, and sprinkle it evenly over the vegetables. Gently pour the custard filling over all. Bake the pie for 40 to 45 minutes, adding a crust shield or foil around the edges for the final 20 minutes. Remove the quiche from the oven and let it rest for about 45 minutes before serving. Refrigerate any leftovers.

NUTRITION INFORMATION PER SERVING (1/10 QUICHE, 136G): **9g whole grains,** 270 cal, 22g fat, 7g protein, 13g complex carbohydrates, 1g sugar, 3g dietary fiber, 120mg cholesterol, 281mg sodium, 185mg potassium, 312RE vitamin A, 6mg vitamin C, 1mg iron, 77mg calcium, 117mg phosphorus.

Roasted Corn Quiche

YIELD: One quiche, 8 to 10 servings
BAKING TEMPERATURE: 400°F
BAKING TIME: 35 to 40 minutes

We hope the recipe for this dish will be just a starting point for those of you who find it intriguing; we're sure you can think of lots of ways to make this recipe your own. Make it just as it is and serve slices as a side dish. Add some cooked crumbled bacon and call it supper, with a salad on the side. Make it Southwestern, with some cumin in place of the thyme, a cup of grated cheese and a smattering of sliced jalapeño peppers. Got some extra barbecued chicken? Sure, mix it in! One caveat: Too many add-ins might yield an excess of filling for the crust. Just roll the crust more thinly and use a deeper pie pan if you foresee this becoming an issue.

Crust

⅔ cup (2¼ ounces) old-fashioned rolled oats
¾ cup (3⅛ ounces) unbleached all-purpose flour
¼ teaspoon salt
½ cup (1 stick, 4 ounces) cold unsalted butter
3 to 5 tablespoons (1½ to 2½ ounces) ice water

Filling

4 ears fresh corn (2 to 2½ cups kernels)
1½ tablespoons unsalted butter
1½ cups (7½ ounces) diced sweet onion (1 medium-to-large onion) 1 medium (about 5 ounces) red bell pepper, diced (about 1½ cups)
3 large eggs
1½ cups (12 ounces) half-and-half
1 teaspoon dried thyme
½ teaspoon Worcestershire sauce
½ teaspoon salt
¼ teaspoon pepper
1 cup (2¼ ounces) sliced scallions, white and green parts
¼ cup (⅜ ounce) snipped fresh chives

TO PREPARE THE CRUST: Grind the oats in a food processor (mini, if you have one) for about 30 seconds. Transfer the oats to a medium bowl, and stir in the flour and salt. Cut the butter into small cubes, and work it into the dry ingredients using your fingers, a pastry blender or fork, or a mixer till the

---

WHEN IS A PIE A QUICHE?

A quiche is an open-faced (single-crust) pie, usually comprised of a custard-based filling containing cheese, along with meat, fish and/or vegetables. Often quiches are baked in a shallow fluted tart pan; but since the standard American pie pan is much more likely to grace the kitchen cupboard of the typical American baker, we've chosen to use a 9-inch pie pan for the quiches in this chapter, rather than a quiche pan. Do feel free to substitute a 10-inch quiche pan, if you own one, for any of these quiche recipes. The ingredient quantities can remain the same, but you'll want to reduce the baking time just a bit.

dough is unevenly crumbly. Sprinkle in the water a tablespoon at a time, continuing to mix till the dough is cohesive. Grab a handful; if it holds together willingly and doesn't seem at all dry or crumbly, you've added enough liquid.

Shape the dough into a disk. Roll on its edge along a floured work surface, as though the disk were a wheel, to smooth the edges out. Pat the disk till it's about 1 inch thick, wrap it in plastic wrap and refrigerate for at least 30 minutes or for up to 3 days.

About 30 minutes before you're ready to assemble the quiche, remove the dough from the refrigerator. If it's been chilled longer than 30 minutes, allow it to warm a bit and become flexible, 15 to 30 minutes.

Flour your work surface, and roll the dough into a 12-inch circle. Transfer the dough to a regular (not deep-dish) 9-inch pie pan that's at least 1¼ inches deep. Trim and crimp the edges, making a tall crimp. Place the crust in the refrigerator to chill while you're preparing the filling.

Preheat the oven to 450°F or fire up the barbecue grill.

TO PREPARE THE FILLING: Shuck the corn, and remove the silk. Spray the ears lightly with nonstick vegetable oil spray, and place on a baking sheet. Roast the corn in the oven, turning occasionally, till the kernels are golden brown, 20 to 25 minutes. If using the grill, cook the ears over medium heat, turning frequently, till evenly colored all over. Remove the corn from the heat and cool to room temperature. Cut the kernels from the cobs, using a serrated knife. You should have between 2 and 2½ cups.

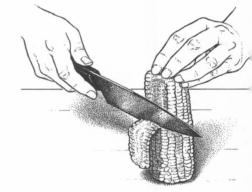

Hold the corncob vertically, stem-end down, on a flat surface. Placing a serrated knife between corn kernels and cob, gently saw downward to remove kernels.

Melt the butter in a large skillet over medium heat. Add the onion and bell pepper, and cook till the vegetables are soft, 5 to 7 minutes. Remove the pan from the heat, and set it aside to cool.

Whisk together the eggs, half-and-half, thyme, Worcestershire sauce, salt and pepper in a large mixing bowl. Stir in the scallions, chives, corn and sautéed onion-pepper mixture.

Preheat the oven to 400°F (or reduce the oven heat to 400°F, if it was at 450°F for the corn).

TO ASSEMBLE AND BAKE THE QUICHE: Remove the crust from the refrigerator, and pour the filling into it. (If you have too much filling, simply pour the excess into a custard cup, and bake it along with the quiche, removing it from the oven when a cake tester inserted into the center comes out clean.) Bake the quiche for 35 to 40 minutes, covering the crust with a pie shield or foil after 25 minutes. When the quiche is done, the center won't wobble when you jiggle the pan, and a knife inserted 1 inch from the edge will come out wet but clean. Remove the quiche from the oven and cool for at least 30 minutes before serving.

NUTRITION INFORMATION PER SERVING (1/10 QUICHE, 191G): 6g whole grains, 271 cal, 18g fat, 6g protein, 23g complex carbohydrates, 3g dietary fiber, 108mg cholesterol, 206mg sodium, 261mg potassium, 274RE vitamin A, 34mg vitamin C, 2mg iron, 66mg calcium, 143mg phosphorus.

VARIATION: *To make this pie with a golden cornmeal crust, substitute ¼ cup (2½ ounces) whole grain cornmeal for the oats. One caveat: we've found that piecrust made with whole cornmeal inevitably has a somewhat gritty texture. If you don't mind this signature "grittiness" that cornmeal sometimes imparts, go for it. Or, if you're willing to eschew whole grains in favor of a more processed grain (just this once!), use regular fine-grind cornmeal, or masa harina.*

Beef and Portobello Mushroom Turnovers

YIELD: 10 large turnovers
BAKING TEMPERATURE: 375°F
BAKING TIME: 35 minutes

These entrée-size turnovers feature a wine-scented stir-fry of beef, mushrooms and onions inside a buttery 100 percent whole wheat crust. Serve them with a garnish of sour cream and a "kitchen sink" salad: lettuce with every possible salad-type item you can find in the fridge!

Crust
3 cups (12 ounces) traditional whole wheat flour
2 tablespoons (7/8 ounce) buttermilk powder (optional)
1 tablespoon confectioners' sugar
3/4 teaspoon salt
1/2 teaspoon baking powder
1 cup plus 2 tablespoons (2 1/4 sticks, 9 ounces) cold unsalted butter
1/3 cup (2 5/8 ounces) orange juice
2/3 cup (5 3/8 ounces) ice water

Filling
1 1/2 pounds London broil, 1 inch thick
1/4 cup (1 ounce) unbleached all-purpose flour
1 teaspoon dried parsley
1/2 teaspoon dried thyme
1 teaspoon salt
1/2 teaspoon coarsely ground black pepper
3 tablespoons (1 1/4 ounces) olive oil or vegetable oil, divided
Scant 5 cups (13 3/4 ounces) sliced portobello or white mushrooms
2 1/4 cups (11 1/4 ounces) chopped sweet or yellow onion
Generous 3/4 cup (6 1/2 ounces) red wine

TO PREPARE THE CRUST: Whisk together the flour, buttermilk powder (if using), sugar, salt and baking powder in a medium bowl. Cut the butter into small cubes, and work it into the dry ingredients using your fingers, a pastry blender or fork, or a mixer till the dough is unevenly crumbly. Sprinkle in the orange juice, mixing to combine. Then add ice water a tablespoon at a time, continuing to mix till the dough is cohesive. Grab a handful; if it holds together willingly and doesn't seem at all dry or crumbly, you've added enough liquid.

Divide the dough into 10 pieces. Shape each piece into a disk. Roll each disk on its edge along a floured work surface, as though the disk were a wheel, to smooth the edges out. Wrap the disks in plastic wrap, and refrigerate overnight or for up to 3 days. The filling can be made ahead of time and refrigerated for up to 3 days or it can be made just prior to filling the pockets.

TO PREPARE THE FILLING: Cut the beef into ½-inch pieces. The easiest, neatest way to do this is to cut it into ½-inch slices, then use a pair of scissors to cut each slice lengthwise into two long ½-inch-wide strips. Use the scissors to snip all the strips into ½-inch cubes. Toss the beef in a large bowl with the flour, parsley, thyme, salt and pepper. Set it aside while you prepare the vegetables.

In a large skillet (preferably 12-inch), heat 1 tablespoon oil. Add the mushrooms, and sauté, stirring frequently, until they're golden brown, about 10 minutes. Transfer them to a large bowl. Add another tablespoon of oil, and sauté the onions, stirring frequently, until they're a mottled light gold and darker brown, about 10 minutes. Transfer them to the bowl with the mushrooms.

Heat the remaining tablespoon of oil in the skillet, and add the beef. Sauté for several minutes, stirring frequently, until it's evenly browned. Return the mushrooms and onions to the pan, then add the wine. Cook over medium-low heat, scraping the bits up from the bottom of the pan, until the wine has thickened and coats the beef and vegetables about 10 minutes. Remove from the heat; refrigerate the filling until you're ready to use it.

About 30 minutes before you're ready to assemble the turnovers, remove the dough from the refrigerator. Allow it to warm a bit and become flexible, 15 to 30 minutes.

Preheat the oven to 375°F. Lightly grease 2 baking sheets or line with parchment paper.

TO ASSEMBLE AND BAKE THE TURNOVERS: Flour your work surface, and roll each piece of dough into an 8-inch circle, making the circles as round and even as possible. Trim the edges, if you're feeling particularly neat.

Spread about ½ cup of the filling on half of the circles, placing it just off-center so that you have room to fold the dough in half and have the edges meet. Paint halfway around the edge of each circle with some milk; this will help the turnovers stay sealed. Fold the rounds into half-circles, pressing down with the tines of a fork to seal them shut around the edges. Prick each turnover several times with a fork, to let the steam escape, and place them on the prepared baking sheets.

Bake the turnovers till they're lightly browned, 35 minutes. If they appear to be browning too quickly, tent them with foil for the final 10 minutes of baking. Remove them from the oven and serve hot or warm. Refrigerate any leftovers.

NUTRITION INFORMATION PER SERVING (1 TURNOVER, 230G): 34g whole grains, 550 cal, 32g fat, 20g protein, 33g complex carbohydrates, 1g sugar, 5g dietary fiber, 108mg cholesterol, 446mg sodium, 643mg potassium, 177RE vitamin A, 6mg vitamin C, 4mg iron, 76mg calcium, 358mg phosphorus.

NO PEEKING!

The amount of willpower needed to *not* immediately cut into a hot-from-the-oven pie or quiche is daunting. But however much it takes: summon it. The result can only be disappointing. Sure, you're dying to see how it looks inside, whether it thickened properly, if the bottom crust is nice and brown. But pie isn't finished setting up until it cools, at least a bit. A hot fruit pie, cut immediately, will release its filling into the hole you've opened. The bigger the wedge you cut, the larger the amount of fruit will flow into the breach, robbing the remainder of the pie of its filling. A custard pie or quiche may ooze or settle. And aside from all that, the pie will be too hot to taste without burning your mouth. So walk away, finish some chores, do whatever it takes; but once you take that pie out of the oven, don't cut into it for at least 30 minutes, preferably 45 minutes or an hour or even longer, if the recipe directs. You'll have a beautiful pie, ready to eat, and you'll be happy you waited.

PASTRY
ethereal & wholesome

When you walk into a bakery, you see these beauties beaming at you from a lighted case. They look impossibly tender and light, their crisp surfaces shiny with glaze. What could be further from most people's idea of whole grain baking than a croissant, whose ethereal layers of dough and hauntingly flaky texture epitomize baking's highest expression?

We have found, much to our delight, that using whole grains in pastry dough means no compromise in quality at all. In fact, the complex, rich flavors that whole grains bring to pastries more than compensate for the little bit of extra attention the dough needs. Adding whole grains to classic, buttery puff pastry has been a revelation, giving more to taste and enjoy in each bite.

Every whole grain brings with it its own set of baking characteristics. When we looked at which whole grains to use in pastry, we discovered that some grains just didn't have the right temperament for the job. Cornmeal, no matter how finely ground, retains a grittiness that just doesn't belong in pastry. The assertive flavor and lack of gluten in rye make it suitable only for very limited and specific pastry applications. But when we turned to oats, whole wheat pastry flour and barley, we found ourselves in much friendlier territory. The type of whole grain you choose can alter the personality of the finished pastry. Of the three grains we settled on, whole wheat flour makes a pastry dough that's easiest to roll out and has the most elasticity. Oat or whole barley flour gives crunchier or more flaky results, respectively, but you have to be a little more patient with the dough.

If you're interested in making your own pastry and defying every preconceived notion of what whole grain baking is like, this is the place to start. It takes a little extra time, but the steps are simple and the results are immensely satisfying.

499

CLASSIC WHOLE GRAIN PUFF PASTRY

Its ingredients are basic: flour, butter, water, salt. What you do with them is where classic puff pastry departs from everyday baking. First, you surround a prepared block of butter with dough. Then you roll out this package and fold it over on itself, creating layers of butter and dough. Each set of folds, or "turns," multiplies the number of layers, until you've created 729 separate layers of dough and butter, all within six turns. This process, easier than it sounds, creates "laminated" dough. The dough can be portioned and frozen for up to three months, ready to work its magic.

Classic puff pastry uses no yeast: the "puff" comes from the heat of the oven working on the layers of butter to create steam. The steam separates the layers of dough, giving rise (literally) to the distinct texture and flakiness for which puff pastry is known.

Because of its unique characteristics, we found whole wheat pastry flour to be the whole grain of choice for laminated dough. When paired with the higher gluten content of bread flour and a little bit of nonfat dry milk for mellowness, the dough rolled nicely and created a very light, tender croissant. Pastry dough that includes yeast, or that doesn't require so much rolling and folding, can accommodate other whole grain flours that have little or no gluten, such as barley and oat, as featured in Yeasted Whole Grain Puff Pastry (p. 515) and Whole Grain Blitz Puff Pastry Dough (p. 509).

LIGHT DOUGH NEEDS A LIGHT TOUCH...

Let's face it, kneading by hand can be a sticky business, especially at the beginning of the process. Yet adding a lot of extra flour during kneading to cut down on the stickiness makes for heavy, stiff, dense baked goods. Instead, try using a dough scraper or baker's bench knife in one hand while you're kneading. Push the dough down and away from you with your free hand, then scrape it back on top of itself and give it a quarter turn with a lightly greased dough scraper or baker's bench knife in the other hand. A little squirt of nonstick spray on the work surface will help too. Keep using the scraper to fold the dough on itself, using your free hand for kneading, and you'll see how quickly the dough develops from sticky mess into a lovely, smooth ball.

The dough becomes easier to handle as the water in it is more evenly distributed and absorbed. This takes a few minutes, but a little patience, nonstick spray and the indispensable dough scraper or baker's bench knife will pay off in a big way when you see the wonderfully light texture of the croissants you've baked. These tools also help with any moist dough and you'll notice we refer to them often in this book. We wouldn't knead dough without them in our test (or home) kitchens.

Whole grain doughs can be sticky at first; use a baker's bench knife or dough scraper to help you turn it over while kneading. That way, you'll be less likely to add too much flour.

Classic Whole Wheat Puff Pastry: A Primer

YIELD: 3³⁄₄ pounds dough, enough for 24 croissants

While puff pastry isn't something you can make from scratch on short notice, it's a simple process. You already learned most of the skills you need to make this dough in kindergarten: folding, making a straight line, matching edges and rolling are all that's required. Just as it did then, neatness counts, but you get to throw a lot of flour around too. Just follow the steps and pictures here, and take your time.

Step 1: Making the Dough
3 cups (10¹⁄₈ ounces) whole wheat pastry flour
3 cups (12³⁄₄ ounces) unbleached bread flour
2 tablespoons (¹⁄₂ ounce) nonfat dry milk
4 tablespoons (¹⁄₂ stick, 2 ounces) chilled unsalted butter
2 teaspoons salt
1¹⁄₂ cups plus 2 tablespoons (13 ounces) water

Whisk together the flours and nonfat dry milk in the bowl of an electric stand mixer. Add the chilled butter and blend with the mixer's paddle attachment, or by hand with a pastry blender, until the mixture resembles cornmeal. Add the salt to the water, stir well, then add to the flour mixture. Mix gently with a fork, or the mixer's paddle at a low speed, until you have a rough dough that pulls away from the sides of the bowl. If you need to add more water, do so a tablespoon at a time until the dough holds together.

Turn out the dough onto a lightly floured surface and knead until it's smooth and a bit springy; this will take 2 to 3 minutes. Avoid adding extra flour if possible; a baker's bench knife or dough scraper can help you with the kneading process (see sidebar, facing page). If the dough seems a little wet or tacky, that's OK; the whole wheat takes a little extra time to absorb the water in the dough.

Pat the dough into a square about 1 inch thick and wrap it in plastic wrap or place it in a large plastic bag. Refrigerate the dough for at least 1 hour.

Step 2: Preparing the Butter
2 cups (4 sticks, 1 pound) unsalted butter, softened but still cool to the touch
¹⁄₃ cup (1¹⁄₈ ounces) whole wheat pastry flour
Unbleached all-purpose flour for dusting

Using a mixer, food processor or spoon, combine the butter and whole wheat pastry flour until smooth and well blended, with no lumps. Lightly flour a piece of plastic wrap or wax paper, place the butter/flour mixture on it and pat it into an 8-inch square. Cover the square and place it on a flat surface in the refrigerator for at least 30 minutes. (Adding flour to the butter helps stabilize it so it won't "flow" out the seams when rolled.)

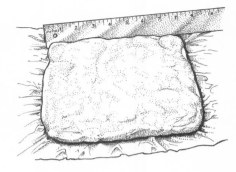

Combine the cool butter and flour until smooth, then form into an 8-inch square on a piece of lightly floured plastic wrap. It will be about ³⁄₄ inch thick.

Step 3: Rolling and Folding
Have on hand:
Unbleached all-purpose flour for dusting
Rolling pin
Yardstick or tape measure
Pastry brush
Water

Remove the dough from the refrigerator and place on a lightly floured surface. Gently roll it into a square about 12 inches across. Put the butter square in the center of the dough at a 45-degree angle.

Place the butter so it looks like a diamond in the square of dough.

Pull the flaps of the dough over the edges of the butter until they meet in the middle. Pinch and seal the edges together, moistening them with water if necessary. Press out any air bubbles before sealing the last seam. Dust the top of the dough with flour, then turn it over and tap it gently with the rolling pin into a rectangular shape. Make sure the dough isn't sticking underneath—dust with more flour if necessary—and roll it out from the center into a larger rectangle, 20 x 10 inches. The barrel of most standard-size rolling pins is 10 inches long, so when the dough is as wide as the rolling pin and twice as long, you're in good shape. Use a yardstick or tape measure to double-check the rectangle's length.

When the dough is the right size, lightly sweep off any excess flour from the top with your pastry brush, wet the long edges just a little with your fingers, then fold the bottom third up to the center and the top third over (like a business letter). The dough may be a little floppy, so take care to gently line the edges up on top of each other, and even up the corners so they're directly above one another, before taking the next step. Turn the dough 90 degrees to the right, so it looks like a book ready to be opened. You have completed the first turn.

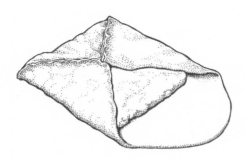

Bring the flaps of dough up and over the butter like an envelope around a letter, pinching the seams together. Wet the edges of the dough before pinching to ensure a tight seal. Press out any air bubbles before closing the last seam.

Roll the dough-butter package from the center out to form a 20 x 10-inch rectangle.

If the dough is still cool to the touch and relaxed, roll out to 20 x 10 inches again, fold, and turn 90 degrees to the right once more. If the dough springs back when you roll it, it isn't relaxed, so cover it and let it rest in the refrigerator for 20 minutes before trying again.

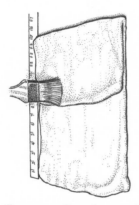

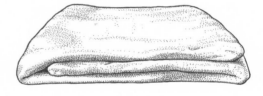

Brush off any excess flour, then wet the long edges of the dough lightly with your fingers. Fold the dough in thirds, like a business letter. Take care to line up the outside edges directly over each other.

After turning the dough 90 degrees to the right, it looks like a book ready to be opened.

When you've successfully rolled out the dough and folded it twice, you've completed two turns. Make a note of how many turns you've completed, and the time, and then put the dough back in the refrigerator. Classic puff pastry dough gets six turns, total, before being formed into finished shapes. Dough made with whole wheat needs longer rests (at least 1 hour) between turns than dough made with all white flour. Since this dough has no yeast, you can even let it rest overnight before turning it again. Just let it sit for 10 minutes after taking it out of the refrigerator to let the butter temper. Otherwise the butter will break when you start to roll it, instead of bending with the dough. Once you've completed six turns, you're ready to shape the dough into the pastries of your dreams.

The inclusion of whole wheat flour in laminated dough makes it a bit less forgiving and flexible as you push it with your rolling pin. You may see patches of butter peeking through the surface of the dough. Sprinkle those places liberally with some all-purpose flour and carry on, after first making sure there's no butter on your rolling pin to make things worse. Any butter already on the pin will stick to the dough and open it up in more places.

Also, be sure to stop and sprinkle flour underneath the dough often, turning it over if necessary. If you find your pin is still sticking to the surface, place a piece of plastic over the dough (we like food-storage bags, slit open, since they're heavier than wrap) and roll on top of that; there's no need to grease the plastic. You'll find even temperamental dough will be much easier to work with this way.

WHAT TO DO WITH ALL THAT DOUGH?

This recipe makes enough dough for 24 pastries, which can be more than you need at one time. We suggest cutting the chilled dough in half or quarters, and wrapping each piece well, first in plastic, then in foil. The dough will keep for 3 to 6 months, as long as it's shielded from exposure to air and the freezer door isn't opened too frequently.

To use frozen pastry dough, take it out of the freezer and thaw overnight in the refrigerator. If you see any dry spots or edges after opening the package, trim them off with a sharp knife before proceeding with the recipe.

Classic Whole Wheat Croissants

YIELD: 1 dozen croissants
BAKING TEMPERATURE: 425°F, then 350°F
BAKING TIME: 25 to 30 minutes

The spiral shape of a croissant in profile shows off puff pastry's hundreds of layers to their best advantage. By rolling the dough up, the layers surround each other, yielding an incredible combination of crisp outer layers with tender inner ones.

Puff pastry requires a hot oven initially, because the high temperature turns the moisture in the dough to steam, forcing the layers to separate. Having done its job, the steam then needs to be cooked away so the pastry isn't damp and underdone in the center. That takes a while, so be sure the croissants are a deep golden brown where the dough overlaps itself before taking them out of the oven.

½ recipe Classic Whole Wheat Puff Pastry (p. 501)
1 egg beaten with 1 tablespoon water, to glaze

Lightly grease a baking sheet or line with parchment paper.

TO SHAPE THE CROISSANTS: On a lightly floured surface, roll the dough to a 19 x 13-inch rectangle. Trim and discard the edges of the dough on all sides by using a ruler and cutting straight down with a very sharp knife or a pizza wheel. This cuts off the folded edges that would inhibit the "puff."

Cut the dough in thirds lengthwise and in half through the middle. This will give you six 4 x 9-inch rectangles. Cut these pieces in half diagonally, and arrange them so the points of the triangles are facing away from you. It's okay to stretch them out gently to elongate them when you do this. Cut a ½-inch notch in the short side of the triangle.

Roll up each triangle, starting at the notched edge and working toward the tip. Make sure the point is tucked under the bottom of the croissant. Form the crescent by bending the two ends toward the center where the dough's tip is tucked under.

Place the croissants on the prepared baking sheet. Cover and chill for at least 30 minutes; this keeps the butter in the layers from running out too quickly once in the oven.

Preheat the oven to 425°F.

TO BAKE THE CROISSANTS: Take the croissants out of the refrigerator, uncover them, and brush the tops with the beaten egg mixture. Bake for 15 minutes; reduce the heat to 350°F and bake for 10 to 15 minutes more. The croissants should be a deep golden brown all over. Remove from the oven and cool completely on a rack.

NUTRITION INFORMATION PER SERVING (1 CROISSANT, 70G): 14 g whole grains, 265 cal, 18g fat, 4g protein, 23g complex carbohydrates, 2g dietary fiber, 47mg cholesterol, 185mg sodium, 92mg potassium, 163RE vitamin A, 1mg iron, 21mg calcium, 77mg phosphorus.

FINISHING

It's traditional to finish a croissant in a way that signals what's inside. Plain croissants need no more than the shine they acquire in the oven from the egg wash. Fruit-filled croissants are often glazed with sugar or honey, or drizzled with a thin ribbon of confectioners' sugar icing. Almond-filled pastries should be glazed and sprinkled with toasted sliced or chopped almonds. Chocolate croissants get striped with melted chocolate. Savory filled croissants are usually made in a rectangular shape, with just enough filling showing at the ends to let the diner know what's inside.

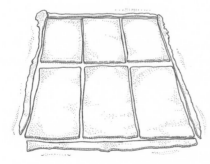

Roll the dough to a 19 x 13-inch rectangle, then trim the edges with a sharp knife or pizza cutter. Cut the dough in thirds lengthwise, and in half across the middle.

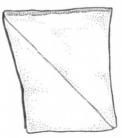

After cutting each piece of dough into two triangles, cut a ½-inch notch in the center of the short side, nearest you.

PALMIERS

Often affectionately called elephant ears, these pastries take a sheet of puff pastry, coat it with a sweet or savory topping, and roll it up like a scroll from both sides. Palmiers can be as big as your hand or in tidy half-dollar-size pieces, great for snacking, as a dessert accent next to mousse or ice cream. The savory version makes perfect hors d'oeuvres.

Sweet Palmiers

YIELD: 48 to 50 palmiers
BAKING TEMPERATURE: 425°F
BAKING TIME: 18 to 20 minutes

Sprinkling pastry dough with sugar, inside and out, gives it a satisfying crunch once baked. The sugar melts, then caramelizes; as soon as it takes on some color in the oven it goes very quickly, so keep a close eye on the baking time.

¼ recipe Classic Whole Wheat Puff Pastry (p. 501)
½ cup (3⅞ ounces) Demerara or maple sugar, plus more for dredging

TO ASSEMBLE: On a lightly floured work surface, roll the dough out to an 18 x 12-inch rectangle. Pick it up from time to time to make sure it doesn't stick to the countertop. Sprinkle the top evenly with sugar until it's completely covered. Starting with the long edges, roll the dough up from each side like a scroll, until the two sides meet in the middle.

Cut the long piece of dough in half, and transfer both halves to a baking sheet. Cover the dough and freeze for 30 minutes.

TO BAKE: Preheat the oven to 425°F.

Line a baking sheet with parchment paper. Remove the palmier dough from the freezer. Cut each log into ⅜-inch slices, and coat each slice in more sugar on both sides. Place the palmiers on the prepared baking sheet, leaving an inch of space between them. Bake until the tops are just beginning to brown on the edges, 12 minutes. Remove the pan from the oven, and turn the palmiers over using a fork and a spatula.

Return the palmiers to the oven and bake until the bottoms are nicely browned, 6 to 8 minutes more. Remove from the oven and cool on a rack before serving. The palmiers will become crunchier as they cool.

NUTRITION INFORMATION PER SERVING (2 PALMIERS, 22G): 3g whole grains, 81 cal, 4g fat, 1g protein, 6g complex carbohydrates, 4g sugar, 12mg cholesterol, 47mg sodium, 34mg potassium, 41RE vitamin A, 9mg calcium, 19mg phosphorus.

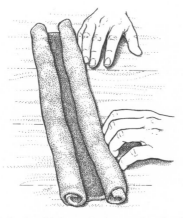

Roll the dough's long edges toward each other, forming a scroll shape when they meet in the center.

Turn the palmiers over after the first 12 minutes of baking; this will make them evenly crisp all over.

Savory Palmiers

YIELD: 48 to 50 palmiers
BAKING TEMPERATURE: 400°F
BAKING TIME: 18 to 20 minutes

Substituting a savory paste for sugar turns palmiers into a terrific appetizer, especially when the dough includes the more assertive flavors of whole grains. Start simply, sprinkling on some freshly grated Parmesan cheese before rolling, cutting and baking. From there it's easy to branch out: we've tried sundried tomato pesto, basil pesto and a purée of spinach, artichokes and goat cheese, to name a few possibilities. The key is to use a filling that has the consistency of a paste; if it's too wet, the center of the dough won't bake through and become crisp.

¼ recipe Classic Whole Wheat Puff Pastry (p. 501)
½ to ¾ cup (4 to 6 ounces) pesto or grated cheese, your choice of flavors

TO ASSEMBLE: Roll out the dough as for sweet palmiers (see recipe, previous page), and spread with the savory filling of your choice. Roll up the dough, freeze, cut, and bake the same way, adding a few minutes of baking time if necessary to cook the palmiers all the way through to the center.

NUTRITION INFORMATION PER SERVING (2 PALMIERS, MADE WITH BASIL PESTO, 23G): 3g whole grains, 96 cal, 7g fat, 2g protein, 6g complex carbohydrates, 13mg cholesterol, 83mg sodium, 50RE vitamin A, 33mg potassium, 50RE vitamin A, 22mg calcium, 22mg phosphorus.

WHOLE GRAIN BLITZ PUFF PASTRY

As the name implies, this is a quicker method of achieving almost as much of the distinctive flakiness of laminated dough without dirtying more than one mixing bowl (always a good thing). The butter is mixed into the dough in large chunks before folding. Since the dough doesn't have to stretch and encapsulate a large slab of butter as it does in classic puff pastry, it's possible to use other whole grain flours that don't have significant amounts of gluten. The trick is to give the dough a good rest after mixing (see sidebar, below). This extra time pays off, because the texture and flavor you get will be cause for amazement and delight.

GIVING BARLEY AND OAT FLOURS A TIME-OUT

The secret of using these flours in pastry is to give them a nice, long nap after the dough is mixed. This extra time allows the bran in the flour to absorb water, softening the dough as a result. When first mixed, pastry dough that includes these flours will be on the soft, sticky side: not something you can roll and fold easily. Like a recalcitrant child, the dough benefits from being left to itself for a while to think it over. An hour's rest will make the dough much easier to work with. An overnight nap (in the refrigerator) will do even more.

Whole barley flour is our preferred whole grain when looking for the flakiest results possible; it gives us the classic "shatter" you expect from traditional croissant dough. We found whole barley flour's flavor to be a good match for savory or meat-filled pastry.

Oat flour lends a hint of nutty sweetness to the dough, and we found ourselves pairing it with fruit fillings with excellent results.

The feel of pastry dough made with these flours is different from what you may be used to: it won't stretch as smoothly as a dough made with whole wheat pastry flour, and it isn't nearly as elastic. A wheat flour recipe made with whole barley flour instead won't roll out to as large a rectangle. Just keep this in mind and you'll be okay.

Whole Grain Blitz Puff Pastry Dough

YIELD: 2¼ pounds dough, enough for 32 (4-inch) squares or 2 tarts

The mixer does most of the work of putting this dough together. After giving it four letter folds, divide it in two and freeze half to use later.

1 cup (3¼ ounces) oat or whole barley flour
2½ cups (10⅝ ounces) unbleached bread flour
1½ cups (3 sticks, 12 ounces) chilled unsalted butter, cut into ½-inch pieces
1 cup (8 ounces) cold water
2 teaspoons salt

Using an electric mixer with a paddle attachment, mix the flours and cold butter at low speed until the mixture forms large chunks. Combine the water and salt and add to the flour-butter mixture. Mix on low speed just until the dough begins to come together into a shaggy mass. Turn out the dough onto a floured surface or a piece of parchment paper (see illustration) and fold it over on itself until it comes together. If you're not using parchment paper, a baker's bench knife can be helpful with gathering the dough (see sidebar, p. 500).

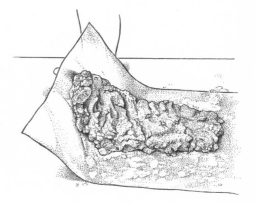

Use the parchment paper to help you pick up the shaggy dough and fold it over on itself.

Pat the dough into a block, roughly 8 x 10 inches. Sprinkle both sides with flour, then wrap in plastic wrap or a large plastic bag. Refrigerate the dough on a flat surface for at least 1 hour and as long as overnight.

After the dough has rested, remove it from the refrigerator and give it four letter folds, using the rolling and folding technique as described and illustrated on pages 502 to 503. After the last fold, chill the dough for 1 hour before using.

Nectarine Galette

YIELD: One galette, 10 servings
BAKING TEMPERATURE: 400°F
BAKING TIME: 35 to 40 minutes

You've just come back from the orchard or farmstand with an abundant supply of fragrant nectarines or peaches. What next? While you're budgeting your slices for cereal, or gearing up for pie or jam, consider making a quick and very simple galette. Start with Whole Grain Blitz Puff Pastry Dough (p. 509), and your dessert is in the oven as soon as you can roll it into a circle and slice up the fruit. The oat streusel underneath soaks up the wonderful juices from the fruit, while adding to the flavor (and fiber) in this dessert. Serve with heavy cream, Devon cream or ice cream.

Dough
½ recipe Whole Grain Blitz Puff Pastry Dough (p. 509)

Filling
1½ pounds (4 to 6 medium) nectarines, peaches or plums (not peeled), sliced thin
1 tablespoon fresh lemon juice
¼ cup (1¾ ounces) granulated sugar
½ teaspoon ground cinnamon
⅛ teaspoon ground nutmeg

Oat streusel
6 tablespoons (¾ stick, 3 ounces) unsalted butter, softened
½ cup (3¾ ounces) packed light or dark brown sugar
1 teaspoon ground cinnamon
¼ teaspoon salt
⅛ teaspoon ground nutmeg
½ cup (1⅝ ounces) whole wheat pastry flour
1 cup (3½ ounces) old-fashioned rolled oats

Lightly grease a baking sheet or line with parchment paper.

ROLLING THE DOUGH: On a floured work surface, roll the dough into a 13-inch circle. Transfer the dough to the prepared baking sheet. The edges will overlap the sides; that's OK for now, they'll be folded over the filling later.

TO MAKE THE FILLING: Slice the fruit and sprinkle with lemon juice. Combine the sugar, cinnamon and nutmeg in a small bowl.

Preheat the oven to 400°F.

TO MAKE THE STREUSEL: Stir together the butter, sugar, cinnamon, salt and nutmeg in a medium bowl until combined. Stir in the flour until the mixture is evenly moistened; stir in the oats to form a crumbly mixture.

TO ASSEMBLE: Place the streusel in the center of the dough, sprinkling it to an even thickness and leaving a 2-inch border of bare dough. Starting at the outer edge of the streusel, shingle the fruit slices in concentric circles until they form a high, domed center. Sprinkle the sugar-spice mixture over the fruit, then fold the edges of the dough up over the filling, making pleats as you go around the circle. For a shiny top, brush the dough with milk and sprinkle with granulated sugar if you like.

Bake the galette until the pastry is golden brown, the juices are bubbling and the sugar on the fruit has caramelized, 35 to 40 minutes. The juicier the fruit, the longer it will need to bake. Remove from the oven and cool on the pan on a rack for 20 minutes before slicing.

NUTRITION INFORMATION PER SERVING (1 SLICE, 1/10 GALETTE, 191G): 12g whole grains, 194 cal, 13g fat, 3g protein, 17g complex carbohydrates, 5g sugar, 1g dietary fiber, 34mg cholesterol, 196mg sodium, 109mg potassium, 143RE vitamin A, 3mg vitamin C, 1mg iron, 12mg calcium, 44mg phosphorus.

Chicken and Mushroom Pastry Pockets

YIELD: 9 pastries, 3 x 4 inches each
BAKING TEMPERATURE: 400°F
BAKING TIME: 23 to 25 minutes

These flaky pastries are filled with a tasty mixture of chicken, mushrooms and herbs. With a cup of soup and a salad, they are excellent light fare.

Filling
1 tablespoon vegetable oil
¾ pound ground chicken, turkey or pork
1 cup (2¾ ounces) chopped fresh mushrooms
½ cup (2½ ounces) diced onions
1 teaspoon ground sage
1 teaspoon dried thyme
1 teaspoon dried parsley or 2 teaspoons fresh
¾ teaspoon salt
¼ teaspoon pepper
½ cup (4 ounces) heavy cream or nonfat sour cream

Dough & egg wash
½ recipe Whole Grain Blitz Puff Pastry Dough (p. 509)
1 egg beaten with 1 tablespoon water

FOR THE FILLING: Heat the vegetable oil in a large skillet until you see ripples on its surface. Add the meat, breaking it up with a spoon into small chunks. Cook until the meat is browned. Add the mushrooms and onions and stir well. Cook until the onions are clear and most of the moisture has evaporated from the pan. Stir in the herbs, salt and pepper. Add the cream (or sour cream) and cook over medium-high heat until the bubbles in the liquid are ½ inch across. Remove the pan from the heat and let the filling mixture cool completely.

Preheat the oven to 400°F. Lightly grease a baking sheet or line with parchment paper.

TO ASSEMBLE: Roll out the dough on a floured work surface to a 19 x 13-inch rectangle. With a ruler and a pizza cutter or sharp knife, trim the edges to make an 18 x 12-inch rectangle. Cut the rectangle in thirds in both directions, to make 9 squares, 4 x 6 inches each.

Place 3 tablespoons of filling on one half of each rectangle. Brush the edges with some of the beaten egg mixture, fold the rectangle in half, and seal the edges of the pockets with the tines of a fork (see below).

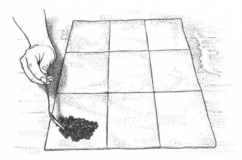

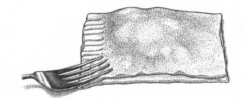

After trimming the edges, cut the dough into 9 rectangles, 4 by 6 inches each. Place 3 table-spoons of filling on one half of each rectangle.

Fold the uncovered half of the pastry over the filling, and seal the edges with the tines of a fork.

Transfer the pastries to the prepared baking sheet. Brush the tops with the remaining egg wash. Bake until the pastries are deep golden brown, 23 to 25 minutes. Remove from the oven and let cool for 10 minutes before serving.

NOTE: The pastries can be made ahead and frozen for up to 1 month. Remove the pastries from the freezer and defrost for 30 minutes before baking. Baking time may need to be increased by 5 minutes to make sure the filling is completely warmed through.

NUTRITION INFORMATION PER SERVING (1 PASTRY, 147G): 6g whole grains, 411 cal, 26g fat, 17g protein, 27g complex carbohydrates, 1g sugar, 2g dietary fiber, 107mg cholesterol, 411mg sodium, 253mg potassium, 229RE vitamin A, 1mg vitamin C, 2mg iron, 44mg calcium, 190mg phosphorus.

Peach and Ginger Turnovers

YIELD: 16 turnovers
BAKING TEMPERATURE: 400°F
BAKING TIME: 23 to 25 minutes

The mellow sweetness of ripe peaches is enhanced by the nip of crystallized ginger. A little drizzle of cinnamon glaze makes these turnovers look as good as they taste. The dough is good for tart shells or pastry crusts too.

Dough
¾ cup (2½ ounces) whole wheat pastry flour
¾ cup (3⅛ ounces) unbleached bread flour
½ teaspoon baking powder
¼ teaspoon salt
1 cup (2 sticks, 8 ounces) cold unsalted butter
½ cup (4 ounces) sour cream

Filling
2 cups (12 ounces) peeled, diced peaches
½ cup (3½ ounces) sugar
⅓ cup (2¼ ounces) diced crystallized ginger
3 tablespoons (1⅛ ounces) quick-cooking tapioca
½ teaspoon ground cinnamon
⅛ teaspoon ground nutmeg
Pinch of salt
¼ teaspoon almond extract (optional)

Egg wash
1 egg beaten with 1 tablespoon water

Cinnamon glaze (optional)
2 ¼ cups (9 ounces) confectioners' sugar
2 tablespoons plus 1 teaspoon (1¼ ounces) milk
2 tablespoons (1⅜ ounces) light corn syrup
1 teaspoon ground cinnamon

TO MAKE THE DOUGH: Whisk together the flours, baking powder and salt in a medium bowl. Cut in the butter, leaving it in chunks the size of your thumbnail. Stir in the sour cream; the dough will be blotchy and uneven in texture at this point. Turn it out onto a floured work surface or a piece of parchment paper (see the illustration for the shaggy texture of Whole Grain Blitz Puff Pastry Dough, p. 509) and bring it together with a few quick kneading strokes.

Pat the dough into a square, and roll it out to an 8 x 10-inch rectangle. Dust both sides of the dough with flour and fold it in thirds as you would a business letter. Flip the dough over and turn it 90 degrees; roll it out and fold it in thirds again. Wrap the dough and chill in the refrigerator for 30 minutes.

FOR THE FILLING: Place all the ingredients in a small saucepan. Let the mixture sit for 10 minutes, stirring occasionally, to allow the tapioca to soften. Place over medium heat, stirring constantly, until the sugar dissolves and the fruit begins to give up its juice. Bring to a simmer, and cook until the mixture thickens and becomes clear, 3 to 5 minutes. Remove from the heat and set aside to cool before using to fill turnovers.

Preheat the oven to 400°F. Lightly grease a baking sheet or line with parchment paper.

TO ASSEMBLE: Roll out the pastry dough on a floured surface to a 17-inch square. With a ruler and a pizza cutter or sharp knife, trim the edges to make a 16-inch square. Cut the square into 4 rows of 4-inch squares. Spoon 2 tablespoons of filling onto the center of each square. Brush the edges of the squares with some of the egg wash, and fold one corner of the pastry over the filling to the opposite corner to form a triangle. Repeat for all 16 turnovers. Seal the edges of the pastries together with a fork (see illustration p. 512, for pastry pockets). Transfer the turnovers to the prepared baking sheet. Brush the tops with more of the egg wash.

Bake the turnovers until deep golden brown, 23 to 25 minutes. Remove from the oven and let cool for at least 15 minutes before serving (the filling will be hot enough to burn your mouth if you try them too soon!), or cool completely before decorating with cinnamon glaze.

TO MAKE THE GLAZE (IF USING): Whisk together all the ingredients in a medium bowl until smooth; drizzle over the cooled turnovers.

NUTRITION INFORMATION PER SERVING (1 TURNOVER, UNGLAZED, 66G): 6g whole grains, 214 cal, 14g fat, 2g protein, 13g complex carbohydrates, 9g sugar, 1g dietary fiber, 36mg cholesterol, 57mg sodium, 88mg potassium, 136RE vitamin A, 2mg vitamin C, 1mg iron, 27mg calcium, 41mg phosphorus.

Yeasted Whole Grain Puff Pastry

YIELD: 3¾ pounds dough, enough for 24 croissants or 18 filled rectangular croissants

While classic puff pastry does wonderful things for tart shells, palmiers and potpie toppings, the croissants you're most likely to find at any American bakery are made from a laminated dough that includes yeast. The addition of yeast to pastry dough gives it an extra boost in the oven, adding a dimension of cloudlike centers to the shatteringly crisp layers of pastry.

Once yeast enters the picture, you need to allow for some rising time after shaping before the croissants go into the oven. Whole wheat pastry dough doesn't rise dramatically while being proofed, but when it gets into the oven it more than makes up the difference, reaching impressive heights.

Dough

2½ cups (10 ounces) whole wheat flour, traditional or white whole wheat, or whole barley flour

3 cups (12¾ ounces) unbleached bread flour

2 tablespoons (⅞ ounce) sugar

2 tablespoons (½ ounce) nonfat dry milk

2 teaspoons salt

1½ teaspoons instant yeast

1 large egg

1½ cups plus 2 tablespoons (13 ounces) water

Butter

2 cups (4 sticks, 1 pound) butter, softened but still cool to the touch

⅓ cup (1⅛ ounces) whole wheat pastry flour

FOR THE DOUGH: Combine the flours, sugar, dry milk, salt and yeast in a large mixing bowl using the paddle attachment of your mixer. Beat together the egg and water, and add to the dry ingredients with the mixer running at low speed. Mix until the dough comes together, cleaning the sides of the bowl. Turn the dough out onto a floured surface, and knead lightly to make sure the moisture is evenly distributed throughout. Pat the dough into a 9-inch square, and wrap loosely in plastic. Place in the refrigerator for 1 hour.

FOR THE BUTTER: Mix the butter and flour until smooth and well blended. You can do this with a mixer, a food processor or by hand with a spoon. Take care not to incorporate too much air into the butter; you don't want it to be fluffy.

Lightly flour a piece of plastic wrap or parchment paper, place the butter/flour mixture on it, and pat it into an 8-inch square (see illustration, p. 502). Cover the square and place it on a flat surface in the refrigerator for at least 30 minutes. (Adding flour to the butter helps stabilize it so it won't "flow" out the seams when rolled.)

MAKING THE TURNS: Follow the procedure for Classic Whole Wheat Puff Pastry, p. 501, giving a total of four turns to the dough. (Yeasted dough needs fewer turns than nonyeasted dough.) Wrap the dough loosely after its last turn, since the yeast will cause it to expand. Refrigerate for at least 2 hours, but preferably overnight. Before you put the dough in the refrigerator this time, decide if you want to freeze some of it for future use. If so, divide it in half, wrap one half tightly in plastic, then again in foil, and freeze for up to 1 month. Put the other half in the refrigerator for its second, slow rise.

Use the dough to make croissants or pastry pockets.

Cinnamon-Sugar Croissants

YIELD: 12 curved croissants
BAKING TEMPERATURE: 425°F, then 350°F
BAKING TIME: 30 to 35 minutes

Whole grains pair well with spices, and the wafting smell of cinnamon is the perfect complement to the buttery croissant dough. For the flakiest croissants, make your dough with whole barley flour instead of whole wheat. The dough will be a bit stiffer to handle, but barley flour gives a satisfying shatter to the outer layers of the pastry.

Dough & egg wash
½ recipe Yeasted Whole Grain Puff Pastry (p. 515)
1 egg beaten with 1 tablespoon water

Filling
¼ cup (1¾ ounces) granulated sugar
½ teaspoon ground cinnamon

Cinnamon glaze
2¼ cups (9 ounces) confectioners' sugar
2 tablespoons plus 1 teaspoon (1¼ ounces) milk
2 tablespoons (1⅜ ounces) light corn syrup
1 teaspoon ground cinnamon

Lightly grease a baking sheet or line with parchment paper.

Roll and cut the dough as for Classic Whole Wheat Croissants, p. 504. After cutting the dough into triangles and notching the base, brush the center of the dough with the egg wash.

Combine the granulated sugar and cinnamon. Sprinkle ½ teaspoon of the sugar mixture over the egg wash as shown. Roll up each triangle, starting at the notched edge and working toward the tip. Make sure the point is tucked under the bottom of the croissant. Form the crescent by bending the two ends toward the center where the dough's tip is tucked under.

After the croissants are formed, transfer them to the prepared baking sheet. Cover lightly with greased plastic wrap, and allow the croissants to rise for 30 minutes. They won't get much taller, but they will get puffy-looking.

Preheat the oven to 425°F.

Brush the tops of the croissants with beaten egg mixture. Bake the croissants for 15 minutes. Lower the oven temperature to 350°F, and bake until the dough is deep golden brown, even where it overlaps itself, 15 to 20 minutes more. Remove from the oven and transfer to a rack to cool completely.

Whisk together all the glaze ingredients in a medium bowl until smooth; drizzle over the cooled turnovers.

Brush the center of the croissant above the notch with egg wash; sprinkle ½ teaspoon cinnamon sugar over the area.

NUTRITION INFORMATION PER SERVING (1 CROISSANT, WITH CINNAMON GLAZE, 72G): 14g whole grains, 262 cal, 8g fat, 4g protein, 19g complex carbohydrates, 13g sugar, 2g dietary fiber, 47mg cholesterol, 153mg sodium, 78mg potassium, 129RE vitamin A, 1mg iron, 21mg calcium, 66mg phosphorus.

Chocolate Croissants

YIELD: 9 filled croissants
BAKING TEMPERATURE: 425°F, then 350°F
BAKING TIME: 30 to 35 minutes

These are the first to disappear from any pastry tray; the glimpse of chocolate peeking out from the end is all it takes to attract chocolate lovers of all ages. We like to turn heads even further by giving the tops a zebra stripe of chocolate glaze as well.

For the filling, you can use any chocolate you like, from chips to chunks of a chocolate bar to chocolate batons made expressly for croissants.

Dough
½ recipe Yeasted Whole Grain Puff Pastry (p. 515)

Filling
1 cup (6 ounces) chocolate chips or 6 ounces of your favorite chocolate pieces or
   9 chocolate batons

Egg wash
1 egg beaten with 1 tablespoon water

Glaze
¼ cup (2 ounces) heavy cream
1 tablespoon light corn syrup
½ cup (3 ounces) chopped chocolate or chocolate chips

Lightly grease a baking sheet or line with parchment paper.

Roll out the dough on a floured surface into a 12 x 18-inch rectangle. Cut in thirds both lengthwise and across, to make nine 4 x 6-inch rectangles.

Place 2 tablespoons (about ¾ ounce) of chocolate or one chocolate baton in the center of a rectangle. Fold the rectangle like a letter, then turn the croissant over so the seam is on the bottom. Press the croissant down with the palm of your hand to flatten the top.

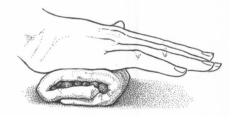

After the croissants are formed, transfer them to the prepared baking sheet. Cover lightly with greased plastic wrap, and allow the croissants to rise for 30 minutes. They won't get much taller, but they will get puffy-looking.

Press the filled croissant to flatten it slightly; this will help keep it from unwinding when it bakes.

Preheat the oven to 425°F.

Brush the tops of the croissants with the egg wash. Bake for 15 minutes. Lower the oven temperature to 350°F, and bake until the dough is deep golden brown, even where it overlaps itself, 15 to 20 minutes more. Remove from the oven and transfer to a rack to cool completely.

TO MAKE THE GLAZE: Bring the cream and corn syrup to a simmer in a small saucepan or in the microwave at medium power. Pour over the chocolate and stir until the mixture is smooth. Drizzle the glaze over the cooled croissants.

NUTRITION INFORMATION PER SERVING (1 CROISSANT, WITH CHOCOLATE GLAZE, 115G): 19g whole grains, 458 cal, 29g fat, 7g protein, 27g complex carbohydrates, 17g sugar, 3g dietary fiber, 71mg cholesterol, 205mg sodium, 191mg potassium, 199RE vitamin A, 2mg iron, 36mg calcium, 120mg phosphorus, 22mg caffeine.

VARIATION: CHEESE AND APRICOT CROISSANTS *Substitute 1 tablespoon each diced dried apricots and Cheese filling for Cheese Danish, page 522, for the chocolate. Glaze with Apricot glaze, page 522, to finish.*

Spinach Croissants

YIELD: 9 filled croissants

BAKING TEMPERATURE: 425°F, then 350°F

BAKING TIME: 30 to 35 minutes

Croissant dough is a wonderful vehicle for savory pastries, which can be filled any number of ways for a grab-and-go meal that's more special than a sandwich.

This filling is very simple and the flavor can be customized anyway you like: add sautéed mushrooms or onions, change the cheese, add some spices or olives. There's just one constraint for your personal variations: any ingredient you add or substitute shouldn't be too wet.

Filling

1 (10-ounce) package frozen chopped spinach, thawed and squeezed very dry

½ cup (2 ounces) grated Swiss cheese

¼ cup (2 ounces) garlic herb cheese

½ teaspoon salt

¼ teaspoon pepper

½ to 1 teaspoon chopped garlic (optional)

Dough & Egg wash

½ recipe Yeasted Whole Grain Puff Pastry (p. 515)

1 egg beaten with 1 tablespoon water

Lightly grease a baking sheet or line with parchment paper.

Combine all the filling ingredients in a small mixing bowl. Refrigerate until ready to use.

Roll out the dough on a floured surface into an 18 x 12-inch rectangle. Cut in thirds both lengthwise and across, to make nine 4 x 6-inch rectangles.

Place 1½ tablespoons of the filling in the center of a rectangle. Fold the rectangle like a letter, then turn the croissant over so the seam is on the bottom. Press the croissant down with the palm of your hand, to flatten the top (see illustration, p. 518).

After the croissants are formed, transfer them to the prepared baking sheet. Cover lightly with greased plastic wrap, and allow the croissants to rise for 30 minutes. They won't get much taller, but they will get puffy-looking.

Preheat the oven to 425°F.

Brush the tops of the croissants with the egg wash. Bake for 15 minutes. Lower the oven temperature to 350°F, and bake until the dough is deep golden brown, even where it overlaps itself, 15 to 20 minutes more. Remove from the oven and transfer to a rack to cool completely.

NUTRITION INFORMATION PER SERVING (1 CROISSANT, 108G): **19g whole grains,** 319 cal, 21g fat, 7g protein, 26g complex carbohydrates, 1g sugar, 3g dietary fiber, 72mg cholesterol, 382mg sodium, 175mg potassium, 348RE vitamin A, 3mg vitamin C, 2mg iron, 91mg calcium, 122mg phosphorus.

VARIATION: PROSCIUTTO, FONTINA AND ARTICHOKE CROISSANTS *This hearty flavor combination is well suited to whole wheat pastry.*

> **5 ounces fontina cheese**
> **3 ounces thinly sliced prosciutto**
> **1 (14-ounce) can artichoke hearts, well drained, quartered**
> **¼ cup (2 ounces) roasted red peppers, well drained (optional)**

Roll and cut the dough as for spinach croissants. Fill the center of each croissant with ½ ounce of cheese, ½ slice of prosciutto, 2 pieces of artichoke and a strip of red pepper, if using.

Proof and bake the same as above.

Whole Grain Danish Pastry Dough

YIELD: 3 pounds 14 ounces, enough for 32 filled Danish or 4 dozen sticky buns

Whole wheat pastry flour makes this dough amazingly tender and light, as do the eggs in the dough. Danish dough uses more eggs and spices than other laminated pastries, making it ideal for sweet rolls as well as the classic filled rounds we recognize as Danish pastries.

> *Dough*
> **3 cups plus 2 tablespoons (10⅝ ounces) whole wheat pastry flour**
> **1½ cups (12 ounces) water**
> **2 large eggs**
> **2 tablespoons (1 ounce) butter, melted**
> **¼ cup (1¾ ounces) sugar**
> **1 scant tablespoon salt**
> **2 teaspoons instant yeast**
> **1 teaspoon vanilla**
> **½ teaspoon ground cardamom**
> **¼ teaspoon ground nutmeg**
> **⅛ teaspoon ground cloves**
> **¼ cup (1 ounce) nonfat dry milk**
> **3 to 3½ cups (12¾ to 14⅞ ounces) unbleached bread flour**

Butter

2 cups (4 sticks, 1 pound) butter, just cool to the touch

¼ cup (1 ounce) unbleached bread flour

Unbleached all-purpose flour for sprinkling

TO MAKE THE DOUGH: Combine the whole wheat pastry flour and water in the large mixing bowl of an electric stand mixer. Let this mixture rest for 30 minutes to soften the wheat bran.

After 30 minutes, mix in the eggs, melted butter, sugar, salt, yeast, vanilla and spices. Whisk the dry milk into 1 cup of the bread flour, and mix into the dough. Switch to a dough hook, add the rest of the bread flour, and knead the dough until it comes together and is smooth, 4 to 6 minutes. Remove the dough from the mixing bowl, pat it into a 9-inch square, wrap loosely, and refrigerate for 30 minutes while you prepare the butter.

TO MAKE THE BUTTER: Mix the butter and flour until smooth and well blended. You can do this with a mixer, a food processor or by hand with a spoon. Take care not to incorporate too much air into the butter; you don't want it to be fluffy.

Lightly flour a piece of plastic wrap or wax paper, place the butter/flour mixture on it, and pat it into an 8-inch square (see illustration, p. 502). Cover the square and place it on a flat surface in the refrigerator for at least 30 minutes. (Adding flour to the butter helps stabilize it so it won't "flow" out the seams when rolled.)

MAKING THE TURNS: Follow the procedure for Classic Whole Wheat Puff Pastry, page 501, giving a total of four turns to the dough. Wrap the dough loosely after its last turn, since the yeast will cause it to expand. Refrigerate for at least 2 hours, but preferably overnight. Use to make Cheese Danish (p. 522) or Raspberry Sticky Buns (p. 524). We recommend that you divide the dough into halves or quarters, use what you need and wrap the rest in plastic, then in foil, and freeze for 3 to 6 months. See "What to do with all that dough?," page 504.

Cheese Danish

YIELD: 16 (3-inch) pastries
BAKING TEMPERATURE: 400°F
BAKING TIME: 18 to 22 minutes

Including whole grains in Danish dough brings a subtle, nutty wheat flavor to the pastry that shows off the luxurious cheese filling, Cinnamon-Sugar swirl and apricot glaze to great advantage.

Cinnamon filling
¼ cup (1¾ ounces) sugar
1 teaspoon ground cinnamon

Cheese filling
6 ounces (two 3-ounce packages) cream cheese, softened
2 tablespoons (⅞ ounce) sugar
1 tablespoon unbleached all-purpose flour
1 teaspoon vanilla extract
1 teaspoon lemon zest or 2 drops lemon oil
1 teaspoon fresh lemon juice

Dough & Egg wash
½ recipe Whole Grain Danish Pastry Dough, p. 520
1 egg beaten with 1 tablespoon water

Apricot glaze
½ cup (6 ounces) apricot preserves
¼ cup (2 ounces) water
1 tablespoon light corn syrup

TO MAKE THE CINNAMON FILLING: Combine the sugar and cinnamon; set aside.

TO MAKE THE CHEESE FILLING: Combine all the ingredients until smooth using a food processor or a whisk. Refrigerate until ready to use in pastry dough.

Lightly grease 2 baking sheets or line with parchment paper.

TO ASSEMBLE: Roll out the pastry dough on a floured surface to a 22 x 12-inch rectangle. Brush one half of the dough with some of the egg wash, and sprinkle with the cinnamon filling, leaving a ½-inch border around the edge. Fold the uncoated dough over the filling, lining up the edges as closely as possible. Lightly roll with a rolling pin to seal. With a ruler and pizza cutter or sharp knife, trim the edges to make them straight. Cut the dough into 16 strips ¾ inch wide (see illustration, p. 523).

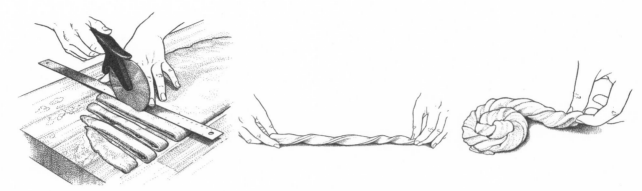

After filling with cinnamon sugar, use a ruler and a pizza cutter to cut 16 strips, 11 inches long by ¾ inch wide.

Twist the ends of each strip of dough in opposite directions to form a spiral.

Wind the twisted dough around itself like a snail to form a round Danish.

Twist the strips to make spirals, then wind the spirals to form pinwheel-shaped rounds. Pinch the end of the strip under the round to seal it.

Place the Danish on the prepared baking sheets. Let rise, uncovered, for 30 minutes; they'll begin to get puffy-looking.

Preheat the oven to 400°F.

Press the center of each Danish down with your fingers, and scoop 1 level tablespoon of cheese filling into the indentation. Brush the outside edges (not the filling) with egg wash.

TO BAKE: Bake until the Danish are deep golden brown, 18 to 22 minutes. Remove from the oven and let cool for 10 minutes before glazing.

TO MAKE THE APRICOT GLAZE: Combine all the ingredients in a small saucepan. Bring to a simmer over medium heat. Break up the jam with a spoon as you stir the mixture. When the glaze bubbles in the center, remove from the heat and pour through a strainer to remove any chunks of fruit. Brush the glaze over the warm Danish, covering the filling to seal it.

NUTRITION INFORMATION PER SERVING (1 CHEESE DANISH, WITH APRICOT GLAZE, 64G): 9g whole grains, 221 cal, 16g fat, 3g protein, 8g complex carbohydrates, 10g sugar, 1g dietary fiber, 61mg cholesterol, 220mg sodium, 85mg potassium, 163RE vitamin A, 1mg vitamin C, 1mg iron, 31mg calcium, 67mg phosphorus.

VARIATION: FRUIT-FILLED DANISH *Any prepared fruit pie filling will work as a filling for Danish; use it instead of or in addition to the cheese. We've enjoyed raspberry, apple, apricot and canned lekvar (prune filling). The Peach and Ginger Turnover filling, page 513, is a memorable choice.*

Raspberry Sticky Buns

YIELD: 1 dozen buns
BAKING TEMPERATURE: 400°F
BAKING TIME: 22 to 25 minutes

Everyone has his or her own idea of perfect sticky buns. We make them here with a swirl of raspberry jam in the center, and place each bun in its own muffin cup. That way every single bun is bathed in glaze and topped with nuts, while baking evenly through to its center. This is just one of the many delicious ways to use scraps and trimmings from cutting and shaping Danish or puff pastry dough.

Dough
¼ recipe Whole Grain Danish Pastry Dough, page 520, or 16 ounces Yeasted Whole
    Grain Puff Pastry, page 515

Filling
½ cup (6 ounces) raspberry pie filling

Glaze
½ cup (5½ ounces) light corn syrup or golden syrup
3 tablespoons (1½ ounces) unsalted butter, melted
1 cup (3¾ ounces) chopped pecans or walnuts
1 cup (7½ ounces) packed light brown sugar

TO FILL THE DOUGH: On a well-floured work surface, roll out the dough to a 16 x 10-inch rectangle, with a long side facing you. Spread the dough with the pie filling, leaving ½ inch of one long side uncovered; the side closest to you is easiest. Wet the uncovered strip of dough with your fingers or a pastry brush. Starting with the far edge, roll the dough toward you, creating a long spiral. Pinch together the long edges, cover loosely with greased plastic wrap and refrigerate the dough while you prepare the baking pan.

TO MAKE THE GLAZE: Combine the corn syrup (or golden syrup) and melted butter, and spoon a generous tablespoon of the mixture into each cup of a greased 12-cup muffin pan. Divide the nuts and brown sugar equally among the cups.

TO ASSEMBLE: Remove the dough from the refrigerator (chilling makes slicing it a bit easier), and slice the log into 12 equal pieces. A sharp knife can do the job, but we prefer to use dental floss for this, because it makes much neater slices, especially with soft dough.

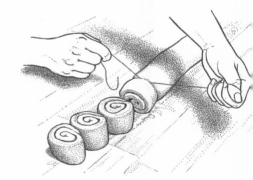

Slide unflavored dental floss under the roll of dough. Cross the ends, and pull gently to slice the dough.

Place one slice in each cup of the prepared pan, and cover with greased plastic wrap. Let rise for about 30 minutes; they'll become puffy-looking.

Preheat the oven to 400°F.

When the buns have risen, remove the plastic and place the muffin pan on a rimmed baking sheet to catch any drips. Bake until the buns are an even golden brown, 22 to 25 minutes. Remove from the oven, and place the pan on a rack for 5 minutes. Place a piece of parchment paper on top of the buns and a baking sheet or large serving platter over that. Using a potholder to handle the muffin pan, hold the two together and flip everything over. Let the muffin pan sit on top of the buns for a few minutes to allow the glaze to drip down, then carefully remove it. Rearrange any nuts or glaze that have gone astray, and let cool for 15 minutes more before serving.

NUTRITION INFORMATION PER SERVING (1 STICKY BUN, 69G): 6g whole grains, 265 cal, 15g fat, 2g protein, 8g complex carbohydrates, 26g sugar, 2g dietary fiber, 31mg cholesterol, 153mg sodium, 129mg potassium, 84RE vitamin A, 1mg iron, 28mg calcium, 70mg phosphorus.

WHOLE GRAIN PÂTE À CHOUX: ÉCLAIR OR CREAM PUFF PASTRY

Any éclair starts with pâte à choux (paht ah SHOO), which literally means cabbage paste (and refers to the similarity in shape between cream puffs and small cabbages). Cream puffs are leavened by steam, which expands them quickly and leaves large holes in their middles, ready to hold your choice of fillings. Bringing whole grains into this equation gave us a chance to answer a baking question we'd had for a while: what's more responsible for forming and holding that distinctive cavity, the protein in the egg or the protein in the flour?

The eggs have it, folks. We made perfectly formed cream puffs and éclairs with half of the flour in a conventional recipe replaced with oat flour or whole wheat pastry flour. The oat flour gave a crunchier texture, more suitable for savory applications. The whole wheat pastry flour gave us an éclair that was virtually indistinguishable (except for its more complex, robust flavor) from a standard recipe. Whole barley flour, which we found efficacious for flaky pie dough and crispy croissants, didn't fare as well in pâte à choux: éclairs made with barley flour were just plain hard, so it's not an ingredient we recommend for this type of pastry.

Whole Grain Éclair Pastry

YIELD: **1 dozen (5-inch) éclairs**
BAKING TEMPERATURE: **425°F, then 375°F**
BAKING TIME: **30 minutes**

This dough is also used to make cream puffs or profiteroles. If the idea of using a pastry bag fills you with dread, simply scoop the finished dough with a tablespoon-sized cookie scoop for cream puffs or a teaspoon scoop for profiteroles. If you plan to make a sweet pastry, we recommend using whole wheat pastry flour. Savory fillings pair best with éclairs made with oat flour.

> ¾ **cup (2½ ounces) whole wheat pastry or oat flour**
> ½ **cup (2⅛ ounces) unbleached bread flour**
> **1 cup (8 ounces) water**
> ½ **cup (1 stick, 4 ounces) unsalted butter**
> ¼ **teaspoon salt**
> **4 large eggs**

TO MAKE THE DOUGH: Combine the whole wheat pastry flour (or oat flour) and bread flour.

Combine the water, butter and salt in a saucepan, and bring the mixture to a rolling boil. Remove it from the heat, and add the flours all at once. Stir vigorously. Return the pan to the burner and cook over medium heat, stirring all the while, until the mixture forms a ball; this should only take about 1 minute. Remove the pan from the heat, and let the mixture cool for 5 to 10 minutes, to 140°F. It will still feel hot, but you should be able to hold a finger in it for a few seconds. Transfer the dough to a mixer, and beat in the eggs one at a time; the mixture will become fluffy. Beat for at least 2 minutes after adding the last egg.

Preheat the oven to 425°F. Line 2 baking sheets with parchment paper and mark the paper with two 4-inch-wide lines (see illustration at right).

TO SHAPE AND BAKE: Place the dough in a pastry bag with a ¾-inch opening. Pipe the dough in 1 x 4-inch strips on the prepared baking sheets. Be sure to leave at least 1 inch of space between each strip of dough, since the éclairs will expand as they bake.

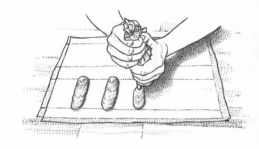

Mark parallel lines 4 inches apart on the parchment paper, then turn it over. Use the lines as a guide to make your éclairs. Hold the pastry bag straight up and down and move slowly in a straight line. Release the pressure on the bag before picking it up to start the next éclair.

Bake the éclairs for 15 minutes. Reduce the oven temperature to 375°F, and bake for 15 minutes more. Turn off the oven, open the door a crack, and leave the éclairs inside to cool for 30 minutes. Remove from the oven to cool completely.

NUTRITION INFORMATION PER SERVING (1 UNFILLED ÉCLAIR, 59G): 6g whole grains, 139 cal, 10g fat, 4g protein, 10g complex carbohydrates, 1g dietary fiber, 92mg cholesterol, 23mg sodium, 59mg potassium, 103RE vitamin A, 1mg iron, 14mg calcium, 63mg phosphorus.

Peanut Butter Éclairs

Crisp pastry shells with smooth filling and a blaze of chocolate on top: éclairs are the rare dessert that can be formal and fun at the same time. The filling for these pastries is based on pastry cream, flavored with peanut butter. If you wish, you can divide the warm pastry cream in half and flavor it two ways (see the éclair variations that follow for some ideas) for even more variety.

2 dozen baked Whole Grain Éclair shells (2 batches Whole Grain Éclair Pastry, p. 526)

Peanut butter filling
3 cups (24 ounces) whole milk, divided
¾ cup (5¾ ounces) sugar
4 large egg yolks
¼ cup (1 ounce) cornstarch
1 tablespoon unbleached all-purpose flour
4 tablespoons (½ stick, 2 ounces) butter
2 teaspoons vanilla extract or vanilla bean paste
1 cup (9½ ounces) smooth peanut butter (see Note)
1 cup (8 ounces) heavy cream, whipped to soft peaks

Chocolate glaze
½ cup (4 ounces) heavy cream
1 tablespoon light corn syrup
1 cup (6 ounces) semisweet chocolate chips
Chopped peanuts for garnish (optional)

TO MAKE THE FILLING: Stir together 2½ cups of the milk and the sugar in a medium saucepan. Bring the mixture to a boil over medium heat.

Meanwhile, whisk the remaining ½ cup milk, egg yolks, cornstarch and flour in a medium bowl. Whisk some of the boiling milk mixture into the egg yolk mixture, then pour it all back into the hot milk mixture and return to the heat. Bring to a boil, stirring constantly, and boil for 30 seconds. Remove from the heat, strain through a fine sieve, and stir in the butter and vanilla extract (or paste).

Stir the peanut butter into the hot pastry cream until evenly blended. Rub a pat of butter over the surface to keep it from forming a skin, top with a piece of plastic wrap, then refrigerate until cool. To complete, fold the whipped cream into the cooled pastry cream.

NOTE: If you choose to make more than one flavor, divide the warm pastry cream into two bowls. Mix ½ cup peanut butter into one bowl, and the specified amount of other flavoring—caramel and pistachio are mentioned in the variation below—into the other half. Before using, fold half the whipped cream into each chilled flavor.

TO MAKE THE GLAZE: Bring the cream and corn syrup to a simmer in a small saucepan or at medium power in the microwave. Pour over the chocolate, and stir the mixture until smooth. Hold at room temperature until ready to glaze the éclairs.

TO ASSEMBLE: Spoon the filling into a pastry bag that has been fitted with a large-holed writing tip. Poke three holes in the bottom of the éclair shell with a skewer, and pipe some filling into each hole. If you aren't using a pastry bag, slice off the top third of the éclair shell, spoon filling into the cavity, and replace the top.

Working over the bowl, spoon the chocolate glaze over the éclair, letting the excess run back into the bowl.

Holding the filled éclair at an angle, pour the glaze on the uphill edge.

Refrigerate éclairs until ready to serve.

NUTRITION INFORMATION PER SERVING (1 ÉCLAIR, 67G): 6g whole grains, 174 cal, 11g fat, 5g protein, 5g complex carbohydrates, 10g sugar, 1g dietary fiber, 52mg cholesterol, 71mg sodium, 141mg potassium, 66RE vitamin A, 1mg iron, 47 mg calcium, 90mg phosphorus, 4mg caffeine.

VARIATIONS: CARAMEL ÉCLAIRS *To half of the warm pastry cream, add ¼ cup (2½ ounces, 7 individual) caramels. Stir until the caramels melt; finish as the recipe directs. Finish the éclairs with caramel glaze: melt 3 ounces caramel with 1 tablespoon heavy cream, stirring until smooth.*

PISTACHIO ÉCLAIRS *To half of the warm pastry cream, add ⅓ cup (4⅛ ounces) pistachio paste, and stir until no lumps remain. Finish the éclairs by sprinkling chopped pistachio nuts on top of the chocolate glaze before it hardens.*

DOUGHNUTS

No matter where you go in this country, doughnuts are part of the landscape. From beignets with coffee at a sidewalk café to the box on the tailgate of a pickup truck, they bring sustenance, comfort and smiles wherever they go. Doughnuts and fried dough have a long tradition on these shores; whether it's the crullers in Grandma's kitchen or the Zeppole stands on Atlantic boardwalks, the smell of doughnuts frying is instantly recognizable.

Many of the recipes in our collection used whole wheat flour all along; it was easy to find ways to include other whole grains. Two recipes start with a simple dough that stirs together easily. These use baking powder, a light touch when kneading and a rest in the refrigerator to bring the dough to its peak for frying. The other two recipes use yeast to make light, crisp treats that can be brushed with glaze or filled with preserves.

While doughnuts aren't something we indulge in every day, most of the recipes here sport fewer calories than a protein bar, muffin or brownie. A properly fried doughnut absorbs roughly a teaspoon of fat, which translates to about 40 calories. Including whole grains in doughnut recipes is one way to tip the scales (literally) back to a more moderate stance.

So when it's time for a treat on a cold winter's day, or you have a crowd around to help you make them disappear, we hope you'll indulge in the warm, irresistible pleasure of a freshly made, stirred-with-love doughnut.

FRY SAFELY

The most important thing you can do to fry food safely is to keep the oil at a consistent temperature (this also ensures the best results). The recipes in this chapter call for dough to be cooked at temperatures of 365°F to 375°F. The easiest way to do this is with a small tabletop fryer or electric frying pan whose thermostat will monitor the oil's temperature for you. If you're using a heavy pan on the stove to fry in, we strongly recommend you have a thermometer on hand. You can use a clip-on candy or deep-frying thermometer, or an instant-read thermometer that's rated for temperatures up to 500°F.

Before you start a recipe that calls for frying, make sure you have an uncluttered workspace, absorbent paper on a baking sheet for draining the doughnuts, a thermometer, a slotted spoon and a lid that can tightly cover the pan you're frying in, in case of a flame-up.

When oil gets too hot, it begins to smoke; if left unattended the oil can reach its flash point, and burst into flame. If you see the oil begin to smoke, immediately turn off the heat, cover the pan, and let the pan cool down. Dispose of the oil, clean the pan, and start again with fresh oil. Never try to put out an oil fire with water; it will spatter the oil everywhere, making a bad situation much worse.

Jelly Doughnuts

YIELD: 13 doughnuts
FRYING TEMPERATURE: 365°F
FRYING TIME: 5 minutes

Nothing, but nothing, will bring people to the kitchen faster than a warm jelly doughnut. This recipe created a stampede and a lot of happy exclamation points from our taste testers. You can make the dough with a mixer or by hand, but we found the dough cycle of our bread machine to be just the ticket.

1 cup (4 ounces) whole wheat flour, traditional or white whole wheat
½ cup (4 ounces) water
⅓ cup (2⅓ ounces) granulated sugar
2 tablespoons (½ ounce) nonfat dry milk
2 teaspoons instant yeast
½ teaspoon salt
Grated zest from 1 lemon or ½ teaspoon lemon oil
¼ cup (½ stick, 2 ounces) softened butter
2 large eggs plus 1 egg yolk, at room temperature (reserve the egg white)
2 cups (8½ ounces) unbleached all-purpose flour
½ cup (6 ounces) strawberry, raspberry or blackberry jam

5 to 6 cups (about 2 pounds) vegetable oil or lard for frying
¼ to ½ cup (1 to 2 ounces) confectioners' sugar or granulated sugar

FOR THE DOUGH: Combine the whole wheat flour and water in a mixing bowl or the bucket of your bread machine, and let the mixture sit, covered, for 30 minutes to soften the bran.

After the flour's had a good soak, add the granulated sugar, dry milk, yeast, salt, lemon zest (or oil), butter, eggs and egg yolk, and stir vigorously. The butter may want to stay in lumps but don't worry. It will blend in nicely when the dough is kneaded.

Mix in the all-purpose flour, and let your bread machine finish its dough cycle. If you're using a mixer, knead the dough for 6 to 8 minutes, until it becomes smooth and elastic. Place the dough in a greased bowl, turning it so the top has a thin film of grease on it. Cover with greased plastic wrap and let rise for 1½ to 2 hours.

TO ASSEMBLE: Flour a baking sheet or line it with parchment paper. After the dough has risen, deflate it and turn it out onto a lightly floured surface. With a floured rolling pin, roll out the dough until it is about ¼ inch thick. With a floured biscuit cutter about 2½ inches in diameter, cut out rounds of dough and place them on the prepared baking sheet. On half of the dough pieces, place 1 teaspoon jam. Lightly beat the reserved egg white and moisten the edges of the circles with it. Place the plain dough circles over those with jam and pinch the edges together. Cover with lightly greased plastic wrap and let rest for about 30 minutes.

Heat vegetable oil (or lard) to 365°F. You should have at least 2 inches of oil in the pan. Carefully slip 2 or 3 doughnuts at a time into the fat and cook for 2 or 3 minutes a side. Remove and drain on a paper towel. Cool and then dredge both sides in sugar.

NUTRITION INFORMATION PER SERVING (1 DOUGHNUT, 83G): 13g whole grains, 287 cal, 14g fat, 5g protein, 22g complex carbohydrates, 13g sugar, 2g dietary fiber, 59mg cholesterol, 104mg sodium, 118potassium, 2mg iron, 25mg calcium, 88mg phosphorus.

Yeast-Raised Beignets

YIELD: 32 beignets
Frying temperature: 365°F
Frying time: 2½ to 3 minutes

Beignets are often served simply, with a little something sweet on the side to dip them in (we confess our partiality for maple syrup) or perhaps a light dusting of confectioners' sugar. Their light, airy texture is reminiscent of a glazed doughnut, so we've included a versatile glaze if you'd like to finish them that way.

Beignets
¾ cup (6 ounces) water
2 cups (8 ounces) whole wheat flour, traditional or white whole wheat
½ cup (4 ounces) half-and-half
1 large egg
2 tablespoons (1 ounce) butter, melted
¼ cup (1¾ ounces) sugar
1 teaspoon salt
2 teaspoons instant yeast
2 cups (8½ ounces) unbleached all-purpose flour

5 to 6 cups (about 2 pounds) vegetable oil for frying
⅓ to ½ cup (1⅜ to 2 ounces) confectioners' sugar for dusting

Beignet glaze
2 cups (8 ounces) confectioners' sugar
¼ cup (2 ounces) water, coffee or milk
One of the following: 1 teaspoon vanilla or other extract of your choice;
or 1 teaspoon lemon juice or 1 tablespoon grated lemon peel or ½ teaspoon lemon oil;
or 2 tablespoons warmed honey

TO MAKE THE DOUGH: Pour the water into a mixing bowl or the bucket of your bread machine. Add the whole wheat flour and let the mixture soak for 30 minutes, to soften the bran in the flour.

Beat the half-and-half, egg, butter, sugar and salt in a small bowl. Stir this into the flour mixture. Add the yeast and all-purpose flour, program your bread machine for the dough cycle, and press Start. Whether you're mixing by hand or machine, once a soft dough forms, knead for 6 to 8 minutes. Cover the dough with greased plastic wrap, and let rise until it has doubled in bulk, 1½ to 2 hours.

After the dough has risen, deflate it and turn it out onto a floured work surface. Knead out any stray bubbles and let rest for about 5 minutes to relax the gluten. While you roll out and shape the beignets, start heating the oil to 365°F. You should have at least 2 inches of oil in the pan.

TO CUT THE BEIGNETS: Roll the dough out to a rectangle roughly 12 x 20 inches and ¼-inch thick. Use a flour-sprinkled bench knife or bowl scraper to keep the dough free from the kneading surface. You may need to throw a bit of flour underneath from time to time to keep the dough from sticking. With a pizza cutter or a sharp knife, cut the dough into 4 long strips, 3 inches wide. Cut each of the strips into 8 pieces. Cover with greased plastic wrap and let them relax while the oil heats.

TO FRY: Once the oil is hot, slip in 4 or 5 beignets at a time and cook for about 1 minute before you flip them over. Let them cook another 1½ to 2 minutes, flipping them back and forth so they brown evenly. Every once in a while you'll have one that doesn't want to turn over because its "tummy" is so fat. Use your spoon to turn it and gently hold it in place until the underside is brown enough. When the beignets are done, remove them with a slotted spoon and drain on a paper towel. Continue with the remaining dough.

After the beignets have cooled, toss them in a paper or plastic bag with ⅓ to ½ cup of confectioners' sugar, or brush with glaze (below).

TO MAKE THE GLAZE: Mix the confectioners' sugar and your choice of liquid and flavoring in a small bowl. You can dip one or both sides of your beignets or brush some glaze over the tops.

NUTRITION INFORMATION PER SERVING (2 BEIGNETS, DUSTED WITH CONFECTIONERS' SUGAR, 45G): 18g whole grains, 177 cal, 7g fat, 4g protein, 22g complex carbohydrates, 2g sugar, 2g dietary fiber, 20mg cholesterol, 141mg sodium, 101mg potassium, 28mg vitamin A, 15mg calcium, 83mg phosphorus.

Molasses Doughnuts *(Beignets à la Mélasse)*

YIELD: 1 dozen doughnuts, 1 dozen doughnut holes and some scraps for tasting
Frying temperature: 365°F
Frying time: 2 minutes

This Canadian recipe is very similar to ones you find in old New England cookbooks. Although molasses sounds heavy and strong, these are lightly flavored and not overly sweet. They're just plain good! A coating of confectioners' sugar is tasty but not necessary.

½ cup (4 ounces) buttermilk
1 large egg
½ cup (6 ounces) molasses
½ cup (3½ ounces) sugar
2 tablespoons (1 ounce) melted butter
1 cup (4 ounces) whole wheat flour, traditional or white whole wheat
1 cup (3¼ ounces) oat flour or whole barley flour
2 cups (8½ ounces) unbleached bread flour
4 teaspoons baking powder
1 teaspoon salt
½ teaspoon baking soda
½ teaspoon ground ginger
¼ teaspoon each ground cinnamon and nutmeg

5 to 6 cups (about 2 pounds) vegetable oil for frying
Confectioners' sugar for sprinkling (optional)

TO MAKE THE DOUGH: Beat together the buttermilk, egg, molasses, sugar and butter in a large mixing bowl either by hand or with an electric mixer. Mix together the dry ingredients in another bowl. Add the dry ingredients to the wet ingredients and mix by hand for 2 minutes, or at low speed for 1 minute, until the dough comes together. Cover and refrigerate the dough for 2 hours.

TO CUT THE DOUGHNUTS: Turn the dough out onto a floured board, knead gently 4 or 5 times, flatten with the palms of your hands and then roll out until the dough is about ⅜ inch thick. You'll need to keep sprinkling flour around because this dough is sticky. Dip your doughnut cutter in flour and begin cutting out the doughnuts. Don't twist the cutter when you cut through the dough. This tends to press the dough together instead of shearing through it. It's better to move the cutter back and forth on the surface of the table to make sure it is all the way through the dough. Flour the cutter each time you make a cut so you don't wind up with a stuck doughnut hole.

Because this is a baking powder dough, it's best not to reroll any of the scraps—rerolled dough will make for tough doughnuts. Go ahead and cook the odd-shaped pieces as is. They're great for testing and for fending off enthusiastic children or other circling parties.

Heat your cooking oil to 365°F. You should have at least 2 inches of oil in the pan.

TO FRY: Slide the dough pieces gently into the hot fat and cook for about 1 minute on each side. Keep the temperature as close to 365°F as possible, since molasses can go quickly from tasting good to tasting a bit burned. Remove the doughnuts with a slotted spoon to drain and cool on two or three layers of paper towel. Doughnut holes will take about 1 to 1½ minutes total to cook. Sprinkle with confectioners' sugar if desired.

NUTRITION INFORMATION PER SERVING (1 ROUND DOUGHNUT, 50G): 15g whole grains, 207 cal, 10g fat, 4g protein, 21g complex carbohydrates, 6g sugar, 2g dietary fiber, 17mg cholesterol, 300mg sodium, 70mg potassium, 63mg vitamin A, 1mg iron, 79mg calcium, 96mg phosphorus.

WHICH OIL TO USE?

In times gone by, lard was the fat of choice for frying doughnuts. It was relatively inexpensive and widely available. Given today's consciousness of saturated fats, lard has fallen out of favor. Until recently, solid vegetable shortening was the preferred fat for frying, because its hydrogenated state kept it from oxidizing and picking up any "off" flavors for a long period of time. These days, solid vegetable shortening is also out of favor, because the trans fats it contains increase "bad" cholesterol while depleting "good" cholesterol.

What's a responsible doughnut maker to do? For frying, we recommend a liquid fat with a high smoke point and a neutral flavor, such as canola, safflower or peanut oil. All these oils have smoke points higher than 450°F. It's best to buy the smallest amount you'll need and start with a fresh bottle. The longer oil stays open in your pantry, the more likely it is to bring "off" flavors with it.

Western Doughnuts

YIELD: 1½ dozen plus 4 to 5 dozen small pieces

Frying temperature: 375°F

Frying time: 5 minutes

This recipe's granddaddy came from a chuck wagon, way out West. Cake-style, simple and without any highfalutin' airs, these doughnuts are perfect with a cup of cocoa or cider, while sitting around a campfire and telling tall tales.

1 cup (4 ounces) whole wheat flour, traditional or white whole wheat

½ cup (1⅝ ounces) oat flour or whole barley flour

2 cups (8½ ounces) unbleached bread flour

1 tablespoon baking powder

1 teaspoon salt

1 teaspoon ground cinnamon

½ teaspoon ground nutmeg

2 large eggs

2 tablespoons (1 ounce) butter, melted and cooled

1 cup (7 ounces) sugar

1 cup (8 ounces) milk

5 to 6 cups (about 2 pounds) vegetable oil for frying

TO MAKE THE DOUGH: Whisk together the flours with the baking powder, salt, cinnamon and nutmeg in a medium bowl.

Lightly beat the eggs in a large bowl. Beat in the melted butter and sugar. Add about 1 cup of the flour mixture, and beat until the mixture comes together. Stir in one-third of the milk. Add 1 cup of the flour mixture and half the remaining milk, then repeat the process once more until all the ingredients are combined. Cover the dough and refrigerate for 30 minutes.

TO CUT THE DOUGHNUTS: Line 2 large baking sheets with parchment paper. Remove the dough from the refrigerator and cut it in half. Place one half on a lightly floured surface. Sprinkle the dough with flour and roll it out until it's ½ inch thick. Using a 2¾-inch doughnut cutter, cut out as many doughnuts as you can, and transfer them to the prepared baking sheets with a spatula. Use a 1-inch round cutter to make small doughnuts from the scraps; don't reroll, or the doughnuts will be tough. Refrigerate the doughnuts while the oil heats.

TO FRY: Heat 2 to 3 inches of vegetable oil in a deep, heavy skillet until it reaches a temperature of 375°F. Deep-fry the doughnuts, 3 or 4 at a time, turning them over after about 3 minutes. Remove the doughnuts from the oil and drain on paper towels. Repeat with the other half of the dough.

NUTRITION INFORMATION PER SERVING (1 DOUGHNUT, 50G): **5g whole grains,** 190 cal, 11g fat, 3g protein, 14g complex carbohydrates, 8g sugar, 1g dietary fiber, 20mg cholesterol, 154mg sodium, 59mg potassium, 23RE vitamin A, 1mg iron, 52mg calcium, 66mg phosphorus.

THE WHOLE GRAINS

Each grain variety brings its own special attributes to the recipes in this book, and the more you know, the more you'll be able to mix-and-match specific grains to your own family recipes. We've given you some background on common grains, and at the end of each description of the major grains, we've included a recipe that we think highlights the very best qualities of that grain. As you begin experimenting with various grains, you may want to try these recipes to become familiar with the grain's absorption and baking qualities and its flavor.

537

Wheat

Triticum aestivum

Wheat is, without question, the heart and soul of American baking, the foundation upon which we build delicious constructions of butter and eggs and chocolate and yeast. Without wheat, there would be no high-rising sandwich loaves, no beautifully domed, tender muffins, no light-textured butter cakes. Gluten, a structure-building combination of proteins, is the magic that transforms batter and dough into beautifully risen treats. And of all the grains in the world, wheat is the mother lode of gluten, the only grain with sufficient amounts to successfully make the baked goods we all know and love.

The array of foodstuffs using wheat is vast, stretching way beyond yeast bread to include breakfast cereal and pasta; baked sweets, from brownies to biscotti; crêpes and burritos; tabbouleh (wheat salad), and couscous, the Middle East's pancake-like flatbreads, and more. Wheat is the second-largest cereal crop in the world, behind corn (maize), and ahead of rice, with over 600 million tons produced annually. China is the world's largest wheat producer, followed by India, the United States (where wheat is grown on more acreage than any other crop), and the area formerly known as the Soviet Union.

Without wheat, the world would be a far different place. It was wheat and its cultivation that made it possible for our ancestors to give up wandering the world in search of food, and to begin to put down roots in one place. This made it possible to create a more stable and complex society. In the genetic material that makes up wheat—its cultivation, and subsequent hybridization—is the history of human civilization.

Archaeological evidence of the three varieties of so-called "ancient wheat"—einkorn, the progenitor of every variety of wheat grown today, emmer, and their first-generation descendant, spelt—dates back to the Neolithic era (the New Stone Age), around 10,000 BC. In that era in Mesopotamia, along the eastern shore of the Mediterranean and east to the valley of the Tigris and Euphrates, people stopped searching for randomly growing patches of wild wheat and started to sow it, grow it and harvest it. Although this "domesticated" wheat was still essentially wild, the fact that it was consciously tended was of great significance. The next step was even more momentous. These ancient farmers noticed that much of their wild wheat cast its seeds to the wind as soon as it ripened, much like a dandelion. But a few kernels of wheat in those crops of wild wheat weren't released. By collecting and planting these stick-in-the-mud wheat berries, people found that the next crop would produce more of the same: wheat that could be harvested at the will of humans, not the wind. Thus very slowly began the manipulation of the genetic codes of wild wheat, and the beginnings of real wheat husbandry and "domestication." This planting and harvesting of wheat spelled an end to the nomadic, food-gathering lifestyle necessary up to that point. Communities were established, and as more wheat was grown it became a commodity, building trade relationships between communities and cultures.

By 3,000 BC, wheat was being farmed all over Europe, North Africa, and Asia. In China, wheat was made not into bread, but noodles; wheat was an important food crop in China long before rice.

ORGANIC PLASTIC?

One of the newest uses of wheat is in the manufacture of plastic. Engineers have discovered that the straw left over, once the wheat kernels have been removed from the wheat stalk, can be ground into a fine powder, and mixed $^{50}/_{50}$ with plastic resins. This results in a "bio-composite" that can then be molded into automobile parts, trash cans, and other hard or soft plastic products.

WHO EATS THE MOST WHEAT?

When you think of bread and pastry, the main products made from wheat flour, what country springs immediately to mind? Italy, with its pasta and bread? France, with its wide array of baked goods? America, with the "billions and billions" of hamburgers (accompanied by their wheat-flour buns) sold at McDonald's? The answer is: none of the above. Latest available statistics (circa 2000) show that the residents of Turkmenistan, bordering the Caspian Sea just north of Iran and Afghanistan, each consume a whopping 210kg (463 pounds) of wheat products yearly. Italians enjoy about 330 pounds of wheat products per person per year; the French, only 213 pounds (must be those light and airy baguettes); and Americans, a mere 188 pounds. (Source: *FAOSTAT, the Food and Agricultural Organization of the United Nations*)

The popularity of wheat remained constant as the centuries went on. Wheat was introduced to the New World by Christopher Columbus; in 1520, it was brought to Mexico by Spanish explorers. English colonists carried wheat to Virginia in the early 1600s, and from there it spread throughout America as the settlers moved west.

A key turning point in the history of wheat in America came just after the Civil War. Mennonites from Holland left that country during Europe's religious reformation, and in their travels passed through the Russian Crimea, where they discovered a wheat variety called Turkey Red. In 1874, a wave of Mennonite emigrants came to America, bringing with them their prized Turkey Red wheat. Turkey Red was an entirely new variety of wheat in America; unlike the typical American wheat, planted in the spring and harvested in the fall, Turkey Red was planted in the fall, wintered over, and harvested the following summer. The resulting crop was bounteous, easy to mill, and had tremendous baking qualities, thus pleasing all three of its constituents: farmers, millers, and bakers. Today's premium American baking flours are still based on strains of that original Turkey Red.

Another landmark era for wheat worldwide came after World War II. A variety of wheat from war-ravaged Japan, Norin-10, was brought to North America, where various scientists crossed it with other wheat strains to produce new varieties that increased yield up to 300% per acre. An American plant breeder, Norman Borlaug, brought Norin-10 to Mexico, where he worked with it tirelessly, producing an array of natural hybrids.

In the decade between 1953 and 1963, Mexico's wheat harvest grew 600%. Some of the high-producing Mexican wheat was brought to famine-threatened India in 1963, again by Borlaug. By 1974, India's harvest was up 300%, and the country was feeding itself. A similar story played out in Pakistan. These incredible improvements in yield were dubbed the Green Revolution, and Borlaug was awarded the Nobel peace prize in 1970 for his work.

Types of wheat

After eons of farmers and then scientists isolating and encouraging the genetic development of more "user friendly" characteristics, there are over 30,000 varieties of wheat today, each with its own merits. Most simply, we can classify current wheat varieties as some combination of each of the following: hard or soft, red or white, winter or spring.

- Hard wheat is high-protein wheat; i.e., it produces more gluten than soft wheat. Physically, a hard wheat berry tends to be longer and more bullet-shaped than soft wheat berries, which are plumper. Hard wheat is critical for yeast-leavened baked goods, but is also appropriate for a wide range of baking.

- Soft-wheat varieties, the plump ones, have a larger percentage of carbohydrates and thus less gluten-forming ability. Soft wheat has less protein, can be red or white, and is called winter wheat, as it "winters over" in a state of dormancy in areas where the weather is less severe. Soft winter wheat is grown primarily east of the Mississippi, from Missouri and Illinois east to Virginia and the Carolinas in the South and New York in the North. There are also important crops of soft white wheat in the northern Pacific states. Soft wheat is used to make cake flour and pastry flour.

- The color of the wheat relates to pigments found primarily in the bran. Hard-wheat varieties are predominantly red, though a new variety of hard white wheat has been working its way into the market since the 1980s. Soft wheat can be either red or white.

- Winter wheat is planted in the fall, mainly in Texas, Kansas, Nebraska and other prairie states. It grows until it's about 5 inches tall, and then with the onset of winter and cold weather, it becomes dormant under (hopefully) a good snow cover, and continues growing the following spring. It's harvested in late spring and early summer.

- Spring wheat grows predominantly in the northern plains states and in Canada, where the climate is more rigorous. It's planted in the spring and harvested in late summer and early fall.

- Hard-wheat varieties are usually red, higher in protein and can be either winter or spring varieties. Hard red winter wheat is grown from Texas north through Kansas, the largest wheat state, and into mid-Nebraska. Generally, the farther north you go, the more spring wheat you'll find and the greater the levels of protein. Spring wheat is grown primarily in the Dakotas, Minnesota and Montana into Canada. There are many more acres planted to hard wheat than soft wheat in this hemisphere. Hard wheat is used to make all-purpose flour and bread flour.

Nutrition

To understand wheat's nutritional attributes, it's helpful to understand its anatomy. A wheat berry is made up of three parts. The bran layer (seed coat) comprises about 15 percent of the total wheat berry. It contains about 86 percent of the berry's niacin, 33 percent of its thiamine, 42 percent of the riboflavin, and 19 percent of the protein. It's also an important source of insoluble dietary fiber. Because fiber tends to move quickly through the body, some of the nutrients present in high-fiber foods never make it into our systems; thus these figures don't necessarily represent what we actually get out of the bran.

The germ is only 2½ percent of the wheat berry; it's the wheat embryo that would have produced a new wheat seedling, had it been planted. It contains about 2 percent of the berry's niacin, 64 percent of the thiamine, 26 percent of the riboflavin and 8 percent of the protein.

Wheat germ is also a source of polyunsaturated oil, in which is found iron and vitamins B and E. Because of the presence of this oil, whole wheat flour is more sensitive to storage conditions than white flour, and should be stored in the refrigerator or freezer when you get home from the grocery.

The endosperm makes up about 83 percent of the wheat berry, and is the initial food source for the wheat seedling after it has sprouted. White flour (unbleached all-purpose flour) is the ground endosperm of the wheat berry, without its bran and germ. Before white flour is enriched (see below), it contains 12 percent of the niacin, 3 percent of the thiamine, 32 percent of the riboflavin and 70 to 75 percent of the protein (with soft wheat having the smaller percentage of protein).

In the early 1940s, the United States Food and Drug Administration mandated the addition of certain nutritional ingredients to all-purpose white flour. Because consumption of flour was so widespread, it was felt that its "enrichment" was the most direct and effective way to alleviate certain diseases caused by vitamin deficiencies (pellagra, beriberi, rickets, etc.). Tiny amounts of iron, niacin, thiamine, riboflavin, and folic acid thus were added to white flour to enrich it, much as vitamins A and D are added to enriched milk. As a result, all-purpose white flour contains added amounts of riboflavin, niacin and thiamine, plus iron, equal to or exceeding those found in whole wheat flour.

Flavor

One major sticking point for many people is whole wheat's strong flavor. This flavor derives in part from phenolic acid in the bran layer of red wheat. Phenolic acid is responsible for the "tannic" flavor some people taste; it makes your mouth pucker, much like the sensation you sometimes get from the dregs of a glass of red wine, or in a cup of strong black tea. While many folks appreciate this taste, feeling it's whole wheat's "signature" flavor element, others don't care for it. If you're in the latter group, try white whole wheat flour. Phenolic acid has been bred out of the bran layer.

Unfortunately, the second element of whole wheat's flavor that's not so easily dealt with is the bitterness brought on by rancidity. Freshly milled whole wheat flour is delightfully "sweet," with a fresh, nutty flavor. However, as soon as the germ is cracked open and exposed to air during the milling process, the oil in it begins to oxidize, turn rancid, and taste bitter. The more finely ground the wheat, the more quickly it'll "turn"; keep that in mind, when looking at different types of whole wheat flour.

The best solution to wheat's rancidity is twofold. First, store whole wheat flour in the freezer. Not after a few weeks, not when you think it's been out on the counter awhile, but immediately, as soon as you purchase it—even if it's unopened. Stick the bag of flour in a plastic zip-top bag; or transfer the flour to an airtight container, and put it in the freezer. When you're ready to use the flour, take out what you need, and return the rest to the freezer. Wait 15 minutes or so for the flour to come to room temperature before using it.

Second, we've found that orange juice seems to counter the bitter flavor of flour that's a bit rancid. Try substituting ¼ cup or so of orange juice for the liquid in your recipe. You won't taste any orange flavor; but the bitterness of the whole wheat will be tempered.

The germ is only 2½ percent of the wheat berry; it's the wheat embryo that would have produced a new wheat seedling, had it been planted. It contains about 2 percent of the berry's niacin, 64 percent of the thiamine, 26 percent of the riboflavin and 8 percent of the protein.

Cooking and baking with wheat

The most common form of wheat used in baking is flour. But there are many other forms wheat takes, and all can be used in your baking. Keep in mind that any of these forms of wheat that require softening or cooking in water will release some of their liquid into bread dough (or cookie batter, or anything mixed) as you stir or knead the batter or dough. You'll want to reduce the liquid in your recipe a bit to account for this.

- Wheat berries can be used intact if cooked first. You may cook them according to the chart on page 583, or in a slow cooker on low for 8 to 12 hours.

- It's also possible to sprout wheat berries and add them to bread dough. Sprouted wheat is even higher in certain vitamins than whole wheat flour, and the sprouts lend texture and a slight sweetness to your loaf (p. 186).

- Cracked wheat is the whole wheat berry cracked into pieces. It can be cooked and added to bread dough for delicious chewy texture.

- Bulgur is wheat that's been steamed (partially cooked), dried, and cracked. It can be added to bread dough after soaking. For each cup of dry bulgur, add 1½ cups

ADDING UNBLEACHED FLOUR TO YOUR WHOLE WHEAT RECIPES: IT'S NOT A SIN!

Whole wheat flour is good for you, no argument there. But it's wrong to dub "white" flour (unbleached all-purpose flour) nutritionally useless. That's just plain hogwash. And we'll show you why. Take a look at the following comparison between King Arthur Unbleached All-Purpose Flour and King Arthur Traditional Whole Wheat Flour (values are per cup):

	Enriched All-Purpose	Whole Wheat
Calories	400	400
Fat	1.4g	2.4g
Protein	13g	16g
Carbohydrates	86g	80g
Fiber	3g	15g
Sodium	0mg	4mg
Potassium	140mg	444mg
Iron	5mg	4mg
Thiamine	.80mg	.66mg
Riboflavin	.34mg	.14mg
Niacin	6mg	5mg
Calcium	19mg	41mg
Magnesium	28mg	166mg
Phosphorus	135mg	415mg
Selenium	42mg	85mg

Clearly, whole wheat flour's the big winner in the fiber category; much of that fiber is insoluble, meaning it provides bulk and roughage in your diet, which we all need. Whole wheat is also noticeably higher in potassium, calcium, magnesium, phosphorus and selenium, and a bit higher in protein. All-purpose flour is lower in fat and sodium. They're about equal in iron and carbohydrates.

boiling water, cover, and let the mixture rest for 20 minutes or so, until the water is absorbed. This will yield about 2½ to 3 cups soft, fluffy bulgur. Add to bread dough sparingly, perhaps ½ cup in a 3-cup-of-flour recipe.

Bulgur also makes a very tasty substitute for rice, and can be a key element in cold salads. Tabbouleh, the Middle Eastern mint-flavored salad, is based on bulgur.

• Wheat flakes are the wheat equivalent of oatmeal or oat flakes. They can be added to a bread dough for texture, up to about 1 cup per 3 cups of flour. Also, try substituting wheat flakes for oats in a granola recipe.

• Wheat bran, an excellent source of fiber, vitamins and minerals; and wheat germ, high in vitamin E and folic acid, among other nutrients, can be added to whatever you're baking to increase that product's nutritional attributes. Stabilized or toasted wheat germ is wheat germ that's been specially prepared to oxidize more slowly, thus staying fresh longer. Add about ¼ cup of either to a typical 3-cup-of-flour bread recipe; try slightly larger percentages in cookies and muffins.

- Vital wheat gluten (or "gluten flour") is flour that's been mixed with water to activate the gluten-producing proteins, washed to remove the starchy part of the flour, and then dried and milled back to a flourlike consistency. ("High-gluten flour," not the same thing, contains the starchy endosperm). It can be added, about a tablespoon per loaf, to bread dough that contains low-protein flours or meals (ryes, oats, corn, etc.), or a lot of extras (such as cheese, onions, dried fruit or nuts) to produce lighter loaves.

Baking with whole wheat flour

There are two main types of whole wheat flour available to the home baker: hard whole wheat flour, labeled "traditional" or "white whole wheat;" and soft whole wheat flour, called whole wheat pastry flour. Graham flour was a common name for whole wheat flour in the 1800s; today, the equivalent is a coarsely ground hard whole wheat flour.

Traditional (hard) whole wheat flour can range in grind from very coarse, with noticeable flakes of bran and specks of germ: to extra-fine, a smooth, tan-colored version of white flour. The recipes in this book were tested using a medium-grind whole wheat: King Arthur Traditional Whole Wheat Flour, or King Arthur 100% White Whole Wheat Flour. If you use a more coarsely ground flour, one you might get from a local miller or find in a health-food store, you may find the dough or batter you stir up is unexpectedly wet. That's OK; just let it rest awhile so the flour has more of a chance to absorb the liquid.

Hard whole wheat flour is the equivalent of all-purpose flour: good for anything from cookies and brownies to sandwich bread and pizza crust. Whole wheat pastry flour, made from soft wheat, is ideal for muffins and biscuits, scones and pancakes, piecrust and cake... anytime you're looking for tenderness rather than chew.

A combination of whole wheat flours—traditional and pastry—will give you a protein level (and a gluten level, and thus a degree of tenderness vs. chew) somewhere in between the two. Adding all-purpose flour to traditional whole wheat flour lightens the color and texture, and increases the rise of whatever you're baking. Adding all-purpose flour to whole wheat pastry flour adds stability and strength to the baked good's structure. The following recipe showcases whole wheat flour at its best. Traditional whole wheat's rich, nutty flavor is a pleasant contrast to the sweetness of banana and honey in this tender, moist loaf.

> **FROM FIELD TO TABLE**
>
> A bushel of wheat weighs about 60 pounds and yields 42 pounds of flour, once milled. That 42 pounds of flour will yield about 56 one-pound loaves of bread.

Easy Banana-Walnut Bread

YIELD: One 9 x 5-inch loaf, 12 servings
BAKING TEMPERATURE: 350°F
BAKING TIME: 1 hour to 1 hour 5 minutes

This deep-brown bread is extremely moist, and pleasantly dense; whole wheat flour lends just the right touch of hearty texture and taste. The flavor of bananas is a strong base supporting hints of honey and spice, and walnuts round out the experience.

Be sure to use ultra-ripe bananas for this; their skins should be mottled black, and they should feel very soft to the touch. Using what you normally consider to be ripe bananas will diminish the bread's rich flavor.

½ cup (1 stick, 4 ounces) unsalted butter
½ cup (3¾ ounces) packed light or dark brown sugar
¾ teaspoon baking soda
½ teaspoon salt
½ teaspoon ground cinnamon
¼ teaspoon ground nutmeg
1 teaspoon vanilla extract
1½ cups (12 ounces) mashed ripe banana (about 3 medium-to-large bananas)
¼ cup (3 ounces) honey
2 large eggs
2 cups (8 ounces) whole wheat flour, traditional or white whole wheat
½ cup (2 ounces) chopped walnuts

Preheat the oven to 350°F. Lightly grease a 9 x 5-inch loaf pan.

Beat together the butter, sugar, baking soda, salt, cinnamon, nutmeg and vanilla in a medium bowl until smooth. Add the banana, honey and eggs, beating until smooth. Add the flour and nuts, stirring until smooth. Spoon the batter into the prepared pan and let it rest at room temperature, uncovered, for 10 minutes.

Bake the bread for 50 minutes. Lay a piece of foil gently across the top, and bake until a cake tester inserted into the center comes out clean, 10 to 15 minutes more. Remove the bread from the oven, and allow it to cool for 10 minutes before turning it out of the pan onto a rack to cool completely.

NUTRITION INFORMATION PER SERVING (1 SLICE, 87G): 19g whole grains, 258 cal, 12g fat, 5g protein, 21g complex carbohydrates, 15g sugar, 3g dietary fiber, 56mg cholesterol, 185mg sodium, 258mg potassium, 79RE vitamin A, 3mg vitamin C, 1mg iron, 61mg calcium, 108mg phosphorus.

Banana-Chocolate Chip Muffins

YIELD: 1 dozen muffins

BAKING TEMPERATURE: 350°F

BAKING TIME: 23 to 28 minutes

The combination of banana and chocolate may seem odd at first glance, but remember the flavor of a banana split; now do you get the picture?

Preheat the oven to 350°F. Line a 12-cup muffin pan with muffin cups, and grease the muffin cups with nonstick vegetable oil spray.

Prepare the Easy Banana-Walnut Bread batter (p. 545), replacing the walnuts with ⅔ cup (4 ounces) chocolate chips. Divide the batter among the muffin cups; they'll be nearly full. Bake the muffins until a cake tester inserted in the center of one comes out clean, 23 to 28 minutes. Remove them from the oven, and after a couple of minutes transfer the muffins to a rack to cool.

THE RISE, FALL, AND RISE OF WHOLE WHEAT BREAD

The first record of "bread," an unleavened wheat-and-water cake, was found in Switzerland and dates to about 6,700 BC. It was thousands of years after that, around 3,000 BC, that the Egyptians baked the first yeast-leavened bread, thus creating the serendipitous marriage of yeast and wheat that's provided bread to the world ever since. By the time of Jesus Christ, Roman bakeries were baking and selling a wide variety of yeast-leavened breads, and flour milling had progressed to the point where it was possible to produce "white" flour, which quickly became a very desirable status symbol. White flour was prized for its rarity and baking qualities, and thus saved for high-ranking members of society. In addition to its ability to produce lighter, whiter baked goods, it became desirable over the years simply because of its "noble" associations. By the 14th century, London had two separate bread bakers' guilds: one for brown bread bakers, one for white; one for peasants, one for nobility.

Since then, bread made from white flour has been seen as superior to whole-wheat bread, if not nutritionally, then texturally and flavor-wise. And certainly white bread as "status symbol" has remained strong, at least until the past 50 years or so, when the rise of "all-natural," the concepts of organic farming and sustainable living and, most recently, the new USDA Food Pyramid, have cast a new and favorable light on whole wheat bread.

THE MAGIC OF GLUTEN

Shortly after wheat came under cultivation, one variety—emmer—was accidentally crossed with wild goat grass, and thus was born a new strain of wheat with a very important attribute: two proteins, gliadin and glutenin, which together form gluten, the elastic network that allows baked goods to trap and hold air as they rise. It was goat grass that threw these proteins into the mixture, and we can thank that wild grass for the soft, high-rising sandwich bread we enjoy today.

While wheat flour is mainly starch, it also includes three water-soluble protein groups, and two non-water-soluble protein groups. When water is added to flour, the soluble proteins dissolve, leaving the two nonsoluble proteins: the bread-baker's friends, glutenin and gliadin. When the flour-water mixture is kneaded, the glutenin forms long, thin, elastic strands, while the gliadin connects the strands, holding them together in a cohesive structure. This entire protein structure is called gluten.

Whole wheat flour actually has more protein—more gliadin and glutenin—than white flour, and it's able to form a significant amount of gluten. Then why doesn't whole wheat bread rise as nicely as white bread? Because the bran in whole wheat flour is sharp, and it cuts some of the gluten strands as they develop, thus rendering the structure fragile, rather than strong. This fragile structure "leaks" air as bread dough rises, and that's why whole wheat bread is denser than white bread.

Oats

Avena sativa

For a grain that has turned out to be such a nutritional powerhouse, it's ironic that oats were the last of the major cereal crops to be domesticated. They're native to central Asia; and for centuries were considered to be a pernicious weed in fields of wheat and barley. Finally, farmers realized if you can't beat 'em, eat 'em, and oats began to be cultivated for their own sake. It soon became apparent that oats were well suited for marginal soils and cool, humid growing conditions that would be too harsh for corn or wheat.

Oats are an annual that can be planted in the fall for next summer's harvest, or in the spring, to be harvested in early autumn. Sometimes oats are sown as an off-season ground cover, and plowed under in spring as a green fertilizer.

Oats were considered horse feed in most European cultures, with the exception of Scotland and Ireland. This prejudice goes back pretty far in time. The Roman historian Pliny wrote disparagingly about Germanic, oat-eating people (the same people who would later overrun the Empire); to the Romans, oats were "animal food." The Middle English name for oats was "haver" (the word is still used in Dutch); the word survives in the English term "haversack," which originally meant a livestock feeding bag.

Before the potato became Ireland's staple food, oats were the mainstay of the Irish table. The Scots have always considered oats to be one of the sources of their considerable strength. Over the centuries the Scots have found ways to weave oats into hundreds of dishes for every course at the table. Oatcakes are everyday constants, served with any meal. For desserts, Scotland has gone way beyond oatmeal cookies to the lofty realm of cream crowdie, a mixture of whisky, cream, oats and fruit, also known as cranachan. Skirlie is a savory side dish of oats cooked in butter or roast beef drippings.

Oats first landed on American shores in 1602 with a sea captain who planted them off the southern coast of Massachusetts. Oats grew well in North American coastal areas, but were never as popular as corn, partly because their yield per acre was lower, and partly because the first settlers were English and weren't great fans of eating oats in the first place.

Demand for oats in the human diet has steadily increased in the last 10 to 15 years, as repeated scientific studies have found the soluble fiber in oats to lower blood serum cholesterol. What the Scots have always known, the rest of the world has begun to embrace: that oats are an excellent food. They're occasionally used in brewing beer, oatmeal stout in particular.

Forms of oats

Oat grains as they come off the plant have an outer husk that must be removed. To be processed, the grains are cleaned and toasted, husked and scoured, leaving a whole oat kernel called groats.

- Steel cut, Scottish, Irish, porridge or pinhead oats are groats that have been cut into two or three pieces.

- Old-fashioned rolled oats are steamed oat groats that have been flattened by a roller. Since rolled oats can be eaten raw, they're a chief ingredient in minimally cooked recipes, such as granola.

- Quick-cooking rolled oats get the same treatment as old fashioned, but the groats are cut in pieces before being steamed and rolled, so the resulting flakes are smaller.

- Instant oats are finely chopped before the steaming and rolling process, making them small enough to be "cooked" merely by adding boiling water. They're generally prepackaged, with added sugar, salt and flavors.

- Oat flour is made of oat groats, ground to a powder. It's used in many manufactured breakfast cereals. For example, Cheerios were originally called "Cheeri-Oats."

Nutrition

Oats look very much like wheat in structure, with a bran covering over a starchy endosperm and a germ sitting at the bottom of the grain. But oats are different in that the outer parts of the kernel are soft, and the nutritious bran is not removed during processing. The soluble fiber in oat bran is one of the things that makes it such a dietary hero. Oat bran lowers LDL (the "bad" cholesterol); the beta glucans in the bran responsible for this benefit has also been shown to enhance the human immune system's response to bacterial infection.

One ounce of oats has twice the protein of wheat or corn flakes. They're considered a gluten grain, although some research is accumulating that oats may be safe for those who have celiac disease, if processed in a gluten-free facility. Celiac disease is a rare condition that results in damage to the lining of the small intestine when foods with gluten are eaten.

Oats are 70 percent starch by weight and 12 to 24 percent protein (the highest among the cereal grains). Oats have the highest fat content of any cereal crop except corn; and four times the fatty acids of wheat. Oats are high in lysine, which is often missing in other cereal grains. The fats in oats are relatively healthy: 21 percent saturated, 37 percent monounsaturated, and 43 percent polyunsaturated.

Since oats are a high-fat grain, keep them in an airtight container, and store them in a cool dry place for up to 2 months.

Flavor attributes

Oats have a comforting, nutty, slightly sweet flavor that most people find appealing; rolled oats have a texture that's chewy without being hard. Oats are neutral enough to pair well with savory and sweet; they're often used as a meat extender. Oat flour is a good thickener for soups, gravies and stews.

Baking with oats

While oats have some gluten, their protein is water-soluble, like spelt's, so it won't help the structure of baked goods. Instead oats and oat flour are often added to make dough more moist, or to give a nice nubby texture to the finished product. Oats make a wonderful addition to yeast breads, both for their moisture retention and their flavor; they can make up to one third of the volume of the flour in a loaf before they begin to weigh it down too much.

Oats are wonderful as the primary component of cookies. When combined with butter, sugar, spices and fruit, they make a delicious, chewy treat. With less liquid in the recipe you'll get a crispy oatmeal cookie. See *The King Arthur Flour Cookie Companion* (The Countryman Press, 2004) for directions on creating every kind of texture you could want in an oatmeal cookie.

Oats are a natural for scones. Their tweedy texture and moisture-retaining qualities lend a lot of interest to this sweetened form of biscuit. Oat flour and rolled oats work well in most quickbreads, from pancakes to loaves to muffins.

Crisps and streusels often include oats, for their looks, texture and flavor. When combined with nuts they create a nice crunchy counterpoint to the soft pool of baked fruit underneath.

We found that oat flour was a little too dense for classic foam cakes, like genoise or jelly rolls. It excelled as an ingredient in some cakes that relied on creaming butter and sugar together (although not in pound cakes; oats have too much fat, which curdled the batters) and in the stir-together cakes that included lots of moist ingredients.

The recipe below highlights the purity of oats' flavor and the marvelous way the texture and flavor combine with fruit. The variations that follow show just how versatile and oatmeal base can be.

Baked Oatmeal

YIELD: 16 servings
BAKING TEMPERATURE: 350°F
BAKING TIME: 35 to 40 minutes

This dish presents some of the comforting and familiar traits of morning oatmeal in an unusual way. It's an easy way to put breakfast on the table for a crowd or on a brunch buffet: just assemble it and let the oven do the work. Serve with milk or half-and-half for a breakfast that's incredibly nourishing and a bit more special than the usual morning bowl of hot cereal. This dish is so versatile, it will also serve as a healthful dessert. You could serve Baked Oatmeal warm, like a pudding, with whipped cream or ice cream (or frozen yogurt) on top. Vary the additions of fruit to your taste or try the Banana Walnut/Banana Split variation that follows.

1 cup (5³⁄₄ ounces) steel-cut oats
4 tablespoons (¹⁄₂ stick, 2 ounces) unsalted butter
4 cups (1 quart) water
3 cups (10¹⁄₂ ounces) old-fashioned rolled oats
³⁄₄ cup (5⁵⁄₈ ounces) packed light or dark brown sugar
1¹⁄₂ cups (6 ounces) peeled and diced apple (1 large)
¹⁄₂ cup (3 ounces) diced dried apricots
¹⁄₄ cup (1⁵⁄₈ ounces) diced crystallized ginger
1 teaspoon salt
2 teaspoons ground cinnamon
¹⁄₄ teaspoon ground nutmeg
2 large eggs
¹⁄₂ cup (4 ounces) milk
1 teaspoon vanilla extract

Preheat the oven to 350°F. Butter a 9-inch-square baking dish.

Place the steel-cut oats and butter in a large bowl. Bring the water to a boil, and pour over the oats. Cover and let stand for 20 minutes.

After 20 minutes, stir in the old-fashioned oats, brown sugar, apple, apricots, ginger, salt and spices. In a separate bowl, whisk together the eggs, milk, and vanilla. Stir into the oat mixture. Transfer to the prepared baking dish.

Bake, until the center is set, 35 to 40 minutes. Remove from the oven, and serve warm with milk or cream for breakfast, or warm with whipped cream, ice cream or frozen yogurt for dessert.

NUTRITION INFORMATION PER SERVING (APPROXIMATELY ¾ CUP, ¹⁄₁₆ OF RECIPE, 138G): 29g whole grains, 224 cal, 6g fat, 6g protein, 26g complex carbohydrates, 12g sugar, 4g dietary fiber, 35mg cholesterol, 155mg sodium, 268mg potassium, 160RE vitamin A, 1mg vitamin C, 2mg iron, 52mg calcium, 167mg phosphorus.

VARIATIONS: BLUEBERRY OATMEAL *Omit the apricots, and substitute 2 cups of fresh blueberries for the diced apples.*

BANANA-WALNUT OATMEAL *Substitute 1½ cups diced bananas for the apples, and ½ cup chopped walnuts for the apricots.*

BANANA SPLIT OATMEAL *Make substitutions as for Banana-Walnut Oatmeal, and stir in 1 cup chocolate chips before baking.*

CRANBERRY-APPLE OATMEAL *Substitute ½ cup dried cranberries for the apricots; replace 2 cups of the water with apple juice or cider.*

Corn

Zea Mays

For over 7,000 years, native peoples throughout the New World have made the bounty of corn the center of their cultures, finding countless ways to incorporate it into their cuisines and rituals. Corn's life-giving status as a staple crop, coupled with its height (often as tall as a human, or taller) and its outstretched leaves that looked like arms reaching toward the heavens made it a short step to anthropomorphize corn into a symbol of the gods.

This relationship between man and plant has ensured the survival of both.

Of the three biggest cereal grains grown worldwide, corn is the only one that can't propagate itself without our help. Grains of corn as they grow on the ear are completely enclosed in the husk. If left on the stalk in the wild, the ear would rot on the stalk before it had a chance to germinate. Even if an ear of corn was put in the ground, the kernels are so close together that they'd crowd each other out, prohibiting the growth of a new plant.

Zea mays has been cultivated for so long, no one is positive about its precise origins. Theories abound, but the most commonly held is that corn evolved from a complex cross of several related New World grasses. Teosinte is the earliest known ancestor to still be found growing in the wild in Peru; its seeds are each surrounded by an individual husk. For this reason Teosinte is sometimes referred to as "pod corn."

What to call it?

When Columbus arrived in the Caribbean, he heard the word *mahiz* from the Arawak Indians, as they pointed to ears of corn and the cakes they'd made from them. Corn's spread through Europe was faster than the development of a vocabulary to keep up with it in the scientific community. It was labeled "Turkey Wheat" by a Parisian botanist in 1536, a name that still occasionally crops up today (*granturco* in Italian, *blé de Turquie* in French). The Portuguese named it "milho," which is a derivative of their word for millet (*milhete*).

The word "corn" in Old English meant a small worn-down particle, like a grain of sand or salt. This term was eventually applied to cereal grains in general. In Britain, the principal grains were wheat, barley and oats, any of which could be referred to as "corn." British colonists never took up the word "maize"; instead they called it "Indian corn" to distinguish it from the grains they already knew.

Corn was in many ways the salvation of the first colonists; had the Indians not shared their knowledge and stores of native flint corn with the first European residents of the New World, getting through their early winters would have been even more difficult. Corn traveled everywhere the Spanish, Italian and Portuguese explorers went after the discovery of the Americas. Corn reached China in 1516, spread through Africa and was embraced in Northern Italy within a generation of Columbus's return, because it would grow on colder hillsides that wouldn't support wheat. Corn has been grown in India, China, Africa and Turkey for so many centuries, to many people in these places it's considered a native grain.

As happened with so many cereal crops, those that were eaten of necessity rather than choice often suffered from a lack of status. The early American colonists saw corn as the food of "savages," and despaired of making light, soft bread with it, so they considered it inferior. They ate it as mush, as "hasty pudding," popped as a breakfast cereal and as a flatbread cooked on their hearths.

Corn has more varieties than any other crop species, since it cross-pollinates so readily, needing only the wind to move its pollen from one plant to another once its seeds have been planted. New varieties are being bred continually, but it's useful to identify six major types of corn: flint, flour, dent, sweet, pop and waxy.

Flint corn (*zea mays indurate*) is the type of corn that the eastern American Indians were growing when the first colonists arrived. It has small ears, and hard seed kernels that were mostly dried for storage and ground as needed. The colorful, decorative stalk ears that we buy to decorate with at harvest time are a variety of flint corn. It can come in the full range of colors found in corn, from white to yellow to red to blue. White Rhode Island flint corn is considered to be the only acceptable corn for making the traditional Rhode Island jonnycake. These simple cakes were formed from a paste of ground corn and water, then baked on a hearth, hoe or plank in the fireplace. What the native peoples of Central America call an *arepa* took on an entire family of names as it spread throughout early America, including journey cake, Shawnee cake, ash cake, corn-pone and hoe cake. Flint is the corn variety used to make polenta in Italy, as well as hominy and masa harina. Flint corn can be eaten fresh when it's very young, and the kernels are still translucent.

Flour corn (*zea mays amylacea*) a.k.a. soft or squaw corn, contains mostly soft starch, and the soft kernel breaks apart easily. This corn is used to grind fresh for tortillas, and is also used to make pancake and quickbread mixes. The blue corn that's used for tortilla chips is a flour corn.

Dent corn (*zea mays indentata*) is a tall variety (it can reach 15 feet high at maturity) with high yields. It came about by crossing flint and flour corns. As a result, it contains both hard and soft starches. The hard starches form the sides of the kernel, and the softer starch is on the top. When the seed ripens, the soft starch shrinks, creating the characteristic dent on top. Of all the types of corn, more dent is grown in the United States than any other. Sometimes called field corn, dent is the major livestock feed corn grown in America. Dent is also used to make corn-based whiskies, fuel ethanol and corn syrup and sweeteners. White varieties of dent corn are used mostly for human consumption, in breakfast cereals and grits.

Sweet corn (*zea mays rugosa*) can be dried and used as a seed corn or ground into flour, but by far its most common use is for eating on the cob or for canning, more like a vegetable than a grain. The sugars in old-fashioned types of sweet corn would rapidly convert to starch once picked, which lead to the much-quoted folk wisdom of walking out to the cornfield and running back, in order to get the ears into the pot of boiling water as quickly as possible. The current varieties of super-sweet hybrids are selected for a mutation in one of their genes that inhibits the conversion of sugar to starch for as long as 10 days after picking.

Popcorn (*zea mays everta*), one of the first widely accepted whole grain foods, began its march to popularity in Colonial times, when it was eaten with sugar and cream as the first puffed breakfast cereal. With it's rigid outer hull and soft starch within, it literally turns itself inside out when heated, creating a white, fluffy kernel more than double its original size.

A sweetened version of popcorn that endures to this day is Cracker Jack, which made its debut at the 1893 World's Columbian exposition in Chicago. Popcorn as a snack food got a big boost during World War II, when most candy was shipped to our soldiers overseas, and popcorn filled the void. Orville Redenbacher raised popcorn's profile once again in the 1980s with his Gourmet Popping Corn (a hybrid he developed called Snowflake, which popped to higher volume and left fewer unpopped kernels). Today flavored popcorn cakes and microwave bags are everywhere, favored by dieters for their low-calorie, filling qualities, and by snackers who crave a sweet or salty crunch.

Waxy corn is a variant that was found in China in 1908. It's distinguished by its high oil content (2 to 3 percent higher than normal corn), and the fact that its starch is composed of 100 percent amylopectin, which features branched chains of starch that are favored for thickening liquids. The kernels have a waxy appearance when cut from the cob. Cornstarch is used as a thickener for cooking, a source of corn syrup and corn sugar, and in hundreds of other products, from paper sizing to laundry starch to foam packing peanuts. Corn sweeteners, in the form of high-fructose corn syrup, are pervasive throughout the foods we see on our grocery-store shelves.

Nutrition

Corn is a good source of vitamin A, manganese and potassium, and it contains protein, but not to the same degree as rice or wheat. Like most whole grains, corn's proteins are incomplete. Tryptophan and lysine (two of the eight essential amino acids humans need) are present in corn, but inaccessible (unable to be absorbed by humans) when the corn is eaten fresh or in dried form. The native peoples of the Americas discovered the process of ash or lye cooking to remove the hulls of the corn kernels, yielding the product we know as hominy or *posole*. Processing corn with alkaline substances changes its nutritional profile, making the tryptophan able to be absorbed by the body. The lime from wood ashes also brought more calcium to the diet.

Ground hominy was used to make masa harina, the principal ingredient in tortillas and tamales. These breads have the unusual characteristic of being more nutritionally complete than they would be if made with the whole grain.

Storage

How long freshly ground whole cornmeal stays fresh depends on a number of factors. How long ago was it milled? How long did it sit on a store shelf? Try to find a source of whole cornmeal that turns over its inventory regularly. For longest life, whole cornmeal should be stored in an airtight container in the freezer, to keep the oils in the germ from going rancid. Depending on how frequently the container is opened, it should last in the freezer for 4 to 6 months.

If you're storing dried whole corn kernels or popcorn, place them in sealed plastic or glass containers, and store in a cool, dry place for up to a year.

Flavor attributes

Almost all of us can conjure the taste of sweet, buttery corn on the cob, sprinkled with a bit of salt. That flavor can be brought over to baking by putting fresh corn kernels into corn bread or muffins, or stirring them into batter and frying up some fritters. Corn and whole cornmeal have a wonderful round flavor. Whole cornmeal has a much richer taste than the stuff in the cylinder at the grocery store, which has had its germ removed, to assure a longer shelf life. Since whole cornmeal is often stone ground, its texture can be a bit grittier, as larger chunks of the kernel are retained in the milling process.

Corn and cornmeal are equally comfortable in savory company or sweet. Cheese, spices, and vegetables of all kinds pair well with corn in polentas, savory muffins or spicy cornbreads. Any food you can think of, from your breakfast scrambled eggs to tofu and beans to barbecued pork fits just fine inside a warm corn tortilla or on top of a fried tortilla shell.

Baking with corn

Whole cornmeal is most successful in quick or flat breads, especially if it's the only grain being used. Tortillas are pressed thin, then baked on a griddle. *Arepas* are a thicker version, crispy on the outside, creamy on the inside. Moistened whole cornmeal can be mixed with eggs and baked like a soufflé, to make spoonbread, or mixed into a thick batter and fried up as hush puppies.

To make lighter baked goods with cornmeal, it needs to be joined by some wheat flour to lend some structure and lift, since cornmeal has no gluten. Cornmeal's gritty texture calls for preparations that have a higher amount of moisture. For that reason, cornmeal isn't very well suited to a wide range of cookies.

When mixed with other whole grains such as rye and whole wheat, cornmeal makes wonderful steamed bread; prolonged moist heat softens the corn and eliminates any grittiness. Boston Brown Bread (p. 62) was known in Colonial times as "Thirds" bread, since it called for ⅓ wheat flour, ⅓ rye and ⅓ "Indian meal." Cornmeal in yeast dough lends a nice yellow color and a bit of crunch; it can be substituted for as much as one-third of the other flour without weighing down the loaf too much.

When it comes to cakes, cornmeal pairs very well with lemon in our Lemon-Cornmeal Pound Cake (p. 386) and with cranberries in Cranberry-Cornmeal Cake (p. 378). The underlying sweetness of corn's flavor provides just the right backdrop for tart fruits.

Whole cornmeal really shines in quick breads; be it combined with cheese or chiles, blueberries or bacon, whole cornmeal is a dependable, delightful way to bring whole grains to baking. It's wonderful in muffins and in cornbread, both of which can be amended in an infinite number of ways. The recipes that follow showcase why cornmeal has been so popular in the Americas through the centuries.

Cornbread

YIELD: **One 9-inch-square pan or 9-inch round cast-iron skillet, 8 or 9 servings**
BAKING TEMPERATURE: **400°F**
BAKING TIME: **30 to 35 minutes for the square pan, 25 to 30 for the skillet**

This cornbread combines lots of corn flavor with a subtle assist from whole wheat pastry flour, which helps the bread stay moist, even hours after its baked. A touch of honey adds just a bit of sweetness, allowing the flavor of the corn to stay up front. If you prefer sweeter cornbread, we give you lots of options for adapting the versatile recipe below.

Preheating the pan gives a satisfying crunchy crust to the bottom and edges of the bread. If you don't want to heat the pan in advance, grease and fill it as you would any other quick bread, and add 3 to 5 minutes to the baking time.

2 cups (9¾ ounces) whole cornmeal
1 cup (3⅜ ounces) whole wheat pastry flour
1 cup (4¼ ounces) unbleached all-purpose flour
2 teaspoons baking powder
1 teaspoon baking soda
1 teaspoon salt
2 cups (16 ounces) buttermilk
¼ cup (3 ounces) honey
2 large eggs
½ cup (1 stick, 4 ounces) unsalted butter, melted
1 tablespoon butter or grease for the pan

Preheat the oven to 400°F. For a crispy crust, place a 9-inch-square pan or 9-inch cast-iron skillet in the oven. Otherwise, butter (or grease) your chosen baking pan and set it aside.

TO MAKE THE BATTER: Whisk together the cornmeal, flours, baking powder, baking soda and salt in a large bowl. Whisk together the buttermilk, honey, eggs and melted butter in a separate bowl. Add, all at once, to the dry ingredients, stirring quickly and lightly just until the batter is evenly combined.

TO BAKE IN A PREHEATED PAN: Remove the pan or skillet from the oven and place the tablespoon of butter (or grease) into it. Swirl the pan around so the butter melts and covers the bottom and sides. Carefully transfer the batter to the hot pan, and return it to the oven to bake until the top is golden brown and a cake tester inserted in the center comes out clean, 25 to 30 minutes. Remove from the oven and serve warm.

TO BAKE IN A GREASED PAN: Pour the batter into the prepared pan and bake until the top is golden brown and a cake tester inserted into the center comes out clean, 30 to 35 minutes. Remove from the oven and serve warm.

NUTRITION INFORMATION PER SERVING (1 SERVING, ⅑ OF RECIPE 161G): **37g whole grains,** 409 cal, 13g fat, 11g protein, 55g complex carbohydrates, 8g sugar, 6g dietary fiber, 77mg cholesterol, 538mg sodium, 322mg potassium, 133RE vitamin A, 3mg iron, 141mg calcium, 281mg phosphorus.

VARIATIONS: CORN STICKS *Grease a cast-iron corn-stick pan. Fill the indentations with a scant ¼ cup muffin batter each, and bake at 375°F for 8 to 10 minutes.*

RICH CORNBREAD *Substitute half-and-half for the buttermilk, omit the baking soda and increase the baking powder to 1 tablespoon.*

SWEET CORNBREAD *Decrease the honey to 2 tablespoons, and add ¼ to ⅓ cup brown sugar, according to taste, to the buttermilk mixture before adding.*

CREAMED CORNBREAD *Decrease the buttermilk to 1½ cups, stir in one (14.75 ounce) can creamed corn along with the wet ingredients, or use 1 cup fresh corn kernels and ½ cup heavy cream.*

MAPLE CORNBREAD *Omit the honey, and decrease the buttermilk to 1½ cups. Add ½ cup Grade B maple syrup and ½ teaspoon maple flavor to the batter along with the wet ingredients.*

BACON-CHEDDAR CORNBREAD *Cook, drain, and crumble ½ pound of bacon. Stir into the batter with 1½ cups grated Cheddar cheese.*

JALAPEÑO-CHEESE CORNBREAD *Stir in 1½ cups grated Monterey Jack cheese and ½ cup canned, drained sliced jalapeño peppers (one 7-ounce can) or ⅓ cup diced fresh jalapeños.*

CAST-IRON AND CORN

We know a lot of bakers for whom one and only one kind of pan will do for cornbread: a cast-iron pan. Many have cherished their grandmother's skillets, corn stick, or gem pans, lovingly preserving their glossy, seasoned surfaces (the original nonstick). The appeal of cast-iron bakeware is so strong that the Lodge Company in South Pittsburg, Tennessee, is still turning out biscuit pans, wedge pans, muffin pans and corn stick pans nearly 200 years after Joseph Lodge first forged skillets in the early 1800s. Other classic names in cast-iron such as Wagner and Griswold live on as well, under the umbrella of the American Culinary Corporation.

Cast-iron is an excellent conductor of heat, and for many that's the secret of its appeal for baking cornbread. The time-honored technique for a crispy bottom crust on your cornbread with moist, creamy insides goes like this: Preheat a cast-iron pan in a hot (400°F) oven for 15 minutes. When the batter is mixed, take the pan out of the oven, and swirl a flavorful fat in the bottom, such as bacon grease or butter. Carefully add the batter, and return the pan to the oven to bake. This method gives an unforgettable toasted cornmeal flavor to the bottom crust, and the quick initial heat gives the batter a boost as it activates the leavening. After the bread is done, bring the skillet or pan to the table, where the trusty cast-iron pan will keep the bread warm for as long as it lasts.

Next time you've a hankering for cornbread, dig out Grandma's skillet and give it a whirl. Once you've tried cornbread in cast-iron, you'll see why this beloved baking tool has endured for generations.

Barley

Hordeum vulgare

Barley, the world's fourth-largest cereal crop in number of acres planted (following wheat, rice, and corn) is also one of civilization's oldest cultivated crops. Evidence of cultivated barley has been found in present-day Syria, in sites dating back to 10,000 BC, just about the time that wheat came under cultivation.

Barley is an extremely hardy grain, and grows in areas that are too cold, too dry, or too salty for wheat, or even for rye, another robust grain. Because of its tough double husk, as well as an additional undercoating of bran between husk and endosperm, barley is very resistant to insects. It's ready for harvesting in just three months, and will grow in multiple climatic zones, ranging from the Arctic to the desert. In fact, the only conditions barley doesn't tolerate are those prized by most other growing things: heat and humidity. To this day, barley remains a staple food grain in Tibet, Finland, the Netherlands (where its resistance to saline soil is key) and Ethiopia, among others. Together, Russia and the Ukraine are the world's largest barley producers, harvesting more than double the amount of Canada, the next largest grower.

Barley was a major food source for the ancient Greeks and Romans, the Egyptians and the Chinese. The Babylonians, who used barley as their main currency, are also responsible for the world's oldest barley wine recipe, dating to 2,800 BC. Barley is mentioned often in the Bible; one of the famous 10 plagues of Egypt is the destruction of its barley crop by hailstones. (And since slaves building the pyramids were fed three loaves of barley bread and a portion of barley beer daily, this was indeed a disaster!)

In Europe, barley very early became the chief grain used for bread, a distinction it held into the 16th century. Since barley has very little productive gluten and makes a flat, dense loaf, it was fashioned into "trenchers," edible plates into which the rest of the meal was ladled. Barley water—water in which barley had been boiled—was used to calm upset stomachs, and was also sweetened and cooked to make barley sugar candy, a popular European sweet in the 1600s. As wheat grew more common, barley was gradually relegated to other uses, including animal fodder and brewing.

In 13th-century Great Britain, barley was the basis for the antecedent of whisky, called *uisge beata*—"water of life," in Gaelic. It wasn't drunk for pleasure, but was considered an all-purpose medicine; it was even rubbed on aching muscles. Eventually, this potent drink was used for pleasure, and the name *uisge beata* segued to *uisge*, then to whiskey. Scots poet Robert Burns famously wrote of whisky (as it's spelled in Scotland) in verse, referring to John Barleycorn—whisky—as "a hero bold, of noble enterprise, for if you do but taste his blood, 'twill make your courage rise."

Barley was brought to the New World by Christopher Columbus and by the early 1600s was being cultivated in America. Since wheat and corn were both easily accessible and grew well in North America, barley wasn't used for bread; instead, it was mainly fed to animals, and eventually used to brew beer.

Barley is currently grown in 27 U.S. states; of the domestic crop, about half is used to feed animals, and half processed for human consumption in various forms, the chief of which is malt.

Nutrition

Barley comes in several forms, including hulled barley (barley that's had just its outer hull removed); barley flakes (hulled barley that's been steamed and flattened, like oatmeal), barley flour (hulled barley that's been milled into flour); and pearled barley, which has not only the hull, but also some of the inner bran layer removed. Hull-less barley, a new barley whose hull is so loose it falls off easily during the threshing process, is a variety gradually making its way into the mainstream.

One of barley's chief nutritional assets is its protein; a cup of cooked hulled barley contains as much protein as a glass of milk. It's also low in fat, and high in antioxidants and fiber, particularly soluble fiber, which helps lower cholesterol; the FDA has authorized marketers of barley products to advertise barley's role in reducing the risk of coronary heart disease, the same claim made for oat bran. Barley and oats are the only two whole grains with a significant amount of soluble fiber. And while fiber is found in the bran layer of most whole grains, in barley it's dispersed throughout the grain, meaning even pearled barley offers some fiber benefit.

Pearled barley is the form most commonly found on your supermarket shelf; cooks add it to soups or stews, or cook and serve it as a side dish. However, pearled barley is nutritionally inferior to hulled barley; hulled barley has about 33 percent more vitamins, minerals and fiber than pearled. And since its bran has been removed, it's not classified as a whole grain. Nevertheless, cooked pearled barley contains nearly twice the amount of fiber as the same size serving of cooked brown rice.

Barley is digested quite slowly, and has a low glycemic index (GI). This is important for those watching their blood-sugar levels, as it means eating barley will raise the blood's glucose and insulin levels more slowly. And, for those trying to lose weight, this long, slow digestion process translates into reduced hunger.

Taste

Barley's flavor, like that of many whole grains, is often characterized as "nutty." In taste tests, we found barley flour very mild-tasting, a great way to add whole grains to your baked goods without affecting their flavor. Because it's low in useable gluten, wheat flour—either whole wheat or all-purpose flour—is a good complement, adding the structure most baked goods need and that barley alone can't provide.

When cooked, barley's soluble fiber becomes viscous. This viscosity translates to a "buttery" or "fat" feeling in your mouth, making barley flour a pleasing addition to most baked goods.

Cooking with barley

Barley is a wonderful filler or extender—it has a mildly nutty taste of its own, and also takes on the flavor of whatever food it's combined with. Thus you'll find cooked barley berries adding starch and body to many vegetable soups, or teaming with vegetables to make a nice stuffing for turkey or chicken. In the winter, when you're eating heartier foods, it's nice to keep some cooked barley on hand in the refrigerator to add to soup or stew.

Though the barley you'll find most often at the supermarket is pearled barley, we prefer to use hulled barley when cooking whole berries. Though pearled barley cooks much more quickly, it's not difficult to cook hulled barley. It makes a delicious side dish, akin to rice; and can be refrigerated (for up to a week) and used in a hearty salad.

Barley that's been steamed, then rolled and cut becomes barley flakes, the barley equivalent of oats. Cook barley flakes exactly as you would oatmeal; they can also stand in for oats in granola, cookies, meatloaf or anywhere else you use oats as an ingredient.

Baking with barley flour

Although barley is a high-protein whole grain, the gluten it produces is weak and unsuitable for building structure. Thus it's nearly always paired with wheat flour—either whole wheat or all-purpose flour—in baked goods. An exception, as you'll see in the recipe on page 562, is pancakes, in which eggs provide all the structure these flat cakes need.

Cookies

Since cookies don't rise very much, they don't require a lot of help, structurally speaking. And most of what they need is provided by an egg or two, an exception being some eggless cookies, such as shortbread (which rises barely at all). Try substituting barley flour for up to half the flour in your cookie recipe; it'll add whole grain nutrition, and with barley's fine grind (meaning no "gritty" feel in the mouth), and mild flavor, your family probably won't be able to tell the difference. For a great example of barley flour in cookies, see our recipe for Classic Crunchy Chocolate Chip Cookies, p. 305.

Muffins, quickbreads, and cake

These higher-rising baked goods can't take as large a percentage of barley flour as cookies can. While it adds very mild background flavor, and enhances their tender texture, muffins, quickbreads and cake tend to crumble very easily if they're made with too much barley flour. Try substituting barley flour for one-fourth of the all-purpose or whole wheat flour in your recipe.

Piecrust

With its mild taste, barley allows the flavor of butter to shine through in piecrust. It makes a tender crust that's nearly as flaky as one made with all-purpose flour. The downside? Again, it's that lack of usable gluten and the problem with structure inherent in barley flour. A piecrust made with barley flour, water, butter, and salt will roll out nicely, look

BARLEY, BREAD AND BEER

Barley is the world's top crop for feeding livestock, and the majority of barley grown in the world goes to that end. But its second most popular use is in making malt, which is then used as a sweetener or flavoring (e.g., barley syrup, malted milk); is added to flour as yeast food; is the basis for a variety of caffeine-free hot beverages (e.g., Caffix); and serves as a key ingredient in beer and whisky.

Any grain can be "malted" (transformed into malt) by soaking the grain berries in water, allowing them to germinate (just as if you were making sprouted wheat berries), then dried, cured and ground into powder. Malting first converts the proteins in the grain into enzymes, and then those enzymes work to turn the grain's starch into sugar. The resulting sweet product is prized by flour millers, beer brewers and whisky distillers. Since barley is one of the least expensive grains to produce, creates a lot of enzymes during germination, and thus produces a large amount of sugar when it's malted, it's the grain of choice for industries that use malt in their products.

What does malt do in flour? As a simple sugar, it provides growing yeast with an ongoing source of easily accessible food. Diastatic malt, prepared in a slightly different manner, is used by professional bread bakers. High in enzymes, it's added to bread dough, where those enzymes speed up the process of converting the starch in flour to sugar, again providing growing yeast with an easy food source.

How does malt help turn vegetables or grains into beer or whisky? Malt provides instant food for yeast, which feeds on the starches in the vegetable or grain mash to which it's added. As the yeast grows, it produces carbon dioxide and alcohol, and from there it's the manufacturer's job to distill or brew that alcohol into Glenfiddich whisky or Budweiser beer.

great going into the oven, then go to pieces as it bakes, literally: the edges will break and fall off.

Our solution? Add an egg to barley piecrust. The protein in an egg white is sufficient to hold the crust together, and the fat in the yolk adds its own tenderness. Or try piecrust with half whole wheat or all-purpose flour, half barley flour. Less barley means less of its mild flavor, but more stability.

Yeasted baking

The higher you expect your yeast bread to rise, the less barley flour you should use. Pan (sandwich) loaves can handle the least amount of barley flour; any amount beyond about 10 percent of the flour total will noticeably affect the bread's rise, so use barley flour sparingly in high-rising sandwich bread.

Flatbreads, since their rise is lower, can take more barley flour. Substituting barley for about one-third of the wheat flour in your recipe should produce an acceptable (though lower rising) loaf. For barley bread reminiscent of those dense "trenchers" used in 16th-century England, make a loaf that's half barley flour, half all-purpose flour. The loaf will be a rich mahogany color, and pleasantly dense and moist. You can also make pizza crust that's half barley, half wheat flour; it'll be dense and chewy, rather than light and crisp.

The following recipe showcases barley's best baking attributes: tender texture; a mild, pleasing taste; and warm color.

Barley Cakes

YIELD: 10 large (3½-to 4-inch) pancakes
COOKING TIME: 5 to 6 minutes

These light and fluffy, tender pancakes are the muted gold color of an autumn sunset. Their mild flavor features a hint of orange, and a touch of honey. To bring this dish full circle, serve them with a drizzle of barley syrup.

3 large eggs
¾ cup (6 ounces) milk
½ cup (4 ounces) orange juice
1 teaspoon vanilla extract
3 tablespoons (1½ ounces) unsalted butter, melted
2 tablespoons (1½ ounces) honey
¾ teaspoon salt
1½ cups (6 ounces) whole barley flour
2 teaspoons baking powder

Whisk together the eggs, milk, orange juice, vanilla, melted butter, honey and salt in a batter bowl (a bowl with a pouring spout), extra-large measuring cup or medium bowl. Stir in the barley flour. (Don't add the baking powder yet.) Allow the mixture to rest at room temperature while you preheat your griddle, about 15 minutes. If you're using an electric griddle, set the temperature to 300°F.

When you're ready to cook the pancakes, add the baking powder, stirring the batter for about 15 seconds, until the leavening is completely dispersed throughout. Pour the batter onto the griddle by the ¼-cupful; a muffin scoop works well here.

Cook the cakes until they're golden brown underneath, 3 to 3½ minutes. Unlike white-flour pancakes, you won't see bubbles forming and popping on top of these, so don't wait for that to happen. Gently flip the cakes over, and cook till they're golden brown on the bottom, 2 to 2½ minutes more. Serve hot, with butter and barley syrup or maple syrup, if desired.

NUTRITION INFORMATION PER SERVING (1 PANCAKE, 71G): **17g whole grains,** 138 cal, 5g fat, 4g protein, 15g complex carbohydrates, 4g sugar, 2g dietary fiber, 73mg cholesterol, 275mg sodium, 125mg potassium, 61RE vitamin A, 6mg vitamin C, 1mg iron, 104mg calcium, 190mg phosphorus.

From the 5th century right up through the 1700s, barley was used as the basis for measurement, first in Great Britain, then in America. One grain of barley, called a barleycorn, equaled ⅓ inch. Thus, 12 inches (1 foot) equaled 36 barleycorns. Shoe sizes were often quoted in barleycorns; as late as the late 19th century, a shoe size might be listed as "Size 13, 39 barleycorns." Barley was also used as a weight measurement; the word "gram," used in the metric system, evolved from the word "grain," referring to barley.

Rye

Secale cereale

Rye was a relative latecomer on the grain scene, with first evidence of cultivation dating back only about 5,000 years ago. While there's some evidence rye may have predated wheat cultivation, it's still generally accepted that rye first arrived as a weed in early wheat fields. Rye originated in Asia Minor, near the Fertile Crescent, but its ability to survive cold and dry conditions guaranteed a spread north.

Rye can survive subzero winters and will grow and even germinate in near-freezing temperatures. It's capable of thriving in fields that have been exhausted by overproduction of wheat. Over the next few thousand years, rye traveled north through Greece and Rome, where it was used in bread and porridge but was less valued than wheat for baking. By the Middle Ages, rye had reached northern Europe, where its hardy nature made it the predominant grain. From Europe, it spread across Russia and, in the other direction, made the trip to America with the early settlers.

Despite rye's agricultural and nutritional attributes, rye bread was never as highly esteemed as wheat bread, most likely because it's so much lower in gluten than wheat. Even the best rye breads are dark and dense in comparison with wheat bread, so rye became the bread of the masses, while wheat, which was harder to grow and more expensive, was reserved for the upper classes. As is often the case with "peasant" food, rye bread was more nutritious and kept better than the refined bread consumed by the elite.

While rye is hardy and nutritious, it's also very susceptible to ergot, a fungus that affects the human nervous system. Ergot poisoning can cause muscle spasms, hallucinations and convulsions, and some believe that ergot-infested rye may have been a contributing factor to historic episodes of witchcraft, such as happened during the Middle Ages and at Salem. In more recent times, ergot was a base in the development of lysergic acid and is now deliberately cultivated for use in a number of medicines.

Nutrition

Not only is rye easier to grow than wheat, it retains more nutrients in milling than wheat does. Rye's germ and bran are harder to separate from the endosperm, so more of them remain in the flour during milling than when milling wheat. Rye flour is usually milled first and then sifted to remove different degrees of germ and bran. The darker the flour, the more of the germ and bran remain, and the more nutrition is available. Rye flour is usually sold as light or white rye, medium rye, dark rye (which is still not whole rye), and whole rye, or pumpernickel.

Rye flour is higher in calcium, iron, fiber, lysine and manganese, among other nutrients. Because some of the germ and bran are present after sifting, even light rye will provide you with significant nutrients, though the fiber is lower, and the flavor is milder than dark rye.

Although rye flour has significantly less gluten than wheat flour, it's not low enough for those who must adhere to a gluten-free diet. It has a high level of bran, fiber and minerals, which results in a higher absorption of water than wheat flour. Rye is relatively high in lignans and other antioxidants that may offer additional health benefits.

Rye is very high in amylase enzymes, the enzymes that convert starches to sugars, with the result that rye is quick to ferment and makes a hospitable environment for yeast. Rye is also high in pentosans, which contribute to the gummy quality often associated with baked goods made with rye.

Rye flour should be stored in the freezer if you plan to keep it for longer than 6 months.

Flavor

When it comes to rye, people usually fall into two categories: rye lovers and rye haters. This is a shame, because what people are often responding to is not the rye itself, but the flavors they associate with it. If you dig a little deeper you generally find that what people actually object to is the caraway or sour flavor you find in typical, American-style rye bread. The sour flavor so many people hate in rye bread is often not a true rye sour, but the chemical flavor of shortcuts used by some bakers to make a sour-flavored wheat bread with a little rye added. There's often an acidic aftertaste with these products, and that metallic tone can be increased by adding caraway seeds, whose aromatic flavor can turn chemical if it's overused.

Rye itself, high in sugars, has a sweet, grassy flavor. Next time you try a rye muffin or biscuit, see if your tongue doesn't detect a faintly tacky texture. That's the pentosans. In some things, this can be an appealing component of the product, because there's a fine line between tender and gooey. This gummy characteristic is even more pronounced in bread, where the rye is heated for a longer period of time. To successfully make bread that's not overwhelmingly gummy, bakers acidify the rye flour through the sourdough process.

Baking with rye

Rye is easy and inexpensive to grow, rye flour is good for you, and it has a sweet taste—so why don't we see more of it in baked goods? As we noted above, that gummy quality of rye flour doesn't disappear with baking. This can be manageable in some smaller baked goods—crackers spring to mind, where the rye is rolled so thin, that you're eating mostly crust, and the sweet, caramelized flavor comes through without the gummy texture. Rye works pretty well in waffles (see Cornmeal-Rye Waffles, p. 21) and biscuits (see Onion-Rye Biscuits, p. 80), too, where the crust dominates and a very tender interior is welcome.

Rye bread

In bread, though, rye can be tricky to manage for a variety of reasons. First of all, rye flour is low in gluten, so it's more dense than bread made with wheat flour. The higher the proportion of rye, the more dense the bread.

Second, rye flour has this gummy quality (pentosans) mentioned earlier. These are chains of sugars, or polysaccharides. They work to hold moisture in the bread and to hold the bread together as it bakes. The trick is that they're very fragile, so when you try to develop the bread with vigorous kneading, they break, and the moisture they've been holding floods back into the dough, making it even gummier. The solution is to knead very gently, just enough to bring the dough together and allow the flour to absorb the liquid.

The final challenge is the increased presence and activity of amylase enzymes. These work to convert starches into sugar, and in rye flour they continue this activity well past the temperature at which wheat flour amylases stop. This means that in the oven, rye bread is madly converting starch to sugar, and the structure of the bread, tenuous to start with since there's so little gluten, begins to disintegrate. The solution here is sourdough. Sourdough actually works to slow the amylase activity, keeping it in check long enough for the bread's structure to set as it bakes.

So, for the rye bread baker, this means the higher the level of rye, the more water you'll add because of its increased bran and fiber. You'll want to mix part of the rye flour with a sourdough starter to slow the amylase activity. You'll mix the dough more gently, so the pentosans can do their work holding the bread together. Let the dough rise for a shorter period of time, to keep the amylase activity under control, and to keep the bread from getting too sour. Then, when you bake the bread, bake it at a higher initial temperature to get it hot enough to stop amylase activity early in the baking period, then let it finish baking at a lower temperature, to help the bread crumb set and the flavor develop. Rye bread will be gummy if you cut it too early. It's best to let rye bread cool completely and, for breads that are entirely rye, even age for a day or two before you cut, to let the structure set and the flavor develop.

All in all, to make great rye bread, you need a different body of knowledge and experience. It takes some practice, and likely some failures before you're making rye bread you truly love. Of course, that's just part of the allure of baking.

Volkornbrot

YIELD: **One 8¹⁄₂ x 4¹⁄₂-inch loaf, about 25 slices**
BAKING TEMPERATURE: **475°F, then 375°F**
BAKING TIME: **1¹⁄₄ hours**

Voll means "full" in German, korn means "grain" and brot *means "bread," so this bread is translated as full grain bread, which is exactly what it contains. This version comes to us from Jeff Hamelman, director of our bakery and true lover of great rye bread. It's the ideal recipe to represent rye since it's made entirely with rye flour, and it illustrates how to turn the drawbacks of rye into assets. Part of the rye here comes as cracked rye, which can be made by running whole rye berries through your grain mill at its coarsest setting. The bread uses a rye starter to slow the high amylase activity, and it's barely kneaded. Though it's not a high riser, it does get some spring in the oven. It's a long process to make the bread, because it really needs to sit for a day or two after it's baked, but the flavor and texture are rich and intense. It's easy to double, triple or quadruple the recipe, and it keeps for a long time.*

Rye sour
1¹⁄₂ cups (5⁵⁄₈ ounces) whole rye (pumpernickel) flour
³⁄₄ cup (6 ounces) cool water
1¹⁄₂ teaspoons ripe rye starter (see Sourdough, p. 273)

Grain soaker
³⁄₄ cup (4 ounces) cracked rye
¹⁄₂ cup (4 ounces) cool water

Final dough
All of the rye sour
All of the grain soaker
1¹⁄₄ cups (4⁵⁄₈ ounces) whole rye (pumpernickel) flour
¹⁄₄ cup (2 ounces) cool water
¹⁄₂ cup (2¹⁄₂ ounces) sunflower seeds
1¹⁄₄ teaspoons salt

TO MAKE THE DOUGH: The night before you're ready to bake, combine the ingredients for the sour into a thick paste. Cover the container and let it sit overnight at room temperature, or up to 15 hours. Pour the water over the cracked rye for the soaker, cover it and let it soak overnight.

The next morning, the soured rye should have a fresh, astringent aroma. Combine it with the soaker in the bowl of your mixer. Add the remaining dough ingredients. Mix the dough for 10 minutes, stopping frequently to scrape down the sides. You want to mix on the lowest speed possible to make sure the pentosans don't break down. The dough won't look like any other bread dough; instead, it looks like a thick paste, and it will lighten in color a bit.

After you've finished the dough, cover the bowl and let it sit while you prepare the oven and the pan.

TO BAKE THE BREAD: Grease an 8½ x 4½-inch pan and dust it with whole rye flour. Spray your hands and your work surface with water to help keep the dough from sticking. Shape it into a rough log, and put it in the prepared pan. Sprinkle the loaf with a light dusting of pumpernickel, cover the pan with plastic wrap, and let the loaf rise for 1 hour.

Preheat your oven to 475°F and prepare it for steam (see p. 284).

Just before you bake the bread, slash it with a sharp knife—a diamond pattern is nice. Put the loaf in the oven and steam it. Bake for 15 minutes, then turn the heat down to 375° and bake for 1 hour more. Remove the bread from the pan, and cool it thoroughly on a wire rack. When it's completely cool, wrap it loosely and set aside for 1 or 2 days before slicing it. Serve it sliced very thin, about ¼ inch.

NUTRITION INFORMATION PER SERVING (1 SLICE, 32G): 16g whole grains, 69 cal, 2g fat, 3g protein, 12g complex carbohydrates, 4g dietary fiber, 107mg sodium, 138mg potassium, 1mg iron, 13mg calcium, 122mg phosphorus.

Spelt

Triticum aestiva var. spelta

Imagine yourself traveling through time, back to the Stone Age, about 6000 BC. Life then centered entirely around the food supply: while men were hunting, women were gathering. And one of the foods women gathered was spelt, one of the founding members of the wheat family. Crushed spelt mixed with water and cooked over fire is an original antecedent of the bread we enjoy today.

Sibling to emmer and einkorn (which you may have heard of, if you're a whole grains aficionado), spelt has a lighter, nuttier flavor than wheat. Of these three so-called "ancient wheat" varieties, spelt is probably the easiest for the home baker to obtain; look in natural-foods markets or health-food stores for spelt flour. Ancient wheats, also known as ancestral wheats, are the progenitors of the modern wheat hybrids created over the past 150 years or so, wheats that were bred for higher yield and easier threshing. Still, these unhybridized "pure" wheat varieties, possessing all their original attributes, have something to offer the modern baker: a higher nutritional profile and better flavor.

Spelt probably originated in present-day Iran and then spread throughout Europe over the next couple thousand years. One of the seven original grains mentioned in the Bible, spelt remains an important European grain today. In Germany, spelt *(dinkle)* is used in a variety of foods, from beer to bread. In Italy, spelt (*farro*) is often found in pizza crust, bread and cake.

Spelt was introduced to the United States by Swiss immigrants in the late 19th century, and for a while enjoyed quite a bit of popularity. But it has a very poor yield per acre, compared to wheat. And its tough, thick husk not only takes up much of the grain berry, but also makes threshing difficult. Thus spelt's short reign as a popular wheat among American farmers came to an end in the 1920s. Today, the same characteristic— a tough, thick hull—that made it anathema to farmers 80 years ago makes spelt attractive to those interested in organic farming. Because the inner endosperm and germ of the berry are so well protected, spelt is considered very hardy, and is resistant to insects and disease without the use of chemical pesticides.

Nutrition

Whole spelt flour is very high in fiber, with more than four times the amount of fiber in a single serving than whole wheat flour. It's also high in protein (up to 40 percent higher than wheat), B-complex vitamins and manganese. Partially due to its super-protective hull, spelt is extremely water-soluble, meaning its nutrients can be absorbed by the body more easily than those of other grains. The hull also keeps spelt's nutrients fresher for a prolonged period, much longer than other grains. Because the vitamins and minerals in spelt are more evenly distributed throughout the grain berry than those of wheat (which are found mainly in the berry's outer layers and in its germ), even white spelt, while not a whole grain, will provide you with a healthy measure of nutrients.

At one time, it was thought spelt might be able to be tolerated by individuals with wheat allergies. However, spelt has more protein than wheat, and thus is capable of making more gluten, so it's not suitable for those with gluten allergies.

To keep spelt (and its nutrients) as fresh as possible, store spelt flour airtight in the freezer, where it will stay good for 6 months or so. Spelt berries can be stored at room temperature or, preferably, in a closed container in the freezer.

Flavor

Spelt tastes milder than wheat; it is often characterized as smooth, "nutty," and "sweeter" than wheat. In testing baked goods here at King Arthur Flour, we've found that the majority of tasters prefer spelt to whole wheat, noting its "mild" flavor. Spelt is missing an element in wheat's bran layer, phenolic acid, which gives wheat its characteristic bitter or tannic flavor. Without the phenolic acid, spelt's delicious "wheaty" flavor is able to shine through.

Cooking spelt berries

If you find a source for spelt berries and want to experiment, try cooking them as a stand-in for the usual starch on your plate, such as rice or potatoes. (See chart, p. 583.)

Baking with spelt flour

With spelt's great flavor and sound nutritional attributes, why not just use it exclusively, and forgo whole wheat? Not so fast, partner. The same water solubility that makes spelt's nutrients so accessible to us also gives baked goods made with spelt a more fragile structure. And, though spelt is higher in protein and forms more gluten than wheat, that gluten is more delicate. The bottom line? Spelt is a pleasure to bake with, but don't expect it to do everything wheat does; and do expect to "baby" your baked goods during their preparation, more than you would those made with whole wheat flour.

We've found that spelt absorbs liquid readily, but also lets it go just as readily. At first we believed it just took spelt longer to absorb liquid, but eventually we discovered that liquid is absorbed, then let go as the dough is kneaded or mixed. The solution? Just take your time, giving dough or batter a rest (to reabsorb liquid) before baking.

Cookies

For cookie dough, an overnight rest in the refrigerator allows the dough to stabilize, with any excess liquid gradually being absorbed. Cookie dough refrigerated overnight before baking will spread less when baked, and not just because it's been chilled; there'll actually be less "free" liquid in the dough, meaning less opportunity for the cookies to spread.

Muffins, quickbreads and cake

We've found spelt is delicious in whole grain muffins, quickbreads and cakes, where it makes a lighter, more tender product than traditional whole wheat flour. As with cookies, a resting period before baking seems to help spelt's performance. We recommend letting prepared batters made with baking powder rest overnight in the refrigerator before baking. If your muffin or cake recipe calls for only baking soda, we don't suggest using spelt, as the necessary overnight rest will cause the baking soda to lose its punch.

Yeasted baking

For yeast bread, including pan breads, rolls, braids, pizza and flatbreads, we've had good luck using an overnight starter. Use 1 cup spelt flour, ½ cup water and a pinch of instant yeast. The starter gives the yeast a good head start by breaking down some of spelt's carbohydrates into simple sugars, which is what yeast needs in order to grow. In addition, the overnight rest stabilizes the liquid in at least some of the spelt flour, making the resulting dough easier to work with. Next day, continue with the recipe (accounting for the amount of flour and water you've used in the starter, of course).

You may be thinking: If spelt bread made with a starter is successful, how about sourdough bread made entirely with spelt flour? We don't recommend it. The long rests dough undergoes as sourdough bread develops its characteristic flavor destroys spelt's fragile gluten structure. However, if you're willing to add some all-purpose or bread flour in place of some of the spelt, it's possible to make a very nice spelt sourdough loaf (p. 299).

EAT SPELT BEFORE YOUR MARATHON!

The glycemic index (GI) of any particular food is an emerging benchmark for those watching their weight, as it's long been for endurance athletes, and those tracking their blood-sugar levels, such as people with diabetes. The GI measures how fast carbohydrates break down in the body once a certain food is consumed, and how quickly blood sugar rises. In general, the more slowly carbohydrates break down and blood sugar rises, the better for your body.

Spelt has a lower GI than most whole grains, due to its higher percentage of both simple and complex carbohydrates. The combination of spelt's array of different carbohydrates, the length of those carbohydrate chains (meaning it takes awhile to digest them), and their easy digestibility have made it a special favorite of endurance athletes (such as marathoners and triathletes) who "carbo-load" before competition. In addition, some of these carbohydrates, mucopolysaccharides, do double duty, aiding in blood clotting, and stimulating the body's immune system.

Spelt yeast dough handles beautifully. It's supple and extensible, rolling out easily without snapping back or shrinking. While our pan breads didn't rise as high as whole wheat breads, they had lovely flavor. Characteristically, a spelt pan bread will look beautiful going into the oven, will rise high, then will settle a bit in the final phase of baking.

On the other hand, a braid made with spelt dough bakes into a lovely loaf. Braided dough made from all-purpose flour sometimes splits or unravels as it bakes, due to the strength of the flour and its very tight gluten. But braids made with spelt seem to relax just enough in the oven to hold their shape.

We've found spelt makes wonderful pizza crust and flatbreads. Since it's not required to rise as high, it's more successful in these applications than in pan breads or free-form artisan loaves.

The following recipe showcases spelt's ancient heritage, its wonderfully nutty taste and its golden color.

Vineyard Focaccia

YIELD: One 13 x 18-inch focaccia, 16 servings
BAKING TEMPERATURE: 350°F
BAKING TIME: 25 to 30 minutes

We pay tribute to spelt's long history here by combining it with other time-honored ingredients—salt, water, honey, olive oil, yeast and rosemary—to make a delicious, tender flatbread.

Our taste-testers fell into two camps around the toppings we offered. Oven-roasted onions and kalamata olives were a slam dunk; everyone loved that combination. But we wanted to bring wine into the equation—how can you possibly speak of ancient culinary history without including wine?—and Merlot-poached grapes, while a tremendous hit with some of our more daring taste-testers, fell flat with the mainstream crowd, who deemed the combination of bread and cooked grapes "too weird." The lesson: Assess the "hipness" of your audience before making this bread, and choose the appropriate topping.

Starter
1 cup (3½ ounces) whole spelt flour
⅓ cup (2⅝ ounces) cool water
Pinch of instant yeast

Dough
All of the starter
¼ cup (1¾ ounces) olive oil
1 tablespoon honey
⅔ cup (5⅜ ounces) lukewarm water
2½ cups (8¾ ounces) whole spelt flour
2 teaspoons instant yeast
1¼ teaspoons salt
1 to 2 teaspoons dried rosemary, to taste

Grape topping
1¼ pounds seedless red grapes
½ cup (4 ounces) red wine; choose something smooth and nonassertive, like Merlot

Onion and olive topping
2 tablespoons (⅞ ounce) olive oil
2 pounds sweet onions, peeled and coarsely chopped
1½ cups (8 ounces) pitted kalamata olives

TO PREPARE THE GRAPE TOPPING: This topping requires an overnight stay in the refrigerator, so start a day ahead. Place the grapes and wine in a wide, shallow sauté pan. Bring the mixture to a gentle simmer, and cook until the wine has mostly evaporated and what's left has become syrupy, about 30 minutes. Transfer the grapes and liquid to a shallow dish, cover, and refrigerate overnight.

TO PREPARE THE STARTER: Mix the starter ingredients in a small (2- to 3-cup) bowl, cover the bowl, and let rest overnight at room temperature.

TO PREPARE THE DOUGH: Combine all the ingredients, and mix and knead them—by hand, mixer or bread machine—until you have a soft, smooth dough. Cover and allow the dough to rise until it's puffy and nearly doubled in bulk, 1 to 2 hours. If you've chosen the onion and olive topping, prepare it while the dough is rising.

TO PREPARE THE ONION AND OLIVE TOPPING: Preheat the oven to 350°F. Spread 1 tablespoon olive oil in a large baking sheet; a half-sheet pan is a good choice. Spread the onions in the pan, and drizzle them with the remaining 1 tablespoon oil. Roast the onions, stirring occasionally, until they're a light golden brown interspersed with darker brown, 1 hour. Remove them from the oven, and set aside.

At the same time the onions are roasting, prepare the olives. Lightly grease a 9-inch round cake pan, and spread the olives in the pan. Roast them in the oven with the onions for 30 minutes; they'll be dry, but still fairly soft. Remove them from the oven, transfer them to a bowl, and set aside.

TO SHAPE AND TOP THE FOCACCIA: Use nonstick vegetable oil spray to lightly grease a 13 x 18-inch half-sheet pan or similar-size pan with edges. Spread 2 tablespoons olive oil in the pan. Yes, you really do want to grease the pan first, then spread it with olive oil. Gently deflate the dough, and transfer it to the pan. Flatten it in the pan, gently patting it into the corners. Don't be obsessive about making it cover the entire bottom of the pan, just make a good effort. Spread your filling of choice over the dough.

Cover the focaccia with well-greased plastic wrap or a proof cover, and let it rise until it's puffing up around the topping, about 1½ hours. Preheat the oven to 375°F.

TO BAKE THE FOCACCIA: Bake the focaccia till it's golden brown, 25 to 30 minutes. Remove it from the oven, use a spatula to loosen the edges and bottom, and slide it onto a rack to cool; if you let it cool in the pan, its crisp bottom will become soggy. Serve the focaccia warm or at room temperature.

NUTRITION INFORMATION PER SERVING WITH GRAPE TOPPING (1 SLICE, 84G): 22g whole grains, 124 cal, 4g fat, 4g protein, 21g complex carbohydrates, 1g sugar, 4g dietary fiber, 168mg sodium, 180mg potassium, 2RE vitamin A, 1mg vitamin C, 1mg iron, 7mg calcium, 86mg phosphorus.

NUTRITION INFORMATION PER SERVING WITH ONION TOPPING (1 SLICE, 107G): 22g whole grains, 147 cal, 7g fat, 4g protein, 20g complex carbohydrates, 1g sugar, 4g dietary fiber, 293mg sodium, 177mg potassium, 6RE vitamin A, 3mg vitamin C, 2mg iron, 25mg calcium, 96mg phosphorus.

Buckwheat

Fagopryum esculentum var. Moench

Pioneers have been carrying buckwheat with them for over 6,000 years. From its birthplace in the mountainous regions of southwestern Asia in the neighborhood of 4,000 BC, this triangular-shaped seed spread throughout China and Russia. It eventually reached Europe in the Middle Ages, and there are records of it being grown in what is modern-day Czech Republic as early as the 12th century. Since buckwheat produces well under extreme weather conditions (it actually likes cold, wet weather, as long as drainage is good), it was a reliable staple to bring along when venturing into uncharted territory. To give you an idea of how hardy this plant is, there is a genus of buckwheat (Koeniga) that has only one species, but it can be found growing in the Arctic, the Himalayas, and Tierra del Fuego in Argentina.

Buckwheat's name is likely derived from the Middle Dutch *boecweit*: "Beech Wheat" (because the kernel is shaped like the three-sided, rust-colored beechnut). Buckwheat isn't a grass, like wheat. It's related to sorrel and rhubarb; the buckwheat kernel is actually a fruit seed. Buckwheat is often considered to be a cereal, however, because of the ways in which it's used. It cooks like a cereal: it's popular as a porridge and pilaf grain in Europe. In China it's used as a bread grain, and in Japan it's the key ingredient in soba noodles.

Buckwheat came to American shores with the Dutch in the 1620s, and again with the Germans in the late 1600s and early 1700s. These pioneers brought buckwheat with them during America's westward expansion, where it provided many a reliable meal. As America grew, buckwheat pancakes gained a following that endures to this day in the southern states.

The whole kernel of buckwheat has a tough outer hull, consisting of 18 to 20 percent of the kernel's weight, which must be removed before eating. This hull helps it to naturally resist pests. Buckwheat also thrives without fertilizers; another characteristic that makes it a good candidate for an organic food crop. It's planted in Eastern Europe for its weed-killing properties, as an interim crop before flax. Buckwheat is popular as a host plant for honeybees; its pollen yields honey with dark, rich flavor. It's sometimes underplanted in orchards, to increase fruit pollination while also giving a second crop of distinctly flavored honey from orchard bees.

Buckwheat has taken up a beloved place in the cuisines of many of the countries where it can be grown. It's used as a base for stuffing meats and pastries throughout Europe. The most familiar buckwheat recipe to most Americans (besides buckwheat pancakes or flapjacks) are the Russian pancakes called blinis. Traditionally, blini are eaten at Maslenitsa, the pre-Lenten feast where meat is prohibited, and butter and seafood (yes, caviar, too) take the stage.

The French (who call buckwheat *sarrasin*) also treasure a buckwheat pancake (*galette*). In northern Italy, puréed cooked buckwheat (*grano saraceno, frumentone*) is used to make black polenta (*polenta nera*). Most of North America's production of buckwheat is exported to Japan for its soba noodles. In Japan, the darkest buckwheat flour is used to make yabu soba. The most refined (sifted) buckwheat flour is used for gozen soba (*gozen* meaning "to be served before nobles"). In India, buckwheat is used during the nine-day Navrata fast in spring and autumn, where wheat is to be avoided.

Nutrition

Buckwheat is high in magnesium, and has twice the B-vitamins of wheat. In combination with wheat flour, it provides a good balance of the eight essential amino acids our bodies need, including lysine. A classic dish in the Jewish culinary tradition of Eastern Europe capitalizes on this combination: *kasha varnishkas* is a mixture of kasha pilaf and thick egg noodles.

There is some evidence that compounds in buckwheat inhibit production of melanin in the skin; it is an accepted bit of farmer's wisdom that light-colored horses or livestock should not eat buckwheat, since they may get sunburned! Buckwheat contains a substance called rutin, which has been shown to be beneficial for controlling high blood pressure.

Storage

Buckwheat has a significant amount of volatile essential fats that can go rancid quickly after the hulls are removed. It's best to store buckwheat in an airtight container in the freezer to slow down the oxidation of those fats. Use buckwheat flour within 2 months of purchase.

Flavor

Buckwheat has a distinctive taste. It's strong enough, and unfamiliar enough to many to make it an acquired one. But there were a lot of enthusiastic buckwheat fans among our tasters, and their excitement over the recipes we made was gratifying.

Unroasted buckwheat has a soft, nutty flavor; cracked, unroasted buckwheat is sold as buckwheat grits. Roasted buckwheat groats are called kasha. Roasting gives the hulls a darker color and a stronger taste, which has been described as "earthy" and "mushroomy." After roasting, the buckwheat groats may be packaged as is, or cut to smaller pieces: coarse, medium and fine kasha are produced.

Cooking buckwheat groats

Traditionally, kasha (roasted buckwheat) was coated with egg, toasted, then simmered. The egg is supposed to keep the grains of kasha from clumping together. We tried the egg method, and next to it we tried cooking the kasha with a tablespoon of butter, like a pilaf. We were much happier with the flavor, texture and consistency of the butter version.

Baking with buckwheat

Buckwheat flour can be found in light or dark forms, the darker being more nutritious because it retains more of the buckwheat kernel. Buckwheat has no gluten, so when it's used in baking it has to be combined with a higher protein flour. Substitute buckwheat flour for up to one-third of the flour in a bread recipe, pairing it with unbleached bread flour for the remainder.

When we tried buckwheat in cakes and quick breads, we found its pronounced taste to be so strong that it got in the way; it wasn't very popular in those recipes. Biscuits and pancakes did much better. We've found that making buckwheat pancakes with a sponge greatly improves the flavor of the finished product; the slow fermentation of the batter mellows the taste of the buckwheat.

Buckwheat Pancakes *(Blini)*

YIELD: 20 (3-inch) pancakes
COOKING TIME: 3 minutes

American pioneers made a batter like this, fried it up, and called it flapjacks. When made as a smaller, silver-dollar size, they become the classic Russian pancake, called blini. Blini are the perfect vehicle for caviar, if you happen to have it. We serve our blinis with smoked salmon, grated hard boiled eggs, capers, chopped red onions and sour cream.

Sponge
½ cup (2⅛ ounces) buckwheat flour
½ cup (2⅛ ounces) unbleached all-purpose flour
1 cup (8 ounces) water
½ teaspoon instant yeast

Batter
All of the sponge
2 large eggs, separated
¼ cup (2 ounces) milk
1 teaspoon sugar
½ teaspoon salt
½ cup (2⅛ ounces) buckwheat flour
4 tablespoons (½ stick, 2 ounces) unsalted butter, melted

TO MAKE THE SPONGE: Combine all the sponge ingredients, cover and let rest at room temperature for 4 hours or in the refrigerator overnight.

TO MAKE THE BATTER: Whisk the egg yolks, milk, sugar and salt into the sponge; stir in the additional buckwheat flour. Set the mixture aside to rest for 30 minutes.

After 30 minutes, heat a heavy cast-iron frying pan over medium heat, or preheat an electric griddle to 350°F. Stir the melted butter into the batter. Whip the egg whites to medium peaks, and fold them into the batter.

TO COOK THE PANCAKES: Lightly grease the pan or griddle. Pour 2 tablespoons of the batter for each pancake at a time onto the hot griddle. Cook until bubbles rise that don't break and the edges of the pancakes look dry, 1½ minutes. Turn the pancakes over, and cook for another 1½ minutes on the second side; the pancakes will be a nice, medium brown. Remove from the griddle and hold, uncovered, on a plate in a low (175°F) oven, until ready to serve..

NUTRITION INFORMATION PER SERVING (2 PANCAKES, 65G): 12g whole grains, 123 cal, 6g fat, 4g protein, 13g complex carbohydrates, 1g dietary fiber, 56mg cholesterol, 125mg sodium, 106mg potassium, 68RE vitamin A, 1mg iron, 19mg calcium, 74mg phosphorus.

VARIATION: ONION BLINI *Add 1 heaping tablespoon of onion powder and 2 tablespoons dry chives (or ¼ cup fresh chives) to the batter before cooking.*

Rice

Oryza sativa, oryza glaberrima

Archaeologists have found evidence of rice cultivation along the Yangtze River in China as early as 11,500 years ago. Today there are thousands of rice varieties cultivated around the globe, supplying as much as 600 million tons of rice, and accounting for half the calories of more than half the world's population. With such a distinguished pedigree, it's hardly surprising that in some Asian countries the verb "to eat" is translated as "to eat rice," the word for "food" is "rice," and in China, "agriculture" is "rice," an indication that rice cultivation was developing at the same time as language.

When you think of rice, most likely what springs to mind is the Asian variety, *oryza sativa*. This is the rice that sustains much of the world in one form or another. Africa, too, has its own species, *oryza glaberrima*, with cultivation on that continent beginning around 1500 BC. Then of course, there's North America's native, wild rice, with three species (*zizania aquatica, zizania palustris* and *zizania texana*), none of which were actually cultivated until the 1970's. Wild rice was harvested by a number of Native American tribes, but it's not really rice at all, rather a seed of a different species of grass. Asian rice made its way slowly across the globe, spreading throughout Asia and the Middle East by 200 BC. It had spread through Europe by the 13th century, and from there it made the trip to North America by the end of the 17th century.

Although most of us think of rice as an exclusively wetland crop, growing in swamp areas, there are actually a variety of cultivation techniques, including some techniques that rely on rainfall rather than irrigation for their development. Most rice, though, is grown in standing water, requiring five months of warm, wet conditions to reach maturity. In the United States and Europe it's harvested mechanically, but in much of the world, rice is still cultivated and harvested the way it has been for generations—by hand, with very little mechanization at any point in the process. Despite what might be viewed as a primitive process, rice requires a complex system of fields and irrigation that could only be supported by a stable community.

Nutrition

Most of the rice consumed in the world is polished white rice, rice that has been processed to remove the bran and germ, drastically reducing its nutritional value. White rice, like white flour, is not a whole grain, and has to be enriched to prevent vitamin deficiencies in those for whom it's a dietary mainstay. Brown rice, on the other hand, is a whole grain, with a germ, endosperm and bran, even though the outermost hull has been removed to make the grain edible. Brown rice is slightly higher in protein and fat than white rice, because it retains the germ and bran, but it's significantly higher in B vitamins, magnesium, iron and fiber. While many of these are added back to white rice in the enrichment process, those enrichments are often water-soluble and wash away when you wash the rice.

Rice protein is one of the best and most digestible proteins in the grain world, but rice is especially valuable as a complex carbohydrate. Here, too, brown rice is superior to white, in that it's digested more slowly and therefore has a lower glycemic index. Rice is also one of the least allergenic of the grains and is fine for those on gluten-free diets.

Rice flour is available in both white and brown forms, with brown rice flour, like whole brown rice, being nutritionally superior, but also more subject to rancidity because of the oil present in the germ and bran. Store brown rice flour in the refrigerator or freezer. In the refrigerator it will last up to 5 months, in the freezer up to 1 year.

Flavor

Within the domesticated Asian variety of rice, *oryza sativa*, there are two broad categories; short-grained rice, *japonica*, and long-grain rice, *indica*. Short-grained rice, because of the nature and percentage of its starch, cooks into a stickier product than long-grain rice, which makes a "fluffier" finished dish. There are also categories based on flavor, such as jasmine or basmati rice.

Brown rice has a nuttier flavor than its white counterpart and a much chewier texture. It's probably the difference in texture that makes people think of brown rice as "nutritious" rather than "delicious." You may substitute brown rice for white rice in many recipes, but be aware that unless it's a quick cooking variety it'll take longer to cook than white, and will still retain its chewy quality. Brown rice flour, too, has a nuttier flavor and because its texture is similar to white rice flour, it's easy to substitute it in recipes calling for white rice flour.

When making rice pudding, we had better results using brown rice that was already cooked. Raw brown rice cooked directly in milk tended to curdle the milk before it was able to absorb it and become tender. The double cooking also seemed to give it a more tender bite.

Baking with rice flour

Rice flour is a traditional ingredient in foods from many cultures including rice cakes in the Philippines (very unlike the rice cakes made of puffed rice we see in the United States), rice noodles, rice drinks and shortbread. With the recent emergence of food allergies and intolerances, rice's nonallergenic properties have made it a popular base for a number of gluten- and dairy-free products, from bread to ice cream.

Because rice flour is gluten-free it really doesn't work in yeast breads unless you're mixing it with other flours. In cookies and crackers, rice flour can give a sandy, crumbly texture that's pleasing. Be aware, however, that baked goods made completely from rice flour can be too crumbly to hold together. That same sandy quality that's pleasing when you combine it with wheat flour in a shortbread cookie can seem grainy or gritty if you're using nothing but rice flour in the recipe. Letting baked goods rest overnight helps cut down on the grit, but it never completely disappears.

# Brown Rice Shortbread

YIELD: 2 (9-inch) rounds, 32 cookies
BAKING TEMPERATURE: 375°F
BAKING TIME: 12 to 15 minutes

Rice flour is a traditional ingredient in shortbread, where its characteristically sandy texture is welcome. This version cuts down on the gritty quality by giving the dough an overnight rest. The shortbread keeps for days, and even improves as it ages. We've added crystallized ginger in acknowledgment of rice's Asian origins, but it's also delicious plain, or lightly spiced with cardamom or cloves.

1 cup (2 sticks, 8 ounces) unsalted butter, room temperature
½ cup (3¾ ounces) packed light or dark brown sugar
1 tablespoon orange juice
2 teaspoons vanilla extract
1 cup (4½ ounces) brown rice flour

1 cup (4¼ ounces) unbleached all-purpose flour
¼ teaspoon baking powder
¼ teaspoon salt
¼ cup (1⅝ ounces) minced crystallized ginger

Cream the butter and brown sugar until light. Beat in the orange juice and vanilla. Add the flours, baking powder and salt, and mix to combine, scraping down the sides of the bowl with a spatula. Stir in the crystallized ginger.

Divide the dough in half, and form each half into a flat, 4- to 5-inch disk. Wrap tightly with plastic wrap and refrigerate overnight.

Half an hour before you're ready to bake, preheat the oven to 375°F. Remove the shortbread dough from the refrigerator, and let it come to room temperature.

To bake the shortbread, unwrap the dough and, with your hands, press each disk onto a piece of parchment paper. Push and press the pieces, using the palm of your hand, to a flat round about 9 inches across. Place the parchment and shortbread on a baking sheet. Use a bench knife or other sharp knife to cut each round in half and in half again and so on until you have 16 equal, pie-shaped wedges.

Bake the shortbread rounds until golden brown around the edges, 12 to 15 minutes. Remove the pan from the oven and allow it to cool for 5 minutes. The cuts you made with your bench knife now will be faintly visible. Use a knife or a bench knife to gently cut through the lines, being careful not to crumble the cookies. Let the cookies cool completely before serving. These improve as they age; store them in a tin.

NUTRITION INFORMATION PER SERVING (1 COOKIE, 17G): 4g whole grains, 101 cal, 6g fat, 1g protein, 6g complex carbohydrates, 4g sugar, 16mg cholesterol, 23mg sodium, 32mg potassium, 51RE vitamin A, 9mg calcium, 24mg phosphorus.

OTHER GRAINS

These grains are sometimes used in baking, with great success. Their comparative lack of availability led us to not rely on them for our recipes. But we encourage you to try them out, when you come upon fresh-ground flour from any of these grains.

Amaranth

Amaranthus cruentis, Amaranthus hypochondriacus

Amaranth is not really a cereal grain, but the tiny seed of a leafy plant, a member of the pigweed family. It was cultivated in Central America as long as 7,000 years ago, and despite the attempts of Cortez to eradicate it, it survived and is still commonly eaten in Mexico, and in the Himalayas, where it's also quite popular. Amaranth is beginning to be cultivated more widely in the United States, largely because of its hardy nature and terrific nutritional profile. Amaranth seed is the highest in protein of all the grains, and is especially high in lysine. Lysine is the amino acid many grains lack, and its presence improves the quality of the protein for human consumption.

In Mexico, amaranth seeds are popped and mixed with syrup to make a sweet called *alegria*; it's also milled and made into *atole*, a traditional Mexican drink. Amaranth flour has no gluten, so doesn't work as the sole flour in a yeasted bread, but it's often a component of gluten-free baked goods or pasta. In conventional baked goods, it's usually paired with other ingredients to help it behave like all-purpose flour. Amaranth has a mild, nutty flavor, with a slight hint of grass, and the flour is apt to get bitter if not used right away. Because of its high oil content, store amaranth and amaranth flour in the refrigerator or freezer to keep it from going rancid.

Teff

Eragrostis tef

Teff is a very small grain cultivated in Ethiopia for as long as 5,000 years. Because it's so small (about the size of a poppy seed), it's difficult to harvest, which has made it slow to spread outside of its native area. Teff is very high in protein, calcium and iron and is the main nutrient in the Ethiopian diet. It's now beginning to be cultivated in other parts of the world, including the United States, but is still not widely available.

The grain itself can be cooked into a porridge or pilaf and is relatively quick to prepare. Its small size makes it difficult to grind into grain at home, so flour must be purchased. Teff has no gluten, so it's fine for those with celiac disease, but can't be made into yeast bread without being paired with other flours. There are recipes for cookies, pancakes and other baked goods, but it's most often used as an additive to baked goods, in combination with other flours. The one exception to this is *injera*, a fermented Ethiopian flatbread with a distinctively sour flavor, which typically takes 2 to 3 days to make. Teff flour should be stored in the refrigerator or freezer.

Triticale

X Triticosecale

Triticale is a cross between rye and wheat and was bred to have the best attributes of both grains. Early attempts to crossbreed the two grains resulted in infertile plants, but in the 1930s scientific advances in breeding technology made it possible to create plants that could reproduce. It's now grown in several countries around the world, though primarily for animal feed rather than human consumption.

Triticale is hardy like rye, with a lysine content better than that of wheat, making it a source of more complete protein. It's got the baking attributes of wheat, with a strong, nutty flavor, and can be used in baked goods. It does have gluten, so can be used in yeast breads, but the gluten is somewhat more delicate and apt to degrade with overdevelopment. If you're making yeast bread with triticale flour, knead it only enough to incorporate the flour, and give it a single rise before baking.

Like most whole grains, triticale flour should be stored in the refrigerator or freezer to keep it from going rancid.

Quinoa

Chenopodium quinoa

Quinoa, a native of South America, is not really a grain, but the seed of a leafy plant related to spinach and beets. The plant has been cultivated in the Andes region for 8,000 years and was an important part of the Inca's diet. Quinoa is remarkably hardy, able to grow in poor soil at high elevations. Quinoa is now grown in North America, although the flavor of quinoa grown at the lower elevations of North America is inferior to that of the grain from the Andes.

Quinoa is known for its terrific nutritional profile; it may contain as much as 20 percent protein, and that protein is high quality, with a balance of amino acids that is exceptional in the grain world. It's also notably high in B vitamins, iron, fiber, potassium and phosphorus. Because it has no gluten, it's a good choice for those on gluten-free diets.

One possible reason for quinoa's hardiness may be the fact that it has a natural coating of saponin, a bitter, soapy-tasting substance that repels birds and other potential pests. While most of the saponin is usually removed in processing, it's pretty potent and traces may remain. For this reason, quinoa must be thoroughly rinsed before cooking.

Quinoa is most often consumed whole, in a pilaf or pudding, but because it's gluten-free, more consumers are looking to add quinoa flour to their baked goods. Quinoa flour has a higher fat content than wheat flour, which can translate to a moister mouthfeel, and it has a nutty, grassy flavor that is complimented by aromatic spices, like ginger. Quinoa flour should be stored in the freezer to keep it from going rancid.

Before cooking quinoa, be sure to rinse it thoroughly. Place the grain in a sieve and run cold water through it as you rub it with your fingers. Continue to run the water until the water coming out the bottom of the sieve is clear. Taste a grain to check for a soapy flavor; if it's still soapy continue to rinse it until the soapy flavor is gone.

Millet

Panicum miliaceum

"Millet" is the loose term used for a number of grains found all over the world. There's evidence of millet cultivation in China as early as 7000 BC, and it was a sacred grain in the Chinese culture, though not as highly valued as rice. Millet can be grown in drier climates than wheat or rice, so it has spread to other parts of the world and in its different forms provides sustenance for several cultures. Because there are so many varieties, the flavor can vary significantly from one type to another. The *Panicum miliaceum*, or broomcorn millet, is the one we're most apt to find in this country for human consumption, and the flavor is mild, sweet and nutty."

Since the entire germ is contained in the millet, hulling the grain doesn't affect its nutritional profile. Millet is high in lysine and a great source of B vitamins and iron. It's also nonallergenic and easy to digest, a popular combination for baby food in some parts of the world. Millet contains no gluten, so can't be used for yeast breads, unless in combination with other flours.

Millet is most frequently prepared whole, in porridges or pilafs, although India and Africa have a tradition of flatbreads made with millet flour. Millet flour gives a soft, crumbly texture to baked goods like cakes, quick breads and cookies. Millet is high in fat and therefore the flour is subject to rancidity; it's important to find a source with fresh flour and high turnover or simply grind your own as you need it. Store millet flour in the freezer.

Kamut

Triticum turanicum

There's been some buzz about Kamut over the last few years. Kamut is the brand name for a type of wheat. Although it was originally thought to date back to ancient Egypt, it's now accepted that this type of wheat was not grown in ancient Egypt, but was cultivated more recently in that area, since the only type of wheat the ancient Egyptians grew was emmer.

Kamut, also known as QK-77, or Khorasan, is related to durum wheat, but is larger, sweeter and higher in protein than conventional wheat, making it easy to substitute successfully in recipes calling for whole wheat flour. Because Kamut has a lower proportion of bran, its gluten is stronger than that of wheat; because it's sweeter, it can be used without additional sugar to counteract the traditionally bitter flavor of whole wheat. Kamut is thought to be more easily tolerated by some people who suffer from gluten intolerance, but because it's a wheat, it isn't acceptable for people who have true wheat allergy or celiac disease. Despite its many apparent assets, Kamut is considerably harder to find than wheat and has failed to catch on as a crop or an ingredient. As Kamut becomes more widely available, we hope to see it appear in more recipes and products.

Cooking Grains

Cooked grains are a great resource for the home baker; many can be added to your recipes in their cooked form with great success. This chart shows that different grains have different rates of absorption and cooking times, and we found that some variation exists from producer to producer and even batch to batch. That makes sense—grain is a natural product subject to the environment in which it is grown. It might have been harvested after a very wet growing season or a very dry one, for example, and that will affect the end product. In each case, we combined the grains with the water in the pot, brought the mixture to a boil and turned the heat down as low as it would go to finish cooking. Salt is optional and the amount you use to salt to taste will vary considerably from grain to grain. The first time you cook an unfamiliar grain, salt it to taste after you've cooked it. Most grains will cook more quickly if you soak them ahead of time, preferably overnight, but even an hour or two will make a difference. This chart is formulated for raw, unsoaked grain, with the exception of the larger whole grains—oats, rye, spelt and wheat.

Grain (1 cup)	Water Quantity	Cooking Time	Yield
Amaranth	2½ cups	20 minutes	2¼ cups
Barley, hulled	3½ cups	2 hours	4 cups
Barley, flakes	1½ cups	12 to 15 minutes	2 cups
Brown rice	2½ cups	40 minutes	3 cups
Buckwheat groats (kasha)	2 cups	11 to 14 minutes	3 cups
Kamut, whole	3 cups	1¼ hours	3 cups
Millet, whole	3 cups	25 to 30 minutes	4 cups
Oats, groats	3 cups	1 hour	3 cups
Oats, rolled (flakes)	1½ cups	8 to 10 minutes	1½ cups
Oats, steel-cut	2½ cups	25 minutes	2½ cups
Quinoa, whole	2 cups	15 minutes	3 cups
Rye, whole	3½ cups	1¼ hours	3 cups
Rye, chops	3 cups	20 to 25 minutes	2½ cups
Rye, flakes	1¾ cups	15 to 18 minutes	2 cups
Spelt, whole	3 cups	1 hour	3 cups
Teff, whole	4 cups	20 minutes	3¾ cups
Triticale, whole	3½ cups	1 hour 20 minutes	3 cups
Wheat, whole berries	3½ cups	1½ hours	3 cups
Wheat, cracked	3 cups	25 to 30 minutes	2¾ cups
Wheat, flakes	2 cups	15 minutes	2 cups

Ingredient Weights

Weighing ingredients is a more accurate way of determining amounts than measuring by volume. When it comes to volume measurements, there are many variables that can affect actual amounts. Measuring cups and spoons can vary significantly (we've discovered this over and over in our test kitchen). Cooks everywhere use varying techniques, and one person's idea of "full" or "packed" is usually different from the next person's.

Ingredients can vary significantly too. Flour weighs less when the air is drier than it does in humid months. Raisins from an opened box that's been in the pantry or refrigerator for months won't weigh as much as fresh ones. Off-brand versions of many ingredients weigh less by volume than name brands. Vegetables and berries can have a wide range of water contents, so they may weigh different amounts at any given time. You get the idea.

This chart gives average weights for amounts commonly used in our recipes. It can help you plan your shopping, as well as being handy if you want to convert recipes to significantly larger amounts.

Item	Measurement	Ounces
Almond flour, toasted	1 cup	3⅜
Almond paste, packed	1 cup	9⅛
Almonds, sliced	½ cup	1½
Almonds, slivered	½ cup	2
Almonds, whole, unblanched	1 cup	5
Amaranth flour	1 cup	3⅝
Apples, dried, diced	1 cup	3
Apples, peeled, sliced	1 cup	4
Applesauce	½ cup	4
Apricots, dried, diced	½ cup	3
Bananas, mashed	1 cup	8
Barley flour	1 cup	4
Barley, pearled, raw	1 cup	6½
Basil pesto	2 tablespoons	1
Berries, frozen	1 cup	5
Blueberries, fresh	1 cup	5
Bread crumbs, dried (seasoned or plain)	½ cup	2
Bread crumbs, fresh	½ cup	¾
Brown rice, cooked	1 cup	6
Brown rice flour	1 cup	4½
Buckwheat flour	1 cup	4¼
Buckwheat, whole (kasha)	1 cup	6
Bulgur, uncooked	1 cup	5⅜
Butter	½ cup, 1 stick	4
Buttermilk	1 cup	8
Buttermilk powder	2 tablespoons	⅞
Candied peel	½ cup	3

Item	Measurement	Ounces
Caramel, 14 to 16 individual pieces	1/2 cup	5
Carrots, grated	1 cup	3 1/2
Cashews, chopped	1 cup	4
Cashews, whole	1 cup	4
Cheese, grated (Cheddar, Jack, mozzarella, Swiss)	1 cup	4
Parmesan, grated	1/2 cup	1 3/4
feta	1 cup	4
ricotta	1 cup	8
Cheese powder	1/2 cup	2
Cherries, dried	1/2 cup	2 1/2
Cherries, frozen	1 cup	4
Chives, fresh	1/2 cup	3/4
Chocolate, chopped	1 cup	6
Chocolate chips	1 cup	6
Cocoa, unsweetened	2 tablespoons	3/8
	1/4 cup	3/4
	1 cup	3
Coconut, grated, unsweetened	1 cup	4
Coconut, sweetened flakes	1 cup	3
Coffee powder	2 teaspoons	1/8
Cookie crumbs	1 cup	3
Cornmeal, whole	1 cup	4 7/8
Cornstarch	1/4 cup	1
Corn syrup, light, dark or brown sugar	1 cup	11
Cottage cheese	1 cup	8
Cranberries, dried	1/2 cup	2
Cranberries, fresh or frozen	1 cup	1/2
Currants, packed	1 cup	5
Dates, chopped	1 cup	5 1/4
Egg white, fresh	1 large	1 1/4
Egg yolk, fresh	1 large	1/2
Flax flour	1/2 cup	1 3/4
Flaxseed	1/4 cup	1 1/4
Garlic cloves, in skin for roasting	1 large head	4
Garlic, minced	2 tablespoons	1
Garlic, peeled and sliced	1 cup	5 1/4
Ginger, crystallized	1/2 cup	3 1/4
	1/3 cup	2 1/4
Ginger, fresh, sliced	1/4 cup	2
Graham crackers, crushed	1 cup	5
Granola	1 cup	4
Hazelnut flour	1 cup	3 1/8
Hazelnuts, whole	1 cup	5
Honey	1 tablespoon	3/4
	1 cup	12
Jam or preserves	1/4 cup	3
	2/3 cup	7 1/4
Lard	1/2 cup	4

Item	Measurement	Ounces
Macadamia nuts, whole	1 cup	5¼
Malted milk powder	¼ cup	1¼
Malt syrup	2 tablespoons	1½
Maple sugar	½ cup	2¾
Maple syrup	½ cup	5½
Marshmallows, mini	1 cup	1½
Meringue powder	¼ cup	1½
Milk	1 cup	8
Milk, evaporated	½ cup	4½
Milk, nonfat dry	¼ cup	1
Milk, sweetened condensed	¼ cup	2¾
Millet, whole	½ cup	3⅝
Molasses	¼ cup	3
Mushrooms, sliced	1 cup	2¾
Oat bran	½ cup	1⅞
Oat flour	1 cup	3¼
Oats, old-fashioned rolled	1 cup	3½
Oats, quick-cooking	1 cup	3⅛
Oats, steel-cut, cooked	1 cup	9
Oats, steel-cut, raw	½ cup	2⅞
Oil, vegetable	1 cup	7
	⅓ cup	2⅜
	⅔ cup	4⅝
Olives, sliced	1 cup	5
Onions, canned French-fried	½ cup	1⅜
Onions, fresh, diced	1 cup	5
Peaches, peeled and diced	1 cup	6
Peanut butter, smooth or crunchy	½ cup	4¾
Peanuts, whole, shelled	1 cup	5
Pears, peeled and diced	1 cup	5¾
Pecans, chopped	½ cup	1⅞
	1 cup	3¾
Pineapple, dried	½ cup	2½
Pine nuts	½ cup	2½
Pistachio nuts	½ cup	2⅛
Popped corn	4 cups	¾
Potato flakes	½ cup	1⅛
Potato flour	¼ cup	1⅝
Praline paste	½ cup	5½
Prunes	1 cup	5½
Pumpkin, canned	1 cup	9½
Quinoa flour	1 cup	3⅞
Quinoa, cooked	1 cup	6½
Quinoa, whole, uncooked	1 cup	6¼
Raisins, loose	1 cup	5¼
Raisins, packed	½ cup	3
Raspberries, fresh	1 cup	4¼
Rhubarb, fresh, medium dice	1 cup	4¼
Rye flakes	1 cup	4⅜

Item	Measurement	Ounces
Rye flours		
Medium rye	1 cup	3 5/8
Whole rye (pumpernickel)	1 cup	3 3/4
White rye	1 cup	3 3/4
Scallions, sliced	1 cup	2 1/4
Semolina	1 cup	5 3/4
Sesame seeds	1/2 cup	2 1/2
Shallots, peeled and sliced	1 cup	5 1/2
Sour cream	1 cup	8
Soy flour	1/4 cup	1 1/4
Spelt flour, whole	1 cup	3 1/2
Sugar, brown, light or dark, packed	1 cup	7 1/2
Sugar, confectioners'	1 cup	4
	1/3 cup	1 3/8
	2/3 cup	2 5/8
Sugar, Demerara	1 cup	7 3/4
Sugar, granulated white	1 cup	7
	1/3 cup	2 3/8
	2/3 cup	4 3/4
Sun-dried tomatoes (dry pack)	1 cup	6
Sunflower seeds	1/4 cup	1 1/4
Tahini paste	1/2 cup	2 1/2
Tapioca flour	1/4 cup	1 1/4
Tapioca, quick-cooking	2 tablespoons	3/4
Teff flour	1 cup	4 3/4
Toffee chunks	1 cup	5 1/2
Vegetable shortening	1/4 cup	1 3/4
	1/3 cup	2 3/8
	1/2 cup	3 1/4
Walnuts, chopped		
whole	1 cup	4
	1 cup	3 3/4
Water	1/3 cup	2 5/8
	2/3 cup	5 3/8
Wheat bran	1/2 cup	1 1/8
Wheat, cracked	1/2 cup	2 5/8
Wheat flakes, malted	1/4 cup	1
Wheat flours		
All-purpose, unbleached (white)	1 cup	4 1/4
Bread flour, unbleached (white)	1 cup	4 1/4
Durum flour	1 cup	4 1/2
Pastry flour (white)	1 cup	3 3/4
Whole wheat pastry	1 cup	3 3/8
Whole wheat (traditional or white)	1 cup	4
Wheat germ	1/4 cup	1
Yeast, instant	2 1/4 teaspoons	1/4
Yogurt	1 cup	8
Zucchini, shredded	1 cup	8 1/4

Where to Buy

As you work your way through the recipes in this book, you'll become familiar with at least three sources for ingredients that will be of immense help to you:

- **The Baker's Catalogue, where you can find baking ingredients and utensils mentioned in this book.** *The Baker's Catalogue* is owned by King Arthur Flour and strives to have available just about everything the home baker would ever want or need. The catalogue's products can be found at www.bakerscatalogue.com, where you can type in the name of the product you're searching for in the "keyword" box or you can call and place an order, or request a catalogue, at 1-800-827-6836.

- **The Baker's Store in Norwich, Vermont.** This is a baker's mecca, with whole grain flours, wheat berries, mills, ingredients and tools for every baker. The store is owned by King Arthur Flour and it carries everything offered in *The Baker's Catalogue* plus a few extra odds and ends.

- **Your local food co-op, natural foods market or health-food store.** We found most of the ingredients readily available at Whole Foods Markets and Wild Oats Markets. Good retail merchants will be willing to order items for you if their distributors carry them. Before you cruise the aisles and perhaps give up, ask to speak with a store manager and request a special order. Show the retailer the cookbook and impress upon him or her that these ingredients are going to become popular as more and more home bakers get comfortable with whole grains.

- **The Internet.** If you type in just about any ingredient in this book, you'll find a source for it. It may be worth your while to make a phone call to assure that the inventory turns over frequently so you are not buying stale ingredients, including flour or grains. We used Google for our searches and we found this a very efficient way to buy things we wanted to use in our test kitchen (if we didn't have them already).

Glossary

AUTOLYSE (pronounced *auto-leeze*): A process in bread baking during which flour and water are combined then allowed to rest, usually for 20 to 30 minutes, before the remaining ingredients are added. This gives the flour a chance to absorb the water, and the gluten in the flour time to relax a bit, both of which make the resulting dough easier to knead.

BAKER'S BENCH KNIFE: A 6-inch-long rectangle of stainless steel with a handle across the top, used to divide kneaded dough into pieces and to help knead wet ("slack") dough without adding too much additional flour (see p. 500). Also very useful for cutting brownies and other bars, and for cleaning crusted dough off your work surface.

BAKING SHEETS: see Pans.

BAKING STONE: A ½-inch-thick piece of porous stone that, when hot, draws moisture away from the bread or pizza dough placed on it. When baked on a baking stone, hearth breads and pizza crusts acquire a crisp, crunchy crust.

BANNETON: A woven wooden basket lined with linen or canvas, used for the final rising of traditionally shaped European breads (see illustration, p. 280). The liner, which is liberally floured before use, draws moisture away from the dough as it rises, making the bread's lovely crust chewy.

BARLEY MALT EXTRACT (BARLEY MALT SYRUP OR MALT SYRUP OR MALT POWDER): A sweetener made from sprouted barley grain.

BISCUIT CUTTERS: One of the keys to high-rising flaky biscuits is how they are cut—honestly! Cutting biscuits with the edge of a drinking glass compacts their sides, meaning they won't rise as well as biscuits cut with a sharper edge. Sharp biscuit cutters made from tin, stainless steel, nylon or plastic slice right through the dough and promise a high-rising biscuit you'll be proud to serve. Make sure the cutters are at least 1 inch tall to accommodate your thickest biscuit dough. You'll see them in round, square and hexagonal shapes; they can be used to cut cookies and scones, too, or small, personal-size cakes.

BOWL SCRAPER: A flexible piece of plastic about 4 x 6 inches that is straight on one edge and curved on the other. Use it to scoop sticky batter or scrape yeast dough out of a bowl, cut cinnamon roll dough quickly and easily, and scrape crusted dough off the counter.

BRAN: The outer coating of a wheat berry that holds it together and protects it. Bran, no matter how finely ground, has sharp edges that tend to shred strands of gluten in developing dough. This leads to a denser dough. The bran is also the part of the wheat that makes whole wheat flour a good source of fiber.

BREAD MACHINE: A great tool for kneading bread dough and for letting it have its first rise at a perfect temperature. We love bread machines for kneading—they take the guesswork out of the process. Just make sure you look at the dough as it is being kneaded to ensure it forms a smooth ball. If the dough is too wet (slack), add a bit of flour. If the dough is too dry (crumbly), add a bit of liquid, usually water. Of course you can also bake your bread in the machine, which is very convenient but doesn't allow you to hand-shape the loaf. Still, baking in the machine can be done while you're busy or away, and that's a powerful attribute.

CAKE PANS: see Pans.

CHICKPEA FLOUR: A flour made of dried chickpeas, commonly used in Indian cooking and also referred to as besan.

CHILLING: After cookie or pie dough is mixed, chilling firms up the fat and gives the flour time to absorb liquid evenly. This allows dough to roll out more evenly, without sticking as much, and to hold its shape while being cut and transferred to a baking sheet for cookies or a pie pan for pies.

CHOCOLATE, MELTING: Chocolate scorches easily, and can seize (become hard and unmixable) if it comes in contact with water when melting. We recommend melting chocolate at medium power in the microwave, in a heatproof container. One cup of chocolate chips melted at half power should be heated for $1\frac{1}{2}$ to 2 minutes, depending on how powerful your microwave is. Chocolate can also be melted at low heat in a double boiler set over simmering water, tightly covered so steam doesn't come in contact with it.

COOKIE CUTTERS: Made of tin, plastic, copper or copper-plated aluminum, these should be at least 1 inch deep and have a sharp side for cutting and a dull side for holding.

COOKIE SCOOPS: Also called food dishers or depositors, these are sized-down ice cream scoops that deposit a traditional size ("teaspoon" or "tablespoon") onto a baking sheet, quickly and cleanly. When a recipe calls for dishing out a rounded tablespoon or teaspoon of dough, the tablespoon or teaspoon scoop approximates that size. A teaspoon scoop will make cookies about $1\frac{1}{2}$ inches in diameter and a tablespoon scoop will make cookies about $2\frac{1}{2}$ inches round. These scoops come in various sizes and can be used to dish out scones and drop biscuits as well. A larger size ($\frac{1}{4}$-cup) scoop is perfect for muffins, pancakes and cupcakes. If dough starts to stick to the scoop, clean it out and spray with cooking spray (or simply dip in water) to allow dough or batter to release more easily.

COOKIE SHEETS: see Pans, baking sheets.

COOKIES, COOLING: When baking whole grain cookies, especially if you like chewy ones, leave the cookies on the baking sheet for 5 minutes after you take the pan out of the oven. This gives the cookies a chance to firm up a bit before you slide a spatula underneath them. After 5 minutes, transfer the cookies to a cooling rack (see below) to finish cooling.

Bar cookies should cool in their baking pans on a rack. Don't cut them while they're warm; you'll make bars with very ragged edges, their texture will suffer and they're much more likely to fall apart when you're taking them out of the pan.

COOLING RACKS: If fresh-from-the-oven baked goods are cooled on or in a pan, their crusts can become soggy and, in the case of muffins, tough, due to condensation. Racks prevent this. They also are helpful when you're drizzling icing or chocolate over pastries and don't want the cookie or cupcake to sit in a puddle of icing. Choose racks that have a grid design rather than parallel strips of metal; a grid offers better support.

CRACKED WHEAT: The whole wheat berry that has been broken into coarse pieces.

CREAM, WHIPPING: Whipping cream is 31.3 percent fat (compared to half-and-half, which is 12 percent fat, and heavy cream, about 37.6 percent fat). It is used in baked goods and also as a garnish. When you whip cream, you are incorporating air. If possible, keep the bowl you're using cool so that your cream doesn't turn to butter, which happens at warmer temperatures.

CREAMING: Creaming is responsible for creating the texture of cookies, cakes and some muffins. Sugar and fat are beaten together to form and capture air bubbles, when the sugar crystals cut into fat molecules to make an air pocket. When you first start beating sugar and fat together, the mixture is thick and somewhat lumpy. As you continue to beat, the mixture becomes creamier in texture, more uniform, and lighter in color as air is beaten in.

CRÊPE PAN: A shallow, flat-sided sauté pan that looks like an undersized skillet. Nonstick or regular, always use a thin film of butter before adding the batter. After adding the batter, pick up the pan and swirl it around to cover the bottom of the pan with batter. This takes a little practice. Cook the crêpe on one side, turn over carefully with tongs or a thin spatula, cook on the other side, and the crêpe should slide out of the pan easily.

CUTTING BUTTER INTO FLOUR: The technique combines fat and flour in a way that preserves irregular-size pieces of butter in the mixture. When these shards of butter melt during baking, they create a flaky, tender piecrust, cookie or scone. Cutting in can be accomplished with your fingers, a pastry fork, two knives, a pastry blender, a mixer or a food processor (pulsed gently). Leave the biggest pieces of butter larger than you are tempted to (we suggest the size of your thumbnail); they really do create a flake that is divine.

DOCKING: Pricking holes in a "short" dough (one that's high in fat and has a flaky or crisp texture after cooking) helps to vent the steam created in the oven during baking. You can use a fork or a dough docker (below) to prick small holes all over the surface of the dough. By venting the steam, docking keeps the dough from billowing or heaving as it bakes. It's an important step for crisp crusts, cookies or crackers.

DOUGH, GATHERING INTO A COHESIVE BALL: This process is usually easily accomplished by combining the ingredients, liquid and dry (see Well, below), then using your hands to shape the mixture into a ball that can be kneaded. With whole grains, dough can start out quite messy because of the flour's slowness in absorbing the liquid. We describe on page 500 how to knead this sticky dough using a dough scraper or baker's bench knife to fold it over on itself several times, until it starts to come together. Keep at it; with a bit of patience, the mess will become a mass that can be kneaded.

DOUGH DOCKER: Looking like a small (3- to 4-inch) spiked rolling pin, the dough docker cuts even rows of holes into cracker dough or thoroughly pricks the bottom of a pie or tart shell to help vent steam. See illustration, page 168.

DOUGH SCRAPER: see Bowl scraper.

EGGS, ADDING ONE AT A TIME: After creaming together butter and sugar (see Creaming, above), the next ingredient in many cookie and cake recipes is eggs. They should be added one at a time, each one thoroughly beaten in before the next is added, to allow the creamed butter/sugar mixture to most effectively retain its trapped air. Be sure to scrape the sides of the bowl so all the butter/sugar mixture is incorporated.

EGGS, SEPARATING: Crack the shell in the middle and use the two halves to pass the yolk from one side to the other, letting the white drip out of the shell and into a bowl.

EGG WHITES, BEATING: Beating egg whites properly is the key to creating certain extra-light cookies, such as meringues or ladyfingers. Three things to remember: The bowl and beaters must be clean and grease-free. Use a stainless-steel, ceramic or glass bowl, not plastic. Egg whites will whip higher if they're at room temperature before beating.

When beating egg whites, at first you'll have a puddle of clear liquid with some large bubbles in it. Continue beating, and soon the whisk will begin to leave tracks in the bowl. Eventually, the whites will form stiff peaks. To test the character of your whites, pull your whisk or beaters straight up out of the foam. It's extremely easy to go too far. When you start to see grainy white clumps, you're beyond stiff peaks, and every stroke of the whisk or beater is tearing apart the network of air, water and protein you've worked so hard to create. You'll also see a pool of clear liquid under the foam. The good news is that the foam on top of the liquid will essentially still work. The bad news is that you can't really fix what's happened, other than to start over with new egg whites.

ELECTRIC STAND MIXER: see Mixer.

EMULSIFY: To mix two ingredients together that might not normally go together willingly, such as oil and water. This is done by slowly adding one ingredient to the other while vigorously mixing or whisking.

FERMENT: Fermentation is fundamental to bread baking, as well as other wonderful foods, such as cheese, yogurt, wine and beer. During fermentation, yeast converts starches and sugars present in the dough into carbon dioxide, as well as alcohol and other acids, giving bread both flavor and rise.

FILLING A PASTRY BAG: see Pastry bag, filling.

FOLDING: When ingredients with air beaten in, such as beaten egg whites or whipped cream, are combined with other ingredients in a batter, you want to preserve as much of the added air as possible. We do this very gently with a wire whisk or spatula, because gentle combining—folding—promotes a light texture in the finished product.

GHEE (OR CLARIFIED BUTTER): Ghee is the Indian version of clarified butter, which is butter that has all the water and milk solids removed. It is 100 percent fat and can be stored for considerably longer than butter. Store-bought ghee can be stored at room temperature for many months; clarified butter that you make yourself can be stored in the refrigerator for several months.

HAZELNUTS, BLANCHING: Unblanched whole hazelnuts have a papery skin that's easily removed by toasting the nuts in a single layer for 20 minutes at 325°F. Remove the nuts from the oven and wrap them in a clean dishtowel. Rub the nuts together inside the towel to remove the brown skins.

HIGH-ALTITUDE BAKING: Most baking recipes, including those made with whole grains, require adjustments to their ingredients when made at high altitudes (3,000 feet or above). The following are general guidelines for changes to make for different types of whole grain baking recipes. Individual microclimates in the mountains can vary greatly; it's best to try adjustments one at a time, and keep notes on your results.

- Keep whole grain doughs and batters well covered while resting; dry air at high altitudes can draw the moisture out, leaving less water available to soften the bran.

- **Cakes:** Increase the baking temperature 15°F to 25°F to set the batter's structure before the gases created by leavening expand too much. You may also get better results if you decrease the amount of sugar (start by removing 1 tablespoon of sugar from each cup the recipe calls for). In very rich cake recipes (such as pound cakes) it may be beneficial to decrease the amount of fat by 1 to 2 tablespoons for each cup in the recipe. With some recipes, adding another egg will reinforce the cake's structure. If the cake uses chemical leaveners, you may have better results if you decrease the leavening as described in Quick breads, below.

- **Cookies:** The dough may need an extra tablespoon of liquid to help it come together.

- **Quick breads:** Increase baking temperatures by 15°F to 25°F. Some of the baking soda in the leaveners may not be fully used up at these faster baking temperatures; therefore try decreasing the amount of baking powder or soda by ⅛ to ¼ teaspoon for every 1,500 feet of increased elevation. Try the smaller decrease first.

- **Yeast breads:** Whole grain yeast breads take time to be at their best; the bran in the flour needs time to absorb the dough's moisture. At higher altitudes, breads tend to rise faster, because there is less air pressure for the dough to push against. In many cases, letting the dough rise three times before baking will give it the chance to fully develop its flavor. Try putting the dough in the refrigerator for its first two rises. You may choose to use less flour, depending on the air's humidity and the look of the dough.

INSTANT-READ THERMOMETER: Useful for lots of baked goods, these thermometers help you monitor the internal temperature of custard pies (done at 165°F), bread (done between 190°F for most yeast breads and 210°F for denser yeast breads with a higher percentage of whole grains in them), lava cake (done at 165°F) and the optimal bread-rising temperature (76°F to 78°F). They usually work within 15 seconds, and thermometers with an extra-thin probe don't leave a noticeable hole in the item.

KNEADING MAT: This mat, either 100 percent silicone or fiberglass treated with a nonstick silicone, makes kneading and cleanup a snap. Sometimes marked with circle or inch measurements, it's good for rolling piecrust, especially whole grain crusts, which tend to be a bit more delicate due to their lower gluten content. Be sure to use only plastic utensils when working with this type of mat, as it can be cut with sharp tools.

LACTOBACILLUS: Bacteria that are resident in sourdough starters that help give sourdough its distinctive sour flavor.

LAME (pronounced *lahm*): A curved razor blade set into a handle used to slash the top crust of risen country loaves and baguettes. The slash allows the bread to expand fully. A small, very sharp paring knife or serrated knife can be used instead.

LOAF PANS: see Pans.

MALT EXTRACT: see Barley malt extract.

MEASURING: see Scale.

MEASURING CUPS: There are two types of measuring cups—one type for measuring liquids and another for measuring dry ingredients. A liquid measure has a pouring spout and is usually made of clear plastic or glass, with clear markings on the side. Markings should include as many in-between markings as practical, such as ¼, ⅓, ½, ⅔ and ¾. Some measuring cups are marked from the inside, allowing you to set the cup on the counter and read while looking down on the cup. This is quite handy. To read a regular measuring cup, fill it, place it on the counter, and crouch down to see where the top of the liquid falls, at eye level. The accurate measurement is where the line touches the side of the measuring cup. Microwave-safe liquid measuring cups are a great idea; they allow you to melt butter or warm milk right in the cup.

Dry measures come in cup measurements, and a full set—while a bit of an extravagance—can be very handy. A full set includes ⅛-, ¼-, ⅓-, ½-, ⅔-, ¾-, 1-, 1½-, 2- and 3-cup measures. Fill these right up to the top (if measuring flour or baking mix or pancake mix, see page xii for measuring tips) and level off with the flat edge of a knife. When measuring flour, don't pack it in. However, when measuring brown sugar, we assume a packed measuring cup.

MEASURING SPOONS: You would be amazed at the inaccuracy among measuring spoons. The best way to test yours is to see if 3 teaspoons add up to 1 tablespoon, or two ½ teaspoons equal 1 teaspoon, and so on. If you treat yourself to a new set, you might want to look for the oblong type that fit nicely into spice canisters or that can sit on a counter without spilling. Our favorites are stainless steel, but the colored plastic ones can help you identify the right size (red = teaspoon and yellow = tablespoon, for example).

MELTING CHOCOLATE: see Chocolate, melting.

MIXER, ELECTRIC STAND: Maybe your mother did without one of these, but we see no reason you should have to. Look for one with some heft to it but that you can move around the counter if you need to. We like ones that can handle 5-quart (or greater) bowls, and the bowl should have a handle on it—this makes it much easier to scoop out a stiff or thick dough. Make sure the lowest speed is slow enough to prevent flour from flying out of the bowl when you turn on the machine. The machine should have a motor heavy-duty enough to handle 20 minutes of mixing or kneading without overheating and/or shutting down. A dough hook, whisk and flat beater should all be included with the machine.

NUTS: see Hazelnuts, blanching; or Toasting nuts.

OAT BRAN: The outer casing of the oat, it is high in soluble fiber and thought to be the cholesterol-lowering attribute of oats.

OAT FLOUR: Flour that is simply finely ground groats (the oat with the tough outer hull removed).

OATS, STEEL-CUT OR IRISH: Oat groats (the part of the oat berry that is left after the hard hull is removed) that have been cut in half by a steel blade.

OVERNIGHT RESTS: Because whole grain flours are generally more coarsely ground than all-purpose flour, they don't absorb liquid as readily as all-purpose flour. The result? Cookies may spread too much as they bake, piecrust may be difficult to roll out and yeast dough may be challenging to knead. Some recipes advise you to give the dough a rest, anywhere from half an hour to 3 days. In addition, baked goods made with whole grains may benefit from an overnight rest before serving. These extra hours allow the bran in the flour to soften, improving the mouthfeel of the baked good and making it easier to slice. This is particularly true with one-step bars (such as brownies) and quick breads.

PANS:

- **Baking sheets:** For best heat circulation around the pan, use pans that have at least a 2-inch clearance on all sides when they're in your oven. Substantial baking sheets won't warp or develop hot spots. Light-colored shiny baking sheets will be less likely to burn the bottoms of your cookies. Using parchment paper or a silicone liner can really make your life easier—no need to grease the pan and your cookies will not stick, period; baked for the proper time, they will not dry out and the bottoms will be just right.

- **Cake pans:** Choose cake pans made from light-colored aluminum because cakes need quick, steady heat to rise properly, and a dark pan may burn their crust. The most popular shapes for cake pans are round and square/rectangular. Layer cakes almost always call for an 8-inch or 9-inch round pan. Make sure the pans are at least 2 inches deep, and don't fill them to the tip-top or your cake will overflow while baking, making a terrible mess. Note: Using a 9-inch round cake pan is an excellent way to bake freeform whole grain yeast breads, as the pan gives the rising loaf the support it needs to hold its shape.

- When making a single layer cake, you'll use either a 9 x 13-inch pan or a 9-inch-square pan. You can also bake a cake in a half-sheet pan (13 x 18 x 1 inch deep) using 6 to 8 cups of batter, and cut the cake into shapes or strips to create special, multilayered confections (see p. 393) or a special shape. For best cleanup, look for pans that have inside corners that are slightly rounded to avoid trapping crumbs.

- **Bundt pans, tube pans or angel-food cake pans** are used to bake cakes a bit fancier than a layer or sheet cake. Usually these are 8- to 12-cup capacity and are made from nonstick aluminum or aluminum-steel, with Bundt pans creating lovely, fancy shapes (so nice that icing is not required to make it look good!).

- **Loaf pans:** These make the quintessential sandwich loaf. There are 2 popular sizes: 8½ x 4½-inch pans and 9 x 5-inch pans. The smaller pan accommodates a recipe that calls for 3 to 3½ cups of flour in total. For a recipe that uses 4 cups of flour in total, use a 9 x 5-inch loaf pan. Using the proper size pan will give you a nicely domed loaf. For sandwich breads, we prefer dark-colored pans to promote good browning. For sweet breads, use a light-colored pan to keep the bread's crust from burning.

• **Pie pans:** Most recipes call for a 9- or 10-inch pie pan and the recipes in this book assume the pan is at least 1¼ inches deep. Cheaper aluminum pans bought in the grocery store, while convenient, may not be deep enough for the recipes in this book. Smaller-diameter pans (4½ to 5 inches) are great for individual pies or potpies; just make sure they aren't too shallow. Dark-colored metal pie pans tend to become hotter faster and transfer heat better than ceramic pans, though ceramic pans look great. The point of fast heat is to firm up the bottom crust quickly so that the filling doesn't seep through and make the crust soggy. Clear glass pie pans have the advantage of allowing you to see when the bottom crust is browned.

PARCHMENT PAPER: A traditional pan liner to keep cookies, cakes, scones, etc., from sticking to the pan, these sheets are coated with silicone or vegetable oil to render them nonstick. They can be used more than once and won't burn in a typical home oven. Parchment comes in pre-cut sheets for cake pans and sheet pans, and in rolls. You can also purchase silicone or flexible fiberglass pan liners that last much longer. All of these avoid the aggravation of cookies, cakes or other baked goods stuck to the bottom of the pan, and they make cleanup a breeze. In recipes calling for a pan to be both greased and floured, grease the pan, put the parchment on top, and grease the parchment. No need to flour.

PASTRY BAG, FILLING: Most people wish they had three hands when it comes to filling a pastry bag! A tall, narrow container with a heavy base, such as a large beer mug, is a great holder to steady and support the bag as you fill it, so your hands are free to put frosting or batter into the bag. Fill the bag no more than three-quarters full. Overfilling makes the bag hard to close and hard to control. It should fit comfortably in your hands. Use a twist tie to keep the top of the bag closed, so the filling doesn't back up onto your hand when you squeeze the bag.

PEEL, PIZZA OR BAKER'S: A flat, beveled-edge square of wood or aluminum (with a wooden handle) used to transfer large, flat loaves or pizzas from your work surface to a hot baking stone. If your dough sticks to the peel, place a piece of parchment on the peel, then the dough, and transfer parchment and dough to the stone all at once—the parchment won't affect the ability of the stone to crisp the crust.

PIE PANS: see Pans.

PIZZA WHEEL: Also known as a rolling pizza cutter, it is a sharp wheel with a handle that cuts pizza, of course, but also cuts dough for crackers, lattice piecrust, dough for croissants and breadsticks. Use it whenever you want to cut a long, straight line.

PLASTIC WRAP: Use greased plastic wrap as a proof cover for rising bread dough.

PRE-FERMENT: Usually a mixture of flour, water and some yeast that is allowed to ferment before being added to the rest of the ingredients.

PROOF COVER: Shaped yeast dough needs to be covered as it rises, to protect it, help keep it warm and prevent it from drying out. Choose something clear and tall as a proof cover: a large glass or clear plastic bowl, turned upside down over the dough, or the tall, clear plastic cover from a large takeout party platter.

RESTING BATTER: The consistency of whole grain batters often benefits from extra time between mixing and baking. During this rest, the bran from the whole grain slowly absorbs some of the moisture in the batter. The result is a muffin or pancake with a smoother, less gritty texture, one that holds itself together better after being cooked. You'll see many recipes in this book that recommend letting batter rest before baking; simply cover and refrigerate for the recommended amount of time before proceeding with the recipe.

ROLLING PIN: These come in a variety of materials, especially wood and marble, but our favorite is either stainless steel or silicone coated. Whatever you're rolling sticks less to these two materials.

RYE FLAKES: These are rye berries that are steamed, then rolled into flakes, similar to rolled oats.

SAUTÉ: To cook quickly in a small amount of fat in a skillet.

SCALDING MILK: Heating milk just below the boiling point; scalding retards souring and incapacitates some of the enzymes that might otherwise retard yeast growth.

SCALE: All the recipes in this book contain volume and weight measurements. Weight measurements are more accurate than volume measurements, especially when scaling a recipe up or down (making it larger to serve more people or smaller to serve fewer). Look for a battery-powered digital scale with a flat platform that most of the bowls you'll be using, such as your mixer bowl, will fit on. Make sure the switch is easy to locate and use, and that you can easily see the weight when your bowl is on the platform. Look for a scale with the "tare" feature so that you can measure one ingredient into your bowl, then reset the weight to zero, add the desired weight of the next ingredient, and so forth. Our favorite scales stay on through at least 5 minutes of inactivity before shutting off, to allow for those ever-present distractions.

SCRAPING THE BOWL: Recipes that combine creamed fat and liquids can be difficult to mix thoroughly, because the butter/sugar mixture sticks to the sides of the bowl. The only sure remedy for this is to stop mixing partway through and scrape the sides and bottom of the mixing bowl with a rubber spatula.

SEPARATING EGGS: see Eggs, separating.

SERRATED KNIFE: Serrated edges are perfect for slicing through either soft sandwich breads or crusty baguettes, especially knives with a larger "wave" serration. The blade should be 8 to 10 inches long and made of high-carbon stainless steel.

SILICONE MAT: see Kneading mat.

SILICONE SPATULA: A spatula whose blade is made of, or covered with, silicone to prevent sticking.

SIMMER: Bringing a cooked liquid, broth or soup to just below the boiling point. You'll know when it reaches that stage because small bubbles appear on the surface.

SLASHING: Many bread loaves, especially country or European loaves, are slashed on top with a lame (see p. 284) just before being baked. This allows the bread to expand and gives the loaf its distinctive look.

THERMOMETER: see Instant-read thermometer.

TOASTING FLOUR: Some flours, such as amaranth, quinoa and teff, benefit from being toasted before you bake with them. The toasting helps counteract the grassy flavor present in some of the more obscure grains. You may toast flour on a sheet pan in a low oven (300°F) until the flour begins to smell toasty and is a shade or two darker than when you began. For small amounts, it's even easier to toast the flour in a skillet on top of the stove. Place the pan over low heat and stir constantly until the flour is evenly toasted, just a few minutes.

TOASTING NUTS: Toasting nuts enhances their flavor. Since nuts are high in fat, they can scorch easily. Always toast nuts in a shallow container in a single layer. A low to moderate oven (300°F to 350°F) is best. The nuts are done when you can smell their aroma and they've become golden brown. Remove them from the oven when their color is just a shade lighter than what you're looking for, as they'll continue to cook a bit as they cool. Transfer them to a cool surface immediately, to minimize this carryover cooking.

TUBE PAN: see Pans.

WEIGHING, WEIGHTS: see Scale; also Ingredient Weights (see p. 584).

WELL: Forming a well in dry ingredients and adding wet is a way to combine dry and wet ingredients without overmixing and without creating lumps, useful when making pancake, muffin or cake batters. Move the dry ingredients to the sides of the bowl, leaving a depression in the center in which the wet ingredients can pool. You can do this with a spoon, a spatula or your fingers. Once you've added the wet ingredients, you mix them into the dry ingredients gradually, by stirring around the edges of the pool until the ingredients are thoroughly combined.

WHEAT FLAKES: This is the wheat equivalent of oat flakes—the whole wheat berry steamed, then rolled flat.

WHEAT GERM: The embryo of the wheat berry, which is high in fat and contains a lot of nutrients. You can buy wheat germ and add it to some baked goods. Look for stabilized wheat germ, which stays fresher longer.

WHIPPING CREAM: see Cream, whipping.

WHIPPING EGG WHITES: see Egg whites, beating.

Index